MEAT-EATING &
HUMAN EVOLUTION

MEAT-EATING &
HUMAN EVOLUTION

EDITED BY
Craig B. Stanford & Henry T. Bunn

OXFORD
UNIVERSITY PRESS

2001

OXFORD
UNIVERSITY PRESS

Oxford   New York
Athens   Auckland   Bangkok   Bogotá   Bombay   Buenos Aires
Calcutta   Cape Town   Dar es Salaam   Delhi   Florence   Hong Kong
Istanbul   Karachi   Kuala Lumpur   Madras   Madrid   Melbourne
Mexico City   Nairobi   Paris   Shanghai   Singapore   Taipei   Tokyo   Toronto   Warsaw

and associated companies in
Berlin   Ibadan

Copyright © 2001 by Oxford University Press, Inc.

Published by Oxford University Press, Inc.
198 Madison Avenue, New York, New York 10016

Oxford is a registered trademark of Oxford University Press

Library of Congress Cataloging-in-Publication Data
Meat-eating and human evolution / edited by Craig B. Stanford and Henry T. Bunn.
p.   cm.
Includes bibliographical references and index.
ISBN 0-19-513139-8
1. Prehistoric peoples—Food.   2. Fossil hominids.   3. Meat—History.
4. Human evolution.   I. Stanford, Craig B. (Craig Britton), 1956–
II. Bunn, Henry T.
GN799.F6 b M43   2001
599.93'8—dc21   00-036745

9 8 7 6 5 4 3 2 1

Printed in the United States of America
on acid free paper

C. S. dedicates the volume to his parents,
Jacqueline and Leland Stanford, Jr.

H. B. dedicates the volume to his family

and we both dedicate the book to the memory of Glynn Isaac

Contents

IV. Theoretical Considerations

Contributors

Michael Alvard
Department of Anthropology
380 MFAC
State University of New York at Buffalo
Buffalo, NY 14261

Henry Bunn
Department of Anthropology
5240 Social Building
Univ. of Wisconsin
Madison, WI 53706-1395

Robert Foley
Department of Biological Anthropology
University of Cambridge
Downing Street
Cambridge, CB2 3DZ
United Kingdom

Kristen Hawkes
Department of Anthropology
University of Utah
Salt Lake City, UT 84112

William McGrew
Departments of Biology and Anthropology
Miami University
Oxford, OH 45056

Jim Moore
Department of Anthropology
University of California, San Diego
La Jolla, CA 92093

Katherine M. Moore
American Section, Museum of Archaeology
   and Anthropology
University of Pennsylvania
33rd and Spruce Streets
Philadelphia, PA 19104

Shawn Murray
Department of Anthropology
University of Wisconsin
Madison, WI 53706-1395

Travis Pickering
University of Witwatersrand Medical
   School
Department of Anatomical Sciences
7 York Road, Parktown 2193
Johannesburg, South Africa

John Rick
Department of Anthropology
Stanford University
Stanford, CA 94305-2145

Lisa Rose
Department of Anthropology
Washington University
Box 1114
St. Louis, MO 63130-4899

Margaret Schoeninger
Department of Anthropology
University of Wisconsin
Madison, Wl 53706-1395

Jeanne Sept
Department of Anthropology
Indiana University
Bloomington, IN 47405

John Speth
Museum of Anthropology
4009 Museums Building
University of Michigan
Ann Arbor, MI 48109

Craig Stanford
Jane Goodall Research Center
Department of Anthropology
University of Southern California
Los Angeles, CA 90089-0032

Martha Tappen
Department of Anthropology
University of Minnesota
395 HHH Center
301 19th Ave. South
Minneapolis, MN 55455

Eitan Tchernov
Department of Evolution, Systematics,
  and Ecology
Hebrew University-Jerusalem
91904 Jerusalem
Israel

Blaire van Valkenburgh
Department of Biology
U.C.L.A.
Los Angeles, CA 90095-1606

Natalia Vasey
Department of Anthropology
409 Carpenter Building
Penn State University
University Park, PA 16802

Alan Walker
Department of Anthropology
409 Carpenter Building
Penn State University
University Park, PA 16802

Bruce Winterhalder
Department of Anthropology
CB #3115 Alumni Biding.
University of North Carolina
Chapel Hill, NC 27599

MEAT-EATING &
HUMAN EVOLUTION

Introduction

Craig B. Stanford
Henry T. Bunn

More than 30 years after the publication of *Man the Hunter*, the role of meat in the early human diet remains a central topic of human evolutionary research. There is little doubt that meat-eating became increasingly important in human ancestry, despite the lack of direct evidence in the fossil record of how meat was obtained, or how much was eaten, or how often, or how exactly increasing importance of meat-eating may have contributed to the rise of the genus *Homo*. Although the fossil evidence is becoming clearer on these issues, we still lack key evidence about early hominid behavioral ecology. Information about meat-eating patterns from modern nonhuman primates, from modern foraging people, and from the fossil record could all contribute to a clearer picture of early humanity than we have at present.

With this goal in mind, a workshop was held October 2–5, 1998, on the campus of the University of Wisconsin, Madison. "The Early Human Diet: The Role of Meat," sponsored by the Wenner-Gren Foundation for Anthropological Research, brought together 18 participants representing several subfields of human origins research. Papers were presented at the workshop by Michael Alvard, Henry Bunn, Robert Foley, Kristen Hawkes, William McGrew, Katharine Milton, Travis Pickering, John Rick, Lisa Rose, Margaret Schoeninger, Jeanne Sept, John Speth, Craig Stanford, Mary Stiner, Martha Tappen, Blaire Van Valkenburgh, Alan Walker, and Bruce Winterhalder.

Why publish a volume on meat-eating at this time? Despite its importance in the evolutionary ecology of the Hominidae, scholars from different disciplines have only rarely gathered to discuss the topic. Few of the contributors to this volume had sat in the same group to discuss the crosscutting aspects of their work before the Madison workshop. Most of the participants work in the field of biological anthropology or archaeology; lack of intellectual crossfertilization may simply reflect increasing specialization within the discipline.

Each era in the study of human behavioral origins has treated meat-eating in its own way, based on the most reasonable interpretations of the available data. Since Raymond Dart (1953), reconstructions of early hominid behavior have revolved around dietary issues, due to the recognition that among many social animals including nonhuman primates, social behavior and grouping patterns are profoundly influenced by the need to balance energy output with nutrient energy intake. The diet of most higher primates consists largely of leaves and fruit, and foraging for these consumes most of each day. Including a highly concentrated packet of nutrients and calories, such as meat represents, may have provided emerging humans with a key nutritional supplement that favored the evolution of other key traits, such as cognition.

From the 1960s until the early 1980s, consideration of meat-eating generally focused on the importance of hunting to early human social patterns (Washburn and Lancaster 1968; Tiger and Fox 1971; Suzuki 1975; Lovejoy 1981; Hill 1982; Tooby and DeVore 1987). In this earlier era, the most influential and ultimately infamous body of theory related to meat-eating was Man the Hunter. The idea that hunting was the seminal behavior accounting for the expansion of the human brain neocortex and higher intelligence emerged from a conference of the same name held in April, 1966, in Chicago. About 75 scholars gathered to discuss the behavior and status of foraging people ("hunter-gatherers") in the world at that time. The volume that followed, edited by Richard Lee and Irven DeVore, included a chapter by Sherwood Washburn and Chet Lancaster entitled "The Evolution of Hunting," in which Washburn and Lancaster hypothesized that hunting was among the most fundamental of human behavioral adaptations. They proposed that the importance of communicating and coordinating big game hunting placed a premium on intelligence and the expansion of the brain's neocortex. Because hunting is primarily a male activity in modern, and presumably ancient, human societies, this would have accounted for the large size of the human brain in males. By ignoring the role of females in the evolution of human brain size, Washburn and Lancaster unleashed a firestorm of criticism. Some anthropologists (e.g., Tanner and Zihlmann 1976) took issue with the assumption that meat composed a substantial or important portion of the early human diet. Others argued that a predatory view of human cognitive origins was rooted in male-biased science. Ironically, the consensus of opinion at the Man the Hunter conference was that meat is of relatively little nutritional importance in the diets of the same modern tropical foragers.

The legacy of Man the Hunter was long-lasting in academic discussions of meat-eating and human origins. The debate may have even accounted in part for the rise of feminist theory in anthropology in the 1970s (Stanford 1999). The backlash against Man the Hunter led many anthropologists to reject hunting as an important subsistence mode among early hominids and led others to reject meat-eating as an important part of the early human diet.

Beginning in the 1980s, the hunting paradigm fell victim to reinterpretations of archaeological sites, which suggested that the cooperative, predatory tendencies of early humans had been misinterpreted. Data from Plio-Pleistocene sites were increasingly interpreted as evidence of meat procurement by scavenging rather than by hunting (Binford 1981; Isaac and Crader 1981; Shipman 1986; Blumenschine

1987; Potts 1988). Bunn (1982) and Bunn and Kroll (1986) advocated both scavenging of large ungulate carcasses and hunting of smaller prey based on their analysis of Plio-Pleistocene material from Olduvai Gorge. Some early advocates of the importance of scavenging (Howell 1968; Schaller and Lowther 1969) had proposed this behavior as an adjunct to hunting, but for the more recent work scavenging was often proposed as the primary or even sole means of carcass acquisition. Shipman and Potts (1981) and Shipman (1986) showed that some Pliocene bone assemblages had unambiguous evidence of hominid cutmarks made on top of carnivore toothmarks, supporting a scavenging foraging mode for early genus *Homo*. Binford (1981) took the most extreme view, rejecting the possibility that any taxon of hominid prior to earliest *Homo sapiens* would have had the cognitive capacity for cooperative hunting or food-sharing. Isaac's seminal (1978) work on food acquisition and food-sharing among early hominids was part of a movement to consider the Pliocene past by use of analogy with the better-understood present. During the workshop we returned time and again to Isaac's ideas and agreed that his food-sharing model, put aside during the rush to "dehumanize" early hominids during the 1980s, accords as well with field data today as it did then.

In the 1990s, a more balanced view of hunting and scavenging has prevailed, which this volume attempts to represent. The current perspective has been based on research in the three areas covered by this volume: meat-eating by nonhuman primates and their analogs, meat-eating by modern foragers, and evidence of meat-eating in the fossil record. There is a growing consensus among researchers studying the fossil record that earlier dichotomies between hunting and scavenging were simplistic and ultimately false. This perspective was evident at the Wenner-Gren workshop, in which the long-standing debate over the occurrence and importance of hunting and scavenging by early hominids was rarely at issue. There is a recognition today that this dichotomy has eroded with the collection of data from a variety of research sites. Thus, Blumenschine's (1986) argument for an exclusive scavenging niche based on a reconstruction of the ecology of Pliocene Serengeti was extremely valuable, but no longer accords well with data from reconstructions of hominid behavioral ecology from other habitats (e.g., Tappen, this volume). There are no obligate scavengers among living mammals; carnivores from lions to hyenas typically acquire meat by either hunting or scavenging as the opportunity arises. Bunn and Ezzo (1993) and Bunn (this volume) argue for a mode of hominid subsistence based on the opportunistic hunting and pirating ("power scavenging") of large mammalian carcasses in a manner that resembles what many carnivores do today. This does not mean that passive scavenging might not have been important in some periods and among some taxa in hominid evolution; only that the strict hunting versus scavenging debate of the 1980s seems to have given way to a more realistically complex view of Pliocene hominid behavioral ecology.

Approaches to the Study of Meat-Eating

Some definitions are in order before we proceed further with a discussion of meat-eating. First, by meat-eating we refer to the consumption of vertebrate fauna (but see McGrew, this volume, for invertebrate faunivory), including muscle, viscera, the skeleton, and associated body tissues. "Meat" is thus more properly referred to as "carcass biomass," but for purposes of this volume it is understood that meat-eating encompasses all body tissues. The nutrient and caloric values of mammalian carcasses have been studied by a range of scholars in fields ranging from biochemistry and nutritional sciences to archaeology, and for an equal variety of reasons. This volume contains a number of chapters that discuss the nutrient and caloric properties of meat but none that examines in detail the biochemical basis for meat as a valuable nutrient source (that is, the amino acids, fats, etc., contained in a carcass). This is perhaps a necessary failing in that all the chapters herein accept the (admittedly incomplete) received wisdom about why carnivores and omnivores live on diets that are partially or wholly the meat of other animals.

We include both scavenged carcasses and hunted live prey when discussing meat-eating as a dietary/behavioral adaptation. Considering these as separate foraging modes makes sense, even though there are no living mammals that do one without at least sometimes also doing the other.

The lines of evidence that were presented at the conference encompassed the three fields below, with many chapters crosscutting two or more of these. In addition, two theoretical issues directly related to meat-eating in human evolution were included that did not fall neatly into any of the three areas below.

Meat-Eating by Nonhuman Analogs

Recent field data on hunting behavior by wild chimpanzees, building on Teleki (1973) and Goodall's (1986) work, have shown that chimpanzees consume more meat, at least at some study sites, than previously thought (Stanford 1996, 1998). At some sites, chimpanzees hunt cooperatively (Boesch and Boesch 1989, Boesch 1994). The level of predatory cooperation seen among wild chimpanzees refutes Binford's argument that early hominids would not have been cognitively able to engage in cooperative hunting and food-sharing. In addition, the growing realization that chimpanzee populations display cultural diversity paralleling that of the most technologically simple human societies (McGrew 1992) provides much insight into the likely cultural aspects of early human technologies and other behaviors.

Using nonhuman primates to interpret the meat-eating behavior of our ancestors is, however, fraught with problems. Chimpanzees and modern humans share an ancestor that lived some six million years ago; we cannot assume that modern chimpanzees are very similar to the ancestral chimpanzee any more than we would think that modern people are very much like the ancestral hominid. The chimpanzee dietary adaptation reflects life in a wide variety of habitat types, some of which may never have been inhabited by Pliocene hominids. Moreover, among the four great apes, only the chimpanzee is an avid hunter and consumer of meat. Using the chimpanzee as a presumptive model of meat-eating patterns in an early australopithecine necessarily ignores other living exemplars, like the bonobo, that offer a contrasting view.

Nevertheless, chimpanzees are valuable referential models of early human behavioral ecology because they enable us to go beyond the one-dimensional portrait that the fossil record provides of extinct taxa. Because it is in most cases extremely fragmentary, the fossil record can deceive us into accepting a single, well-documented site as representative of a species' biology. Chimpanzee behavioral diversity across wide geographic areas, due to both ecological influences and local cultural traditions, offers an important lesson for students of early hominid behavioral ecology. Chimpanzee behaviors from tool use to hunting techniques to grooming styles vary from population to population. Likewise, we should expect that a species of *Australopithecus* or early *Homo* may have been an avid scavenger of large carcasses at one site and an avid hunter but not a scavenger at a contemporaneous site 100 km away. Chapters in this volume by McGrew, Rose, and Schoeninger et al. present ideas and data related to the consumption of meat by nonhuman primates.

We need not limit ourselves to primates when attempting to reconstruct the behavior and ecology of the earliest hominids. Van Valkenburgh reconstructs Pliocene African ecosystems in which early *Homo* would have been one component and, using data on diet and body weight, argues that feeding competition from other, larger, meat-eating species would have been major factors in the behavioral ecology of these taxa.

Meat-Eating by Modern Foraging People

Field studies of modern foraging societies have done much to show how and why they obtain meat. Meat may compose only a small part of the diet, but the composition of the overall diet and its seasonal variation provide opportunities for hypothesis testing. Likewise, the ways in which prey are caught, or carcasses scavenged, and then butchered and distributed to group members are still poorly understood for many foraging societies. Studies of tropical and subtropical foragers, especially of the behavioral ecology of the Hadza in East Africa (Hawkes et al. 1991), the !Kung in southwestern Africa (Lee 1979), the Efe in eastern Congo (Bailey and Peacock 1988), and the neotropical Aché of Paraguay (Hill and Hawkes 1983; Kaplan and Hill 1985), have tested hypotheses about the pattern and purpose of meat-eating. These studies have shown that elements of the behavioral ecology of modern people, such as nutrient/caloric costs and benefits of foraging for plant versus animal foods (Hawkes 1993) and the pattern and sequence of carcass transport and consumption (O'Connell and Hawkes 1988), provide appropriate and valuable comparisons with analogous behaviors among other living primates having similar energetic exigencies.

There is a long-standing debate about the utility of modern foragers in studying human evolution; some scholars assert that studying modern people with an eye toward the past is inherently useless and possibly even racist. Humans living with relatively simple technologies, who forage for a living from their forest or grassland environment, make decisions every day about which foods to forage for and which to pass by, or about which parts of an animal carcass they will relish and which they will discard. These decisions, no matter how culturally influenced, are tied to the nutritional health and reproductive lives of the men and women in the group. As such they can be examined, and questions can be asked about the decisions themselves. There is no doubt that even among the most remote foraging groups in the world today, outside cultures have played an influential role. Nevertheless, foraging decisions have biological, reproductive consequences. The chapters in this volume (see further discussion by Bunn) and elsewhere that examine forager behavioral ecology use this rationale and ask whether a cautiously applied Darwinian paradigm can explain aspects of what foraging people do regarding meat.

In this volume, Hawkes, Bunn, and Alvard discuss studies of foragers that have implications for early human faunivory. Rick presents data from a Holocene population of hunter-gatherers whose hunting behavior can be reconstructed from the bone assemblages they left behind. Winterhalder presents a review and analysis of the literature on food-sharing and the theoretical models that are available to interpret meat-eating.

Meat-Eating in the Human Fossil Record

The fossil record provides the only direct evidence for human evolution, although the clues it contains are often difficult to interpret. Perhaps the major advance of the 1980s was the increasing attention paid to natural processes that may give an appearance of early human influence to fossil assemblages. Such taphonomic studies were crucial in allowing archaeologists to reconstruct the past by analogy with the present. Evidence of stone tools has long been available, but their purpose and which species of early human used them have been debated. It is important to note that we have a fossil record, albeit fragmentary, of more than four million years of evolution. Within that span there have been numerous taxa and many more populations, and we should not expect to be able to categorize patterns of meat-eating neatly by time period or taxon. It is likely that hunting and scavenging have both characterized the behavior of early hominids of a wide variety of taxa, from early to recent, varying across wide geographic areas.

Early hominid diets have been reconstructed using patterns of tooth wear (Teaford and Walker 1984), associated tool artifacts (Bunn and Kroll 1986; Shipman 1986) and more recently through the study of isotopic signatures in the fossilized bone material made by ingestion of different forms of carbon (Sponheimer and Lee-Thorp 1999; Schoeninger et al. this volume). In all cases the results are open to debate because major gaps in our information remain. How often was meat eaten? Was meat a regular part of the diet of early hominids, or was it a very small part of the diet that happens to have a high archaeological visibility? Hunting and scavenging have been interpreted on the basis of archaeological signatures of tool use by hominids and tooth damage to bone assemblages by carnivores. The relative importance of scavenging, and the degree to which it could have created a dietary niche without hunting, have been questioned.

There are many ways to make sense of the fossil record for hominid meat-eating. In this volume Pickering discusses taphonomic explanations for the faunal assemblages at Swartkrans. Tappen considers the widely invoked Serengeti model for scavenging by early *Homo* and finds it lacking. Bunn compares Hadza cutmarks with those found at Pliocene fossil sites in East Africa. Speth and Tchernov offer views on Neandertal diet from Israel and Italy, respectively. Sept brings the meat-eating picture into ecological focus with an examination of the likely plant food diet against which australopithecines and early Homo would have foraged for meat. Foley examines large-scale patterns of environment, encephalization, and the hominid phylogeny. Finally, Vasey and Walker present a theoretical article in which they consider the rapid expansion of the Plio-Pleistocene brain in relation to concomitant changes that would have occurred evolutionarily in other organ systems, in this case gestation.

Key Questions

We organized the workshop in Madison according to a set of key questions about the role of meat in the early human diet. These questions were addressed at length in the workshop, although they could not necessarily be answered in any definitive way at present:

1. How is hominid behavior distinguished from natural processes in the fossil record? How is hunting distinguished from scavenging in the fossil record?
2. What are the costs and benefits associated with meat-eating compared to relying on a herbivore's diet?
3. How do hunters hunt? What is the role of cooperation and communication during the hunt for both human and nonhuman animal hunters?
4. What is the nature of the variation crossculturally in the nutritional importance of meat to modern foraging people? When and why does meat represent more than just a source of nutrition for modern foraging people?
5. What is unique about the pattern of meat-eating in modern people compared to great apes?
6. What was the role of meat-eating in the geographic radiation of the genus *Homo*?
7. What aspects of meat-eating and foraging for meat may have influenced the evolution of human intelligence?
8. In what ways can meat-sharing among modern primates and human foragers inform us about sharing in early humans?

These questions were the focus for our discussions in Madison, and they recur throughout the following chapters. The reader should find, if not the final answers to the questions, at least the state of the field data, laboratory data, and theoretical advances that are currently available.

Acknowledgments

The preparation of this book and the conference on which it is based could not have been accomplished without the help of many people. First and foremost, we gratefully acknowledge the Wenner-Gren Foundation for Anthropological Research for their sponsorship of the conference at the University of Wisconsin in October 1998 from which this edited volume emerged. At Wenner-Gren, we especially thank Dr. Sydel Silverman and Laurie Obbink. The conference itself was an dynamic mix of perspectives and personalities, and we thank the participants and contributors themselves for their involvement in this project from beginning to completion.

During the editing process, both of our academic departments of anthropology, at the University of Southern California and the University of Wisconsin, Madison, provided secretarial and other support that facilitated the preparation of this book. We are grateful for the time that many anonymous reviewers took to help the 17 authors revise and improve their individual chapters. We especially thank Sadie S. Moore for her editorial assistance, Rita R. Jones for secretarial help, and Kirk Jensen for the invitation to publish the book with Oxford University Press.

Part I

Meat-Eating
and the
Fossil Record

1

Deconstructing the Serengeti

Martha Tappen

Introduction

The expansion of meat-eating by hominids beyond the level of extant apes had repercussions for hominid ecology, anatomy, and social behavior. In recent years many have attempted to develop explicit models of hominid behavior based on the ecological distribution of animal and plant foods in modern African savannas. The modern environments used as analogs by most workers emphasize very dry, very seasonal areas of modern Africa. This has limited our view of the spatial and temporal distribution of available animals. However, the true variety of modern African savannas demonstrates greater variability that would influence meat-eating. In wetter savannas scavenging would be much less predictable, with very high search costs and relatively low returns.

The Savanna Hypothesis

The "savanna hypothesis," with us since the time of Dart (1925), has been the most influential theory in paleoanthropology. Nearly every major hypothesis of the origins of bipedalism in some way incorporates the idea of dry habitats replacing wetter ones. Recently it has become popular to critique the hypothesis (e.g., Cerling 1992; Clarke and Tobias 1995; Berger and Tobias 1996), justified by a weakening of the dichotomy of rainforest-ape/savanna-hominid (McGrew et al. 1981; Moore 1996). It now appears that the common ancestor of living apes and humans may not have been restricted to a continuous rainforest and probably had terrestrial locomotion as a part of its positional repertoire (e.g., Rose 1991; Gebo 1996; Pilbeam 1996).

13

Likewise, early australopithecines were not restricted to dry seasonal savanna. While on average the Miocene (22–5 myr [million years ago]) was wetter than the Pliocene (5–1.7 myr), and the Pliocene wetter than the Pleistocene (beginning about 1.7 myr), Miocene habitats were not exclusively lowland rainforest but of mixed structure. Within a clear drying trend through time (deMenocal 1995), mixed habitats have a long antiquity going back into the Miocene (e.g., Kingston et al. 1994). Mounting paleoenvironmental and anatomical evidence suggests that Pliocene hominids frequently occupied mixed woodland. This is supported by the association of some forest and/or woodland dwelling fauna with hominids and the long-term maintenance of climbing adaptations in australopithecines. These facts have dampened enthusiasm for the savanna hypothesis.

The savanna hypothesis has been linked to ideas of the origins of meat-eating. After all, savannas have less fruit than forests, and hominids would have had to change their diets in response. Independent of this, early australopithecines may be expected to eat meat at least to the degree that living chimpanzees do (by argument from phylogeny and parsimony), and taphonomists need to continue to search to see if any evidence of that survives (e.g., Pickering and Wallis 1997; Plummer and Stanford 2000; Tappen and Wrangham in press). Here I would like to distinguish between this more general "savanna hypothesis" and the "Serengeti hypothesis" as the early hominid "Environment of Evolutionary Adaptiveness" (EEA).

The Serengeti Hypothesis

The savanna hypothesis in paleoanthropology has been much more specific than a vision of the effects of hominids leaving the forest for the savanna and the logical outcome of that; in reality, it has usually been what I call the "Serengeti hypothesis." The Serengeti ecosystem, lying mainly in northern Tanzania and extending into southern Kenya, is well known (Sinclair and Norton-Griffiths, 1979, 1995). The Serengeti has a rainfall gradient of increasing dryness from the northwest corner (woodlands) to the southwest (grass plains). Seasonal dry periods are such that grass in general does not grow from July to October (Sinclair 1979). The problem is that the Serengeti is not a representative sample of African savannas. It is spectacular, dramatic, photogenic, relatively accessible, and Olduvai Gorge is there— these facts have contributed to it dominating our research perspectives. There have been some studies of wetter, less seasonal savannas, such as by Sept (1992, 1994), but these are few and far between and are less well incorporated into paleoanthropological models.

One critique of the influential Wenner-Gren " Man the Hunter" conference was that the bushmen of the Kalahari became the quintessential model for Paleolithic foragers, despite much evidence for variation in environments, material culture, and social systems in hunter-gatherers. In a similar way, the Serengeti has become the quintessential savanna in which we evolved, despite much evidence of variation in modern savannas and climate fluctuations in the past. One of the predominant aspects of the Serengeti is the large migratory herds that create seasonal gluts and dearth of large mammal biomass as they move between their wet season range on the plains and their dry season range in the woodlands. The huge migratory herds and intense dry seasons are central to many models of human evolution. For example, Sinclair et al. (1986) hypothesize that bipedalism evolved as a means of long-distance travel, with hominids forced to follow migratory herds in order to scavenge their dead. Foley (1987) suggested that the split of the genera *Homo* and *Paranthropus* from *Australopithecus* reflected differing coping strategies to intense dry seasons—and used the Serengeti and an even dryer semidesert from Kenya (Amboseli) as models for differing habitats that the two genera adapted to. Speth made a series of predictions about hominid meat-consumption strategies based on the extreme seasonal stress of modern ungulates and hunter-gatherers in the Serengeti and South Africa (and also the presumably less extreme but seasonal stress on modern chimpanzees) (Speth and Spielman 1983; Speth 1987, 1989). The Serengeti is indeed a good place for study of modern ecosystems as a first step of model-building foraging and site formation there—it is simply incomplete.

When researchers make reference to other ecosystems as analogs for hominid habitats, they usually include habitats that are *even dryer* than the Serengeti. Binford used the Serengeti ecosystem to model bone deposition rates based on natural deaths of ungulates and the even dryer semidesert in South Africa to model his waterhole hypothesis of bone accumulations (Binford 1981, 1983). Additionally, models of hunter-gatherers living in desert environments such as the Kalahari form the basis of much of the social environment of the EEA. For example, the seasonal foraging strategies of Kalahari bushmen have been used to identify what seasons hominids occupied Olduvai sites (Speth and Davis 1976).

Finally, the Serengeti ecosystem has been used to model where on the landscape hominids could most effectively scavenge (Schaller and Lowthar 1969; Blumenschine 1986, 1987, 1989; Blumenschine and Peters 1998). According to the Serengeti model, scavenging would be most profitable for hominids in certain parts of the ecosystem and during certain times of the year. Scavenging from lions is more profitable than from hyenas because lions feed incompletely upon large carcasses. In the open grass plains hyenas are more common, and carcasses are more completely consumed. So, hominids would have the most success scavenging in riparian woodlands where lions predominate. Furthermore, seasonality is such that scavenging would be most profitable during the dry season because attritional mortality is high. This general model has been expanded to include the seasonal and spatial predictability of wildebeest drownings in Lakes Masek and Ndutu in the Serengeti Ecosystem (Capaldo and Peters 1994), as well as predictably located tree-stored leopard kills in woodlands (Cavallo and Blumenschine 1989).

The predominance of the Serengeti model cannot be understated, and it has penetrated a variety of subfields. Evolutionary psychologists have often incorporated it as the model for the "Environment of Evolutionary Adaptiveness" where we evolved (see Foley 1995/96 for review). The EEA is modeled to involve a particular social environment (much like that of extant hunter-gatherers) and also particular habitats: "If we assume that the evolution of our species includes the development of psychological mechanisms that aid adaptive response to the environment, then savanna-like habitats should generate positive response in people, much as the "right" habitat motivates exploration and settling behaviors in other species" (Orians and Heerwagen 1992: 556). So we are not only from the savanna, we should "feel good" about the savanna, too. But not just the savanna, high-quality savanna: "We have been testing people's response to tree shapes and have found that tree shapes characteristic of high-quality savanna are preferred over those found in lower-quality savanna" (p. 559). Our very psychology has been shaped by savannas such as the Serengeti, no matter what part of the world we come from.

It is reasonable to assume that people may prefer safe, comfortable environments over the desert, but to suggest that we know what kind of environment we *evolved in* is not reasonable. Fossil site distribution does not delimit or systematically sample the geographic range or environmental variability of the habitats that hominids occupied: obviously, it is largely determined by gross taphonomic features such as rifts and karstic caves. Because Olduvai is located near the Serengeti does not mean we evolved in the Serengeti, yet often we treat as if it is the sacred spot where we evolved. The expansion of the known geographic range of australopithecines to include Chad (Brunet et al. 1995) is clear evidence that early hominids were not severely restricted geographically and in fact may be characterized as cosmopolitan.

Deconstructing the Serengeti Hypothesis

There are many anthropogenic influences on all modern African environments; for example, there are still lingering effects of the European big-game hunters (Little 1996). The herding strategies by pastoralists have modified the proportion of annual and perennial species of the Serengeti. Poaching has essentially eliminated rhinoceros, and elephants have been reduced by 80% in the Serengeti; Roan antelope and wild dogs have become very rare (Sinclair and Arcese 1995). Much of the grassland today in Africa can be termed "secondary grasslands," as they are anthropogenically created or maintained in a subclimax state, usually by fire (Vesey-Fitzgerald 1963).

While seasonality is a ubiquitous characteristic of savannas, huge migratory herds are not. In some African savannas migratory ungulates significantly outnumber sedentary ones (Fryxell et al. 1988), but this is not always the case, and Africa today tends to be more arid than in many periods in the past. Even in our modern arid period, savanna bovids and equids vary greatly in their ranging patterns, both within and between species. In the Serengeti, the spectacular migration of one and a half million wildebeest is a recent phenomenon. Once there were only 200,000 wildebeest; in 1972 there were 850,000, and in 1979 there were 1.3 million because humans eradicated the exotic virus rinderpest in the region and increased proportions of grass cover with burning (Norton-Griffiths 1979; Sinclair 1979).

Being migratory is not a species-specific characteristic but a response to the ecological demands of some environments. For example, the Uganda kob (*Kobus kob thomasi*) is a year-round residential lek breeder; individuals spend the majority of their lives within a few square kilometers. However, its conspecific, *K.k. leucotis*, of the more arid southern Sudan, migrates several hundred kilometers each year. A subspecies of topi (*Damaliscus lunatus tiang*) is also migratory and much more mobile than other topi (Fryxell and Sinclair 1988). The wildebeest herds

(*Connochaetes taurinus*) of the Serengeti migrate seasonally, covering thousands of square kilometers, whereas most members of the same species in Ngorongoro Crater almost never leave the 18-km diameter crater, and some members of the western, wetter part of the Serengeti are also sedentary (Maddock 1979). Furthermore, migrations occur at a continuum of distances, and many ungulates have systems of seasonal concentration—dispersion, for example in the near-desertic conditions at Amboseli Park, Kenya (Western 1973). Some populations of wildebeest, such as most in Kenya (e.g., Athi-Kapiti plains) also migrate but go much shorter distances than those in the Serengeti. In contrast, the closely related black wildebeest of southern Africa is generally sedentary.

Migratory behavior in ungulates is facultative and depends on environmental conditions (McNaughton 1990; Murray 1994; McNaughton et al. 1997). For example, when water and food suddenly become available year round (e.g., when a bore hole is dug), migratory wildebeest will split off and begin to lead residential lives (observed in Kalahari Gemsbok Park and in Wankie National Park). The presence of permanent water allows the wildebeest of Ngorongoro to be residential. If adverse conditions arise, the "formation of sedentary colonies from migratory populations is reversible" (Estes 1969: 363). Janis and Wilhelm (1993) suggested that the major migratory systems first evolved in the Plio-Pleistocene and Holocene because of relatively cooler and more arid conditions, noting that extant taxa that exhibit migratory behavior (reindeer, zebra, and wildebeest) do not exist earlier than this time. Even if secondary grasslands occurred as early as 2 million years ago (Spencer 1997) it does not necessarily indicate migratory behavior. Could ungulates have been more residential during wet periods and more migratory during dry periods? For example, if Olduvai Gorge received a few hundred more millimeters of rain a year in lower Bed I than it does today, as near Tuff IB (Kapplemen 1984), would that have been sufficient to have more residential ungulates? Could the more arid conditions around Tuff 1F have resulted in an increase in migratory behavior?

The paleoenvironmental record includes ample evidence for climate fluctuations through time. Although monsoonal rainfall patterns already existed (Prell and VanCampo 1986; Quade et al. 1989), it does not indicate that the hominid habitats were dominated by major migrations of animal populations. The modern monsoon system of seasonal rainfall produces migratory populations in some but not all savannas. In addition to the pattern of highly seasonal rainfall, people often practice burning, so many environments are dominated by fire-adapted species. There are many areas of overgrazing, and the decrease in the vegetation itself causes further decreases in moisture, resulting in extremely dry seasons. The paleoenvironmental evidence from $\delta^{13}C$ and $\delta^{18}O$ records in paleosol carbonates from Olduvai and East Turkana indicate that the modern environment is both as hot and as dry as *at any earlier time recorded in either sequence* (Cerling and Hay 1986; Cerling et al. 1988; Cerling 1992).

As techniques for paleoenvironmental reconstruction become more refined and sample sizes get larger, we find the early Pleistocene was more wooded than previous reconstructions, but the evidence has been there all along. In lower Bed I, between Tuffs IB and ID at Olduvai (FLK Zinj times), rainfall was about 300 mm a year higher than today (about 8–900 mm), there were more montane plant species, mean annual temperature was much lower (15 versus 22 degrees), reduncines were common, and the lake was high (Bonnefille and Riollet 1980; Kappelman 1984, 1986; Cerling and Hay 1986; Hay 1990). Near Tuff 1F things began to get dryer. And although there is an increase in grasses at the beginning of the Pleistocene, sites were not overwhelmingly grassland until 1 myr (Cerling 1992). Furthermore, recent analyses of taxonomic indices and of community structure in Bed I of Olduvai, including small and large mammals, suggest "that although they form part of the spectrum of savanna ecosystems as observed in present-day habitats, the faunas from most of the Olduvai Bed-I sequence represent well wooded environments, which are different but richer than any part of the present-day savanna biome. None of the Olduvai faunas represent environments as open as the Serengeti ecosystems today" (Fernandez-Jalvo et al. 1998: 165–166).

A wooded environment is consistent with more recent data on soil carbonates at the Olduvai FLK Zinj site and in a basal Bed II paleosol (Sikes 1994). Taxon-free analyses of bovid limb morphology indicate the Olduvai sites had more intermediate and closed habitats than predicted by taxonomic analyses (Plummer and Bishop 1994), although new ecomorphological studies of bovid femora indicate there was a full range of habitats present, closed to open (Kappelman et al. 1997). Hay (1976, 1990) believes that it was wetter than Olduvai today but still semiarid, based on the presence of Urocyclid slugs below 1D. They are most abundant below 1B, but also found at Zinj level, beneath 1C. Olduvai lake levels fluctuated in a similar manner—generally higher earlier with a dry interval between 1D and just before 1F. However, I do not suggest there was never a dry season or period at this locality. The saline nature of Paleolake Olduvai indicates that evaporation was high at times. Inflow and evaporation regulates salinity, and the lake is thought to have had no outlet (Hay 1976). This indicates a lack of congruence between paleoenviromental data. How much was controlled by the changing geomorphology? Does it suggest that these pieces of data are not really contemporary? Were there very rapidly shifting environmental contexts?

PNV: A Central African Savanna

Park National des Virunga (PNV), located in the Western Rift Valley adjacent to the Central African rainforest in the Democratic Republic of the Congo, offers an important comparison to the Serengeti (Figure 1.1). The Northern Secteur of the park borders the great lowland rainforest to the west, the Rwenzori Mountains to the north, and Lake Edward to the south. Mean annual rainfall is within the range of the wettest part of the Serengeti (900 mm) and includes two dry seasons, though the dry seasons are less severe (Figure 1.2). There is abundant permanent fresh water in Lake Rutanzige (ex-lake Edward) and the Semliki River (Figure 1.3). The result is a nonmigratory ecosystem, dominated by reduncines (Uganda kob, waterbuck, reedbuck), buffalo, warthog, and hippopotamus. The large carnivores include lion, spotted hyena, and leopard; there are no cheetahs or wild dogs. Grasses, *Acacia*, and *Euphorbia* trees are predominant in the vegetation. PNV is not immune to anthropogenic influences; for example, the decimation of elephants by poachers has caused encroachment of bushland on grassland.

The study area can be divided into two main habitats: the Plateau and Southern Plateau. The Plateau is a relatively open grass plain with scattered *Euphorbia* and

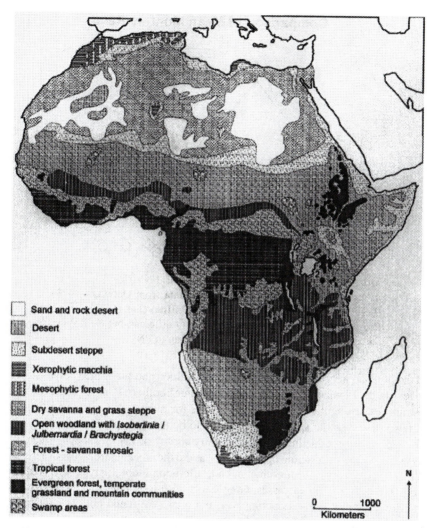

Figure 1.1. Location of Parc National des Virunga (1) and the Serengeti Ecosystem (2) in relation to major vegetation zones in Africa (Graphic adapted from Clark 1982).

Acacia trees, while in the Southern Plateau and near the lake and river, tree density is about of four times higher (Tappen 1995). Taller grass gives lions sufficient cover for ambush even in the open Plateau. Beause there is also year-round occupation by kob and reedbuck, the lions prefer this habitat. One of the most important ecological differences between PNV and the Serengeti is that in the Serengeti lions are much more successful at ambushing in wooded areas than in grassy areas that they tend to prefer the trees and bushes (Schaller 1972: Table 56). Also, because they have altricial young, they are unable to follow migratory herds, so they stick to the regions with residential prey (Schaller 1972). There are no comparable hunting success data for PNV, but in PNV the grass is long and thick nearly everywhere,

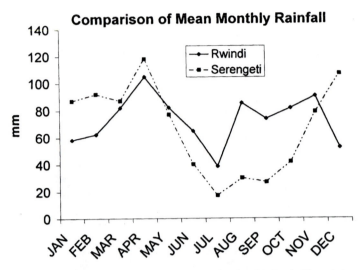

Figure 1.2. Comparison of monthly rainfall, PNV (Rwindi) and the Serengeti. Rwindi (PNV, Secteur Sud) data from Delvingt (1978), 1963–1972; Serengeti Data from Norton-Griffiths et al. (1975) between 1962 and 1972. The two areas are not very different, but the dry season is longer and drier in the Serengeti than in PNV.

and the lions do not require bush to be totally hidden and place themselves near the kob leks in the Plateau. In contrast, in the bushier Southern Plateau, and near water, there are fewer ungulates, more denning sites for hyenas due to changes in slope, and fewer lions, so the spotted hyenas tend to be there most often.

In addition to conducting the bone density survey of PNV (Tappen 1995), I actively searched for scavenging opportunities, as did the other anthropologists who were in the field with me. In the morning and late afternoon I took forays in the land rover to look for vultures and carcasses. Greg Laden also took independent forays in the Land Rover while I was conducting bone transects. We found only one scavenging opportunity during such active search but found most of the "scavengable food" while going about the business of conducting a pedestrian survey for bones. This research involved walking transects in different geomorphological and vegetation areas in the park for most of the day, nearly every day. Two or three Nande assistants who were very familiar with the park and one park guard usually accompanied me. All of these individuals kept an eye out for scavenging opportunities. If we saw any indication of a fresh carcass while conducting the pedestrian survey we dropped the bone survey to investigate. We did this at every opportunity that presented itself. The two other researchers working in the area most of the time were also constantly alert in separate areas to scavenging opportunities. This system of spotting scavenging opportunities is an analogy for early hominids that would opportunistically scavenge while out conducting other activities (e.g., foraging for other foods), as opposed to strategically searching for carcasses. The addition of the two other researchers finding carcasses is analogous to party members who had fissioned off on their own foraging forays. We found 14 carcasses in all (including carcasses nearly completely consumed except skin,

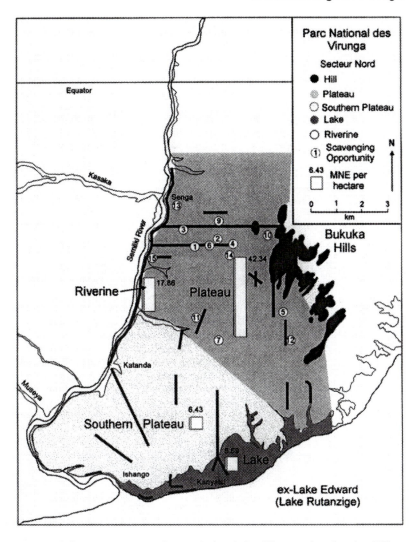

Figure 1.3. Secteur Nord of Parc National des Virunga showing the different zones in the park (defined in Tappen 1995), location of transects surveyed on foot for bones, average Minimum Number of Elements per hectare for each zone. The spatial distribution of scavenging opportunities (circles) partly reflects my own land-use patterns during my survey in PNV, but also a real lack of scavenging in the Southern Plateau and Lake zones.

brains, and marrow, but still fresh) and searched for one that was never found (Table 1.1). Late-access scavenging after carnivores are finished with a carcass is less dangerous and more opportunistic than "power scavenging" (e.g., Potts 1988; Bunn and Ezzo 1993), so these data can be used to model late-access scavenging. In such a model, a hominid uses the savanna for other foraging activities but will exploit any scavengable animal remains encountered, perhaps because of their relatively high proportion of fat and/or protein.

Table 1.1. Scavenging opportunities found in Parc National des Virunga.

Date		Species	Age	Sex	Method of Location	Food Available
7-16	1	Kob	Adult	M	Vultures landed while I drove to survey area	Brain, skin, marrow of all long bones except fem + hum
7-24	2	Kob	Adult	F	Vultures landed while surveying T3	All meat except viscera
7-28	3	Buffalo	Adult	F	Heard the kill from camp, then lions seen while driving by	All except anus
7-31 to 8-14 camp at Kanyatsi instead of Senga						
8-26	4	Kob	Juvenile		Vultures landed while I was surveying T7	all marrow + skin + brain
9-6	5	Kob	Adult		Found while I was surveying T9 then followed vultures	all marrow + skin + brain
9-9 to 9-14 renewing visa in Goma						
9-20	6	Kob	Old adult	M	Found by active searching for carcasses	all marrow + skin + brain
9-22	7	Kob	Neonate		Vultures landed while driving to T14	Marrow, organs, some flesh + brain
9-23	8	Followed 24 vultures in riverine area, but carcass never found				
10-5	9	Kob	Juvenile		Vultures landed while driving to T17	marrow + skin, no brain
10-22	10	Reedbuck	Adult	M	Found by Bellomo's workers during his experiments	All but internal organs + upper limb flesh
10-25	11	Kob	Adult	M	Heard the Kill during survey of T25 scared off 3 lions	Meat present, except upper limbs; brain, skin, marrow present
10-29	12	Kob	Adult	M	Vultures landed while I was excavating on T25	marrow, skin, brain only
10-30	13	Reedbuck	Adult	M	Found in water hole near Bellomo's fire experiments	All, later scavenged by hyena
11-10	14	Kob	Old adult	F	Vultures landed while driving to T25	Some rib meat, skin, brain all marrow except in hum + fem
11-22	15	Kob	?	?	Found by Laden	Marrow, brains, + skin, a little flesh

Scavenging in PNV

Foraging returns are usually thought of in terms of return per unit of time as a proxy for energy expenditure. This type of information is often lacking in studies of scavenging, making it difficult to assess return rates. Here, the mean number of days between scavenging opportunities was 9.3 (s.d. = 7.565 days). Using this experiment as an analog, a hominid conducting other activities in the savanna would encounter an average of less than one scavenging opportunity per week at the cost of minimal extra time. These encounters were distributed through time in a clumped pattern (rather than uniformly or randomly: Index of Dispersion of days between encounters is 6.14, $\chi^2 = 73.8$, $p < 0.05$; Ludwig and Reynolds 1988). Because of this clumpiness, there were periods when scavenging opportunities were frequent (e.g., 1 or 2 days apart) and periods when there were substantial gaps of time between the scavenging opportunities (e.g., 29 days between S.O #3 and S.O. #4). The longest gap occurred during the period we were camped in the Lake Zone at Kanyatsi. This lake zone also had very low bone deposition rates (Tappen 1995; and below). (One could argue that the marrow and brain-seeking hominids would have stayed in the Senga base camp, avoiding Kanyatsi, thus raising encounter rates and decreasing clumpiness. However, these low return periods constitute less than 10% of the total period of study.)

Twelve of the carcasses were found while conducting other types of research: four were found while driving/to or from a survey transect, five while working on bone transects themselves, and three during the research of the other members of my "foraging team." Two kills happened so close to us that we *heard* them occur, and with Land Rovers and park guards it was easy to call these scavenging opportunities, but early hominids may or may not have been able to confront the lions at these kills. More than half of the carcasses (eight) were found by spotting vultures landing on or near the animal while we were doing other research.

Only one carcass was found by active search in the Land Rover. Unfortunately, I did not collect data on the total amount of time I spent exclusively searching for carcasses by Land Rover, but it was about an hour or two several days a week, or about 6 hours per week. Only 1 of the 14 scavenging opportunities was found as the result of this active searching. In this study, active searching for carcasses was relatively unproductive (it had a high cost in terms of time and distance with low rates of return). Passive scavenging had dramatically lower costs.

It is possible that I lacked special knowledge that hominids would have employed to increase returns by active searching. On the other hand, I was able to cover large distances quickly in the Land Rover, so I may have actually been *better* than early hominids at surveying for carcasses. Nonetheless, even if hominids employed knowledge such as "I know that lion kills are most frequent in the open grassland area," the sporadic locations of individual kills almost certainly means hominids would have had to endure high costs of covering large distances to find them. It seems that the way hominids could increase their scavenging returns would be to deliberately center their activities around the lions' activities, and the risks of this could have been enormous. If hominids used special knowledge of the locations of tree-stored leopard kills, leopards would have likely changed their strategy of hiding carcasses in response (Lewis 1997). If these inferences are true, the costs of search are too high for active search by an early hominid. Scavenging opportunities are too unpredictable and rare to be highly ranked food items for early hominids. On the other hand, opportunistic late-access scavenging has low costs and returns that are not as high.

The spatial distribution of scavenging opportunities found during the PNV bone survey is shown in Figure 1.3. The concentration of scavenging opportunities just to the south and east of Senga reflects both my surveying behavior and the "real" distribution of scavenging opportunities. The concentration is along the car track I took to and from bone transects and to initiate active search for carcasses (our home base was at Senga 5) and so reflects places we were most often. However, we also spent a good deal of time in the Southern Plateau and Lake areas of the park, we were based for 2 weeks at Kanyatsi instead of Senga, we were often at Ishango, and many days were spent conducting transects in that part of the park—yet there are no scavenging opportunities recorded there. The more wooded areas are areas of poor availability of scavengable food because of two factors: hyenas are more common there, and ungulates are rare there. This pattern is in direct contrast to that observed in the Serengeti (Tappen 1995).

The Amount of Food

How important would this type of encounter scavenging be in the diet of hominids? Long bone marrow, brain, and skin were the only consumable portions left for half of these opportunities (Numbers 1, 4, 5, 6, 9, 12, and 15), and four more had some flesh in addition to this minimum (Numbers 7, 10, 11, and 14). Three of these included most of the carcass (Numbers 2, 3, and 13).

The modal scavenging opportunity at PNV is an adult kob with all marrow bones intact, which would yield at least 1600 kcal of high-quality fat (estimated by using the numbers for Grant's gazelle, which are the size of female kob (Blumenschine and Madrigal 1993). Add to this the fatty brain (e.g., Stiner 1991), and it seems reasonable to use the round number of 2,000 kcal as an estimate of the late-access, passive scavenging opportunity. According to the encounter rate of this study, this late-access scavenging would yield about 215 calories a day in marrow and brains. Depending on foraging group size and other resources in the environment, this could be considered anywhere from a large to a small patch. Being sympatric with the superpredators, it may be that hominids foraged in reasonably large groups rather than as isolated individuals as predator defense (van Schaik 1983). Nonetheless, the importance and rarity of fat in savanna ecosystems suggests that these patches would indeed be exploited (Speth and Spielman 1983; Speth 1989).

In addition to the scavenging opportunities, the proportion of whole versus broken marrow bones and whole to broken skulls found on the bone survey indicate of the amount of marrow and brain left behind by lions and hyenas in PNV (Table 1.2). Large carnivores (including secondary scavengers) leave behind 57% of the ungulate brains and 55% of the long bone marrow in PNV.

Which elements are most likely to contain marrow for the postcarnivore scavenger? In both the front and the hind limbs, the upper, more meaty bones (the humerus and femur) are broken open most frequently, the mid-leg bones (radius and tibia) are broken open less frequently, and finally the metapodials are broken open least often by the primary carnivores. Therefore, a late-access scavenger would get marrow most often from the mid to lower limb bones. Would it be reasonable to suggest that this would be the pattern in the past? To assess this it is best to understand the underlying mechanism as to why carnivores are breaking the bones in this order at PNV.

There are several factors that are involved in a carnivore's decision to break open a limb bone. Because carnivores can break their teeth while cracking bones (Van Valkenburgh 1988), the thickness of the cortical bone may cause the carnivores to

Table 1.2. Minimum Number of Elements (MNE) of bones with embedded food (marrow or brains), and the number left whole by the carnivores in PNV.

Skeletal Element	Total MNE	# Whole	% Whole
Cranium	139	79	57
Humerus	151	60	40
Radius	135	79	58
Metacarpal	97	62	64
Femur	133	60	45
Tibia	122	70	57
Metatarsal	104	77	74
Total Marrow Bones	742	408	55

avoid the lower bones. The humerus and femur are thinner walled and thus easier to break open [they tend to have a lower bulk density (Lyman 1984)], and even lions can break open these bones in ungulates the size of kob [they are at the upper end of size class 2 of Bunn (1982); they weigh between 50–120 kg (Haltenorth and Diller 1977)]. Breaking thick bones would not have been a problem for hammerstone wielding hominids, of course (Blumenschine 1986).

The amount of bone grease in the bone could be another motivating factor. Bone grease in kob long bones has not been measured, so I compared measurements from bison (while total amounts would certainly be different, basic anatomical similarities indicate that they are probably similar in rank order; this, of course, needs to be measured directly to be sure). The percentage of grease varies greatly with each portion of any skeletal element, making it difficult to generalize to whole bones. However, the breakage rank of the six marrowbones at PNV correlates well with rank order of the average weight of fat in the amount of "bone grease" found in each element (Brink 1997). (Only the metacarpal and metatarsal are switched in order, i.e., the metatarsal is broken less often than the metacarpal, but it has more bone grease.) Because bones need to be crushed and consumed for bone grease to be digested, and these bones were found in an identifiable state, amount of bone grease may not be the cause of the observed patterns.

The amount of bone marrow within the skeletal element varies between species and by age, sex, and condition of the animal (e.g., Blumenschine and Madrigal 1993; Bunn and Ezzo 1993). The amount of bone marrow in kob long bones has not been measured to my knowledge. However, bovid species are fairly consistent in rank order of marrow amounts, for example, of five African bovid species measured, wet weight of marrow (for adults) was consistently highest in the tibia, then in the femur, and the lowest amounts are most often in the metapodials (Blumenschine and Madrigal 1993: Table 1.2). Bone marrow amounts do not correlate with the bone-breaking strategies of the carnivores in PNV because the carnivores do not prefer the femur and tibia over the humerus and radius, although they do break the metapodials the least often (Table 1.3).

Rather than focusing on the amount of marrow, carnivores could exhibit preference in breaking open the bones based on the quality of the marrow. The percent-

Table 1.3. Comparison of the rank order in which marrow bones are left intact by carnivores in PNV compared to their rank order in bulk density and amount of marrow.

	% Whole-PNV	Bulk Density Midshaft-Bison (Lyman, 1984)	Bulk Density Midshaft-Deer (Lyman, 1984)	Amount of Marrow (Blumenschine and Madgrial, 1993)
Humerus	6	5.5	5	3
Femur	5	5.5	4	5
Tibia	4	1	1.5	6
Radius	3	4	3	4
Metacarpal	2	2	2	2
Metatarsal	1	3	1.5	1

age of lipids in bone marrow in reedbuck, buffalo, and waterbuck have been measured, and varies between 0.5% to well over 90%, depending on the state of the animal and the specific bone (e.g., Brooks et al. 1977; Blumenschine and Madrigal 1993). Marrow fat is mobilized last when animals are extremely stressed [perhaps bone grease is metabolized even after that (Brink 1997)]. Speth has pointed out that marrow in the lower limbs tends to contain more unsaturated fat than the upper limbs. Marrow is often metabolized progressively from the upper limb bones to lower limb bones, and is more quickly metabolized in the upper forelimb than upper hindlimb when animals are stressed (Speth 1983, 1987). Because the carnivores in PNV break the upper limb bones most often, the order of metabolism does not determine their choice of bones to break open for marrow. This is not surprising, given the lack of intense seasonal stress on the PNV ungulates, so the fat content of their marrow may be relatively high most of the time.

An explanation that fits the data well is that the PNV carnivores break open those bones that are most easily broken, jumping to the relatively dense tibia earlier in the sequence than expected, because of its high volume of marrow. This sequence does not correlate with the consumption sequence of carnivores in the Serengeti. There, carnivores consume marrow in the hindlimb first, then the forelimb (Blumenschine 1986). However, carnivores there tend to eat the marrow of all the bones of an animal if they eat any at all (Blumenschine 1986). This suggests that the skeletal elements containing marrow left for late-access scavengers can vary among habitats.

Blumenschine and Madrigal (1993: 580) suggest such scavenging "would not be sufficient to sustain an active system of food-sharing of the sort envisioned by Isaac (1978)" While early hominids may well have, and were even likely to have conducted such passive scavenging, its importance in creating selection pressures that resulted in changes in adaptations may have been minimal. It may have provided fat in lean times, but the rarity, and most important the unpredictability, of the locations and times of these scavenging opportunities would deem them impossible to strategically exploit without very high search costs or sprouting wings for soaring (Houston 1979). Strategic scavenging is unlikely because given such high search time, such scavenging opportunities are unlikely to be a highly ranked food item (Pyke et al. 1977).

It is interesting to consider whether such a late-access patch could cause conflict or cooperation if the foraging group size was larger than the amounts that could reasonably be shared between all of its members. In situations where large patches of food occur such that the same individual is unlikely to consistently find them, but rather, different individuals will come across them at different times, conditions arise for the evolution of reciprocal altruism *sensu* Trivers (1971) and food-sharing, *sensu* Isaac (1978) (Blurton-Jones 1984, 1987). Finding scavengable patches by spotting vultures landing on carcasses has an interesting characteristic: unlike fruit in a forest that can be relatively cryptic, these patches are often found from distances of more than a kilometer away. Foraging hominids spread out over a large area could all become aware of a scavengable patch more or less simultaneously. How they would then proceed to determine ownership and access would probably be determined by the rules of reciprocal and kin altruism (Winterhalder, this volume), who could get there the fastest, and rank.

I argued that scavenging opportunities would be more abundant in the open plains, away from the river and the lake in PNV today because (1) lions are more common in the open and hyenas are more common in the wooded riparian setting; (2) there were many more antelope in the open plains than in the more wooded areas; and (3) bone deposition was highest in these areas. The scavenging opportunities described here further support this hypothesis; there were 12 found in the open Northern Plateau, only 2 in the Riverine Zone, and none in the Lake Zone or Southern Plateau. There is further evidence: carnivores leave more whole bones in the open northern Plateau than along the river, lake, and more wooded Southern Plateau. Kob bones are used in this analysis because kob are by far the most abundant species found here, and by using one species I held more variables constant, such as body mass and bone density. The Southern Plateau, River, and Lake zones are lumped together as hyena-preferred habitats. In the Plateau, 43.28% of the long bones are whole ($N = 201$) while in the Southern Plateau, River and Lake habitats only 36.36% of the long bones are whole ($N = 44$, $\chi^2 = 6.037$, $p = 0.014$). Even more important than the proportion of broken to whole bones is the overall abundance of bones (reflected in N). To illustrate, compare the magnitude of the difference between the lion frequented Plateau and hyena-frequented Southern Plateau, Lake, and River Zones. Although the area surveyed for the Plateau was less than the other zones combined (56 hectares versus 126.05 hectares), it had nearly four times more bones in total [MNE (Minimum Number of Elements) = 2371 versus MNE = 1365] than the hyena habitat (Tappen 1995). Thus, although the sample size of scavenging opportunities is small, regarding spatial distribution, it concurs with the results of my bone deposition survey (where sampling is extensive) and with observations of the ecology of the park. In PNV scavenging would be more profitable in the open grassland.

In a study in the Maasai Mara area of Kenya, Dominguez-Rodrigo (ms) also found that scavenging would be more difficult in riparian woodlands than out in the open. There lions leave less meat in the riparian area than in the open plains. Furthermore, sporadic surplus killing and restricted consumption that would leave more food for scavengers was found to be highly unpredictable and so unlikely to be part of strategic foraging by hominids. I also found it very difficult to detect scavenging opportunities in the PNV woodlands—it is too difficult to follow vultures because trees block the view, and one cannot see where they land. There is no basic principle that scavenging is easier in woodlands near watercourses than in open grasslands.

Concluding Comments

I do not argue that the ecology of PNV should replace Serengeti ecology as our model of early hominid habitats. In some ways PNV is a better model, and in some ways, the Serengeti is a better model. For example, the species diversity in the Serengeti is higher than at PNV, which more closely approaches the Plio-Pleistocene—which was even more diverse (Fernandez-Jalvo et al. 1998). There are very dry periods in the fossil record for which the Serengeti may be a closer analog than PNV. I do suggest that it is time for us to stop emphasizing that the Serengeti is the best modern analog for the entire EEA.

The Serengeti model is too specific, and data from a wetter savanna indicate that it is unlikely that hominids were strategically scavenging. There are phylogenetic, biogeographic and archaeological (Bunn this volume) reasons to expect hunting. Scavenging opportunities are too unpredictable and rare to be a highly ranked food item for early hominids because deliberate search for them has a high rate of failure. If habitats have a dry season that is not as intense as that of the Serengeti, then seasonal deaths caused by starvation and drought will be more rare, and seasonal prediction becomes less reliable. It has proven extremely difficult to tell hunting from scavenging from the taphonomic and archaeological evidence from early sites such as FLK Zinj, mostly because of equifinality and complex taphonomic histories (Behrensmeyer 1987). There are many ways to interpret the data of skeletal part frequencies, age profiles, and cut mark frequencies at archaeological sites. Perhaps some evidence will come to light that clearly denotes hunting (as in the freak preservation of wooden weapons). Until then, other pieces of evidence such as tooth wear, stable carbon isotopes, and Sr/CA ratios can help us to address questions of the degree of meat consumption.

Acknowledgments   I thank Greg Laden for his help in all aspects of this work, and for many thought-provoking discussions on these issues. This work has been improved by discussions over the years with Ofer Bar-Yosef, Kay Behrensmeyer, Irv and Nancy DeVore, David Pilbeam, and Catherine Smith. However, I take full responsibility for its contents. I thank the members of the Semliki Research Expedition, the Conservateurs of Parc National des Virunga, and many local Nande from Kavinyunge, Democratic Republic of the Congo, for assistance in fieldwork. The L. S. B. Leakey Foundation, Sigma Xi, the Holt Family Charitable Trust, and a National Science Foundation grant to the Semliki Research Expedition funded this research.

REFERENCES

Behrensmeyer, A. K. 1987. Taphonomy and hunting. In *The Evolution of Human Hunting* (M. H. Nitecki and D. V. Nitecki, eds.), pp. 423–450. New York: Plenum Press.

Berger, L. R., and P. V. Tobias. 1996. A chimpanzee-like tibia from Sterkfontein, South Africa and its implication for the interpretation of bipedalism in *Australopithecus africanus*. *Journal of Human Evolution* 30:343–348.

Binford, L. R. 1981. *Bones: Ancient Men and Modern Myths*. New York: Academic Press.

Binford, L. R. 1983. *In Pursuit of the Past*. New York: Thames and Hudson, Inc.

Blumenschine, R. J. 1986. Carcass consumption sequences and archaeological distinction of scavenging and hunting. *Journal of Human Evolution* 15:639–660.

Blumenschine, R. J. 1987. Characteristics of an early hominid scavenging niche. *Current Anthropology* 28:383–407.

Blumenschine, R. J. 1989. A landscape taphonomic model of the scale of prehistoric opportunities. *Journal of Human Evolution* 18:345–371.

Blumenschine, R. J., and C. T. Madrigal. 1993. Variability in long bone marrow yields of East African ungulates and its zooarchaeological implications. *Journal of Archaeological Science* 20:555–587.

Blumenschine, R. J., and C. R. Peters. 1998. Archaeological predictions for hominid land use in the Paleo-Olduvai Basin, Tanzania, during lowermost Bed II times. *Journal of Human Evolution* 34:565–607.

Blurton Jones, N. G. 1984. A selfish origin for human food sharing: tolerated theft. *Ethology and Sociobiology* 5:1–3.

Blurton Jones, N. G. 1987. Tolerated theft, suggestions about the ecology and evolution of sharing, hoarding, and scrounging. *Social Science Information* 26:31–54.

Bonnefille, R., and G. Riollet, 1980. Palynologie, vegetation et climat de Bed I et Bed II a Olduvai, Tanzanie. In *Proceedings of the Eighth Pan-African Congress of Prehistory*, pp. 123–127. Nairobi.

Brink, J. W. 1997. Fat content in leg bones of *Bison bison*, and applications to archaeology. *Journal of Archaeological Science* 24:259–274.

Brooks, P. M., J. Hanks, and J. V. Ludbrook. 1977. Bone marrow as an index of condition in African ungulates. *South African Journal of Wildlife Research* 7:61–66.

Brunet, M., A. Beauvilain, C. Yves, E. Heintz, A. Moutaye, and P. David. 1995. The first australopithecine 2,500 kilometres west of the Rift Valley (Chad). *Nature* 378:273–275.

Bunn, H. T. 1982. Archaeological evidence for meat-eating by Plio-Pleistocene Hominids from Koobi Fora and Olduvai Gorge. *Nature* 291:574–577.

Bunn, H. T., and J. A. Ezzo. 1993. Hunting and scavenging by Plio-Pleistocene hominids: nutritional constraints archaeological patterns, and behavioral implications. *Journal of Archaeological Science* 20:365–398.

Capaldo, S. D., and C. R. Peters. 1994. Skeletal inventories from wildebeest drownings at Lakes Masek and Ndutu in the Serengeti ecosystem of Tanzania. *Journal of Archaeological Science* 22:385–408.

Cavallo, J. A., and R. J. Blumenschine. 1989. Tree stored leopard kills: expanding the hominid scavenging niche. *Journal of Human Evolution* 18:393–399.

Cerling, T. E. 1992. Development of grasslands and savannas in East Africa during Neogene. *Palaeogeography, Palaeoclimitology, Palaeoecology* 97:241–247.

Cerling, T. E., J. R. Bowman, and J. R. O'Neil. 1988. An isotopic study of a fluvial-lacustrine sequence: the Plio-Pleistocene Koobi Fora sequence, East Africa. *Paleogeography, Paleoclimatology, Paleoecology* 63:335–356.

Cerling, T. E., and R. L. Hay. 1986. An isotopic study of paleosol carbonates from Olduvai Gorge. *Quaternary Research* 25:63–78.

Clark, J. D. 1982. *The Cambridge History of Africa*. Cambridge: Cambridge University Press.

Clarke, R. J., and P. V. Tobias. 1995. Sterkfontein Member 2 foot bones of the oldest South African hominid. *Science* 269:521–524.

Dart, R. A. 1925. *Australopithecus africanus*: the man-ape of South Africa. In *Nature* 115:195–199.

deMenocal, P. B. 1995. Plio-Pleistocene african climate. *Science* 270:53–59.

Delvingt, W. 1978. *Ecologie de L'Hippopotame* (Hippopotamus amphibius. *L.*) *Au Parc National des Virunga (Zaire)*. Belgique: Faculte des Sciences Agronomiques de L'Etat Gembloux.

Dominguez-Rodrigo, M. ms. Flesh availability and bone modification in carcasses consumed by lions.

Estes, R. D. 1969. Territorial behavior of the wildebeest (*Connochaetes taurinus* Burchell, 1823). *Zeitschrift fur Tierpsychologie* 26:284–370.

Fernandez-Jalvo, Y., C. Denys, P. Andrews, T. Williams, Y. Dauphin, and L. Humphrey. 1998. Taphonomy and palaeoecology of Olduvai Bed-I (Pleistocene, Tanzania). *Journal of Human Evolution* 34:137–172.

Foley, R. 1987. *Another Unique Species*. New York: John Wiley & Sons.

Foley, R. 1995/96. The adaptive legacy of human evolution: a search for the environment of evolutionary adaptedness. *Evolutionary Anthropology* 4:194–203.

Fryxell, J. M., and A. R. E. Sinclair. 1988. Seasonal migration by white-eared kob in relation to resources. *African Journal of Ecology* 26:17–31.

Fryxell, J. M., J. Greever, and A. R. E. Sinclair. 1988. Why are migratory ungulates so abundant? *The American Naturalist* 131:781–798.

Gebo, D. L. 1996. Climbing, brachiation, and terrestial quadrupedalism: historical precursors of hominid bipedalism. *American Journal of Physical Anthropology* 101:55–92.

Haltenorth, T., and H. Diller. 1977. *A Field Guide to the Mammals of Africa Including Madagascar*. London: Williams Collins Sons and Co., Ltd.

Hay, R. L. 1976. *Geology of the Olduvai Gorge*. Berkeley: University of California Press.

Hay, R. L. 1990. Olduvai Gorge; a case history in the interpretation of hominid paleo-environments in East Africa. *Geological Society of America Special Paper* 242:23–37.

Houston, D. C. 1979. The adaptations of scavengers. In *Serengeti: Dynamics of an Ecosystem* (A. R. E. Sinclair and M. Norton-Griffiths, eds.), pp. 263–286. Chicago: University of Chicago Press.

Isaac, G. L. 1978. Food sharing and human evolution: archaeological evidence from the Plio-Pleistocene of East Africa. *Journal of Anthropological Research* 34:311–325.

Janis, C. M., and P. B. Wilhem. 1993. Were there mammalian pursuit predators in the tertiary? Dances with wolf avatars. *Journal of Mammalian Evolution* 1:103–125.

Kappelman, J. 1984. Plio-Pleistocene environments of Bed I and lower Bed II, Olduvai Gorge, Tanzania. *Paleogeography, Paleoclimatology, Paleoecology* 48:171–196.

Kappelman, J. 1986. Plio-Pleistocene Marine-continental correlation using habitat indicators from Olduvai Gorge Tanzania. *Quaternary Research* 25:141–149.

Kappelman, J., T. Plummer, L. Bishop, S. Appleton, and A. Duncan. 1997. Bovids as indicators of Plio-Pleistocene paleoenvironments of East Africa. *Journal of Human Evolution* 32:229–256.

Kingston, J. D., B. Marino, and A. Hill. 1994. Isotopic evidence for neogene hominid paleoenvironments in the Kenya Rift Valley. *Science* 264:955–959.

Lewis, M. E. 1997. Carnivoran paleoguilds of Africa: implications for homind food procurement strategies. *Journal of Human Evolution* 32:257–288.

Little, P. D. 1996. Pastoralism, biodiversity and the shaping of savanna landscapes in East Africa. *Africa* 66:37–51.

Ludwig, J. A., and J. F. Reynolds. 1988. *Statistical Ecology*. New York: John Wiley & Sons.

Lyman, R. L. 1984. Bone density and differential survivorship of fossil classes. *Journal of Anthropological Archaeology* 3:259–299.

Maddock, L. 1979. The migration and grazing succession. In *Serengeti: Dynamics of an Ecosystem* (A. R. E. Sinclair and M. Norton-Griffiths, eds.), pp. 104–129. Chicago: University of Chicago Press.

McGrew, W. C., P. J. Baldwin, and C. E. G. Tutin. 1981. Chimpanzees in a hot, dry and open habitat: Mt. Assirik, Senegal, West Africa. *Journal of Human Evolution* 10:227–244.

McNaughton, S. J. 1990. Mineral nutrition and seasonal movements of African migratory ungulates. *Nature* 345:613–615.

McNaughton, S. J., F. F. Banyikwa, and M. M. McNaughton. 1997. Promotion of the cycling of diet-enhancing nutrients by African grazers. *Science* 278:1798–1800.

Moore, J. 1996. Savanna chimpanzees, referential models and the last common ancestor. In *Great Ape Societies* (W. C. McGrew, L. F. Marchant, and T. Nishida, eds.), pp. 275–292. Cambridge: Cambridge University Press.

Murray, M. G. 1994. Specific nutrient requirements and migration of wildebeest. In *Serengeti II—Research, Management and Conservation of an Ecosystem* (A. R. E. Sinclair and P. Arcese, eds.), pp. 231–256. Chicago: University of Chicago.

Norton-Griffiths, M. 1979. The influence of grazing, browsing, and fire on the vegetation dynamics of the Serengeti. In *Serengeti: Dynamics of an Ecosystem* (A. R. E. Sinclair and M. Norton-Griffiths, eds.), pp. 310–352. Chicago: University of Chicago Press.

Norton-Griffiths, M., D. Herlocker, and L. Pennycuick. 1975. The patterns of rainfall in the Serengeti ecosystem, Tanzania. *East African Wildlife Journal* 13:347–374.

Orians, G. H., and J. H. Heerwagen. 1992. Evolved responses to landscapes. In *The Adapted Mind: Evolutionary Psychology and the Generation of Culture*. (J. H. Barkow, L. Cosmides, and J. Tooby, eds.), pp. 555–579. New York: Oxford University Press.

Pickering, T. R., and J. Wallis. 1997. Bone modifications resulting from captive chimpanzee mastication: implications for the interpretation of Pliocene archaeological faunas. *Journal of Archaeological Science* 24:1115–1127.

Pilbeam, D. 1996. Genetic and morphological records of the hominoidea and hominid origins: a synthesis. *Molecular Phylogenetics and Evolution* 5:155–168.

Plummer, T. W., and L. C. Bishop. 1994. Hominid paleoecology at Olduvai Gorge, Tanzania as indicated by antelope remains. *Journal of Human Evolution* 27:47–75.

Plummer, T. W., and C. Stanford. 2000. Analysis of a bone assemblage by chimpanzees at Gombe National Park, Tanzania. *Journal of Human Evolution* 39:245–265.

Potts, R. 1988. *Early Hominid Activities at Olduvai*. New York: Aldine.

Prell, W. L., and E. Van Campo. 1986. Coherent response of Arabian Sea upwelling and pollen transport to late quaternary monsoonal winds. *Nature* 323:526–528.

Pyke, G. H., H. R. Pulliam, and E. L. Charnov. 1977. Optimal foraging: a selective review of theory and tests. *The Quarterly Review of Biology* 52:137–154.

Quade, J., T. E. Cerling, and J. R. Bowman, 1989. Developed Asian monsoon revealed by marked ecological shift during the latest Miocene in Northern Pakistan. *Nature* 342:163–165.

Rose, M. 1991. The process of bipedalization in hominids. In *Origine(s) de la Bipedie chez les Hominides* (Y. Coppens and B. Senut, eds.), pp. 37–47. Paris: CNRS.

Schaller, G. B. 1972. *The Serengeti Lion: A Study of Predator-Prey Relations*. Chicago: University of Chicago Press.

Schaller, G. B., and G. P. Lowther. 1969. The relevance of carnivore behavior to the study of early hominids. *Southwestern Journal of Anthropology* 25:307–340.

Sept, J. M. 1992. Was there no place like home? A new perspective on early Hominid archaeo-
    logical sites from the mapping of chimpanzee nests. *Current Anthropology* 33:187–207.
Sept, J. M. 1994. Beyond bones: archaeological sites, early hominid subsistence, and the
    costs and benefits of exploiting wild plant foods in east African riverine landscapes.
    Journal of Human Evolution 27:295–320.
Sikes, N. E. 1994. Early hominid habitat preferences in East Africa: paleosol carbon isoto-
    pic evidence. *Early Hominid Behavioural Ecology* 27:25–45.
Sinclair, A. R. E. 1979. Dynamics of the Serengeti ecosystem. In *Serengeti: Dynamics of
    an Ecosystem* (A. R. E. Sinclair and M. Norton-Griffiths, eds.), pp. 1–30. Chicago:
    University of Chicago Press.
Sinclair, A.R.E. and P. Arcese. 1995. Serengeti in the context of worldwide conservation
    efforts. In *Serengeti II: Dynamics, Management and Conservation of an Ecosystem*,
    pp. 31–46. Chicago: University of Chicago Press.
Sinclair, A.R.E., M. D. Leakey, and M. Norton-Griffiths, 1986. Migration and hominid
    bipedalism. *Nature* 324:307–308.
Sinclair, A. R. E., and M. Norton-Griffiths. 1979. *Serengeti: Dynamics of an Ecosystem.*
    Chicago: University of Chicago Press.
Sinclair, A. R. E., and M. Norton-Griffiths, ed. 1995. *Serengeti II: Dynamics of an Ecosys-
    tem.* Chicago: University of Chicago Press.
Spencer, L. M. 1997. Dietary adaptations of Plio-Pleistocene Bovidae: implications for
    hominid habitat use. *Journal of Human Evolution* 32:201–228.
Speth, J. D. 1987. Early hominid subsistence strategies in seasonal habitats. *Journal of
    Archaeological Science* 14:13–29.
Speth, J. D. 1989. Early hominid hunting and scavenging: the role of meat as an energy
    source. *Journal of Human Evolution* 18:329–343.
Speth, J. D., and D. D. Davis. 1976. Seasonal variability in early hominid predation. *Sci-
    ence* 192:441–445.
Speth, J. D., and K. Spielman. 1983. Energy source, protein metabolism, and hunter-gatherer
    subsistence strategies. *Journal of Anthropological Archaeology* 2:1–31.
Stiner, M. C. 1991. Food procurement and transport by human and non-human predators.
    Journal of Archaeological Science 18:455–482.
Tappen, M. 1995. Savanna ecology and natural bone deposition. *Current Anthropology*
    36:223–260.
Tappen, M., and R. W. Wrangham. in press. Recognizing hominoid modified bones: the
    taphonomy of red colobus bonespartially digested by free-ranging chimpanzees in the
    Kibale Forest, Uganda.
Trivers, R. L. 1971. The evolution of reciprocal altruism. *Quarterly Review Biology* 46:35–57.
van Schaik, C. P. 1983. Why are diurnal primates living in groups? *Behavior* 85:91–117.
Van Valkenburgh, B. 1988. Incidence of tooth breakage among large, predatory mammals.
    American Naturalist 131:291–302.
Vesey-Fitzgerald, D. F. 1963. Central African Grasslands. *Journal of Ecology* 51: 243–274.
Western, D. 1973. *The Structure, Dymamics, and Changes of the Amboseli Ecosystem.* Ph.D.
    Dissertation, University of Nairobi.

2

Taphonomy of the Swartkrans Hominid Postcrania and Its Bearing on Issues of Meat-Eating and Fire Management

Travis R. Pickering

Introduction

The Plio-Pleistocene cave site of Swartkrans (Gauteng, South Africa) has long been a valuable source for evidence of early hominid evolution and behavior. Most recently, the meticulous excavations and analyses of Swartkrans fossils under the direction of C. K. Brain (1965–1986) have prompted exciting new ideas about the behavioral and technological capabilities of early hominids in South Africa (summarized in Brain 1981, 1993a, 1993b; Brain et al. 1988). Particularly, the juxtaposition of cutmarked and burned bones, with stone tools and hominid fossils in Swartkrans Member 3 raises an important question. The question is whether the spatial association between stone tools, cutmarked and burned bones, and the remains of hominid individuals implicates these particular individuals as the parties completely or partially responsible for these cultural traces that indicate the utilization of large mammal carcasses and a mastery of fire.

While all the hominid craniodental remains from Member 3 are attributed to *Australopithecus (Paranthropus) robustus* (Grine 1993), is it reasonable to assume that *Homo* cf. *erectus* was also present in the vicinity at this time because this species is represented along with *A. robustus* in the earlier Members 1 and 2 (Grine 1993)? Traditionally, it has been assumed that *A. robustus* was the less adept of the two species, both culturally and technologically (e.g., Robinson 1972), and that this "disadvantage" may have accounted for the extinction of the robust australopithecines. Referring specifically to the Swartkrans evidence, Brain (1988: 315) has stated, "It may be surmised that the management of fire by early human [*Homo*] populations could have contributed to the extinction of the 'robust' australopithecines if these two kinds of hominids had been in direct competition. Therefore, it may be more than a coincidence that the last glimpse of . . . *A. robustus* in Member 3 at Swartkrans coincides with the first appearance of evidence for controlled fire in the cave's stratigraphic record."

Although fire can be employed effectively as a defensive tool against predators, evidence presented in this paper does *not* directly support the notion that the hominid individuals represented in Swartkrans Member 3 were technologically competent fire managers capable of warding off large carnivores. Patterns of hominid postcranial skeletal part representation and bone surface modifications on hominid specimens at Swartkrans are consistent from the earliest, prefire/precutmark Members 1 (Lower Bank, LB) and 2 to the later-occurring Member 3. This consistency indicates that the mode of hominid carcass part deposition was likely identical through all three members at Swartkrans. I will argue that the predominant mode of hominid carcass part deposition was via the defecation and regurgitation by large carnivores that had consumed the hominid carcasses elsewhere on the landscape. Because, as with the previous two members, hominid postcranial remains were deposited in Member 3 as by-products of carnivore ingestion, their spatial association with cutmarked and burned bones also recovered from Member 3 may be entirely fortuitous. The Discussion section of this chapter will address whether or not this indicates that just these particular hominid individuals were merely unfortunate. Alternatively, a particular species of hominid may have been less adept at predator evasion than another possessing a culture more like that of modern humans, which included meat-eating and the ability to harness the power of fire.

The Swartkrans Cave Site

Historical Overview of the Hominid Taphonomy at Swartkrans

The Swartkrans cave site's complex stratigraphy (see Brain 1993c) spans much of the Plio-Pleistocene and preserves the fossilized remains of numerous animals (Brain 1981). This chapter is concerned with the hominid components of the most recently excavated (1979–1986) faunal assemblages from Swartkrans Member 1 (LB) (1.8 million years old, m.y.), Member 2 (1.5 m.y.), and Member 3 (1.0 m.y.). Based on his analyses of the Swartkrans fauna, Brain (e.g., 1981, 1993b) maintains that during Member 1 and Member 2 times carnivores were largely responsible for the deposition of the macrovertebrate faunal assemblages in the cave. Specifically, with regard to the primate fossil subassemblages, Brain (1993b: 260) contends that, ". . . hominids and baboons used the entrance of the cave as a sleeping site and that they were preyed upon there occasionally by leopards and, possibly, sabre-toothed cats, which ate their victims in the cavern itself." In support of this contention, Brain (1981) described numerous fossil hominid specimens from the earlier excavated Member 1 Hanging Remnant with certain and probable carnivore-inflicted feeding damage.

Although it is well documented that extant cercopithecines and hominids are preyed upon by carnivores such as leopards (*Panthera pardus*), lions (*Panthera leo*), and spotted hyenas (*Crocuta crocuta*) (reviewed in Rose and Marshall 1996; see references therein), only a few systematic studies of carnivore consumption of primate carcasses have been undertaken. Brain (1981) conducted experiments, feeding baboons (*Papio anubis*) to three captive cheetahs (*Acinonyx jubatus*), to a captive leopard, to two wild brown hyenas (*Hyaena brunnea*), and to an unknown number of spotted hyenas. Based on his observations of these feeding episodes and analyses of the resultant bone refuse, Brain (1981) concluded that primate skeletons are more completely destroyed by feeding carnivores than bovid skeletons of comparable size. Further, Brain (1981, 1993b) intimated that this may be the explanation for the relative abundance of primate craniodental remains and a paucity of their postcranial bones in Swartkrans Member 1 Hanging Remnant (and in the Lower Bank and Member 2).

Swartkrans Member 3 is more complex taphonomically. Brain (1993b) argued that because of the presence of cutmarked bones, hominids, in addition to carnivores, were also partially responsible for the accumulation of bones in this member. Brain (1993b, 1993d) also presented evidence, in the form of burned bones, that he believes indicates Member 3 hominids managed fire. He has alternated his opinion on the taxonomic identity of the presumed fire-tenders in Member 3. [See the quote above from Brain (1988: 315) in which he implicates early *Homo*, and compare it to his later statement: "The Swartkrans investigation has been characterized by surprises, so an australopithecine [*A. robustus*] fire-tender would not be out of character for this remarkable cave . . ." (Brain 1993b: 263)].

An Alternative Interpretation of Hominid Skeletal Part Deposition at Swartkrans

The present study is supportive of Brain's primary hypothesis that carnivores were major accumulators of the macrovertebrate fauna in Swartkrans Members 1, 2, and 3. But the results of this study do not support the suggestion that complete hominid carcasses were introduced into the cave only to have most of the postcrania deleted and/or rendered unidentifiable by carnivore feeding at the site. Rather, it is argued that hominid postcranial skeletal part representation in the fossil assemblage is probably a nearly accurate reflection of the elements originally deposited in the site in all three members under consideration.

In 1995, Janette Wallis and I collected large carnivore scats at Ugalla, a chimpanzee (*Pan troglodytes*) field site in western Tanzania. I observed an anecdotal similarity between skeletal part representation of cercopithecine bones extracted from these carnivore scats and the hominid fossil postcrania from Swartkrans. This observed similarity prompted me to test the hypothesis that carnivore regurgitation and/or defecation may have been the taphonomic mechanism responsible for the deposition of much of the hominid postcrania at Swartkrans. To test this hypothesis I analyzed: (1) an assemblage of cercopithecine bones derived from carnivore scat; and (2) what I refer to as a "refuse" assemblage of cercopithecine bones. The refuse assemblage consists of those bones not ingested by the feeding carnivores. Considering the *broad* similarities between cercopithecine and hominid physiques, if the Swartkrans hominid fossils were deposited in the manner hypothesized by

Brain, the fossils should then bear similarities to the modern refuse assemblage in terms of skeletal part representation and bone surface modifications. If, on the other hand, the hypothesis that the hominid postcrania was deposited mainly by carnivore defecation and/or regurgitation is correct, then the Swartkrans hominid assemblages should more closely resemble the modern, scat-derived assemblage in terms of skeletal part representation and bone surface damage.

My experimental findings support the carnivore-voiding hypothesis rather than Brain's original bone-refuse hypothesis. Based on these findings, I contend that a predominance of hominid metapodials and phalanges at Swartkrans indicates that these elements entered the faunal assemblages, at least in part, through large carnivore regurgitation and/or defecation.

Materials

The Modern Samples

This study utilizes two modern samples of cercopithecine bones extracted from large carnivore waste material. These samples are combined and hence referred to collectively as the scat sample. Part of the scat sample consists of baboon (*P. anubis*), blue monkey (*Cercopithecus mitis*), and redtail monkey (*C. ascanius*) bones derived from five separate carnivore (primarily leopard) regurgitation and scat piles collected at the chimpanzee field site of Ugalla (Tanzania) in 1995. The second component of the scat sample consists of baboon bones extracted from the scats of a large male leopard housed at the Moholoholo Wildlife Rehabilitation Centre, South Africa, and from the scats of a leopard and a spotted hyena housed at African Game Services, South Africa. These captive carnivores were fed the baboon carcasses under controlled, experimental conditions (described below).

The other modern sample that this study includes is referred to as the refuse sample. This is an assemblage of noningested primate bone residues from the large carnivore feeding experiments conducted at the Moholoholo Wildlife Rehabilitation Centre and African Game Services. Thus, I have the "complete" package of feeding residues (i.e., both carcass refuse and scats) for the South African baboon carcasses.

The Fossil Sample

The fossil sample analyzed in this study consists of the Swartkrans hominid postcranial remains excavated under the direction of C. K. Brain between 1979–1986, and described by Susman (e.g., 1988a, 1988b, 1989, 1993; Brain et al. 1988; see Susman 1993: 118, Table 1 for a specimen list). Three specimens require brief discussion here. The cervical vertebra specimen, SKW 4776, was included in the skeletal part analysis but was excluded from the bone surface modification analysis because it was missing from the collection at the time of my study and could not be examined. Two other specimens originally described by Susman, SKX 12814 and

SKX 31117, were excluded from *both* the skeletal part and bone surface modification analyses because I consider them nonhominid.

Methods

Tanzania

A landscape taphonomy study was conducted at the chimpanzee field site of Ugalla, Tanzania, in 1995. Belt transects were established throughout the area and surveyed for carcasses, bones, and carnivore waste material. A total of 30 carnivore regurgitations and feces were collected from Ugalla, five (16.7 %) of which contained the remains of blue monkeys and/or redtail monkeys and baboons.

South Africa

Ten baboons were culled using a large caliber rifle in late 1997 and early 1998 on the Bergpaan Soutwerke near Vivo, South Africa. Each culled primate was weighed, eviscerated (gastrointestinal tract only was removed per the request of the carnivore keepers, leaving the respiratory and cardiovascular systems in place) and weighed again. Intact weights ranged from 14.2–32.6 kg (mean, 22.0 kg), and eviscerated weights ranged from 11.2–26.6 kg (mean, 17.44 kg). The carcasses were then frozen for transport to the Moholoholo Wildlife Rehabilitation Centre in the Northern Province and African Game Services in the Northwestern Province.

At Moholoholo, six of the baboon carcasses were thawed and presented one at a time to a captive male leopard (3 years old, 75 kg). In each experimental feeding episode, an individual baboon carcass was presented to the leopard, which had not eaten for 48 hours. After inducing the leopard into a smaller, attached holding cage, the baboon carcass was placed in the larger, outdoor enclosure where the leopard is typically held. The leopard was then reintroduced into the larger enclosure and allowed to feed on the baboon carcass for as long as it desired. Depending on the size of the carcass, the leopard would feed intermittently for about 12–72 hours. After cessation of leopard interest in an individual carcass, the leopard was induced back into the holding cage and all primate remains (soft tissues and bones) were collected for study. In addition, all leopard regurgitations and feces resulting from a feeding episode were collected for study. The baboon carcasses were fed concurrently, so there are no other types of "prey" remains mixed with the collected primate materials. A similar procedure was undertaken at African Game Services, with two carcasses going to a large leopard and two going to a spotted hyena (ages and weights of the carnivores unknown).

All collected regurgitations and scats from both the Tanzanian and South African samples were disaggregated manually, using dental picks and tweezers. "Prey" bones and soft tissues were removed and separated into two categories— identifiable specimens and nonidentifiable specimens. Identifiable specimens from the wild-collected Tanzanian sample were divided further into primate and nonprimate categories. The primate remains were included in the analyses reported on here.

Swartkrans

Each fossil specimen was examined both macroscopically and under a low power stereomicroscope at various magnifications.

Observations, Analyses, and Results

Experimental Results

Based on observations of the experimental feeding episodes, a "typical" pattern of baboon carcass consumption was as follows. The carnivore entered the thorax via the incision cut by me earlier to remove the gastrointestinal tract, consuming the heart and lungs along with whole upper ribs (first through third), sternal ends of lower ribs, clavicles, and the sternebrae. As feeding continued on the trunk, vertebrae, ribs, scapulae, and pelves were damaged and sometimes consumed. Limb musculature was consumed, and joints were often destroyed. When consumed, hands and feet were eaten starting with the fingers and proceeding proximally towards the wrist and ankles. Often, articulated digits from the proximal to distal phalanx were removed from the hand or foot at the articulation of the metapodial and first phalanx. These digit units were swallowed whole without mastication, as Willey and Synder (1989) have described for wolf (*Canis lupus*) consumption of articulated cervid phalangeal units. In addition, entire carpal and tarsal masses were sometimes swallowed whole, as Marean (1991) has described for spotted hyena consumption of bovid skeletons. Skull elements were never eaten, although the carnivores often moved the baboon carcasses by the heads, inflicting puncture marks on the crania and mandibles.

Comparison of Postcranial Skeletal Element Abundance

Metapodials and phalanges make up a large proportion of the total hominid postcranial material from all three members at Swartkrans, whether considered as a proportion of the postcranial total number of identified specimens (tNISP) or the postcranial total minimum number of elements (tMNE) (see Susman 1993: 118, Table 1). Two-by-two table tests (chi-square) were conducted to evaluate the significance of differences in the percentages of digit elements (i.e., combined MNE of metapodials plus phalanges) versus all other postcrania (i.e., combined MNE of all nonmetapodial/phalanx specimens) between the modern and fossil assemblages (see Tables 2.1 and 2.2 for raw NISP and MNE estimates in the modern refuse and scat assemblages). Results of these tests indicate that the modern refuse and scat assemblages are significantly different in their proportion of digit elements versus all other postcrania ($\chi^2 = 51.728$, $p < 0.001$). Further, the scat assemblage is significantly different in proportions of digit elements and all other postcrania from

Table 2.1. Modern refuse assemblage skeletal part representation (NISP/MNE).

Element	Carcass Number										
	1	2	3	4	5	6	7	8	9	10	Total
CRAN	1/1	1/1	1/1	1/1	1/1	1/1	1/1	1/1	1/1	1/1	10/10
1/2MAN	2/2	2/2	2/2	2/2	2/2	2/2	2/2	2/2	2/2	2/2	20/20
ATLAS	1/1	1/1	0	1/1	0	1/1	1/1	0	1/1	0	6/6
AXIS	1/1	1/1	0	1/1	0	1/1	0	0	1/1	0	5/5
CERV	0	3/2	1/1	0	0	0	0	0	4/4	0	8/7
THOR	1/1	0	0	4/3	0	10/10	6/4	3/2	13/8	2/2	39/30
LUM	1/1	0	2/2	3/3	0	9/6	1/1	0	4/4	4/3	24/20
VERT	0	3/1	0	4/1	0	0	3/1	0	5/2	1/1	16/6
SAC	0	0	0	1/1	0	1/1	1/1	1/1	1/1	0	5/5
CAUD	0	0	4/4	0	0	0	5/5	0	0	3/3	12/12
RIB	1/1	0	5/3	12/8	6/5	21/20	13/9	9/9	17/14	5/3	89/72
CLAV	0	0	0	0	0	0	0	0	0	0	0
STERN	0	0	0	0	0	0	0	0	0	0	0
SCAP	1/1	0	3/2	1/1	0	1/1	2/1	2/2	2/2	2/2	14/12
HUM	2/2	2/2	2/2	1/1	2/2	3/2	2/2	2/2	2/2	1/1	19/18
RAD	0	1/1	2/2	2/1	2/2	2/2	1/1	2/2	2/2	0	14/13
ULN	1/1	0	2/2	1/1	2/2	2/2	1/1	2/2	2/2	1/1	14/14
CARP	0	0	0	0	0	18/18	0	9/9	0	0	27/27
MTC	0	0	0	0	0	10/10	0	9/9	0	0	19/19
PHLX I	0	0	0	10/10	0	15/15	9/9	9/9	0	6/6	49/49
PHLX II	0	0	0	8/8	0	12/12	8/8	7/7	2/2	6/6	43/43
PHLX III	0	0	10/10	0	0	15/15	10/10	5/5	3/3	7/7	50/50
1/2PEL	0	0	0	2/2	2/2	2/2	2/2	2/2	2/2	0	12/12
FEM	1/1	2/2	2/2	2/2	2/2	2/2	2/2	2/2	2/2	3/2	20/19
PAT	0	0	0	0	0	0	0	0	0	0	0
TIB	1/1	2/2	0	2/2	2/2	2/2	2/2	2/2	2/2	2/2	19/19
FIB	0	1/1	2/2	2/2	2/1	1/1	2/2	2/2	2/2	3/2	17/15
TAR	0	0	0	14/14	0	7/7	14/14	0	14/14	14/14	63/63
MTT	0	0	0	10/10	0	5/5	6/6	0	7/7	4/4	32/32
LBS	1/-	0	1/-	3/-	3/-	1/-	0	6/-	5/-	0	20/-
FRG	0	6/-	8/-	6/-	1/-	11/-	16/-	3/-	4/-	8/-	63/-

Abbreviations: NISP, number of identified specimens; MNE, minimum number of elements; CRAN, cranium; 1/2MAN, hemimandible; CERV, cervical vertebra; THOR, thoracic vertebra; LUM, lumbar vertebra; VERT, indeterminate vertebra; SAC, sacrum; CAUD, caudal vertebra; CLAV, clavicle; STERN, sternebra; SCAP, scapula; HUM, humerus; RAD, radius; ULN, ulna; CARP, carpals; MTC, metacarpal; PHLX I, first phalanx (manual + pedal); PHLX II, second phalanx (manual + pedal); PHLX III, third phalanx (manual + pedal); 1/2PEL, os coxae; FEM, femur; PAT, patella; TIB, tibia; FIB, fibula; TAR, tarsals; MTT, metatarsal; LBS, unidentifiable long bone shaft fragment; FRG, unidentifiable bone fragment.
    Sesamoids are excluded from this table and all analyses.

that expected in a hypothetical bone assemblage composed of 10 complete baboon skeletons ($\chi^2 = 62.085$, $p < 0.001$); while the refuse assemblage is not significantly different in these proportions when compared to the hypothetical assemblage of 10 complete baboons ($\chi^2 = 1.5765$, $0.5 > p > 0.2$). In other words, the refuse assemblage retains a roughly similar proportion of digit elements ($n = 193$, 33.98%) as that expected in complete carcasses (for 10 complete carcasses, $n = 760$, 36.84%), while the

Table 2.2. Modern scat assemblage skeletal part representation (NISP/MNE).

Element							Scat Occurrence									Total
	1	2	3	4	5	6	7	8	9	10	11	12	13	14	15	
CRAN	0	15/1	0	0	0	0	0	0	0	0	0	0	0	0	0	15/1
1/2MAN	0	2/1	0	0	0	0	0	0	0	0	0	1/1	0	0	0	2/1
ATLAS	0	0	0	0	0	1/1	0	0	0	1/1	0	0	0	0	0	2/2
AXIS	0	0	0	0	0	0	0	0	0	1/1	0	0	0	0	0	1/1
CERV	0	1/1	0	0	0	2/1	0	3/1	0	0	0	0	0	2/1	0	7/4
THOR	4/2	4/4	7/4	3/2	3/2	2/2	3/2	3/3	0	0	0	0	1/1	0	0	31/22
LUM	5/2	6/2	4/2	0	2/2	3/1	5/2	0	1/1	0	0	0	1/1	0	0	27/13
VERT	14/2	5/1	10/3	4/2	20/4	11/3	3/1	14/3	13/2	6/2	0	0	3/1	1/1	0	104/25
SAC	1/1	1/1	0	0	0	0	0	0	0	0	0	0	0	0	0	2/2
CAUD	0	8/6	3/3	0	2/2	1/1	0	1/1	1/1	4/3	3/1	0	5/1	0	1/1	21/18
RIB	13/4	6/3	15/2	3/1	6/2	5/2	5/1	12/4	2/2	7/4	0	0	1/1	0	0	82/27
CLAV	0	1/1	0	0	0	0	0	0	0	0	1/1	0	0	0	0	2/2
STERN	0	0	0	0	0	0	0	0	0	0	0	0	0	0	0	0
SCAP	2/1	1/1	0	0	1/1	0	0	0	0	0	1/1	0	1/1	0	0	6/5
HUM	1/1	2/2	0	0	2/2	0	0	0	0	0	0	0	2/1	0	0	7/6
RAD	1/1	0	0	0	0	0	0	0	0	0	0	0	0	0	0	3/2
ULN	0	2/1	0	0	0	0	0	0	0	0	0	0	0	0	0	2/1
CARP	6/6	0	4/4	7/7	20/18	0	16/16	3/3	19/18	8/8	3/3	0	0	0	1/1	87/84
MTC	0	0	2/1	3/2	10/6	0	8/5	0	11/9	4/2	0	0	1/1	0	1/1	37/26
PHLX I	6/4	11/9	2/1	3/2	17/14	1/1	10/6	11/9	12/10	9/7	1/1	0	8/8	0	1/1	92/73
PHLX II	5/4	10/10	8/7	3/3	14/14	1/1	8/8	6/6	8/8	8/8	3/3	0	7/7	4/4	1/1	86/84
PHLX III	5/5	12/12	12/12	4/4	15/15	2/2	9/9	10/10	9/9	5/5	3/3	0	6/6	3/3	1/1	96/96
1/2PEL	0	1/1	0	0	0	0	0	0	0	0	0	0	0	0	0	1/1
FEM	0	0	0	0	1/1	1/1	0	0	1/1	0	0	0	1/1	0	0	5/5
PAT	0	2/2	0	0	1/1	0	0	0	0	0	0	0	0	0	0	3/3
TIB	0	0	0	0	2/2	0	0	0	0	0	0	0	0	0	0	2/2
FIB	0	0	0	0	0	0	0	0	0	0	0	0	0	0	0	0
TAR	0	1/1	5/5	0	9/9	1/1	0	12/12	0	0	1/1	0	0	0	0	29/29
MTT	0	0	0	0	0	12/5	0	11/8	0	0	1/1	0	0	0	0	24/14
MTP	10/6	4/2	4/3	0	8/5	0	0	1/1	0	6/3	0	0	0	0	0	33/20
LBS	45/-	22/-	9/-	21/-	13/-	0	18/-	26/-	3/-	46/-	0	0	6/-	2/-	0	211/-
FRG	83/-	104/-	79/-	59/-	124/-	34/-	77/-	102/-	33/-	21/-	14/-	0	12/-	36/-	22/-	800/-

See legend to Table 2.1 for abbreviations.

Scat occurrences 1–10 are associated with Carcasses 1–10 (see Table 2.1), while occurrence 11–15 were recovered from the scat of wild, free-ranging carnivores and have no analyzed, associated refuse remains.

Sesamoids are excluded from this table and all analyses.

scat assemblage diverges from the "complete carcass" proportions in possessing a higher relative representation of digit elements ($n = 313$, 55.2%) (Figure 2.1).

Results of chi-square tests between the Swartkrans assemblages demonstrate that there is not a significant difference between Members 1 (LB) and 2 in terms of relative digit element proportions ($\chi^2 = 0.566$, $0.5 > p > 0.2$). The Member 3 assemblage could not be included in chi-square analyses because it lacks any nondigit postcranial specimens, and the chi-square test cannot be conducted with cell frequencies of less than 1. The Member 3 assemblage, being composed *entirely* of metapodial and phalanx specimens, is an extreme of the general pattern evident in all three members of a preponderance of digit elements over other postcranial bones. Raw NISP and MNE estimates are calculated from Susman (1993: 118, Table 1), with digit element proportions (based on postcranial tMNE) as follows: Member 1 (LB), 68.75% ($n = 11$); Member 2, 54.55% ($n = 6$); Member 3, 100% ($n = 10$) (Figure 2.1).

Comparisons of the modern assemblages to the Swartkrans samples indicate that the modern scat assemblage is not significantly different from the Swartkrans Member 1 (LB) and Member 2 assemblages in its proportion of digit elements versus all other postcrania. Chi-square values are: Scat vs. Swartkrans Member 1 (LB), 1.156 ($0.5 > p > 0.2$); scat vs. Swartkrans Member 2, 0.00172 ($p > 0.5$).

In contrast to the modern scat assemblage, the modern refuse assemblage is significantly different from the Swartkrans Members 1 (LB) and 3 assemblages in its proportion of digit elements versus all other postcrania, while there is not a significant difference between the refuse assemblage and Member 2. Chi-square values

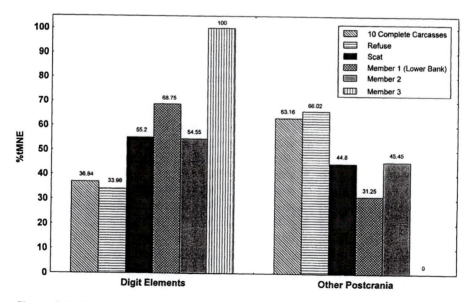

Figure 2.1. Comparison of proportion of digit elements (metapodials + phalanges) versus all other postcranial in: a hypothetical assemblage of complete baboon carcasses; the modern refuse assemblage; the modern scat assemblage; Swartkrans Member 1 (Lower Bank); Swartkrans Member 2; Swartkrans Member 3.

are as follows: refuse vs. Swartkrans Member 1 (LB), 8.27 ($0.01 > p > 0.001$); refuse vs. Member 2, 2.023 ($0.2 > p > 0.1$).

In summary, the modern experimental assemblages differ significantly from one another, with the refuse sample retaining proportions of digit element specimens comparable to that expected in an assemblage composed of complete primate carcasses. In contrast, the modern scat assemblage displays digit element specimen proportions higher than that expected in an assemblage of complete carcasses. In this regard, the scat assemblage is similar to the Swartkrans assemblages, two of which (Members 1 and 3) also display digit element proportions higher than those expected in an assemblage composed of complete carcasses ([10 Complete Carcasses versus Member 1(LB), 6.94 ($0.01 > p > 0.001$); 10 Complete Carcasses versus Member 2, 1.474 ($0.5 > p > 0.2$)]. This pattern is taken to an extreme in the Member 3 assemblage, in which the *only* postcranial elements represented are phalanges and metapodials (Pickering 1999).

Comparison of Bone Surface Modifications

Taphonomists are well aware that the action of carnivore gastric acid can corrode, etch, smooth, and destroy bone tissue (see, e.g., d'Errico and Villa 1997). These types of obvious bone damage have been documented in both modern and fossil assemblages that had voiding carnivores as contributing taphonomic agents.

Many bone specimens from the modern scat assemblage are modified by carnivore digestive processes. The scat assemblage has a postcranial tNISP of 792. Of this tNISP, 628 specimens display bone surface damage attributes resulting from carnivore digestion. The only scat assemblage specimens to remain completely unscathed *derive from the hands and feet*. One hundred sixty-four metapodials and phalanges recovered in the scat assemblage show *no* traces of cortical bone damage. Many of the recovered phalanges were articulated and covered by skin, soft tissues, and/or nails (Figure 2.2), which completely protected the underlying bone from the destructive forces of carnivore digestive acids.

A total MNE of 99 phalanges from the scat assemblage were modified by carnivore digestive acids. The majority of these damaged phalanges ($n = 62$) do *not* display intensive corrosion of the bone surfaces (again, probably because for most of their passage through the carnivore digestive tract they were protected by overlying skin and ligaments), as do other recovered postcranial specimens. Rather, these 62 phalanx specimens show only light erosion of bone cortex along one or both metaphyses, occurring alternatively on the ventral, dorsal, or both aspects of the specimens.

Phalangeal metaphyses are porous and thus perhaps more susceptible than other bone portions to being damaged by gastric acids. d'Errico and Villa (1997: 16) describe a similar phenomenon of gastric acid excavating out the "predisposed" nutrient foramina of long-bone specimens.

Subtle metaphyseal erosion is apparent on five Swartkrans specimens (SKX 5016, SKX 13476, SKX 19576, SKX 27431, and SKX 27504), and I interpret this damage as also resulting from these pieces being modified moderately by carnivore digestion. In addition, three other Swartkrans specimens are heavily corroded (SKW 2954, SKX 5020) and rounded (SKX 5019) on their heads, probably as the result of passing through the digestive tracts of carnivores.

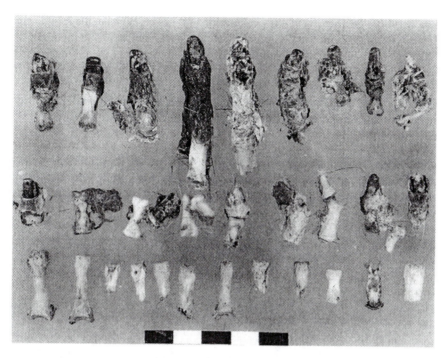

Figure 2.2. Sample of phalanges recovered from the modern scat assemblage in various states of preservation and articulation. Note the presence of outer soft tissue and keratinous nails on some specimens, which protected many of these pieces from corrosion by carnivore digestive acids.

Summary and Interpretation of Experimental Results

This study has confirmed that carnivore defecation and regurgitation are important taphonomic processes, creating discrete concentrations of often highly identifiable bones, bone fragments, and other indigestible tissues of prey animals. Metapodials and phalanges as well as hand/foot skin and finger/toe nails are especially well represented in these concentrations as identifiable body parts.

The skeletal part composition of the scat-derived assemblage seems to be the result of a combination of factors. First, while various postcranial body parts were ingested, many of the recovered hand and foot bones are phalanges that entered the carnivores' digestive systems as whole, articulated digits. These articulated units were often sheared off orally at the articulation of the metapodial and proximal phalanx but not masticated, merely swallowed whole.

Greater relative digit element representation is also partly a result of the relative identifiablity of the recovered bone specimens. Bones and bone portions from other regions of the postcranial skeleton were also consumed in addition to hand and foot bones. But, because most metapodials and phalanges were not heavily masticated before swallowing, as with ingested bone from other body regions, there was little destruction and fragmentation of these elements in the initial stages of carnivore ingestion. Finally, greater relative survivability of metapodials and phalanges in an identifiable condition is, in part, a function of the protection from gastric juices afforded by a predominance of tough, ligamentous connective tissues in this body region, as well as the indigestible, keratinous nails that partially sheath the third phalanges. A paucity of stomach acid-etched phalanges in the scat assemblage supports this contention, as well as the presence of hand/foot skin and finger/toe nails.

Thus, it seems that in addition to preferential consumption by carnivores, inherent properties of hand and foot elements likely increase the probability not only of their survival through a carnivore's digestive system, but also of their identifiability once through the system. Numerous researchers report a predominance of prey metapodials and phalanges in large carnivore scats of disparate taxonomic and geographic origins (e.g., Binford 1981; Siegfried 1984; Willey and Synder 1989; Fay et al. 1995). The observations of these workers support the supposition presented here, that—in addition to other factors—it is intrinsic aspects of these body parts that account for their surviving carnivore ingestion in identifiable states.

Summary and Interpretation of Comparative Results

The results of the analyses discussed above support the hypothesis that the Swartkrans postcranial material was deposited by voiding carnivores rather than by carnivores feeding in the cave. Proportions of metapodials and phalanges are similar between the modern scat assemblage and all three Swartkrans assemblages, while these proportions are different between the modern refuse assemblage and the Swartkrans materials. Few bones display ancient surficial modifications in the Swartkrans assemblages (see below). Most of those fossil specimens that are damaged are phalanges and metapodials that appear only moderately affected by carnivore digestive acids, as do most of the modified phalanges in the modern scat assemblage.

In anticipation of various arguments that my interpretations of these data may raise, I have chosen to address two here. First, my study indicates that carnivore-created refuse assemblages should contain high proportions of primate head and limb bones, with percentage survival (%survival) values (for derivation of %survival values, see Brain 1981) for crania, mandibles, and all limb bones at or above 65% (Figure 2.3). However, the experimental derivation of my results may have conditioned this outcome more than "typical" carnivore feeding behavior. There are at least two variables that if altered could have differentially affected the experimental outcome. First, individual baboon carcasses were presented to individual carnivores; this procedure eliminated feeding competition, a factor known to condition the completeness of carcass consumption (e.g., Blumenschine 1986). Second, although the carnivores fed on the baboons until satiated, there was no subsequent scavenging of carcass remains after initial consumer interest ceased; secondary scavenging could have destroyed and/or removed skeletal elements containing within-bone nutrients.

Modification of these variables, rendering the refuse assemblage the result of more intensively exploited resources, could well have altered the consequent skel-

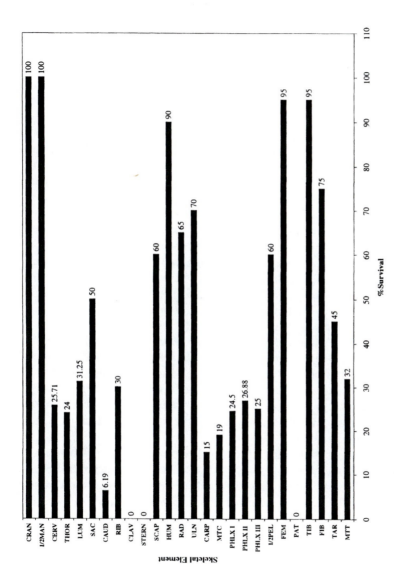

Figure 2.3. Baboon skeletal part percentage survival values (% survival) in the modern refuse assemblage. See legend to Table 2.1 for skeletal element abbreviations. Derivation of percentage survival values is described in Brain (1981). It is based on expected values of skeletal elements found in a complete skeleton. Thus in an assemblage composed of 10 complete baboon carcasses, there is expected to be 10 complete crania, one for each baboon represented—and so forth for each element category. Expected values for *Papio* cervical vertebrae, thoracic vertebrae, lumbar vertebrae, caudal vertebrae, sternebrae, and ribs are derived from Schultz (1961).

etal part ratios. I was able to examine two of the baboon skeletons from Brain's (1981) cheetah-primate feeding experiments. Skeletal part representation conforms broadly to the pattern evident in my larger refuse sample. However, these skeleton remnants, like my refuse sample, were also derived under experimental conditions.

In contrast to the experiments conducted independently by Brain and myself with large cats, wild brown hyenas consumed nearly completely a baboon carcass tied to a tree by Brain (1981)—leaving only skull fragments behind. While these results are suggestive, they still only represent a single, artificial event and are enigmatic, especially when compared to the less extensive destruction imparted by the jaws of the more powerfully equipped spotted hyenas used in my experiments. At this point, I can only suggest that more naturalistic field observations must be made of the taphonomic fate of dead primates—but, until this occurs, the experimental results presented here provide the most complete and well-reported data available on the subject.

A second argument that can be raised against my interpretations is that the modern, comparative assemblages were conditioned by only two cycles of destructive processes—carnivore consumption, and carnivore digestion. In contrast, the skeletons that contributed to the Swartkrans fossil assemblages were subjected to an unknown number of destructive cycles and forces during their transitions through death assemblages and deposited assemblages into fossil assemblages. It is well documented that less dense bones and bone portions are deleted more frequently from faunal assemblages at various postmortem stages, regardless of the agent(s) of destruction and the effector(s) applied to the bones (reviewed in Marean and Frey 1997; see references therein). Thus, it may be argued that the observed hominid skeletal part ratios at Swartkrans are merely the product of attritional processes eliminating less-dense bones from whole skeletons over time.

There have been a few studies of modern human (*Homo sapiens*) skeletal part densities (e.g., Boaz and Behrensmeyer 1976; Ricklan 1986; Morden 1991; Willey et al. 1997). The results of none of these studies are ideal for testing whether the Swartkrans hominid skeletal part ratios are correlated with relative bone density. The results are inadequate because of weaknesses in density calculation methods and because most studies did not calculate density values for all skeletal elements and/or element portions.

Morden (1991) has conducted the most complete study, which included most human skeletal parts but, unfortunately, excluded the sternum, patella, and hand and foot sesamoids. In addition, Morden did not differentiate between the various podial bones, lumping all carpals together and all tarsals together for her study. Still, her "suspended density" (i.e., suspended weight/volume of wet bone) values are informative heuristically for the question at hand.

Because the data manipulated in this case contains so many ties (Table 2.3), the Gamma statistic was calculated rather than Spearman's R. While there is a weak positive correlation between Morden's density values and %survival values for the Swartkrans postcrania (Gamma = 0.355), this correlation is not significant at the $p < 0.01$ level ($p = 0.033$). This suggests that density-mediated processes had only a minimal effect on the resultant skeletal part ratios.

Table 2.3. Swartkrans hominid percentage survival
values versus density of human postcranial elements.

Element	%Survival	Density
CERV	0.332	1.05
THOR	0.193	1.04
LUM	0	1.12
SAC	0	1.05
RIB	0	1.09
CLAV	0	1.09
SCAP	0	1.13
HUM	2.33	1.15
RAD	3.49	1.22
ULN	1.16	1.40
CARP	0.145	1.03
MTC	0.698	1.07
mPHLX I	1.395	1.14
mPHLX II	2.616	1.09
mPHLX III	0.698	1.20
1/2PEL	0	1.03
FEM	0	1.08
TIB	0	1.06
FIB	0	1.18
TAR	0	1.19
MTT	0.698	1.11
pPHLX I	0.233	1.11
pPHLX II	0.581	1.12
pPHLX III	0	1.03

See legend to Table 2.1 for abbreviations. Additional abbreviations included
here: mPHLX I, manual phalanx I; mPHLX II, manual phalanx II; mPHLX III,
manual phalanx III; pPHLX I, pedal phalanx I, pPHLX II, pedal phalanx II;
pPHLX III, pedal pahalanx III.

Derivation of percentage survival values is described in Brain (1981). Expected values are based on a total hominid minimum number of individuals,
MNI (all three assemblages combined) of 43. Based on teeth, Grine (1993)
calculated the following MNI estimates: Member 1 (Lower Bank), 13; Member 2, 21; Member 3, 9.

Density measures are suspended density values for modern human skeletal parts from Morden (1991: 125, Table 13).

Finally, it is necessary to address the issue of the abundant hominid skull remains from Swartkrans Members 1 (LB), 2, and 3. The assumption that hominid
postcranial taphonomy is at variance with hominid craniodental taphonomy in these
members is implicit in the preceding sections of this chapter, but will now be explored in more detail.

Of the 69 hominid craniodental specimens recovered from Swartkrans Members 1 (LB) ($n = 12$), 2 ($n = 37$), and 3 ($n = 20$) (Grine 1993), *none* display evidence
of mammalian tooth damage (Pickering unpublished data). Based on the behavioral observations made during the experiments reported here, it is not unexpected
that primate heads would be ignored by carnivores from a nutritional standpoint.

In none of the experiments did the carnivores feed on baboon head soft tissues nor did they breech the crania and mandibles to gain access to within-bone nutrients. Regardless, 8 of 10 baboon crania in the modern refuse assemblage display obvious tooth marks in the form of punctures and scores. This damage resulted from the carnivores moving the baboon carcasses by the primates' heads.

It is unreasonable to expect direct comparability between the crania in the modern refuse sample and the Swartkrans hominid crania in terms of bone damage. Most of the skull punctures in the modern sample are through baboon neurocrania and eye sockets, while these regions are not even represented in the fossil samples. Thus, while the Swartkrans hominid skull parts *could* be the residue of carnivores feeding on complete carcasses, there are no independent lines of evidence available (e.g., bone surface modifications on skull remains) to support or refute this idea; skeletal part representation alone is not sufficient.

In addition, because there is no strong indication of skeletal part density mediating the relative survival of postcrania in the Swartkrans assemblages, it does seem that the hominid skull and postcranial samples were deposited as the result of separate processes. If the skulls and postcrania arrived together as whole skeletons at the site, and density mediated processes were subsequently responsible for the resulting pattern of skeletal part representation, it would be expected that in addition to the abundant teeth, there should also be a pattern of dense postcranial parts preserved. As discussed above, there is only a weak, positive correlation between postcranial %survival values and suspended density that is not significant.

In summary, it appears that skull and postcranial elements recovered from Swartkrans Members 1 (LB), 2, and 3 have varying taphonomic histories. The carnivore-voiding hypothesis seems to best explain the postcranial deposition while the origin of the craniodental material is more enigmatic.

Discussion

R. L. Susman (e.g., 1988a, 1988b, 1989) has argued that hominid manus elements recovered from Swartkrans display all the requisite morphology for Oldowan stone tool production. While the finding that these same bones were deposited (at least in part) as by-products of carnivore ingestion might seem to contradict a posited causal association of these particular hominids with stone tools in all three members and with cutmarked and burned bones in Member 3, there are scenarios that can reconcile Susman's conclusions with mine. Most obviously, technological competency may not have been necessary to effectively evade predation. Or, perhaps predation is not the issue, but rather the deposited hominid postcrania derived from the scavenged carcasses of individuals who had died on the veld of other causes.

Unfortunately, it is not possible to attribute the carnivore-deposited postcrania to a particular hominid species. Based on craniodental evidence, at least two species of early hominids, *Australopithecus robustus* and *Homo* cf. *erectus*, are represented in Members 1 (LB) and 2 (Grine 1993). And while Member 3 contains only *A. robustus* skull remains (Grine 1993), it seems reasonable to assume that early *Homo* was also present in the vicinity at this time. The presence of two contemporaneous hominid species in the Swartkrans deposits has complicated matters when attempting to attribute responsibility for the material evidence of hominid culture preserved at the site. Did only one of the hominid species possess a "human-like" adaptation, including fire technology and regular meat-eating, while the other was behaving in a decidedly less human-like fashion, being preyed upon in the open veld near the cave? Or, were both *A. robustus* and *Homo* individuals endowed with the morphological and cognitive abilities to exploit large mammalian prey and to harness fire for defensive purposes, implying that the individuals preyed upon were simply unfortunate souls, regardless of their degree of technological competency?

There *is* a predominance of *A. robustus* over *Homo* individuals at Swartkrans based on counts of skull elements (e.g., Grine 1993). But, the findings presented here suggest that the hominid craniodental remains have a separate (and comparatively unclear) taphonomic history from the postcrania, most of which was deposited in Swartkrans as an end-product of carnivore digestion. By extension, there is no longer a compelling basis to argue that "simple statistical probability" requires that isolated postcrania from Swartkrans are attributed to *A. robustus* simply because of the predominance of this species at the site in skull remains (*contra* Susman 1989, 1991, 1993). Trinkaus and Long (1990: 420) are correct in stating that such an argument "relies on the assumption that the [species] frequency distribution of craniodental remains determines the underlying frequency distribution of postcranial remains, since no 'statistical probability' exists without knowledge of, or the reasonable assumption of, the underlying distribution." Separate taphonomic histories for the skulls and postcrania preclude access to this knowledge. Thus, the findings reported here indicate that it is still unclear if one species of early hominid was preferentially preyed upon (or scavenged) and deposited at Swartkrans over the other. This conclusion prohibits attributing archaeological evidence (i.e., burned and cutmarked bones) that indicates modern, human-like behavior such as fire management and meat-eating to one early hominid species over another.

Acknowledgments   I thank Henry Bunn and Craig Stanford for the invitation to this conference and for financial support of my attendance. Fieldwork in Tanzania was supported by the LSB Leakey Foundation and Sigma Xi. Many thanks go to my co-workers at Ugalla: Janette Wallis, Jeanne Sept, Frank Mbago and Jim Moore, who invited me to participate and made it possible by his generous financial support. Work in South Africa was supported by the Wenner-Gren Foundation and the National Science Foundation. I thank Phillip Tobias, Ron Clarke, Lee Berger, and Francis Thackeray for permission to study fossils in their care. I thank the following people for their help with the feeding experiments: Robbie Emmerich, Theuns Broekman, Brian Jones, Ricardo Ghiazza, Simon Hall, and Lex Hes. I thank Ron Clarke and Kathy Kuman for their support of my research and for their friendship. Thanks to Lucinda Backwell and Heidi Fourie for everything. I thank Randy Susman for useful discussions on Swartkrans. For various pieces of advice and assistance, I thank Leslie Eisenberg, Margaret Schoeninger, Matt G. Hill, and Colin Menter. I thank the other conference participants and two anonymous reviewers for many helpful suggestions. Thanks to Tim White and Nick Toth for their kindness in sharing data. As always, I thank my family, Evelyn, Robert, and Lance. A very special thanks goes to my wife, Anneliese. Finally, I wish to thank Bob Brain and the whole Brain family for all the hospitality and kindness they have shown to me while I've been in South Africa and for their interest in my work. Bob, you blazed a wide trail, I'm just trifling with details. I dedicate this chapter to you.

REFERENCES

Binford, L. R. 1981. *Bones: Ancient Men and Modern Myths.* New York: Academic Press.

Blumenschine, R. J. 1986. Carcass consumption sequences and the archaeological distinction between hunting and scavenging. *Journal of Human Evolution* 15:639–659.

Boaz, N. T., and A. K. Behrensmeyer. 1976. Hominid taphonomy: transport of human skeletal parts in an artificial fluvial environment. *American Journal of Physical Anthropology* 45:53–60.

Brain, C. K. 1981. *The Hunters or the Hunted? An Introduction to African Cave Taphonomy.* Chicago: University of Chicago Press.

Brain, C. K. 1988. New information from the Swartkrans Cave of relevance to "robust" Australopithecines. In *Evolutionary History of the "Robust" Australopithecines* (F. E. Grine, ed.), pp. 311–316. New York: Aldine de Gruyter.

Brain, C. K. ed. 1993a. *Swartkrans: A Cave's Chronicle of Early Man.* Pretoria: Transvaal Museum.

Brain, C. K. 1993b. A taphonomic overview of the Swartkrans fossil assemblages. In *Swartkrans: A Cave's Chronicle of Early Man* (C. K. Brain, ed.), pp. 257–264. Pretoria: Transvaal Museum.

Brain, C. K. 1993c. Structure and stratigraphy of the Swartkrans Cave in the light of the new excavations. In *Swartkrans: A Cave's Chronicle of Early Man* (C. K. Brain, ed.), pp. 23–33. Pretoria: Transvaal Museum.

Brain, C. K. 1993d. The occurrence of burnt bones at Swartkrans and their implications for the control of fire by early hominids. In *Swartkrans: A Cave's Chronicle of Early Man* (C. K. Brain, ed.), pp. 229–249. Pretoria: Transvaal Museum.

Brain, C. K., C. S. Churcher, J. D. Clark, F. E. Grine, P. Shipman, R. L. Susman, A. Turner, and V. Watson. 1988. New evidence of early hominids, their culture and environment from the Swartkrans cave, South Africa. *South African Journal of Science* 84:828–835.

d'Errico, F., and P. Villa. 1997. Holes and grooves: the contribution of microscopy and taphonomy to the problem of art origins. *Journal of Human Evolution* 33:1–31.

Fay, J. M., R. Carroll, J. C. Kerbis-Peterhans, and D. Harris. 1995. Leopard attack on and consumption of gorillas in the Central African Republic. *Journal of Human Evolution* 29:93–99.

Grine, F. E. 1993. Description and preliminary analysis of new hominid craniodental fossils from the Swartkrans Formation. In *Swartkrans: A Cave's Chronicle of Early Man* (C. K. Brain, ed.), pp. 75–116. Pretoria: Transvaal Museum.

Marean, C. W. 1991. Measuring the post-depositional destruction of bone in archaeological assemblages. *Journal of Archaeological Science* 18:677–694.

Marean, C. W., and C. J. Frey. 1997. Animal bones from caves to cities: reverse utility curves as methodological artifacts. *American Antiquity* 62:698–711.

Morden, J. L. 1991. *Hominid Taphonomy: Density, Fluvial Transport, and Carnivore Consumption of Human Remains with Application to Three Plio/Pleistocene Hominid Sites.* Ph.D. dissertation. Rutgers, The State University of New Jersey, New Brunswick, NJ.

Pickering, T. R. 1999. *Taphonomic Interpretations of the Sterkfontein Early Hominid Site (Gauteng South Africa) Reconsidered in Light of Recent Evidence.* Ph.D. dissertation. University of Wisconsin, Madison.

Ricklan, D. E. 1986. The influence of mass, volume and density on the frequency of recovery of fossil hominid hand and wrist bones. *Human Evolution* 1:399–404.

Robinson, J. T. 1972. *Early Hominid Posture and Locomotion*. Chicago: University of Chicago Press.

Rose, L., and F. Marshall. 1996. Meat-eating, hominid sociality, and home bases revisited. *Current Anthropology* 37:307–338.

Schultz, A. H. 1961. Vertebral column and thorax. In *Primatologia: Handbook of Primatology* (H. Hofer, A. H. Schultz, and D. Starck, eds.), pp. 1–66. New York: S. Karger.

Siegfried, W. R. 1984. An analysis of faecal pellets of the brown hyaena on the Namib coast. *South African Journal of Zoology* 19:61.

Susman, R. L. 1988a. Hand of *Paranthropus robustus* from Member 1, Swartkrans: fossil evidence for tool behavior. *Science* 240:781–784.

Susman, R. L. 1988b. New postcranial remains from Swartkrans and their bearing on the functional morphology and behavior of *Paranthropus robustus*. In *Evolutionary History of the "Robust" Australopithecines* (F. E. Grine, ed.), pp. 149–172. New York: Aldine de Gruyter.

Susman, R. L. 1989. New hominid fossils from the Swartkrans Formation (1979–1986 excavations): postcranial specimens. *American Journal of Physical Anthropology* 79:451–474.

Susman, R. L. 1991. Species attribution of the Swartkrans thumb metacarpals. *American Journal of Physical Anthropology* 86:549–552.

Susman, R. L. 1993. Hominid postcranial remains from Swartkrans. In *Swartkrans: A Cave's Chronicle of Early Man* (C. K. Brain, ed.), pp. 117–136. Pretoria: Transvaal Museum.

Trinkaus, E., and J. C. Long 1990. Species attribution of the Swartkrans Member 1 first metacarpals: SK 84 and SK 5020. *American Journal of Physical Anthropology* 83:419–424.

Willey, P., A. Galloway, and L. Synder. 1997. Bone mineral density and survival of elements and element portions in the bones of the Crow Creek Massacre victims. *American Journal of Physical Anthropology* 104:513–528.

Willey, P., and L. Synder 1989. Canid modification of human remains: implications for time-since-death estimations. *Journal of Forensic Sciences* 34:894–901.

3

Neandertal Hunting and Meat-Processing in the Near East
Evidence from Kebara Cave (Israel)

John D. Speth
Eitan Tchernov

Introduction

Few would question the assertion that by the end of the Upper Paleolithic (about 10,000 years ago) humans were highly competent hunters, going about the business of hunting much as any modern forager would, and probably employing a broadly similar range of techniques, strategies and decision-making criteria. While much less is known about the foraging behavior of Plio-Pleistocene hominids, most would also probably agree that their behavior was quite unlike that of modern hunter-gatherers, differing not just because early hominids possessed a far more rudimentary technology, but also because they probably went about it in ways that have few analogues among contemporary foragers. Thus, we seem to have fairly clear notions about the nature of human foraging at either end of the Pleistocene—scavenging and small-game hunting at the beginning, highly skilled large-game hunting by the end (see Bunn this volume).

In contrast, our view of what foragers were like during the intervening 1.5 to 2.0 million years remains shrouded in controversy. Not long ago, it was widely accepted that *Homo erectus* and Neandertals were both accomplished big-game hunters, slaughtering mammoth, bison, aurochs, and other large and dangerous prey. Then, about two decades ago, this "modern myth," as Binford (1981) bluntly called it, came under harsh attack, the victim of new taphonomic approaches that were joining the standard arsenal of archaeological tools. The big-game hunters of the Lower and Middle Paleolithic found themselves demoted to bumbling scavengers (Binford 1981, 1984) and, in the most extreme view, came to be seen as dimwitted proto-humans lacking planning depth, language, food-sharing, and a gender-based division of labor. Within the last decade, however, we have seen the beginnings of another about-face in our perceptions of premodern human foraging as a growing number of faunal studies, now making full use of taphonomic approaches, are once again elevating at least the later Neandertals to the rank of hunter, though *Homo erectus* and perhaps earlier Neandertals still remain suspended in limbo.

In fact, our understanding of Neandertal hunting behavior is now in an exciting state of flux although much of the recent progress on this front has been obscured by the attention surrounding modern human origins (Lewin 1993). Nevertheless, the picture that is unfolding is one of a formidable hunter, capable of killing even the adults of Eurasia's largest and most dangerous Ice Age animals (e.g., Jaubert et al. 1990; Farizy et al. 1994). We certainly do not wish to imply that there is any clear consensus on this issue—far from it. Although few continue to see Neandertals as dimwitted scavengers, the field is still divided when it comes to deciding whether Neandertal hunting was merely a "technologically challenged" variant of what modern hunters do or instead a fundamentally different way of going about one's subsistence pursuits that reflects an unbridgeable behavioral or cognitive chasm between "them" and "us."

One way to begin to resolve this conundrum is to move beyond the initially productive, but ultimately rather limiting, focus on whether Neandertals hunted or scavenged big game to consider the broader complex of behaviors involved in Neandertal use of animal resources, big or small (see Stiner this volume). In other words, we need to look not just at how megafauna were procured, but also at such things as the seasonal timing of procurement, the determinants of prey choice, the role of utility and other factors in the selection of particular carcass parts for transport, the manner in which animals were processed and cooked, and so forth. Obviously this list is far from exhaustive, but these are a few of the core issues that provide a reasonable place to begin such an expanded inquiry.

This chapter explores some of these issues, using the Middle Paleolithic ungulate remains from Kebara Cave (Israel) as a case study. The success of such an endeavor, of course, ultimately hinges on first conducting a thorough taphonomic evaluation of the assemblage to determine to what extent and in what ways the material has been altered by natural agencies unrelated to human behavior. However, to keep this chapter within reasonable bounds, we touch upon these issues only briefly, referring the reader to other reports that deal head-on with the nuts and bolts of Kebara's taphonomy (Bar-Yosef et al. 1992; Speth and Tchernov 1998). Instead, we jump quickly into the heart of the matter, looking at the fauna as a source of insight about several interrelated aspects of Neandertal use of animal resources. What emerges from this study are glimpses of subsistence-related behaviors and shifting site functions that will seem very familiar to archaeologists who work with Upper Paleolithic and more recent foragers. While we certainly cannot conclude on this basis alone that Levantine Neandertals and modern foragers possessed comparable behavioral or cognitive wherewithal, we find nothing in these data to suggest that Neandertals differed in their use of animal resources in fundamental ways that would set them apart either from their anatomically more modern-looking quasi-contemporaries or from their Upper Paleolithic successors in the region.

Background and Methods

Kebara is a large cave on the western face of Mt. Carmel, 30 kilometers (km) south of Haifa and 2.5 km east of the Mediterranean shoreline. Two major excavations at the site—the first by Stekelis between 1951 and 1965 (Schick and Stekelis 1977), the second by a French-Israeli team codirected by Bar-Yosef and Vandermeersch between 1982 and 1990 (Bar-Yosef et al. 1992)—yielded thousands of animal bones from a 4-m deep sequence of Middle Paleolithic deposits dating between 60,000 and 48,000 years ago.

The present study examines a sample of about 21,000 ungulate bones. Because details concerning the nature of the faunal sample, its taphonomic history, and our methods of coding and analysis have been presented elsewhere (Davis 1977; Speth and Tchernov 1998), only a brief recap is provided here. Most of the ungulate remains derive from two taxa—mountain gazelle (*Gazella gazella*, 60%) and Persian fallow deer (*Dama mesopotamica*, 21%). Other animals, represented by small numbers of specimens, include roe deer (*Capreolus capreolus*, <1%), red deer (*Cervus elaphus*, 6%), wild goat (*Capra* cf. *aegagrus*, 1%), wild boar (*Sus scrofa*, 5%), and aurochs (*Bos primigenius*, 7%). A few equid remains are also present, though these have not yet been coded.

Nearly half of Kebara's Middle Paleolithic ungulate remains came from a single dense concentration close to the cave's north wall. In the central part of the cave, bones were encountered in smaller, discrete patches, separated from each other by zones with few or no bones. Mineralogical studies of the sediments on the cave floor indicate that these localized bone concentrations reflect the original burial distribution, not the effects of selective dissolution following burial (Weiner et al. 1993).

Although there is compelling evidence throughout the cave's Middle and Upper Paleolithic sequence for the intermittent presence of carnivores (Dayan 1994), most notably spotted hyenas (*Crocuta crocuta*), the hundreds of cutmarked and burned bones, as well as hearths, ash lenses, and large numbers of lithic artifacts, clearly testify to the central role played by humans in the formation of the bone accumulations. In fact, as we show later, the dense concentration of bones along the north wall is the remains of a midden that accumulated when Neandertals used the site as a long-term seasonal basecamp.

Our handling of the stratigraphy deserves comment. Stekelis excavated the site in arbitrary horizontal spits, providing upper and lower elevations for each level in centimeters (cm) below an arbitrary datum set in the wall of the cave. The French-Israeli team excavated the deposits according to the site's natural stratigraphy, recording depths below the same datum used by Stekelis. However, because the deposits in some parts of the cave are not horizontal, it has been nearly impossible to correlate the horizontal spits of the older excavations to the natural strata recognized by the more recent excavations. Nevertheless, to maximize our sample sizes, we have been forced to pool the Stekelis and French-Israeli material, using depth below datum to subdivide the material into arbitrary, horizontal half-meter- or 1-meter-thick levels. Despite the obvious short-comings of this procedure, by using thick levels, by focusing only on the most robust patterning, and by emphasizing the convergence of results generated by independent lines of evidence, we feel we can draw some reasonable inferences about Middle Paleolithic hunting practices and site function that are not just artifacts of our sampling and pooling procedures.

In determining the statistical significance of our results, we evaluate the difference between percentages using the arcsine transformation (t_s), as defined by Sokal and Rohlf (1969: 607–610). In addition, we use standard unpaired t-tests (t) to evaluate differences between means, and Spearman's rank correlation coefficient (r_s) for correlations.

Animal Resource Use at Kebara

Elsewhere, using a variety of taphonomic evidence, we have shown that most of the bones in Kebara were brought there by humans, not hyenas (Bar-Yosef et al. 1992; Speth and Tchernov 1998). Using mortality data, as well as indices of skeletal completeness and head-to-limb-part ratios (Stiner 1994), we have also shown that the Kebara Neandertals were effective hunters, targeting prime adults of large and dangerous prey like wild boar and aurochs (Speth and Tchernov 1998). There is no indication in these data that Kebara's inhabitants engaged in scavenging to any significant extent. We now broaden our perspective to examine other aspects of animal resource use at Kebara, and we track the shifting nature of these activities over the last 12,000 years of the Levantine Middle Paleolithic (60,000–48,000 years ago). We do this in four brief sections. The first looks at the sex ratio of the gazelle and fallow deer and uses this information to infer the seasonality of hunting activities. The second section looks at the way animal resources were prepared for transport to the cave and the way they were processed for cooking and consumption. The third section examines the spatial distribution of bones within the cave, demonstrating that the north wall bone concentration is actually a midden that accumulated during periods of intensive habitation. The final section looks at temporal changes in settlement function, showing that the earliest and latest occupations were quite ephemeral, perhaps devoted largely to hunting, whereas the occupations during the mid-portion of the sequence were far more intensive and probably represent extended cool-season basecamps. We conclude with a brief discussion of the implications of the Kebara evidence for our broader understanding of Neandertal economic behavior.

Sex Ratios and Season of Occupation

Among recent foragers, procurement, butchering, and transport decisions are strongly conditioned by the sex of the prey (Speth 1983). It is not unreasonable to suppose, therefore, that the sex structure of prey taken by Neandertals might also be of interest, as it may provide us with insights into the seasonality of site use and reveal aspects of the decision-making strategies employed by these archaic humans. Unfortunately, determining the sex of fragmentary skeletal elements in taxa that are only moderately dimorphic is very difficult. As a consequence, we succeeded in sexing only the horn cores and pubis in gazelle, and the acetabulum, distal humerus, distal metacarpal, astragalus, and of course, antlers in fallow deer. The procedures used for sexing these elements are presented in Speth and Tchernov (n.d.).

The sex ratio for gazelle is shown in Figure 1 [based on total number of identifiable specimens (NISP) for horn cores and pubis]. The proportion of males steadily declines from somewhat over 45% in the early part of the sequence to a low of about 20% midway through the sequence and then rises again to nearly 40% at the end of the Mousterian and to nearly 60% in the Upper Paleolithic. Female gazelle, therefore, predominate throughout much of the Middle Paleolithic sequence but are least abundant at the beginning and end of the sequence. In modern gazelle populations, adult males typically comprise between 35% and 45% of the total adult population (Dunham 1997; Baharav 1983a: 66). If roughly comparable proportions characterized Middle Paleolithic herds, Figure 3.1 suggests that Kebara hunters, on average, took male and female gazelle more or less in proportion to their availability.

The proportion of immature gazelle, estimated on the basis of teeth, is also shown in the same figure. We expected the frequency of young individuals to be positively correlated with the proportion of adult females. In other words, if hunters targeted females, they might also encounter and take more young animals. This turned out to be the case although the trend is barely perceptible in the figure when plotted at the same scale as adult sex ratio. The proportion of immature individuals rises from a low of 3.2% in the early part of the sequence to a maximum of 6.4% and then falls off again toward the end of the Mousterian. Although differences between adjacent levels are small, the difference between the highest value in level 600–650 cm and the lowest value near the base of the sequence in level 750–800 cm is significant ($t_s = 2.11, p < 0.05$). Other pairwise comparisons are not significant, but this is not surprising given the small sample sizes.

Figure 3.1 also shows the sex ratio for fallow deer. The proportion of males falls off steadily from a high point of 100% early in the sequence to a low value of about 20% toward the end of the sequence and then rises again to nearly 40% in the Upper Paleolithic. This pattern of change is broadly similar to the one shown for gazelle. In modern European fallow deer, as in gazelle, adult males again compose between 35% and 45% of the total adult population (Chapman and Chapman 1975: 159; Putman 1988: 105–107; Focardi et al. 1996). If roughly comparable proportions characterized Middle Paleolithic deer herds in the Levant, Figure 3.1 would suggest that Kebara hunters took male and female fallow deer in proportions more or less according to their availability.

The proportion of immature fallow deer, estimated on the basis of teeth, is also shown in Figure 3.1. As in gazelle, we expected the frequency of young animals to be positively correlated with the proportion of adult females. This again turned out to be the case, and the trend in fallow deer is more clear-cut than in gazelle. The proportion of immature individuals rises from a low of 2.9% early in the sequence (level 700–750 cm) to a maximum of 16.7% in the latter part of the sequence (level 450–500 cm). Again, differences between adjacent levels are small and not statistically significant, but the difference between the highest and lowest values is significant ($t_s = 1.96, p = 0.05$). The value in level 550–600 cm (10.6%) also differs significantly from the lowest value ($t_s = 2.48, p = 0.01$).

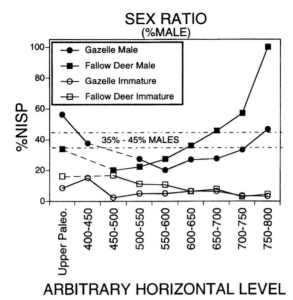

Figure 3.1. Sex ratio (% male) and proportion of immature gazelle and fallow deer (based on dentitions) plotted against arbitrary horizontal half-meter levels (NISP).

Up to this point, we have emphasized the fact that Kebara's Neandertal hunters generally killed higher proportions of females than males and that, on average, they probably took both sexes more or less in accordance with their availability. We now consider the distinctly U-shaped form of the curves shown in Figure 3.1. In both taxa, the proportion of males is high in the early part of the sequence, declines in the mid-portion, and then rises again toward the close of the Mousterian and in the Upper Paleolithic. We suspect that these curves reflect changes in the seasonality of hunting although the information presently available to demonstrate this is far from ideal.

Modern human hunters are keenly aware of the behavior and physiological condition of their prey (Speth and Spielmann 1983), which in large part are determined by the annual reproductive cycle of the animals, seasonal changes in the availability of food and cover, and photoperiod length (Baharav 1974, 1981, 1983a, 1983b; Asher 1985; Asher et al. 1987, 1996; Lincoln 1992; Loudon and Brinklow 1992; Jopson 1993; Carranza et al. 1996; Focardi et al. 1996; Mulley et al. 1996; Jopson et al. 1997). Thus, the shifts seen at Kebara in the proportions of male and female gazelle and fallow deer very likely reflect changes in the season of the year when most hunting took place. Our difficulty lies in pinpointing the precise nature of the behavioral and condition changes in these two taxa that would make one or the other sex easier to capture or more suitable as prey at a particular time of year. Unfortunately, for gazelle, we have only a limited amount of information about their behavior and almost nothing on their physiological condition; for fallow deer we have extensive data on both behavior and condition, but only for the European *Dama dama*, not for the Near Eastern *D. mesopotamica*, and most information relates to northern Europe and New Zealand rather than Mediterranean habitats. Thus, the discussion that follows should be viewed as a very tentative first step toward explaining the intriguing changes in sex ratio seen at Kebara.

The timing of the reproductive cycle in fallow deer is tightly constrained, endogenous, and cued by photoperiod length (Asher 1985; Asher and Langridge 1992; Lincoln 1992; Loudon and Brinklow 1992). Thus, fallow deer in the northern and southern hemispheres have nearly identical reproductive cycles but offset by 6 months. Interestingly, the timing of the cycle appears to be quite insensitive to differences in latitude and habitat, allowing one to infer the timing of the reproductive cycle in the Near East even in the absence of direct observations (Caughley 1971). The rut in European fallow deer takes place primarily in October (Chapman and Chapman 1975: 131). One of the striking things about rutting male fallow deer is that they essentially stop eating and lose 15% to 25% of their body weight, even when food is abundant (Chapman and Chapman 1975: 82–83; Asher et al. 1987; Jopson 1993; Jopson et al. 1997). Thus, in northern temperate habitats males commonly enter winter in a seriously depleted physical state and do not recover until the following spring.

In Mediterranean environments, the rut coincides with the dry season and hence a time of year when resources are poor (Braza et al. 1988; Carranza et al. 1990, 1996; Focardi et al. 1996; San Jose and Braza 1997). However, winters are less harsh and renewed plant growth accompanies the onset of the winter rains. Thus, male condition might be expected to begin improving by late winter, somewhat earlier than in deer in more northerly habitats. In Israel today the rainy season extends from about October to May, with the first heavy rains generally in late December and most precipitation in January and February (Baharav 1981). The entire reproductive cycle of Persian fallow deer appears to be advanced by 4 to 5 weeks compared to that of the European form (Chapman and Chapman 1975: 228; Asher et al. 1996: 213). Thus, the rut in Persian deer takes place in late August and September, which coincides with the height of the dry season in Mediterranean environments (Carranza et al. 1996). One might speculate, therefore, that male Persian deer would be in their worst physiological condition, and hence most likely to be avoided by hunters, during the late summer and fall and in increasingly better condition during the winter and especially in the spring and early summer (prior to the rut) when they might become the prime targets.

The most probable timing can be narrowed down even further by considering the cycle of antler casting and regeneration in fallow bucks. Antler casting disrupts the male dominance hierarchy; males disperse and become very secretive after shedding their antlers (Putman 1988: 90). In Persian deer casting takes place in February and early March. Because it takes about 15 to 17 weeks until the velvet of the new antlers is shed (Chapman and Chapman 1975: 107–108), males would become increasingly vulnerable targets toward the end of the spring and during the summer up until the rut.

Female European fallow deer have a highly synchronous birth period; over 70% of fawns are born in June (Caughley 1971; Hamilton and Blaxter 1980; Asher and

Langridge 1992). Because the birth season in Persian deer is 4 to 5 weeks earlier, most fawning in the Levant would occur in late April or May, more or less coincident with the onset of the dry season. Given the high caloric demands of late pregnancy and lactation, females at this time of year are likely to be in their poorest condition. Female fallow deer apparently lactate for up to 7 months (Putman 1988: 99). Thus, late spring, summer, and early fall would be times of the year when pregnant or nursing females would be least desirable as prey. Their value to hunters would increase in late fall, once the fawns are weaned, and they would probably attain their peak condition in the winter and early spring.

In sum, male and female Persian fallow deer appear to have broadly overlapping condition cycles with both sexes in prime condition in the winter and early spring. Significant differences between the sexes may not emerge until the late spring and summer. Female condition probably declines first, in the spring, in response to the increasing demands of pregnancy and lactation, whereas male condition may persist somewhat longer, not declining significantly until the rut in late summer. The dispersed, secretive behavior of fallow bucks after their antlers have been cast suggests that their vulnerability to hunting would increase markedly once their new antlers were fully developed, a process that normally would be completed by late spring or early summer.

Thus, on the basis of these observations in modern fallow deer, we can suggest that the male-dominated earlier and later Mousterian assemblages at Kebara, as well as those from the Upper Paleolithic, reflect hunting activities that occurred after female condition had begun to decline significantly, and after the new antlers of the males had developed, but before the rut; in other words, during the late spring and/or early summer. In contrast, the female-dominated mid-sequence assemblages probably reflect hunting that occurred somewhat earlier in the year and were centered most heavily on the winter, perhaps continuing into the early spring.

Let us turn now to gazelle. Unfortunately, there is much less information on seasonal changes in the physiological condition of this animal, and our safest approach is to focus on the birth season as the period of the year when females are likely to be in poorest condition. According to Baharav (1983a, 1983b), some mountain gazelle populations breed in December and give birth in June while others produce young all year but with two distinct peaks, conceptions occurring in October and May and births in April and November. Even in the population with two birth peaks, however, the earlier spring peak is the major one (Baharav 1983b). Shortage of water appears to be the critical factor determining whether there are one or two birth peaks (Baharav 1983b). Thus, the majority of young are born during the spring or early summer, coincident with the dry season, making the late spring, summer, and early fall the times of year when pregnant or nursing females are most likely to be avoided by hunters. Winter and perhaps early spring would appear to be the best times to target females. These suggestions broadly mirror our conclusions for female fallow deer.

The behavior of female gazelle dovetails reasonably well with these conclusions. If group size exerts any influence on the probability of finding and successfully killing gazelle, the largest aggregations occur during the winter and early spring (i.e., December–March; Baharav 1974, 1983a). The animals are more dispersed and much harder to detect during the dry season between April and November. Thus, females would probably be most successfully hunted during the winter.

The breeding season in gazelle occurs during the autumn and early winter, in some populations as early as October and in others not until December and January (Baharav 1983a, 1983b). Although we have found no data concerning the extent of fat mobilization in reproductively active male gazelle, it is very likely that these animals would be in poorest condition following the breeding season. How long it takes for their condition to rebound is not clear either, but they probably would become increasingly desirable targets by late spring, a time when the condition of pregnant and nursing females would be declining. Thus, as in fallow deer, our reconstruction suggests that female condition would begin to decline somewhat earlier than that of reproductively active males.

Fortunately, our ideas about seasonality can be checked to some extent by comparing our reconstruction with the seasonality determinations made by Lieberman (1993a, 1993b, Lieberman and Shea 1994) on the basis of an extensive dental cementum study of Kebara gazelle. He analyzed 41 thin sections, 26 from the Mousterian levels and 15 from the Upper Paleolithic levels. Lieberman (1993a: 213) recognized seven season-of-death categories in the thin sections: fall (October–November); fall/winter (October–February); winter (December–February); spring (March–May); spring/summer (March–September); and summer (June–September). He acknowledges that the accuracy of the seasonal determinations is relatively low, in the best of circumstances only to within about three months ($N = 21$) and in a number of specimens ($N = 5$) only to the nearest half year (i.e., wet season versus dry season).

On the basis of the cementum annuli, Lieberman concluded that the Middle Paleolithic occupation of Kebara was multiseasonal, with evidence for Neandertal use of the cave during both the wet and dry seasons and perhaps during all four seasons of the year. While he may be correct, we note that over 75% (16 out of 21) of the samples that he assigned to a single 3-month season are either winter (7) or spring (9). Moreover, among the five specimens that he could only assign to a 6-month interval, two are fall/winter and three are spring/summer. In other words, it is possible that over 80% (21 out of 26) of his samples relate to just winter or spring. Lieberman's Upper Paleolithic samples are even more tightly clustered, with 14 specimens (93%) attributed to either spring, spring/summer, or summer, and only one (7%) assigned to the fall. Thus, Lieberman's results accord reasonably well with our seasonality reconstructions based on sex ratios, pointing to heavy winter and spring use of the site during the Middle Paleolithic and primarily spring or spring/summer use during the Upper Paleolithic.

Transport and Processing

We now look briefly at the way ungulates were exploited and processed at Kebara. In this discussion, we treat the Mousterian fauna as a single, composite assemblage. We add the spatial and temporal dimensions later. These data provide interesting insights into the procurement, transport, and processing strategies employed by Levantine Neandertals. For example, Figure 3.2 shows the proportion of maxillae

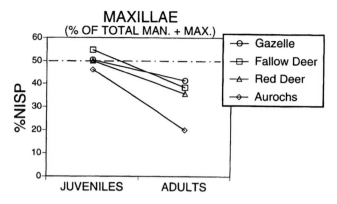

Figure 3.2. Juvenile and adult maxillae expressed as proportion of total maxillary and mandibular fragments (NISP, including isolated teeth).

(crania), calculated as a percentage of total mandibles and maxillae. There are two interesting patterns that emerge from this figure. First, most animals are better represented by mandibles than by crania, and in the largest species—aurochs—almost no crania were returned to the site. Second, elimination of bulky crania is evident only in adult animals; juvenile mandibles and maxillae were brought back to the cave in nearly equal proportions. Both patterns point to the importance of bulk in Neandertal transport decisions.

Figure 3.3 shows the proportional distribution of cutmarks by anatomical unit for gazelle, fallow deer, and red deer (the sample of aurochs postcranial elements is too small for inclusion). Again, two patterns are noteworthy. First, all three taxa

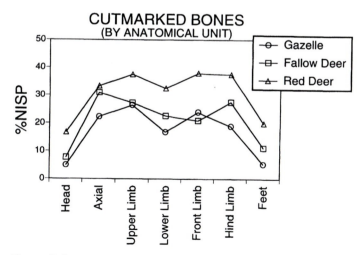

Figure 3.3. Cutmarked bones by anatomical unit (NISP, including isolated teeth).

show broadly similar distributions of cutmarks—few on the head, high numbers on the limb bones, with fewer on the less meaty lower limbs than on the meatier upper limbs, and few on the feet. Second, the proportion of elements (excluding isolated teeth) displaying cutmarks increases with body size, with fewest in gazelle (12.8%), intermediate values in fallow deer (18.5%), and high proportions in red deer (25.6%). These differences are significant (gazelle versus fallow deer: $t_s = 6.57$, $p < 0.001$; fallow deer versus red deer: $t_s = 3.87$, $p < 0.001$). This result implies that larger carcasses necessitated more thorough dismembering prior to transport and probably also during preparation as food.

The proportion of cutmarked bones observed in different anatomical units is significantly and positively correlated with the average utility of the elements in those units, as measured by Binford's (1978: 74) Modified General Utility Index or MGUI (gazelle: $r_s = 0.82$, $p < 0.05$; fallow deer: $r_s = 0.82$, $p < 0.05$). Thus, Neandertals invested greater effort in dismembering, defleshing, and processing carcass parts of higher overall utility.

The proportion of burned bones by anatomical unit is shown in Figure 3.4. The patterning displayed in this figure is intriguing because it may shed light on an issue in Paleolithic studies that has been difficult to address (Stiner et al. 1995). At issue is whether burned bones in sites such as Kebara became charred as they were being cooked or only after they had been discarded, when they were exposed to heat or flames from hearths that were repositioned or rekindled by later occupants. Stiner et al. (1995) conclude that much of the burning found in Italian Middle Paleolithic faunas relates to postdiscard exposure of the bones to fire, not to food preparation. While their conclusion may be correct in the Italian cases, the patterning shown in Figure 3.4 suggests that at Kebara much of the burning may be the result of cooking-related activities, not accidental postdiscard exposure to fire. This is suggested by the fact that the probability of elements being burned varies in a sys-

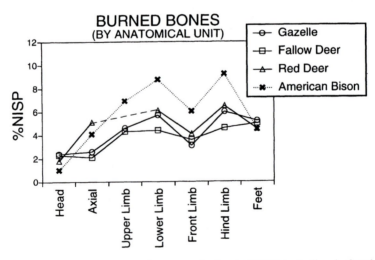

Figure 3.4. Burned bones by anatomical unit (NISP, including isolated teeth).

tematic fashion across anatomical units with the incidence of burning being low in head, axial and front-limb elements and high in rear-limb elements, especially in those of the lower portion of the hind leg (head versus axial: $t_s = 4.46$, $p < 0.001$; upper versus lower limb: $t_s = 2.18$, $p < 0.05$; upper front versus upper rear limb: $t_s = 2.40$, $p = 0.01$; lower front versus lower rear limb: $t_s = 3.15$, $p = 0.001$; all species combined). If most burning occurred by accident after bones had been tossed aside, one would expect a random, or perhaps a uniform, distribution across anatomical units. For comparative purposes, we have included data in Figure 3.4 for the anatomical distribution of burning on bones of American bison (*Bison bison*) from a late prehistoric (AD 1300) Indian village in New Mexico (Speth, unpublished data). The patterning is remarkably similar.

The nonrandom distribution of burning on bones at Kebara can be documented in another way as well. If we compare the proportion of burned limb epiphyses (5.6%) to the proportion of burned shaft fragments (2.3%), the values are significantly different ($t_s = 2.83$, $p < 0.01$; all species combined). If fragmentary bones were burned by accidental exposure to fire after they had been discarded, shaft fragments and articular ends should have similar burning frequencies, which they clearly do not.

Spatial Patterning

Up to this point we have focused on the procurement, transport, and processing of ungulates at Kebara. We now look at a few aspects of the spatial distribution of these faunal remains to gain further insights into the functional nature of Kebara as a settlement. As in the previous section, we continue to ignore the temporal dimension, treating all of the material as though it came from just one component. In the final section, we add the temporal dimension and examine the manner in which settlement function changed over the roughly 12,000 years that the cave was frequented by Neandertals.

Our approach here is to compare the assemblages from the central floor area of the cave with the masses of bone that accumulated close to the cave's north wall. Stekelis (Schick and Stekelis 1977: 102) was struck by the sheer volume of bone near the wall, and concluded that it probably represented ". . . the kitchen midden of the Mousterian inhabitants." The stone tools found there, according to Bar-Yosef et al. (1992: 526), are consistent with Stekelis's view, as the assemblage is "comprised of larger pieces than elsewhere in the cave and includes an abundance of cores, cortical elements, flakes, and other waste." Keeping habitation areas clear of debris is, of course, commonplace among contemporary hunter-gatherers. In modern forager camps, trash gradually accumulates along the peripheries of the habitation area, a pattern that becomes increasingly apparent the longer the occupation (O'Connell 1987). In this section, we present several lines of evidence in support of the view that the concentration of bones along Kebara's north wall does, in fact, represent a Middle Paleolithic midden.

One such line of evidence is the fact that the average MGUI value for the bones in the north wall concentration (26.34) is significantly lower than the value for the central floor area (28.22, $t = 3.78$, $p < 0.0001$; all taxa combined). In addition, bulky, low-utility elements are more abundant in the midden area. This is clearly illustrated by heads, the bulkiest element in the ungulate skeleton; over 60% of the heads are found in the midden, regardless of taxon, and the highest proportion, not surprisingly, is for aurochs (73%), by far the largest animal.

One of the most interesting patterns to emerge from the spatial analysis concerns the distribution of burned specimens. The proportion of burned bones is consistently higher in the north wall area (5.9%) than out on the floor of the cave (4.1%), despite the fact that most of the hearths are located away from the wall ($t_s = 3.59$, $p < 0.001$; all taxa combined). This, of course, adds another element to the argument made earlier that burning is not largely a fortuitous result of discarded bones becoming charred as later visitors to the cave repositioned or rekindled hearths. One could argue, however, that this result is merely an artifact of taphonomic processes. Because burned bones are more fragile than unburned ones (Stiner et al. 1995), the higher proportion of charred items in the midden could simply indicate that more of the burned elements in this part of the site had broken apart into smaller pieces. To check this, we recomputed the percentages of burned bones in the two areas, looking only at complete elements (e.g., phalanges, carpals, tarsals). The difference between midden and floor area persists. In the north wall zone, 6.6% of the complete bones are burned compared to only 3.8% in the central area ($t_s = 2.89$, $p < 0.01$; all taxa combined).

If the concentration of bones close to the north wall represents a genuine midden, and if much of the burning at Kebara is the result of cooking, then the higher incidence of burning close to the wall indicates that Neandertals periodically cleaned their cooking and eating areas and dumped this debris in the midden. Although such behavior is commonplace among contemporary foragers (O'Connell 1987), this small element of fastidiousness may surprise those who still view Neandertals as subhuman dimwits.

Temporal Change

In this final section, we look at the faunal data from a temporal perspective to explore the ways in which the site's function changed over the course of the Mousterian. We have already discussed one temporal pattern that very likely reflects changing seasonal use of the cave—the shift in gazelle and fallow deer sex ratios from an elevated proportion of males in the early part of the sequence, to a predominance of females and young during the middle portion of the sequence, then a return to higher numbers of males toward the end of the Mousterian. There are many other changes in the fauna that occur hand in hand with the shift in sex ratio, and, taken together, they suggest that the site's function changed from an ephemeral late spring/summer camp early in the sequence, perhaps largely for hunting, to an intensively occupied winter/early spring basecamp during the period of midden accumulation and then back once more to a short-term late spring/summer camp, again perhaps primarily for hunting.

Figure 3.5 shows clearly that the period of midden formation was confined to the mid-portion of the sequence. Early in the sequence the incidence of burning is higher in gazelle bones from the central floor area and lower on bones found close

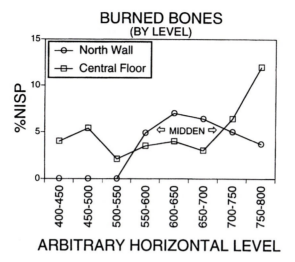

Figure 3.5. Burned bones in north wall and central floor areas plotted against arbitrary horizontal half-meter levels (gazelle only, NISP, excluding isolated teeth).

to the north wall. Then, during the mid-portion of the sequence, the burning frequency rises in the north wall assemblage to values that exceed those near the hearths, indicating that material was being cleaned from cooking and eating areas and dumped at the periphery of the habitation. Finally, toward the end of the sequence, burning frequencies in the north wall zone decline to zero, denoting the end of midden formation (a very similar pattern, not shown, is seen in fallow deer).

The period of midden accumulation appears to have been a time of intensive, probably long-term, seasonal occupation of the cave. This is best seen in Figure 3.6, which tracks the shifting proportion of carnivore-damaged bones over the course of the Mousterian. If hyena visitation to the cave was predicated on the human occupants being elsewhere, this figure suggests that the period of midden formation was indeed a time of fairly extended and intensive Neandertal presence.

One major reason for transporting heavy limb bones back to a settlement is for their marrow. The next figure plots the average marrow utility of the major limb elements, for all taxa combined, by stratigraphic level (Figure 3.7). We measure marrow utility, an index of the amount of marrow in each element, using Binford's "Standardized Marrow Index" for caribou (1978: 27) although the simplified index developed by Jones and Metcalfe (1988) could also be used here with similar results. As expected, the highest values are seen during the period of midden development.

Figure 3.8 shows the *Index of (Relative) Skeletal Completeness* (tMNE/MNI), as defined by Stiner (1994: 242), plotted by arbitrary horizontal 1-meter levels for gazelle and fallow deer. This index is obtained by dividing the total number of skeletal elements (tMNE) by the minimum number of individuals (MNI) represented in the assemblage. Higher values of the index denote greater relative skeletal completeness. Figure 3.8 reveals that the period of midden formation is also the period with the high-

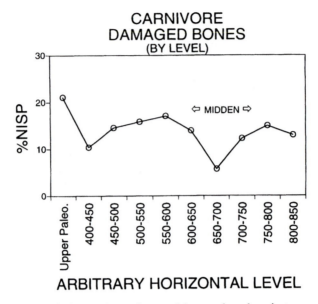

Figure 3.6. Carnivore damaged bones plotted against arbitrary horizontal half-meter levels (all taxa combined, NISP,
excluding isolated teeth).

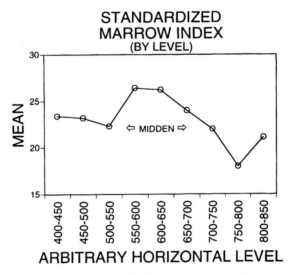

Figure 3.7. Mean standardized marrow index (Binford
1978: 27, Table 1.9, Caribou) plotted against arbitrary
horizontal half-meter levels (all taxa combined).

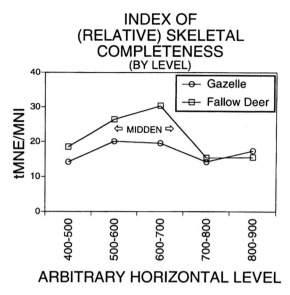

Figure 3.8. *Index of (Relative) Skeletal Completeness* (tMNE/MNI) for gazelle and fallow deer plotted against arbitrary horizontal 1-meter levels.

est values of the index in both taxa. In other words, during the early and late parts of the sequence, there are proportionately fewer skeletal elements per animal than during the intensive occupations in the mid-portion of the sequence. As already discussed, one major difference between the midden period and the early and late segments of the sequence is that the latter assemblages are dominated by lower utility elements, whereas the midden has a much greater representation of higher utility parts (Figure 3.7). Taken together these observations imply that during the more ephemeral visits to the cave, either a narrower range of carcass parts, of lower average food utility, was brought back to the site, or, as seems more likely, many of the carcass parts that did make it to Kebara during these short-term encampments were butchered and processed only to the extent necessary to prepare the higher utility parts for transport elsewhere, leaving behind mostly lower utility skeletal parts that had been culled and discarded. In contrast, during the period of midden formation, a time of much more intensive occupation of the cave, a broader range of carcass parts, including many more parts of moderate to high utility, were brought into the cave, where they were cooked and eaten, and the bones then discarded in the midden.

Summary and Conclusions

It will be useful at this point to pull together some of the more interesting findings concerning Kebara's ungulate fauna. The evidence for the first point is presented in Speth and Tchernov (1998).

1. The Middle Paleolithic inhabitants of Kebara Cave, presumably Neandertals throughout, were very capable hunters, taking prime adults of gazelle, fallow deer, red deer, wild boar, and aurochs. Although they may have scavenged animals now and then, there is no evidence that scavenging was a major component of their procurement strategies.

2. Overall, the hunters took male and female gazelle and fallow deer in proportions similar to their availability in living populations. Nevertheless, there is clear temporal patterning in the sex ratio for both species, with more males being taken at the beginning and toward the end of the sequence, and more females and young during the mid-portion of the sequence. These temporal shifts in sex ratio probably reflect changes in the time of year when most hunting took place. Drawing on behavioral and physiological studies of modern gazelle and fallow deer, it appears that the cave was occupied in the late spring and/or summer during the early and late portions of the sequence, whereas during the mid-portion of the sequence Kebara was occupied somewhat earlier in the year, most likely during the winter and/or early spring.

3. Neandertal transport decisions were conditioned by both bulk and utility. Thus, bulkier elements were more likely to be abandoned at a kill than smaller, more portable ones, and higher utility parts of larger prey were more thoroughly dismembered and butchered than lower utility ones in preparation for transport, cooking, and consumption.

4. Bones may have become burned largely as a result of cooking, not accidental postdiscard exposure to fire. The proportion of burned bones varies in a systematic fashion across anatomical units such that limbs have higher burning frequencies than heads, axial elements, or feet. The Kebara pattern is very similar to the anatomical distribution of burning in bison from a late prehistoric (AD 1300) Indian village in New Mexico (USA). Unfortunately, we lack sufficient comparative data from contemporary contexts to guide us in interpreting the Mousterian patterning. In fact, although numerous ethnoarchaeological studies among contemporary foragers have focused on hunting, butchering, transport, and final discard (e.g., Binford 1978; Hill et al. 1987; Bunn et al. 1988; O'Connell et al. 1990), there are surprisingly few that look at what happens to animal bones in the intermediate stages of cooking and consumption (Yellen 1991a, 1991b; e.g., Gifford-Gonzalez 1993; Jones 1993; Kent 1993; Oliver 1993; Lupo 1995). To interpret evidence such as that from Kebara, we first need a far more systematic look at the cooking technologies of modern foragers and the nature of their effects on bone.

5. Spatial analysis shows that a substantial midden developed along the north wall of the cave. Several lines of evidence point to this conclusion: (a) the unusually high density of bones close to the north wall; (b) the elevated proportions of bulky, low-utility elements in this area of the site; and (c) the higher frequency of burned bone near the wall than in the vicinity of the hearths. This last observation demonstrates that Neandertals periodically cleaned their cooking and eating areas, dumping the debris near the wall.

6. The faunal remains also display some striking temporal patterns: (a) the season of occupation when most hunting was done may have changed over the course of the Mousterian, from a late spring/summer emphasis during the earliest and latest occupations, to a winter/early spring emphasis during the mid-portion of the

sequence; (b) midden development occurred during the mid-portion of the sequence; and (c) the intensity of occupation was clearly greatest during the period of midden development, as indicated by reduced levels of carnivore damage, elevated proportions of higher utility elements, and the presence of more complete skeletons. Because of increased carnivore activity in the cave during the early and late portions of the sequence, the precise nature of the more ephemeral visitations to the cave remains unclear and in need of further scrutiny.

We obviously cannot reconstruct an entire settlement system on the basis of a single site, or on the basis of just the fauna. Nevertheless, the results of this preliminary assessment make it clear that Levantine Neandertals were mobile foragers who used a variety of different settlement types in their annual round (Marks 1989; see also Henry 1992). Over the course of the Mousterian, Kebara's functional position within the settlement system was far from static, changing from a limited-activity hunting station, to a basecamp, then back again to a more limited-activity hunting station. It is impossible at this point to tell whether these changes reflect a complete restructuring of the settlement system, or whether Kebara merely became less suitable for winter habitation during certain segments of the Middle Paleolithic, perhaps because the cave's interior became too damp.

The Kebara data also suggest that Neandertals, like modern foragers, were concerned about the physiological condition of their prey, targeting male or female animals depending on which sex was in better condition at the time of year when the hunting took place. Moreover, like modern foragers, the Kebara Neandertals transported considerable quantities of meat over the landscape, and their transport decisions were conditioned by the bulk and food utility of the parts. It is hard to reconcile these findings with the extreme view, still persuasive in some circles, that Neandertals were utterly lacking in planning depth. Of course, it is impossible with just the Kebara data to show that Neandertal planning depth was on a par with the levels of foresight and planning seen in modern foragers. We make no such claim here. We hasten to add, however, that the issue of Neandertal planning depth remains largely at the level of speculation, with little hard evidence upon which to build a case one way or the other.

Finally, the faunal data from Kebara show that it is premature to conclude, as Lieberman did, that the site's Neandertal inhabitants adapted to the rapidly changing ecology of the Late Pleistocene Levant by means of a single system of land use (Lieberman 1993a; Lieberman and Shea 1994). What our data do show is that the settlement system of which Kebara was a part was dynamic and changing and that we need to know much more about the overall structure of the system before we can conclude that Levantine Neandertals organized their use of space in a manner that was qualitatively distinct from the land-use systems employed by anatomically modern humans.

In conclusion, what we have described here are subsistence-related behaviors that are very familiar to archaeologists who work with Upper Paleolithic and later foragers. Although we in no way mean to imply on this basis that Levantine Neandertals were already fully modern in their behavioral or cognitive capacities, we have found nothing as yet in the faunal data that clearly sets Neandertals apart either from their anatomically modern quasi-contemporaries or their Upper Paleolithic successors in the region.

Acknowledgments   We thank O. Bar-Yosef, A. Belfer-Cohen, S. Davis, T. Dayan, P. Gold-berg, N. Goren-Inbar, L. Horwitz, E. Hovers, R. Klein, L. Meignen, R. Rabinovich, M. Schiffer, M. Stiner, M. Wolpoff, an anonymous outside reviewer, and the editors of this volume for their helpful comments and suggestions. Support for the research was received from the U.S.–Israel Binational Science Foundation, L. S. B. Leakey Foundation, National Endowment for the Humanities, Irene Levi-Sala CARE Archaeological Foundation, Hebrew University of Jerusalem, and the University of Michigan.

REFERENCES

Asher, G. 1985. Oestrous cycle and breeding season of farmed fallow deer, *Dama dama*. *Journal of Reproduction and Fertility* 75:521–529.

Asher, G., D. Berg, S. Beaumont, C. Morrow, K. Oneill, and M. Fisher. 1996. Comparison of seasonal changes in reproductive parameters of adult male European fallow deer (*Dama dama dama*) and hybrid Mesopotamian × European fallow deer (*D. d. mesopotamica* × *D. d. dama*). *Animal Reproduction Science* 45:201–215.

Asher, G., A. Day, and G. Barrell. 1987. Annual cycle of liveweight and reproductive changes of farmed male fallow deer (*Dama dama*) and the effect of daily oral administration of melatonin in summer on the attainment of seasonal fertility. *Journal of Reproduction and Fertility* 79:353–362.

Asher, G., and M. Langridge. 1992. Seasonal pattern of births, female reproductive success and causes of neonate mortality of farmed red deer and fallow deer in northern New Zealand (Abstract). In *The Biology of Deer* (R. Brown, ed.), p. 217. New York: Springer Verlag.

Baharav, D. 1974. Notes on the population structure and biomass of the mountain gazelle, *Gazella gazella gazella*. *Israel Journal of Zoology* 23:39–44.

Baharav, D. 1981. Food habits of the mountain gazelle in semi-arid habitats of eastern lower Galilee, Israel. *Journal of Arid Environments* 4:63–69.

Baharav, D. 1983a. Observations on the ecology of the mountain gazelle in the upper Galilee. *Mammalia* 47:59–69.

Baharav, D. 1983b. Reproductive strategies in female mountain and Dorcas gazelle (*Gazella gazella* and *Gazella dorcas*). *Journal of Zoology* (London) 200:445–453.

Bar-Yosef, O., B. Vandermeersch, B. Arensburg, A. Belfer-Cohen, P. Goldberg, H. Laville, L. Meignen, Y. Rak, J. Speth, E. Tchernov, A. Tillier, and S. Weiner. 1992. The excavations in Kebara Cave, Mt. Carmel. *Current Anthropology* 33:497–550.

Binford, L. 1978. *Nunamiut Ethnoarchaeology*. New York: Academic Press.

Binford, L. 1981. *Bones*. New York: Academic Press.

Binford, L. 1984. *Faunal Remains from Klasies River Mouth*. Orlando: Academic Press.

Braza, F., C. San Jose, and A. Blom. 1988. Birth measurements, parturition dates, and progeny sex ratio of *Dama dama* in Doñana, Spain. *Journal of Mammalogy* 69:607–610.

Bunn, H., L. Bartram, and E. Kroll. 1988. Variability in bone assemblage formation from hadza hunting, scavenging, and carcass processing. *Journal of Anthropological Archaeology* 7:412–457.

Carranza, J., F. Alvarez, and T. Redondo. 1990. Territoriality as a mating strategy in red deer. *Animal Behaviour* 40:79–88.

Carranza, J., P. Fernandez-Llario, and M. Gomendio. 1996. Correlates of territoriality in rutting red deer. *Ethology* 102:793–805.

Caughley, G. 1971. The season of births for northern-hemisphere ungulates in New Zealand. *Mammalia* 35:204–219.

Chapman, D., and N. Chapman. 1975. *Fallow Deer*. Lavenham, Suffolk: Terence Dalton.

Davis, S. 1977. The ungulate remains from Kebara Cave. In *Moshé Stekelis Memorial Volume* (B. Arensburg and O. Bar-Yosef, eds.), pp. 150–163. Eretz-Israel: Archaeological, Historical and Geographical Studies 13. Jerusalem: The Israel Exploration Society.

Dayan, T. 1994. Carnivore diversity in the late quaternary of Israel. *Quaternary Research* 41:343–349.

Dunham, K. 1997. Population growth of mountain gazelle *Gazella gazella* reintroduced to central Arabia. *Biological Conservation* 81:205–214.

Farizy, C., F. David, and J. Jaubert. 1994. *Hommes et Bisons du Paléolithique Moyen à Mauran (Haute-Garonne)*. Supplément à Gallia Préhistoire 30. Paris: CNRS Editions.

Focardi, S., S. Toso, and E. Pecchioli. 1996. The population modelling of fallow deer and wild boar in a Mediterranean ecosystem. *Forest Ecology and Management* 88:7–14.

Gifford-Gonzalez, D. 1993. Gaps in zooarchaeological analyses of butchery: is gender an issue? In *From Bones to Behavior* (J. Hudson, ed.), pp. 181–199. Occasional Paper 21. Carbondale: Southern Illinois University, Center for Archaeological Investigations.

Hamilton, W., and K. Blaxter. 1980. Reproduction in farmed red deer, 1. Hind and stag fertility. *Journal of Agricultural Science (Cambridge)* 95:261–273.

Henry, D. 1992. Transhumance during the late Levantine mousterian. In *The Middle Paleolithic: Adaptation, Behavior, and Variability* (H. Dibble and P. Mellars, eds.), pp. 143–162. Monograph 78. Philadelphia: University of Pennsylvania, The University Museum.

Hill, K., H. Kaplan, K. Hawkes, and A. Hurtado. 1987. Foraging decisions among Ache hunter-gatherers: new data and implications for optimal foraging models. *Ethology and Sociobiology* 8:1–36.

Jaubert, J., M. Lorblanchet, H. Laville, R. Slott-Moller, A. Turq, and J. Brugal. 1990. *Les Chasseurs d'Aurochs de la Borde: Un Site du Paléolithique Moyen (Livernon, Lot)*. Documents d'Archéologie Française 27. Paris: Editions de la Maison des Sciences de l'Homme.

Jones, K. 1993. The archaeological structure of a short-term camp. In *From Bones to Behavior* (J. Hudson, ed.), pp. 101–114. Occasional Paper 21. Carbondale: Southern Illinois University, Center for Archaeological Investigations.

Jones, K., and D. Metcalfe. 1988. Bare bones archaeology: bone marrow indices and efficiency. *Journal of Archaeological Science* 15:415–423.

Jopson, N. 1993. *Physiological Adaptations in Two Seasonal Cervids*. PhD Dissertation, Department of Animal Science, University of New England, Armidale, NSW, Australia.

Jopson, N., J. Thompson, and P. Fennessy. 1997. Tissue mobilization rates in male fallow deer (*Dama dama*) as determined by computed tomography: the effects of natural and enforced food restriction. *Animal Science* 65:311–320.

Kent, S. 1993. Variability in faunal assemblages: the influence of hunting skill, sharing, dogs, and mode of cooking on faunal remains at a sedentary Kalahari community. *Journal of Anthropological Archaeology* 12:323–385.

Lewin, R. 1993. *The Origin of Modern Humans*. New York: Scientific American Library.

Lieberman, D. 1993a. *Mobility and Strain: The Biology of Cementogenesis and Its Application to the Evolution of Hunter-Gatherer Seasonal Mobility During the Late Quaternary in the Southern Levant*. Unpublished Ph.D. Dissertation. Department of Anthropology, Harvard University, Cambridge, MA.

Lieberman, D. 1993b. The rise and fall of seasonal mobility among hunter-gatherers: the case of the southern Levant. *Current Anthropology* 34:599–631.

Lieberman, D., and J. Shea. 1994. Behavioral differences between archaic and modern humans in the Levantine mousterian. *American Anthropologist* 96:300–332.

Lincoln, G. 1992. Biology of seasonal breeding in deer. In *The Biology of Deer* (R. Brown, ed.), pp. 565–574. New York: Springer Verlag.

Loudon, A., and B. Brinklow. 1992. Reproduction in deer: adaptations for life in seasonal environments. In *The Biology of Deer* (R. Brown, ed.), pp. 261–278. New York: Springer Verlag.

Lupo, K. 1995. Hadza bone assemblages and hyena attrition: an ethnographic example of the influence of cooking and mode of discard on the intensity of scavenger ravaging. *Journal of Anthropological Archaeology* 14:288–314.

Marks, A. 1989. Early Mousterian settlement patterns in the Central Negev, Israel: their social and economic implications. In *L'Homme de Néandertal, Vol. 6. La Subsistance* (M. Patou and L. Freeman, eds.), pp. 115–126. Etudes et Recherches Archéologiques de l'Université de Liège 33. Liège: Université de Liège.

Mulley, R., A. English, J. Thompson, R. Butterfield, and P. Martin. 1996. Growth and body composition of entire and castrated fallow bucks (*Dama dama*) treated with zeranol. *Animal Science* 63:159–165.

O'Connell, J. 1987. Alyawara site structure and its archaeological implications. *American Antiquity* 52:74–108.

O'Connell, J., K. Hawkes, and N. Blurton Jones. 1990. Reanalysis of large mammal body part transport among the Hadza. *Journal of Archaeological Science* 17:301–316.

Oliver, J. 1993. Carcass processing by the Hadza: bone breakage from butchery to consumption. In *From Bones to Behavior* (J. Hudson, ed.), pp. 200–227. Occasional Paper 21. Carbondale: Southern Illinois University, Center for Archaeological Investigations.

Putman, R. 1988. *The Natural History of Deer*. London: Christopher Helm.

San Jose, C., and F. Braza. 1997. Ecological and behavioural variables affecting the fallow deer mating system in Doñana. *Ethology, Ecology and Evolution* 9:133–148.

Schick, T., and M. Stekelis. 1977. Mousterian assemblages in Kebara Cave, Mount Carmel. In *Moshé Stekelis Memorial Volume* (B. Arensburg and O. Bar-Yosef, eds.), pp. 97–149. Eretz-Israel: Archaeological, Historical and Geographical Studies 13. Jerusalem: The Israel Exploration Society.

Speth, J. 1983. *Bison Kills and Bone Counts*. Chicago: University of Chicago Press.

Speth, J., and K. Spielmann. 1983. Energy source, protein metabolism, and hunter-gatherer subsistence strategies. *Journal of Anthropological Archaeology* 2:1–31.

Speth, J., and E. Tchernov. 1998. The role of hunting and scavenging in Neandertal procurement strategies: new evidence from Kebara Cave (Israel). In *Neandertals and Modern Humans in Western Asia* (T. Akazawa, K. Aoki, and O. Bar-Yosef, eds.), pp. 223–239. New York: Plenum Press.

Speth, J., and E. Tchernov. n.d. Kebara Cave as a middle paleolithic settlement: a faunal perspective. In *The Middle Paleolithic Archaeology of Kebara Cave, Mt. Carmel (Israel)* (O. Bar-Yosef and L. Meignen, eds.). Unpublished manuscript.

Stiner, M. 1994. *Honor Among Thieves*. Princeton: Princeton University Press.

Stiner, M., S. Kuhn, S. Weiner, and O. Bar-Yosef. 1995. Differential burning, recrystallization, and fragmentation of archaeological bone. *Journal of Archaeological Science* 22:223–237.

Weiner, S., P. Goldberg, and O. Bar-Yosef. 1993. Bone preservation in Kebara Cave, Israel using on-site Fourier transform infrared spectrometry. *Journal of Archaeological Science* 20:613–627.

Yellen, J. 1991a. Small mammals: !Kung San utilization and the production of faunal assemblages. *Journal of Anthropological Archaeology* 10:1–26.

Yellen, J. 1991b. Small mammals: post-discard patterning of !Kung San faunal remains. *Journal of Anthropological Archaeology* 10:152–192.

4

Modeling the Edible Landscape

Jeanne Sept

Introduction

Evaluating how important meat-eating was to early hominid subsistence hinges on the question "compared to what?" The answer lies in the choices that would have confronted each hominid consumer on paleolandscapes scattered with patches of seasonal plant foods. Studies of modern human foragers and nonhuman primates emphasize the dietary importance of dependable and abundant plant foods in savanna habitats. So, despite the lack of direct archaeological evidence for early hominid plant food subsistence, it is important to consider evidence for meat-eating within an omnivorous context. This chapter develops a model of early hominid plant food subsistence choices to help archaeologists think about site landscape contexts in ways that could evaluate hypotheses about meat-eating and human evolution.

Early archaeological evidence for patterns of plant food exploitation is indirect, at best Sept 1986, 1990, 1992, 1994). Therefore, archaeological interpretations of early hominid subsistence strategies are heavily dependent on nonarchaeological information. One common approach relies on dietary hypotheses derived from hominid fossils, when inferences based on tooth microwear, stable isotope chemistry, or anatomy and biomechanics are used to associate particular fossil species with the (as-yet anonymous) archaeological record. However, such inferences are open to considerable debate Sept 1992). For example, tooth morphology and wear indicated a largely vegetarian diet for the South African australopithecines (Kay and Grine 1988). However, bone chemistry studies (e.g., Sponheimer and Lee-Thorp 1999) have suggested that both gracile and robust South African australopithecines were omnivorous, and Susman (1998) argues that South African robusts also had the dexterity to manufacture early stone tools.

A recent East African case has raised a similar subsistence question—which species of hominid used stone tools to butcher the animal remains found at Bouri, a 2.5 million-year-old site in Ethiopia (de Heinzelin et al. 1999)? Currently, two East African hominids are known to be contemporary with this early site, *Australopithecus garhi* and *A. aethiopicus*. Bones of *A. garhi* were found near the archaeological site, giving this species an opportunity to have been the "Butcher of Bouri." Both hominids had very large postcanine teeth, which are commonly interpreted as adaptive for eating a mechanically demanding diet consisting of tough or hard plant foods (Walker 1981; Demes and Creel 1988). However, *A. garhi* lacks facial robusticity and other traits normally associated with megadontia (Asfaw et al. 1999; McCollum 1999), suggesting that perhaps this new species was less well adapted to a heavily chewed vegetarian diet than its contemporaries, and had a potential motive to use tools to acquire meat and marrow. Archaeological evaluation of this hypothesis is moot; the behavioral significance of such early butchery evidence could represent anything from an incidental experiment with meat-eating to evidence of a new, red-blooded, ecological niche due to the ambiguity inherent in such isolated archaeological samples (Isaac 1984; Binford 1987).

Whether or not a site assemblage can ever be attributed to a particular hominid species, we are still left with the question of how any early hominid could have balanced the costs and benefits of acquiring meat in the context of a basic dependence on plant foods. Archaeological inferences about early hominid plant food diet therefore also depend heavily upon principles derived from behavioral ecology and analogies from ethnoarchaeology, actualistic studies, and experiments (Blumenschine 1989, 1992; Bunn 1991; Gifford-Gonzalez 1991; Sept 1992; Bunn and Ezzo 1993). Previous efforts to model early hominid plant food diet in a landscape context have focused on food availability, emphasizing either large-scale, regional comparisons (Peters et al. 1984; Peters 1987) or local contrasts in patchy habitats (Sept 1986, 1990, 1992, 1994). This chapter also addresses questions of food availability, comparing microhabitat data on plant food distribution. But it develops the comparison further by modeling the spatial distribution of foraging costs and benefits that would have faced different hominid consumers foraging for plant foods in different seasons on patchy landscapes.

Landscape Perspectives

There has been a growing recent interest in trying to understand changing patterns of early hominid subsistence behavior in the context of their ancient landscapes. Research efforts have been paced by theoretical developments in evolutionary ecology and by improved methodologies for the recovery and interpretation of paleoenvironmental and paleoanthropological data (Potts 1998). In situ archaeological evidence is uniquely suited to address ecological questions of how early hominid subsistence patterns were shaped by their local landscapes (Sept 1992, 1994). Unlike hominid fossil localities, which mark the final resting places of hominids filtered through taphonomic processes (White 1988), carefully excavated archaeological sites can document the local habitats of specific visits and activities of stone-flaking, bone-breaking hominids (Isaac 1981, 1984). The best in situ archaeological sites document short-term episodes of hominid behavior in a local context. But even these sites represent palimpsests of debris that have undergone considerable taphonomic transformation. Therefore, our ability to generalize about early hominid subsistence patterns or strategies is dependent upon treating archaeological sites as samples of regional or long-term behavior patterns and asking how the residues of short-term events have been winnowed, mixed, and layered through geological time (Stern 1993). This is one of the key goals of "landscape archaeology." While landscape archaeology has developed into a significant subfield among archaeologists working on Holocene sites (e.g., Kelso and Most 1990; Miller and Gleason 1994), a landscape archaeology of human origins faces much stiffer paleogeographic and taphonomic challenges, and is still in its infancy.

In East Africa, three key projects have led the way in developing a landscape approach to the Early Stone Age. Working on the east side of Lake Turkana, Glynn Isaac and Jack Harris developed a two-pronged investigation of "stone age visiting cards" (Isaac 1981). On the one hand, they documented an archaeological record that placed a number of large artifact and faunal assemblages in careful stratigraphic and paleogeographic context (Isaac and Isaac 1997). On the other hand, they also experimented with a nonsite sampling strategy, excavating "minisites" (Isaac 1981), recording artifact "scatters between the patches" (Isaac and Harris 1980; Stern 1993; Rogers et al. 1994), and looking for sites without stone artifacts (Bunn 1994). In the Olorgesailie basin, traditional excavations by Isaac and earlier researchers (Isaac 1977) established foundations for Rick Potts' archaeological sampling across a paleolandsurface and paleobehavioral analyses (Potts 1994, 1996). Finally, decades of work by Mary Leakey and Richard Hay at Olduvai Gorge (Leakey 1971, 1974; Hay 1976) stimulated a number of site–specific paleoenvironmental studies (Sikes 1994), and laid the groundwork for the Olduvai Landscape Archaeology Project (OLAP). Led by Rob Blumenschine (Blumenschine and Masao 1991; Peters and Blumenschine 1993, 1995; Blumenschine and Peters 1998), this project has focused on sampling archaeological materials across a laterally extensive horizon 1.7 MYA in Bed II. Their goal is to interpret these archaeological materials using a paleohabitat model of the Olduvai basin.

Most of the early archaeological sites in the Rift Valley are preserved in semiarid river or lake-margin sediments with ancient vegetation ranging from closed woodlands to open grasslands (Bonnefille 1995). Unfortunately for the would-be landscape archaeologist, these contexts are also noted for their geomorphological instability and dynamic, patchy plant and animal communities (Sept 1984, 1986; Hughes 1988, 1990). Although the large-scale vegetation patterns in such sedimentary environments can persist for hundreds of years, sometimes profound, local changes can occur quite suddenly (Western and Van Praet 1973; Carr 1976). Landscape ecologists stress the complex interplay between ecological processes that operate at different spatial and temporal scales in such settings (Meentmeyer and Box 1987; Allen and Hoekstra 1992). Therefore, the goal of this chapter is only to explore relatively small-scale, short-term patterns that might influence the development of a local archaeological record: the seasonal variability and patchiness of plant foods in semiarid riverine settings. Several related questions will be considered. What were the common associations of different types of food in different microhabitats and seasons? How did keystone or preferred foods of different hominid species probably vary in their spatial and temporal distribution? What were the key habitats for different species—the places that would periodically have met a critical need for survival? How did stratigraphic conditions that frequently preserved sites also intersect with food distribution patterns?

To address such questions, Wiens (1995) advocates viewing landscapes as cost-benefit contour maps, to show how patches of foods produce different cost-benefit contours for different organisms. Foley had similar "off-site archaeology" objectives when he explored the economic value of East African landscapes for Later Stone Age foragers by plotting food "isocal maps" for Amboseli (Foley 1981). This chapter pursues a comparable approach for local, seasonal plant food variability. Incorporating these observations into longer term, regional models, as advocated by Potts (1996, 1998), will be the subject of a separate study.

Methods

Four analytical steps were followed to model early hominid plant food landscapes.

1. Vegetation was surveyed in two Kenyan habitats that were selected as sedimentary and climatic analogs to situations in which early archaeological sites were preserved. Transect samples provided quantitative field data that were used to describe attributes of the plant communities sampled by sedimentary zone in different seasons.

2. Consumer-specific plant food menus were hypothesized (for baboon, chimpanzee, modern hunter-gatherer, early *Homo*, and two australopithecines), and the abundance of foods included in each menu was documented in the vegetation transects as edible kilocalories (kcal) by season.

3. Transect data were used to extrapolate the spatial distribution of different types of foods in different seasons across each study area, generating "edible landscape maps" that model the variable distribution of total potential food energy that would have been available to each consumer at each study site.

4. Differential costs of exploiting each specific food type were then factored into each "edible landscape map" to develop hypotheses about the distribution of productive patches of high ranking plant foods for each consumer.

Vegetation Samples

No modern environment in Africa is a direct analog for a Plio-Pleistocene African environment. Yet we can model ancient vegetation through a combination of direct paleontological and geochemical evidence (Bonnefille 1995; Sikes 1994) and analogy, assuming that variables such as basin geomorphology, soil moisture, and soil chemistry would have structured vegetation in the past the same way they do today (Hughes 1988, 1990; Malanson 1993; Belsky 1995). The availability of plant foods in semiarid riparian habitats follows the structure of vegetation in such settings (Sept 1984, 1986, 1990, 1994). Therefore, simple, quantitative predictions can be made about the relative frequency of different categories of plant foods in ancient riparian habitats based on studies of vegetation in modern sedimentary analogs.

Two sets of riparian vegetation samples were collected in 1981–1982: the Il Sej Naibor channel in the Turkana basin in northern Kenya and the Voi River in the Tsavo region of southwestern Kenya (Sept 1986). The flora of both regions is similar, with vegetation mosaics of dry bushland, edaphic grasslands, and riparian woodlands that are comparable to vegetation patterns reconstructed for archaeological sites in the Turkana basin after 2.5 million years ago (Sept 1986; Isaac and Isaac 1997). Both study sites were small channels that included active sedimentary zones analogous to sedimentary contexts in which archaeological sites from East Turkana had formed (e.g., site FxJj50) (Isaac and Isaac 1997). In fact, the same Turkana channel was used for taphonomic and geomorphological study by several other members of the Koobi Fora Research Project (Kaufulu 1983; Schick 1987). Both channels were effluent, ephemeral streams whose intermittent flow supported some cut and fill depositional regimes and active overbank and floodplain sedimentation along parts of their meandering courses. Their catchment areas were comparable. Yet they differed in aspects of local climate and soils in a way that revealed an interesting contrast in vegetation structure and plant food availability. The Voi soils were derived from quartzite bedrock while the Turkana channel cut through mainly leached, alkaline soils of volcanic origin (and carbonate formation). All else being equal, one might expect the Turkana soils to provide a better nutrient balance for plant growth (Bell 1982). However, the Voi River was located in a more productive, semiarid region with up to 550 mm of rainfall a year (slightly more in its local headwaters) while the Turkana streams were in an arid region with less than 200 mm of rainfall a year. Both channels were sampled along sections of their meandering course, including sections of extensive overbank alluvium and cut banks. The Turkana channel samples included smaller tributaries draining into one section of higher relief upstream and also included a downstream braided section. The Turkana channel had a much narrower floodplain than the Voi River. The Voi River was less sinuous and included more extensive alluvial plains. Because it flooded more frequently, the immediate channel margins were more disturbed. Also, the drainage in the central section of the Voi River had been artificially disturbed, creating a swamp.

The line-intercept transect technique was used as a sampling methodology to allow the simultaneous sampling of herbaceous and woody vegetation layers (Sept 1986). Transects were established perpendicular to the channel course at random intervals along each sampled region (a 5-km length of stream). Segments along each transect were classified into different sedimentary zones based on aerial photographs, topographic data, and field observations, and these were treated as samples of each sedimentary zone for subsequent analysis. Each study site was sampled in separate seasons to monitor the growth patterns and productivity of the different species. Based on bimodal rainfall patterns in both regions, four seasons were distinguished for this analysis: a main rainy season (March–May), a main dry season (June–October), a short rainy season (November–December), a short dry season (January–February). The transect samples produced measures of the relative density, frequency and cover of each species of plant, which were combined to calculate the

Importance Value of each species as well as the floristic richness and diversity of each sampled community. These data were also grouped into structural classes (e.g., "trees," "shrubs") for quantitative analysis of the vegetation structure in each sampling area. Encounter rates for food items presented below were derived from the linear measures of the relative density of individual plants. Field and herbarium data on plant phenology in each region were used to describe the seasonal availability of particular food items in each region.

Consumer Analysis

The edibility of different parts of each plant species sampled in the field was determined from the literature, herbarium records, and discussions with ethnobotanical informants (Sept 1984, 1990). Sample plants had been harvested in the field for a measure of their edible productivity; these harvests were timed and weighed, and nutritional samples of many of these plant foods were also analyzed. The abundance of each species of food plant in different sedimentary zones sampled on the transects was calculated.

To explore how plant food abundance would vary from the perspective of different consumers, I developed six simple consumer models of plant food diet. First, three living species were modeled as consumers to test the approach. Baboons were modeled as eating a wide range of flowers, fruits, and seeds, some immature legume pods, some young leaves, shoots, and shallow roots of monocots, as known for several different populations today (e.g., Norton et al. 1987; Henzi et al. 1992; Whiten et al. 1992). Chimpanzees were modeled as eating a wide range of flowers, fruits, and seeds, including soft, ripe legumes, nuts cracked with tools, and terrestrial hebaceous vegetation, based on a range of research studies (e.g., Schoeninger et al., this volume, McGrew et al. 1981, 1988; McGrew 1992; Tutin et al. 1992; Wrangham et al. 1992; Moore 1996). Human foragers were modeled as dependent on tools and cooking to acquire and eat fruits, nuts, and some other dicot seeds, legumes, tender herbaceous dicot greens, bulbs, corms, and deeply buried tubers, as is commonly observed across ethnographic populations (e.g., Sept 1984; Vincent 1995a, 1995b; Hawkes et al. 1995, 1997). Secondly, three early hominid consumers were modeled. *A1*, an early australopithecine, was modeled as a nontool user with the ability to chew large amounts of any type of fruit or seed eaten by baboons or chimpanzees today, including legumes, as well as hebaceous vegetation, and shallow roots. *A2*, a derived robust australopithecine, was modeled as a hominid with excellent chewing ability, able to use simple tools for digging and pounding/cracking to acquire all the foods of the *A1* australopithecine, plus additional hard dicot seeds, nuts, and deeply buried tubers (Sept 1984; Vincent 1985a; Peters 1987). *H*, an early *Homo*, was modeled as able to chew any type of fruit or legume eaten by chimpanzees today, using containers for efficient collecting and tools for cutting, digging deep tubers, and pounding/cracking legume pods and nuts. These hominid models did not attempt to realistically portray specific fossil taxa but illustrated plausible alternative subsistence models for several of them: *A1* for *Australopithecus anamensis* or *A. afarensis*; *A2* for *Australopithecus boisei* or *A. aethiopicus*; *H* for *Homo habilis* or *Homo rudolfensis*. Using experimental work on harvesting rates (Sept 1984, 1990; Vincent 1985a) I estimated the caloric benefits and costs that each of these model consumers would face exploiting the specific food items counted on the transect samples in each study region. All of these cost/benefit estimates are hypothetical because only one of the consumers, baboons, lives in one of the study areas today (the Voi River). Because the study areas were located in national parks, the only humans that forage along either river are paleoanthropologists.

I chose to use a time/energy currency and simple cost/benefit foraging parameters to model the comparative return rates for each food type. There are good, theoretical reasons for examining energy as a critical resource for early hominids (Foley and Lee 1991; Leonard and Robertson 1992; Aiello and Wheeler 1995). Still, this is a simplistic approach, and more realistic questions of amino acid availability, lipo-protein requirements and other micronutrient constraints would be important to consider in any realistic foraging study (Milton 1987; Bunn and Ezzo 1993). However, bold contrasts have heuristic value in a modeling process, and energy is a useful dietary variable to explore issues of subsistence strategy and time allocation (Hames 1992).

Spatial Modeling

While field data were originally collected in transects, for this analysis these data were extrapolated across a 100-meter grid superimposed on a 4 × 10-km map of each study region. Each 1 hectare (HA) area (100 ×100-meter) grid square was classified into one of the sedimentary zones observed in the field. Data grids of food plant encounter rates were calculated from the average transect frequency values for each species in each sedimentary zone. A spreadsheet (*MS Excel*) was used to assign each grid square a potential seasonal caloric productivity value for each plant species. The mean caloric productivity of each plant food type that I measured in the field was set as the maximum model value. A spreadsheet function was used to assign each grid square a random percentage of that mean value (from 0 to 1), to represent a random probability of actually encountering that type of food when moving through that hectare at any given time. These assumptions produce a conservative estimate of the available plant foods, because abundance is only allowed to vary below the average values measured in the field. Areas of 1 hectare were chosen for the analysis because they are large enough to include more than one stand of shrubs or trees in both semiarid channel margin (highest density) and floodplain (lowest density) zones yet small enough to demonstrate heterogeneous patterns across the region. They are also comparable to grid surveys done of chimpanzees in open country (McGrew et al. 1981, 1988).

These caloric productivity distribution values were then filtered through the plant food menus for each consumer. This generated data for each hectare of the total amount of edible plant food calories (kcal/HA) potentially available for each consumer in each season. Thematic maps of the data matrices were generated and manipulated using a simple GIS program (*MapInfo*) to display the seasonal distribution of calories for each consumer across each landscape grid, and map the differences between consumers. Finally, net return harvesting rates for each plant species were used to generate cumulative matrices of the distribution of easily accessible calories that each hypothetical consumer would encounter on the different seasonal model landscapes. Seasonal landscape maps were generated based on the harvesting costs (kcal/HA) each consumer would incur in each grid unit but cannot be presented here because of space limitations. These maps illustrated patches or zones where each hominid consumer could expect to find the best (most energy/least cost) foraging, compared to the overall abundance of foods in each area,

Results

Comparing Habitats As Consumer Menu Landscapes

The Voi channel is in a higher rainfall area with greater stream flow and thus has the expected greater overall species richness and total biomass than the Turkana channel (Sept 1986). However, when viewed in terms of the seasonal distribution of edible calories (kcal) available to the six modeled consumers, the two habitats reveal some surprising similarities and differences. Some of these are illustrated below in maps (Figures 4.1 and 4.2) that represent the potential edible productivity

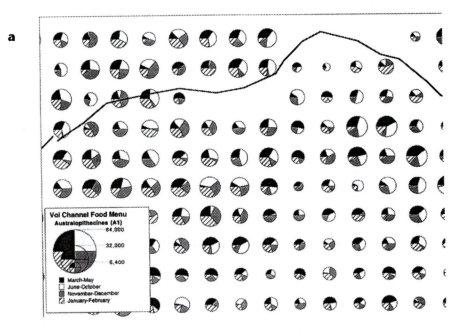

Figure 4.1. (a–c) Voi Channel food menus for (a) *A1* australopithecine 1 (without tools), (b) *A2* robust australopithecine (with simple tools) (c) *H* early *Homo*. These are landscape maps of the seasonal food availability modeled for early hominids, based on the landscape Voi River. A 670-hectare area of the model is illustrated. The solid line represents the center of the river channel. Each circle represents the abundance of edible plant foods in 1 hectare. The size of the circles is proportional to the total annual energy value (kilocalories) of plant food in the hectare available to the model hominid. Each circle energy total is subdivided into the proportions of energy that would be available to that hominid in each season.

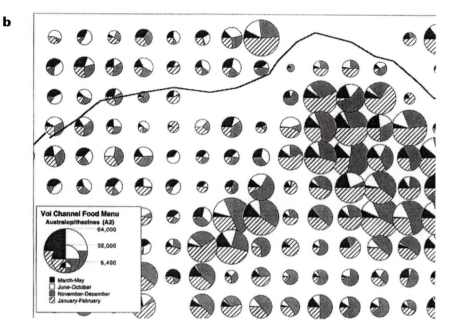

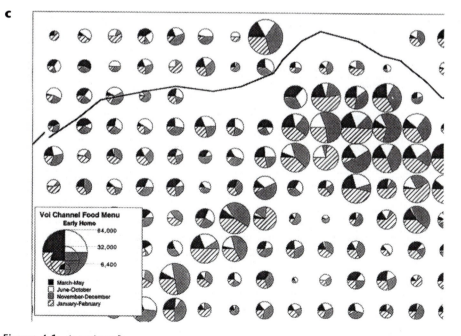

Figure 4.1. (*continued*)

(total kcal distribution) of the two landscapes as modeled for the hominid consumers. However, it is important to note that these maps only illustrate the overall abundance of foods available to each consumer and do not reflect differential foraging costs, which are described in a later section.

Baboon Menu Landscapes

One troop of baboons lived in the Voi River territory sampled during the study and was observed feeding on different plant foods, including ripe berries and some shoots and rhizomes. Note that detailed vegetation plots were not collected for baboon foods, as would be necessary for an ecological study (Norton et al. 1987; Whiten et al. 1992). Major baboon foods that occurred in the transect samples included figs, small fruits such as *Azima tetracantha*, *Maerua* spp., *Securinega virosa*, flowers of *Abutilon* spp, and roots and stems of sedges. As measured in the samples for this study and extrapolated for the model, the distribution of resource energy available

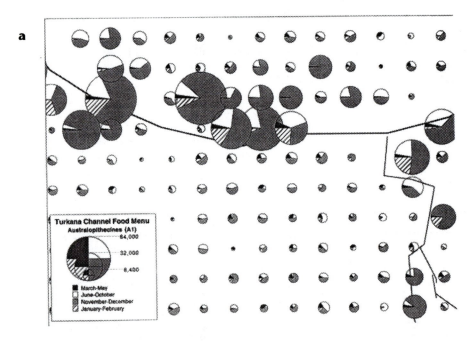

Figure 4.2. (a–c) Turkana Channel food menus for (a) *A1* australopithecine 1 (without tools), (b) *A2* robust australopithecine (with simple tools) (c) *H* early *Homo*. These are landscape maps of the seasonal food availability modeled for early hominids, based on the Turkana landscape near the Il Sej Naibor channel. A 670-hectare area of the model is illustrated. The solid line represents the center of the river channel. Each circle represents the abundance of edible plant foods in one hectare. The size of the circles is proportional to the total annual energy value (kilocalories) of plant food in the hectare available to the model hominid. Each circle energy total is subdivided into the proportions of energy that would be available to that hominid in each season.

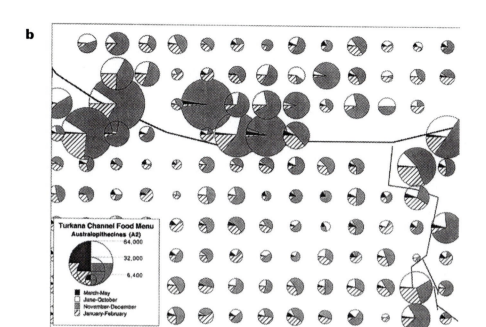

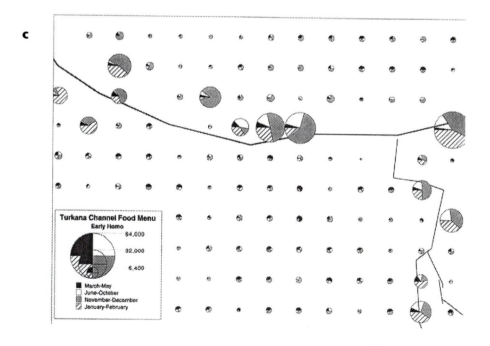

Figure 4.2. (*continued*)

to baboons across this landscape is low (averaging less than 3000kcal/HA) but quite evenly distributed between different sedimentary zones and seasons. The alluvial plains included a few more grid squares with relatively high baboon food densities. Compared to other baboon habitats (e.g., Norton et al. 1987; Henzi et al. 1992; Whiten et al. 1992), such resource patterning would not be unusual, and this provides some validation for the estimates and assumptions of the model. Although evidently adequate for baboons, the Voi habitat has a relatively low productivity of baboon foods when compared to the other consumer models. In contrast, baboons were not observed living along the Turkana channel. The model predicts that baboon plant foods would be encountered more rarely in this habitat than at Voi, especially before and during the beginning of the normal rainy season. The Turkana food species considered to be edible by baboons included ripe fruits such as the species of *Maerua*, *Grewia tenax*, *Salvadora persica*, *Boscia coriacea*; green pods of small Acacias; and bulbs and grass corms. Some productive patches of baboon foods (e.g., green legume seeds and berries) would be available along the riparian channel in this Turkana landscape throughout the growing season and both dry seasons (but would have disappeared by the time the rainy season began in March). This suggests that January through March or April would be a season of extreme food scarcity for *Papio* baboons in this habitat, and would limit their ability to live there.

Chimpanzee Menu Landscapes

Chimpanzee plant food productivity in the Voi habitat is modeled as comparable to or less than the range of baboon foods. For example, fruits and flowers from small, widely distributed plants eaten by baboons, such as *Abutilon* and *Withania somnifera*, were not included in this model chimp menu. Spatial distribution of the modeled chimpanzee foods varied significantly with season. During the main rainy season and subsequent dry season, the alluvial plains adjacent to the Voi River included more fruits and shoots from a chimpanzee menu than the surrounding unflooded areas. However, during other times of the year few foods would have been available to chimps anywhere in this landscape, precluding their survival there. Overall, the arid Turkana landscape would offer few plant food foraging opportunities for chimpanzees, except for patches of green legumes and small fruits and berries available along the main channel. January through March or April would be a season of extreme food scarcity for chimpanzees in this habitat. Thus, this model predicts that chimpanzees, which are dependent on the soft fruits and seeds of forests, woodlands, and wooded savannas (see Schoeninger et al., this volume), probably could not survive in either of these dry bushland habitats.

Human Forager Menu Landscapes

This model predicts that the Voi River floodplains would support abundant patches of plant foods for a modern human forager, particularly during the main dry season when relatively few kcal would be available from plant foods in the surrounding terrain. The fewest foods would be available during the main rains, but there would be some available. Key hunter-gatherer plant food species that were included in the Voi transects were the fruits and tubers of selected cucurbits and other vines, berries from various shrubs, and commonly eaten fruits of large trees such as tamarind, fig, and *Dobera glabra*, as well as less frequently eaten "famine foods" such as *Kigelia* fruit. Modern human foragers would find stronger spatial contrasts in plant food availability near the Turkana channel. Almost no foods would be available during the rains or early dry season anywhere in the region. Extensive patches of berries and cookable legume seeds would be available along the channel and tributaries by the end of the dry season and short rains (e.g., between August and December) with negligible plant foods to be encountered away from this narrow ribbon of riparian foods. Edible species in the samples included cooked legume seeds, such as *Acacia tortilis* and *Cadaba farinosa*; fruits and berries such as *Ziziphus sp.*, Cordia sinensis, and *Grewia tenax*; and tubers such as *Vatovoea pseudolablab*.

Australopithecine (A1) Menu Landscapes

A1 hominids were modeled as generalized australopithecines that did not use tools but had the ability to chew a wide range of tough plant foods including soft seeds. This model predicts that they would have encountered a significantly different range of plant food foraging opportunities in the Voi landscape than either the living baboon, chimp, human, or other early hominids modeled. Figure 4.1a maps a sample of the Voi landscape feeding opportunities for *A1* with the size of the circles representing the total annual Kcal abundance of *A1* plant foods in each hectare and slices of each pie showing seasonal proportions. In particular, the riparian zone along the Voi River would have had fewest plant food calories available for *A1* compared to the other hominid models although the surrounding terrain would have had opportunities comparable to *H*. Without access to deeply buried tubers, *A1* would have encountered the fewest foods between September and February and thus might have been forced to eat a plant food diet of greens, shallow roots, and small fruits similar to that of baboons during this half the year. The Voi landscape would have provided at best a marginal, seasonal subsistence base for this australopithecine model. In contrast, in the Turkana habitat *A1* would have encountered abundant foraging opportunities for relatively soft seeds, especially *Acacia* and other legume tree pods, in the late dry season/short rainy season that would have offered a significant supplement to the small fruits and berries that ripen that time of year (Figure 4.2a). Thus, the Turkana channel margins would have been abundant sources of plant foods for *A1* hominids. Even without tools, *A1* consumers in the Turkana area would have encountered more abundant plant foods across the landscape and a wider range of foraging opportunities in all seasons than *H*. Comparing both habitats, these patches of trees in the dry riparian zones would have offered the most foraging opportunities for *A1* hominids.

Robust Australopithecine (A2) Menu Landscapes

A2 hominids are modeled as specialized megadonts with the ability to use some tools, similar to some suggestions for robust australopithecines in South Africa

(Brain 1993; Sussman 1998). *A2* hominids are assumed to have had the ability to dig up and chew a wide range of roots, including tubers and woody rootstocks, as well as ripe legume seeds—a wider diet breadth than the other consumers modeled here. Therefore, *A2* australopithecines would have encountered a greater abundance of plant food foraging opportunities on both landscapes than the other hominids. The Voi alluvial plains would have been an abundant source of diverse plant foods for these consumers, but the ability of *A2* to dig up and chew a wide range of roots would have made the surrounding terrain a good territory for plant foods as well, as illustrated by the dense distribution of plant food pies in Figure 4.1b. *A2* consumers would also have encountered a wider range of foraging opportunities in the Turkana habitat and along the Turkana channels in particular. Rainy season plant foods would have been the most limited, but dry season foraging opportunities for roots and seeds would have been widely distributed and abundant (Figure 4.2b). As mapped, both habitats appear to be dense carpets of diverse plant food feeding opportunities from the *A2* perspective.

Early *Homo* (*H*) Menu Landscapes

Early *Homo* (*H*) was modeled without the cooking ability of modern human foragers but with the ability to dig up and chew more fibrous roots, and eat more raw, herbaceous vegetation than modern foragers normally do. The relative size of the circles in Figure 4.1c illustrates how more foods would have been more abundant over large areas of the alluvial plains at Voi compared to either the channel margins or the surrounding, unflooded habitats. The model predicts that, compared to modern hunter-gatherers, *H* would have encountered comparable plant food foraging opportunities in the riparian zone and significantly more plant food foraging opportunities away from the Voi channel. Thus, particularly during the main rains and early growing season, Voi would have been a productive habitat for *H*. In contrast *H* would have found fewer plant food foraging opportunities in the Turkana area than modern human foragers. *H* might have exploited small patches of herbaceous growth dispersed across this landscape during the rains and early dry season (Figure 4.2c). However, without the ability to cook the hard, ripe pods of *Acacia tortilis* and other common legumes as modern humans do, the only large patches of edible plant food calories available to *H* would have occurred at widely spaced intervals immediately along the channels. Thus, small differences in the vegetation between these two, semiarid bushland habitats seem to have major consequences for the plant food availability modeled for early *Homo*.

The average seasonal patterns of food availability modeled for the three hominids can be summarized as follows. First, during the main rainy season, no significant differences in average food availability are predicted between the different hominids although australopithecines would always have had a few more feeding opportunities because they are modeled as eating a wider range of shoots, pith, and stems. During the main dry season, average foraging opportunities for the three hominid consumers would have been comparable at Voi but would have diverged at Turkana. Robust australopithecine tool users (*A2*), in particular, would encounter more plant food energy sources across such an arid landscape during this season. By the end of the dry season and during the short rains, dramatic contrasts in food availability would have existed for the different hominid consumers, particularly in the driest habitat at Turkana. The abundance of seeds along the Turkana channels would provide a bounty to *A1* and *A2* during this season unavailable to *H*. On the other hand, lack of access to tubers during this same season would limit the foods available to nontool-using australopithecines (*A1*) at Voi. During the short dry season, as foods in both habitats become scarce, tool-using hominids (*H* and *A2*) would have encountered the most feeding opportunities overall, particularly in the arid Turkana habitat.

Early Hominid Cost/Benefit Landscapes

To evaluate how landscape differences in plant food abundance might influence general foraging strategies of *H*, *A1*, and *A2*, both the costs and benefits of foraging for plant foods must be taken into account. The handling costs of exploiting different plant foods vary with the morphology, phytochemistry, and growth habit of the plant and with the skill, anatomical adaptations, and technology·of the consumer. Cost/benefit ratios influence whether modern foragers like the Hadza, for example, decide to dig for tubers or collect berries (Hawkes et al. 1995, 1997). A megadont, such as *A2*, would be expected to be able to process tough foods more efficiently than smaller toothed *H*. Alternatively, the use of a simple sling container would allow *H* to snack and collect foods simultaneously and thus forage for some foods more efficiently than *A1* feeding merely hand to mouth. Therefore, consumer-specific handling rates were estimated for each food type and habitat zone to reflect the anatomical and behavioral differences. These handling rates were then used to calculate the time it would take for each consumer to harvest the food available in each grid square.

This approach can be used to suggest approximately when and where the different hominid consumers could have foraged most efficiently for plant foods. During the rainy season, the return rates for plant foods would have been extremely low across both landscapes for all three hominids, ranging from 400–600kcal/hour at Turkana and 400–900kcal/hour at Voi. *H* could have foraged equally inefficiently away from the channels as near them during the rains while both *A1* and *A2* would have had marginally better return rates on the alluvial plains, especially in a habitat like Voi. During the main dry season, all three hominids in the Voi habitat would have found the best foraging patches in the unflooded hinterlands away from the channel with average return rates over 1700kcal/hour, despite the menu model showing foods would have been abundant in the alluvial plains of Voi. During the main dry season as Turkana, the australopithecine return rates would have been marginally better along the channels, up to 600kcal/hour, but *H* returns would have been genrally higher, particularly in the unflooded Turkana zones (1250kcal/hour). The most significant differences emerge in these cost/benefit landscapes during four months at the end of the year—the short rains and short dry season (October through February). At Voi, *A1* would have faced the lowest return rates overall: 400–600kcal/hour in a relatively undifferentiated landscape. *A2* foraging would have been more productive and cost effective anywhere away from the Voi channel margins with return rates averaging over 1500kcal/hour on the broad alluvial plains. The Voi alluvial floodplains would also have provided the best foraging patches for *H*, during this time but with lower return rates (1000–1400kcal/hour) than the robust australopithecines. At Turkana, during this same season, the channel margins and floodplains would have provided the only adequate foraging zone for *A1* and *H* (100–900kcal/hour). In contrast, this model suggests *A2* would have had better return rates during these seasons at Turkana, including efficient foraging patches near the channels (200–1000kcal/hour) and return rates averaging 500kcal/hour away from the channels. *A2* thus would have faced less of a contrast in return rates across the landscape than the other two consumers. The options available for the two australopithecines diverge most markedly during the short dry season (January–February) when *A2*'s ability to dig for tubers would have helped them survive.

Table 4.1 summarizes the main patterns of foraging efficiency predicted by this model, compared in terms of the amount of time it would take each consumer to acquire a daily allowance of 2500kcal by foraging at the predicted rates on the foods actually available in each hectare. This comparison highlights patterns of potential overlap and competition. During the main dry season, while foods are abundant near the channel, the most efficient foraging patches for hominid plant food consumers would have been dispersed across landscapes. This is a nonintuitive result and leads to an interesting question. Would hominids have been lured away from the channel during this period, incurring greater travel costs while searching for "cheap" plant foods? The answer to this would depend upon what other foods would have been available in the different habitats, as discussed below. The model also suggests that the greatest food stress, and potential competition among hominids for plant foods, would have occurred in riparian zones at the end of the main dry season/short rains. During the short, hot dry season in January–Feburary and into March, with the onset of the rains, australopithecines without tools and early *Homo* would have faced their worst times foraging for plants. However, during this same season robust *A2* australopithecines could have used their cheek teeth and digging tools to maintain good plant food return rates in the riparian zones and modest return rates elsewhere. This short dry season would have been a season when selection pressures would have encouraged hominid consumer strategies to diverge.

Discussion: Incentives for Omnivory

To what extent can a study of plant food foraging options help us pursue research on early hominid subsistence strategies or meat-eating? It can do so in the context of site formation processes, due to the economics of resource competition and habitat preference. Despite its simplicity, this edible landscape model makes several predictions about the early hominid edible landscape that may prove to be a useful springboard for research.

First, this model has explored semiarid riverine woodlands as likely loci of hominid competition for plant foods. For example, at the end of the long dry season and during the short rains (October–December), such riparian zones would have been distinctive, cost-effective patches where hominids might have converged in search

Table 4.1a. Voi foraging zones compared.

Season	Australopithecine 1		Australopithecine 2		Early *Homo*
March–May	No zonal focus for either robust hominid: Alluvial plains: 2.5–5 hours for 2500 kcal in all zones Hinterland: > 25 hours			> <	No zonal focus: Alluvial plains: 5–10 hours Hinterland: 5–10 hours
June–Oct	Hinterland excellent: Alluvial plains: 2.5–5 hours Hinterland: 1–2.5 hours	> =	Hinterland excellent: Alluvial plains: 2.5–5 hours Hinterland: 1–2.5 hours	 = 	Hinterland excellent: Near channel: 2.5–5 hours Hinterland: 1–2.5 hours
Nov–Dec	No zonal focus: good overall Alluvial plains: 2.5–5 hours Hinterland: 2.5–5 hours	 < <	No zonal focus: overall excellent: Alluvial plains: 1–2.5 hours Hinterland: 1–2.5 hours	 = >	Alluvial plains excellent: Alluvial plains: 1–2.5 hours Hinterland: 2.5–5 hours
Jan–Feb	Alluvial plains fair: Alluvial plains: 5–10 hours Hinterland: > 15 hours	 < <	Alluvial plains excellent: Alluvial plains: 1–2.5 hours Hinterland: 5–10 hours	 > >	Alluvial plains fair: Alluvial plains: 2.5–5 hours Hinterland: > 15 hours

Seasonal ranking, based on the average amount of time it would take to harvest 2,500 kcal, of the foraging zones for each hominid model for the Voi channel (Table 4.1a) and Turkana channel (Table 4.1b) landscape models. The symbols > < and = are used to highlight which hominids would have faced better foraging options in each season and habitat zone.

Table 4.1b. Turkana foraging zones compared.

Season	Australopithecine 1		Australopithecine 2		Early Homo
March–May	No zonal focus for either robust hominid: 2.5–5 hours for 2500 Kcal in all zones			>	No zonal focus: 5–10 hours in all zones
June–Oct	No zonal focus:		Channel margins good:		Hinterland excellent:
	Near channel: 5–10 hours	<	Near channel: 2.5–5 hours	=	Near channel: 2.5–5 hours
	Hinterland: 5–10 hours	=	Hinterland: 5–10 hours	<	Hinterland: 1–2.5 hours
Nov–Dec	Channel margins good:		Channel margins excellent:		Channels good:
	Near channels: 2.5–5 hours	<	Near channels: 1–2.5 hours	>	Near channel: 2.5–10 hours
	Hinterland > 10 hours	<	Hinterland 2.5–5 hours	>	Hinterland > 15 hours
Jan–Feb	Poor foraging everywhere:		Channel margins good:		Poor foraging everywhere:
	Near channels: > 25 hours	<	Near channels: 2.5–5 hours	>	Near channels: 10–15 hours
	Hinterland: > 25 hours	<	Hinterland 5–10 hours	>	Hinterland: > 25 hours

of plant foods. The drier the region, the higher the resource valence of such gallery forest patches; riparian zones could have acted as magnets to draw in hominids foraging for plant foods. Because many early archaeological sites have been found in channel margin and floodplain sediments, it would be interesting to test this seasonal hypothesis with empirical evidence. However, finding paleontological or sedimentological evidence to demonstrate seasonality in early site formation remains an elusive goal.

Seasonal feeding competition within and between primate groups under such circumstances could lead to long-term socio-ecological divergence in features such as group size and composition, mobility, or food selectivity (Tutin et al. 1992; Isbell and Young 1996). If competition for fleshy fruits was seasonally high in riparian settings, then the ability to switch and chew energy-rich, hard ripe seeds instead, would have given robust australopithecines a selective advantage (also see arguments in Schoeninger et al. this volume). However, hominids could also have faced increased risks of predation if they had limited their preferred ranging to such zones. Are such seasonal plant food patches common in other riparian settings in East Africa, or are the predictions of these models unusual? Previous actualistic research (Sept 1994) and ethnographic analogy (Vincent 1985a, 1985b; Hawkes et al. 1995, 1997) both suggest that the end of the year may be a prime time to forage for many arboreal fruits and seeds. So, this may be a common pattern, but further fieldwork is needed to demonstrate its variability in different phytogeographic zones. In particular, it would be useful to model the details of plant food foraging opportunities in regions with a single, long dry season, or in deciduous woodland zones with more extensive legume and nut tree species (Peters et al. 1984; Peters 1987; Moore 1996; Schoeninger et al. 1999).

Second, the edible landscape model also points to circumstances in which plant food exploitation patterns might have led early hominids to visit habitats with different frequencies. If hominids like *A2* and *H* had been sympatric, *A2* would have always had plant food foraging returns equal to or better than *H* in riparian settings. What are the implications of this? While their adaptations would afford them many choices, *A2* australopithecines would almost always have been able to forage for plant foods most economically in riparian habitats. In contrast, during much of the year early *Homo* could have foraged most efficiently for plant foods away from riparian zones, especially during the dry season, lured by higher plant food returns in unflooded terrain. While early *Homo* might have been tethered to riparian zones for shade, refuge, or water, this model suggests that they would have needed to travel more extensively searching for smaller patches of plant foods than *A2* australopithecines. Any contrasts between the seasonal land use patterns of these types of plant food consumers also would be expected to be larger in drier settings. Reed's suggestions (Reed 1997) of habitat divergence for robust and gracile hominids during the Plio-Pleistocene fit the predictions of this landscape model.

Because archaeological sites sample the channel margin and alluvial zones almost exclusively, this model also reminds us of the fact that our sedimentary samples likely derive from intermittent, fluctuating, and incomplete series of activities, perhaps from several different hominid species. For example, if *A2* australopithecines contributed to the archaeological record preserved in such settings, this model would predict that their stone or bone contributions would derive from a relatively local catchment, particularly between September and February. The more wide-ranging foraging activities predicted for early *Homo* during the dry seasons would only be represented in the sedimentary samples if transported back to the riparian habitat for some reason such as refuge, shade, water exploitation, or provisioning/sharing. As these diverse debris patterns could become superimposed as palimpsests in the sediments, it might prove impossible for archaeologists to distinguish sites with "local" signatures from sites with "regional" signatures, but it would be a worthwhile objective for small sites.

Finally, plant food foraging models should help predict the times and places when early hominids would be most dependent on nonplant foods. Zooarchaeologists have focused on the long dry season as a stressful time for early hominids, a season when small game or carcasses scavenged during periods of high natural mortality would have assisted survival (cf. Sept 1992; Bunn and Ezzo 1993). As modeled here, plant foods would have been available during this period, but *H*, in particular, would have faced relatively low foraging returns for plant foods in the riparian zones, particularly in the drier, Turkana habitat. Thus, early *Homo* would have had an economic incentive to search further afield for plant foods. Such a strategy could have led to more frequent encounters with hunting or scavenging opportunities away from the riparian zone (refer to Tappen, this volume, for a discussion of alternative models of scavenging opportunities). Remembering the earlier prediction that long dry season sites created by early *Homo* would be expected to demonstrate a "regional" signature, this would imply that such seasonal sites should include greater numbers of butchered, transported large mammal remains. Also, for such foragers traversing floodplains during the late dry season, fish could have been collected in dessicating pools on alluvial plains and in shallow oxbow lakes (Stewart 1994), particularly if the streams flowed seasonally, as happens at both Voi and Turkana today.

This study suggests that hominids would have experienced their most marginal plant food returns from January through March or April. While a number of small fruits ripen intermittently throughout this period, it would have been a tough transition period before a new growing cycle would begin again with the main rains. Roots, though increasingly bitter, would have been a staple food during this period. But what types of alternative foods would have been available during this time of year? Several types of animal foods could have been acquired during this stressful period with the same foraging strategies used to search for plant foods. Insects and honey would have been good options in gallery woodlands, particularly because they are both energy and protein rich, but would probably have required a basic level of technology for efficient foraging (see McGrew this volume). Honey is prized by chimpanzees in dry habitats (McGrew 1992) and is also collected by Hadza during a similar season (Hawkes et al. 1995, 1997). On the other hand, with the ability to eat a few more seeds and dig up a wide range of roots, this model suggests that robust australopithecines could have specialized on plant food foraging and achieved fair return rates without a dependence on animal foods. Early *Homo* would have faced relatively low foraging returns for plant foods during this season before the main rains, increasing the selective advantage of supplementing a plant-based diet with foods from insects and animals. The riparian zone would have yielded equal or slightly better plant food returns to *H* during this period, so this may have been a good season to steal cached leopard kills or develop systematic strategies to take advantage of other riparian scavenging opportunities (Cavallo and Blumenschine 1989; Blumenschine 1994).

Conclusions

As paleoanthropologists take up the challenge of landscape archaeology, we face special constraints of taphonomic process, and spatial and temporal resolution not faced by colleagues working in later time periods. However, I believe that a cautious approach to using actualistic studies to model habitat variation can help develop hypotheses about the behavioral processes that led to site formation that may be testable with the archaeological record. The plant food perspective of this study suggests that avenues of renewed archaeological investigation should include: evidence of seasonal site formation in different paleohabitat zones, evidence of the relative distances of resource transport at different sites, and evidence of the exploitation of small game or insect resources.

The model of plant food foraging parameters developed here is relevant for interpreting sites in small-scale, semiarid, or arid channel settings comparable to sites in East Africa such as East Turkana sites FxJj50 and FxJj20 (Isaac and Isaac 1997). Integrating empirical data from other riparian habitats (e.g., Sept 1984, 1990) would help strengthen this modeling approach. However, even this preliminary comparison can help bracket the likely direction and dimensions of plant food variability through time within one stratigraphic sequence, such as the small-scale variations between sites documented for the East Turkana record (Isaac and Isaac 1997).

The next stage in this modeling process should increase the variety of information layers in the GIS. For example, it would be useful to include the importance values of trees and shrubs as proxies for refuge availability and some types of predation risk (Sept 1984). This would help develop models of hominid mobility strategies as well as site formation processes. Also, including comparable food distribution and harvesting data on insect and animal foods from the same study sites as the plant foods would be valuable. Obviously animal foods are livelier than sessile plant foods, so it would be important to make the landscape models of animal foods more dynamic and probabilistic.

The edible landscape models presented here are based on static sedimentary classifications. A logical next step could develop spatial models that explore how plant and animal foods would vary with the short-term sedimentary shifts that shape site formation processes. To evaluate larger scale, longer term patterns of foraging choices in settings of fluctuating climate or basin geomorphology, more dynamic and probabilistic models are needed. It would be a mistake to simply aggregate the short-term, localized predictions of this model to form a longer term record, both for taphonomic reasons (e.g., Stern 1993), and for reasons of scalability and shifting mosaics, as landscape ecologists have argued (Turner 1990; Rastetter et al. 1992; Delcourt and Delcourt 1992; Pickett and Cadenasso 1995).

Finally, it is important to emphasize that many of the implications for hominid behavior produced by this preliminary model could not be derived from simply comparing descriptions of the gross abundance of plant foods in each region. Developing hypotheses of the cost/benefit ratios of specific foods for specific consumers was an important step in building this model and should be a critical element in future models of consumer landscapes aimed to address paleoanthropological questions.

Acknowledgments   I would like to thank the Wenner Gren Foundation for Anthropological Research and the organizers Craig Stanford and Henry Bunn for the invitation to participate in a stimulating conference. The research that laid the foundation for this chapter was supported by the National Science Foundation and the L. S. B. Leakey Foundation. Thanks to Craig Stanford and the other reviewers for providing insightful and helpful comments. Additional ideas were honed through discussions with the conference participants, as well as M. K. Holder and Jim Moore.

REFERENCES

Aiello, L. C., and P. Wheeler. 1995. The expensive-tissue hypothesis. *Current Anthropology* 36(2):199–222.

Allen, T. F. H., and T. W. Hoekstra. 1992. *Toward a Unified Ecology*. New York: Columbia University Press.

Asfaw, B., et al.. 1999. *Australopithecus garhi*: a new species of early hominid from Ethiopia. *Science* 284:629–635.

Bell, R. H. V. 1982. The effect of soil nutrient availability on community structure in African ecosystems. In *Ecology of Tropical Savannas* (B. J. Huntley and B. H. Walker, eds.), pp. 193–216. Berlin: Springer.

Belsky, A. J. 1995. Spatial and temporal landscape patterns in arid and semi-arid African savannas. In *Mosaic Landscapes and Ecological Processes* (L. Hansson et al., eds.), pp. 31–56. London: Chapman and Hall.

Binford, L. R. 1987. Researching ambiguity: frames of reference and site structure. In *Method and Theory for Activity Area Research: An Ethnoarchaeological Approach* (S. Kent, ed.), pp. 449–512. New York: Columbia University Press.

Blumenschine, R. J. 1989. A landscape taphonomic model of the scale of prehistoric scavenging opportunities. *Journal of Human Evolution* 18:345–371.

Blumenschine, R. J. 1992. Hominid carnivory and foraging strategies, and the socioeconomic function of early archaeological sites. In *Foraging Strategies and Natural Diet of Monkeys, Apes and Humans. Proceedings of a Royal Society Discussion Meeting held on 30 and 31 May 1991* (A. Whiten and E. M. Widdowson, eds.), pp. 211–221. Oxford: Clarendon.

Blumenschine, R. J., et al. 1994. Competition for carcasses and early hominid behavioral ecology: a case study and conceptual framework. *Journal of Human Evolution* 27:197–213.

Blumenschine, R. J., and F. Masao. 1991. Living sites at Olduvai Gorge, Tanzania? Preliminary landscape archaeology results in the basal Bed II lake margin zone. *Journal of Human Evolution* 21:451–462.

Blumenschine, R. J., and C. R. Peters. 1998. Archaeological predictions for hominid land use in the paleo-Olduvai basin, Tanzania, during lowermost Bed II times. *Journal of Human Evolution* 34:565–607.

Bonnefille, R. 1995. A reassessment of the Plio-Pleistocene pollen record of East Africa. In *Paleoclimate and Evolution, with Emphasis on Human Origins* (E. S. Vrba et al., eds.), pp. 299–310. New Haven, CT: Yale University Press.

Brain, C. K., ed. 1993. *Swartkrans: A Cave's Chronicle of Early Man*. Pretoria: Transvaal Museum.

Bunn, H. T. 1991. A taphonomic perspective in the archaeology of human origins. *Annual Review of Anthropology* 20:433–467.

Bunn, H. T. 1994. Early Pleistocene hominid foraging strategies along the ancestral Omo River at Koobi Fora, Kenya. *Journal of Human Evolution* 27(1–3):247–266.

Bunn, H. T., and J. A. Ezzo. 1993. Hunting and scavenging by Plio-Pleistocene hominids: Nutritional constraints, archaeological patterns, and behavioral implications. *Journal of Archaeological Science* 20(4):365–398.

Carr, C. J. 1976. Plant ecological variation and pattern in the lower Omo basin. In *Earliest Man and Environment in the Lake Rudolf Basin* (Y. Coppens et al., eds.), pp. 432–470. Chicago: Chicago University Press.

Cavallo, J. A., and R. J. Blumenschine. 1989. Tree-stored leopard kills: expanding the hominid scavenging niche. *Journal of Human Evolution* 18:393–399.

de Heinzelin, J., et al. 1999. Environment and behavior of 2.5-million-year-old Bouri hominids. *Science* 284:625–629.

Delcourt, P. A., and H. R. Delcourt. 1992. Ecotone dynamics in space and time. In *Landscape Boundaries. Consequences for Biotic Diversity and Ecological Flows* (A. J. Hanson and F. di Castri, eds.), pp. 19–54. New York: Springer Verlag.

Demes, B., and N. Creel. 1988. Bite force, diet and cranial morphology of fossil hominids. *Journal of Human Evolution* 17:657–690.

Foley, R. 1981. *Off-Site Archaeology and Human Adaptation in Eastern Africa: An Analysis of Regional Artifact Density in the Amboseli, Southern Kenya*. Cambridge: British Archaeological Reports.

Foley, R. A., and P. C. Lee. 1991. Ecology and energetics of encephalization in hominid evolution. *Philosophical Transactions of the Royal Society of London* B:63–73.

Gifford-Gonzalez, D. 1991. Bones are not enough: analogues, knowledge, and interpretive strategies in zooarchaeology. *Journal of Anthropological Archaeology* 10(3):215–254.

Hames, R. 1992. Time allocation. In *Evolutionary Ecology and Human Behavior* (E. A. Smith and B. Winterhalder, eds.), pp. 203–235. New York: Aldine de Gruyter.

Hawkes, K., et al. 1995. Hadza children's foraging: juvenile dependency, social arrangements, and mobility among hunter-gatherers. *Current Anthropology* 36(4):688–700.

Hawkes, K., et al. 1997. Hadza women's time allocation, offspring provisioning, and the evolution of long postmenopausal life spans. *Current Anthropology* 38(4):551–577.

Hay, R. L. 1976. *The Geology of Olduvai Gorge*. Berkeley: University of California Press.

Henzi, S. P., et al. 1992. Patterns of movement by baboons in the Drakensburg Mountains: primary responses to the environment. *International Journal of Primatology* 13(6):601–629.

Hughes, F. M. R. 1988. The ecology of African floodplain forests in semi-arid and arid zones: a review. *Journal of Biogeography* 15:127–140.

Hughes, F. M. R. 1990. The influence of flooding regimes on forest distribution and composition in the Tana River floodplain, Kenya. *Journal of Applied Ecology* 27:475–491.

Isaac, G. L. 1977. *Olorgesailie: Archaeological Studies of a Middle Pleistocene Lake Basin in Kenya*. Chicago: University of Chicago Press.

Isaac, G. L. 1981. Stone age visiting cards: approaches to the study of early land-use patterns. *Patterns in the Past* (I. Hodder, et al., eds.), pp. 37–103. Cambridge: Cambridge University Press.

Isaac, G. L. 1984. The archaeology of human origins: studies of the lower Pleistocene in East Africa 1971–1981. *Advances in World Archaeology* (F. Wendorf, ed.), vol. 3, pp. 1–87. New York: Academic Press.

Isaac, G. L., and J. W. K. Harris. 1980. A method for determining the characteristics of artefacts between sites in the Upper Member of the Koobi Fora Formation, East Lake Turkana. In *8th Panafrican Congress on Prehistory and Quaternary Studies*. Nairobi, Kenya: TILLMIAP.

Isaac, G. L., and B. Isaac, eds. 1997. *Koobi Fora Research Project Vol 5. Plio-Pleistocene Archaeology*. Oxford: Oxford University Press.

Isbell, L. A., and T. P. Young. 1996. The evolution of bipedalism in hominids and reduced group size in chimpanzees: alternative responses to decreasing resource availability. *Journal of Human Evolution* 30:389–397.

Kaufulu, Z. 1983. *The Geological Context of Some Early Archaeological Sites in Kenya, Malawi, and Tanzania*. Berkeley: Univerisity of California.

Kay, R. F., and F. E. Grine. 1988. Tooth morphology, wear and diet in Australopithecus and Paranthropus from southern Africa. *Evolutionary History of the "Robust" Australopithecines* (F. E. Grine, eds.), pp. 427–448. New York: Aldine de Gruyter.

Kelso, W., and R. Most, eds. 1990. *Earth Patterns: Essays in Landscape Archaeology*. Charlottesville: University of Virginia Press.

Leakey, M. D. 1971. *Olduvai Gorge, Vol. 3 Excavations in Beds I and II, 1960–1963*. Cambridge: Cambridge University Press.

Leakey, M. D. 1994. *Olduvai Gorge, Vol 5 Excavations in Beds III, IV and the Masek Beds, 1968–1971*. Cambridge: Cambridge University Press.

Leonard, W. R., and M. L. Robertson. 1992. Nutritional requirements and human evolution: a bioenergetics model. *American Journal of Human Biology* 4:179–195.

Malanson, G. P. 1993. *Riparian Landscapes*. Cambridge: Cambridge University Press.

McCollum, M. A. 1999. The robust australopithecine face: a morphogenetic perspective. *Science* 284:301–305.

McGrew, W. C. 1992. *Chimpanzee Material Culture. Implications for Human Evolution*. Cambridge: Cambridge University Press.

McGrew, W. C., et al. 1988. Diet of wild chimpanzees (*Pan troglodytes verus*) at Mt. Assirik, Senegal. I. Composition. *American Journal of Primatology* 16:213–226.

McGrew, W. C., et al. 1981. Chimpanzees in a hot, dry, and open habitat: Mt Assirik, Senegal, West Africa. *Journal of Human Evolution* 10:227–244.

Meentemeyer, V., and E. O. Box. 1987. Scale effects in landscape studies. *Landscape Heterogeneity and Disturbance*. (M. G. Turner, ed.), pp. 15–36. New York: Springer-Verlag.

Miller, N. F., and K. L. Gleason, eds. 1994. *The Archaeology of Garden and Field*. Philadelphia: University of Pennsylvania Press.

Milton, K. 1987. Primate diets and gut morphology: implications for hominid evolution. In *Food and Evolution: Toward a Theory of Human Food Habits* (M. Harris and E. Ross, eds), pp. 93–115. Philadelphia: Temple University Press.

Moore, J. 1996. "Savanna" chimpanzees, referential models and the LCA. In *Great Ape Societies* (W. C. McGrew, L. Marchant, and T. Nishioa, eds.). New York: Cambridge University Press.

Norton, G. W., et al. 1987. Baboon diet: a five-year study of stability and variability in the plant feeding and habitat of the yellow baboons (*Papio cynocephalus*) of Mikumi National Park, Tanzania. *Folia Primatologica* 48:78–120.

Peters, C. R. 1987. Nut-like oil seeds: food for monkeys, chimpanzees, humans, and probably ape-men. *American Journal of Physical Anthropology* 73:333–363.

Peters, C. R., and R. J. Blumenschine. 1993. Modeling resource distributions and hominid land use in the Olduvai Basin during lowermost Bed II times. In *Four Million Years of Hominid Evolution in Africa. An International Congress in Honour of Dr. Mary Douglas Leakey's Outstanding Contribution in Palaeoanthropology.* Arusha, Tanzania.

Peters, C. R., and R. J. Blumenschine. 1995. Landscape perspectives on possible land use patterns for Early Pleistocene hominids in the Olduvai Basin, Tanzania. *Journal of Human Evolution* 29:321–362.

Peters, C. R., et al. 1984. Plant types and seasonality of wild plant foods, Tanzania to southwestern Africa: resources for models of the natural environment. *Journal of Human Evolution* 13:397–414.

Pickett, S. T. A., and M. L. Cadenasso. 1995. Landscape ecology: spatial heterogeneity in ecological systems. *Science* 269:331–334.

Potts, R. 1994. Variables versus models of early Pleistocene hominid land use. *Journal of Human Evolution* 27:7–24.

Potts, R. 1996. Evolution and climatic variability. *Science* 273:922–923.

Potts, R. 1998. Evironmental hypotheses of hominid evolution. *Yearbook of Physical Anthropology* 41:93–136.

Rastetter, E. B., et al. 1992. Aggregating fine-scale ecological knowledge to model coarser-scale attributes of ecosystems. *Ecological Applications* 2(1):55–70.

Reed, K. E. 1997. Early hominid evolution and ecological change through the African Plio-Pleistocene. *Journal of Human Evolution* 32:289–322.

Rogers, M. J., et al. 1994. Changing patterns of land use by Plio-Pleistocene hominids in the Lake Turkana basin. *Journal of Human Evolution* 27:139–158.

Schick, K. D. 1987. Modeling the formation of Early Stone Age artifact concentrations. *Journal of Human Evolution* 16(7/8):789–808.

Schoeninger, M. J., et al. 1999. Subsistence strategies of two "savanna" chimpanzee populations: the stable isotope evidence. *American Journal of Primatology.*

Sept, J. M. 1984. *Plants and Early Hominids in East Africa: A Study of Vegetation in Situations Comparable to Early Archaeological Site Locations.* Berkeley: University of California Press.

Sept, J. M. 1986. Plant foods and early hominids at site FxJj50, Koobi Fora, Kenya. *Journal of Human Evolution* 15:751–770.

Sept, J. M. 1990. Vegetation studies in the Semliki Valley, Zaire as a guide to paleoanthropological research. *Virginia Museum of Natural History Memoire* 1:95–121.

Sept, J. M. 1992. Archaeological evidence and ecological perspectives for reconstructing early hominid subsistence behavior. In *Archaeological Method and Theory* (M. B. Schiffer, ed.), vol. 4, pp. 1–56. Tucson: University of Arizona Press.

Sept, J. M. 1994. Beyond bones: archaeological sites, early hominid subsistence, and the costs and benefits of exploiting wild plant foods in east African riverine landscapes. *Journal of Human Evolution* 27:295–330.

Sikes, N. 1994. Early hominid habitat preferences in East Africa: paleosol carbon isotope evidence. *Journal of Human Evolution* 27:25–45.

Sponheimer, M., and J. A. Lee-Thorp. 1999. Isotopic evidence for the diet of an early hominid, *Australopithecus africanus. Science* 283:368–336.

Stern, N. 1993. The structure of the lower Pleistocene archaeological record: a case study from the Koobi Fora formation. *Current Anthropology* 34(3):201–226.

Stewart, K. M. 1994. Early hominid utilisation of fish resources and implications for seasonality and behavior. *Journal of Human Evolution* 27:229–246.

Susman, R. L. 1998. Hand function and tool behavior in early hominids. *Journal of Human Evolution* 35:23–46.

Turner, M. G. 1990. Spatial and temporal analysis of landscape patterns. *Landscape Ecology* 4(1):21–30.

Tutin, C. E. G., et al. 1992. Foraging profiles of sympatric lowland gorillas and chimpanzees in the Lope Reserve, Gabon. In *Foraging Strategies and Natural Diet of Monkeys, Apes and Humans* (A. Whiten and E. M. Widdowson, eds.), pp. 19–24. Oxford: Clarendon Press.

Vincent, A. 1985a. Plant foods in savanna environments: a preliminary report of tubers eaten by the Hadza of northern Tanzania. *World Archaeology* 17:1–14.

Vincent, A. 1985b. *Underground Plant Foods and Subsistence in Human Evolution*. Ph.D. dissertation. University of California, Berkeley.

Walker, A. 1981. Dietary hypotheses and human evolution. *Philosophical Transactions of the Royal Society of London* 292:57–64.

Western, D., and C. Van Praet. 1973. Cyclical changes in the habitat and climate of an east African ecosystem. *Nature* 241:104–106.

White, T. D. 1988. The comparative biology of "robust" *Australopithecus*: clues from context. In *Evolutionary History of the "Robust" Australopithecines* (F. E. Grine, ed.), pp. 449–484. New York: Aldine de Gruyter.

Whiten, A., et al. 1992. Dietary and foraging strategies of baboons. In *Foraging Strategies and Natural Diet of Monkeys, Apes and Humans* (A. Whiten and E. M. Widdowson, eds.), pp. 449–484. Oxford: Clarendon Press.

Wiens, J. A. 1995. Landscape mosaics and ecological theory. In *Mosaic Landscapes and Ecological Processes* (L. Hansson et al., eds.), pp. 1–26. New York: Chapman and Hall.

Wrangham, R. W., N. L. Conklin, C. A. Chapman, and K. D. Hunt. 1992. The significance of fibrous foods for Kibale Forest chimpanzees. In *Foraging Strategies and Natural Diet of Monkeys, Apes and Humans* (A. Whiten and E. M. Widdowson, eds.), pp. 11–17. Oxford: Clarendon Press.

Part II

Living Nonhuman Analogs
for Meat-Eating

5

The Dog-Eat-Dog World of Carnivores

A Review of Past and Present Carnivore Community Dynamics

Blaire Van Valkenburgh

Introduction

Approximately 2 million years ago, individuals of early *Homo* began to incorporate meat in their diets, and within 1 million years, they were likely active hunters (cf. Foley 1987; Bunn and Ezzo 1993; Potts 1996; Walker and Shipman 1996). The shift to omnivory with a greater reliance on vertebrate prey placed *Homo* partially within a dangerous and highly competitive guild, that of large carnivores. Because guilds are groups of coexisting species that share a similar resource, members of the same guild are expected to compete more intensely than those of separate guilds. Predatory guilds, whether invertebrate or vertebrate, often are characterized by both competition and intraguild predation, most often by larger species on smaller (Polis and Holt 1992). Indeed, among mammalian carnivores, intraguild killing might be a more appropriate term, as the victims are often uneaten, suggesting the motivation was competition rather than hunger. Consequently, when *Homo* took up carnivory, sympatric predators might have expanded their view of *Homo* from prey item to competitor as well, adding a new incentive for killing them.

To better understand how the acquisition of meat-eating might have influenced subsequent evolution in *Homo*, it is useful to examine the dynamics within the guild of mammalian carnivores in some detail. I begin by reviewing the evidence concerning intraguild interactions among extant predators worldwide in a range of environments from forest to savannah. My emphasis is on repeated patterns of dominance within guilds and the effect of dominant taxa on subordinate taxa. The composition of the African Plio-Pleistocene predator guild is then examined, and the position of *Homo* within it is evaluated. The threat of intraguild predation would have favored several behavioral attributes of early *Homo*, including larger body size, cooperative behavior, diurnal activity, the ability to rapidly dismember large carcasses, and the hunting of small prey. Finally, the question of predator densities and how those might have affected scavenging opportunities for hominids is addressed. I argue that predators likely were more abundant as well as more diverse in the Plio-Pleistocene of Africa and that this would have reduced the availability of undefended carcasses in both closed and open vegetational settings. Consequently, if early *Homo* was consuming large prey regularly, it is probable that prey were often acquired by confrontational scavenging (i.e., stealing), as well as perhaps hunting, and this would have been possible only because *Homo* had sufficient intelligence to overcome the superior strength, speed, and weaponry of other predators.

The Dog-Eat-Dog World

Eaton (1979) was one of the first biologists to promote the importance of interference competition among coexisting large mammalian carnivores. In his review, he focused on interspecific interactions over carcasses and noted that larger carnivores tended to displace smaller ones from carcasses but that grouping behavior could reverse this relationship. He noted as well that interspecific battles over kills occurred and often resulted in injury or death to one of the participants. In a study of adaptations to coexistence among carnivores, Van Valkenburgh (1985) pointed out the additional pressure of interspecific predation among sympatric carnivores, noting that both juveniles and adults are killed but not always eaten.

Carcass theft (kleptoparasitism) and predation constitute strong interference competition, but most of the work cited in Eaton and Van Valkenburgh concerns East African savannah species, and it could be that interference competition is only significant in such open environments where it is more difficult to sequester kills. Even in the savannah, some might argue that interference interactions occur too infrequently to have any impact on the behavioral and morphological evolution of the participants. This is a difficult problem to address with extensive quantitative data because the animals are difficult to observe and the causes of mortality are troublesome to resolve; in many instances, individuals simply disappear. However, the past decade of mammal research has produced a wide array of examples from around the world, which are reviewed hereafter (all literature cited in the following review is listed in an appendix to this chapter). Evidence in support of the importance of interference competition among predators can be either direct or indirect. Direct evidence includes data on intraguild predation and carcass loss to competitors. Indirect evidence includes documentation of spatial and/or temporal separation among sympatric species, the presence of behaviors and/or morphological characters that minimize the likelihood of interspecific encounters (Van Valkenburgh 1985), and the occurrence of interspecific aggression when no food is present (e.g., mobbing of spotted hyenas, *Crocuta crocuta*, by wild dogs, *Lycaon pictus*). If interference competition is common among coexisting predators worldwide, in relatively forested as well as more open environments, tropical as well as temperate climates, then it seems probable that the Plio-Pleistocene carnivore community was similar and that consequently, a meat-eating *Homo* incurred a significant risk by either scavenging or hunting.

Africa

As noted above, most of our observations concerning carcass theft and intraguild predation have come from studies of large mammals of the African savannah. This is because they are more easily observed than forest species and consequently have been the subject of more work. Lions (*Panthera leo*) and spotted hyenas are the primary "troublemakers" in both eastern and southern African communities. Unless they have been removed by humans, these two species always greatly outnumber all other large carnivore taxa (Creel and Creel 1996). They are the largest species, and both will scavenge kills from each other and any of the smaller carnivores, such as leopards (*Panthera pardus*), cheetahs (*Acinonyx jubatus*), and wild dogs. Lions tend to dominate hyenas in most situations and can be a major cause of juvenile and adult mortality (Table 5.1). For example, Hofer and East (1995) found that male lions were responsible for 20% (*n* = 45) of all Serengeti hyena deaths where the cause was known, and in Botswana, Cooper (1991) observed male lions suffocate seven adult hyenas within 2 years, making them responsible for more than 50% of the known deaths. The hyenas were not consumed. In that same study, Cooper noted that spotted hyenas were able to drive lionesses from a carcass if they outnumbered them by at least four to one and no male lion was present. She argued that this presents an excellent justification for lionesses to share food with nonhunting males and favors the evolution of group living to defend carcasses in both species.

The impact of lions and spotted hyenas on smaller predators can be severe. Creel and Creel (1996, 1998) documented a strong and significant negative relationship between wild dog density and lion or spotted hyena densities in six ecosystems. As they pointed out, wild dogs have almost disappeared from the Serengeti over the last 25 years, during which spotted hyena numbers have doubled. Hyenas were present at over 85% of all Serengeti wild dog kills (*n* = 62) observed by Fanshawe and FitzGibbon (1993) and stole food from the dogs in over half of these instances (Table 5.2). Wild dogs are no longer present in the Ngorongoro Crater, where Kruuk (1972) documented a 60% loss of carcasses to hyenas between 1964 and 1968. Lions kill wild dogs regularly, accounting for 33–39% of all pup deaths and 43% of all adult deaths in studies of Kruger park dogs (South Africa; van Heerden et al. 1995; Mills and Gorman 1997), and 50% in a similar study in Moremi National Park (Botswana; McNutt 1995; Creel and Creel 1998). In response, Kruger park dogs avoid areas where lions are common even though these areas also have the greatest density of prey, and both cheetah and wild dog tend to hunt at times when lions are least likely to be hunting (Mills and Gorman 1997).

Similarly, cheetah densities are lower in parks where lions and hyenas are more abundant (Laurenson 1995). In the Serengeti and Kruger, cheetahs lose from 12–14% of their kills to hyenas (Schaller 1972; Mills and Biggs 1993). Notably Kruger National Park is much more heavily wooded than the Serengeti, and yet the Kruger cheetahs appear to do no better at retaining their kills (Table 5.2). Although klepto-

Table 5.1. Percent of observed deaths caused by interspecific predation.

Locality	Victim	Aggressor(s)	Total of Observed Deaths Due to all Causes	% Total Mortality Due to Aggressor	Comments on Victims	Sources
Selous, Tanzania	Lycaon pictus	Panthera leo	45	9	pups and adults	Creel and Creel 1998
		Crocuta crocuta	45	4		
Kruger, S. Africa	L. pictus	P. leo	56	34	pups and adults	van Heerden et al. 1995
	L. pictus	P. leo	32	44	pups and adults	Mills and Biggs, 1993
Moremi, Botswana	L. pictus	P. leo	14	50	pups and adults	McNutt in Creel and Creel 1996
Chobe, Botswana	Crocuta. crocuta	P. leo	13	54	cubs and adults	Cooper 1991
Ngorongoro/Serengeti, Tanzania	C. crocuta	P. leo	28	55	cubs and adults	Kruuk 1972
Serengeti, Tanzania	Acinonyx jubatus	P. leo	119	42	cubs only	Laurenson 1994
		C. crocuta	119	7		
Montana, British Columbia	Canis latrans	Puma concolor	7	43	adults only	Koehler and Hornocker 1991
	Lynx rufus	P. concolor	8	62		
Kern Co., California	Vulpes macrotis	Canis latrans	23	65	pups and adults	Ralls and White 1995
Royal Chitawan, Nepal	Panthera pardus	Panthera tigris	6	83	cubs and adults	McDougal 1988

104

Table 5.2. The frequency and outcome of competition between predators over kills.

Locality	"Owner" of Kill	Total Kills Observed	% Kills Detected	Potential Thief	% Kills Where Thief Ate	Comments	Sources
Selous, Tanzania	*Lycaon pictus*	404	18	*Crocuta crocuta*	2	Moderate hyena density	Creel and Creel 1996
Serengeti, Tanzania	*L. pictus*	62	86	*C. crocuta*	86	High hyena density	Fanshawe and Fitzgibbon 1993
Ngorongoro/ Serengeti	*L. pictus*	62	74	*C. crocuta*	60	High hyena density	Kruuk 1972
Kruger, S. Africa	*L. pictus*	52	frequent	*C. crocuta*	0	Low hyena density	Mills and Biggs 1993
Serengeti, Tanzania	*Crocuta crocuta*	244	21	*Panthera leo*	19		Kruuk 1972
Chobe, Botswana	*Panthera leo*	134	79	*C. crocuta*	63		Cooper 1991
Kruger, S. Africa	*Panthera pardus*	55	50	*C. crocuta*	few	Hyenas were unable to access kills in trees	Bailey 1993
Kruger, S. Africa	*Acinonyx jubatus*	29	not reported	*C. crocuta*	14		Mills and Biggs 1993
Serengeti, Tanzania	*A. jubatus*	238	not reported	*C. crocuta* *P. leo* *P. pardus*	12		Schaller 1972
Idaho	*Puma concolor*	33	40	*Canis latrans, Lynx rufus*	not reported		Koehler and Hornocker 1991
Idaho	*Lynx rufus*	7	43	*C. latrans, Puma concolor*	not reported		Koehler and Hornocker 1991
Yellowstone Wyoming	*Puma concolor*	122	27	*C. lupus*	3		Murphy 1998
Glacier, Montana	*P. concolor*	25	36	*Ursus arctos*	not reported		Murphy 1998

The column labeled "% kills detected" includes the number of kills observed where a potential thief appeared but may or may not have eaten.

parasitism is harmful because it forces cheetahs to hunt more frequently, it has less of an impact on cheetah populations than does intraguild predation. In the Serengeti, over 70% of all cub deaths with known causes were due to predation, mostly by lions, who almost never ate the cubs (Laurenson 1994, 1995). Lions clearly went out of their way to kill cheetah cubs and will kill adults as well if they can catch them (Caro 1987).

Because of their tree-climbing abilities, leopards are not as vulnerable as wild dogs and cheetahs. Nevertheless, they are often the targets of attempted klepto-parasitism. In Kruger Park, spotted hyenas discovered about half of 55 leopard kills but were unable to steal them if the carcass was in a tree (Bailey 1993). Lions have been known to steal leopard kills that were not placed high enough in trees (Turnbull-Kemp 1967; Schaller 1972), and wild dogs are able to chase leopards off kills on the ground (Pienaar 1969; Schaller 1972; Creel and Creel 1996). Thus it appears that the tree-caching ability of leopards is critical to their success. African leopards occasionally engage in intraguild predation on hyenas, cheetahs, and jackals and have themselves been the victims of spotted hyenas (Pienaar 1969; Caro 1987; Bailey 1993).

India and Nepal

There are three, reasonably well-studied large predators in Asia—tiger (*Panthera tigris*), leopard (*P. pardus*), and dhole (*Cuon lupinus*). The three coexist in tropical forest habitats that include both moist deciduous and dry deciduous forest such as Bandipur and Nagarahole, southern India. As is the case in Africa, the largest predator, the tiger, is the dominant species, and the others appear to modify their behavior in response to its presence. Published observations of kleptoparasitism and intraguild predation are much less frequent than for African carnivores, and this is expected given the environment. The combination of lower population densities and thick vegetation make forest carnivores much more difficult to observe. Nevertheless, dholes were seen harassing leopards and stealing their kills on several occasions in the Mudumalai Sanctuary, Tamil Nadu, India (Venkataraman 1995). As in Africa, leopards were unlikely to lose prey that they had placed in trees. Interestingly, leopards do not cache their prey in trees in Sri Llanka where tigers and dholes are absent (Muckenhirn and Eisenberg 1973).

Both leopards and tigers will kill dholes (Karanth and Sunquist 1995), and resting dholes always have a sentinel individual who responds to the alarm calls of primates and deer (Venkataraman 1995). Tigers kill leopards occasionally (McDougal 1988; Johnsingh 1992), but more often leopards appear to avoid areas where tigers are common (Seidensticker 1976; Seidensticker et al. 1990; Stoen and Wegge 1996).

North America

Data on interspecific competition among North American large (weighing more than 7 kg) carnivores have come from studies of communities that typically include only three or four of the continent's 12 predators. This is because there are almost no North American parks or reserves that contain their historical richness of predators, probably as a result of persistent human persecution. The only exceptions are parts of Alaska and perhaps Yellowstone National Park, where gray wolves (*Canis lupus*) were reintroduced only 3 years ago. However, even in Alaska and Yellowstone, the numbers of some species, such as the gray wolf, brown bear (*Ursus arctos*), and puma (*Puma concolor*), are low, and consequently, interspecific interactions are rarely observed and likely occur less frequently than among their African counterparts. Nevertheless, there are some dramatic examples, with the Yellowstone reintroduction of wolves being one of the most prominent. After 60 years of being absent from the park, approximately 35 gray wolves from Canada were reintroduced in 1995. Within 3 years, they organized themselves into eight packs and nearly tripled their numbers (Robbins 1997). Simultaneous with the wolves' success, coyote (*Canis latrans*) numbers plummeted, and numerous wolf-killed coyotes were documented (Robbins 1997; Miller 1998). In the northern part of the park, the coyote number was halved, from 80 to about 36 in just 3 years (Robbins 1997). Not all deaths were associated with the presence of a contested carcass; in one instance, coyote pups in a den were dug out and killed (D. Smith, pers. comm.). The negative impact of wolves on coyotes was not a surprise; several previous studies of these two canids in sympatry had documented avoidance of wolves by coyotes as well as wolf-killed coyotes, often left uneaten near prey carcasses (Fuller and Keith 1981; Carbyn 1982; Pacquet 1989, 1991; Johnson et al. 1996).

The dominant predator in North America is likely the brown or grizzly bear. Weighing some 250 kg, this species is more than twice the size of any other predator, except the more omnivorous black bear (*Ursus americanus*). Grizzly bears occasionally will prey on hibernating adult black bears, digging them out of their dens and feeding on them prior to their own hibernation (Jonkel and Cowen 1971; Smith and Follman 1993; Assoc. Press 1997). Numerous interactions between grizzlies and wolves have been recorded and are summarized in Carbyn (in press). For example, Murie, working in Denali National Park (formerly Mt. McKinley) in the 1940s, reported that grizzlies often stole kills from gray wolves (Murie 1944), and Ballard (1982) records the death of a wolf at a carcass due to an interaction with a grizzly. As is true of lion–hyena and leopard–dhole interactions, the smaller species (wolf) has been observed to attack or harass the larger species (bear) when it outnumbers the larger in situations where there is no provocation such as a carcass (Ballard 1982; Kehoe 1995; Carbyn in press), suggesting that the wolf considers the grizzly a threat.

Gray wolves also interact negatively with black bears and wolverines, with the wolves being the aggressors in most instances. Like grizzlies, wolves will dig hibernating black bears from their dens and kill and eat them; at least five such instances are recorded, with three occurring in a single year in one study (Rogers and Mech 1981; Horejsi et al. 1984; Pacquet and Carbyn 1986; Carbyn in press). Wolves have been known to attack black bears over a carcass (Gehring 1993), and not surprisingly, black bears occasionally succeed in killing a wolf (Joslin 1966; Gehring 1993). Carbyn (in press) reports several instances of wolves killing wolverines, usually in the presence of a carcass.

Pumas are highly secretive big cats that are thought to avoid interactions with other large predators including man. However, ongoing studies have revealed that regular contact between wolves and pumas, and grizzly bears and pumas does occur. In Yellowstone, wolves were present at 27% of 122 puma kills, displaced the cat in four instances, and were responsible for three puma deaths (Murphy 1998). Similarly, in Glacier National Park, grizzly bears were present at 36% of 25 observed kills and were responsible for a single puma mortality (Murphy 1998). Pumas are not always the victims of an interspecific predator encounter; they will kill and not consume coyotes and bobcats (*Lynx rufus*). In a 5-year study in Idaho, five of eight bobcat deaths and three of seven coyote deaths were due to puma predation, usually near a food cache (Koehler and Hornocker 1991). Remarkably, nearly 40% of puma kills were scavenged by bobcats or coyotes, suggesting that carcass detection is not that difficult in a temperate forest (Table 5.2). Supplementary reports of puma-killed coyotes come from additional studies in Idaho (Hornocker 1970), Montana (Boyd and O'Gara 1985), Yellowstone Park, Wyoming (Murphy 1998), and possibly southern California (Sauvajot et al. in press).

Just as the gray wolf appears to control coyote numbers and distribution in many places, the coyote performs a similar function for other smaller canids such as kit foxes (*Vulpes macrotis*), swift foxes (*V. velox*), gray foxes (*Urocyon cinereoargenteus*), and perhaps red foxes (*V. vulpes*). In some cases, such as the kit and swift foxes, coyotes are the predominant cause of mortality, accounting for 50–87% of all deaths (Table 5.1) (White and Garrott 1997). Ironically, the removal of gray wolves from Canada's prairies may have allowed coyotes to proliferate and decimate swift fox populations there (Carbyn 1994; Herrero 1998). The impact of coyotes on red foxes and gray foxes appears not to be as severe but is still significant. Red fox and coyote territories tend not to overlap, and coyotes are known to kill red foxes (Johnson et al. 1996). Coyote and gray fox home ranges often overlap (Wooding 1984; Johnson et al. 1996), and intraguild predation occurs. A recent study of sympatric carnivores in southern California reported six to seven gray foxes killed and partially eaten by coyotes within a year, constituting 100% of all known fox deaths (Sauvajot et al. in press).

The medium-sized North American cats, the bobcat and lynx (*Lynx canadensis*), appear to avoid interactions with larger sympatric carnivores. Occasionally, lynx are killed by wolves and coyotes (O'Donoghue et al. 1995, 1997), and bobcats are preyed upon by coyotes with some regularity in southern California (Sauvajot et al., in press). In fact, as I was writing this chapter at my home in the Santa Monica Mountains of southern California, a bobcat was mauled by a coyote on my property—a vivid inspiration to continue my essay. Bobcats and lynxes are not only the victims of intraguild predation; lynxes prey fairly often on red foxes when their preferred prey, snowshoe hares, are rare (Stephenson et al. 1991; O'Donoghue et al. 1995), and bobcats are occasional predators on kit foxes in California's San Joaquin Valley (Ralls and White 1995).

South America

Relatively few studies are available on the larger predators of the Neotropics. Two large cats, the jaguar (*Panthera onca*) and the puma, coexist extensively. Several workers have documented mutual avoidance with no evidence of intraguild predation or kleptoparasitism (Rabinowitz and Nottingham 1986; Emmons 1987), but Crawshaw and Quigley (1984) observed that jaguars kill pumas. Both cats exhibit considerable geographic variation in size, but when sympatric, jaguars are typically larger than pumas (Hoogesteijn and Mondolfi 1996).

Given the remarkable richness of canids (10 species) in South America, it is unfortunate that so little is known of their natural history. Two medium-sized species, the gray zorro (*Dusicyon griseus*) and the culpeo fox (*D. culpaeus*), have been examined in sympatry in southern and north-central Chile (Jaksic et al. 1983; Johnson and Franklin 1994; Johnson et al. 1996). In both regions, the larger culpeo appears to displace the smaller zorro, but no instances of intraguild predation or kleptoparasitism have been documented (Fuentes and Jaksic 1979; Johnson et al. 1996).

Summary of Interspecific Interactions Among Sympatric Predators in Modern Environments

Several important points emerge from the above review. First, most interspecific interactions between predators occur as contests for the possession of a kill. The motivation for intraguild predation appears to be hunger in many instances, particularly when the body size difference between the two species is fairly large (e.g., coyote–kit fox, brown bear–black bear, lynx–red fox). However, equally or more often, the victim is not eaten, and the likely motivation is to remove a competitor who might also prey on the agressor's young. Second, body size is the usual determinant of rank within the guild; larger species tend to dominate smaller ones (e.g., lion–hyena, hyena–wild dog, brown bear–wolf, wolf–coyote, tiger–leopard, jaguar–puma). Third, the body size rule can be overturned by the smaller species acting as a group (e.g., hyenas versus lions, wolves versus bears, wild dogs versus hyenas). Fourth, intraguild predation and kleptoparasitism occur in both forested and open environments. Although these events have been observed less frequently in forested environments, the behavior of some species strongly suggests that they have had a significant impact (e.g., spatial segregation of leopards versus tigers and pumas versus jaguars, presence of sentinels in dholes, absence of tree-caching behavior in leopards when tigers and dholes are absent).

The Plio-Pleistocene East African Predator Guild

The East African Plio-Pleistocene guild of large (>20 kg) mammalian carnivores included at least 11 species, as opposed to just six today (Table 5.3). The increased diversity was due to additional big cats and hyaenids, the two families that include the dominant species of the modern African savannah (e.g., lion and spotted hyena). If early *Homo* was fairly carnivorous, it would have found itself in the middle of the guild with five species smaller than it and six that were nearly equal or greatly exceeded it in size, based on an estimated body weight of approximately 60 kg for *Homo habilis* (Ruff et al. 1997) (Figure 5.1). This would not appear to be a very comfortable position given the potential for exploitative competition from carnivores smaller than *Homo* and predation and kleptoparasitism from the larger spe-

Table 5.3. Species composition of the Plio-Pleistocene predator guild of East Africa, excluding *Homo*.

Species	Description	Estimated Body Mass (KG)
Felidae		
Homotherium crenatidens	sabertooth cat	170
Panthera leo	lion	170
Dinofelis sp.	"false" sabertooth cat	150
Megantereon cultridens	sabertooth cat	95
Acinonyx jubatus	cheetah	60
Panthera pardus	leopard	45
Canidae		
Canis sp.	wolf-like canid	30
Hyaenidae		
Crocuta crocuta	spotted hyena	52
Hyaena brunnea	brown hyena	39
Hyaena hyaena	striped hyena	32
Chasmoporthetes nitidula	running hyena	21

This is a minimum list as there are one or two unresolved species of *Panthera* (leopard size) and a bear (L. Werdelin, pers. comm.) that may also have been present. Sources for species list: Lewis 1997; Werdelin and Barthelme 1997. Estimated body masses are based on Lewis (1995, 1997).

cies, some of which were likely social (e.g., lion and spotted hyena). Moreover, all the other species could run faster than the hominids and were better equipped with claws and/or sharp teeth (Shipman and Walker 1993). Thus, even though early *Homo* may have weighed as much or more than some species, such as leopards and hyenas, they may not have dominated them in a one-to-one encounter.

Examination of the body size distribution for the extant East African and North American guilds suggests that species in the lower two-thirds of the distribution are likely to have their movements, numbers, and survivorship affected by the larger species (Figure 5.2). In Africa, lions and spotted hyenas limit where cheetahs and wild dogs can survive. In India, the tiger does the same to the leopard, and in North America, the wolf similarly affects the coyote. Which species performed these roles in the Plio-Pleistocene of Africa? It would seem likely that they would have been the spotted hyena and some or all of the four largest felids (*Homotherium*, *P. leo*, *Dinofelis*, and *Megantereon*). Two key pieces of evidence necessary to determine which of these cats likely had the most impact on other species are relative abundance and social behavior. Unfortunately, the fossil record almost never preserves an accurate picture of relative abundance, especially for rare taxa such as carnivores. Group living probably can be inferred for both the lion and hyena based on their extant representatives, but is difficult to determine for the other big cats. Given these uncertainties, I will consider all of these species to have been relatively dominant members of the guild. These dominant taxa would have chosen their preferred habitats and activity times, and the smaller or less well armed (e.g., cheetah) would have likely worked around them.

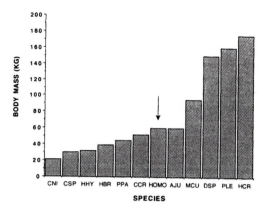

Figure 5.1. Body size distribution of species within the Plio-Pleistocene predator guild of Africa. Arrow points to *Homo habilis*. Abbreviations: CNI, *Chasmoporthes nitidula*; CSP, *Canis sp.*; HHY, *Hyaena hyaena*; HBR *Hyaena brunnea*; PPA, *Panthera pardus*; CCR, *Crocuta crocuta*; HOMO, *Homo habilis;* AJU, *Acinonyx juba-tus*; MCU, *Megantereon cultridens*; DSP, *Dinofelis sp.*; PLE, *P. leo*; HCR, *Homotherium crenatidens*.

Where and When Would Homo Have Foraged?

Except for the spotted hyena, the putative dominant species were ambush hunters although the long limbs of *Homotherium* suggest an ability to run greater distances than is typical of lions (Anyonge 1997; Lewis 1997; Turner and Anton 1997). All five of these species probably preferred to hunt at night given that the hunting success of extant lions and hyenas is greater at night than day, with moonless nights providing the best cover (Stander and Albon 1993; Holecamp et al. 1997). Habitat choice is more difficult to discern, especially given that large carnivores tend to be relatively flexible in their habitat choice. Wild dogs and hyenas live in open savannah in the Serengeti but choose *Acacia* thickets in Kruger Park. Leopards exist in a wide array of habitats, from rainforest to woodland to Kalahari desert. Predators follow their prey and adapt their hunting style to the vegetation structure (Tappan this volume). Thus, species recognizable as ambush predators by their limb structure are not confined to forest habitats; all that is required is some cover. Similarly, long-limbed cursors can hunt in dense woodland as well as on the plains, as evidenced by dholes in India and wild dogs in Kruger. This habitat flexibility makes it difficult to match limb structure with habitat choice in carnivores.

Limb structure does indicate hunting style, ambush as opposed to cursor, and provides information on locomotor abilities such as climbing and digging but should not be used to narrowly predict habitat choice in carnivores (Van Valkenburgh 1987; Taylor 1993). Although Marean (1989) has argued on the basis of limb proportions that both *Megantereon* and *Dinofelis* inhabited dense forest, I am not convinced

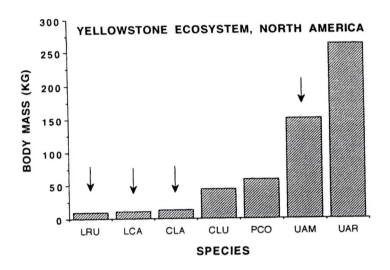

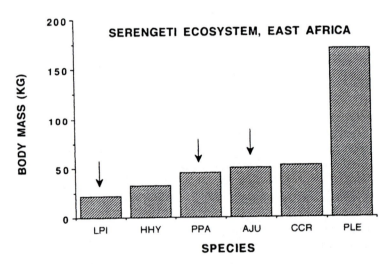

Figure 5.2. Body size distribution of the extant North American Yellowstone predator guild limited to species ≥10 kg), (top), and East African Serengeti predator guild, limited to species ≥20 kg (bottom). Arrows indicate species that appear especially vulnerable to interference competition. Abbreviations: LRU, *Lynx rufus;* LCA, *Lynx canadensis*; CLA, *Canis latrans;* CLU, *Canis lupus*; PCO, *Puma concolor*; UAM, *Ursus americanus*; UAR, *Ursus arctos;* LPI, *Lycaon pictus*; HHY, *Hyaena hyaena*; PPA, *Panthera pardus*; AJU, *Acinonyx jubatus*; CCR, *Crocuta crocuta*; PLE, *P. leo.*

they can be so constrained. Rather, it seems probable that the dominant taxa would have chosen to reside where prey biomass was greatest, which would have tended to be more open areas that contained groups or herds of ungulates. This would have made diurnal foraging within the forest and at the forest edge the safest strategy for early *Homo,* no matter whether foraging for meat or plant matter.

An added incentive to remain near woodlands would be the refuge offered by trees. Encounters with the more terrestrial hyenas, large canids, and two largest cats could be easily avoided by climbing out of their reach. This may have been less effective against the four remaining cats; all but the cheetah could probably climb to some degree. However, a treed early *Homo* was probably safe from attack given that extant leopards rarely hunt in trees (Bailey 1993). Because of the dangers of falling while attempting a kill, the big Plio-Pleistocene felids probably behaved similarly.

How Available Were Undefended Carcasses?

Two key parameters that affect carcass availability are: (1) the array of carnivore feeding types that are present, and (2) the density of carnivores, especially bone-cracking species (Blumenschine 1987, 1988). There were nine highly carnivorous species in the Plio-Pleistocene predator guild (all but the striped and brown hyenas) as opposed to five today, and this might be expected to have affected carcass availability. Of the nine, only the spotted hyena would have regularly consumed an entire carcass, including all bones. Others (Ewer 1954; Blumenschine 1987; Marean 1989) have suggested that the presence of so many big cats, three of which were sabertooths (*Megantereon, Homotherium, Dinofelis*), would have resulted in a predictable supply of carcasses for early *Homo* to scavenge. Marean (1989) argued that the dental specializations of sabertooths would have precluded them from dismembering carcasses and consuming all the flesh; thus, they would have left behind substantial amounts of protein for scavengers. This is likely an overstatement. A recent analysis by Marean and Ehrhardt (1995) of a North American Pleistocene cave deposit containing numerous individuals of *Homotherium* and juvenile mammoths (*Mammuthus columbi*) contradicts this view of sabertooths. The mammoth bones are mostly disarticulated limb elements that appear to have been transported to the cave for feeding. Many of the bones have gnaw marks that were likely made by the big cat. Other evidence concerning sabertooth cat feeding behavior comes from a study of tooth fracture in *Smilodon fatalis* from the Pleistocene Rancho La Brea deposits of California (Van Valkenburgh and Hertel 1993). Tooth fracture in extant carnivores is associated with heavy carcass utilization and bone-eating (Van Valkenburgh 1988), and *Smilodon* broke its teeth regularly, especially its incisors. Given this evidence, and the fact that modern big cats often use their rough tongues to rasp flesh off bones, it seems probable that sabertooths were quite capable of both dismembering and thoroughly finishing a kill up to the bone-cracking stage.

So, what were the scavenging opportunities available to early *Homo*? It is possible that at least three of the cats, the leopard, *Dinofelis,* and *Megantereon,* cached their kills in trees, although recent postcranial studies by Lewis (1997) suggest that the two extinct felids were not adept tree climbers. As pointed out by Cavallo and

Blumenschine (1989), carcasses in trees persist longer than those on the ground because they are ignored by vultures and unavailable to terrestrial predators. Moreover, African leopards typically abandon their carcasses for an extended period during the day, returning eventually to feed. Because hominids could climb, these abandoned carcasses would have been accessible and may have served as an important source of meat. However, there are two problems with this view. First, as noted by Lewis (1997), Plio-Pleistocene leopards might have guarded their kills more diligently when there was a threat of losing the kill to hominids or other big cats. Second, even if leopards did abandon kills fairly regularly, *Dinofelis* and *Megantereon* might have competed with *Homo* for these tree treasures, and it is guaranteed that tree caches disappeared more quickly in the Plio-Pleistocene than they do at present.

The opportunities for nonconfrontational scavenging on the ground seem less plentiful, given the presence of spotted hyenas and the overall high diversity of extremely carnivorous species. Spotted hyenas are remarkably efficient at finding kills. For example, spotted hyenas were present at 85.5% of 62 wild dog kills in the Serengeti (Fanshawe and Fitzgibbon 1993), 78.5% of 135 lion kills in Chobe National Park, Botswana (Cooper 1991), and described as frequently seen in the vicinity of wild dog kills in Kruger Park (Table 5.2) (Mills and Biggs 1993). Notably, the wild dog kills were all made in daylight, whereas the Chobe lions were observed at night only. Even in the dark, without the help of circling vultures, hyenas had little trouble arriving at kills within 30 minutes of their occurrence (Cooper 1991). Spotted hyenas are attracted by the sounds associated with kills (e.g., bleating wildebeest, lion and hyena vocalizations), so much so that audiotapes of such noises can used to census hyenas (Mills 1996). Consequently, unless hyena densities were considerably less than at present, hyenas probably would have been present at most kills soon after they were made. Given that most kills occurred at night, there would have been relatively little left for a diurnal scavenger such as *Homo*.

In addition to diversity, predator density can influence levels of interspecific competition within the guild. If densities are high, then the likelihood of interspecific encounter is greater, and therefore, intraguild predation and kleptoparasitism are more frequent, thus reducing carcass availability. In most scenarios of the past, we tend to assume that species existed at population densities similar to what we observe today in so-called pristine environments such as the Serengeti National Park, Tanzania, or Denali National Park, Alaska. Although this may be near the truth for some herbivores, it is much less likely to be true for large predatory mammals. Large predators are and have been persecuted heavily by humans because they are considered competitors for prey and threats to our livestock and ourselves (Woodroffe and Ginsberg 1998). For the last several centuries, it was common practice to kill predators to promote herbivore numbers, and it still occurs today (e.g., wolves in Alaska and Canada). Even in the Serengeti where hunting is banned, snares placed by poachers for ungulates are a major cause of mortality for hyenas and lions (Hofer and East 1995; M. Roelke pers. comm.), and a recent review of the impact of humans on carnivores in various protected areas revealed that 74% of 635 known-cause deaths were caused directly by people (Woodroffe and Ginsberg 1998). In most cases, humans will not tolerate even moderate densities of large carnivores near their communities. For example, pumas were eradicated from the eastern and much of the western United States within 200 years of European colonization (Nowell and Jackson 1996). Bans placed on hunting in the 1960s have allowed this elusive cat to persist and even increase its numbers recently. In some areas, contacts between humans and pumas have become more frequent, although still very rare, and there have been several human fatalities. Even though the risk to a hiker of being killed by a puma is much less than that of being killed by a rattlesnake or lightning, the cry has gone out for a return to hunting pumas (Brooke 1997). If an action can be taken to reduce a risk, humans are likely to take it, even if it means reducing predator numbers below what is sustainable.

Although it is difficult to be certain, it appears likely that carnivore densities were much higher when human numbers were much lower and persecution of predators was less common, as would have been the case in the Plio-Pleistocene. Indirect evidence in support of formerly higher predator densities can be found in the predators of the late Pleistocene Rancho La Brea deposits of California. Four large carnivores are well represented at La Brea—the sabertooth cat *Smilodon fatalis*, the giant American lion, *Panthera atrox*, the dire wolf, *Canis dirus*, and the coyote, *C. latrans*. All four exhibit a remarkably high incidence of teeth that fractured in life, three to five times the incidence observed in extant large predators such as the lion and spotted hyena. As mentioned above, frequent tooth fracture is associated with heavy carcass utilization. Carnivores finish carcasses more fully when food is difficult to obtain, and this can result from low prey densities and/or frequent kleptoparasitism. Because there was little reason to assume low prey densities in the late Pleistocene, Van Valkenburgh and Hertel (1993) favored kleptoparasitism as the explanation for the high incidence of broken teeth in Rancho La Brea carnivores. They argued that high predator densities led to more frequent kleptoparasitism, which favored increased carcass utilization and thus tooth fracture. Unfortunately, there are no comparable data for the East African Plio-Pleistocene predators, but dire wolves from a Mexican late Pleistocene site have a similarly high tooth fracture incidence, suggesting that the pattern might be typical of the late Pleistocene.

It seems likely that overall carnivore biomass was higher in the Plio-Pleistocene than at present, but it may have been distributed differently among species. Today, the lion and spotted hyena are the most abundant predators in most, if not all, African game reserves (Creel and Creel 1996) and appear to suppress the numbers of some other species such as the wild dog and cheetah. In the Plio-Pleistocene, this lion-spotted hyena hegemony may not have been the case; in fact, their numbers could have been limited by some other more abundant species. This could have affected carcass availability for hominids, especially if the bone-cracking species were very rare. As noted earlier, it is difficult to estimate the relative abundance of carnivore species from the fossil record, but even a crude assessment (i.e., a simple ranking) might prove useful. If hyenas are among the most common fossils, it would suggest that they were not rare in the community and consequently that hominids rarely may have found an undefended carcass with uncracked long bones and much flesh remaining.

The Impact of Carnivores on the Evolution and
Behavior of Early *Homo*

In the Plio-Pleistocene of East Africa, predator diversity was high, and predator densities were likely greater than at present given the absence of modern, technology-assisted human persecution of large carnivores, as discussed above. Consequently, meat acquisition would have been difficult for early *Homo*. Nevertheless, the species clearly utilized meat to some degree (Shipman and Walker 1993; Brantingham 1998a, 1998b; Bunn this volume). The dual threats of intraguild predation and kleptoparasitism were significant and would have favored behaviors to decrease competition and reduce the chance of predation. Diurnal activity patterns would have minimized encounters with the largest, most dangerous species. The hunting of small (e.g., gazelle fawns) rather than large prey might have been favored because such prey could have been discretely killed and rapidly consumed without catching the attention of potential thieves (cf. Brantingham 1998a, 1998b). As noted by others in this volume and elsewhere, foraging in groups would have been advantageous for a number of reasons (Shipman and Walker 1993; Brantingham 1998a, 1998b; Foley, Winterhalder this volume). Predators tend to be detected by groups more quickly than by solitary individuals, and groups can defend themselves and a carcass more easily than solitary individuals. Like young ravens who improve their ability to defend a carcass by attracting other ravens to the kill (Winterhalder this volume), individuals of early *Homo* may have been able to retrieve more from a carcass when they shared the booty. Moreover, interference competition among carnivores favors the ability to process carcasses rapidly before being discovered. Hyenas use their massive jaws and teeth to do so, whereas the weaker-jawed wild dogs work together to rapidly pull apart a carcass. A group of early *Homo* might have cooperated as wild dogs do, using their simple tools to begin dismembering a carcass and then pulling against one another to rip the carcass into pieces that could be transported to a safer place, such as up a tree.

Life within or at the edges of the guild of predatory mammals would have placed strong selection pressures on hominids to improve their defensive and agonistic capabilities (Shipman and Walker 1993; Foley this volume) as well as their ability to avoid dangerous encounters with aggressive carnivores. Because body size is an important determinant of rank within the predator guild, we could expect to see size increase within *Homo* or at least between *Australopithecus* and *Homo* if the latter is becoming relatively more carnivorous. In fact, it is clear from the fossil record that by 1.7 million years ago, if not earlier, *Homo* was some 50% larger than *Australopithecus* (McHenry 1994). In addition to larger size, because the relatively small-toothed and soft-pawed hominids joined a guild full of heavily armed species such as sabertooth cats and spotted hyenas, the development of weapons was essential. Although perhaps first developed as a defense against predation, weapons could then have been used to take larger prey. The ability to throw rocks with force and accuracy would have been a major innovation and might have allowed groups of *Homo* to become kleptoparasites, actively driving smaller groups of larger predators from their kills as lions, hyenas and wild dogs do today.

The evidence for the importance of interference competition in shaping extant carnivore communities is now substantial and incontrovertible in some cases. Consequently, the impact of large mammalian predators on the evolution of a meat-eating hominid cannot be ignored (cf. Brantingham 1998a, 1998b). If it can be demonstrated that by 2 million years ago, *Homo* was regularly consuming some of the most nutritious parts of relatively large prey animals, then it seems likely that this was done by active, confrontational scavenging and perhaps hunting (as argued by Bunn this volume). Prime, undefended carcasses would have been rare given the diversity and probable high density of carnivorous species. Stealing from saber-tooths, lions, or hyenas would have required teamwork and intelligence, as well as perhaps weapon use, and thus early *Homo* would have been a very clever primate that dominated larger, faster, dangerous species by its wit rather than its brawn. As a part-time meat-eater, early hominids might have found that big cats such as *Homotherium* and *P. leo*, which occasionally hunted the large primates when they were herbivorous, now traveled out of their way to kill them and their young because they perceived them as competitors for the same prey or potential predators on their juveniles. The price of entering the dog-eat-dog world of the carnivore guild was undoubtedly high, and therefore, the rewards must have been substantial.

REFERENCES

Publications cited concerning interference competition and intraguild predation in extant large-predator guilds.

Associated Press. 1997. A grizzly meal. *Bozeman Daily Chronicle.* December 28:13.

Bailey, T. N. 1993. *The African Leopard.* New York: Columbia University Press.

Ballard, W. B. 1982. Brown bear kills gray wolf. *Canadian Field-Naturalist* 94:91.

Boyd, D., and B. O'Gara. 1985. Cougar predation on coyotes. *The Murrelet* 66:17.

Carbyn, L. N. 1982. Coyote population fluctuations and spatial distribution in relation to wolf territories in Riding Mountain National Park, Manitoba. *Canadian Field-Naturalist* 96:176–183.

Carbyn, L. N. 1994. Swift fox reintroduction program in Canada from 1983 to 1992. In *Restoration of Endangered Species* (M. L. Bowles and C. J. Whelan, eds.), pp. 247–271. Cambridge: Cambridge University Press.

Carbyn, L. N. in press. Wolf interactions with non-prey. In *The Wolf, Vol. 2.* (D. L. Mech, ed.) Chicago: University of Chicago Press.

Caro, T. M. 1987. Cheetah mothers' vigilance: looking out for prey or for predators. *Behavioral Ecology and Sociobiology* 20:351–361.

Cooper, S. M. 1991. Optimal hunting group size: the need for lions to defend their kills against loss to spotted hyaenas. *African Journal of Ecology* 29:130–136.

Crawshaw, P. G., and H. B. Quigley. 1984. A ecologia do jaguar ou onca pintada no Pantanal. In *Relatorio final, Instituto Brasiliero de Desenvolvimento Florestal.* Brasilia D. F.

Creel, S., and N. M. Creel. 1996. Limitation of African wild dogs by competition with larger carnivores. *Conservation Biology* 10:526–538.

Creel, S., and N. M. Creel. 1998. Six ecological factors that may limit African wild dogs, *Lycaon pictus. Animal Conservation* 1:1–9.

Emmons, L. H. 1987. Comparative feeding ecology of felids in a neotropical rainforest. *Behavioral Ecology and Sociobiology* 20:271–273.

Fanshawe, J. H., and C. D. Fitzgibbon. 1993. Factors influencing the hunting success of an African wild dog pack. *Animal Behaviour* 45:479–490.

Fuentes, E. R., and F. M. Jaksic. 1979. Latitudinal size variation of Chilean foxes: tests of alternative hypotheses. *Ecology* 60:43–47.

Fuller, T. K., and L. B. Keith. 1981. Non-overlapping ranges of coyotes and wolves in northeastern Alberta. *Journal of Mammalogy* 62:403–405.

Gehring, T. M. 1993. Adult black bear, *Ursus americanus*, displaced from a kill by a wolf, *Canis lupus*. *Canadian Field-Naturalist* 107:373–374.

Herrero, S. 1998. Canada's swift fox reintroduction an experiment in ecological restoration. *First North American Swift Fox Symposium, Saskatoon, Saskatchewan, Feb. 18–19, 1998*, Abstracts: 18.

Hofer, H., and M. East. 1995. Population dynamics, population size, and the commuting system of Serengeti spotted hyenas. In *Serengeti II: Dynamics, Management, and Conservation of an Ecosystem* (A. R. E. Sinclair and P. Arcese, eds.), pp. 332–363. Chicago: University of Chicago Press.

Hoogesteijn, R., and E. Mondolfi. 1996. Body mass and skull measurements in four jaguar populations and observations on their prey base. *Bulletin of the Florida Museum of Natural History* 39:195–219.

Horejsi, B. L., G. E. Hornbeck, and R. M. Raine. 1984. Wolves, *Canis lupus*, kill female black bear, *Ursus americanus*, in Alberta. *Canadian Field-Naturalist* 98:368–369.

Hornocker, M. 1970. An analysis of mountain lion predation upon mule deer and elk in the Idaho Primitive Area. *Wildlife Monographs* 21:1–39.

Jaksic, F. M., J. L. Yanez, and J. R. Rau. 1983. Trophic relationships of the southernmost populations of Dusicyon in Chile. *Journal of Mammalogy* 64:697–700.

Johnsingh, A. J. T. 1992. Prey selection in three large sympatric carnivores in Bandipur. *Mammalia* 56:517–526.

Johnson, W. E., and W. L. Franklin. 1994. Spatial resource partitioning by sympatric grey fox (*Dusicyon griseus*) and culpeo fox (*Dusicyon culpaeus*) in southern Chile. *Canadian Journal of Zoology* 72:1788–1793.

Johnson, W. E., T. K. Fuller, and W. L. Franklin. 1996. Sympatry in canids: a review and assessment. In *Carnivore Behavior, Ecology and Evolution, Vol. 2.* (J. L. Gittleman, ed.), pp. 189–218. Ithaca, NY: Cornell University Press.

Jonkel, C. J., and I. McT. Cowen. 1971. The black bear in the spruce-fir forest. *Wildlife Monographs* 27:1–57.

Joslin, P. W. B. 1966. *Summer Activities of Two Timber Wolf* (Canis lupus) *Packs in Algonquin Park*. M.S. Thesis, University of Toronto.

Karanth, K. U., and M. E. Sunquist. 1995. Prey selection by tiger, leopard and dhole in tropical forests. *Journal of Animal Ecology* 64:439–450.

Kehoe, N. M. 1995. Grizzly bear, *Ursus arctos*, wolf, *Canis lupus*, interaction in Glacier National Park, Montana. *Canadian Field-Naturalist* 109:117–118.

Koehler, G. M., and M. G. Hornocker. 1991. Seasonal resource use among mountain lions, bobcats, and coyotes. *Journal of Mammalogy* 72:391–396.

Kruuk, H. 1972. *The Spotted Hyena*. Chicago: University of Chicago Press.

Laurenson, M. K. 1994. High juvenile mortality in cheetahs (*Acinonyx jubatus*) and its consequences for maternal care. *Journal of Zoology* 234:387–408.

Laurenson, M. K. 1995. Implications of high offspring mortality for cheetah population dynamics. In *Serengeti II: Dynamics, Management, and Conservation of an Ecosystem* (A. R. E. Sinclair and P. Arcese, eds.), pp. 385–399. Chicago: University of Chicago Press.

McDougal, C. 1988. Leopard and tiger interaction at Royal Chitwan National Park Nepal. *Journal of the Bombay Natural History Society* 85:609–611.

McNutt, J. W. 1995. *Sociality and Dispersal in African Wild Dogs*, Lycaon pictus. Ph.D. dissertation. University of California, Davis.

Miller, A. A. 1998. Call these canines . . . Survivors. *Bozeman Daily Chronicle*, March 12.

Mills, M. G. L. 1996. Methodological advances in capture, census, and food-habits studies of large African carnivores. In *Carnivore Behavior, Ecology and Evolution, Vol. 2.* (J. L. Gittleman, ed.), pp. 223–242. Ithaca, NY: Cornell University Press.

Mills, M. G. L., and H. C. Biggs. 1993. Prey apportionment and related ecological relationships between large carnivores in Kruger National Park. In *Mammals as Predators* (N. Dunstone and M. Gorman, eds.), pp. 253–268. Symposia of the Zoological Society of London 65. Oxford: Oxford University Press.

Mills, M. G. L., and M. L. Gorman. 1997. Factors affecting the density and distribution of wild dogs in the Kruger National Park. *Conservation Biology* 11:1397–1406.

Muckenhirn, N. A., and J. F. Eisenberg. 1973. Home ranges and predation of the Ceylon leopard. In *The World's Cats 1* (R. L. Eaton, ed.), pp. 142–175. Winston, OR: Winston Wildlife Safari.

Murie, A. 1944. *The Wolves of Mount McKinley*, vol. 5, pp. 1–238. United States National Park Service. Fauna Series.

Murphy, K. M. 1998. *The Ecology of the Cougar* (Puma concolor) *in the Northern Yellowstone Ecosystem: Interactions with Prey, Bears, and Humans*. Ph.D. dissertation. University of Idaho.

O'Donoghue, M., E. Hofer, and F. I. Doyle. 1995. Predator versus predator. *Natural History* 104:6–9.

O'Donoghue, M., S. Boutin, C. J. Krebs, and E. J. Hofer. 1997. Numerical responses of coyotes and lynx to the snowshoe hare cycle. *Oikos* 80:150–162.

Pacquet. P. C. 1989. *Behavioral Ecology of Sympatric Wolves* (Canis lupus) *and Coyotes* (Canis latrans) *in Riding Mountain National Park, Manitoba*. Ph.D. dissertation. University of Alberta, Edmonton.

Pacquet. P. C. 1991. Winter spatial relationships fo wolves and coyotes in Riding Mountain National Park, Manitoba. *Journal of Mammalogy* 72:397–401.

Pacquet, P. C., and L. N. Carbyn. 1986. Wolves, *Canis lupus*, killing denning black bears, *Ursus americanus*, in the Riding Mountain National Park area. *Canadian Field-Naturalist* 100:371–372.

Pienaar, U. de V. 1969. Predator-prey relationships among the larger mammals of Kruger national park. *Koedoe* 12:108–176.

Rabinowitz, A. R., and B. G. Nottingham. 1986. Ecology and behaviour of the jaguar (*Panthera onca*) in Belize, Central America. *Journal of Zoology* 210:149–159.

Ralls, K., and P. J. White, 1995. Predation of San Joaquin kit foxes by larger canids. *Journal of Mammalogy* 76:723–729.

Robbins, J. 1997. In two years, wolves reshaped Yellowstone. *New York Times* 147, December 30:B13, F1(l).

Rogers. L. L. and L. D. Mech. 1981. Interactions of wolves and bears in northeastern Minnesota. *Journal of Mammalogy* 62:434–436.

Sauvajot, R. M., E. C. York, T. K. Fuller, H. S. Kim, D. A. Kamradt, and R. K. Wayne. in press. Distribution and status of carnivores in the Santa Monica Mountains, California: preliminary results from radio telemetry and remote camera surveys. In *Proceedings of the Second Conference on the Interface between Ecology and Land Development in California.* (J. Keeley, ed.), Southern California Academy of Sciences.

Schaller, G. B. 1972. *The Serengeti Lion*. Chicago: University of Chicago Press.

Seidensticker, J. 1976. On the ecological separation between tigers and leopards. *Biotropica* 8:225–234.

Seidensticker, J., M. E. Sunquist, and C. McDougal. 1990. Leopards living at the edge of Royal Chitawan National Park, Nepal. In *Conservation in Developing Countries: Problems and Prospects* (J. C. Daniel and J. S. Serrao, eds.), pp. 415–423. Bombay: Bombay Natural History Society.

Smith, M. E., and E. H. Follman. 1993. Grizzly bear, *Ursus arctos*, predation of an adult denned black bear, *Ursus americanus*. *Canadian Field-Naturalist* 107:97–99.

Stephenson, R. O., D. V. Grangaard, and J. Burch. 1991. Lynx, *Felix lynx*, predation on red foxes, *Vulpes vulpes*, caribou, *Rangifer tarandus*, and Dall sheep, *Ovis dalli*, in Alaska. *Canadian Field-Naturalist* 105:255–262.

Stoen, O. G., and P. Wegge. 1996. Prey selection and prey removal by tiger (*Panthera tigris*) during the dry season in lowland Nepal. *Mammalia* 60:363–373.

Turnbull-Kemp, P. 1967. *The Leopard*. San Francisco: Tri-Ocean Books.

van Heerden, J., M. G. L. Mills, M. J. van Vuuren, P. J. Kelley, and M. J. Dreyer. 1995. An investigation into the health status of wild dogs (*Lycaon pictus*) in the Kruger National Park. *Journal of South African Veterinary Association* 66:18–27.

Venkataraman, A. B. 1995. Do dholes (*Cuon alpinus*) live in packs in response to competition with or predation by large cats? *Current Science* 69:934–936.

White, P. J., and R. A. Garrott. 1997. Factors regulating kit fox populations. *Canadian Journal of Zoology* 75:1982–1988.

Wooding, J. B. 1984. *Coyote Food Habits and the Spatial Relationships of Coyotes and Foxes in Mississippi and Alabama*. Master's thesis. Mississippi State University, State College.

Other publications cited

Anyonge, W. N. 1997. Locomotor behaviour in Plio-Pleistocene sabretooth cats: a biomechanical analysis. *Journal of Zoology* 238:395–413.

Blumenschine, R. J. 1987. Characteristics of an early hominid scavenging niche. *Current Anthropology* 28:383–407.

Blumenschine, R. J. 1988. A landscape taphonomic model of the scale of prehistoric scavenging opportunities. *Journal of Human Evolution* 18:345–371.

Brantingham, P. J. 1998a. Mobility, competition, and Plio-Pleistocene hominid foraging groups. *Journal of Archaeological Method and Theory* 5:57–98.

Brantingham, P. J. 1998b. Hominid–carnivore coevolution and invasion of the predatory guild. *Journal of Anthropological Archaeology* 17:327–354.

Brooke, J. 1997. Too often, cougars and people clash. *New York Times*, September 3:A12.

Bunn, H. T., and J. A. Ezzo. 1993. Hunting and scavenging by Plio-Pleistocene hominids: nutritional constraints, archaeological patterns, and behavioural implications. *Journal of Archaeological Science* 20:365–398.

Cavallo, J. A., and R. J. Blumenschine. 1989. Tree-stored leopard kills: expanding the hominid scavenging niche. *Journal of Human Evolution* 18:130–136.

Eaton, R. L. 1979. Interference competition among carnivores: a model for the evolution of social behavior. *Carnivore* 2:9–16.

Ewer, R. F. 1954. Some adaptive features in the dentition of hyaenas. *Annals and Magazine of Natural History* 7:188–194.

Foley, R. 1987. *Another Unique Species: Patterns in Human Evolutionary Ecology*. Essex, England: Longman Group.

Holekamp, K. E., L. Smale, R. Berg, and S. M. Cooper. 1997. Hunting rates and hunting success in the spotted hyena (*Crocuta crocuta*). *Journal of Zoology* 242:1–15.

Lewis, M. E. 1995. *Plio/Pleistocene Carnivoran Guilds: Implications for Hominid Paleoecology.* Ph.D. dissertation. State University of New York at Stony Brook.

Lewis, M. E. 1997. Carnivoran paleoguilds of Africa: implications for hominid food procurement strategies. *Journal of Human Evolution* 32:257–268.

Marean, C. W. 1989. Sabertooth cats and their relevance for early hominid diet and evolution. *Journal of Human Evolution* 18:559–582.

Marean, C. W., and M. Ehrhardt. 1995. Paleoanthropological and paleoecological implications of the taphonomy of a sabertooths den. *Journal of Human Evolution* 29:515–547.

McHenry, H. M. 1994. Behavioral ecological implications of early hominid body size. *Journal of Human Evolution* 27:77–87.

Nowell, K., and P. Jackson. 1996. *Wild Cats. Status Survey and Conservation Action Plan.* IUCN/SSC Cat Specialist Group. Gland, Switzerland: IUCN Press.

Polis, G. A., and R. D. Holt. 1992. Intraguild predation: the dynamics of complex trophic interactions. *Trends in Ecology and Evolution* 7:151–154.

Potts, R. 1996. *Humanity's Descent: The Consequences of Ecological Instability.* New York: Avon Books.

Ruff, C. B., E. Trinkaus, and T. W. Holliday. 1997. Body mass and encephalization in Pleistocene *Homo. Nature* 387:173–176.

Shipman, P., and A. Walker. 1983. The costs of becoming a predator *Journal of Human Evolution* 18:373–392.

Stander, P. E., and S. D. Albon. 1993. Hunting success of lions in a semi-arid environment. In *Mammals as Predators* (N. Dunstone and M. Gorman, eds.), pp. 127–144. Symposia of the Zoological Society of London 65. Oxford: Oxford University Press.

Taylor, M. E. 1993. Locomotor adaptations by carnivores. In *Carnivore Behavior, Ecology and Evolution, Vol. 1* (J. L. Gittleman, ed.), pp. 382–409. Ithaca, NY: Cornell University Press.

Turner, A., and M. Anton. 1997. *The Big Cats and Their Fossil Relatives.* New York: Columbia University Press.

Van Valkenburgh, B. 1985. Locomotor diversity within past and present guilds of large predatory mammals. *Paleobiology* 11:406–428.

Van Valkenburgh, B. 1987. Skeletal indicators of locomotor behavior in living and extinct carnivores. *Journal of Vertebrate Paleontology* 7:162–182.

Van Valkenburgh, B. 1988. Incidence of tooth breakage among large, predatory mammals. *American Naturalist* 131:291–300.

Van Valkenburgh, B., and B. Hertel. 1993. Tough times at La Brea: tooth breakage in large carnivores of the late Pleistocene. *Science* 261:456–459.

Walker, A., and P. Shipman. 1996. *The Wisdom of the Bones.* New York: Alfred A. Knopf.

Werdelin, L., and J. Barthelme. 1997. Brown hyena (*Parahyaena brunnea*) from the Pleistocene of Kenya. *Journal of Vertebrate Paleontology* 17:758–761.

Woodroffe, R., and J. R. Ginsberg. 1998. Edge effects and the extinction of populations inside protected areas. *Science* 280:2126–2128.

6

A Comparison of Social Meat-Foraging by Chimpanzees and Human Foragers

Craig B. Stanford

Introduction

Chimpanzees and traditional human foragers are among the few higher primates that actively hunt mammalian prey for a part of their subsistence. Both hunt socially, and meat is a relatively small part of the overall diet for both chimpanzees and most human hunter-gatherers. Most attempts to understand the hunting and meat-eating behavior of chimpanzees have likened these apes to social carnivores, such as wolves and lions. Those species are, however, obligate meat-eaters and, therefore, make hunting decisions daily based on where to find prey and how to capture, not whether to forage for it versus plant foods. A more appropriate comparison is with traditional human foragers of the tropics and subtropics because both hunter-gatherers and chimpanzees forage primarily for plant foods, making decisions about whether to pursue meat on an hourly or daily basis. Seeing both chimpanzees and humans as omnivores that have evolved separate suites of adaptations valuable for foraging, including meat foraging, allows us to pose a number of theoretical questions relating to the ecology of meat procurement. Because the last common ancestor of chimpanzees and modern humans likely resembled a chimpanzee in at least some important ways (Wrangham 1987; Moore 1996), a comparison of the meat-foraging adaptations of the two species should help us understand key behaviors involved in the divergence of the hominid phylogeny as well as the behavioral ecology of the common ancestor.

This chapter explores the rationale for considering both chimpanzees and humans as omnivorous foragers and uses the results to suggest trends in the evolution of the human diet and the role of meat in it. I ask what the essential differences are between the predatory patterns of humans compared to those of great apes and how these may be related to our divergence from our common ancestor; in particular, I consider (1) the ecology of meat-foraging, (2) the strategies and tactics used in hunting, and (3) the division of meat. My sample consists of the three chimpanzee populations in which hunting has been well documented plus four forager societies whose behavioral ecology and meat-eating patterns are well known.

It should be stated clearly at the outset that any comparison that uses information from living apes and hunter-gatherers in the hope of building a portrait of early humans is prone to serious error for at least two reasons. First, the sample of available chimpanzee populations in which hunting has been well studied is very small and that of foragers only slightly larger. Second, the inferred similarities between modern chimpanzees and the last common ancestor are somewhat conjectural, given the near absence of a fossil record for extinct apes between 5 and 10 million years ago. Chimpanzees therefore provide a window onto the range of possible behavioral ecologies of early humans rather than being an accurate portrait of what the earliest hominids were like.

O'Connell et al. (1988) have pointed out that recent efforts to reject hunter-gatherers as sources of inference about the human past have been premised on the uniqueness of early hominids while acknowledging that modern foragers are the only large-brained, technologically proficient hominids to use as referential models. Instead of assuming that early humans and modern foragers are very similar, we might better use foragers as case studies in how humans with subsistence technologies cope with their habitat. This is in fact what a number of current hunter-gatherer researchers do.

The Sample

Chimpanzees

To examine aspects of the meat-eating ecologies of the two species, I employ a sample drawn from the human and ape populations on which the most extensive comparable meat foraging data exist (Table 6.1). There are three well studied chimpanzee populations for which published hunting data exist: Gombe National Park and Mahale National Park in Tanzania, and Taï National Park in Ivory Coast. A fourth site, Ngogo in Kibale National Park in Uganda, is also beginning to produce detailed hunting records. These populations, Gombe in particular, have produced detailed information about the behavioral ecology and social behavior of chimpanzees that can inform research into predatory behavior.

The hunting ecology of the great apes is one of the few pieces of evidence available in interpreting the meat-eating behavior of prearchaeological hominids. Of the four great apes, only chimpanzees eat meat on a frequent basis, and their hunting patterns and tactics have been the topic of much research. Studies of Gombe chimpanzees by Goodall (1968) and Teleki (1973) showed that these apes hunt and eat the meat of other mammals and that meat is shared in strategic ways. Recent field research has shown that while mainly frugivorous, the quantity of carcass biomass eaten by wild chimpanzee communities can exceed 700 kg in some years, most of which is composed of small mammals whose remains do not leave an archaeological trace (Stanford 1996). Moreover, the entire prey carcass, including bones, hair,

Table 6.1. Aspects of the meat-foraging ecology of some human and chimpanzee populations.

Population	% Meat in Annual Diet	% Kills by Males[a]	Prey Age Classes	Actively Search for Meat?	Home Range Size (sq.km)
Chimpanzee					
Gombe	3-5	91	76% immatures	No	10–18
Mahale	?	79	57% immatures	No	20–25
Taï	?	81	> 50% adults	Rarely	27
Ngogo	?	98	?	No	25
Human					
Aché	45	100	Mainly adults (monkeys)	Yes	
Hadza	20	100?		Yes	2,520
!Kung	15	100		Yes	260–2,500
Efe	9 (% of calories)	100	?	Yes	150–780

[a]For all prey over 5 kg.

Sources: Gombe: Goodall 1986; Stanford 1998; Stanford et al. 1994a. Mahale: Uehara 1997; Takahata et al. 1984; Uehara et al. 1992. Taï: Boesch 1994; Boesch and Boesch 1989. Ngogo; Mitani and Watts in press. Aché: Hill and Hawkes 1983. Hadza: O'Connell et al. 1988; Hawkes et al. 1991. !Kung; Less 1979. Efe: Bailey 1985; Bailey and Peacock 1988.

and skin, is typically consumed. Chimpanzees in Gombe hunt a variety of small mammals; red colobus monkeys compose more than 80% of the meat portion of the diet. More than 90% of kills are made by males, and most hunting is social, with hunting success correlated with the number of hunters (Goodall 1986; Stanford et al. 1994a). Although they are mainly frugivorous, and meat composes less than 5% of the diet annually, chimpanzees may consume enough red colobus to be the controlling factor on red colobus group size, population size, and age structure in forests where the two species cooccur (Stanford 1995). There is no evidence that Gombe chimpanzees actively search for prey; instead, prey are encountered opportunistically while foraging for plant foods.

In Mahale National Park, about 100 km south of Gombe, red colobus are also consumed avidly, along with duiker antelope and other mammals (Takahata et al. 1984; Uehara et al. 1992). Following early work by Nishida (1968) and others, studies of predatory patterns of Mahale chimpanzees have paralleled findings at Gombe, with some notable exceptions. Unlike Gombe, the diminutive blue duiker (*Cephalophus monticola*) is a frequent prey item at Mahale; it does not occur at Gombe. Little information exists on the ecology of potential prey species at Mahale, so predator–prey relationship are little known. Although the overall sample size of hunts is smaller than at Gombe, Mahale chimpanzees also appear to hunt seasonally (Takahata et al. 1984). The hunting season peaks in the late dry/early wet season of October and November, somewhat later than Gombe, where hunting peaks in August and September (which is the peak dry season at Gombe).

In Taï National Park, some 5000 km to the west, patterns of hunting described by Boesch and Boesch (1989) and by Boesch (1994) are quite different from those at Gombe and Mahale. Hunting at Taï is cooperative, with males taking roles to drive colobus and other monkeys toward other hunters who act as ambushers. Females are more involved in making the kill and in dividing it than at Gombe or Mahale. Boesch (1994) has suggested that the forest structure at Taï, in which a tall, continuous tree canopy provides escape routes for colobus, has led to greater cooperation than is seen in other chimpanzee study sites.

Hunting by chimpanzees has also been studied more recently at Ngogo in Kibale National Park. This work (Mitani and Watts 1999) constitutes a new valuable database to compare with hunting patterns at Gombe, Mahale, and Taï.

Human Foragers

The Aché are a traditional foraging people of the subtropical forests of eastern Paraguay. The northern Aché of the region of Ygatimi have been studied for the past 18 years by a team of anthropologists who have documented their behavioral ecology and demography (Hawkes et al. 1982; Hill and Hawkes 1983; Kaplan and Hill 1985; Hill et al. 1987; Hill and Hurtado 1996). Over the past 2 decades they have been forced to settle on missions, but the Aché continue to forage in the forest regularly, and while on these forays, groups of men pursue and eat mammalian prey. Shotguns have been introduced in recent years, but hunting is still often done with bows and arrows. They do not use toxins on their arrows and rarely use dogs. Among tropical and subtropical foraging people, the Aché include more meat in their diet than nearly any other group; up to 45% of the diet consists of the meat of about 50 species of vertebrates (Hill and Hawkes 1983). The Aché environment is a mosaic of habitat types; in each habitat a different selection of mammalian prey is available.

The single most important prey by weight is the collared peccary (*Pecari angulatus*), a species of wild pig. The prey that is most often and most profitably hunted (when bow hunting) is the brown capuchin monkey (*Cebus apella*). These are 4-kg monkeys that live in the forest canopy and flee at the approach of humans. The Aché either pursue the animals and then wait for a clear bow shot or ambush the monkeys after attracting them with imitated infant capuchin distress calls. When a hunter encounters a capuchin group, he solicits the help of other hunters, and if enough hunters are present, large numbers of monkeys may be killed in a single hunt.

The Hadza of northern Tanzania have also been used extensively as exemplars of aspects of early human behavioral ecology. They hunt and scavenge both big game and smaller animals, eating an average of more than 1 kg per individual per day (Hawkes et al. 1991). The Hadza per capita meat intake per year far exceeds that of other well-studied foraging people, such as the Dobe San, or !Kung (Lee 1979). Because the Hadza live in the same geographic region in which crucial stages of human evolution occurred, and because they consume relatively large quantities of meat, varying seasonally depending on availability, they have been widely used reconstructing aspects of the meat-foraging and carcass division in human evolutionary ecology.

The Efe are a Bantu people of the lowland rain forests of the easternmost Congo basin. They have been studied for many years, and much is known about their dietary habits (Turnbull 1961; Bailey 1985; Bailey and Peacock 1988). Efe men hunt a variety of forest animals though their hunting return rates and overall percentage of meat in the diet are quite low, which may be related to a lack of prey.

The Ecology of Meat Foraging

Researchers have tried to understand the behavioral ecology of both nonhuman primates and traditional foraging people using paradigms taken from evolutionary theory and modern behavioral ecology (reviews in Kaplan and Hill 1992). This is not controversial when applied to nonhuman animals; it is widely accepted that food of adequate quantity and quality is needed to enable a wild animal to survive and reproduce. When applied to humans, these models do not dispute the role of cultural traditions in shaping hunter-gatherer behavior. Instead, they argue that the expenditure of time and energy by people engaged in a subsistence life must be offset by the caloric and nutrient return they receive from the foods they eat. Because meat is an ideal source of protein and fat, much research has focused on the role of hunting in foragers' behavioral ecology. Most tropical hunter-gatherers eat mainly plant foods, but even when meat is a small part of the diet it is highly desired. *Valued* resources may not be the same as nutritionally *valuable* resources due to cultural influences, but as a starting point to frame research questions, we can infer that there are functional reasons for many aspects of the behavior of foraging people. The question of how meat is procured has occupied research on tropical foragers for decades. In this section I examine some of the distinguishing features of the ecology of chimpanzee versus human meat-foraging. I ask two questions. First, why don't chimpanzees actively search for sources of meat as human foragers do? Second, why don't chimpanzees scavenge? I use these two questions to elucidate key differences in the evolutionary ecology of hominoid meat-foraging.

During the past 2 decades, it became a common practice to use patterns in modern ecosystems and the fauna and flora therein to reconstruct a portrait of extinct ecosystems. Despite the earlier prevalence of chimpanzee models within primatology, archaeologists looked at chimpanzees as outliers of the process of human meat-foraging because their meat intake was reported to be far less than that of any tropical forager society. We know today that this is not necessarily the case; although chimpanzees eat relatively little meat compared to most hunter-gatherer groups, their annual meat consumption at some sites rivals that of some forager diets. Data from Gombe from the 1970s (Wrangham and Bergmann-Riss 1990) through the 1980s and 1990s (Stanford et al. 1994a) showed that meat intake could be much greater than previously thought. Stanford (1996) showed that in the dry months of peak hunting at Gombe, adult and adolescent chimpanzees increased their meat intake to approach the levels of some forager societies. Numerous researchers have hypothesized nutritional (Wrangham 1975) and social (Teleki 1973; Goodall 1986; Stanford 1998) explanations for hunting at Gombe.

The key aspects of meat foraging that influence behavioral ecology are (1) the nutritional and caloric value of meat, and (2) its patchy, unpredictable distribution. Nutritionally, the meat of small mammals can be a valuable package of protein and fat but not necessarily more so than some plant foods in the same forest. At Gombe, chimpanzees harvest fruits of the oil palm (*Elaeis guineensis*), which provide more than eight times as many calories per gram and also more fat than monkey meat (Leung 1968). Palms are of course sedentary, and although each tree has a fruiting season, there are generally some fruits available on at least some trees in all months of the year. Animal prey are, by contrast, highly mobile, require cooperative action to capture (see Boesch 1994 and the next section), and are capable of causing injuries to the chimpanzees in the course of capture.

Chimpanzees are highly frugivorous; over 70% of the diet of most populations consists of ripe fruit (Wrangham 1975; Goodall 1986; Nishida 1990). Fruit tends to be patchily distributed on the landscape both temporally and spatially. Feeding on ripe fruit means, therefore, that chimpanzees must continually monitor, and also remember, where and when fruit crops are ripening throughout the year. Fruit trees are stationary, and chimpanzees can navigate to them over many kilometers when needed. Locomotion by wild chimpanzees is largely terrestrial and always quadrupedal. This form of travel is less efficient energetically than bipedal locomotion (Taylor and Rowntree 1973; Rodman and McHenry 1980). Steudel (1996) recently argued that compared to other quadrupeds, chimpanzees are not remarkably inefficient, though in comparison to habitual bipeds they are. Rodman and McHenry argued that chimpanzees are unable to actively search for very widely scattered resources (which would include both carcasses and prey) due to their quadrupedal mode of locomotion.

The rate at which chimpanzees hunt monkeys is partially determined by how often they encounter them in the forest (Stanford 1998). The encounter rate is determined largely by the distance that chimpanzee parties travel each day combined with the use of food sources in which the prey are also feeding. Even though chimpanzees are mainly frugivores and red colobus are mainly folivores, half of both species' 10 most important plant food species are the same (Stanford 1998). Chimpanzees would have to dramatically increase their day range to bump opportunistically into monkey groups often enough to raise their meat intake to approach human forager levels. The energetic constraint imposed by the chimpanzees' inefficient mode of quadrupedal travel probably precludes doing so, and so may also preclude active searching for prey or for carcasses.

Janson and Goldsmith (1995) showed that in large primate groups the distance each group member must travel in a day to obtain sufficient food increases. Therefore, we expect a positive correlation between group size and day range, especially in species whose diets are high in widely dispersed foods. This suggests that meat foragers must either have large home ranges or else small foraging groups to be energetically efficient while eating meat that is searched for rather than encountered opportunistically. Using data from Kelly (1995), I compared hunter-gatherer societies to see if travel distance between resource patches is related to the consumption of meat (Figure 6.1). The regression uses only tropical and subtropical foraging people to minimize confounding effects from the dramatically lower pro-

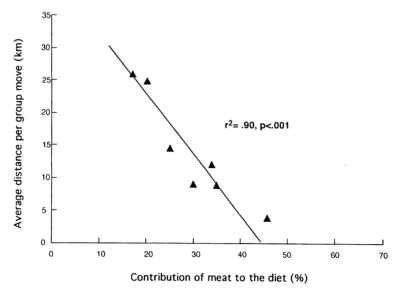

Figure 6.1. Regression of the average travel distance between residential sites (as a proxy for interresource patch distance) and the contribution of hunting to the diet. Data cited from Kelly 1995.

ductivity of the ecosystem in which boreal and arctic hunter-gatherers live. Many tropical and subtropical foragers have large home ranges, presumably so they can follow mobile or migratory prey, and because some habitats, such as the Kalahari desert, support only a low population density of large ungulates. This leads to a prediction that those populations for whom hunting is important should travel the furthest between resource patches. The opposite, however, turned out to be the case for the sample of seven forager groups (the G/Wi, Ju/Hoansi, Penan, Semang, Hadza, Mbuti, Siriono) in the analysis (the only groups for which travel data could be found). There was a strongly significant negative correlation ($r^2 = 0.90$, $p < 0.001$) between the average distance between residential sites (a proxy figure used for ranging) and the percentage of meat in the diet.

Although there are no directly comparable data for chimpanzees, hunting is more frequent in larger foraging parties and in parties containing many males (Stanford 1998). Both males and mixed-sex larger parties tend to have longer day ranges than parties of other compositions. Day range and encounter rate with prey also tend to be positively correlated (Stanford 1998). This suggests that hunting contributes more to the chimpanzee diet when their foraging parties travel furthest per day. It is important to caution, however, that the chimpanzees' unpredictable fission–fusion social system makes the comparison difficult to interpret because party sizes are highly variable even in the course of a single day.

Human foragers may search for meat because they can afford the expenditure of calories to do so while chimpanzees do not search for meat because it is not energetically feasible for them to do so. Other factors are involved as well; the likelihood of obtaining meat may depend on possibilities for reciprocal sharing (see the next section). Meat consumption at Gombe is disproportionately by the adult males, especially those who made the kill plus their close allies, plus any adult female with whom there is a familial, political, or sexual incentive to share. For members of the hunting party not connected socially to either the captor or the dominant male who controls the carcass, the amount of meat received can be negligible.

Scavenging opportunities from carcasses may present a different equation because there is a cost of location but not of capture (although piracy from other would-be carnivores may compose a large percentage of scavenging opportunities). Contrary to Schaller and Lowther (1969), Blumenschine (1987) argued that carcass availability and edible lifespan was great enough in early hominid habitats to have formed the basis for early genus *Homo* subsistence. However, because the locations of carcasses themselves are unpredictable and detectable only by visual cues (vultures) or by foraging for them, they probably represent a food source far patchier and less reliable than fruit.

O'Connell et al. 1988 point out that scavenging among the Hadza is simply an aspect of their ongoing meat-foraging strategy. The Hadza are always attentive to scavenging opportunities that arise; they cannot be categorized as occupying either a scavenging or hunting niche. Their success at obtaining scavenged meat relies on two main factors: encounter rates and ability to successfully compete for carcasses with carnivores such as lions and hyenas. Encounter rate depends on distance traveled and on cues to the presence of carcasses; it places a premium on long distance walking. O'Connell et al.'s observations show clearly that the Hadza are effective at driving these large and dangerous predators off their kills to claim them for themselves. Bunn and Ezzo (1993) and O'Connell et al. (1988) argue that early hominids could have been very efficient, active pirates of carcasses without necessarily being dangerous hunters, although most modern carnivores are both efficient killers and also effective scavengers.

Meat-eating patterns by wild chimpanzees lend little support to hypotheses for scavenging as a major component of the early human diet. In nearly 4 decades of field research, only a handful of passive scavenging episode have been recorded, although the piracy of freshly killed prey from other predators has been witnessed more often (Morris and Goodall 1977). Why chimpanzees do not scavenge while early hominids apparently did has been discussed previously (e.g., Hasegawa et al. 1983; McGrew 1992), but there are confounding factors that limit the conclusions that we can draw from the comparison. Chimpanzees live mainly in forested habitats that do not hold large populations of ungulates, which are the most frequent source of scavenging opportunities inferred from the fossil record. Chimpanzee populations living in lightly wooded miombo or savanna woodland analogous to those of early hominids have not been studied intensively due to difficulties of habituation and observation in the large home ranges that those populations occupy. But chimpanzees often fail to regard scavenging opportunities as having edible meat (Muller et al. 1995). This could be due to cultural traditions of meat-eating in the same way that chimpanzees at Gombe eat pigs while they are ignored by chimpanzees at Taï. Although the database is very small, female and juvenile chimpanzees may be more likely to show an interest in carcasses than males. Males appear to be interested mainly in living prey, including prey that they have seen killed by other predators.

When a foraging party of either humans or apes looks for food, the search image can include both living prey and carcasses. The main difference between human foragers and chimpanzees in this regard may be that the latter does not treat carcasses as highly desired food in the way that they regard potential prey. Human foragers prize meat of all types as long as it is edible. When the Hadza search for game, they readily scavenge carcasses, to which they are cued by the presence of vultures (O'Connell et al. 1988). The Hadza live in a prime habitat for scavenging, unlike the Aché who live in a densely forested habitat in which scavenging opportunities are presumably limited by a lower biomass of ungulates plus a shorter lifespan of carcasses.

Hunting Patterns

In this section I examine the predatory strategies used by chimpanzees versus those used by human foragers. I focus on the role of cooperation in shaping hunting strategies in the two species, evidenced by the relationships between hunting party size and composition and hunting success. Related to this issue is the role of males in hunting and why females are not more involved in the hunt. I also consider prey choice by species and age class as an element of the hunting strategy.

A comparison of hunting behavior between humans and chimpanzees must begin by stressing the differences between them (Table 6.2). Hunter-gatherers take prey in much greater size classes than chimpanzees do, and even though chimpanzees may kill multiple monkeys in one hunt, their meat consumption never approaches that of human groups such as the Aché or Hadza. Humans forage bipedally and with an active search plan for both meat and plant foods. Humans also use weapons extensively in making a kill while chimpanzees do not (but see Plooij 1984 for a rare exception). The use of weapons, even in the procurement of small game, creates an equation entirely different from that in chimpanzee hunting.

One way to enhance odds of success in a hunt is by cooperating. When the hunting success rate increases with increased party size, cooperation is suggested. This benchmark has been used in studies of lions (Packer and Ruttan 1988) and African wild dogs (Fanshawe and Fitzgibbon 1993). To examine the effect of party size on the amount of meat available to hunters, I compared the return rate in kilograms of meat per hunter during hunts of monkeys by both Aché foragers and Gombe chimpanzees (Figure 6.2). In both cases the prey is an arboreal monkey living in fairly large (20–30 individuals) social groups. In both cases nearly all hunting is done by males. To adjust for the energetic costs incurred by the Aché as they search for meat (Hill and Hawkes 1983), I used only hunts in which the Aché had hunted monkeys and omitted forays in which meat was not encountered. The comparison is thus based on how much meat is harvested in kilos per hunter for each species when a monkey hunt has been undertaken. The results show that the amount of meat taken is much greater for the Aché than for Gombe chimpanzees. However, the effect of hunting party size on per capita return rates is somewhat similar. In both cases hunters obtain the most meat in very small (fewer than three hunters) or large (more than eight

Table 6.2. Comparison of chimpanzee and human meat-foraging ecology.

I. *Chimpanzee–Human Similarities*
1. Largely plant food diet.
2. Sex role division in hunting.
3. Meat is shared strategically (interpopulational variation in both species).

II. *Chimpanzee–Human Differences*
1. Chimpanzee forage quadrupedally; human forager bipedally.
2. Chimpanzees forage for plant food and hunt opportunistically without searching for meat; humans search for both meat and plant foods.
3. Chimpanzees hunt prey in small size classes (under 20 kg) compared to human hunting.
4. Humans often use weapons in hunting, without which arboreal foods would be unavailable.
5. Chimpanzees eat and share meat from hand to mouth; humans may transport meat great distances from the kill site.
6. Humans coordinate hunts with vocal and/or gestural communication.
7. In most chimpanzee populations, dominance and status play a more important role in the division of meat than they do in most human forager societies.

hunters) parties. Hunters in medium-sized parties obtain the lowest amount of meat per hunter. A comparison between Gombe chimpanzees and Efe foragers (Figure 6.3) shows that these two populations have a similar relationship between individual return rates and hunting party size.

How does cooperation or the lack of it affect hunting in foragers and chimpanzees? Among hunter-gatherers, cooperation involves not just numerical strength, but actively coordinated action, including vocal or hand signals used during the hunt to enhance its odds of success. Cooperation among chimpanzees can include

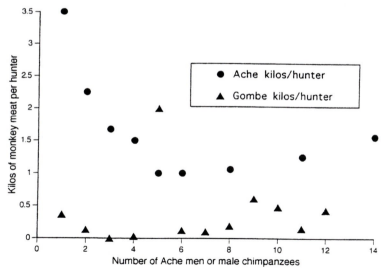

Figure 6.2. Comparison of Aché foragers and Gombe chimpanzees: hunting return rates and hunting party size.

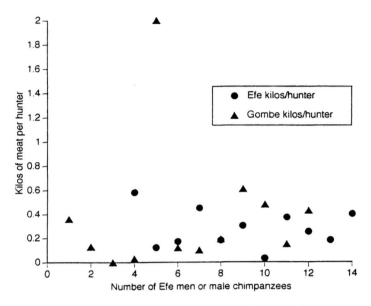

Figure 6.3. Comparison of Efe foragers and Gombe chimpanzees: hunting return rates and hunting party size.

coordinated action (Boesch and Boesch 1989) but more often involves only the additive benefits of more animals hunting together. This effect may increase the odds of each individual making a kill, or it may simply increase the chances that someone in the hunting party will succeed. In this sense, ascribing cooperation to social hunting among chimpanzees is problematic. Although regressions of party size and success rates show the same results between Gombe and Taï (Stanford 1996), observers in the field have gained very different impressions about the levels of cooperation at the two sites.

Data from a wide range of human and nonhuman primate societies clearly show that nearly all hunting is done by males. Among chimpanzee populations, the percentage of kills made by males ranges from 71% (Taï) to 91% (Gombe). At Gombe, one-half of the 9% of kills by females were by Gigi, a female presumed infertile, who often hunted with the males. Among human societies, it is an indisputable fact that nearly every human population on which ethnographic data have been collected is strongly male biased in the acquisition of mammalian prey (Kelly 1995).

Why do males do most of the hunting? Among chimpanzees, it is clear that females desire meat as much as males do but rarely hunt for it. Hunting by females may be dangerous when they are carrying dependent offspring or have young offspring following closely behind them. The canine teeth of a male red colobus could certainly injure or kill an immature chimpanzee. For humans, Hill and Hawkes (1983) suggest that women do not accompany hunting parties because of the potential danger to their children and because of the sexual division of labor; women break the camp from the previous night and then follow the men as they forage. If meat serves a strong social function for men in that the control and distribution of meat serves male sociopolitical and sexual purposes (Hawkes 1991), then men should desire to be the acquirers and possessors of meat.

The size and age of prey choice among chimpanzees may be dependent on simple size relationships between predator and prey. The largest prey recorded is about 20 kilos, ruling out the adults of most small ungulates, including duikers and pigs. The largest prey that are eaten frequently at all sites is monkeys (with the exception of some years in Mahale in which blue duiker have been preferred). At Gombe, chimpanzees kill mainly immatures: about ¾ of all red colobus monkey kills over the past 20 years have been of juveniles and infants (Goodall 1986; Stanford et al. 1994a). Taï chimpanzees, by contrast, kill mainly adults; 47% of their colobus kills are adult males compared to 6% of Gombe colobus killed (Stanford 1996). The reasons for this are many and have been debated. Boesch (1994) argued that the structure of the forest canopy at Taï made kills more difficult without active cooperation but that such cooperation enabled the capture of adults rather than infants, providing the hunters with a better return rate in kilograms of meat. It is unclear, however, whether the choice of 75% juveniles and infants at Gombe is because they are unable to kill adults or because they prefer to capture immatures. The chimpanzee hunters at Gombe who are (based on researchers' impressions) the most skilled and fearless hunters of colobus are also those who capture the highest percentage of infants. Frodo, for example, typically takes neonate infants from their mother's abdomens even though of all the Gombe chimpanzees today he is the most willing to withstand the counter-attack of male colobus to make a kill. Infant colobus provide far less meat than adults but require a similar level of risk and effort to capture.

If infants are preferred for taste reasons, they would also be more useful as social barter than adult prey. Occasional observations at Gombe of chimpanzees killing adults during the course of a hunt then dropping them in favor of pursuing immatures, lends support to the possibility that infants are more valued catches despite their small biomass because of their political value to offer to allies and desired females. It thus appears that both extrinsic constraints and individual strategic choices determine the age composition of kills among chimpanzees.

Interspecific and intraspecific prey choice among foragers is strongly influenced by the habits of the prey and by the weapons technology employed to capture them. Hill and Hawkes (1983) showed that when the Aché use firearms, 87% of their take is big game such as tapirs, peccaries, and deer; these animals are only 24% of the take when bow hunting. The effectiveness of these weapons allows for a greater return rate and therefore preferential hunting of large prey. When bow hunting, the Aché take mainly capuchin monkeys. This may be because there is no enhanced return rate for small game such as monkeys and paca while they are using firearms. Hill and Hawkes hypothesized that small game were not taken by shotgun hunting because their pursuit, even if successful, would decrease, not increase, the return rate for the hunting. For bow hunting the equation was the opposite; bow hunters increased their return rates by hunting monkeys. Alvard and Kaplan (1991) and Alvard (1995) found similar differences in return rates and prey choice in relation to weapons technology among the Piro and the Machiguenga in the Amazon basin. Hunters thus appear to make strategic choices about the optimal size of prey in relation to expected return rates.

This indicates the profound importance of the use of tools and weapons in the procurement of food. Meat-getting technologies alter the energetic equation enough that the introduction of a new weapon or a new hunting tactic using that weapon may markedly change the meat-eating patterns of a population. Stiner (1991, and this volume) documented the change in predatory patterns in the Upper Pleistocene that led to a more specialized prey choice, from an earlier pattern of more indiscriminate predation. This shift may have been brought about by a greater degree of cooperation or by the use of a new weapon, such as better stone projectile points.

Although archaeologists have argued for only a very recent innovation of high levels of cooperation (e.g., Binford 1987), the evidence from chimpanzees is that cooperative hunting occurred even in earliest hominid evolution. It probably showed interpopulational variation due to both ecological pressures and local traditions of hunting. The fundamental difference between foragers and chimpanzees with respect to prey choice may be that chimpanzees, limited in the size of prey that they can kill by their lack of weapons, show a much smaller magnitude in the difference between small prey and large prey (from a fraction of a kilo up to 20 kilos) than human foragers do.

Division of Carcass Meat

If the function of hunting by chimpanzees is even partly to obtain meat for strategic purposes, then we must consider carcass distribution as a key aspect of meat-foraging. The division of captured meat by chimpanzees at Gombe follows largely nepotistic lines. Kin are the main recipients of meat following a kill (Goodall 1986), and high-ranking or sexually swollen females also preferentially receive scraps of meat (Teleki 1973). The females who are the major recipients have greater reproductive success than other females (McGrew 1992). The decision to hunt may be influenced by the availability of fertile females in the hunting party with whom to share meat. Stanford et al. (1994b) showed that a swollen female's presence was a robust predictor of undertaking a hunt in encounters with red colobus. Males share liberally with females who are in estrus; females who obtain meat virtually never share with other females (Goodall 1986). Dominance rank plays an important but not consistent role in meat distribution at Gombe.

Nishida et al. (1992) have shown that the alpha male at Mahale shared meat with his allies more liberally than with other community members and that alphas tend to share meat more generously at the start of their reign than they do later. These results suggest a political motivation for sharing, similar to the pattern seen at Gombe. Following a capture at Taï, division of meat follows lines of reciprocity for participation in the hunt rather than nepotism (Boesch 1994); dominance rank appears to be largely set aside during apportioning of the kill.

Most researchers have seen meat-sharing by human foragers as a strategy of risk reduction; successful hunters give some of their catch away to provide themselves with a safety net of reciprocal sharing when they fail in the future (Kaplan and Hill 1992; Winterhalder 1996). Among the Aché, men from the hunting party distribute meat liberally to other families following a successful hunt. Neither the captor nor his family obtains a disproportionate share of meat. This pattern is seen widely among foraging people (Hawkes 1990). Kaplan and Hill (1985) saw this transfer of resources as an exchange system and suggested that sharing patterns follow predictions from evolutionary theory based on supporting kin and enhancing the hunter's reproductive success. Hawkes (1990, 1991) offered an alternative model to explain Aché hunting. She argued that men may not hunt with the primary goal of provisioning their family members because if nutritional benefits of foraging were all important, men could obtain more calories more efficiently by gathering palm starch. Instead, Hawkes argued that men hunt in hopes of obtaining an occasional bonanza of meat that can be strategically shared to obtain status and sexual favors.

Among the Hadza, the distribution of meat is also controlled by members of the foraging party other than the captor of meat himself. Hawkes et al. (1991) and Hawkes (n. d.) link the distribution pattern of meat in Hadza society, and the egalitarian nature of hunter-gatherer societies, to prey size. Chimpanzee prey are very small; modal prey at Gombe is only 1 kg and mean prey size is 4.4 kg. The modal prey size among the Hadza ($N = 12$) is 237 kg of edible meat (O'Connell et al. 1988). Hawkes et al. found that when carcass weight was over 100 kg, the hunter's family received a larger share than other households did; when prey weight was under 100 kg there was no significant difference in the amount shared between the hunter's household and other households.

The difference in carcass transport patterns between foragers and chimpanzees—that humans can carry food back to camp for distribution and also can dry meat for later consumption—creates opportunities for remote sharing that chimpanzees lack. Meat-sharing by chimpanzees is more limited in its social network of exchange. This is mainly because, since long distance food transport does not occur, sharing takes place only with those community members who are present at the kill (scraps are sometimes taken in to the night nest if the kill is made late in the day). The opportunities for individual enhancement through intragroup transfer of resources are thus reduced relative to human foragers (Winterhalder 1996, 1997) and at the same time are enhanced due to the very small parcels of meat available for distribution due to the small prey size in chimpanzee kills. Meat is therefore a highly desired food item for chimpanzees, even though individual survival does not depend on its acquisition. Meat in chimpanzee societies plays a role in the dominance arena in that high-ranking males control meat whether or not they are skilled hunters. Wilkie, the alpha male at Gombe from 1989 to 1993, rarely killed his own colobus prey but was able to take kills from other hunters with impunity. These were often shared with favored hunting party members. Meat-sharing among chimpanzees is not based on risk reduction because the parcels of meat are rarely large enough to provide substantial sustenance to other hunting party members.

Although there is much variation among human and great ape societies in the sharing pattern, a central paradox exists. What is the relationship, if any, between sharing of key resources such as meat and the egalitarian nature of human forager societies versus the hierarchies of chimpanzee societies? Chimpanzee and hunter-gatherer societies differ in their social networks in one striking way; the importance of status. Forager societies have long been described as relatively egalitarian, and much recent work has attempted to explain how their lack of hierarchy may be related to other aspects of a subsistence lifestyle (Boehm 1993, 2000; Erdal and Whiten

1994, 1996). Chimpanzees, meanwhile, live in status-driven hierarchical societies in which males spend their lives trying to rise in rank. Erdal and Whiten see a U-shaped curve of the evolution of human societies in which a status-driven ape ancestor evolved into hierarchical modern people, while earlier foraging forms of hominids may not have lived in hierarchical societies.

Hawkes (n.d.) argues that social conventions for sharing become a feature of human groups because fighting is too costly, in that an imposed asymmetry of distribution is better for all parties than no convention at all. These conventions become necessary as group size increases. Other researchers have argued that social cognition, group size, and sociality are linked (Dunbar 1992). In larger groups social networks, including sharing patterns, become more complex. Some of the key advantages of cognitive evolution, such as the retention of debts and credits, may lie in the need to remember the distribution web of highly valued resources and the opportunities for using these resources in selfishly manipulative ways.

Conclusions

Figure 6.4 presents a schematic view of the possible evolutionary trajectory of meat-eating and meat-sharing relationships among human group members. I hypothesize

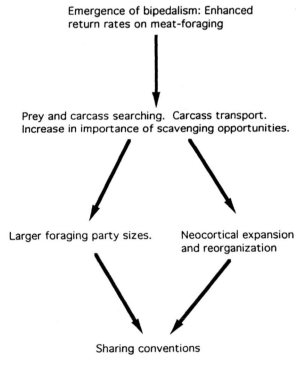

Figure 6.4. An evolutionary trajectory of the role of meat-eating in earliest hominid behavioral ecology.

that meat-foraging became energetically feasible for early hominids due to bipedality, at which point active searching for meat began. This included both scavenging opportunities and small game: meat in any available form was taken. The total biomass of meat eaten was sizable even though the prey may have been taken individually in small parcels. The enhanced profitability of meat-foraging afforded by habitual bipedal locomotion allowed social group sizes to increase without compromising individual foraging success. Group size increase was correlated with neocortical expansion, which enabled increasingly complex sociality and sharing conventions to emerge.

Acknowledgments Research on chimpanzee hunting ecology in Gombe National Park was funded by the L. S. B. Leakey Foundation, the National Geographic Society, the Fulbright Foundation and the James Zumberge Faculty Research Fellowship fund of the University of Southern California. I am also grateful for the assistance and cooperation of Tanzania National Parks (TANAPA), the Tanzanian Commission for Science and Technology (COSTECH), the Serengeti Wildlife Research Institute, and Drs. Anthony Collins, Jane Goodall, and Janette Wallis.

REFERENCES

Alvard, M. 1995. Intraspecific prey choice by Amazonian hunters. *Current Anthropology* 36:789–818.
Alvard, M., and H. Kaplan. 1991. Procurement technology and prey mortality among indigenous Neotropical hunters. In *Human Predators and Prey Mortality* (M. C. Stiner, ed.), pp. 79–103. Boulder, CO: Westview Press, Inc.
Bailey, R. C. 1985. *The Socioecology of Efe Pygmy Men in the Ituri Forest, Zaïre*. Ph.D. dissertation. Harvard University.
Bailey, R. C., and N. Peacock 1988. Efe pygmies of Northeast Zaïre: subsistence strategies in the Ituri Forest. In *Coping with Uncertainty in Food Supply* (I. de Garine and G. Harrison, eds.), pp. 88–117. Oxford: Oxford University Press.
Binford, L. R. 1987. Were there elephant hunters at Torralba? In *The Evolution of Human Hunting* (M. H. Nitecki and D. V. Nitecki, eds.), pp. 47–105. New York: Plenum Press.
Blumenschine, R. J. 1987. Characteristics of an early hominid scavenging niche. *Current Anthropology* 28:383–407.
Boehm, C. 1993. Egalitarian society and reverse dominance hierarchy. *Current Anthropology* 34:227–254.
Boehm, C. 2000. *Hierarchy in the Forest*. Cambridge, MA: Harvard University Press.
Boesch, C. 1994. Cooperative hunting in wild chimpanzees. *Animal Behaviour* 48:653–667.
Boesch, C., and H. Boesch. 1989. Hunting behavior of wild chimpanzees in the Taï National Park. *American Journal of Physical Anthropology* 78:547–573.
Bunn, H. T. and Ezzo, J. A. 1993. Hunting and scavenging by Plio-Pleistocene hominids: nutritional constraints, archaeological patterns, and behavioral implications. *Journal of Archaeological Science* 20:365–398.
Dunbar, R. I. M. 1992. Neocortex size as a constraint on group size in primates. *Journal of Human Evolution* 20:469–493.
Erdal, D., and A. Whiten. 1994. On human egalitarianism: an evolutionary product of Machiavellian status escalation? *Current Anthropology* 35:175–178.

Erdal, D., and A. Whiten. 1996. Egalitarianism and machiavellian intelligence in human evolution. In *Modelling the Early Human Mind* (P. A. Mellars and K. R. Gibson, eds.), pp. 139–150. Cambridge, Eng.: McDonald Institute for Archaeological Research.

Fanshawe, J. H., and C. D. Fitzgibbon. 1993. Factors influencing the hunting success of an African wild dog pack. *Animal Behaviour* 45:479–490.

Goodall, J. 1986. *The Chimpanzees of Gombe: Patterns of Behavior*. Cambridge, MA: Harvard University Press.

Hasegawa, T., M. Hiraiwa, T. Nishida, and H. Takasaki. 1983. New evidence on scavenging behavior in wild chimpanzees. *Current Anthropology* 24:231–232.

Hawkes, K. 1990. Why do men hunt? Benefits of risky choices. In *Risk and Uncertainty in Tribal and Peasant Economies* (E. Cashdan, ed.), pp. 145–166. Boulder, CO: Westview Press.

Hawkes, K. 1991. Showing off: tests of an hypothesis about men's foraging goals. *Ethology and Sociobiology* 12:29–54.

Hawkes, K. n.d. Hunting and the evolution of egalitarian societies: lessons from the Hadza. Unpublished manuscript.

Hawkes, K, K. Hill, and J. F. O'Connell. 1982. Why hunters gather: optimal foraging and the Aché of eastern Paraguay. *American Ethnologist* 9:379–80.

Hawkes, K., J. F. O'Connell, and N. G. Blurton-Jones. 1991. Hunting income patterns among the Hadza: big game, common goods, foraging goals and the evolution of the human diet. *Philosophical Transactions of the Royal Society of London* (*B*) 334:243–251.

Hill, K., and K. Hawkes. 1983. Neotropical hunting among the Aché of eastern Paraguay. In *Adaptive Responses of Native Amazonians* (R. B. Hames and W. T. Vickers, eds.), pp. 139–188. New York: Academic Press.

Hill, K., and A. M. Hurtado. 1996. *Aché Life History*. New York: Aldine.

Hill, K., H. Kaplan, K. Hawkes, and A. M. Hurtado. 1987. Foraging decisions among Aché hunter-gatherers: new data and implications for optimal foraging models. *Ethology and Sociobiology* 8:1–36.

Janson, C. H., and M. L. Goldsmith. 1995. Predicting group size in primates: foraging costs and predation risks. *Behavioral Ecology* 6:32–336.

Kaplan, H., and K. Hill. 1985. Food-sharing among Aché foragers: tests of explanatory hypotheses. *Current Anthropology* 26:223–246.

Kaplan, H., and K. Hill. 1992. The evolutionary ecology of food acquisition. In *Evolutionary Ecology and Human Behavior* (E. Smith and B. Winterhalder, eds.), pp. 167–202. New York: Aldine.

Kelly, R. L. 1995. *The Foraging Spectrum*. Washington, DC: Smithsonian Institution Press.

Lee, R. B. 1979. *The !Kung San: Men, Women and Work in a Foraging Society*. Cambridge: Cambridge University Press.

Leung, W. W. 1968. *Food Composition Table for Use in Africa*. Rome: Food and Agricultural Organization of the United Nations.

McGrew, W. C. 1992. *Chimpanzee Material Culture*. Cambridge: Cambridge University Press.

Mitani, J. C., and D. Watts. 1999. Demographic influences on the hunting behavior of chimpanzees. *American Journal of Physical Anthropology* 109:439–454.

Moore, J. 1996. Savanna chimpanzees, referential models and the last common ancestor. In *Great Ape Societies* (W. C. McGrew, L. F. Marchant, and T. Nishida, eds.), pp. 275–292. Cambridge: Cambridge University Press.

Morris, K., and J. Goodall. 1977. Competition for meat between chimpanzees and baboons of the Gombe National Park. *Folia Primatologica* 28:109–121.

Muller, M., E. Mpongo, C. B. Stanford, and C. Boehm. 1995. A note on the scavenging behavior of wild chimpanzees. *Folia Primatologica* 65:43–47.

Nishida, T. 1968. The social group of wild chimpanzees in the Mahali Mountains. *Primates* 9:167–224.

Nishida, T. (ed.). 1990. *The Chimpanzees of the Mahale Mountains.* Tokyo: University of Tokyo Press.

Nishida, T., T. Hasegawa , H. Hayaki, Y. Takahata, and S. Uehara. 1992. Meat-sharing as a coalition strategy by an alpha male chimpanzee. In *Topics in Primatology, Volume I: Human Origins* (T. Nishida, W. C. McGrew, P. Marler, and M. Pickford, eds.), pp. 159–174. Tokyo: University of Tokyo Press.

O'Connell, J. F., K. Hawkes, and N. Blurton-Jones. 1988. Hadza scavenging: implications for Plio/Pleistocene hominid subsistence. *Current Anthropology* 29:356–363.

Packer, C., and L. Ruttan. 1988. The evolution of cooperative hunting. *American Naturalist* 132:159–198.

Plooij, F. X. 1984. Tool-use during chimpanzees' bushpig hunt. *Carnivore* 1:103–106.

Rodman, P. S., and H. M., McHenry. 1980. Bioenergetics and the origin of hominid bipedalism. *American Journal of Physical Anthropology* 52:103–106.

Schaller, G. B., and G. R. Lowther. 1969 The relevance of carnivore behavior to the study of early hominids. *Southwestern Journal of Anthropology* 25:307–341.

Stanford, C. B. 1995. The influence of chimpanzee predation on group size and anti-predator behaviour in red colobus monkeys. *Animal Behaviour* 49:577–587.

Stanford, C. B. 1996. The hunting ecology of wild chimpanzees: implications for the behavioral ecology of Pliocene hominids. *American Anthropologist* 98:96–113.

Stanford, C. B. 1998. *Chimpanzee and Red Colobus: The Ecology of Predator and Prey.* Cambridge, MA: Harvard University Press.

Stanford, C. B., J. Wallis, H. Matama, and J. Goodall. 1994a. Patterns of predation by chimpanzees on red colobus monkeys in Gombe National Park, Tanzania, 1982–1991. *American Journal of Physical Anthropology* 94:213–228.

Stanford, C. B., J. Wallis, E. Mpongo, and J. Goodall. 1994b. Hunting decisions in wild chimpanzees. *Behaviour* 131:1–20.

Steudel, K. L. 1994. Locomotor energetics and hominid evolution. *Evolutionary Anthropology* 3:42–48.

Steudel, K. 1996. Limb morphology, bipedal gait, and the energetics of hominid locomotion. *American Journal of Physical Anthropology* 99:345–355.

Stiner, M. C. 1991. An interspecific perspective on the emergence of the modern human predatory niche. In *Human Predators and Prey Mortality* (M. C. Stiner, ed.), pp. 149–186. Boulder, CO: Westview Press, Inc.

Takahata, Y., T. Hasegawa, and T. Nishida. 1984. Chimpanzee predation in the Mahale Mountains from August 1979 to May 1982. *International Journal of Primatology* 5:213–233.

Taylor, C. R., and V. J. Rowntree. 1973. Running on two or four legs: which consumes more energy? *Science* 179:186–187.

Teleki, G. 1973. *The Predatory Behavior of Wild Chimpanzees.* Lewisburg, PA.: Bucknell University Press.

Turnbull, C. 1961. *The Forest People.* New York: Simon and Schuster.

Uehara, S. 1997. Predation on mammals by the chimpanzee (*Pan troglodytes*): an ecological review. *Primates* 38:193–213.

Uehara, S., T. Nishida, M. Hamai, T. Hasegawa, H. Hayaki, M. Huffman, K. Kawanaka, S. Kobayoshi, J. Mitani, Y. Takahata, H. Takasaki, and T. Tsukahara. 1992. Characteristics of predation by the chimpanzees in the Mahale Mountains National Park, Tanzania. In *Topics in Primatology, Vol. 1: Human Origins* (T. Nishida, W. C. McGrew, P. Marler, M. Pickford, and de F. B. M. Waal, eds.), pp. 143–158. Tokyo: University of Tokyo Press.

Winterhalder, B. 1996. Social foraging and the behavioral ecology of intragroup resource transfers. *Evolutionary Anthropology* 5:46–57.

Winterhalder, B. 1997. Gifts given, gifts taken: the behavioral ecology of nonmarket, intragroup exchange. *Journal of Archaeological Research* 5:121–170.

Wrangham, R. W. 1975. *Behavioural Ecology of Chimpanzees in Gombe National Park, Tanzania.* Ph.D. dissertation. Cambridge University.

Wrangham, R. W. 1987. The significance of African apes for reconstructing human social evolution. In *The Evolution of Human Behavior: Primate Models* (W. G. Kinzey, ed.), pp. 51–71. Albany: State University of New York Press.

Wrangham, R. W., and E. van Zinnicq Bergmann-Riss. 1990. Rates of predation on mammals by Gombe chimpanzees, 1972–1975. *Primates* 31:157–170.

7

Meat and the Early Human Diet
Insights from Neotropical Primate Studies

Lisa M. Rose

Introduction

The inclusion of meat as a regular part of the diet has long been seen as a significant development in human evolution, affecting patterns of land use, tool development, social interaction, communication, and cognitive development. By the 1960s,
hunting and its behavioral and technological legacy had gained broad acceptance
as the key human adaptation. However, studies of contemporary hunter-gatherers
such as the !Kung (Lee 1979, 1984) and changes in attitudes shaped largely by the
growth of feminist awareness in the 1970s increasingly emphasized the importance
of plant foods in the human diet and the predominant role of women in providing
these foods (Tanner 1979; Dahlberg 1981; Fedigan 1986). In addition, the development of modern, hypothesis-driven archaeology was accompanied by a tendency
to downplay the cognitive capacity of early hominids, particularly their ability to
hunt large prey (e.g., Binford 1981, 1985). Meticulous work at sites such as Olduvai
and Koobi Fora confirmed the associations between carcass remains, tools, and Plio-
Pleistocene hominids, but by the mid 1980s, meat procurement strategies were increasingly cast in terms of scavenging rather than hunting (reviewed in Rose and
Marshall 1996). However, interpretations have now begun to shift back toward a
mixed strategy of hunting and scavenging, as initially proposed by Leakey (1971)
and Isaac (1971) with an emphasis on "power scavenging" rather than marginal,
passive scavenging (Bunn 1996, this volume; Tappen this volume). There have also
been some recent attempts to integrate nonhuman primate studies and behavioral
ecological principles into reconstructions of early hominid meat-eating and land
use (Rose and Marshall 1996; Stanford 1996).

The use of nonhuman primate models has a long tradition in the study of human evolution (e.g., de Vore and Washburn 1963; Jolly 1970; Galdikas and Teleki 1981; review in Kinzey 1987), and much of the early interest in vertebrate predation and food-sharing in nonhuman primates reflected the view that hunting was a key adaptation in hominid evolution. Baboons became a focus of interest in the mid 1970s, following reports of intense vertebrate predation by olive baboons (Strum 1975, 1981), but chimpanzees have generally received the closest attention. The combination of a close phylogenetic relationship and prominent meat-eating, food-sharing, and tool use inevitably evoke analogies between extant chimpanzees and early hominids (McGrew 1992; Boesch-Achermann and Boesch 1994; Stanford 1996). However, the behavioral ecology of hunting by chimpanzees has also been studied in its own right, with particular reference to the predator–prey relationship between chimpanzees and red colobus monkeys (Teleki 1973; Busse 1977; Boesch and Boesch 1989; Boesch 1994a, 1994b, 1994c; Wrangham and Bergmann-Riss 1990; Stanford et al. 1994a, 1994b; Stanford, 1995, 1998). As the hunting behavior of chimpanzees is well documented in the literature and specifically addressed by Stanford (this volume), I will not elaborate upon it here.

A less widely known source of data regarding meat-eating in nonhuman primates is the Neotropical genus *Cebus*. Although the only detailed studies of hunting to date are for white faced-capuchins, *C. capucinus*, in Costa Rica, predatory behavior is reported across the genus and from a wide range of field sites (review in Rose 1997). Common prey include bird eggs and nestlings, frogs, bats, lizards, rodents, adult birds, nestling coatis, and squirrels. Adult squirrels (*Sciurus variegatoides*) are about one-third the size and weight of an adult capuchin, and are the largest prey taken (Figure 7.1). There are no reports of scavenging by capuchins at any site, and I have seen no cases of scavenging during more than 3,000 hours of observation.

Verterbrate Predation by *Cebus Capucinus* in Costa Rica

White-faced capuchins (*Cebus capucinus*) are medium-sized (2.3–3.2 kg), arboreal monkeys with a geographical range extending from Belize to northern Colombia. They are generalized omnivores, found in habitats ranging from primary rainforest to scrubby deciduous forest, and exploit a broad spectrum of plant and animal foods. Capuchins are well known for their ability to extract and process difficult food items and deal with biting and stinging invertebrates, as well as for predation on small vertebrates (Parker and Gibson 1977; Fedigan 1990). Their diet consists of 65–80% fruit and 20–35% animal foods (including vertebrate prey), with considerable local, monthly, and seasonal variation (Chapman 1987; Chapman and Fedigan 1990; Janson and Boinski 1992; Rose 1998). The social structure is multimale, multifemale, with group sizes ranging from 6 to 30. Capuchins are female bonded, and males typically disperse prior to maturity. Males are about 30% larger than females and are usually dominant over all but the alpha female. Most or all of the adult males in a group mate with receptive females (Fedigan 1993; Manson et al. 1997). Capuchins display considerable problem-solving ability in captivity, which may be related to both their foraging skill and social complexity in the wild, as well

Figure 7.1. Juvenile male white-faced capuchin with a freshly caught juvenile squirrel.

as to their manual dexterity, slow maturation, and large brain to body ratio (Parker and Gibson 1977; Fragaszy et al. 1990; Fedigan and Rose 1995; Fragaszy and Bard 1997; Visalberghi 1997).

The most extensive data on vertebrate predation by capuchins come from a long-term study of habituated, nonprovisioned groups in semideciduous forest at Santa Rosa National Park, Costa Rica (Fedigan 1990; Rose 1997; see Fedigan et al. 1996, for description of study site and population). Vertebrate prey account for 2–3% of overall feeding time and up to 15% of feeding time for some individuals during peak predation months (Rose 1998). The nutritional contribution of meat to the capuchin diet is unknown, but because meat is a rich source of protein and very little is wasted, it is probably more significant than the feeding time data suggest. The average group predation rate is 3.7 events (5.4 prey items) per 100 hours of observation, or one successful event every 2.3 days (Table 7.1). Bird eggs and nestlings account for about 40% of all prey taken, and squirrels (*Sciurus variegatoides*) and nestling coatis (*Nasua narica*) each account for about 25%. When differences in group size are taken into account, rates of predation on mammals are comparable to early estimates for Gombe chimpanzees, and individual male kill rates are very similar (Rose 1997). The capuchins kill squirrels at about half the rate that chimpanzees at Gombe and Tai kill red colobus monkeys, with similar proportions of group hunting but notably lower hunting success (Table 7.2).

Squirrels and nestling coatis are the most interesting prey in the current context because successful kills often involve more than one group member. Some hunts appear to involve strategy and possible collaboration, and squirrel and coati meat

Table 7.1. Predation by *C. capucinus* at Santa Rosa: rates per 100 hours observation.

Year	Group	Total Events ($n = 106$)	Total Prey ($n = 156$)	Birds/Eggs ($n = 63$)	Squirrels ($n = 39$)	Coati Pups ($n = 37$)
1986	CP	6.72	7.91	1.98	1.58	2.37
1991	LV	4.62	8.08	4.62	0.38	1.92
	CP	5.61	9.12	1.40	0.70	5.61
1995	LV	4.23	6.22	3.31	2.38	0.00
	CP	2.11	2.53	1.26	1.26	0.00
1996	LV	2.68	3.45	1.15	1.92	—[a]
	CP	0.87	0.87	0.43	0.43	—[a]
	NC	2.45	4.66	1.72	0.49	2.45
Average rate		3.66	5.35	1.98	1.14	2.06

[a]No observer was present in groups LV and CP during 1996 coati predation season.

is shared more often than any other food. Also, predation on squirrels other than nestlings is the only behavior that can be properly designated hunting, in the sense of actively stalking and pursuing relatively large, mobile prey. Other prey are typically taken and consumed by single individuals, often from nests that are routinely checked during the course of normal foraging. However, this "small-scale" predation is relevant and important for several reasons. First, eggs and other small vertebrate prey items are often regular components of the diet for contemporary hunter-gatherer groups and may well have been so for early hominids. Second, eggs and nestlings are often taken by females. Males take more prey of all types, but the sex difference is most pronounced in the case of squirrels (Figure 7.2). Expanding analy-

Table 7.2. Squirrel hunting by capuchins compared with red colobus hunting by chimpanzees.

	Capuchins Santa Rosa[a]	Chimpanzees	
		Gombe[b]	Tai[c]
Squirrel/colobus as % mammal prey	51%	82%	86%[a]
Observed squirrel/colobus kills	39	350	74[b]
Proportion of kills by males	67%	89%	~ 90%[c]
Number of males (range)	2 to 5	5 to 8	7 to 8
Kill rate per male per 100 hours	0.18	0.42	0.34[d]
Group/community kill rate per 100 hours	1.14	2.52	2.85[e]
Estimated kills per group per year	43–50	92–148	125[f]
Squirrel/colobus encounters per 100 hours	5.9	4.2	39[g]
% of encounters leading to hunts	55%	71.5%	17%[h]
Hunting success	17%	52%	46%[i]
% group hunts	81%	85%[j]	95%[k]

[a]Sources: Fedigan 1990; Rose 1997.
[b]Sources: Stanford et al. 1994; Stanford pers. comm.
[c–k]Sources: Boesch 1994a, 1994b; Boesh-Achermann, and Boesh 1994.

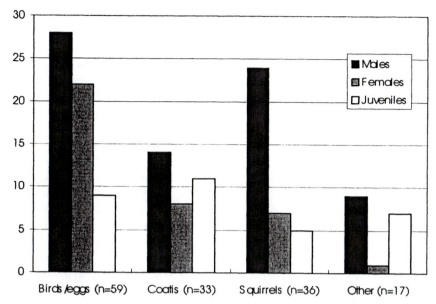

Figure 7.2. Number of prey items taken by adult male, adult female, and juvenile capuchins at Santa Rosa National Park during 2929 observation hours. Values include only prey for which the initial captor could be clearly identified.

ses to include smaller items gives a more complete picture of predatory behavior by both sexes, avoiding the almost exclusive focus on male behavior that dogged the "Man the Hunter" paradigm. Third, the taking of any prey item generates great interest within the group. Generally, the larger the prey the more intense the excitement and the number of individuals that gather around and watch its consumption, but even small eggs attract attention and thus have some impact on group behavior. Finally, although most predation occurs within the context of routine foraging, the monkeys often repeatedly visit and search areas with a high nest density or where prey have recently been captured. This is particularly noticeable in the case of coati nests but probably applies to any prey that tends to be highly concentrated in known or predictable areas. The effect of predation opportunities on range-use patterns and foraging decisions has not been systematically studied, largely because of the difficulty in quantifying "decisions" and identifying those responsible for determining group foraging routes. However, such a study would clearly contribute to our understanding of the circumstances under which occasional opportunistic predation might be a foundation for regular, planned hunting trips and increasing amounts of meat in the diet.

Opportunism versus Intentional Planning

One striking contrast between capuchin and human patterns of meat acquisition is the predominance of opportunism rather than intentional planning and preparation (see Stanford this volume, for similar observations regarding chimpanzee hunting).

The distinction is by no means absolute, as human hunter-gatherers often take prey opportunistically or combine small-game hunting with gathering in a single foraging round in much the same way that capuchins do (Teleki 1975; Southgate 1991; Bunn this volume). Also, our inability to enter the minds of monkeys precludes any certain knowledge as to whether and how they plan foraging activities or communicate any such plans with one another. We can say only that there is no convincing evidence of such forethought. Certainly there is no material preparation such as carrying or stashing tools in anticipation of their use. Tool use is well documented in captive capuchins although it has been studied primarily in *Cebus apella* rather than *C. capucinus* (e.g., Westergaard and Fragaszy 1987; Visalberghi 1993, 1997; Westergaard and Suomi 1997; Visalberghi and Limongelli 1996; McGrew and Marchant 1997). However, there are very few reports of tool use in wild populations (Chevalier-Skolnikoff 1990; Fernades 1991; Panger 1998). The occasional examples that I have observed in *C. capucinus* are very rudimentary: using leaves to obtain water from tree-holes, wipe sticky residue from the hands, or to protect the hands while processing hairy caterpillars or fruits; and breaking and dropping small branches on potential predators (see also Boinski 1988). Capuchins often carry hard nuts or seed cases to sharp rocks or branches to open them, but they bang the item on these hard surfaces rather than using the rock or branch as a hammer (Struhsaker and Leland 1977, pers. obs). There are no behaviors comparable in complexity to the preparation and use of termiting sticks or the transport and use of hammerstones by wild chimpanzees (Goodall 1964, 1986; McGrew 1974, 1992; Nishida and Hiraiwa 1982; Boesch and Boesch 1984, 1990, 1993; Sugiyama 1993) or even the modification of stones or bones reported in captive capuchins (Westergaard and Suomi 1994). Also, although there have been a few reports of chimpanzees using tools to facilitate the capture of prey (Plooij 1978; Huffman and Kalunde 1993), there are no such reports for capuchins.

Studies of capuchins in captivity suggest that it is not lack of cognitive ability or manual skill that inhibits tool use in the wild, but rather a lack of need or motivation to do so, perhaps coupled with an arboreal life-style (McGrew 1989; Visalberghi 1993). Lack of necessity may also apply to complex foraging plans and their communication, although here we are on much more uncertain ground. Captive studies and my own observations suggest that capuchins are not adept at tasks that involve understanding cause-and-effect relationships or abstraction from their immediate surroundings and that their primary approach to problem solving is trial and error rather than obvious reasoning or observational learning (Visalberghi 1993, 1997; Visalberghi and Limongelli 1996). Also, although capuchins have specific calls associated with group movement and coordination (Boinski 1993, 1996), communicating complex ideas involving past experiences or future plans may well be beyond their capacity. Thus, comparisons of early human and capuchin meat-acquisition strategies should consider the likelihood of substantial differences in cognitive and communicative abilities (see also Ingold 1993; Boyd and Richerson 1996).

Despite the predominance of opportunism in capuchin predatory behavior, there are a few indications of a more systematic, intentional approach to meat acquisition. Predation on nestling coatis typically occurs in the last month of the dry season and is often concentrated within a period of a few weeks. Adult female coatis live in groups for most of the year but disperse before the beginning of the birth season (usually in April) and build large tree nests in which their two to six young are born. Most females build several alternate nests in addition to the birth nest and typically move any surviving young if one is raided. The pups are quite defenseless for the first 3–4 weeks of life and are fiercely guarded by their mothers, who remain on the nests for much of the day. However, the nursing females leave at intervals to forage and drink, and the pups are often taken by capuchins at these times. The monkeys will also attempt to raid a nest even when an adult female is present, and although she is sometimes able to drive the monkeys away, almost half of these raids result in the capture of at least one pup. The monkeys repeatedly return to a nest that is successfully defended and try again, or if the female has moved the young to an alternate nest, they find and raid it. The monkeys are so persistent and successful in these raids that in at least some years, they take the entire birth crop of the coati group within their home range (J. Saenz, pers. comm.). The notable aspect of this behavior is that during the peak predation period, the monkeys' movements and foraging patterns are clearly centered around finding, checking, and raiding coati nests. This is particularly noticeable in dry years, when overall food abundance is low and vegetation is sparse, making the coati nests relatively easy to locate.

Squirrel hunting also provides some evidence of deliberate rather than purely opportunistic approaches to meat acquisition. Only about half of the squirrels encountered are chased, suggesting that the monkeys decide whether or not to attempt. A much higher proportion of squirrel encounters lead to chases in the dry season than in the wet season (63% versus 21%), and there is a strong seasonal difference in squirrel hunting success: 19% in the dry season versus 0% in the wet season, excluding nestlings (Rose 1997). Squirrel predation peaks in the mid to late dry season. The monkeys tend to visit and search areas where squirrels are abundant, but the pattern is not as strong as in the case of coati nest predation. In general, it is more similar to the pattern of repeatedly visiting areas where a favored but very patchily distributed fruit is in season. However, in one capuchin group in particular, some individuals engaged in active, specific prey searches that clearly differed from normal foraging behavior. These cases typically involved the group's alpha male and one or two others. The party traveled ahead of the group, moving silently through the trees in an attitude of intense alertness without engaging in any other foraging activity. Squirrels encountered under these conditions were almost always chased immediately. A similar pattern of active prey search is reported for Taï chimpanzees (Boesch and Boesch 1989). This behavior may be recent or idiosyncratic within the Santa Rosa capuchin population and is a striking deviation from the more usual pattern of opportunistic encounters and chases.

Although these examples are limited, they afford some insight into the circumstances under which opportunistic predation becomes more deliberately focused and concentrated. One key condition seems to be that appropriate prey are relatively abundant and that their general location is either known or can be reasonably predicted on the basis of previous encounters. Strum and Mitchell (1987) made similar observations regarding systematic predation by baboons and also noted that a reduction in the abundance of a prey's normal predators may be an important factor.

A second condition promoting systematic predation is that foods that usually provide the bulk of the monkeys' diet are relatively scarce, so there is increasing pressure to seek and invest energy in acquiring alternatives. For capuchins, meat is a highly prized food at the best of times, judging from the excitement that it arouses in the group, the eagerness with which it is consumed, and the frequency of begging and even occasional theft that accompanies its consumption. In times of food scarcity, its value doubtless increases with the level of food stress in the group. In general, there should be a trade-off between the relative abundance and spatial predictability of prey, the energy and risk involved in predation, and overall food availability. A combination of high predictability and low food abundance favors increased investment in predatory behavior, with a trend toward regular, focused prey search rather than simply opportunistic predation.

A third condition that I suggest is of particular importance in respect to the evolution of human hunting is that anticipated prey yields are sufficient that more than one or two individuals are likely to benefit, either by capturing prey themselves or by acquiring a share of prey caught by others. Group members are unlikely to acquiesce in movement patterns centered around vertebrate predation or to participate in group hunting efforts unless there is a reasonable prospect of individual reward. A similar argument follows if indirect benefits such as enhanced mating success or kin survival are gained through food-sharing, as may be true for chimpanzees and particularly humans: the amount of meat acquired must be quite large for sharing to be viable. For capuchins, the type of prey that best meets these conditions are nestling coatis, where the presence of up to five young in a nest present multiple capture opportunities, and adult squirrels, which usually feed three or four monkeys in succession. All three conditions—prey abundance and predictability, low overall food abundance, and prey that provide sufficient meat for more than a few individuals—are maximized in the late dry season, especially in very dry years.

Cooperative versus Individual Hunting

The inclusion of large prey items in the diet is likely to facilitate cooperative hunting, in the sense that joint action produces better results than individual action (Packer and Ruttan 1988; Stanford 1998), and subsequent food-sharing. Cooperation and food-sharing are often seen as crucial in the development of human hunting and tend to be explicitly or implicitly linked. The basis of the linkage may be indirect (large prey simultaneously require cooperation among hunters and afford opportunities for food-sharing) or direct (food-sharing is a necessary condition for cooperative hunting). The latter view is emphasized in Boesch's (1994b) suggested conditions for the emergence of cooperative hunting as an evolutionarily stable strategy: hunters do better by hunting in groups than by hunting alone; the difference compensates for the cost of meat-sharing; and meat is shared in such a way that hunters get a greater share than nonhunters. These conditions are not met in the case of squirrel hunting by capuchins. There is little evidence that group hunts are more successful than individual hunts, and meat is not systematically shared (Rose 1997). The degree to which chimpanzee hunting might be considered cooperative has been debated , but although participating hunters may gain status or allies rather than meat (Nishida et al., 1992), and meat-sharing may be forced rather than voluntary (Busse 1978), the conditional link between cooperative hunting and food-sharing has rarely been challenged (although see Moore 1984).

Whether or not food-sharing is a necessary condition for or an inevitable outcome of cooperative hunting, there can be little doubt that hunting large prey without sophisticated weapons favors the development of cooperation. In capuchins, the extent to which individuals actively cooperate during group hunts is unclear, but the potential for cooperation clearly exists. Some squirrel hunts appear highly coordinated, with individuals observing the position of others relative to the prey, and moving along intersecting trajectories, chasing in relays and/or blocking potential escape routes. However, it is difficult to determine whether this is truly cooperation, or simply individual opportunism (Rose 1997). Equally intriguing but ambiguous behaviors occur during attempted raids on defended coati nests, when some individuals attempt to bait an adult female away from the nest while others attempt to enter it and take pups. Based on our present knowledge, it appears that cooperation in capuchins is less developed than in chimpanzees, and far less developed than we might expect in early hominids. A number of factors are implicated here: differences in cognitive and communicative abilities, a less pressing need for cooperation that could be associated with smaller prey size, less reliance on meat as a food source, and (especially relative to early hominids), less risk from competitors and predators such as large carnivores (Rose and Marshall 1996). It is also likely that in early hominids, cooperative hunting developed in tandem with cooperation in associated activities such as planning and preparation, carcass transport and processing, and food-sharing.

Carcass Transport and Processing

I have already discussed the predominance of opportunism over planning and preparation in capuchin hunting and turn now to the absence of carcass transport and processing subsequent to it. This again is in marked contrast to human hunter-gatherers and archaeological evidence for early hominids. Capuchins rarely move prey more than a few meters from a kill site before eating it. If prey are caught on the ground, the captor moves back into the trees to eat, but otherwise prey are typically consumed in the immediate area that they are caught. The main exceptions are that low-ranking group members attempting to avoid or escape interference from others may carry their prey to a more concealed location (usually high in the canopy) before eating it or flee with it if they are chased by dominants. Dominant individuals (alpha males in particular) make no attempt to find a secluded location but tend to select broad horizontal branches on which to consume coati pups, squirrels, or the very large eggs of guans (*Penelope pupurascens*) or currassows (*Crax rubra*). This allows them to put the prey down and use both hands and teeth to deal with it. Coati pups and squirrels are often rolled or rubbed against the branch prior to consumption, which may help to loosen or tear the skin and soften the meat. The use of large-branch feeding sites also allows other group members, usually infants and juveniles, to approach closely and beg for meat or obtain scraps. However, this is probably a fortuitous rather than deliberate facilitation of food-sharing.

I have never seen capuchins engage in even rudimentary tool use to facilitate prey consumption. Adult males in particular have enlarged, sharp canines, and if the prey has particularly tough skin (as in the case of adult squirrels), the monkeys generally make the first bites and tears in the softer lower belly area. Prey are not deliberately disarticulated, although pieces may fall off during the eating process, and the monkeys seem to have no problem eating bones. Typically, the only parts not eaten are the heads of older coati pups, squirrels, or birds, the skin and tails of squirrels, and the feet and feathers of large birds. The contrast between the lack of carcass processing in capuchins (and also in chimpanzees) and the regular disarticulation and processing of large carcasses by human hunter-gatherers and early hominids probably reflects both prey size (capuchins take no prey that cannot be carried by a single individual) and differences in tooth morphology. Unlike most other primates, neither modern humans nor early hominids have particularly large or sharp canines, and tools were probably essential for disarticulating large carcasses even in Plio-Pleistocene times. Indeed, the regular acquisition of large carcasses by early hominids was almost certainly dependent on, or developed in conjunction with, a basic stone tool technology.

The acquisition of prey or carcasses too large to be captured and dealt with by a single individual and the use of tools to facilitate capture and carcass processing are two major factors that distinguish human and early hominid meat-acquisition patterns from those found in capuchins and chimpanzees. Both of these factors are, in turn, associated with carcass transport and food-sharing, which are also key features of human and hominid meat-eating. Carcass transport by early hominids was probably a response to the joint pressures of competition with large carnivores and other hominid groups, the associated risk of predation by large carnivores, and the need to bring carcasses and stone tools together in a location that was safe and convenient for carcass processing and sharing. Rose and Marshall (1996) suggest that this pattern favored the use of home bases by Plio-Pleistocene hominids, while Potts (1984, 1988) argues in favor of specific "stone cache" sites that were used solely for carcass processing. In either event, the pattern of deliberate carcass transport differs markedly from the general "forage as you go" or "routed foraging" movement patterns of most nonhuman primates, including chimpanzees and capuchins.

Food-Sharing

It cannot be argued that the transport of carcasses to particular locations is a requirement for food-sharing because chimpanzees regularly share meat without transporting it (Teleki 1973; Goodall 1986; Boesch 1994b; Stanford 1998). However, transport and processing might well promote sharing, especially if a number of individuals contribute to the work involved. Regardless of whether meat-sharing is interpreted in terms of reward and incentive for cooperating, kin selection, reciprocal altruism, status gains, or simply as a response to social pressure, it is a behavior that would seem difficult to stop and easy to elaborate once begun. The regular sharing of any sizable amounts of meat is virtually ubiquitous among modern hunter-gatherers. Chimpanzee hunters also share meat on a regular basis, not only among themselves, but also with females. However, capuchins provide a striking exception to this pattern. Meat is shared more often than any other food (Perry and Rose 1994; Rose 1997), but the incidence of sharing is still remarkably low. At Santa Rosa, I estimated the average rate of food-sharing by adults at only 1.7 events per 100 hours, and the rate of meat-sharing at about 1.1 events per 100 hours. The majority of cases involved adults sharing with infants or juveniles, and most were tolerated scrounging or cofeeding on a single carcass rather than active food-sharing.

In capuchins, falling scraps and abandoned carcasses are the most common means by which larger kills are distributed among group members. Except in the few cases that a carcass is stolen (usually from a low-ranking female or juvenile), nestling squirrels and coatis are usually eaten entirely by the captor. However, scraps of meat frequently fall or are pulled from the carcass and are eagerly consumed by monkeys waiting nearby. The carcasses of larger squirrels typically have two to four consecutive owners. When the first owner has finished eating, he or she simply drops the partially eaten carcass or abandons it on a branch, and it is then grabbed by another individual. The chance of acquiring falling scraps or abandoned carcasses is clearly an incentive to stay in close proximity while meat is being consumed. Dominance rank also plays a role, as high-ranking individuals are more likely to obtain and keep abandoned carcasses than those of lower rank. However, infants are the most persistent in their attempts to acquire meat by begging. Although they are rarely rewarded by active sharing, most adults are very tolerant of infants and small immatures, occasionally allowing them to pull small pieces from a carcass and even from the owner's hand or mouth. Adult females are more likely than males to actively share with infants, but they are much less likely to be carcass owners than adult males. Adults very rarely share food with one another. In 1 year that I systematically recorded all occurrences of food-sharing, I noted only three cases of sharing between adults in 1,061 hours of observation: two between males and females and one between adult males. All three cases involved squirrel meat. Rates of meat-sharing at another white-faced capuchin site, Lomas Barbudol, tend to be somewhat higher than at Santa Rosa, but sharing is still predominantly from adults to infants rather than between adults and still occurs at much lower rates than in chimpanzees (Perry and Rose 1994; Rose 1997). There is some evidence of preferential sharing with kin, but the most common interactions are mothers sharing with infants.

The reasons for the rarity of food-sharing among adult capuchins are unclear, but one possible explanation lies in their female-bonded social structure. Adult males take more than half of all prey items captured while females and immatures together take 48%. Adult males make almost all of the adult squirrel kills and take about twice as many coati pups as females (Rose, 1997). In contrast to chimpanzees, capuchins are female bonded rather than male bonded, and in the absence of true cooperative hunting, there may be little incentive for adult males to share meat with one another. Also, capuchins do not have exclusive or prolonged sexual consortships, so males are unlikely to share with females to gain mating advantages, as has been suggested for chimpanzees (Teleki 1973; Tutin 1979; McGrew 1992; Stanford et al.

1994b). However, it is surprising that there is virtually no sharing among adult female capuchins. Capuchins have complex patterns of social interaction and alliance formation (Perry 1996, 1997; Rose 1998), so there would seem to be a potential role for food-sharing as a means of promoting and reinforcing alliances, as suggested for chimpanzees (Nishida et al. 1992). It is possible that in capuchins, the nutritional value of meat outweighs its potential value in social interactions, particularly in times of food scarcity. High rates of voluntary food-sharing are reported in captive *Cebus apella* (de Waal et al. 1993), and coati pups are shared more often at Lomas Barbudol than at Santa Rosa, which may reflect differences in food availability (Perry and Rose 1994).

Another factor underlying the rarity of meat-sharing in capuchins may be the ability to control carcasses, which is related to relatively small prey size and also to dominance relationships. It is easy for high-ranking males to monopolize prey, and females and even juveniles are often able to maintain control of small items. By contrast, large prey are difficult for a single individual to monopolize or defend, especially on the ground where escape routes and defensive positions are more limited than in the canopy. Hawkes (this volume) argues that the lack of control or "ownership" of large carcasses has been a key factor in the evolution of human hunting and meat-sharing, particularly in the elaboration of social pressures and customs related to sharing.

Scavenging

There is very little evidence of scavenging by extant nonhuman primates, but there have been a few cases reported for chimpanzees (Hasegawa et al. 1983; Goodall, 1986; Stanford et al. 1994a; Muller et al. 1995) and baboons (Strum, 1981). By contrast, there are no reported instances of scavenging in *Cebus*. This may be because scavenging opportunities are rare in a tropical forest environment, especially for an arboreal species. Capuchins are the most terrestrial of all New World monkeys, but *C. capucinus* males spend less than 6% of their time on the ground, and females less than 2% (Rose 1994, 1998). However, I have seen the monkeys encounter a few reasonably intact carcasses, including a recently dead howler monkey, a tamandua, a deer, and occasional birds, as well as some older carcasses in advanced stages of decomposition. The monkeys' response, if any, is usually to stare at or briefly threaten the carcass and then ignore it. In the case of the dead tamandua, a few juveniles males poked at it, and one briefly attempted to pull it by the tail. These are quite typical responses to unfamiliar objects, and there were no indications that the monkeys saw the carcasses as potential food. The one exception was that a juvenile male picked up and sniffed a dead parrot and then displayed with it for a few minutes before dropping it on the ground, where several other juveniles subsequently sniffed and poked at it. However, none of them actually attempted to eat the bird, despite its being quite fresh and well within their usual prey size range. Such responses to edible carcasses suggests that scavenging is unlikely, even when opportunities present themselves. It is possible that scavenging occurs in other groups, or could develop in response to food shortage or as a cultural tradition, but at present there is no evidence for it.

Key Differences in Human and Capuchin Meat-Eating

In summary, meat-eating by capuchins differs from that in human hunter-gatherers and early hominids in a number of critical ways. It is predominantly opportunistic, and although group hunting is common in the case of squirrels and coatis, there is little evidence of strategic planning or cooperation between individuals. Vertebrate prey make up only a small part (2–3%) of the overall diet. The prey taken are relatively small, the largest being about one-third the size of an adult capuchin, and none are too large for a single individual to handle or monopolize. Neither hunting nor eating involves tool use, and carcasses are not regularly transported or disarticulated. Some sharing occurs, but meat is not systematically distributed, and most sharing takes the form of tolerated scrounging by infants. Other individuals typically gain access to scraps or abandoned carcasses by virtue of proximity and persistence rather than through active or socially mediated sharing.

In many ways, patterns of meat acquisition in capuchins resemble those in chimpanzees. Prey harvests and the contribution of meat to the diet are quite similar although we do not yet know whether predation by capuchins is regularly sustained over as long a period as it is in chimpanzees. However, there are some notable contrasts, which are probably interrelated. First, there is less evidence of cooperation among capuchins than among chimpanzees. Second, there is occasional evidence of tool-assisted predation in chimpanzees but none for capuchins—and indeed, very little evidence of any tool use at all in wild capuchins. Third, male capuchins and chimpanzees are more active in hunting than females, but the sex difference is less marked in capuchins. Female capuchins often participate in group hunts even though they are not particularly successful, and some females are very active in coati nest predation. Finally, chimpanzees share meat much more frequently than capuchins, and at least some meat-sharing in chimpanzees appears to serve a social function or to be socially mediated.

Overall, patterns of meat acquisition and distribution seem less elaborate or developed in capuchins than in chimpanzees, which are, in turn, less elaborate or developed than those in human hunter-gatherers. This does not imply that meat-eating behavior necessarily follows an evolutionary sequence or that it will eventually converge at a "more human" level in either chimpanzees or capuchins. However, it does suggest that there are stages of development or specialization in meat-eating that are marked by particular behaviors such as planning, tool use, cooperation, carcass transport, and food-sharing and that these stages differ among the three species. These differences are probably associated with cognitive ability, particularly the development of complex communication and the emergence of language in the human lineage. Indeed, it has been argued that meat-eating itself has been critical in the development of human cognitive and social skills (Kitahara-Frisch 1987; Stanford 1998). The energetically expensive increase in brain size in *Homo* may well be linked with increased reliance on meat as a high-quality food source (Foley this volume; Vasey and Walker this volume). However, the rarity of meat-eating in other great apes (and probably in Australopithecines) and its frequency in *Cebus* suggest that brain size and cognitive capacity alone cannot account for the origin of meat-eating in the primate lineage. Clearly, we must look to behavioral ecological factors as well in attempting to explain the origins of meat-eating and the transition from opportunistic predation to systematic, planned strategies of meat acquisition.

Possible Factors Promoting the Evolution of Hunting

The most obvious preconditions for predatory behavior is generalized omnivory. Fedigan (1990) suggests that meat-eating in *Cebus* may have arisen opportunistically through the occasional flushing of vertebrate prey during insect foraging. Harding (1981) and Hladik (1981) also suggest a link between vertebrate predation and the capture of large, mobile invertebrates. As well as catching large, fast-moving insects, capuchins regularly deal with stinging and biting invertebrates in the normal course of foraging. Chimpanzees also deal successfully with stinging and biting invertebrates and often use tools to obtain them (e.g., McGrew 1974; Nishida and Hiraiwa 1982; Boesch and Boesch 1993; Alp 1993). The manipulative and cognitive skills required to overcome invertebrate prey defenses may have played a supporting role in the development of vertebrate predation by both taxa (Janson and Boinski 1992). Also, regular inspection of nests as a source of invertebrates could easily lead to predation on eggs and nestlings, and subsequently extend to larger prey such as squirrels flushed from nests, without any major change in foraging patterns.

A possible factor that may help bridge the gap between invertebrate and nest predation to predation on larger, mobile prey is a tendency to be aggressive toward potential predators, competitors, and other animals (Rose 1997). This opens up the intriguing possibility that there is a psychological factor involved in predation as well as cognitive ability to see other animals in terms of possible food—a possibility that also applies to scavenging behavior. Nutritional requirements and seasonal food stress have also been considered as factors promoting predation in chimpanzees and capuchins (Wrangham 1975; Fedigan 1990; Stanford 1996). At both Gombe and Santa Rosa, vertebrate predation is most common during the dry season, when fruit abundance is typically low. In earlier studies at Santa Rosa, vertebrate predation occurred most frequently in the group with the most marginal habitat (Chapman and Fedigan 1990; Fedigan 1990). However, in more recent years, I found vertebrate predation to be most common in the group with the largest and richest home range, suggesting that food availability alone is not a reliable predictor of predatory behavior (Rose 1997). Stanford (1996,1998) also questions the importance of seasonal food shortage, noting that the peak hunting period for Taï and Mahale chimpanzees is during the wet season and that Gombe chimpanzees have access to oil palm nuts (*Elaeis guineensis*), a good source of calories and fat, during the dry season. Although food availability and marked seasonality probably play a role in promoting predatory behavior, these factors alone do not seem to offer an adequate explanation (see also Foley this volume). Cultural traditions, the influence of particularly avid hunters, and status rewards are also likely to promote hunting, but again do not afford good explanations of its origins. However, all of these factors may be useful in explaining the elaboration of hunting behavior.

I noted earlier that a number of ecological conditions favor a shift from opportunistic predation to systematic hunting and nest-raiding: (1) appropriate prey are relatively abundant and occur in predictable areas; (2) overall food availability is relatively low, and (3) prey yields are sufficient for more than one or two individuals. The single most significant factor responsible for the elaboration of hunting and food-sharing behavior is probably prey size. Obtaining large prey calls for cooperation, and invites or even necessitates carcass transport, disarticulation, and food-sharing. Strategic planning, tool use, and associated cognitive and communicative skills will also be increasingly favored as prey size increases and the logistics of capture and processing become more demanding. Capuchins offer intriguing insights into an early stage of transition from regular but primarily opportunistic predation on nests and small vertebrates to the more systematic and intentional hunting of larger prey. Two directions for future research might be particularly rewarding: (1) comparative behavioral-ecological studies of predation by capuchins, other nonhuman primates, and human hunter-gatherers, and (2) studies of predation by nonhuman primates that integrate findings from field observations, field experiments, and captive studies of cognition and tool use.

Acknowledgments   I thank the Area de Conservacion Guanacaste for permission to conduct research at Santa Rosa National Park, and particularly research coordinator Roger Blanco. Funding for my field work has been provided by the National Science Foundation, National Geographic Society, L. S. B. Leakey Foundation, Sigma XI, Ammonite Ltd., and the National Science and Engineering Research Council of Canada. Additional predation data were contributed by Linda M. Fedigan and Carla Goforth. Many thanks to Craig Stanford and Henry Bunn for organizing this conference and inviting me to participate. Thanks also to Fiona Marshall and Craig Stanford for comments and discussion on an earlier draft of this chapter.

REFERENCES

Alp, R. 1993. Meat-eating and ant dipping by wild chimpanzees in Sierra Leone. *Primates* 34:463–468.
Binford, L. 1981. *Bones: Ancient Men and Modern Myths*. New York: Academic Press.
Binford, L. 1985. Human ancestors: changing views of their behavior. *Journal of Anthropology and Archaeology* 4:292–327.
Boesch, C. 1994a. Chimpanzees—red colobus monkeys: a predator–prey system. *Animal Behavior* 47:1135–1148.
Boesch, C. 1994b. Cooperative hunting in wild chimpanzees. *Animal Behavior* 48:653–657.
Boesch, C. 1994c. Hunting strategies of Gombe and Tai chimpanzees. In *Chimpanzee Cultures* (R. W. Wrangham, W. C. McGrew, F. B. M. de Waal, and P. G. Heltne, (eds.), pp. 77–91. Cambridge, MA: Harvard University Press.
Boesch, C., and H. Boesch. 1984. Possible causes of sex differences in the use of natural hammers by wild chimpanzees. *Journal of Human Evolution* 13:415–440.
Boesch, C., and H. Boesch. 1989. Hunting behavior of wild chimpanzees in the Tai National Park. *American Journal of Physical Anthropology* 78:547–573.

Boesch, C., and H. Boesch. 1990. Tool use and tool making in wild chimpanzees. *Folia Primatologica* 54:86–99.

Boesch, C., and H. Boesch. 1993. Diversity of tool use and tool making in wild chimpanzees. In *The Use of Tools by Human and Non-Human Primates* (A. Berthelet, and J. Chavaillon, (eds.), pp. 158–168. Oxford: Clarendon Press.

Boesch-Achermann, H., and C. Boesch. 1994. Hominization in the rainforest: the chimpanzee's piece of the puzzle. *Evolutionary Anthropology* 3:9–16.

Boinski, S. 1988. Use of a club by a wild white-faced capuchin (*Cebus capucinus*) to attack a venomous snake (*Bothrops asper*). *American Journal of Primatology* 14:177–179.

Boinski, S. 1993. Vocal coordination of troop movement among white-faced capuchin monkeys, *Cebus capucinus*. *American Journal of Primatology* 30:85–100.

Boinski, S. 1996. Vocal coordination of troop movement in squirrel monkeys (*Saimiri oerstedi* and *S. sciureus*) and white-faced capuchins (*Cebus capucinus*). In: *Adaptive Radiations of Neotropical Primates* (M. Norconk, A. L. Rosenberger and P. L. Garber, eds.), pp. 251–269. New York: Plenum Press.

Boyd, R., and P. J. Richerson. 1996. Why culture is common, but cultural evolution is rare. *Proceedings of the British Academy* 88:77–93.

Bunn, H. T. 1996. Reply to Rose and Marshall "Meat-eating, hominid sociality, and home bases revisited." *Current Anthropology* 37:321–323.

Busse, C. D. 1977. Chimpanzee predation as a possible factor in the evolution of red colobus monkey social organization. *Evolution* 31:907–911.

Busse, C. D. 1978. Do chimpanzees hunt cooperatively? *American Naturalist* 112:767–770.

Chapman, C. A. 1987. Flexibility in diets of three species of Costa Rican primates. *Folia Primatologica* 49:90–105.

Chapman, C. A., and L. M. Fedigan. 1990. Dietary differences between neighboring *Cebus capucinus* groups: local traditions, food availability, or responses to food profitability? *Folia Primatologica* 54:177–186.

Chevalier-Skolnikoff, S. 1990. Tool use by wild cebus monkeys at Santa Rosa National Park, Costa Rica. *Primates* 31:375–383.

Dahlberg, F., ed. 1981. *Woman the Gatherer*. New Haven, CT: Yale University Press.

de Vore, I., and S. L. Washburn. (1963). Baboon ecology and human evolution. In *African Ecology and Human Evolution* (F. C. Howell and F. Bourliere, eds.), pp. 335–367. New York: Aldine.

de Waal, F. B. M., L. M. Luttrell, and M. E. Canfield. 1993. Preliminary data on voluntary food-sharing in brown capuchin monkeys. *American Journal of Primatology* 29:73–78.

Fedigan, L. M. 1986. The changing role of women in models of human evolution. *Annual Review of Anthropology* 15:25–66.

Fedigan, L. M. 1990. Vertebrate predation in *Cebus capucinus*: meat-eating in a Neotropical monkey. *Folia Primatologica* 54:196–205.

Fedigan, L. M. 1993. Sex differences and intersexual relations in adult white-faced capuchins (*Cebus capucinus*). *International Journal of Primatology* 14:853–877.

Fedigan, L. M., and L. M. Rose. 1995. Interbirth interval variation in three sympatric species of Neotropical monkey. *American Journal of Primatology* 37:9–24.

Fedigan, L. M., L. M. Rose, and R. M. Avila. 1996. See how they grow: tracking capuchin monkey populations in a regenerating Costa Rican dry forest. In *Adaptive Radiations of Neotropical Primates* (M. Norconk, A. L. Rosenberger and P. L. Garber, eds.), pp. 289–307. New York: Plenum Press.

Fernades, M. E. B. 1991. Tool use and predation of oysters (*Crassostrea rhizophorea*) by the tufted capuchin, *Cebus apella apella*, in brackish water mangrove swamp. *Primates* 3:529–531.

Fragaszy, D. M., and K. Bard. 1997. Comparison of development and life history in *Pan* and *Cebus*. *International Journal of Primatology* 18:683–702.

Fragaszy, D. M., J. G. Robinson, and E. Visalberghi. 1990. Variability and adaptability in the genus *Cebus*. *Folia Primatologica* 54:114–118.

Galdikas, B. M. F., and G. Teleki. (1981). Variations in subsistence activities of female and male pongids: new perspectives on the origins of human labor division. *Current Anthropology* 22:241–256.

Goodall, J. 1964. Tool using and aimed throwing in a community of free-living chimpanzees. *Nature* 201:1264–1266.

Goodall, J. 1986. *The Chimpanzees of Gombe: Patterns of Behavior*. Cambridge, MA: Belknap Press of Harvard University Press.

Harding, R. S. O. 1981. An order of omnivores: nonhuman primate diets in the wild. In *Omnivorous Primates: Gathering and Hunting in Human Evolution* (R. S. O. Harding and G. Teleki, eds.), pp. 191–214. New York: Columbia University Press.

Hasegawa, T., M. Hiraiwa, T. Nishida, and H. Takasaki. 1983. New evidence on scavenging behavior in wild chimpanzees. *Current Anthropology* 24:231–232.

Hladik, C. M. 1991. Feeding strategies of forest primates. In *Omnivorous Primates: Gathering and Hunting in Human Evolution* (R. S. O. Harding and G. Teleki, eds.), pp. 215–254. New York: Columbia University Press.

Huffman, M. A., and M. S. Kalunde. 1993. Tool-assisted predation on a squirrel by a female chimpanzee in the Mahale Mountains, Tanzania. *Primates* 34:93–98.

Ingold, T. 1993. Tools and hunter-gatherers. In *The Use of Tools by Human and Non-human Primates* (A. Berthelet, and J. Chavaillon, eds.), pp. 281–292. Oxford: Clarendon Press.

Isaac, G. L. 1971. The diet of early man: aspects of archaeological evidence from Lower and Middle Pleistocene sites in Africa. *World Archaeology* 2:279–299.

Janson, C. H., and S. Boinski. 1992. Morphological and behavioral adaptations for foraging in generalist primates: the case of the Cebines. *American Journal of Physical Anthropology* 88:483–498.

Jolly, C. 1970. The seed-eaters: a new model of hominid differentiation based on a baboon analogy. *Man* 5:5–26.

Kinzey, W. G. (ed.). 1987. *The Evolution of Human Behavior: Primate Models*. New York: SUNY Press.

Kitahara-Frisch J. 1993. The origin of secondary tools. In *The Use of Tools by Human and Non-human Primates* (A. Berthelet and J. Chavaillon, eds.), pp. 293–246. Oxford: Clarendon Press.

Leakey, M. D. 1971. *Olduvai Gorge. Vol. 3. Excavations in Beds I and II, 1960–1963.* Cambridge: Cambridge University Press.

Lee, R. B. 1979. *The !Kung San: Men , Women and Working in a Foraging Society.* New York: Cambridge University Press.

Lee, R. B. 1984. *The Dobe !Kung.* New York: Holt, Rinehart, and Wilson.

Manson, J. H., S. Perry, and A. R. Parish. 1997. Nonconceptive sexual behavior in bonobos and capuchins. *International Journal of Primatology* 18:767–786.

McGrew, W. C. 1974. Tool use by wild chimpanzees in feeding upon driver ants. *Journal of Human Evolution* 3:501–508.

McGrew, W. C. 1989. Why is ape tool-use so confusing? In *Comparative Socioecology: The Behavioral Ecology of Humans and Other Mammals* (V. Standen and R. Foley, eds.). Oxford: Blackwell Scientific Press.

McGrew, W. C. 1992. *Chimpanzee Material Culture: Implications for Human Evolution.* Cambridge: Cambridge University Press.

McGrew, W. C., and L. F. Marchant. 1997. Using the tools and hand: manual laterality and elementary technology in *Cebus* spp. and *Pan* spp. *International Journal of Primatology* 18:787–810.

Moore, J. 1984. The evolution of reciprocal sharing. *Ethology and Sociobiology* 5:5–14.

Muller, M., E. Mpongo, C. B. Stanford, and C. Boehm. 1995. A note on the scavenging behavior on wild chimpanzees. *Folia Primatologica* 75:43–47.

Nishida, T., and M. Hiraiwa. 1982. Natural history of a tool-using behavior by wild chimpanzees in feeding upon wood-boring ants. *Journal of Human Evolution* 11:73–99.

Nishida, T., T. Hasegawa, H. Hayaki, Y. Takahata, and S. Uehara. 1992. Meat-sharing as a coalition strategy by an alpha male chimpanzee? In *Topics in Primatology: Volume 1: Human Origins* (T. Nishida, W. C. McGrew, P. Marler, M. Pickford, and F. B. M. de Waal, eds.), pp. 159–174. Tokyo: University of Tokyo Press.

Packer, C., and Ruttan, L. 1988. The evolution of cooperative hunting. *American Naturalist* 132:159–198.

Panger, M. A. 1998. Oject-use in free-ranging white-faced capuchins (*Cebus capucinus*) in Costa Rica. *American Journal of Physical Anthropology* 106:311–321.

Parker, C. E., and K. R. Gibson. 1977. Object manipulation, tool use and sensorimotor intelligence as feeding adaptations in *Cebus* monkeys and great apes. *Journal of Human Evolution* 6:623–641.

Perry, S. 1996. Female–female relationships in wild white-faced capuchins, *Cebus capucinus*. *American Journal of Primatology* 40:167–182.

Perry, S. 1997. Male–female relationships in wild white-faced capuchins, *Cebus capucinus*. *Behaviour* 134:477–510.

Perry, S., and L. M. Rose. 1994. Begging and transfer of coati meat by white-faced capuchin monkeys, *Cebus capucinus*. *Primates* 35:409–415.

Plooij, F. X. 1978. Tool-use during chimpanzees' bushpig hunt. *Carnivore* 1:103–106.

Potts, R. 1984. Home bases and early hominids. *American Scientist* 72:338–347.

Potts, R. 1988. On an early hominid scavenging niche. *Current Anthropology* 29:153–155.

Rose, L. M. 1994. Sex differences in diet and foraging behavior in white-faced capuchins (*Cebus capucinus*). *International Journal of Primatology* 15:95–114.

Rose, L. M. 1997. Vertebrate predation and food-sharing in *Cebus* and *Pan*. *International Journal of Primatology* 18:727–765.

Rose, L. M. 1998. *Behavioral ecology of White-Faced Capuchins* (Cebus capucinus) in *Costa Rica*. Ph.D. dissertation. Washington University, St. Louis.

Rose, L. M., and F. Marshall. 1996. Meat-eating, hominid sociality, and home bases revisited. *Current Anthropology* 37:307–338.

Southgate, D. A. T. 1991. Nature and variability of human food consumption. In *Foraging Strategies and Natural Diet of Monkeys, Apes and Humans* (A. Whiten and E. M. Widdowson, eds.), pp. 281–288. Oxford: Clarendon Press.

Stanford, C. B. 1995. The influence of chimpanzee predation on group size and anti-predator behaviour in red colobus monkeys. *Animal Behavior* 49:577–587.

Stanford, C. B. 1998. *Chimpanzee and Red Colobus: The Ecology of Predator and Prey.* Cambridge, MA: Harvard University Press.

Stanford, C. B. 1996. The hunting ecology of wild chimpanzees: implications for the evolutionary ecology of Pleistocene hominids. *American Anthropologist.* 98:96–113.

Stanford, C. B., J. Wallis, H. Matama, and J. Goodall. 1994a. Patterns of predation by chimpanzees on red colobus monkeys in Gombe National Park, 1982–1991. *American Journal of Physical Anthropology* 94:213–228.

Stanford, C. B., J. Wallis, E. Mpongo, and J. Goodall. 1994b. Hunting decisions in wild chimpanzees. *Behaviour* 131:1–18.

Struhsaker, T. T., and L. Leland. 1977. Palm-nut smashing by *Cebus a. apella* in Colombia. *Biotropica* 9:124–126.

Strum, S. C. 1975. Primate predation: interim report on the development of a tradition in a troop of olive baboons. *Science* 187:755–757.

Strum, S. C. 1981. Process and products of change: baboon predatory behavior at Gilgil, Kenya. In *Omnivorous Primates: Gathering and Hunting in Human Evolution* (R. S. O. Harding and G. Teleki, eds.), pp. 255–302. New York: Columbia University Press.

Strum, S. C., and W. Mitchell. 1987. In *The Evolution of Human Behavior: Primate models* (W. G. Kinzey, ed.), pp. 87–104. New York: SUNY Press.

Sugiyama, Y. 1993. Local variation of tools and tool use among wild chimpanzee populations. In *The Use of Tools by Human and Non-human Primates* (A. Berthelet and J. Chavaillon, eds.), pp. 175–187. Oxford: Clarendon Press.

Tanner, N. M. 1979. Gathering by females: the chimpanzee model revisited and the gathering hypothesis. In *The Evolution of Human Behavior: Primate models* (W. G. Kinzey, ed.), pp. 3–27. New York: SUNY Press.

Teleki, G. 1973. *The Predatory Behavior of Wild Chimpanzees*. Lewisburg: Bucknell University Press.

Teleki, G. 1975. Primate subsistence patterns: collector-predators and gatherer-hunters. *Journal of Human Evolution* 4:125–184.

Tutin, C. E. G. 1979. Mating patterns and reproductive strategies in a community of wild chimpanzees (*Pan troglodytes schweinfurthii*). *Behaviour Ecology and Sociobiology* 6:29–38.

Visalberghi, E. 1993. Tool use in a South American monkey species: an overview of the characteristics and limitations of tool use in *Cebus apella*. In *The Use of Tools by Human and Non-human Primates* (A. Berthelet and J. Chavaillon, eds.), pp. 118–131. Oxford: Clarendon Press.

Visalberghi, E. 1997. Success and understanding in cognitive tasks: a comparison between *Cebus apella* and *Pan troglodytes*. *International Journal of Primatology* 18:811–830.

Visalberghi, E. and L. Limongelli. 1996. Acting and understanding: tool use revisited through the minds of capuchin monkeys. In *Reaching into Thought: The Minds of the Great Apes* (A. Russon, K. Bard, and S. Parker, eds.), pp. 57–79. Cambridge: Cambridge University Press.

Westergaard, G. C., and D. M. Fragaszy. 1987. The manufacture and use of tools by capuchin monkeys (*Cebus apella*). *Journal of Comparative Psychology* 101:159–168.

Westergaard, G. C., and S. J. Suomi. 1994. The use and modification of bone tools by capuchin monkeys. *Current Anthropology* 35:75–77.

Westergaard, G. C., and S. J. Suomi. 1997. Transfer of tools and food between groups of tufted capuchins (*Cebus apella*). *American Journal of Primatology* 43:33–41.

Wrangham, R. W. 1975. *The Behavioural Ecology of Chimpanzees in Gombe National Park, Tanzania*. Ph.D. dissertation. Cambridge University, Cambridge.

Wrangham, R. W., and E. V. van Bergmann-Riss. 1990. Rates of predation on mammals by Gombe chimpanzees, 1972–1975. *Primates* 31:157–170.

8

The Other Faunivory
Primate Insectivory and Early Human Diet

William C. McGrew

Introduction

To most palaeoanthropologists, as well as many primatologists and ethnologists, faunivory equals carnivory (e.g., Lee and DeVore 1968; Stanford 1996). That is, the edible tissues of vertebrates is thought to be an important influence on human evolution at levels ranging from nutrition to mate choice to sex roles to communal cooperation. By default, meat equals power equals prominence. This is likely to lead to a skewed picture of early human diet, especially in light of the environment of evolutionary adaptedness in the open habitats of tropical Africa, where hominization began.

Meat, in its most common form of the soft tissues of medium to large mammals, clearly presents physical and cognitive challenges to would-be exploiters. On the hoof, it must be hunted, that is, sought, detected, stalked, pursued, subdued, and dispatched, either solitarily or cooperatively by hunters. If scavenged, the same resource must be sought, detected, and approated or defended from similarly minded scavengers, all quickly, before micro-organisms render the carcass unusable. In either case, both inter- and intraspecific competitors may need to be outwitted, as well as outfought, but the prize is great. So, why should any medium- to large-bodied primate ever bother with humble invertebrates?

The answer is simple, if we think in terms of bites; even the choicest steak is eaten one morsel at a time. Most invertebrates are just bite-sized packets of animal matter distributed widely and superabundantly over the landscape. To a faunivore, to subsist on termites instead of duikers is to solve the problem of efficient assembly, that is, to accumulate enough small units for a meal, while remaining in energetic credit. In principle, a large-brained forager could solve such problems with intelligent strategies of gathering/collection that were equivalently productive to the more eye-catching strategies of hunting.

Accordingly, this chapter aims to explore the likely importance of the non-vertebrate portion of early human diet; to what extent (if at all) did earliest *Homo spp.* eat invertebrates? To tackle this means first considering invertebrates, and especially insects, as prey in terms of costs and benefits. Because the behavioral ecology of early hominids is no longer directly accessible, it is modeled indirectly on the foraging and diet of living nonhuman primates, especially hominoids. Also considered is the entomophagy of living *Homo sapiens* in traditional societies, especially those of tropical gatherer-hunters. Finally, the problems and prospects of recognizing insectivory in prehistory are broached and hypotheses for archaeological testing are proposed.

Edible Invertebrates

Two phyla of invertebrates dominate modern human diets, Mollusca and Arthropoda. (Abrams 1987). Apart from land snails, species of molluscs eaten today come mainly from benthic marine habitats and so cannot be harvested without complex technology. [Only much later do shell middens, e.g. at Klasies River Mouth, play an important archaeological role in defining early anatomically modern humans; (Klein 1977)]. Molluscs figure only occasionally in the diets of nonhuman primates. For example, for wedge-capped capuchin monkeys, snails are more often eaten than are all other invertebrates combined (Robinson 1984).

Among the arthropods consumed, crustaceans and insects are the classes of current choice for modern humans (Abrams 1987). For the Crustacea, the vast majority again are marine forms, such as crabs, lobsters, shrimps, etc.; however tasty they are today, these aquatic creatures likely played no part in the diet of ancestral hominoids or hominids evolving in mosaic terrestrial ecosystems. There seem to be no cases of living nonhuman primates making crustaceans a major dietary item.

This leaves only the insects as genuine alternatives to meat.

Insects as Prey

Table 8.1 shows that insects are the only kind of invertebrate prey that are eaten by primates across the board, from tree shrews to humans. Their basic advantages are many: insect diversity is great, both within and across the range of ecotypes also inhabited by primates. A single tree may contain insects from roots to crown, both on and in every part of the plant. The collective biomass of insects typically exceeds that of all other fauna in any tropical ecosystem, from rain forest to savanna. Nutritionally, insects are of overall high quality, being comparable per unit mass in terms of energy, fat, and protein to mammals or birds (DeFoliart 1989). Mineral content varies, with insects being higher in calcium but lower in potassium than mammals (Eaton et al. 1988). Finally, insects are equal to vertebrates in all known vitamins, including those acquired by humans only from faunivory, for example, Vitamin B_{12}.

Table 8.1. Four grades of insect-eating by primates.

Primate Taxa	Body Size	Frequency Insectivory	Use of Technology[a]	Sex Differences	Prey	Prey Taxa
Callitrichidae Cebidae (some) Cheirogaleidae Galagidae Lorisidae Tarsiidae	small	high	no	no	solitary	Insecta Arachnida Diplopoda Chilopoda Gastropoda
Cebidae (some) Cercopithecidae Hylobatidae	medium	low	no	few (*Cebus*)	solitary, temporary aggregates, social	Insecta Mollusca Arachnida
Pongidae Paninae	large	high/low	instrument	yes	social-defended	Insecta
Homininae	large	high/low	instrument facility	sexual-division of labor	Insecta defended	Crustacea Mollusca (aquati terrestrial

[a]Oswalt (1976).

However, insects as prey for primate predators also have disadvantages. Insects are small. A large insect is no more than one-tenth the mass of a small primate (10 g for a beetle versus 100 g for a bushbaby) while the more usual disparity is much greater (1 g versus 10,000 g). Insects usually fly, often quickly, making them hard to capture for substrate-bound predators. Insects are often well fortified. They tunnel into places accessible only to morphologically specialized predators, such as aardvark, pangolin, or aye-aye. Insects are seasonal. Depending on the extremes of annual climatic cycles, they may be available for only months, weeks, or even days, usually in the wet season (Rhine et al. 1986). Insects are well-armed. They can inflict painful stings or bites, augmented by venom, or sequester toxic substances in glands or irritating hairs. Finally, much of insect adult body mass is tied up in an exoskeleton of chitin that is indigestible to predators lacking chitinolytic enzymes, as is the case with almost all primates (the potto is an exception; see Cornelius et al. 1976).

Thus, insectivory is not to be undertaken lightly. However, two stages of the insect life cycle are avidly sought by predators: larvae (grubs) are fast growing (protein and energy rich) and soft bodied (the only chitin may be in the mouth parts). Reproductives (alates) of truly social insects have much fat stored for dispersal and initial reproductive effort, so they are the highest quality insects eaten.

Finally, many primates, including humans, consume insect products. Prosimian home ranges are sometimes determined by the residual secretions of homopteran larvae (Corbin and Schmid 1995). Termite "earth" from the fortifications of mound-building termites is a mixture of fine-grained clay and saliva; it is consumed by chimpanzees, perhaps to buffer plant-produced toxins. Most notable is honey, the mixture of nectar and saliva produced by social bees and stored in their hives. At

3,232 calories per kg (Hurtado et al. 1985), honey is the highest quality food item available in nature and also contains many constituent trace nutrients.

Primates as Insectivores

There are records of primates eating most of the 28 orders of the Class Hexapoda (or Insecta), but as shown in Table 8.2, five orders are clearly preferred. The Big Five are: Coleoptera (beetles), Hymenoptera (ants, bees, wasps), Isoptera (termites), Lepidoptera (butterflies and moths), and Orthoptera (locusts, grasshoppers, crickets, katydids, etc.). Why this subset? Clearly, it does not reflect mere availability, for the second most numerous and abundant order, Diptera (flies), is notably absent (Figure 8.1).

The Big Five are sometimes large bodied and wingless or slow moving in at least one stage of the life cycle, or clumped, either permanently in colonies or temporarily in aggregations, making them attractive prey packages. On the other hand, they are among the most fortified (termites) and well-armed (stinging bees and wasps, biting ants, poisonous or irritating caterpillars) of insects. Insects also can be a hazard: of the 281 animal-related human deaths in the USA in 1997, 34% were from bee stings, versus only 7% from carnivores and 5% from snake bites (Anonymous 1998). A particular set of features makes only a few forms in each order viable as prey for primates.

Insectivorous primates fall into four ecological types (see Table 8.1).

Obligate Insectivory

As noted by Kay and Hylander (1978), obligatory insect eaters are constrained by energy budgeting to small body weights, usually less than 1,000 g. This applies

Table 8.2. Orders of insects ranked by extent of biodiversity (number of species).

Rank	Order	Common Name
[a]1	*Coleoptera*	beetle
2	Diptera	fly
[a]3	*Lepidoptera*	butterfly, moth
[a]4	*Hymenoptera*	ant, bee, wasp
5	Homoptera	cicada, aphid, hopper
[a]6	*Orthoptera*	locust, cricket, cockroach
7	Hemiptera	bug
8	Odonata	dragonfly
9	Trichoptera	caddisfly
10	Neuroptera	lacewing
. . .	. . .	. . .
??	*Isoptera*	termite

[a]Major order in hominoid diets = Big Five.

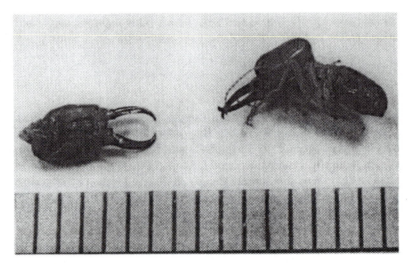

Figure 8.1. Well-armed major soldier termite of *Macrotermes vitrialatus* from the Mahale Mountains, Tanzania (Scale is in mm).

convergently to prosimians (e.g., mouse lemurs, bushbabies, tarsiers) and to some New World monkeys (e.g., squirrel monkeys, marmosets, tamarins). A further convergence occurs in the dietary complementarity of phosphorus-rich insects with calcium-rich plant gums, in both bushbabies (Bearder and Martin 1980) and tamarins (Garber 1984). Bushbabies are eclectic eaters; they consume many types of insects and commonly take spiders, millipedes, centipedes, and snails (Harcourt and Nash 1986). The techniques of capture are the simplest, whether quick snatch or slow stalk, being one-to-one, predator-to-prey encounters. In contrast, tamarins capture katydids by seeing through the cryptic antipredator adaptations of these large, solitary orthopterans; because each prey is as much as 1–2% of the monkey's body weight, only a few insects per day need to be taken (Nickle and Heymann 1996). Finally, the only exclusively faunivorous primates are tarsiers (*Tarsius* spp.), whose overall ratio of invertebrates:vertebrate prey averages 90:10 (Bearder 1987).

Occasional Insectivory

Most species of anthropoid primates are medium-sized monkeys or lesser apes, and most occasionally eat invertebrates (e.g., Moore 1983). These include New World monkeys (capuchins), Old World monkeys (baboons, guenons, langurs, macaques, mangabeys), and gibbons. The emphasis is largely on opportunistic foraging for a wide range of prey, ranging from solitary to social insects, but also including other arthropod classes. Notably, termites or stinging bees are rarely eaten. Wedge-capped capuchins favor caterpillars over ants, grasshoppers, or wasps (Robinson 1984). Guenons also overwhelmingly prefer caterpillars, followed by orthopterans, ants, and spiders (Gautier-Hion 1980). Larger monkeys (>10 kg) make use of insects by focusing on social insects or on transient breeding aggregations (Kay and Hylander

1978) as clumped resources whose patchiness makes their harvesting energetically feasible. Hamilton et al. (1978) described chacma baboons gorging themselves on massive outbreaks of grasshoppers or scale insects and eating little else for days.

Elementary Technological Insectivory

The four living species of great apes show great variation in insect eating. Chimpanzees use instrumental technology (i.e, hand-held implements that impinge directly on nonhazardous goal objects; Oswalt 1976; McGrew 1987) to focus on social insects. Goodall (1968: 186–188) was the first to describe in detail chimpanzee insectivory: at Gombe in Tanzania. The apes fish underground termites from mounds and wood-boring ants from trees, dip driver ants from nests, and lever open and dip honey and bees from nest cavities (McGrew 1992). Apart from these Isoptera and Hymenoptera, they pluck galls from leaves or feast on social caterpillars, both of which are highly seasonal (Goodall 1986: 248–262). Perhaps more importantly, they use their well-developed cerebral cortices to exercise self-control (Goodall 1986: 255) and to adapt clever counterstrategies (McGrew 1974) in the face of pain inflicted by insects. When disturbed, driver ants carpet the forest floor in aggressive defense; then chimpanzees perch on bent-over saplings to dip up the ants while evading their bites (McGrew 1974). Thus, chimpanzees use brains and not brawn to exploit insect resources ignored by sympatric competitors such as baboons or gorillas (Figure 8.2).

Figure 8.2. Chimpanzee fishes for termites at Gombe National Park, Tanzania. Tool is held in right hand (note precision grip) horizontally, and supported by left wrist, as termites are nibbled off.

The calorific and nutritional payoffs for technologically aided insectivory may be great (see Table 8.3). At Gombe, chimpanzees fishing for termites gain about 500 calories, or about 30 g of fat and 50 g of protein, from a typical session. Skillful and persevering individuals may accrue much more, especially when other castes and nonfished soldiers are added to the total. At Mahale, on the other hand, chimpanzees seem to fish for wood-boring ants only as tasty snacks; the amounts taken are too small to be of nutritional significance (Nishida and Hirawa 1982).

Gorillas may eat just as many insects as do chimpanzees at some sites (Tutin and Fernandez 1992), but at high altitudes their insectivory is limited by availability of prey (Watts 1989). Gorillas harvest many of the same "defended" forms of social insects, for example, biting driver ants (*Dorylus* sp.) or mound-building termites (*Cubitermes* spp.), but without instrumental technology (Kuroda et al. 1996). They scoop up driver ants (Watts 1989) and break open termite mounds (Tutin and Fernandez 1983) by hand. At Lopé in Gabon, gorillas and chimpanzees eat similar amounts of weaver ants (*Oecophylla longinoda*). Chimpanzees pluck the leafy nests, crush them, and peel the leaves away one by one, leisurely consuming the contents; gorillas munch the whole nest, leaves and all (Tutin and Fernandez 1992). At Ndoki in the Congo (Brazzaville), neither gorillas nor chimpanzees relish weaver ants, but gorillas eat earthworms (Annelida) (Kuroda et al. 1996). However, gorillas do not tackle stinging hymenopterans anywhere.

Bonobo insectivory is more like that of baboons than of other apes. At Wamba, they feast on short-term outbreaks of caterpillars (Hesperiidae) and spend long hours sifting by hand through mud for earthworms (Kano 1992: 100). At Lomako, bonobos eat a wide variety of invertebrates, including the Big Five orders of insects, plus millipedes and snails, but only hesperiid caterpillars were eaten often (Badrian and Malenky 1984). Notably absent is any instrumental technology and any regular harvesting of defended eusocial insects.

The Asian great ape, the orangutan, shows arboreal insectivory much like that of chimpanzees. Most ants, bees, wasps, and termites are taken from their nests by smash-and-grab techniques (Rijksen 1978: 59ff), but some bees and honey are extracted by probes made of vegetation (Fox et al. 1998). Many of the prey species viciously bite or sting en masse, but these are usually endured, rather than habitually countered by any technological strategy (Rijksen 1978: 89ff).

In summary, great apes are intelligent, specialist insectivores who neutralize or minimize the antipredator defenses of prey that offer great collective, clumped biomass, or the highest quality payoff (honey) or both.

Sex Differences

Across the three grades of insectivory by nonhuman primates (see Table 8.2), small-bodied insectivorous primates and medium- to large-sized monkeys seem to show no sex differences in insect eating (e.g., Rhine et al. 1986, for *Papio cynocephalus*). A conspicuous exception is *Cebus capucinus* (showing yet another convergence with *Pan troglodytes*); females eat more small and immobile invertebrates, while males eat more large invertebrates and vertebrates (Rose 1994, this volume). Among

Table 8.3. Payoffs for a meal of *Macrotermes* spp. termites fished by chimpanzees.

	N	Mean	Range	Reference
A) No. of major soldiers fished/min[a]	16	5.65	2.50–11.21	McGrew and Marchant 1999
B) Duration of termite fishing session (min)	495	26.3	5–200	McGrew 1979
C) Wt. of *M. carbonarius*[b] major soldier (g)	—	0.51 g	—	Redford and Dorea 1984
D) Caloric content of *M. subhyalinus* per 100 g	—	612	—	Santos Oliveira et al. 1976
E) Percent of dry wt. of *M. bellicosus*—fat	—	34%	—	Hladik 1977
F) Percent of dry wt. of *M. bellicosus*—protein	—	59%	—	Hladik 1977

Payoffs for a meal:

			Mean	Range
Energy	A × B × C × (A×B×C/100) (D)	=	465 cal	39–6980 cal
Fat	A × B × C × E	=	26 g	2.2–389 g
Protein	A × B × C × F	=	45 g	3.8–675 g

[a]Excludes minor soldiers and workers eaten from tool, and major soldiers taken other than from tool, e.g., from ground, so underestimates actual intake of termites.

[b]Three species of *Macrotermes* had to be used in calculations, as no single source provided all the necessary information.

great apes, female bias to insects and male bias to mammalian prey is well known for chimpanzees (McGrew 1979; Goodall 1986; Uehara 1986) and orangutans (Rijksen 1978: 93) but not shown for gorillas (Tutin and Fernandez 1992) or bonobos (Kano 1992). This suggests that the degree of sex difference in insectivory is linked to the degree of technology used in extraction of insect prey (Moore, pers. comm.).

Humans Eat Invertebrates

Human entomophagy is embodied in the diversity of species of invertebrates eaten; however, for any given society, the proportion of nonvertebrates in the diet ranges from nil (e.g., when prohibited) to staple (e.g., marine shellfish). Thus, in their great diversity of prey, humans most closely resemble small-bodied, insectivorous primates, with one key difference: while tarsiers, bushbabies, marmosets, and tamarins forage for arthropods and molluscs one at a time, humans usually harvest them *en masse*, either in acquisition or processing. Thus, unlike medium-to-large-sized monkeys or apes, humans fully exploit all of the Big Five, usually aided by technology. The ethnographic literature offers a wealth of data, almost all descriptive, on entomophagy (see Table 8.4; Sutton 1995). Here, I concentrate (when possible) on quantitative data from traditional tropical societies (Winterhalder 1987), or on techniques applicable to an emerging hominid in an ecologically relevant habitat (Foley 1992).

The best data come from Amazonia, where there is a long-standing debate on protein availability and faunivory in indigenous peoples (see review in Beckerman 1979, and summary in Moran 1993). For example, the riverbank-dwelling, fisher-gardening Tukanoan Indians of Columbia eat more than 20 species of insects, focusing on those that form large predictable aggregations: beetles, ants, termites, and caterpillars. During the peak season, 26% of women's and 12% of men's animal protein intake comes from insects (Dufour 1987). The forest-dwelling, forager-horticulturalist Maku Indians of Brazil concentrate on the same orders of insect to augment their hunting of mammals (Milton 1984). The most detailed accounting of insect prey diversity comes from the Yukpa Indians of Venezuela and Columbia who consume seven orders of insects (Ruddle 1973). In a ritual test following the birth of a son, a Yukpa father must gather by hand (without stupefying smoke) nests of wasps that deliver "an extremely painful sting."

Elsewhere in South America, the best data on faunivory come from the Aché, a gather-hunter, forest-dwelling society in Paraguay (Hawkes et al. 1982). They collect 15 types of insect, of which 10 are larvae, and 14 kinds of honey, mostly from honey bees, *Apis mellifera*. For women, 27% of foraging time on average goes to the pursuit of insects, usually chopping out beetle larvae from rotten logs (Hurtado et al. 1985). Men average 5% of foraging time in getting honey by chopping open a nest tree and then smoking out the bees (Hill et al. 1985).

Lizot (1977) presents the most striking data on sex differences in consumption of animal prey. Among the Yanomami of Brazil, men are the sole consumers of mammals while only women eat frogs, crabs, shellfish, termites, and the larvae and pupae of bees and wasps. Both sexes eat caterpillars, but men eat more than 80% of the total biomass collected.

Table 8.4. Insects eaten by various traditional human cultures (+ = eaten; ++ = staple).

Culture	Location	Subsistence	C	H	I	L	O	Other	Reference
New World									
[a]Yanomami	Brazil	Horticult.	+	+	+	++		Crustacea, Mollusca	Lizot 1977
Maku	Brazil	Foragers/Horticult.	+?	+	+	+		Lean season	Milton 1984
[a]Tukanoan	Columbia	Horticult.	+	++	+	++		20 spp.	Dufour 1987
Yukpa	Venezuela	Horticult.	+	++	+	+		Diptera, Neuroptera, Trichoptera	Ruddle 1973
Aché	Paraguay	Foragers	+	+					Hawkes et al. 1982
Paiute	Great Basin, USA	Foragers		+		++	++	Diptera ?	Fowler and Walter 1985
Shoshone									Madsen and Kirkman 1988
overall	Mexico	overall	+	++		+	+	101 spp., Hemiptera, Homoptera, Anoplura	deConconi et al. 1984
Australasia									
Various	New South Wales	Foragers				+		"galls," Crustacea, Mollusca	Flood, 1980
Various	North Queensland	Foragers	+	+	+	+		"fly" = cicada?	Roth 1901
Wailbri	Central	Foragers	+	++				Mollusca	Sweeney 1947
Wanindiljaugwa	Groote Eylandt	Foragers		++				Single species?	Worsley 1961
Alyawara	Central	Foragers				++			O'Connell and Hawkes 1984
Kirwanian	Trobriand Islands	Horticult.	+	+			+	Hemiptera, Anoplura	Meyer-Rochow 1973 Siphonaptera
Chauve	New Guinea	Horticult.	+	+	+	+	+	Hemiptera, Homoptera	Meyer-Rochow 1973
Onabasulu	New Guinea	Horticult.	++	+			+	Odonata	Meyer-Rochow 1973
Africa									
San	Central Kalahari, Botswana	Foragers	+	+	+	+	+	Other orders for noneating	Nonaka 1996
Tongwe	Tanzania	Horticult.	+	+	+		+		Kakeya 1976
Efe	Congo (Zaire)	Foragers		++	+				Bailey and Peacock 1988
overall	Angola	overall	+			+			Santos Oliveira et al. 1976
various	southern Africa	overall				++			DeFoliart 1989

[b]Insect Order

[a]Quantitative data.

[b]C = Coleoptera; H = Hymenoptera; I = Isoptera; L = Lepidoptera; O = Orthoptera.

Comparable data on insectivory from Africa are available for the Efe pygmies of the Congo (Zaïre); they live in the upland rain forest of Ituri, in a mutualistic bond with local Bantu horticulturalists, the Lese (Bailey and Peacock 1988). Honey provides a higher proportion of caloric intake than does meat (13.5% versus 8.5%). In the woodlands of western Tanzania, Tongwe men harvest honey by tying hollowed-out logs in trees to attract wild bees; a "honeyman" may tap up to 300 hives, each of which may yield up to 18 liters of honey (Kakeya 1976). Even in arid environments, the Big Five are paramount: the /Gui and //Gana San of the Central Kalahari of Botswana focus on termite alates, migratory grasshoppers, beetle imagos, moth caterpillars, formicine ants (for seasoning), and honey (Noraka 1996).

Again and again in Africa, the large caterpillars of saturniid moths figure in local cuisine. These 10 cm-long "mopanie worms" are eaten in various forms, from raw to processed and powdered; the latter form is a viable commercial industry (DeFoliart 1989).

In Australia, entomophagy among aboriginal peoples is widespread across the range of habitats from interior desert to coastal rainforest. The Wailbri of the central desert near Alice Springs relish "honey" ants; colonies excavated by women contain worker ants whose distended abdomens act as storage vessels for "honey-dew" collected from aphids. Each of these "repletes" contains about a milliliter of "honey" (Sweeney 1947). In North Queensland, beetle larvae, caterpillars, termites, ants, wasps, and honey are eaten regularly (Roth 1901). In Arnhem Land, the Wanindeljaugwa are so keen on "sugar-bag," the honey of arboreal stingless bees, that fatalities from falling in its pursuit have been recorded (Worsley 1961). O'Connell and Hawkes (1984) showed that Alywara from central Australia foraged optimally for insects; when moth larvae were seasonally abundant, they displaced *Acacia* seeds on the basis of net return rate, as predicted by theory.

The best-documented case is that of the Bugong moths of the Australian Alps eaten by the aboriginal peoples of New South Wales. Millions of the moths (Lepidoptera: Noctuidae) migrate to higher, cooler elevations to hibernate *en masse* in sheltered spots on granite rock faces. Hundreds of people congregate annually to feast for months on the fatted insects. Tons of moths are collected by smoke, net, and stick, then roasted and winnowed, mostly by men (Flood 1980).

It is hard to overestimate the food value of the Big Five as harvested by human foragers. Termite alates average 20–50% fat by dry weight (Redford and Dorea 1984); the species eaten by Angolan humans (and Assirik chimpanzees; McBeath and McGrew 1982), *Macrotermes subhyalinus*, yields 612 cals per 100 g. Migratory locusts in Africa sequester fat to up to 30% of dry body weight; thus the "clumped" stage of the life cycle is also of higher food value than the sedentary, solitary stage (Chen 1952). Caterpillars of two species of saturniid moth, also eaten by Angolans, yield 44 and 49 g of protein per 100 g (Santos Oliveira et al. 1976). Collectively, the nutritional impact of many small units is even more impressive; the Onabasulu of highland New Guinea collect hundreds of kilograms of sago palm beetle larvae *(Rhynochophorus bilineatus)* to stuff giant "sausages" up to 3 m long. These are roasted and shared. Another species of the same genus is eaten in Angola; it yields 42 g of fat, 25 g of carbohydrate, and 20 g of protein per 100 g (Santos Oliveira et al. 1976).

The key difference between human and nonhuman exploitation of insects for food is advanced technology (Sutton 1995). In Oswalt's (1976) terminology, humans go beyond instruments to *facilities*, that is, to a constructed form that controls the movement of prey, often indirectly. Thus, a probe is an instrument, but a snare is a facility; a container may be either depending on the specific function, for example, bucket versus corral. The simplest handheld container of all is probably what makes collecting insects energetically feasible, whether it be made of skin or bark or even leaves, as it allows many small units to be combined and transported.

Hardly more complicated are containers made of wood, bark, woven fibre, etc., used for food processing, whether to mix, compress, pulverize, dry, wet, ferment, store, etc.

Finally, the single most useful facility in entomophagy may be fire, which can be used to drive and to concentrate swarms of locusts, to stupefy bees, wasps, or moths; to depilate hairy caterpillars, and best of all, to cook, that is to roast, boil, fry, etc., a prey item to make it more palatable.

In summary, although human insectivory makes use of the same sort of prey as other primates in many of the same ways, *Homo sapiens* takes the same processes notably further. However, the technological gap in subsistence between chimpanzee and human is tantalizingly small (McGrew 1987) and in captivity, apes are capable of all the cognitive processes underlying the advances outlined above (McGrew 1992). In this "gap," surely, is where the diet of early *Homo* is likely to be found.

Insects in Early Human Diet

The most likely role for insectivory in the diet of early *Homo* falls between that of living chimpanzees (on both phylogenetic and ecological grounds) and living, tropical, open-country human foraging societies (as extant *Homo* in the current habitats most closely resembling the environment of evolutionary adaptedness) (see Sutton 1990, 1995 for similar arguments). Such interpolation yields the following "hypotheses of intermediacy" about early hominid insectivory:

1. It made a notable contribution to diet, nutritionally if not calorifically.
2. It was seasonal but occurred often enough to keep key nutrients such as Vitamin A and Vitamin B_{12} "topped up" (Eaton et al. 1988).
3. It entailed a simple tool kit of intermediate technology, including the container, which was enabled by the advent of bipedal locomotion.
4. It was less risky than hunting or scavenging because competitors were either nocturnal specialist insectivores (aardvark, aardwolf, honey badger, pangolin, etc.) or small-bodied, diurnal generalists (mongoose, meerkat, etc.), unlike the large, at-least-sometimes-diurnal carnivore competitors for larger mammalian or avian prey or their carcasses (wild dog, hyena, lion, sabertooth, cheetah, etc.). Also, because many invertebrate prey (ants, termites) were arboreal, they were safer prey for primates to exploit than are terrestrial ones, which leave the exploiters more vulnerable to large carnivores.

5. It yielded collected products that were reciprocally exchanged for other prized foodstuffs, so enhancing division of labor. Fewer units of invertebrate prey are equal to a portion of meat than are more units of most plant matter (nuts excepted) based on calorific or nutrient (e.g., range of amino acids) content.

6. It was expressed as sexual division of labor, with females specializing in gathering invertebrates and males in hunting or scavenging large vertebrates (McGrew 1981). (Small vertebrates such as tortoises, rodents, or lizards were of intermediate status, available to anyone.) The exception was gathering done by males of *Apis* spp. honey from elevated nests; this precarious foraging activity was incompatible with the carrying of clinging offspring up into the canopy or onto rockfaces, so females avoided it.

The challenge is to test these hypotheses on palaeo-data, that is, to transform them from scenarios into falsifiable propositions (Sutton 1990, 1995; Moore 1996). This is daunting, but there are some possibilities:

1. Archaeologically, any tools used in insectivory were likely perishable, being made of vegetation or of animal soft tissue and so "invisible" in the archaeological record. No reed basket, vine rope, leafy packet, digging stick, twig probe, bark tray, skin bucket, sinew binder, etc., will turn up at a Plio-Pleistocene excavation site.

   The best candidates in nonperishable, lithic materials for confirming the exploitation of invertebrate prey are hammerstones or anvils used to crack open molluscs, but their signs must be distinguishable from percussion marks or wear patterns left from pounding other hard objects such as nuts or bones. Some large arthropods are more readily processed by hammering, but it is doubtful that this would leave a recognizable macrowear signature on the stones. More promising might be microwear patterns on stone tools used to chop, slice, grind, etc. invertebrate prey encased in chitin, calcium carbonate, etc., that would leave a discernable polish (Keeley and Toth 1981, Sutton 1995).

2. Residues of palaeo-foodstuffs may persist on stone tools (Fullagar et al. 1996). Ciochon et al. (1990) recovered phytoliths from fossilized teeth of *Gigantopithecus blacki*, an extinct ape. The opaline particles date from at least 300,000 years ago and are identifiable to taxonomic family level. Blood, hair, cartilage, feathers, etc., may be preserved on artefacts, to be detected by microscopy. Occasionally, chitinous exoskeletal material is also recovered (Hardy 1999). At the biochemical level of analysis, ancient DNA may also be present and can be amplified by the polymerase chain reaction (PCR) and identified (Hardy et al. 1997). Both approaches are amenable to seeking evidence of insect eating.

3. A promising candidate for direct evidence of consumption of arthropods may be dental microwear, the study of which has proven useful in distinguishing broad dietary categories in both fossil (Walker 1981) and living mammals (Teaford 1988). Grine (1986) was able to differentiate the dental microwear, and thus the plant portion of the diets, of two genera of extinct hominids, *Australopithecus* and *Paranthropus*, but made no mention of animal taxa.

There seems to be no study of toothwear in insectivorous versus noninsectivorous primates, but Taylor and Hannam (1987) showed that arthropod-eating mongoose species could be distinguished by microwear from meat-eating species of these African viverrids. As with lithic microwear, the key is whether or not chitin, as opposed to other abrasive substances, leaves a distinctive signature of microwear.

4. Coprolites, either desiccated subfossil or lithified fossil feces, may reveal evidence of insect eating in primates, just as does fresh dung, because with a few exceptions (Cornelius et al. 1976, for prosimians) chitin is passed through the gut undigested. Thus, fragments of exoskeleton, such as wings or mouthparts, may be recovered, although coprophagous taxa, such as dung beetles, must be excluded (Sutton 1995). Bryant and Williams-Dean (1975) found that the most common type of animal remains in human coprolites from a Texas rock shelter dated to 1,000–2,500 years ago were of grasshoppers. Heizer and Napton (1969) recovered remains of both molluscs and insects from Holocene human coprolites from Lovelock Cave, Nevada. Even if the organic material has perished, impressions of hair, feathers, and insects may survive (Chin 1998).

Other alternatives to identifying paleo-insect eating are more tenuous:

5. Subfossil or fossil remains of insects may be recovered directly from sediments at archaeological sites. For example, the cooking method of burying insects in hot sand, in order to roast them collectively by the thousands, may leave detectable residues (Flood 1980; Fowler and Walter 1985).

6. Skeletal features may reveal diet. Skinner (1991) suggested that the pathological apposition of bone on KNM-ER 1808 (*Homo erectus* female) was diagnostic of overconsumption of bee brood, leading to hypervitaminosis A. The larvae and pupae of honeybees are high quality foods, in terms of protein and fat content, as well as Vitamins A and D (Hocking and Matsumura 1960), but it is not clear how much bee brood would have to be eaten to produce osteological abnormality.

7. Stable isotope analysis may reveal diet. Schoeninger et al. (1998) showed for prosimians that nitrogen stable isotope values from hair samples were significantly different between insectivorous bushbabies (*Galago* spp.) and a folivorous sportive lemur (*Lepilemur leucopus*). Even if these methods could be applied to ancient hair, they would not (yet) distinguish among different types of faunivory and so could not shed light on invertebrate versus vertebrate eating.

8. At present, the clearest evidence of entomophagy by early humans is from Upper Paleolithic cave paintings, notably at Altamira in Spain, about 14,000 years old. Depicted on the cave walls are honey combs and ladders (Pager 1976).

In summary, the six hypotheses posed above are amenable to empirical testing by one or more of the eight means just outlined, at least in principle. This is not the first call for such research (see also Sutton 1990, 1995), but it is the most systematic and comprehensive outline so far.

Conclusions

The pursuit, acquisition, processing, distribution, and consumption of vertebrate prey ("meat") may have been a key feature of human origins. Whether this was a function of solitary versus group hunting or scavenging of small- or large-bodied prey, or all of the above, is likely to be only part of the story. Humbler faunivory, based on gathering of invertebrates, likely provided comparable benefits, as set against a different range of costs. Just as woman-the-gatherer-of-plants proved to be an illuminating complement to man-the-hunter-of-animals (Dahlberg 1981 versus Lee and DeVore 1968), so should recognition of the "other" faunivory be useful in reconstructing human origins.

Acknowledgments I thank H. Bunn and C. Stanford for the opportunity to join in this conference; B. Hardy, R. Lee, L. Marchant, J. Moore, and C. Stanford for critical comments on the manuscript; J. Hamill, K. Milton, K. Murphy, J. Speth, L. Walker, and L. Wilson for additional references; C. Kist for manuscript preparation; and A. Collins and C. Tutin for field assistance in research on chimpanzee insectivory.

REFERENCES

Abrams, H. L. 1987. The preference for animal protein and fat: a cross-cultural survey. In *Food and Evolution*, (M. Harris and E. B. Ross, eds.), pp. 207–223. Philadelphia: Temple University Press.

Anonymous. 1998. The killer in your headlights. *Outdoor Life* 201(3):16.

Badrian, N., and R. K. Malenky. 1984. Feeding ecology of *Pan paniscus* in the Lomako Forest, Zaire. In *The Pygmy Chimpanzee, Evolutionary Biology and Behavior* (R. L. Susman, ed.). New York: Plenum.

Bailey, R. C., and N. R. Peacock. 1988. Efe pygmies of northeast Zaire: subsistence strategies in the Ituri Forest. In *Coping With Uncertainty in Food Supply* (I. de Garine, and G. A. Harrison, eds.), pp. 88–117. Oxford: Clarendon Press.

Bearder, S. K. 1987. Lorises, bushbabies, and tarsiers: diverse societies in solitary foragers. In *Primate Societies*, (B. B. Smuts, D. Cheney, R. M. Seyfarth, R. W. Wrangham, and T. T. Struhsaker, eds.), pp. 11–24. Chicago: University of Chicago Press.

Bearder, S. K., and R. D. Martin. 1980. Acacia gum and its use by bushbabies, *Galago senegalensis* (Primates: Lorisdae). *International Journal of Primatology* 1:103–128.

Beckerman, S. 1979. The abundance of protein in Amazonia: a reply to Gross. *American Anthropologist* 81:533–560.

Bryant, V. M., and G. Williams-Dean. 1975. The coprolites of man. *Scientific American* 232(1):100–109.

Chen, S. P. 1952. Changes in the fat and protein, content of the African migratory locust, *Locusta migratoria migratorioides* (R. & F.). *Bulletin of Entomological Research* 431:01–109.

Chin, K. 1998. On the elusive trail of fossil dung. *National Forum* 78(3):36–41.

Ciochon, R. L., D. R. Piperno, and R. G. Thompson. 1990. Opal phytoliths found on the teeth of the extinct ape, *Gigantopithecus blacki*: implications for paleodietary studies. *Proceedings of the National Academy of Sciences* USA 87:8120–8124.

Corbin, G. D., and J. Schmid. 1995. Insect secretions determine habitat use patterns by a female lesser mouse lemur (*Microcebus murinus*). *American Journal of Primatology* 37:317–324.

Cornelius, C., G. Dandrifosse, and C. Jeuniaux. 1976. Chitinolytic enzymes of the gastric mucosa of *Perodicticus potto* (Primate: Prosimian): purification and enzyme specificity. *International Journal of Biochemistry* 7:445–448.

Dahlberg, F., ed. 1981. *Woman the Gatherer*. New Haven, CT: Yale University Press.

de Conconi, J. R. E., J. M. P. Moreno, C. M. Mayandon, F. R. Valdez, M. A. Perez, E. E. Prado, and H. B. Rodriguez. 1984. Protein content of some edible insects in Mexico. *Journal of Ethnobiology* 4:61–72.

DeFoliart, G. R. 1989. The human use of insects as food and as animal feed. *Bulletin of the Entomological Society of America* 35:22–35.

Dufour, D. L. 1987. Insects as food: a case study from the northwest Amazon. *American Anthropologist* 89:383–397.

Eaton, S. B., M. Shostak, and M. Konner. 1988. *The Paleolithic Prescription*. New York: Harper and Row Perennial.

Flood, J. 1980. *The Moth Hunters. Aboriginal Prehistory of the Australian Alps*. Canberra: Australian Institute of Aboriginal Studies.

Foley, R. A. 1992. Evolutionary ecology of fossil hominids. In *Evolutionary Ecology and Human Behavior* (E. A. Smith and B. Winterhalder, eds.), pp. 131–164. New York: Aldine de Gruyter.

Fowler, C. S., and Walter, N. P. 1985. Harvesting Pandora moth larvae with the Owens Valley Paiute. *Journal of California and Great Basin Anthropology* 7:155–165.

Fox, E. A., A. F. Sitompul, and C. P. van Schaik, 1998. Intelligent tool use in wild Sumatran orangutans. *The Mentality of Gorillas and Orangutans* (S. T. Parker, H. L. Miles, and R. W. Mitchell, eds.), Cambridge: Cambridge University Press.

Fullagar, R., J. Furby, and B. L. Hardy. 1996. Residues on stone artifacts: state of a scientific art. *Antiquity* 70:740–745.

Garber, P. A. 1984. Proposed nutritional importance of plant exudates in the diet of the Panamanian Tamarin, *Saguinus oedipus goeffroyi*. *International Journal of Primatology* 5:1–15.

Gautier-Hion, A. 1980. Seasonal variations of diet related to species and sex in a community of *Cercopithecus* monkeys. *Journal of Animal Ecology* 49:237–269.

Goodall, J. v. L. 1968. The behaviour of free-living chimpanzees in the Gombe Stream Reserve. *Animal Behaviour Monographs* 1:161–301.

Goodall, J. 1986. *The Chimpanzees of Gombe*. Cambridge, MA: Harvard University Press.

Grine, F. E. 1986. Dental evidence for dietary differences in *Australopithecus* and *Paranthropus*: a quantitative analysis of permanent molar microwear. *Journal of Human Evolution* 15:783–822.

Hamilton, W. J., R. E. Buskirk, and W. H. Buskirk. 1978. Omnivory and utilization of food resources by chacma baboons, *Papio ursinus*. *American Naturalist* 112:911–924.

Harcourt, C. S., and L. T. Nash. 1986. Species differences in substrate use and diet between sympatric galagos in two Kenyan coastal forests. *Primates* 27:41–52.

Hardy, B. L. 1999. Microscopic residue analysis of stone tools from the Middle Paleolithic site of Starosele. In *The Middle Paleolithic of Western Crimea—Vol. 2* (V. P. Chabai and K. Monigol, eds.), pp. 179–196. Liege: ERAUL 87.

Hardy, B. L., R. A. Raff, and V. Raman. 1997. Recovery of mammalian DNA from Middle Paleolithic stone tools. *Journal of Archeological Science* 24:601–611.

Hawkes, K., K. Hill, and J. F. O'Connell, 1982. Why hunters gather: optimal foraging and the Aché of eastern Paraguay. *American Ethnologist* 9:379–398.

Heizer, R. F., and L. K. Napton, 1969. Biological and cultural evidence from prehistoric human coprolites. *Science* 165:563–568.

Hill, K., H. Kaplan, K. Hawkes, and A. M. Hurtado. 1985. Men's time allocation to subsistence work among the Aché of eastern Paraguay. *Human Ecology* 13:29–47.

Hladik, C. M. 1977. Chimpanzees of Gabon and chimpanzees of Gombe: some comparative data on the diet. In *Primate Ecology* (T. H. Clutton-Brock, ed.), pp. 481–501. London: Academic Press.

Hocking, B., and F. Matsumara. 1960. Bee brood as food. *Bee World* 41:113–120.

Hurtado, A. M., K. Hawkes, K. Hill, and H. Kaplan. 1985. Female subsistence strategies among Aché hunter-gatherers of eastern Paraguay. *Human Ecology* 13:1–28.

Kakeya, M. 1976. Subsistence ecology of the Tongwe, Tanzania. *Kyoto University African Studies* 10:143–212.

Kano, T. 1992. *The Last Ape. Pygmy Chimpanzee Behavior and Ecology*. Stanford: Stanford University Press.

Kay, R. F., and W. L. Hylander. 1978. The dental structure of mammalian folivores with special reference to Primates and Phalangeroidea (Marsupialia). In *The Ecology of Arboreal Folivores* (G. G., Montgomery, ed.), pp. 173–191. Washington, DC: Smithsonian Institution Press.

Keeley, L. H., and N. Toth. 1981. Microwear polish on early stone tools from Koobi Fora, Kenya. *Nature* 293:464–465.

Klein, R. G. 1977. The ecology of early man in southern Africa. *Science* 197:115–126.

Kuroda, S., T. Nishihara, S. Suzuki, and R. A. Oko. 1996. Sympatric chimpanzees and gorillas in the Ndoki Forest, Congo. In *Great Ape Societies* (W. C. McGrew, L. F. Marchant, and T. Nishida, eds.), pp. 71–81. Cambridge: Cambridge University Press.

Lee, R. B., and I. DeVore, (eds.) 1968. *Man the Hunter*. Chicago: Aldine-Atherton.

Lizot, J. 1977. Population, resources and warfare among the Yanomami. *Man* 12:497–517.

Madsen, D. B., and J. E. Kirkman. 1988. Hunting hoppers. *American Antiquity* 53:593–604.

McBeath, N. M., and W. C. McGrew. 1982. Tools used by wild chimpanzees to obtain termites at Mt. Assirik, Senegal: the influence of habitat. *Journal of Human Evolution* 11:65–72.

McGrew, W. C. 1974. Tool use by wild chimpanzees in feeding upon driver ants. *Journal of Human Evolution* 3:501–508.

McGrew, W. C. 1979. Evolutionary implications of sex differences in chimpanzee predation and tool use. In *The Great Apes* (D. A. Hamburg and E. R. McCown, eds.), pp. 440–463. Menlo Park, CA: Benjamin/Staples.

McGrew, W. C. 1981. The female chimpanzee as an evolutionary prototype. In *Woman the Gatherer* (F. Dahlberg, ed.), pp. 35–73. New Haven, CT: Yale University Press.

McGrew, W. C. 1987. Tools to get food: the subsistants of Tasmanian aborigines and Tanzanian chimpanzees compared. *Journal of Anthropological Research* 43:247–258.

McGrew, W. C. 1992. *Chimpanzee Material Culture: Implications for Human Evolution*. Cambridge: Cambridge University Press.

McGrew, W. C., and L. F. Marchant. 1999. Laterality of hand use pays off in foraging success for wild chimpanzees. Submitted for publication.

Meyer-Rochow, V. B. 1973. Edible insects in three different ethnic groups of Papua and New Guinea. *American Journal of Clinical Nutrition* 26:673–677.

Milton, K. 1984. Protein and carbohydrate resources of the Maku Indians of northwestern Amazonia. *American Anthropologist* 86:7–27.

Moore, J. 1983. Insectivory by grey langurs. *Journal of the Bombay Natural History Society* 82:38–44.

Moore, J. 1996. Savanna chimpanzees, referential models and the last common ancestor. In *Great Ape Societies* (W. C. McGrew, L. F. Marchant, and T. Nishida, eds.), pp. 275–292. Cambridge: Cambridge University Press,

Moran, E. O. 1993. *Through Amazonian Eyes. The Human Ecology of Amazonian Populations.* Iowa City: University of Iowa Press.

Nickle, D. A., and E. W. Heymann. 1996. Predation on Orthoptera and other orders of insects by tamarin monkeys, *Saguinus mystax mystax* and *Saguinus fuscicollis nigrifrons* (Primates: Callitrichidae), in north-eastern Peru. *Journal of Zoology* 239:799–819.

Nishida, T., and M. Hirawa. 1982. Natural history of a tool-using behaviour by wild chimpanzees in feeding upon wood-boring ants. *Journal of Human Evolution* 11:73–99.

Nonaka, K. 1996. Ethnoentomology of the Central Kalahari San. *African Study Monographs Supplement* 22:29–46.

O'Connell, J. F., and K. Hawkes. 1984. Food choice and foraging sites among the Alyawara. *Journal of Anthropological Research* 40:504–535.

Oswalt, W. H. 1976. *An Anthropological Analysis of Food-Getting Technology.* New York: Wiley Interscience.

Pager, H. 1976. Cave paintings suggest honey hunting activities in Ice Age times. *Bee World* 57:9–14.

Redford, K. H., and J. G. Dorea. 1984. The nutritional value of invertebrates with emphasis on ants and termites as food for mammals. *Journal of Zoology* 203:385–395.

Rhine, R. J., G. W. Norton, G. M. Wynn, R. D. Wynn, and H. B. Rhine. 1986. Insect and meat-eating among infant and adult baboons (*Papio cynocephalus*) of Mikumi National Park, Tanzania. *American Journal of Physical Anthropology* 70:105–118.

Rijksen, H. D. 1978. *A field study on Sumatran Orang Utans* (Pongo pygmaeus abellii *Lesson 1827*). Wageningen: H. Veenman and Zonen.

Robinson, J. G. 1984. Diurnal variation in foraging and diet in the wedge-capped capuchin Cebus olivaceus. *Folia Primatologica* 43:216–228.

Rose, L. M. 1994. Sex differences in diet and foraging behavior in white-faced capuchins (*Cebus capucinus*). *International Journal of Primatology* 15:95–114.

Roth, W. E. 1901. Food: its search, capture, and preparation. *North Queensland Ethnography Bulletin* 3:7–31.

Ruddle, K. 1973. The human use of insects: examples from the Yukba. *Biotropica* 5:94–101.

Santos Oliveira, J. F., J. Passos de Carvalho, R. F. S. Bruno de Sousa, and M. Madalena Simao. 1976. The nutritional value of four species of insects consumed in Angola. *Ecology of Food and Nutrition* 5:91–97.

Schoeninger, M. T., U. T. Iwaniec, and L. T. Nash. 1997. Ecological attributes recorded in stable isotope ratios of arbored prosimian hair. *Oecologie* 113:222–230.

Skinner, M. 1991. Bee brood consumption: an alternative explanation for hypervitaminosis A in KNM-ER 1808 (*Homo erectus*) from Koobi Fora, Kenya. *Journal of Human Evolution* 20:493–503.

Stanford, C. B. 1996. The hunting ecology of wild chimpanzees: implications for the evolutionary ecology of Pliocene hominids. *American Anthropologist* 98:96–113.

Sutton, M. Q. 1990. Insect resources and Plio-Pleistocene hominid evolution. In *Ethnobiology: Implications and Applications, Volume 1.* (D. A. Posey, W. L. Overal, C. R. Clement, M. J. Plotkin, E. Elisabetsky, C. N. deMota, and J. F. P. deBarros, eds.), pp. 195–207. Belem: Museu Paraence Emilio Goeldi.

Sutton, M. Q. 1995. Archaeological aspects of insect use. *Journal of Archaeological Method and Theory* 1:253–298.

Sweeney, G. 1947. Food supplies of a desert tribe. *Oceania* 17:289–299.

Taylor, M. E., and A. G. Hannam. 1987. Tooth microwear and diet in the African Viverridae. *Canadian Journal of Zoology* 65:1696–1702.

Teaford, M. F. 1988. A review of dental microwear and diet in modern mammals. *Scanning Microscopy* 2:1149–1166.

Tutin, C. E. G., and M. Fernandez. 1983. Gorillas feeding on termites in Gabon, West Africa. *Journal of Mammalogy* 64:530–531.

Tutin, C. E. G., and M. Fernandez. 1992. Insect-eating by sympatric lowland gorillas (*Gorilla g. gorilla*) and chimpanzees (*Pan t. troglodytes*) in the Lopé Reserve, Gabon. *American Journal of Primatology* 28:29–40.

Uehara, S. 1986. Sex and group differences in feeding on animals by wild chimpanzees in the Mahale Mountains National Park, Tanzania. *Primates* 27:1–14.

Walker, A. 1981. Diet and teeth. Dietary hypotheses and human evolution. *Philosophical Transactions of the Royal Society of London, B. Biological Sciences* 292:56–64.

Watts, D. P. 1989. Ant eating behavior of mountain gorillas. *Primates* 30:121–125.

Winterhalder, B. 1987. The analysis of hunter-gatherer diets: stalking the optimal foraging model. In *Food and Evolution* (M. Harris and E. B. Ross, eds.), pp. 311–339. Philadelphia: Temple University Press.

Worsley, P. M. 1961. The utilization of natural food resources by an Australian aboriginal tribe. *Acta Enthnographica* 10:153–190.

9

Meat-Eating by the Fourth African Ape

Margaret J. Schoeninger
Henry T. Bunn
Shawn Murray
Travis Pickering
Jim Moore

Introduction

Two and a half million years ago (de Heinzelin et al. 1999, see also Bunn this volume), hominids processed carcasses of large bodied, terrestrial, group-living ungulates in a savanna woodland or grassland setting. In contrast, modern chimpanzees (the most carnivorous of the extant apes) rarely scavenge and hunt only small- to medium-sized, primarily arboreal prey in forest and woodland settings (Stanford 1998). The ancestral primate diet, seen in most extant species weighing >1 kg, provides energy from simple carbohydrates in fruit (Strait 1997; Fleagle 1999), whereas animal carcasses provide energy from lipids. Carbohydrates are digested in the stomach, whereas lipid digestion takes place in the small intestine (Lambert 1998). The ancestral diet provides the majority of protein from leaves, which package protein within plant cell walls composed of indigestible fiber. Access to this protein requires fermentation by large bacterial colonies housed in expanded stomachs or colons (Chivers and Langer 1994). When eaten at amounts seen in humans, meat contains levels of nitrogen toxic to foregut bacterial colonies and levels of fiber too low to prevent colonic twisting in hindgut fermenters like gorillas or chimpanzees.

Taken together, these facts pose two related questions central to the understanding of hominid origins. First, why were large animal carcasses viewed as food by Plio-Pleistocene hominids? Second, how did hominid digestive systems tolerate the switch from regular fruit- and leaf-eating to regular fat- and meat-eating? To address these questions, we consider the nutritional strategies of extant African hominoids as the successful result of feeding competition in the past. Feeding competition over preferred resources during periods of scarcity is a significant factor in the behavioral ecology of extant nonhuman hominoids (Tutin and Fernandez 1993; Kuroda et al. 1996; Wrangham et al. 1996; Yamagiwa et al. 1996), and the same should be true of ancestral hominoids (McGrew 1992; Moore 1996). We limit discussion to the African hominoids, except for relevant references to fruit-eating in orangutans (e.g., Leighton 1993), because they have been separate from the Eurasian forms since the middle Miocene. Our modern human data derive from the Hadza foragers of Tanzania who exploit an abundance and diversity of wild food resources in an ecological setting similar to that of early hominids. Modern humans, chimpanzees, and gorillas are not identical to their ancestral forms, as all hominoids have followed separate evolutionary paths. Although none can represent ancestral hominids per se, all can contribute to both referential and conceptual hominid models (Moore 1996).

Extant Hominoid Diets

Gorilla (Gorilla gorilla)

Gorillas live in forest-dominated ecosystems where they may eat significant quantities of fruit (Watts 1996; Doran and McNeilage 1998). Mountain gorillas (*Gorilla gorilla beringei*) are the most folivorous with little dietary variation, although bamboo shoots are taken seasonally in some areas (Watts 1996). Lowland gorillas (*graueri* and *gorilla*) take fruit when and where available (Tutin and Fernandez 1993; Watts 1996), adjusting group size to reduce intragroup feeding competition (Remis 1997). When feeding on ripe fruit, ingested seeds are spit out or passed without damage (Rogers et al. 1998), as previously observed in orangutans (Leighton 1993), suggesting that fruit provides energy as carbohydrate without the lipid or protein in seeds. Most protein comes from leaves, as gorillas eat few vertebrates and feed on insects mainly when they are easily available, such as termite-swarming times (Kuroda et al. 1996).

Because gorillas feed on ripe fruit and insects opportunistically (Yamagiwa et al. 1996), such feeding is limited on an annual basis. The majority of their diet can be, and often is, low in protein and high in tannins and fiber. All gorillas increase intake of high fiber foods during periods of fruit scarcity (Watts 1996; Yamagiwa et al. 1996) although, like some monkeys (Glander 1982), they preferentially select portions that are relatively high in protein and low in tannins (Watts 1996). Their large bodies, proportionately large caeca (Chivers and Langer 1994) and long-food retention times (Milton 1999) permit caecal fermentation of cellulose (Watts 1996), similar to some monkeys (Conklin-Brittain et al. 1998). Such fermentation requires long periods of reduced activity (Chivers and Langer 1994; Milton 1999) that limits day-range size (Tutin 1996). The maintenance of caecal bacterial colonies, coupled with their proportionately short small intestines (Milton 1999), may account for their avoidance of fruits with high lipid content (Tutin and Fernandez 1993) and their short bouts of fruit feeding (Kuroda et al. 1996).

Chimpanzees (Pan troglodytes)

In contrast to gorillas, chimpanzees inhabit savannas (McGrew 1992; Moore 1996) and woodlands (Goodall 1986) as well as forests (Boesch and Boesch 1999). Large variations in diet occur but, in contrast to gorillas, chimpanzees show greater and more consistent dependence on ripe fruit (Yamagiwa et al. 1996; Wrangham et al. 1998), which is considered their basic food (McGrew 1992) in all settings. These fruits supply energy in the form of carbohydrate, mostly simple sugars, rather than lipids (Leighton 1993). To a far greater extent than gorillas, chimpanzees forage alone or in small groups (Isbell and Young 1996; Tutin 1996; Wrangham et al. 1996) and increase day range size (Tutin and Fernandez 1993; Doran 1997; Remis 1997) to ensure continued access to these fruits. During times of fruit scarcity in "savannas" (miombo; see Collins and McGrew 1988; Moore 1992), they eat immature seeds (Suzuki 1969; Steklis et al. 1992). In other regions, they can eat limited quantities of stems (McGrew 1992) or pith (Malenky et al. 1994).

Because fruit flesh tends to be low in protein (Chivers and Langer 1994), leaves (Chivers and Langer 1994), seeds (Suzuki 1969), or faunal material (McGrew 1992; Stanford 1998; Boesch and Boesch 1999) provide this dietary component. Ecosystems with predominantly herbaceous vegetation are marginal for chimpanzees (Yamagiwa et al. 1996) although young leaves and herbaceous vegetation, fermented in their relatively large caeca during long food retention times (Milton 1999), are significant sources of protein for them. In contrast to gorillas, however, protein sources other than leaves and herbaceous vegetation are actively pursued (Tutin and Fernandez 1993). All chimpanzee groups observed thus far ingest a wide variety of insects using tools to access them in underground nests (Goodall 1986; McGrew 1992; Tutin and Fernandez 1993; Kuroda et al. 1996; McGrew this volume). Among forest- and woodland-living groups, hunting vertebrate fauna has been directly observed (Stanford 1998; Boesch and Boesch 1999) or indirectly indicated by fecal and stable isotope data (Nishida 1989; Schoeninger et al. 1999b). Although low relative to most human groups, this dependence on fauna may be nutritionally valuable as in some frugivorous ungulates (Bodmer 1989b). Seeds from leguminous trees may provide protein in savanna woodlands (Suzuki 1969; Schoeninger et al. 1999b) although fully mature seeds often contain compounds inhibiting protein digestion (Glander 1982; Stahl 1984; Sept 1990), and they can be surrounded by hard, thick coats (Peres 1991; Grubb et al. 1998). Small frugivorous ungulates and monkeys circumvent these digestive barriers through rumination or powerful mastication (Bodmer 1989a; Kinzey and Norconk 1990; Peres 1991), but the chimpanzee gut does not permit the former, and their thin-enamelled teeth preclude the latter in the absence of processing with tools (Boesch and Boesch 1999).

Bonobos (Pan paniscus)

Far less is known about the diet of this species although like chimpanzees, bonobos are highly dependent on tree fruits, spending most of their time in climax forest (Malenky et al. 1994; White 1996). Fecal evidence, feeding traces, and molar morphology suggest that they are intermediate between gorillas and chimpanzees in extracting sufficient protein and significant energy from herbaceous vegetation (Malenky et al. 1994). This adaptation is associated with larger and more stable social groups than found in chimpanzees (Wrangham et al. 1996). They are considered only in general terms below.

Hadza (Homo sapiens)

In contrast to the other hominoids, human foragers, including the Hadza, often inhabit dry savanna woodland regions (see Collins and McGrew 1988) and open Serengeti-type grasslands (called savanna grasslands in this volume), where available fruits tend to be berry species taken from shrubs (Sept 1990). As among chimpanzees, the Hadza social system is quite fluid and varies with seasonal availability of food resources (Woodburn 1968). During the dry season, they depend mainly on large animals, baobab (*Adansonia digitata*) fruit and seeds, and minor amounts of other fruits and honey. During the wet season they include more small animals, honey, fruit, and baobab seeds (Woodburn 1968; Vincent 1984; Hawkes et al. 1989). Several species of tubers, which provide energy as simple carbohydrates and starch, are also eaten throughout most of the year (Woodburn 1968). In general, however, 20–80% of tuber dry weight is fiber (Vincent 1984; Schoeninger et al. 1999a; see Table 9.1), of which little can be fermented in the human large intestine (Kritchevsky and Bonfield 1997). Further, the majority of the energy produced is used by colonic microbes and the byproducts, volatile fatty acids, provide little energy (Hume and Warner 1980; contra O'Connell et al. 1999). The Hadza expectorate this fiber as a quid rather than swallow it. Fruits and honey provide greater amounts of energy but contain little protein (Murray et al. 1999) and show limited availability in the mid to late dry season (Schoeninger and Bunn, in prep.). Berries have many seeds that are spit out or pass through the digestive system, providing no nutrition.

Baobab fruits, on the other hand, are highly nutritious in terms of both energy and protein, and they are available for a longer period throughout the year than any individual berry species, providing substantial energy on an annual basis. The pulp has energy levels similar to berries (see Table 9.1), and contains significant amounts of calcium and Vitamin C (see Murray et al. 1999). The seeds provide energy on a dry weight basis that is roughly equivalent to honey and higher than that provided by the berries. Significantly, the energy is in the form of lipid rather than simple carbohydrate as in berries and in honeys. The relatively large upper gut (stomach and small intestine) in humans (Milton 1999) and relatively small colonies of colonic bacteria are well suited for lipid digestion. Baobab seed is also a good protein source with adequate levels of five out of eight essential amino acids (see Murray et al. 1999). The Hadza chew young seeds; but when mature, the seeds are cracked individually with a stone or pounded into a coarse flour (see Figure 9.1). Baboons, which have teeth well-shaped for seed cracking (Strait 1997), cannot break the mature seeds and pass them unbroken. Hadza women collect baobab seeds from baboon dung piles, wash them, and prepare them in the normal manner (Bunn and Schoeninger, unpub. obs.). This process extends the annual availability of baobab seeds. Baobab seed flour is winnowed to remove seed coats that apparently contain

Table 9.1. Nutritional composition of foods consumed by Hadza foragers.[a]

Sample	Moisture %	Crude Protein	Fat g/100	Starch g dry weight[b]	Simple CHD	Dietary Fiber	Ash	Energy kcal/100 g Dry Weight[b]
Honey								
Ba'alako (n = 2)	15	3	7	tr	89	nd	1	434
N!ateko (n = 2)	24	3	3	tr	93	nd	1	412
Kanoa (n = 2)	22	2	4	tr	93	nd	1	416
Berries								
Cordia sp (n = 3)	71	14	2	nd	64	14	6	328
Grewia sp (n = 2)	25	10	2	nd	69	13	6	334
Tree Fruit								
Pawe (Sclerocarya birrea)								
Pulp	83	4	nd	nd	50	38	7	232
Baobab (Adansonia digitata)								
Ground seed	5	36	29	tr	11	14	9	454
Pulp	5	2	1	11	36	45	5	203
Tubers								
Vigna frutescens (n = 5)	78	4	nd	26	6	58	5	146
Ipomoea transvaalensis	86	2	nd	24	48	21	6	298
Eminia antennulifera	80	7	nd	20	23	45	6	199

[a]Data taken from Murray et al. 1999 and Schoeninger et al. 1999b, data rounded to closest whole percent; tr is <0.5 %; nd is not determined.
[b]The nutritional compositions, including the calories, are presented for dry weights.

inhibitors of protein digestion (see Murray et al. 1999). The long period of avail-ability and high nutrient quality of baobab fruit pulp and seeds are typical of tree fruits, nuts, and seeds taken by human groups across Africa (Peters 1987).

Feeding Competition and Diet

Gorillas and chimpanzees are sympatric in several regions (overview in Kuroda et al. 1996), with significant differences in the types of foods eaten and in feeding pat-tern. Although they can eat 70–90% of the same fruit species, there is little similar-ity in nonfruit species. Chimpanzees increase intakes of high-fiber foods only dur-ing periods of unusually low fruit availability (Tutin and Fernandez 1993; Kuroda et al. 1996; Yamagiwa et al. 1996; Doran 1997), in disturbed environments (Wrang-ham et al. 1996), or in habitat extremes (Yamagiwa et al. 1996), and never to the extent observed in gorillas. Differences in feeding pattern, which may be related to gastrointestinal constraints, also reduce competition. Where chimpanzees may feed all day in a single fruit patch, gorillas feed for very short periods of time (Kuroda et al. 1996) such that intraspecific encounters are often more aggressive than inter-specific ones (Yamagiwa et al. 1996).

Figure 9.1a & b. Hadza woman pounding baobab seeds to a coarse flour, eaten dry or mixed with water, which contains 36% lipid, 20% protein, and adequate levels of five of the eight essential amino acids. Baobab and other similar high quality tree-fruit seeds are widely available across Africa today in moist savanna woodlands and were more widely spread at the time of hominid divergence from the primitive hominoid ancestor. Photographs by Shawn Murray.

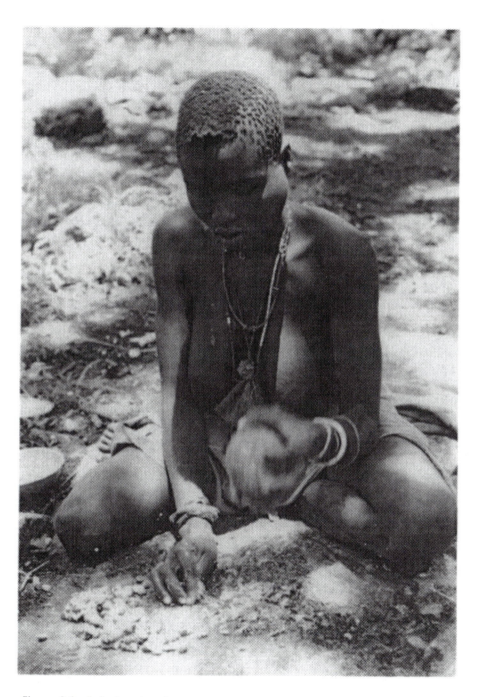

Figure 9.1a & b. (*continued*)

Bonobos are not sympatric with either chimpanzees or with gorillas. The reliance on herbaceous vegetation by bonobos may be due to the absence of competition from gorillas (Wrangham et al. 1996). Similarly, bonobos rely heavily on arboreal fruits for energy, which presumably is permitted by the absence of competition from chimpanzees (White 1996; Wrangham et al. 1996).

Modern humans show no niche accommodation for the other African hominoids. Even though it is not informative to consider the impact of other hominoids on modern human feeding patterns, however, similarities and differences in diet and habitat are suggestive of accommodation in the past. The Hadza use tools to obtain or process three classes of foods (deeply buried tubers, medium to large animals, and hard-shelled nuts), which purportedly separate humans from other primates (Isaac 1980). Gorillas have not been reported eating tubers, and chimpanzee reports are limited to forest settings (Lanjoux, unpub. obs.) where tubers occur at low densities (Chivers and Langer 1994). Deeply buried tubers, such as those used by the Hadza, lack the harmful secondary compounds common in more superficial tubers (Hladik et al. 1984) but require the use of long digging sticks (Vincent 1984). As such, the earliest divergence of the hominid lineage probably did not involve tuber use, although they may have been important later (O'Connell et al. 1999; Wrangham et al. 1999). In terms of meat-eating, gorillas eat little, if any; chimpanzees hunt small-sized animals in forests and woodlands (Stanford 1998), perhaps rarely in savanna woodlands (Moore 1992), and they do not eat larger ungulates. Access to large animals in advance of other predators in open environments (early access scavenging and hunting) probably always required tools, and these postdate the earliest divergence of the hominid lineage (de Heinzelin et al. 1999). In addition, a primitive hominoid gut with large caecal bacterial colonies would not have tolerated a rapid transition to high meat intakes. It seems unlikely, therefore, that large-animal acquisition was important in the divergence of hominids from other hominoids. In terms of nut-eating, chimpanzees eat hard-shelled nuts in forests and woodlands with the assistance of tools (Boesch and Boesch 1999), and they chew immature seeds in savanna woodlands (McGrew 1992). Yet, neither gorillas nor chimpanzees exploit mature seeds and nuts to a great extent (Wrangham et al. 1994; Rogers et al. 1998).

Many Hadza foods are similar to those of the gorilla in the relative difficulty of reducing the food to proteins, carbohydrates, or lipids (see Chivers and Langer 1994). Gorilla vegetation and Hadza tubers are high in fiber; chimpanzees avoid such foods whenever possible. Gorillas and the Hadza eat tree-fruit pulps, which are intermediate in fiber levels (see Table 9.1), when available, but both readily switch to other foods. In contrast, such fruits are basic foods for chimpanzees. The Hadza also depend on mature hard nuts and seeds whereas neither gorillas nor chimpanzees can reduce these foods except with nutting stones.

As for foods swallowed, the Hadza show similarities to chimpanzees rather than to gorillas. Gorillas swallow extremely fibrous vegetation, whereas chimpanzees (Yamagiwa et al. 1996) and Hadza (pers. obs.) spit out wadges. Both chimpanzees and humans separate food items from debris while gorillas swallow all of these (Rogers et al. 1990; Tutin and Fernandez 1993; Kuroda et al. 1996; Yamagiwa et al. 1996). All hominoids swallow seeds, passing small seeds, and chewing some seeds before they are fully mature (Steklis et al. 1992), but gorillas, more commonly than chimpanzees (Corlett and Lucas 1990; Wrangham et al. 1994), also swallow large seeds in ripe fruit and pass them (Rogers et al. 1998). In contrast, the Hadza separate the ripe seeds from the fruit in baobab and other large-seeded fruits and also collect them from baboon dung. The Hadza and some chimpanzee groups also reduce hard seeds by pounding (Boesch and Boesch 1999), using very similar tools (McGrew 1992). Among the Hadza, however, the majority of baobab seed-eating follows reduction to flour that is more extensive than chimpanzee nut-cracking. The Hadza practices relieve their masticatory and gastrointestinal systems.

Gorillas rely on their gastrointestinal tract to do food processing; chimpanzees avoid such foods or ingest them at a lower frequency than gorillas; and the Hadza spit out the fiber in tubers and use tools to process other foods that require reduction. Thus, the Hadza and chimpanzees differ from the gorilla in emphasizing foods that enter the gut with easily extractable energy. These are processed foods in the case of the Hadza; carefully selected foods in the case of the chimpanzee. These are fruits with simple carbohydrates, in the case of the chimpanzee; seeds with lipid and protein or tubers with starch in the case in the Hadza.

In sum, the Hadza are able to eat a gorilla-type plant diet, although higher in lipid and protein, in a chimpanzee-type way because they have tools for obtaining and processing foods that minimize digestive requirements of their masticatory apparatus and gastrointestinal tract. We suggest that the similarities between human and gorilla diets and between human and chimpanzee feeding are longstanding and are diagnostic of the niche divergence between the hominidae and other African hominoids. Before tools, the massive masticatory apparatus of hominids served to process foods thereby reducing demands on the ancestral hominoid digestive tract.

Fossil Hominoid Ecosystems and Diets

The evidence for fossil hominoid nutritional strategies comes from a variety of sources including analogies with living primates, dental morphology, body-size estimates, and ecological reconstructions. Ecological reconstructions are particularly critical because the types of food available for hominoids vary markedly across ecological systems (see Sept, this volume). Recently, the use of carbon-stable isotope ratios ($^{13}C{:}^{12}C$, represented as $\delta^{13}C$ below) in fossil materials has increased the accuracy and specificity of our ecological reconstructions. The method depends on the differential uptake of ^{13}C versus ^{12}C by plants during photosynthesis. Two groups of plants, called C_3 and C_4, have $\delta^{13}C$ values that plot bimodally without overlapping values. Tropical trees, shrubs, and herbaceous plants use the C_3 photosynthetic pathway and have $\delta^{13}C$ values that are significantly lower than those of tropical grasses that use the C_4 pathway. Animals contain the $\delta^{13}C$ values of the plants they eat so that primates eating foods from trees, shrubs, and herbaceous plants have $\delta^{13}C$ values typical of C_3 plants, whereas those feeding on grass seeds have values typical of C_4 plants (see Figure 9.2). Among C_3 plants, those in closed-canopy forests have $\delta^{13}C$ values significantly lower than those in deciduous forests, which, in turn, are significantly lower than plants in savanna woodlands. These differences

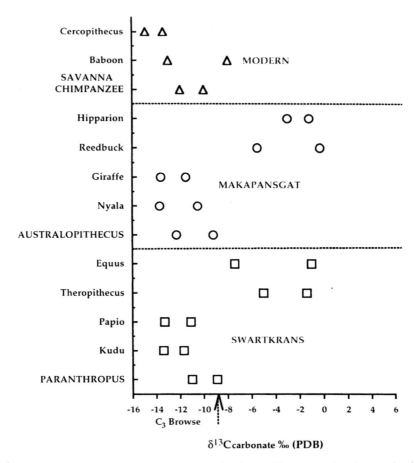

Figure 9.2. Maximum and minimum values of carbon stable isotope data in samples from 1.8–1.0 Ma Swartkrans in South Africa (Lee Thorp et al. 1994), 3 Ma Makapansgat (Sponheimer and Lee Thorp 1999), modern "savanna" chimpanzees (Schoeninger et al. 1999b), and modern nonhominoid primates (Sponheimer and Lee Thorp 1999). The fossil data have been corrected by −1‰ to offset the anthropogenic change of $\delta^{13}C$ in the modern atmosphere and two specimens, whose values suggest diagenetic alteration toward the value in sediments, have not been included. Modern chimpanzee hair data were transformed to expected carbonate values based on an offset of 10.7 ± 2.1‰ between protein carbon and carbonate carbon (Jahren et al. 1998). Fossil browsing species (giraffe, nyala, papio, and kudu) fall within the range expected (−9‰ and below) for modern and fossil browsers (Cerling et al. 1997) and show no overlap with fossil grass-eaters genera (reedbuck, the fossil monkey, *Theropithecus*, and the equids, *Hipparion* and *Equus sp.*). The hominid genera, *Australopithecus* and *Paranthropus,* fall in the range of browsing, C_3-feeding genera that feed in open environments similar to those of "savanna" (i.e., miombo woodland) chimpanzees. The data support hypotheses that hominids supplemented fruit-eating with hard nuts and seeds in open environments.

in $\delta^{13}C$ values across C_3 plants are recorded in soil organics and carbonates (Cerling et al. 1997) and in animal tissues (Schoeninger et al. 1999b) from different ecological systems. Hence, $\delta^{13}C$ values in soil and fossil tooth enamel indicate whether early hominoids fed in closed tropical forests, deciduous woodlands, savanna woodlands, or grasslands (e.g., Sikes 1994; Cerling et al. 1997).

Early Miocene hominoids (~20 Ma), like the majority of today's anthropoid primates, presumably extracted nutrients from C_3 plants in forests (Milton 1984; Chivers and Langer 1994). Unlike chimpanzees and gorillas, however, some species (e.g., *Proconsul major*) had relatively thick tooth enamel (Andrews and Martin 1991), which associates with hard-object feeding in living primate species (Kay 1981). The inclusion of hard objects probably resulted from feeding competition with other hominoid species as well as with early cercopithecoid monkeys (Peters 1987; Benefit 1999; Fleagle 1999).

By the Middle Miocene (~15 Ma), hominoids expanded into woodlands and moist savanna woodlands (Hill and Ward 1988) according to the carbon-stable isotope evidence (Kingston et al. 1994; Morgan et al. 1994; Cerling et al. 1997), and associated ungulate fauna (Kappelman et al. 1997). Dental microwear (Teaford and Walker 1984; Ungar 1998) and molar enamel thickness (Andrews and Martin 1991) indicate some hominoids fed on hard objects as well as soft fruits, suggesting that some species depended on hard seeds and nuts to supplement fruit eating. Other species probably used strategies similar to those of modern chimpanzees and gorillas. Clearly, the range of hominoid dietary adaptations was larger than in today's chimpanzees, gorillas, and bonobos, resulting, in part, from feeding competition among ancestral hominoid species (Kingston et al. 1994).

Several lines of evidence (see Gordon 1993) suggest that the early hominids supplemented fruit-eating with hard seeds and nuts, as proposed previously (Jolly 1970; Kay 1981; Peters 1987; Moore 1992). The adaptation of *Ardipithecus ramidus* (4.4 Ma) cannot be assessed pending further publication (White et al. 1994). But *Australopithecus anamensis* (4.2–3.9 Ma) inhabited woodlands and was bipedal (Coffing et al. 1994; Leakey et al. 1995) with tooth enamel thicker than in chimpanzees and gorillas (Ward et al. 1999). Slightly later, *Australopithecus afarensis* sites at Laetoli, Tanzania (3.6 Ma), Hadar, Ethiopia (around 3 Ma), the Turkana basin, Kenya (3.36–3.0 Ma), and Sterfonktein, South Africa (3.5 Ma) were situated in moist savanna woodlands as well as woodlands (Sikes 1994; Kimbel et al. 1996; Reed 1997; Clarke 1998). Among the most energy-dense foods in such environments are tree fruits with lipid- and protein-rich seeds and nuts (Peters 1987). Early hominids may not have achieved the energetically efficient striding gait of modern humans (Steudel 1996), but they could move long distances with greater energetic efficiency than knuckle-walking species (Rodman and McHenry 1980; Isbell and Young 1996). Hominids could increase range size to access widely spaced woodlands experiencing different mast cycles (Waller 1979) or nonmasting tree species in search of ripe fruit uneaten by monkeys (Wrangham et al. 1998). They could also chew mature seeds and nuts within the fruit or passed by monkeys, gorillas, and chimpanzees. Microdamage on early hominid incisors indicates that they were procuring some foods similar to those eaten by gorillas today (Ryan and Johanson 1989) but their thick molar enamel and woodland setting suggests that they included hard-object feeding along with gorilla-type foods. This implies emphasis on lipids coupled with higher levels of plant proteins with a better mix of essential amino acids. Such an emphasis would affect the small intestine where absorption and lipid digestion occurs. The intermediate level of fiber found in the fruit pulps associated with these seeds (see Table 9.1) would also permit reduction in the size of the caecum.

During the middle to late Pliocene (3–2.5 Ma) several species of hominid are apparent (see Asfaw et al. 1999 for overview), all with massive masticatory systems relative to living hominoids (Andrews and Martin 1991). Their savanna woodland habitats (Reed 1997) supported trees bearing seeds and nuts (see Chivers and Langer 1994), which could be processed dentally (Demes and Creel 1988; Andrews and Martin 1991). Although dental microwear analyses indicate that there was variation in diets across species (Grine and Kay 1988), tooth enamel $\delta^{13}C$ values (see Figure 9.2) are similar (Lee Thorp et al. 1994; Sponheimer and Lee Thorp 1999). All the isotope data overlap those from open country browsing species (Cerling et al. 1997), including extant savanna chimpanzees (Schoeninger et al. 1999b). Although the data do not preclude some level of omnivory, they fit equally well with a diet of tree fruit- and nut-eating, and hominid cranial morphology fits better with the latter than with the former. Pending further microwear and isotopic studies, we concur with Jolly (1970), Kay (1981), and Peters (1987) that early hominid diets were shaped by a reliance on lipid-rich seeds as supplements to fruit pulps.

However, faunal remains associated with 2.5 Ma *Australopithecus garhi* in Ethiopia show both percussion pits and cut marks (de Heinzelin et al. 1999). Thus, at the time that obvious stone tools appear in the fossil record, a hominid species had access to animal fat and meat. The earliest tool use probably improved access to their traditional plant foods, like nuts and seeds, but by the middle Pliocene, this activity had been transferred to cracking long bones and cutting meat of large animals. The 2.5 Ma hominid, unlike extant gorillas and chimpanzees, could subject their gastrointestinal systems to lipid- and protein-dense foods. Although early hominids had relatively small brains, such a diet could provide maternal energy levels throughout the annual cycle which permitted subsequent increases in brain size (Martin 1984) with minimal gastrointestinal requirements (Aiello and Wheeler 1995).

The Third Chimpanzee or the Fourth African Ape?

By the early Pleistocene, *Homo* was regularly obtaining animal meat and fat (Bunn this volume). But, although the regular use of meat represents an increase in diet breadth, the introduction of nutrient-dense foods (high in lipid and protein) came much earlier. We suggest this long-term adaptation to nutrient-dense foods involving food reduction (accomplished orally at first and with tools later) with decreasing reliance on colonic fermentation is the major difference between ancestral hominids and the other African hominoids and characterizes the earliest appearance of hominids. The intermediate level of fiber in tree-fruit pulps would avoid the problem of colonic twisting caused by low-fiber diets in hindgut fermenters like chimpanzees and gorillas. Energy-dense foods, like lipid-rich seeds of the baobab used by the Hadza today, emphasize the lipid-digesting section of the gastrointestinal tract (i.e., the small intestine). The drop in fiber intake coupled with increased dependence on lipids for energy would have favored a larger foregut (small intestine) and a smaller caecum. Subsequently, simple tools, like pounding stones, would have achieved seed coat removal, enhancing access to seed protein by removing digestion inhibitors. These changes would permit an increase in diet breadth to include regular meat-eating within the genus *Homo*.

REFERENCES

Aiello, L. C., and P. Wheeler. 1995. The expensive-tissue hypothesis: the brain and the digestive system in human and primate evolution. *Current Anthropology* 36:199–221.

Andrews, P., and L. Martin. 1991. Hominoid dietary evolution. *Philosophical Transactions of the Royal Society of London B* 334:199–209.

Asfaw, B., T. White, O. Lovejoy, B. Latimer, S. Simpson, and G. Suwa. 1999. *Australopithecus garhi*: a new species of early hominid from Ethiopia. *Science* 284:629–635.

Benefit, B. R. 1999. *Victoriapithecus*: the key to Old World monkey and Catarrhine origins. *Evolutionary Anthropology* 7:155–174.

Bodmer, R. E. 1989a. Frugivory in Amazonian Artiodactyla: evidence for the evolution of the ruminant stomach. *Journal of Zoology, London* 1989:457–467.

Bodmer, R. E. 1989b. Ungulate biomass in relation to feeding strategy within Amazonian forests. *Oecologia* 81:547–550.

Boesch, C., and H. Boesch. 1999. *The Chimpanzees of the Taï Forest*. Oxford: Oxford University Press.

Cerling, T. E., J. M. Harris, S. H. Ambrose, M. G. Leakey, and N. Solounias. 1997. Dietary and environmental reconstruction with stable isotope analyses of herbivore tooth enamel from the Miocene locality of Fort Ternan, Kenya. *Journal of Human Evolution* 33:635–650.

Chivers, D. J., and P. Langer (eds.). 1994. *The Digestive System in Mammals: Food, Form and Function*. Cambridge:Cambridge University Press.

Clarke, R. J. 1998. First ever discovery of a well preserved skull and associated skeleton of Australopithecus. *South African Journal of Science* 94:460–463.

Coffing, K., C. Feibel, M. Leakey, and A. Walker. 1994. Four-million-year-old hominids from East Lake Turkana, Kenya. *American Journal of Physical Anthropology* 93:55–65.

Collins, D. A., and W. C. McGrew. 1988. Habitats of three groups of chimpanzees (*Pan troglodytes*) in western Tanzania compared. *Journal of Human Evolution* 17:553–574.

Conklin-Brittain, N. L., R. W. Wrangham, and K. D. Hunt. 1998. Dietary response of chimpanzees and cercopithecines to seasonal variation in fruit abundance. II. Macronutrients. *International Journal of Primatology* 19:971–998.

Corlett, R. T., and P. W. Lucas. 1990. Alternative seed-handling strategies in primates: seed-spitting by long-tailed macaques. *Oecologia* 82:166–171.

de Heinzelin, J., J. D. Clark, T. White, W. Hart, P. Renne, G. WoldeGabriel, Y. Beyene, and E. Vrba. 1999. Environment and behavior of 2.5–million-year-old Bouri hominids. *Science* 284:625–629.

Demes, B., and N. Creel. 1988. Bite force, diet, and cranial morphology of fossil hominids. *Journal of Human Evolution* 17:657–670.

Doran, D. 1997. Influence of seasonality on activity patterns, feeding behavior, ranging, and grouping patterns in Tai chimpanzees. *International Journal of Primatology* 18:183–206.

Doran, D. M., and A. McNeilage. 1998. Gorilla ecology and behavior. *Evolutionary Anthropology* 6:120–131.

Fleagle, J. G. 1999. *Primate Adaptation and Evolution.* San Diego: Academic Press, Inc.

Glander, K. E. 1982. The impact of plant secondary compounds on primate feeding behavior. *Yearbook of Physical Anthropology* 25:1–18.

Goodall, J. 1986. *The Chimpanzees of Gombe: Patterns of Behavior.* Cambridge, MA: Belknap Press.

Gordon, K. 1993. Reconstructing hominid diet in the Plio-Pleistocene. *Rivista di Antropologia (Roma)* 71:71–89.

Grine, F. E., and R. F. Kay. 1988. Early hominid diets from quantitative image analysis of dental microwear. *Nature* 333:765–768.

Grubb, P. J., D. J. Metcalfe, E. A. A. Grubb, and G. D. Jones. 1998. Nitrogen-richness and protection of seeds in Australian tropical rainforest: a test of plant defence theory. *Oikos* 82:467–482.

Hawkes, K., J. F. O'Connell, and N. G. Blurton Jones. 1989. Hardworking Hadza grandmothers. In *Comparative Socioecology: The Behavioral Ecology of Humans and Other Mammals* (V. Standen and R. A. Foley, eds.), pp. 341–366. Oxford: Blackwell Scientific Publications.

Hill, A., and S. Ward. 1988. Origin of the Hominidae: the record of African large hominoid evolution between 14 My and 4 My. *Yearbook of Physical Anthropology* 31:49–83.

Hladik, A., S. Bahuchet, C. Ducatillion, and C. Hladik. 1984. Les plantes a tubercules de la foret dense d'Afrique centrale. *Refue d' Écolgie (Terre Vie)* 39:249–290.

Hume, I. D., and A. C. I. Warner. 1980. Evolution of microbial digestion in mammals. In *Digestive Physiology and Metabolism in Ruminants* (Y. Ruckebusch and P. Thivend, eds.), pp. 615–634. Westport, CT: AVI.

Isaac, G. 1980. Casting the net wide: a review of archaeological evidence for early hominid land-use and ecological relations. In *Current Argument on Early Man* (L.-K. Königsson, eds.), pp. 226–251. Oxford: Pergamon Press.

Isbell, L. A., and T. P. Young. 1996. The evolution of bipedalism in hominids and reduced group size in chimpanzees: alternative responses to decreasing resource availability. *Journal of Human Evolution* 30:389–397.

Jahren, A. H., L. C. Todd, and R. G. Amundson. 1998. Stable isotope dietary analysis of bone bison samples from Hudson-Meng bonebed: effects of paleotopography. *Journal of Archaeological Science* 25:465–475.

Jolly, C. J. 1970. The seed-eaters: a new model of hominid differentiation based on a baboon analogy. *Man* 5:5–26.

Kappelman, J., T. Plummer, L. Bishop, A. Duncan, and S. Appleton. 1997. Bovids as indicators of Plio-Pleistocene paleoenvironments in East Africa. *Journal of Human Evolution* 32:229–256.

Kay, R. F. 1981. The nut-crackers: a new theory of the adaptations of the Ramapithecinae. *American Journal of Physical Anthropology* 55:141–151.

Kimbel, W. H., R. C. Walter, D. C. Johanson, K. E. Reed, J. L. Aronson, Z. Assefa, C. W. Marean, G. G. Eck, R. Bobe, E. Hovers, Y. Rak, C. Vondra, T. Yemane, D. York, Y. Chen, N. M. Evensen, and P. E. Smith. 1996. Late Pliocene *Homo* and Oldowan tools from the Hadar formation (Kada Hadar Member), Ethiopia. *Journal of Human Evolution* 31:549–561.

Kingston, J. D., B. D. Marino, and A. Hill. 1994. Isotopic evidence for Neogene hominid paleoenvironments in the Kenya Rift Valley. *Science* 264:955–959.

Kinzey, W., and M. A. Norconk. 1990. Hardness as a basis of fruit choice in two sympatric primates. *American Journal of Physical Anthropology* 81:5–15.

Kritchevsky, D., and C. Bonfield, (eds.). 1997. *Dietary Fiber in Health and Disease*. New York: Plenum Press.

Kuroda, S., T. Nishihara, S. Suzuki, and R. A. Oko. 1996. Sympatric chimpanzees and gorillas in the Ndoki Forest, Congo. In *Great Ape Societies* (W. C. McGrew, L. Marchant, and T. Nishida, eds.), pp. 71–81. Cambridge: Cambridge University Press.

Lambert, J. E. 1998. Primate digestion: interactions among anatomy, physiology, and feeding ecology. *Evolutionary Anthropology* 7:8–20.

Leakey, M. G., C. S. Feibel, I. McDougall, and A. Walker. 1995. New four-million-year-old hominid species from Kanapoi and Allia Bay, Kenya. *Nature* 376:565–571.

Lee Thorp, J. A., N. J. van der Merwe, and C. K. Brain. 1994. Diet of *Australopithecus robustus* at Swartkrans from stable carbon isotopic analysis. *Journal of Human Evolution* 27:361–372.

Leighton, M. 1993. Modeling dietary selectivity by Bornean orangutans: evidence for integration of multiple criteria for fruit selection. *International Journal of Primatology* 14:257–313.

Malenky, R. K., S. Kuroda, E. O. Vineberg, and R. W. Wrangham. 1994. The significance of terrestrial herbaceous foods for bonobos, chimpanzees, and gorillas. In *Chimpanzee Cultures* (R. W. Wrangham, W. C. McGrew, F. B. M. de Waal, P. G. Heltne, and L. A. Marquardt, eds.), pp. 59–76. Cambridge, MA: Harvard University Press.

Martin, R. D. 1984. Body size, brain size and feeding strategies. In *Food Acquisition and Processing in Primates* (D. J. Chivers, B. A. Wood, and A. Bilsborough, eds.), pp. 73–103. New York: Plenum Press.

McGrew, W. C. 1992. *Chimpanzee Material Culture: Implications for Human Evolution*. Cambridge: Cambridge University Press.

Milton, K. 1984. The role of food-processing factors in primate food choice. In *Adaptations for Foraging in Nonhuman Primates: Contributions to an Organismal Biology of Prosimians, Monkeys, and Apes* (P. S. Rodman and J. G. H. Cant, eds.), pp. 249–279. New York: Columbia University Press.

Milton, K. 1999. Meat-eating in human evolution: painting one's way out of an evolutionary corner. *Evolutionary Anthropology* 8:11–21.

Moore, J. 1992. "Savanna" chimpanzees. In *Topics in Primatology, Vol. I: Human Origins* (T. Nishida, W. C. McGrew, P. Marler, M. Pickford, and F. B. M. de Waal, eds.), pp. 99–118. Tokyo: University of Tokyo Press.

Moore, J. 1996. Savanna chimpanzees, referential models and the last common ancestor. In *Great Ape Societies* (W. C. McGrew, L. Marchant, and T. Nishida, eds.), pp. 275–292. Cambridge: Cambridge University Press.

Morgan, M. E., J. D. Kingston, and B. D. Marino. 1994. Carbon isotopic evidence for the emergence of C4 plants in the Neogene from Pakistan and Kenya. *Nature* 367:162–165.

Murray, S. S., M. J. Schoeninger, H. T. Bunn, T. R. Pickering, and J. A. Marlett. 1999. Nutritional composition of some wild plant foods and honey used by Hadza foragers of northern Tanzania. *Journal of Food Composition and Analysis* submitted.

Nishida, T. 1989. A note on the chimpanzee ecology of the Ugalla area, Tanzania. *Primates* 30:129–138.

O'Connell, J. F., K. Hawkes, and N. G. Blurton Jones. 1999. Grandmothering and the evolution of *Homo erectus*. *Journal of Human Evolution* 36:461–485.

Peres, C. A. 1991. Seed predation of *Cariniana micrantha* (Lecythidaceae) by brown capuchin monkeys in central Amazonia. *Biotropica* 23:262–270.

Peters, C. R. 1987. Nut-like oil seeds: food for monkeys, chimpanzees, humans, and probably ape-men. *American Journal of Physical Anthropology* 73:333–363.

Reed, K. E. 1997. Early hominid evolution and ecological change through the African Plio-Pleistocene. *Journal of Human Evolution* 32:289–322.

Remis, M. J. 1997. Ranging and grouping patterns of a western lowland gorilla group at Bai Hokou, Central African Republic. *American Journal of Primatology* 43:111–133.

Rodman, P. S., and H. M. McHenry. 1980. Bioenergetics and the origin of hominid bipedalism. *American Journal of Physical Anthropology* 52:103–106.

Rogers, M. E., F. Maisels, E. A. Williamson, M. Fernandez, and C. E. G. Tutin. 1990. Gorilla diet in the Lope' Reserve, Gabon: a nutritional analysis. *Oecologia* 84:326–339.

Rogers, M. E., B. C. Voysey, K. E. McDonald, R. J. Parnell, and C. E. G. Tutin. 1998. Lowland gorillas and seed dispersal: the importance of nest sites. *American Journal of Primatology* 45:45–68.

Ryan, A. S., and D. C. Johanson. 1989. Anterior dental microwear in *Australopithecus afarensis*: comparisons with human and nonhuman Primates. *Journal of Human Evolution* 18:235–268.

Schoeninger, M. J., H. T. Bunn, S. S. Murray, T. R. Pickering, and J. A. Marlett. 1999a. Nutritional composition of tubers used by Hadza foragers of northern Tanzania. *Journal of Food Composition and Analysis* submitted.

Schoeninger, M. J., J. Moore, and J. M. Sept. 1999b. Subsistence strategies of two "savanna" chimpanzee populations: the stable isotope evidence. *American Journal of Primatology* in press.

Sept, J. M. 1990. Vegetation studies in the Semliki Valley, Zaire as a guide to paleoanthropological research. *Virginia Museum of Natural History Memoir Series* 1:95–121.

Sikes, N. E. 1994. Early hominid habitat preferences in East Africa: Paleosol carbon isotopic evidence. *Journal of Human Evolution* 27:25–46.

Sponheimer, M., and J. A. Lee Thorp. 1999. Isotopic evidence for the diet of an early hominid, *Australopithecus africanus*. *Science* 283:368–370.

Stahl, A. B. 1984. Hominid dietary selection before fire. *Current Anthropology* 25:151–168.

Stanford, C. B. 1998. *Chimpanzee and Red Colobus: The Ecology of Predator and Prey.* Cambridge, MA: Harvard University Press.

Steklis, H. D., J. M. Sept, J. W. K. Harris, and S. Cachel. 1992. Ethnoarchaeological investigations of chimpanzees in a gallery forest in eastern Zaire. Research Report submitted to *National Geographic Society*.

Steudel, K. 1996. Limb morphology, bipedal gait, and energetics of hominid locomotion. *American Journal of Physical Anthropology* 99:345–355.

Strait, S. G. 1997. Tooth use and the physical properties of food. *Evolutionary Anthropology* 5:199–211.

Suzuki, A. 1969. An ecological study of chimpanzees in a savanna woodland. *Primates* 10:103–148.

Teaford, M. F., and A. C. Walker. 1984. Quantitative differences in dental microwear between primate species with different diets and a comment on the presumed diet of *Sivapithecus*. *American Journal of Physical Anthropology* 64:191–200.

Tutin, C. E. G. 1996. Ranging and social structure of lowland gorillas in the Lope Reserve, Gabon. In *Great Ape Societies* (W. C. McGrew, L. Marchant, and T. Nishida, eds.), pp. 58–70. Cambridge: Cambridge University Press.

Tutin, C. E. G., and M. Fernandez. 1993. Composition of the diet of chimpanzees and comparisons with that of sympatric lowland gorillas in the Lopé Reserve, Gabon. *American Journal of Primatology* 30:195–211.

Ungar, P. 1998. Dental allometry, morphology, and wear as evidence for diet in fossil primates. *Evolutionary Anthropology* 6:205–217.

Vincent, A. 1984. Plant foods in savanna environments: a preliminary report of tubers eaten by the Hadza of northern Tanzania. *World Archaeology* 17:132–148.

Waller, D. M. 1979. Models of mast fruiting in trees. *Journal of Theoretical Biology* 80:223–232.

Ward, C., M. Leakey, and A. Walker. 1999. The new hominid species *Australopithecus anamensis*. *Evolutionary Anthropology* 7:197–205.

Watts, D. P. 1996. Comparative socio-ecology of gorillas. In *Great Ape Societies* (W. C. McGrew, L. Marchant, and T. Nishida, eds.), pp. 16–28. Cambridge: Cambridge University Press.

White, F. J. 1996. Comparative socio-ecology of *Pan paniscus*. In *Great Ape Societies* (W. C. McGrew, L. Marchant, and T. Nishida, eds.), pp. 29–45. Cambridge: Cambridge University Press.

White, T. D., G. Suwa, and B. Asfaw. 1994. *Australopithecus ramidus*, a new species of early hominid from Aramis, Ethiopia. *Nature* 371:306–312.

Woodburn, J. C. 1968. An introduction to Hadza ecology. In *Man the Hunter* (R. Lee and I. DeVore, eds.), pp. 49–55. Chicago: Aldine.

Wrangham, R. W., C. A. Chapman, and L. J. Chapman. 1994. Seed dispersal by forest chimpanzees in Uganda. *Journal of Tropical Ecology* 10:355–368.

Wrangham, R. W., C. A. Chapman, A. P. Clark-Arcadi, and G. Isabirye-Basuta. 1996. Social ecology of Kanyawara chimpanzees: implications for understanding the costs of great ape groups. In *Great Ape Societies* (W. C. McGrew, L. Marchant, and T. Nishida, eds.), pp. 45–57. Cambridge: Cambridge University Press.

Wrangham, R. W., N. L. Conklin-Brittain, and K. D. Hunt. 1998. Dietary response of chimpanzees and cercopithecines to seasonal variation in fruit abundance. I. Antifeedants. *International Journal of Primatology* 19:949–970.

Wrangham, R. W., J. H. Jones, G. Laden, D. Pilbeam, and N. Conklin-Brittain. 1999. The raw and the stolen: cooking and the ecology of human origins. *Current Anthropology* 40:567–594.

Yamagiwa, J., T. Maruhashi, T. Yumoto, and N. Mwanza. 1996. Dietary and ranging overlap in sympatric gorillas and chimpanzees in Kahuzi-Biega National Park, Zaire. In *Great Ape Societies* (W. C. McGrew, L. Marchant, and T. Nishida, eds.), pp. 82–100. Cambridge: Cambridge University Press.

Part III

Modern Human Foragers

10

Hunting, Power Scavenging, and Butchering by Hadza Foragers and by Plio-Pleistocene *Homo*

Henry T. Bunn

Introduction

The evolutionary significance of meat in human forager diet and adaptations is a long-standing and contentious issue in anthropology. A common view among Plio-Pleistocene archaeologists (e.g., Isaac 1984) acknowledges a marked average difference between the dietary meat percentage among extant nonhuman primates (particularly chimpanzees) and human foragers, with meat percentages of up to several percent versus 20–40%, respectively. From that perspective, central research questions for understanding the early evolution of the genus *Homo* from a more ape-like ancestral hominid are when did such a marked increase in meat-eating occur, and how did that influence the overall behavioral ecology of the genus?

When taphonomic analyses of Plio-Pleistocene archaeological bone assemblages from Olduvai and Koobi Fora were conducted in the late 1970s and 1980s, strong patterning in skeletal element profiles and in bone modifications emerged, prompting diverse behavioral interpretations. Those include: significant meat and fat consumption from hominid hunting and scavenging, with transport and sharing of carcasses (Isaac 1978; Bunn et al. 1980, Bunn 1981); minimal meat and marrow consumption from passive scavenging of already consumed and abandoned carnivore kills (Binford 1981); and scavenging for raw materials (i.e., skin and tendons) rather than for meat (Potts and Shipman 1981). In other words, researchers viewed the Plio-Pleistocene bone patterning as strongly supporting aspects of Isaac's "home base and food-sharing" model, or as seriously undermining it. In the home base model, Isaac (e.g., 1978) argued that because the cooccurrences of stone tools and bones of diverse animals at Plio-Pleistocene archaeological sites resembled the remains discarded by modern human foragers at their base camps, a human-like behavioral package, including a gender-based division of labor, food transport to home bases, and food-sharing, also existed among Plio-Pleistocene hominids.

The ensuing debates encouraged many detailed studies of diverse modern analogues, and that trend is ongoing. As a result, researchers are in a much stronger position than 15 years ago to link taphonomic processes with some of the bone patterning actually documented in Plio-Pleistocene faunal assemblages. This chapter contributes to that research effort by summarizing some of the dynamics of meat acquisition and use by Hadza foragers at Lake Eyasi, Tanzania, and by comparing butchery patterns in bone assemblages generated by the Hadza with relevant data from the 1.75-million-year-old FLK Zinj site at Olduvai (Leakey 1971) to provide insight on meat acquisition and use by early *Homo*.

Hadza Diet

Meat from an abundant and diverse fauna is an unpredictable yet highly valued food resource among the Hadza, whose lifestyle and ecological setting in the Lake Eyasi basin in northern Tanzania are described elsewhere. Meat (used here to include all edible carcass tissues) is their favorite food in a diet that otherwise consists of diverse tubers, berries, baobab, and other fruits, nuts, and honey from several species of bees. Hadza foragers are commonly cited in the literature for subsisting on a diet composed of 20% meat and honey and 80% plants. Cultural anthropologist James Woodburn, whose field research in the late 1950s and early 1960s was the ultimate source of that diet estimate, also identified meat as the favorite food of the Hadza. More recent anthropological studies have added greatly to an understanding of the Hadza adaptation (e.g., Woodburn 1964, 1968a, 1968b, 1972, 1980; Vincent 1985; Bunn et al. 1988; O'Connell et al. 1988; Hawkes et al. 1989), although estimating the actual composition of Hadza diet has proven to be much more complex than Woodburn's percentages indicate. In favorable years, seasons, and areas of the Hadza landscape with a greater abundance of animals than characterized the particular setting of Woodburn's study, meat alone certainly constitutes much more than 20% of the Hadza diet.

Hadza Carcass Acquisition

The Hadza obtain carcasses by a combination of both hunting and scavenging strategies. Hadza men do all of the hunting, using powerful long bows and a variety of wooden and metal-tipped poisoned arrows. Both men and women scavenge, although most scavenging is accomplished by men, probably because their much longer foraging distances provide more scavenging opportunities. Two independent studies have each shown that Hadza hunting produces 80% of the carcasses, while scavenging yields 20% (e.g., Bunn 1993; Bunn et al. 1988; O'Connell et al. 1988). The scavenging figure is significant and helps to establish that scavenging is a viable strategy for obtaining carcasses, rather than some primitive precursor to hunting.

The Hadza practice two methods of hunting. The more common of the two occurs daily, on a year-round basis, any time an individual male or small group of males walks out of camp. Because they are always armed with their bows and a selection of arrows, Hadza men use hunting and scavenging opportunities to shoot animals whenever they are walking. The other hunting technique, ambush hunting from blinds, is productive only in the dry season, when lying in wait at water holes or along game trails leading to water holes yields high-quality shots from close range.

Scavenging for carcasses is a popular subsistence strategy among the Hadza for obtaining essentially cost-free, high-quality food. Hadza scavenging is an opportunistic activity that may occur whenever men or women are out walking around the landscape. Telltale signals, including circling or descending vultures, vultures in a tree, the presence of carnivores, etc., are likely to be investigated by the Hadza. The most productive scavenging strategy is power scavenging, which involves confronting carnivores and forcibly driving them from their kills (Bunn 1996). Depending on the timing relative to the carnivore feeding episode, among other factors, power scavenging can yield essentially fresh, whole carcasses. Power scavenging is easiest to accomplish against small, timid, or solitary carnivores, such as jackals, cheetahs, or leopards, but given prey size preferences, scavenging from lions is more likely to yield quantities of meat. As one Hadza put it to me, "Taking dik-diks from leopards is like drinking chai [tea]" and is a marginal food source. Late-access, secondary scavenging from abandoned carcasses is also generally unproductive for the Hadza because the primary predators, or hyenas, leave little edible tissue to scavenge.

Primary Butchery, Meat Distribution, and Carcass Transport

The substantial investment by Hadza foragers in the acquisition and use of large animal carcasses leads to distinctive bone assemblages on the landscape—at kill sites, snack sites, hunting blinds, base camps—in terms of skeletal element profiles (e.g., Bunn 1993; Bunn et al. 1988; O'Connell et al. 1988). On a finer scale, details in the observed processing of carcasses are preserved as butchery marks on individual bones. Without doubt, that dedicated involvement with carcasses and bones establishes the Hadza, and the bone assemblages they produce, as a prime source of analogue information on the landscape-wide composition of bone assemblages and their behavioral correlates and on bone damage resulting from the work of knowledgeable butchers. Such patterning resulting from known Hadza behavior facilitates comparisons with the principal Plio-Pleistocene archaeological bone assemblages from East Africa, particularly the large assemblage from the FLK Zinj excavation at Olduvai (Leakey 1971).

Although there are obvious limitations to comparisons between the behavior and archaeological residues of modern foragers and those of temporally remote, prehistoric foragers, particularly comparisons that span the entire Pleistocene and involve a different species of hominid, useful insights commonly result. In justification of the use of a Hadza analogue for understanding aspects of the behavioral ecology of early *Homo*, there are some significant parallels between the two. First, there are broad ecological similarities between the two contexts. Both the Hadza and Plio-Pleistocene *Homo* at Olduvai (e.g., Hay 1976; Plummer and Bishop 1994) live(d) in Rift Valley, alkaline lake basins with fresh-water streams providing essential drinking water and a mosaic of savanna-bush-woodland plant communities providing the staple foods in mainly plant-based diets. Both ecosystems include(d) an abundant and diverse fauna, which is/was also utilized in the diet. Even though many of the behavioral responses to similar foraging opportunities by the Hadza and by early *Homo* probably differed, just as occurs among the Hadza themselves on different occasions, both the Hadza and early *Homo* share(d) some of the same basic subsistence challenges, and they certainly overlap in archaeologically visible ways in some behavioral responses.

The utilization of carcasses of large animals as a food source constitutes a prime example. In both cases, the foraging strategy includes a reliance on cutting and pounding tools to butcher carcasses systematically and an energy investment in the repeated transport of carcass portions to favored central locations on the landscape for further butchery and consumption (e.g., Bunn 1997; Bunn and Kroll 1986, 1988). As dedicated butchers with a lifetime of expertise in the efficient skinning, disarticulation, defleshing and marrow-processing of carcasses, the Hadza constitute a far superior analogue than any experimental butchery by inexperienced researchers for understanding the butchery practices of early *Homo*.

There are also some sobering limitations to comparisons between butchery by Hadza and by early *Homo*. Modern human intellect and physical capabilities obviously characterize the Hadza. The Hadza use steel knives and small steel axes as primary butchery tools, and they use rounded granite hammerstones for breaking open marrow-rich bones. They also boil some bones, particularly chopped-up axial skeletal elements, to render the fat contained within them. Hadza social system, group size, and food-sharing networks all influence the degree of carcass and bone segmentation during processing.

In marked contrast, there is early *Homo*. Depending on which species of early *Homo* (or *Australopithecus*) one wishes to implicate as a dominant factor responsible for the butchered bones at the 1.75-million-year-old FLK Zinj site, the contrast varies but is severe in all cases. A smaller and differently organized brain in early *Homo* implies different and lesser intellect than modern people possess. Greater physical strength in early *Homo*, particularly if a large-bodied species such as *H. erectus* was the toolmaker and butcher at FLK Zinj, raises the possibility that some butchery tasks performed with tools by modern people may have been accomplished through physical strength by early *Homo*, without the use of cutting tools and without consequent tool-inflicted bone damage. The tools used in butchery at FLK Zinj were Oldowan stone flakes and hammerstones. For some, but not all, butchery tasks, the stone flakes/knives probably resemble metal knives in functional potential; for example, stone flakes are reasonably efficient in skinning and defleshing tasks, but they are less efficient than metal knives in disarticulating tightly connected joints. Much remains to be learned about the relationships between cutmarks inflicted using stone and metal knives. The lack of a known boiling technology at 1.75 million years ago and unknown social relationships and food-sharing networks also may have influenced carcass-processing decisions and bone damage by early *Homo*.

Finally, and as many have observed elsewhere, there is an inherent risk in employing modern people as an analogue for reconstructing past human behavior, when the basic question being investigated is how did the behavior of prehistoric humans differ from that of modern humanity (e.g., Wobst 1978; Kelley 1995).

With these many analytical and interpretive challenges acknowledged, let us now embark on a specific comparison of the Hadza and early *Homo* and see where it leads. For present purposes, the emphasis will be on butchery patterns with two analytical approaches in mind. First, a visual, qualitative comparison is presented, using composite drawings of cutmarks on bones from FLK Zinj and from two recent Hadza base camps. Then, a quantitative method is used to compare the same data using simple bar graphs.

Cutmarks on Limb Bones: A Comparison of Olduvai and Hadza Bone Assemblages

The behavioral meaning of cutmarks on bones is straightforward enough at first glance. Finding the linear, slicing grooves inflicted by a butcher using a knife logically implies that a carcass was being cut up. From the anatomical location and orientation of cutmarks, it is also reasonable to predict that specific cutmarks can be linked to specific kinds of butchery tasks, such as skinning, dismembering, and defleshing. Twenty years ago, just finding cutmarks for the first time on various skeletal elements from Plio-Pleistocene sites provided a satisfactory, interim means of demonstrating that ancient hominds were involved in all of these steps in animal butchery.

In light of some recent alternative hypotheses about the nature of carcass acquisition and use by early *Homo*, however, it becomes important to seek more explicit information about the meaning of particular cutmark patterns. Carnivore-exploitation hypotheses, for example, envision hominids taking advantage of large carnivores' speed and ability to kill large prey by aggressively driving them from their fresh and largely intact kills. Such power scavenging would yield large quantities of meat and require intensive butchery similar to hunting (Bunn and Ezzo 1993; Bunn 1996). Alternatively, carnivore-avoidance hypotheses envision more timid hominids passively scavenging to obtain edible remnants of meat and fat from carcasses already largely defleshed by primary predators (e.g., Binford 1981, 1984, 1986; Blumenschine 1987; Blumenschine and Cavallo 1993). In that case, much less intensive butchery would be required. Predictions regarding butchery intensity and cutmark patterns are different for the two alternative hypotheses. If there is a direct relationship between butchery intensity and cutmark frequency, then power scavenging, hunting, and more generally, thorough butchery of complete carcasses should produce more cutmarks on bones, while passive, marginal scavenging of largely defleshed carcasses should produce fewer cutmarks. Why, for example, inflict defleshing cutmarks on bones that have already been defleshed by carnivores? Even partial defleshing by carnivores reveals where the surface of the bone is, which enables the butcher to avoid hitting it with the knife (which would only be dulled by contacting the bone and producing a cutmark). It follows from such reasoning that observing different frequencies and patterns of cutmarks on two meat-bearing skeletal elements *could* indicate that the one with fewer cutmarks had less meat on it when it was butchered. To illustrate the implications of these arguments, a series of composite drawings of cutmarks on limb bones from FLK Zinj and from a Hadza base camp are compared.

The bone assemblage from the FLK Zinj excavation conducted by M. D. Leakey (1971) includes approximately 3,500 skeletally identifiable bone specimens, of which more than 200 retain well-preserved cutmarks (Bunn 1981; Bunn and Kroll 1986). Most limb bones were fragmented by hominids during marrow processing, and most of the cutmarks from the assemblage occur on those fragmented limb specimens (Bunn and Kroll 1986, 1988; Capaldo and Blumenschine 1994; Oliver 1994). The composite views were produced by drawing the individual cutmarks to scale and in correct anatomical position from limb specimens of different taxa, different animal sizes, and different sides of the skeleton, all onto one set of whole-bone drawings of the appropriate limb element. For several limb elements, four right-angle views are provided, although each cutmark is drawn only once. For purposes of analyzing patterns in the anatomical clustering of cutmarks, there is some overlap in the bone surface covered in two adjacent views, and there is a degree of arbitrariness in the appearance of a specific cutmark on one view or on the adjacent view; for example, a series of cutmarks occurring on the distal, posteromedial shaft of the humerus could be drawn accurately on either the posterior view or on the medial view of the bone. It is also noteworthy that the representation of different portions of whole limb elements (and any cutmarks on them) is not always equal. In the case of FLK Zinj, that is dictated by the taphonomic history of the assemblage, and the surviving sample is simply all that is available for analysis. Particular limb epiphyses (proximal humerus, proximal and distal femur, and proximal tibia) are underrepresented relative to comprehensive, whole-bone minimum number of element (MNE) estimates, probably resulting from removal by scavenging carnivores, and the paucity of cutmarks in those anatomical areas may reflect only that taphonomic factor. In the case of the Hadza sample, taphonomic loss of bones from scavenging carnivores is greatly reduced. The sample is from two Hadza base camps at localities named Sanola (Bunn 1993) and Bashana (Bunn et al. 1988), where the Hadza residents, by their sustained presence in the camp, unintentionally protected the bones from scavenging carnivores until all but the freshest ones had lost their appeal to scavengers. For this preliminary study, an effort was made to achieve a sample size comparable to FLK Zinj and a representative coverage of all portions of the limb elements, although midshaft specimens are still probably underrepresented.

Figure 10.1 shows composite views of all of the cutmarks on humerus and on femur specimens from the FLK Zinj site at Olduvai. Although the sample sizes (i.e., the comprehensive estimate of the MNE) are comparable for the humeri (MNE = 20) and femora (MNE = 22) at FLK Zinj, there are clearly more cutmarks on humeri than on femora. Using the reasoning outlined above, it *could* be argued that the femora, elements that start with significantly more meat than humeri, had much less meat on them when hominids butchered them. Given the known sequence by which carnivores consume carcasses (abdominal organs and hindlimbs first, chest

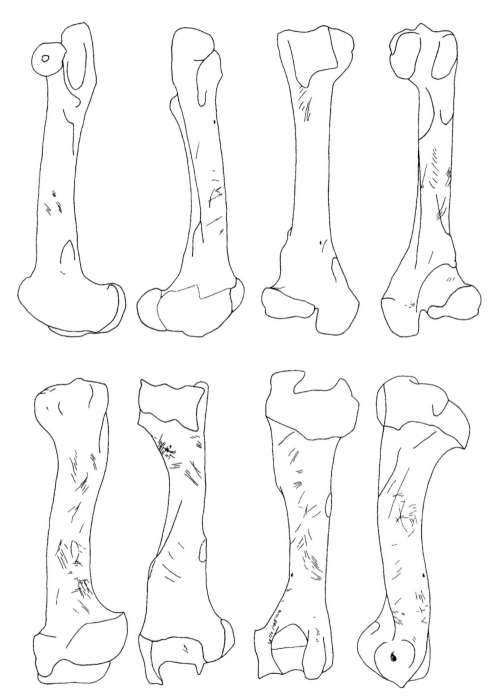

Figure 10.1. Composite cutmarks on humerus (top) and femur (bottom) specimens from FLK Zinj.

organs and forelimbs later) (Kruuk 1972; Schaller 1972; Blumenschine 1987), the humerus-femur pattern of cutmarks at FLK Zinj *could* be viewed as support for the passive, marginal scavenging hypothesis. But is enough known about the form and function of cutmarks to reach that conclusion? The answer is a resounding "No."

Being experienced butchers of complete, intact carcasses, the Hadza generate bone assemblages with the potential to provide useful information on the meaning of different cutmark patterns. Figure 10.2 provides composite views of humerus and femur cutmarks from Hadza butchery of fully fleshed bones, again with sample size held reasonably constant. As at FLK Zinj, there is a marked difference in the frequency of cutmarks on humeri (MNE = 24) and femora (MNE = 22), even though it is known in the Hadza case that all of the meat was present on the bones at the time of butchery. It turns out that there is no simple relationship between cutmark frequency and amount of meat present. Rather, cutmark frequency is directly proportional to the strength of muscle attachments, and those differ significantly for the different limb elements. The meat is more tightly attached to humeri than femora, and many more cutmarks are likely to result from full defleshing of humeri than of femora. The pattern at FLK Zinj is completely consistent with thorough defleshing of both elements by hominids and with hominid access to complete carcasses. Furthermore, comparisons between composite cutmark patterns on the other meat-bearing limb elements from FLK Zinj and from the Hadza also exhibit strong similarities in the clustering of cutmarks around areas of strong muscle attachments [Figure 10.3 shows the tibia (FLK Zinj MNE e= 31; Hadza MNE = 21).

An alternative, quantitative approach to cutmark analysis is presented below. For present purposes, a preliminary analysis of the same cutmark data used in Figures 10.1 and 10.2 is provided, both to illustrate the methodology with the relatively large sample of humerus cutmarks from FLK Zinj and the Hadza camps and to explore whether or not similar or different overall patterns in the anatomical distribution of cutmarks characterize the two contexts.

There are some real theoretical and methodological challenges inherent in this analysis. In theory, it is possible to predict that similar overall patterns in the anatomical distribution of humerus cutmarks in the two samples should indicate overall similarity of the forelimbs being butchered and of the butchery tasks and yields being achieved. More specifically, similar cutmark patterns should indicate similar amounts of meat present, similar conditions of joints, similar defleshing activity and meat yields, similar disarticulating activity, and vice versa. By restricting the comparison to the same skeletal element in the two samples, the strength of muscle attachment is held constant, so that it can be argued that different intensities of defleshing cutmarks imply different amounts of meat present and different meat yields from the defleshing activity. Conversely, similar intensities of defleshing cutmarks imply similar access to and processing of meat. Carcass size should also be incorporated into this reasoning, but because of space limitations, that will be pursued elsewhere.

It is, of course, possible to start with a largely defleshed bone and then experimentally slice away at the visible muscle attachment areas, as Selvaggio (1994) has shown. That would conceivably produce similar patterns of cuts from different

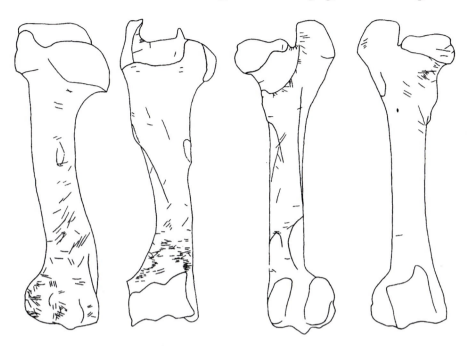

Figure 10.2. Composite cutmarks on humerus (right) and femur (left) specimens from Hadza butchery. For analysis of cutmark distribution, the humerus is divided into five portions (top left margin). The portions are defined as follows: distal epiphysis, which ends at the point of fusion with the shaft; distal shaft, which extends from the point of fusion with the distal epiphysis to a line passing through the posterolateral nutrient foramen and circumscribing the shaft perpendicular to the long axis of the bone; midshaft, which extends from the boundary with the distal shaft to a line passing through the distal end of the deltoid tuberosity and through the proximal end of the teres major tubercle; proximal shaft, which extends from the mid-shaft boundary to the point of fusion with the proximal epiphysis; proximal epiphysis.

amounts of meat being defleshed. I would suggest, however, that butchers with any interest in preserving the sharpness of their knife blades are not going to repeatedly hack into the visible bone surfaces when the adhering meat can be shaved free without hitting the bone directly enough to produce cutmarks. Butchers do not intentionally slice directly into visible bone surfaces. Cutmarks are mistakes; they are accidental miscalculations of the precise location of the bone surface when muscle masses obscure it. As soon as the butcher can see the bone surface, few if any cutmarks will be inflicted thereafter in that area.

From a methodological standpoint, any comparison of cutmarks made by stone tools with cutmarks made by metal tools must acknowledge that for a given butchery task, the quantitative relationship between stone and metal-induced cutmarks is simply not known. There are a few statements in the literature that suggest that metal knives produce more cutmarks than stone knives, but more experimental work with stone-tool butchery, problematic as it is, needs to be conducted. For present

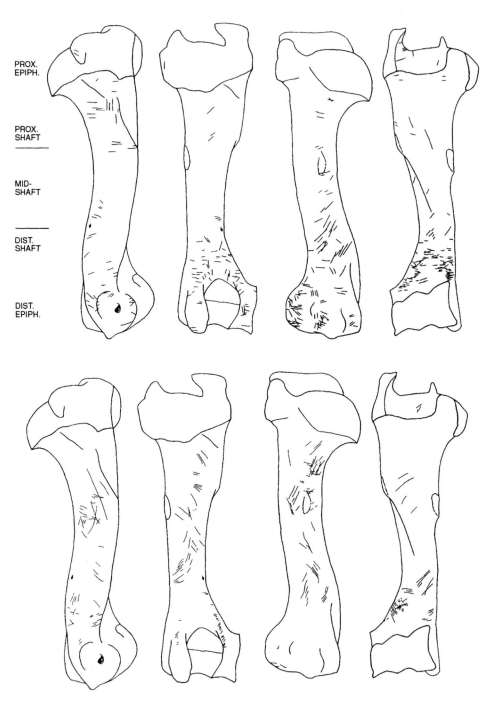

PROX.
EPIPH.

PROX.
SHAFT

MID-
SHAFT

DIST.
SHAFT

DIST.
EPIPH.

Figure 10.3. (TOP) Composite cutmarks on tibia from FLK Zinj; (BOTTOM) Composite cutmarks on tibia from Hadza.

purposes, the analysis relies on the logic that the anatomical locations of clusters of defleshing cutmarks identify areas of muscle attachment and imply, furthermore, that most if not all of the muscle meat was present (and obscuring the precise location of the bone surface) at the time of butchery. Similarly, cutmarks on limb shaft portions lacking muscle meat such as the distal radius shaft, distal tibia shaft, and metapodial shafts, imply skinning or the severing of tendons; cutmarks on or immediately adjacent to the articular facets of limb epiphyses imply disarticulating. Conversely, the lack of cutmarks in locations known from control data (i.e., the Hadza) to require heavy cutting, such as strong muscle attachments or tightly articulated joints, indicates that a particular task was not being done, at least not very thoroughly. A lack of defleshing cutmarks on an area of strong muscle attachment could indicate that the muscle meat was not present at the time of butchery. Some of the more problematic experimental work noted above challenges this simple, basic logic (e.g., Selvaggio 1994; see also Blumenschine 1986).

A final aspect of the logic of the present analysis is that these general relationships between cutmark locations and butchery tasks should apply regardless of the type of hand-held knife being used, at least in terms of the location if not the quantity of cutmarks.

To avoid the uncertainty of the quantitative relationship between stone and metal-induced cutmarks, the two data sets in this analysis are not compared directly as a measure of butchery intensity. Rather, the stone knife-induced cutmarks from FLK Zinj are compared with each other according to their anatomical distribution on different portions of the humerus specimens. Similarly, the metal knife-induced cutmarks from the Hadza camp are compared with each other by anatomical distribution. To achieve the comparison, the humerus was schematically divided into five roughly equal portions using anatomical landmarks as the boundaries between adjacent portions (see Figure 10.2). The number of cutmarks in each humerus portion was then counted and converted to a percentage of the total number of cutmarks on all humerus specimens. That exercise yields two independent sets of percentages, each expressing how cutmarks made by stone knives, and separately those made by metal knives, are distributed along the length of the humerus. Finally, those results are presented as bar graphs and juxtaposed.

Notably, this methodology avoids a serious biasing effect that is inherent in all of the gnaw-mark data from hyena feeding experiments and from small carnivore gnawing at FLK Zinj reported by Blumenschine and colleagues using a related method (Blumenschine 1988; Blumenschine and Selvaggio 1991; Marean et al. 1992; Blumenschine and Marean 1993; Capaldo 1997). By their method, the limb element is divided into the following catergories: epiphyseal fragment, which may or may not include an attached portion of shaft; near-epiphysis fragment of shaft; mid-shaft fragment. Specimens with gnaw marks in any location are counted as gnawed in one of the above categories and eventually converted to a percentage of the total number of gnawed specimens. For example, a specimen comprising an epiphysis plus some shaft, with a single cluster of gnaw marks located only on the shaft (which could easily be a mid-shaft or a near-epiphysis shaft location), would, by the method of Blumenschine and colleagues, be coded and counted as a gnawed epiphyseal specimen. That method does not express where a modification is actually located on the limb element. Interassemblage differences in breakage patterns that are independent of how bones were gnawed would, using the method of Blumenschine and colleagues, produce contrasting results for two assemblages of identically gnawed bones.

Figure 10.4 presents bar graphs showing the percentage distribution of humerus cutmarks by humerus portion for the Hadza sample and for FLK Zinj. The Hadza data, as a control, show the distribution of cutmarks by humerus portion from thorough defleshing and disarticulation of fully fleshed, intact humeri. Most of the Hadza cutmarks occur on the distal shaft, from defleshing, and on the proximal and distal epiphyses, from disarticulating. The FLK Zinj data, as the unknown, show strong similarities to the Hadza data in the distribution of defleshing cutmarks on the distal and proximal shafts but marked differences in the percentages of cutmarks on the epiphyses and on midshafts.

Differences in epiphyseal cutmarks in the two samples result from taphonomic biasing and from actual, known differences in butchery tasks. The FLK Zinj humerus specimens exhibit a taphonomic bias against proximal epiphyses. Those are hammerstone-broken bones and were probably transported as whole bones and whole articulated limb units to the site, where they were then defleshed and broken for marrow. The comprehensive MNE estimates for humeri as a whole are much higher than for the proximal epiphysis portion of the humerus, which indicates taphonomic loss of spongy and greasy proximal portions, probably from removal by scavenging hyenas after hominids abandoned the site (Bunn and Kroll 1986, 1988). Only two proximal humerus epiphyses (both small, size group 1, *Antidorcas recki* specimens) retain cutmarks, and in contrast to the Hadza sample, the extent to which proximal humerus epiphyses from FLK Zinj may have originally exhibited disarticulating cutmarks is simply not known.

The distal humerus epiphysis, being a denser and less greasy portion, is much less affected by such taphonomic biasing, and it is well represented at the Hadza camp and at FLK Zinj. There is a marked difference in the percentage of disarticulating cutmarks on distal epiphyses of humeri in the two contexts, which in this case does reflect a very different emphasis on disarticulating the elbow joint in the two contexts. The Hadza sample (Figure 10.2, medial view) shows abundant disarticulating cuts on the medial surface of the distal epiphysis, where it is necessary to cut during separation of the humerus from the tightly articulated radioulna. Similarly, the Hadza epiphysis bar graph in Figure 10.4 mostly reflects that same abundance of distal humerus cutmarks. Although that same bone portion is well represented at FLK Zinj, comparable disarticulating cutmarks are rare; only one specimen from a large (size group 3) bovid retains disarticulating cuts on the distal humerus epiphysis. Evidently, early *Homo* at FLK Zinj transported intact forelimb units to the site, defleshed them, and usually broke the humerus and radius for marrow without bothering to disarticulate the elbow joint. That result is unsurprising given that Mary Leakey's unpublished plan drawing of the excavation shows five elbow joints of bovids that she found in still-articulated position during the excavation. Interestingly, that also reveals that the abundant cutmarks on distal humerus shafts from FLK Zinj must result from significant defleshing of the bones rather than from disarticulating tasks that were not carried out on those forelimb units. The lower

% CUT MARKS ON HUMERUS SHAFTS

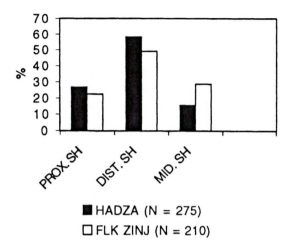

Figure 10.4. Percentage cutmarks on humerus portions from
FLK Zinj and from Hadza butchery.

incidence of midshaft cutmarks in the Hadza data probably reflects underrepresentation of midshaft portions in the Hadza bones used in this preliminary study. The most reasonable conclusions to reach from Figure 10.4 are that less disarticulating of elbow joints occurred at FLK Zinj than at the Hadza camps but that comparable, thorough defleshing of humeri with significant meat yields occurred at both sites.

Discussion and Conclusions

Despite differences in the physical and mental capabilities of the butchers and in their cutting tools, similar anatomical patterning of cutmarks indicates that both the Hadza and early *Homo* at Olduvai had access to intact carcasses of large animals and thoroughly butchered them for meat. Given the quantities of meat obtained, quantities much larger than one individual hominid could consume without drying it for later consumption, it seems probable that, like the Hadza, early *Homo* shared meat.

Both qualitative and quantitative anatomical approaches indicate broad similarities in cutmark patterns between a sample of butchered limbs from a Hadza base camp, where full access to meat and thorough butchery are not in doubt, and the total sample of butchered limb bones from the 1.75-million-year-old FLK Zinj bone assemblage, where access to meat and butchery tasks must be inferred. The virtually identical clusters of defleshing cutmarks on limb shafts and the similar pattern of the distribution of defleshing cutmarks on humeri indicate unambiguously that the emphasis of butchery in both cases was the defleshing of substantial quantities of meat.

Although the Hadza foraging adaptation is in all probability quite different from the foraging adaptation of early *Homo*, there are some significant parallels between the two contexts. In both contexts, repeated carcass transport to particular, favored central locations and thorough, systematic butchery focused on the meatiest limb portions of small and large carcasses are documented. Because both of those behaviors are lacking in chimpanzees, modern foragers provide a more appropriate analogue than chimps for reconstructing some of the foraging adaptations of early *Homo*. That is a simple but important point. The literature is replete with dire warnings about the inadvisability of using modern foragers as analogues for any prehistoric foragers (e.g., Wobst 1978; Kelly 1995). Such blanket dismissals are in serious need of revision so that the kinds of information that are inappropriate for use in prehistoric analogues are specified and distinguished from those that are appropriate. From the results of this study, it is clear that for some specific and significant kinds of information, modern foragers such as the Hadza provide a very appropriate and revealing source of information as analogues for clarifying some of the foraging adaptations of prehistoric foragers, including early *Homo*.

The abundant cutmarks at FLK Zinj provide strong evidence of systematic butchery and significant meat-eating by early *Homo*, but they do not by themselves reveal methods of carcass acquisition. When the cutmark patterns are combined with FLK Zinj skeletal profiles, which show an abundance of mandibles and the upper, meatiest limb bones rather than metapodials, the combination does help to define carcass condition and methods of carcass acquisition. Given the known sequence by which modern African carnivores consume carcasses, the abundance of the very limb elements at FLK Zinj that are defleshed and consumed early by carnivores *and* the abundance of defleshing cutmarks on those same bones in patterns equal to Hadza defleshing of intact limbs indicate that early *Homo* at FLK Zinj had repeated access to complete, intact carcasses of a full range of smaller and larger animals (Bunn and Kroll 1986; Bunn and Ezzo 1993; Bunn 1996).

Repeated access to complete, or even nearly complete, carcasses implies relatively rapid discovery and control of carcasses, probably within minutes or a few hours of the animal's death. Such acquisition could result from hunting, from power scavenging, from active searching (Tappen this volume), from incredible good fortune, or from a combination of the above. An adaptation focused solely on obtaining the relatively small amounts of marrow fat in limb bones of abandoned carnivore kills that had been largely defleshed and consumed after many hours or days of carnivore feeding would not produce the combination of limb proportions *and* defleshing cutmarks documented at FLK Zinj. It is, of course, possible for a relatively slow-moving, diurnal hominid to occasionally find a dead animal's carcass before a carnivore does, but barring incredible good fortune, it is unlikely that early *Homo* routinely outpaced the entire carnivore guild in that fashion. Although hunting of larger animals by early *Homo* remains a possibility, it is difficult to prove, given available evidence and approaches, particularly when a simpler explanation of the evidence—power scavenging—is available. As a form of interference competition, the term power scavenging simply describes the kind of widespread behavior that other carnivores and other primates practice. Individually smaller or weaker carnivores group together to mob larger carnivores at kills (Cooper 1991). Chimps mob and intimidate leopards by banding together (Boesch 1991). As indicated earlier, the Hadza find power scavenging the only productive form of scavenging. The most reasonable explanation of the FLK Zinj evidence is that large-bodied early *Homo*, too, was a power scavenger of large animals. Given the rapidity with which carnivores consume smaller carcasses, which makes *regular* access to them by any form of scavenging unlikely, the hunting of gazelle and smaller sized animals by early *Homo* is probable.

The compelling evidence of skeletal profiles and cutmarks from FLK Zinj provides a firm basis for reconstructing aspects of the meat-foraging strategies of 1.75-million-year-old *Homo*. The basic, patterned, factual evidence is not going away, although as new data and new analytical approaches become available, the interpretations of that evidence are likely to evolve. At one current interpretive extreme, advocates of carnivore-avoidance models attempt to minimize the meat-foraging capabilities and general humanness of 1.75-million-year-old *Homo*. By avoiding the factual evidence, Binford (e.g., 1986, 1988) stridently rejected the comprehensive MNE estimates for FLK Zinj, adhering to his belief that early *Homo* only had access to carcass residues such as metapodials rather than upper limb bones, despite a somewhat tedious, specimen-by-specimen demonstration that the comprehensive MNE patterns are, in fact, incontrovertible (Bunn and Kroll 1986, 1988). Blumenschine and Cavallo (1993) use the comprehensive MNE values from Bunn and Kroll (1986) to support the interpretation of a narrow scavenging niche in which early *Homo* only scavenged passively from largely defleshed carcasses, primarily for marrow fat from limb bones. But in making such an argument, they manage to avoid all reference to the relevant but unsupportive evidence of defleshing cutmarks that was published in the same article that they used for the MNE estimates. Such models would be strengthened if modified to accommodate all of the relevant evidence.

At the opposite interpretive extreme, one could advance an exaggerated version of Isaac's (1978) home base model, maximizing the capabilities and humanness of early *Homo* to the point where early *Homo* becomes virtually indistinguishable from modern humanity. No one advocates such a view, but it is worth pointing out that all current interpretations of the foraging adaptations of early *Homo* may seriously underestimate the actual behavioral sophistication of 1.75-million-year-old early *Homo*. To address that possibility, future models should at least allow for the recognition of more human-like behavior in early *Homo* in case it existed. Big-game hunting, division of labor, sleeping on the ground at base camps, language, etc., may all postdate the 1.75-million-year-old FLK Zinj site, and maybe by a very long time, but care should be taken in the formulation of testable hypotheses to enable recognition of such adaptations when they do first appear in human evolution.

The power scavenging and hunting model advanced herein attempts to identify some of the interpretive middle ground using available archaeological evidence from FLK Zinj. In an evolutionary perspective, the enhanced behavior and diet of early

Homo at 1.75 million years ago, relative to australopithecines, that emerge here, involving aggressive carcass acquisition, carcass transport, systematic butchery, and a marked dietary shift to significant amounts of high-quality meat and fat, are entirely consistent with evolutionary trends discovered in the hominid fossil record. The trends toward encephalization and consequent increased energy requirements (Leonard and Robertson 1994), dental reduction, and gut modification (Aiello and Wheeler 1995), all point to an increase in diet quality, specifically increased meat consumption, in early *Homo*.

Although none of those trends is evident in australopithecines as conventionally defined, Sponheimer and Lee-Thorp (1999) concluded recently from isotopic evidence that 2.5-million-year-old *Australopithecus africanus* may have consumed large quantities of animal tissues from large grazing ungulates. If correct, that would certainly impact understanding of the timing and magnitude of dietary shift to significant meat-eating in human evolution that is more commonly associated with early *Homo* (Schoeninger et al., this volume). But as Sponheimer and Lee-Thorp observe, the isotopic signature may also indicate that *A. africanus* ate grasses or grass-eating insects. The concluding statements of their paper are directly relevant here:

> Therefore, the primary dietary difference between *A. africanus* and *Homo* may not have been the quality of their food but their manner of procuring it. One key difference may have been that stone tools allowed *Homo* to disarticulate bones and exploit bone marrow from large carcasses (obtained through hunting or scavenging) that *A. africanus* could not. (Sponheimer and Lee-Thorp 1999:369)

It is difficult to reconcile that conclusion with their earlier statements on assumed tool use by *A. africanus* or with the evidence of butchery by early *Homo* at FLK Zinj. Sponheimer and Lee-Thorp (1999: 369) suggest that "presently there is no evidence that *A. africanus* used tools, although it is not unreasonable to assume that they could have used tools in the same manner as chimpanzees do today," and that "*P. robustus* . . . may have orally processed foods (such as *Schlerocarya* nuts) that *A. africanus* could only access with hammerstones (like chimpanzees use today)."

If *A. africanus* had hammerstones for cracking nuts, they had hammerstones for cracking large marrow bones, simply because the same hammerstones would be perfectly adequate for both tasks. As for the speculation of stone tools enabling *Homo* to disarticulate bones for accessing marrow, the reasoning needs to be expanded to provide a more balanced view of the possibilities. Cutting tools (which are beyond the known technological repertoire of wild chimps) used in the primary butchery of carcasses serve *three* functions: skinning, defleshing, and disarticulating. If available carcasses were intact, then some skinning and a lot of defleshing would have *necessarily* preceded any exploitation of marrow, which yields an image of *Homo* possessing a lot of meat and fat prior to breaking any bones for marrow fat. If, on the other hand, available carcasses were reduced nearly to bare-bone skeletons from feeding by one or more carnivore taxa prior to acquisition by *Homo*, then hominids focused on marrow processing could proceed directly to breaking limb bones with hammerstones without any need to skin, deflesh, or disarticulate anything; or if transport to another location was desired, then hominids could use cutting tools to disarticulate the bones into transportable portions and then turn to the hammerstones. Notably, neither of those last images involves skinning or defleshing, and neither predicts significant cutmarks from those butchery tasks. In essence, the last images being revisited are the carnivore-avoidance models in which early *Homo* is viewed as only able to exploit marrow fat or marginal tidbits of meat from abandoned, largely eaten carcass residues. Is that a realistic image of early *Homo*, given the physical adaptations and increased energy requirements noted above? The narrowly defined marrow niche yields high-energy fat, but there is simply not a lot of it in marrow bones. Perhaps that is a plausible explanation for how earliest *Homo* or their immediate ancestors may have become involved with exploiting carcasses in the Pliocene, although the abundance of sharp flakes in the oldest tool assemblages suggests otherwise. But the fact is, limb bone marrow constitutes only about 2% of total body fat in wild ungulate carcasses (Bunn and Ezzo 1993). If early *Homo* was interested in that 2% of total body fat, and, given the documentation of systematic hammerstone percussion notches, they were (Bunn 1981; Bunn and Kroll 1986, 1988), then why would they not be under selective pressure to procure more of the high quality food on carcasses, including the other 98% of total body fat and all of the meat? Why encephalize, if not to use the expanded brain to solve foraging challenges such as this? In fact, the compelling evidence from FLK Zinj indicates that early *Homo* at 1.75 million years ago was doing just that!

Acknowledgements   I thank Craig Stanford for inviting me to coorganize the conference and all of the participants for a most informative and enjoyable meeting! The research reported in this chapter was supported by generous grants from the National Science Foundation, the Wenner-Gren Foundation, the National Geographic Society, and the University of Wisconsin Graduate School Faculty Research Committee and Vilas Associate Program. The L. S. B. Leakey Foundation provided partial support for several weeks of museum research in 1989 at the National Museums of Kenya. I thank the Tanzania Commission for Science and Technology for research clearance to study the Olduvai collections and for research clearance to conduct long-term field research with the Hadza. The Hadza research would not have been possible without the cooperation, support, and friendly interest of the Hadza themselves, and I am forever indebted. My chapter has been improved by thoughtful discussions with many people, particularly Ellen Kroll, Travis Pickering, and Margaret Schoeninger. Two anonymous reviewers, whom I wish I could thank by name, greatly improved the chapter, although I am, of course, responsible for all remaining shortcomings in it.

REFERENCES

Aiello, L. C., and P. Wheeler. 1995. The expensive tissue hypothesis. *Current Anthropology* 36:199–222.
Binford, L. R. 1981. *Bones: Ancient Men and Modern Myths*. New York: Academic Press.
Binford, L. R. 1984. *Faunal Remains from Klasies River Mouth*. New York: Academic Press.
Binford, L. R. 1986. Comment on "Systematic butchery by Plio/Pleistocene hominids at Olduvai Gorge" by H. T. Bunn and E. M. Kroll. *Current Anthropology* 27:444–446.

Binford, L. R. 1988. Fact and fiction about the *Zinjanthropus* floor: data, arguments, and interpretations. *Current Anthropology* 29:123–135.

Blumenschine, R. J. 1986. Comment on "Systematic butchery by Plio/Pleistocene hominids at Olduvai Gorge, Tanzania" by H. Bunn and E. Kroll. *Current Anthropology* 27:446.

Blumenschine, R. J. 1987. Characteristics of an early hominid scavenging niche. *Current Anthropology* 28:383–407.

Blumenschine, R. J. 1988. An experimental model of the timing of hominid and carnivore influence on archaeological bone assemblages. *Journal of Archaeological Science* 15:483–502.

Blumenschine, R. J., and J. A. Cavallo. 1993. Scavenging and human evolution. *Scientific American* 267(4):90–96.

Blumenschine, R. J., and C. W. Marean. 1993. A carnivore's view of archaeological bone assemblages. In *From Bones to Behavior* (J. Hudson, ed.), pp. 273–300. Carbondale: Center for Archaeological Investigations, Southern Illinois University, Occasional Paper No. 21.

Blumenschine, R. J., and M. M. Selvaggio. 1991. On the marks of marrow bone processing by hammerstones and hyenas: their anatomical patterning and archaeological implications. In *Cultural Beginnings: Approaches to Understanding Early Hominid Life-Ways in the African Savanna* (J. D. Clark, ed.), pp. 17–32. Bonn: Dr. Rudolf Habelt GMBH.

Boesch, C. 1991. The effects of leopard predation on grouping patterns in forest chimpanzees. *Behaviour* 117:220–241.

Bunn, H. T. 1981. Archaeological evidence for meat-eating by Plio-Pleistocene hominids from Koobi For a and Olduvai Gorge. *Nature* 291:574–577.

Bunn, H. T. 1993. Bone assemblages at base camps: a further consideration of carcass transport and bone destruction by the Hadza. In *From Bones to Behavior* (J. Hudson, ed.), pp. 156–168. Carbondale: Center for Archaeological Investigations, Southern Illinois University, Occasional Paper No. 21.

Bunn, H. T. 1996. Comment on "Meat-eating, hominid sociality, and home bases revisited" by L. Rose and F. Marshall. *Current Anthropology* 37:307–338.

Bunn, H. T. 1997. The bone assemblages from the excavated sites. In *Koobi for a Research Project, Volume 5: Plio-Pleistocene Archaeology* (G. Ll. Isaac, ed.), pp. 402–458. Oxford: Clarendon Press.

Bunn, H. T., and J. A. Ezzo. 1993. Hunting and scavenging by Plio-Pleistocene hominids: nutritional constraints, archaeological patterns, and behavioural implications *Journal of Archaeological Science* 20:365–398.

Bunn, H. T., and E. M. Kroll. 1986. Systematic butchery by Plio/Pleistocene hominids at Olduvai Gorge, Tanzania. *Current Anthropology* 27:431–452.

Bunn, H. T., and E. M. Kroll. 1988. Reply to fact and fiction about the *Zinjanthropus* floor: data, arguments, and interpretations by L. Binford. *Current Anthropology* 29(1):135–149.

Bunn, H. T., L. E., Bartram, and E. M. Kroll. 1988. Variability in bone assemblage formation from Hadza hunting, scavenging, and carcass processing. *Journal of Anthropological Archaeology* 7(4):412–457.

Bunn, H. T., J. W. K. Harris, G. Ll. Isaac, Z. Kaufulu, E. Kroll, K. Schick, N. Toth, and A. K. Behrensmeyer. 1980. FxJj 50: an Early Pleistocene site in northern Kenya. *World Archaeology* 12:109–136.

Capaldo, S. D. 1997. Experimental determinations of carcass processing by Plio-Pleistocene hominids and carnivores at FLK 22 (*Zinjanthropus*), Olduvai Gorge, Tanzania. *Journal of Human Evolution* 33:555–597.

Capaldo, S. D., and R. J. Blumenschine. 1994. A quantitative diagnosis of notches made by hammerstone percussion and carnivore gnawing on bovid long bones. *American Antiquity* 59:724–748.

Cooper, S. M. 1991. Optimal hunting group size: the need for lions to defend their kills against loss to spotted hyaenas. *African Journal of Ecology* 29:130–136.

Hawkes, K., J. F. O'Connell, and N. Blurton Jones. 1989. Hardworking Hadza grandmothers. In *Comparative Socioecology: The Behavioural Ecology of Humans and Other Mammals* (V. Standen and R. Foley, eds.), pp. 341–66. Oxford: Basil Blackwell.

Hay, R. L. 1976. *Geology of the Olduvai Gorge: A Study of Sedimentation in a Semi-Arid Basin*. Berkeley: University of California Press.

Isaac, G. Ll. 1978. The food-sharing behavior of proto-human hominids. *Scientific American* 238:90–108.

Isaac, G. Ll. 1984. The archaeology of human origins: studies of the Lower Pleistocene in East Africa 1971–1981. *Advances in World Archaeology* 3:1–87.

Kelly, R. 1995. *The Foraging Spectrum: Diversity in Hunter-Gatherer Lifeways*. Washington, DC: Smithsonian Institution Press.

Kruuk, H. 1972. *The Spotted Hyena*. Chicago: University of Chicago Press.

Leakey, M. D. 1971. *Olduvai Gorge: Excavations in Beds I and II, 1960–1963*. Cambridge: Cambridge University Press.

Leonard, W. R., and M. L. Robertson. 1994. Evolutionary perspectives on human nutrition: the influence of brain and body size on diet and metabolism. *American Journal of Human Biology* 6:77–88.

Marean, C. W., L. M. Spencer, R. J. Blumenschine, and S. D. Capaldo. 1992. Captive hyena bone choice and destruction, the Schlepp effect, and Olduvai archaeofaunas. *Journal of Archaeological Science* 19:101–121.

O'Connell, J. F., K. Hawkes, and N. Blurton Jones. 1988. Hadza hunting, butchering, and bone transport and their archaeological implications. *Journal of Anthropological Research* 44(2):113–161.

Oliver, J. S. 1994. Estimates of hominid and carnivore involvement in the FLK *Zinjanthropus* fossil assemblage: some socioecological implications. In *Early Hominid Behavioural Ecology* (J. S. Oliver, N. E. Sikes, and K. M. Stewart, eds.), pp. 267–294. London: Academic Press.

Plummer, T. W., and L. C. Bishop. 1994. Hominid paleoecology at Olduvai Gorge, Tanzania as indicated by antelope remains. In *Early Hominid Behavioural Ecology* (J. S. Oliver, N. E. Sikes, and K. M. Stewart eds.), pp. 47–75. London: Academic Press.

Potts, R. B., and P. Shipman. 1981. Cutmarks made by stone tools on bones from Olduvai Gorge, Tanzania. *Nature* 291:577–580.

Schaller, G. B. 1972. *The Serengeti Lion: A Study of Predator–Prey Relations*. Chicago: University of Chicago Press.

Selvaggio, M. M. 1994. Carnivore tooth marks and stone tool butchery marks on scavenged bone: archaeological implications. *Journal of Human Evolution* 27:215–27.

Sponheimer, M., and J. A. Lee-Thorp. 1999. Isotopic evidence for the diet of an early hominid, *Australopithecus africanus*. *Science* 283:368–370.

Vincent, A. S. 1984. Plant foods in savanna environments: a preliminary report of tubers eaten by the Hadza of northern Tanzania. *World Archaeology* 17:132–418.

Wobst, H. M. 1978. The archaeo-ethnology of hunter-gatherers or the tyranny of the ethnographic record in archaeology. *American Antiquity* 43:303–309.

Woodburn, J. C. 1964. *The Social Organization of the Hadza of North Tanganyika*. Ph.D. Dissertation. Department of Anthropology, Cambridge: Cambridge University Press.

Woodburn, J. C. 1968a. An introduction to Hadza ecology. In *Man the Hunter* (R. Lee and I. DeVore, eds.), pp. 49–55. Chicago: Aldine.

Woodburn, J. C. 1968b. Stability and flexibility in Hadza residential groupings. In *Man the Hunter* (R. Lee and I. DeVore, eds.), pp. 103–110. Chicago: Aldine.

Woodburn, J. C. 1972. Ecology, nomadic movement and the composition of the local group among hunters and gatherers: an East African example and its implications. In *Man, Settlement, and Urbanism* (P. Ucko, R. Tringham, and C. Dimbleby, eds.), pp. 193–206. London: Duckworth.

Woodburn, J. C. 1980. Hunters and gatherers today and reconstruction of the past. In *Soviet and Western Anthropology* (E. Gellner, ed.), pp. 95–117. London: Duckworth.

11

Is Meat the Hunter's Property?
Big Game, Ownership, and Explanations of Hunting and Sharing

Kristen Hawkes

Introduction

Meat plays a prominent role in popular scenarios of human evolution. One influential view depicts ancestral males hunting to feed their mates and offspring as the keystone adaptation favoring the spread of features that distinguish us from the other apes (e.g., Washburn and Lancaster 1968; Lovejoy 1981; Lancaster and Lancaster 1983; Tooby and DeVore 1987; Fisher 1992; Ridley 1996; Pinker 1997). This story of human evolution locates the origin of men's work in paternal investment (Trivers 1972). Males in most primate species allocate their reproductive effort largely to mating competition instead of parenting. Any tendency in ancestral human males to shift effort from mating to parental provisioning could only spread if the youngsters a man fed were his own offspring.

But if ancestral hunters targeted large animals, there are good reasons to doubt that a hunter could have maintained ownership of his prey. Among modern tropical foragers, hunters generally do not control the distribution of meat from big animals. Large carcasses are treated more as a communal resource, like a public good from which many claim shares. To the extent this is so, the meat taken by others cannot be counted as part of the hunter's own gain for his effort, and his own family may get no more meat for his work than others do. A hunter cannot exclude other claimants, nor can he exchange portions of meat with other hunters (or anyone else) for obligations to return meat (or anything else), if he does not own the carcass in the first place.

Here I review data from three ethnographic cases that illustrate this absense of ownership, and discuss implications for both causes and consequences of hunting. Parallels between hunting and meat-sharing among chimpanzees and people are instructive. In both species hunting is largely a male specialty, and meat is more widely shared than other foods. I compare an initial phase in the treatment of kills by chimpanzees with the ethnographic examples. Although differences are numerous and important, there is this similarity: more often than not no one has exclusive control of the carcass. The initial phase is quite brief among chimpanzees but not among humans. The expansion of this first phase, both in the duration and extent of meat distribution it encompasses, can be related to prey size.

The arguments developed here distinguish two kinds of sharing. One is the mutual use of a resource that is in the public domain; the other is the voluntary transfer of private property among owners. Chimpanzees often have difficulty exercising ownership over whole prey but do establish possession over smaller pieces. Human hunters take prey in much larger sizes. If larger prey size increases the difficulty of exercising ownership, then more of the meat distribution takes place before portions are small enough to be private property. Hunters capturing larger animals contribute increasingly more to the public domain. Consequently, more of the sharing is not exchange (Woodburn 1998).

Paleoanthropologists have long emphasized maximum prey size as a key feature distinguishing human from chimpanzee hunting (e.g., Isaac 1978, 1984, Issac and Crader 1981). Small-animal hunting as practiced by modern chimpanzees may have been within the behavioral repertoire of all hominids. Stiner (in press) argues that regular hunting of large game may not be indicated in the archaeological record until the late middle Pleistocene.

If the ownership arguments here are correct, the benefits spurring ancestral hunters to target larger prey would not include family provisioning. But those who joined or stayed with more successful big game hunters whenever groups split could expect more meat. The benefit to the hunter himself would depend on a reputation for capturing large prey. Those with reputations for supplying bonanzas would attract more allies. With hunters competing to establish reputations, claiming shares of meat would be a more frequent and rewarding activity for all. Any increased capacity to use conventions to settle contests with reduced conflict costs would be favored as a consequence (Stanford this volume). If Stiner is right about the late dates for large-animal hunting in the archaeological record, then these things may be implicated in the radiation of "archaic" *H. sapiens*.

Ownership

The distinction between sharing that goes on in the absence of ownership and sharing by owners focuses attention on the diagnostic feature of "ownership" and "property" traditionally used in economics (Barzel 1997). Owners have the right of exclusive use and the right to voluntarily transfer their ownership to someone else. This right to exclusive use distinguishes private from public goods. Goods that one cannot exclude from consumption by others are public goods; those that one can keep for exclusive use are private property. Because excludability is more continuous than discrete, few goods are perfectly private or perfectly public. But some are relatively easy to exclude from other users and some are extremely difficult, the costs of exclusion too high to be worth paying.

The cost of exclusion is central to the idea of economic defendability (Brown 1964) that has proven so useful in behavioral ecology and supplies the logic of Blurton Jones' model of tolerated theft (1984, 1987). This model points to a variable that could explain why two phases can more often be distinguished in the sharing of meat than other foods. Game animals come in packages larger than most nongame resources, packages that are large relative to the portion size that one individual (human or chimpanzee) can consume. To get any game meat at all a hunter must down the whole animal. One kilo of kudu may be plenty, but the rest of the kudu comes with it.

Any forager may anticipate large benefits from consuming that first portion (or feeding it to an offspring) and may also anticipate that their own consumption benefits (and those of their children) will begin to diminish long before they have eaten everything. Because the hunter must kill the whole animal, the many portions equal in size and quality that become available when the prey is down will have different value to different potential consumers. The same portion will be worth less to one who has already claimed some. The cost of successfully claiming and defending any portion against other contestants depends on the pressure *they* apply, which, in turn, depends on the value that portion has for others. Division and distribution can thus continue until no one values a portion they do not already hold more than the cost they would have to pay to successfully contest it. At that point, portions are private property: owners can exert exclusive control, consuming them directly or trading them for other goods and services.

This schematic picture is a cartoon, picking out a small handful of variables from the many that must affect real behavior. The purpose of such a simple model is to see whether a few variables could account for systematic variation in others. If economic defendability plays an important role in food-sharing, then resources that are initially acquired in defendable units are not subject to this first phase of sharing. The cost of excluding other claimants from these resources is worth paying from the start. Any sharing is then under the control of the owner. But resources that are acquired in units too large to be successfully defended will initially be divided and distributed as multiple claimants seek shares. No one will be able to control this distribution. Only after enough division results in economically defendable holdings can holders control transfers of their own property.

Meat-Sharing among Modern Human Foragers

Ethnographers have drawn attention to the distinctive ways that people make claims on many resources, including meat, in egalitarian foraging communities (e.g., Erdal and Whiten 1994). Classic characterizations note that claimants do not say "please" or "thank you." Ethnologists interpret the absence of expressions of gratitude to indicate that claimants see shares as their due (Lee 1969; Sahlins 1972). Sometimes claims have an edge of threat. Hunters are often described as "owners" of a carcass, but the label is not used to mean the right of exclusive use (Wiessner 1996).

Other users cannot be refused. Peterson (1993) has labeled such ethnographic patterns as "demand sharing."

The Hadza

Hadza hunters of northern Tanzania (Blurton Jones et al. 1992) specialize in taking big game, and meat is widely shared. Hadza hunters can and sometimes do set snares and take small animals, but usually they do not pursue small prey while hunting, even though they encounter them often. The smallest of the game they regularly take has an adult body weight of about 40 kg. Over a sample of more than 2,000 hunter-days the large prey regularly taken by hunting and competitive scavenging in this population have an average size of 143 kg (live weight) (O'Connell et al. 1988; Hawkes et al. 1991).

Among the Hadza the "demand" style is common. Insistent claims are especially audible at kill sites. Arguments sometimes break out about shares and their size. Claims, not just by men but by women as well, often take the form "where's mine?" The successful hunter is in no position to "relinquish" shares (cf. Hawkes 1993b; Hill and Kaplan 1993) because he does not control them in the first place (Barnard and Woodburn 1988; Woodburn 1998). Neither he nor anyone else tries to exclude other users, except from the share he takes himself.

A sample of 113 shares from 20 large prey weighted at Hadza men's households (Table 11.1, row 1) shows that the successful hunter does not generally get a larger share of the meat. Household share sizes vary widely. They increase with prey size, but so the number of claimants. In this sample residents got shares from only the very largest prey taken by hunters living elsewhere (Table 11.1, row 2). For very large prey(> 180 kg), the hunter's household got a larger share (Table 11.1, row 3a). For prey less than 180 kg the hunter's share was no larger than that of other men (Table 11.1, row 3b). The household share sample included a disproportionate number of the very largest species, an average of 288 kg/prey compared to 143 kg/prey for our total sample of 71 large prey. In the larger sample, 49 of the 71 prey (69%) were less than 180 kg. The sharing sample supports the inference that about 30% of the time (when the prey weigh more than 180 kg) the hunter's household got about 10% of the meat and other men about 5%. More often, when the prey weighed less than 180 kg, both got about 5%.

While the carcass is not owned by the hunter, the shares transported home—the household shares—are better candidates as private property. But there can still be further division by demand. Visitors arrive from other camps on news of a large kill to "help eat meat" and sometimes depart carrying portions. These might be voluntary transfers, the householder trading meat for something else. But nothing indicates he could successfully refuse.[1]

The Ache

The biggest quantitative data set on meat-sharing comes from the Ache of Eastern Paraguay (Kaplan 1983; Kaplan et al. 1984; Kaplan and Hill 1985; Hill and Hurtado

Table 11.1. Hadza household shares of big game.

	n	mean	SE
1. Weight of edible tissue/household w/resident man			
measured in household share sample	113	13.6	1.2
2. Size of prey (edible portion)			
Difference of means (unequal variances) p = 0.85			
a. Hunter a coresident man (boys exluded)	13	114	25.5
b. Hunter living elsewhere	4	285	95.3
3. Hunter a coresident man (boys excluded)			
a. prey > 180 kg, diff. of means *p* = 0.014			
hunter's household	8	29.9	5.1
other men's households	38	13.5	1.2
b. prey < 180 kg, diff. of means *p* = 0.389			
hunter's household	7	2.2	0.8
other men's households	21	3.8	1.0
4. Large animals in household share sample			
a. estimated carcass weight	20	288	57
b. estimated weight of edible tissue	20	173	34
5. Total large animal sample			
a. estimated carcass weight	71	143	19.4
b. estimated weight of edible tissue	71	85	11.6

From Hawkes et al. in press. Weights (kg) of carcasses acquired and shares of edible tissue distributed to house-holds with resident men. Columns list sample size (n), sample mean, and standard errors. Total carcass weights taken from Coe et al. (1976), with carcasses acquired by scavenging estimated at 80% of mean value per taxon. Weight of edible tissue estimated at 60% of total carcass weight. Weights of 113 household shares measured with hanging spring scales plus some estimated portions. "Other men" (rows 5 & 6) are those who did not make the kill. Difference of means are unpaired *t*-tests, one-tailed significance.

1996). The Ache take the largest game available in the Neotropics, but those they encounter in any frequency are about the size of the smallest taken by the Hadza. About 83% of the meat that Ache women and children eat comes from shares of the kills made by men who are *not* their husbands and fathers (Kaplan and Hill 1985). Not only is meat very widely shared among the Ache, but, as with the Hadza, hunt-ers play no proprietary role in meat distributions (Kaplan et al. 1990). Usually an older man takes on the final carving of cooked meat, and all watch as he distributes shares. Observers comment on portion sizes, and agreement among vocal critics directs adjustment. The successful hunter has no special opportunity to control the size or direction of portions.

The Ache are explicit about the virtues of sharing. Because it is extremely im-polite not to share, and in the forest[2] people usually eat in very close proximity, it is difficult to say when a portion of meat becomes someone's property. Children are sometimes teased to give up a piece of food they are consuming with relish. No systematic study has been done of such incidents, but episodes can end with most of the piece (or another) returned to the child. Does the child have the owner's dis-cretion to give or not? One interpretation is that the child's exclusive control is tem-porarily violated for a lesson in manners, perhaps even reciprocity: share with others, and they will share with you. To the extent there *is* individual discretion about whether to give or not, it comes after the meat has been distributed.

The !Kung

The !Kung of the northern Kalahari take the same large animals that the Hadza do, but ungulate densities and hunting success rates are lower there, and hunters do not specialize in big game (Lee 1979). Small animals belong to the hunter. For large ones there is a *nominal* owner, the owner of the arrow that first penetrated the animal, who may or may not be the hunter who took the shot (Marshall 1976; Lee 1979). Marshall (1976) describes the role of this person who carries out some of the distribution but cannot control the destination of shares. This "owner of the animal" may "start off the distribution in the direction of his own relatives." But that distribution is followed by further sharing to include "visitors, even though they are not close relatives," and finally "everybody gets some meat." Marshall emphasizes the many "waves of sharing" (1976: 297ff). Only after repeated division and distribution are the portions under the exclusive control of individuals. Then, she reports, "when an individual receives a portion of meat, he owns it outright for himself. He may give and share it further as he wishes . . . [P]osessing one's piece personally . . . gives one the responsibility of choosing when to eat one's meat and struggling with hunger the best one can when it is finished, without occasion or excuse for blaming others for eating more than their share" (1976: 302). It is only after the "primary distribution and primary kinship obligations have been fulfilled" that a share is private property and subject to the exclusive use of its owner. Then, "the giving of meat *from one's own portion* has the quality of gift giving. . . . The person who has received a gift of meat must give a reciprocal gift some time in future" (1976: 299, emphasis added).

Behavior around the distribution of meat differs in these three ethnographic cases, but in none of them can the hunter, or anyone else, exclude others from shares of a carcass. Among the Ache and !Kung, as among the Hadza, the hunter has no opportunity to control the size or final destination of shares. Only after division and distribution when he controls a share himself could he exchange it for something else. Like anyone else, he can only trade or exchange the portion that is his private property.

Among the Hadza and the !Kung, this absense of control by the hunter applies to large prey, but not small. In the Ache case, even small animals are subject to wide distribution. Perhaps the very tight clustering of people in Ache foraging camps helps explain this. Parties usually camp in the same place for only a single night (Hill et al. 1987), so clearing is not extensive and people are almost within touching distance of all members of the party. When meat is cooked, all members of the camp participate in the same meal. The Ache are adept at dividing even small monkeys into many pieces. Still, not everything is as widely shared. The relationship between package size and the fraction that the acquirer keeps holds across Ache food resources. Even small animals are larger than most plant foods, and the fraction of a resource shared by those outside the acquirer's nuclear family is correlated with package size (Kaplan and Hill 1985; Hawkes 1991).

Chimpanzee Meat-Sharing

Although chimpanzees have been observed to take other prey, they are effectively specialists on colobus monkeys. Mean weights of these prey range from 4.7 to 8.7 kg across three study sites (Stanford 1996). What happens after a chimpanzee hunter captures a monkey has been described by many observers (e.g., Teleki 1973; Goodall 1986; Boesch and Boesch 1989; Wrangham and Riss 1990; Nishida et al. 1992; Uehara et al. 1992). Adult males near the prey rush to seize it. If the initial holder is not the alpha, other males threaten, grab, and sometimes rip the carcass apart. Observers report the extent of aggression displayed here differs depending on the dominance ranks of the males present (W. McGrew and C. Stanford pers. comm.) and among study sites (C. Boesch pers. comm.).

After the initial division aggression is very rare, but clusters of beggars surround those holding portions. The clusters persist sometimes for the hours over which the prey is consumed. During this time possessors may refuse or ignore supplicants. They may allow mutual feeding on the same piece, or actively proffer pieces. Sometimes possessors, having fed for awhile themselves, relinquish the entire remains. Although those holding portions seem able to exclude beggars, the insistent pressure to transfer shares can sometimes seem quite intense. Goodall describes "occasions when the solicitations of begging chimpanzees made it all but impossible for the possessor to feed; at the very least, they are a source of irritation" (1986: 373).

The aggression in the first phase of meat-sharing among chimpanzees is clearly different from what happens initially among human foragers with a large carcass. Although there may be palpable tension, actual physical aggression among claimants is as rare with humans as it is common among chimpanzees. This is an important difference. There is also an important similarity. None of the multiple claimants initially dividing the carcass has discretion over the disposition of shares. In this sense the first divisions are like the scramble competition of many feeders in a fruiting tree. While one individual may have located the bonanza and called others to it, the finder cannot control what or how much others eat, except as one of the claimants taking a share for himself.

Among chimpanzees, the first phase before possession is established is relatively brief. The following phase, in which possessors seem to have control over whether and to whom they transfer ownership of shares, can be extremely lengthy. On grounds of meat ownership, the first short phase among chimpanzees is similar to most of the sharing among humans: a process of multiple claims on a common resource. On those same grounds, the lengthy second phase among chimpanzees, when individuals control shares and can transfer that control or exclude others, is similar to what happens after most of the division is complete among humans: portions of meat are treated as private property.

Social Implications of Prey Size

The picture drawn here highlights similarities between the initial contest for control of prey parts among chimpanzees with the initial divisions and distributions or "waves of sharing" of big animals among human foragers. The protracted "begging circles" of chimpanzees are, on these dimensions, similar only to what happens with humans *after* the "waves of sharing," which encompass most of the substantial division and distribution. In the begging circles, participants seem to obey an ownership convention, as if the meat were the property of the possessor who has discretion about whether and to whom to allow shares. Similar latitude about whether and with whom to share emerges in the human cases only *after* the widespread distribution is over.

Paleoanthropologists have long noted that the difference in prey size targeted by chimpanzees and people must have substantial social implications (e.g., Isaac 1978). The ownership issue highlighted here provides a basis for speculating about those implications and their evolutionary consequences.

Among chimpanzees, prey are very rarely larger than 10 kg (Stanford 1996), but a package less than half that size is still large enough to attract the excited attention of all the chimpanzees in a party. Bigger animals taken by human hunters are even stronger magnets. In Hadza country, even without news from human travelers, the signpost of circling vultures would draw a crowd. The larger the resource piles and the greater the number of interested consumers, the smaller fraction of the total anyone can economically defend. Among the Hadza, household share sizes go up with prey size but not isometrically. The bigger the carcass, the more shares are claimed (O'Connell et al. 1990; Hawkes et al., unpublishedms.).

Where chimpanzees tear prey into a few pieces, a kilo or less each, humans must divide much larger prey many more times to reach even a household share size. I have argued that in one important way division at least to this size is like the initial division that chimpanzees use aggression to accomplish. In both cases multiple users claim shares of a resource from which no one can exclude them.

When Sharing Is Joint Appropriation from the Public Domain

The costs and benefits of exclusion determine economic defendability. If the costs of a contest are greater for some, those for whom it costs less can net a benefit by claiming more (Blurton Jones 1984, 1987; Winterhalder 1996). Models based on these variables do not necessarily predict that multiple contestants will fight over a resource. Those who can anticipate both the appetites and contest capacities of others will do better to refrain from fights that they cannot win. Simple models thus predict that struggles are more likely among those most evenly matched. Among chimpanzees, it is the adult males who participate in the initial tug of war over a carcass. Females and young males, who would surely lose, do not.

But this does not mean that economic defendability can only account for distributions when the bigger and stronger take all and the smaller and weaker get none (cf. Kaplan and Hill 1985; Hawkes 1992). Pressure need not be physical to be an effective contest tool. People everywhere use associations with close kin and allies to improve their bargaining position, a tactic that is not restricted to humans but widely employed among the primates (e.g., de Waal 1982; Aureli et al. 1992). Small juveniles can decrease their cost of engaging in a contest (and increase the cost to those who treat them unfavorably) by crying to mother. These tactics would be no match for physical aggression, but they are often employed, perhaps when physical aggression would clearly be ineffective or especially costly.

When both benefits and costs are potentially high, contestants who are more or less evenly matched can earn substantial net gains over a series of contests by using a convention that settles the matter without the cost of actually fighting (Maynard Smith 1982). If some initially arbitrary asymmetry cues a conditional response, for example, give way to the one on your right, then strategies are coordinated, reducing or eliminating the contest costs. Such coordination is self-enforcing: a slight initial tendency for anyone to bias their response according to such an asymmetry increases the gains for others doing so. Gains for obeying the convention and costs for flouting it increase the more often it is used (Sugden 1986). If meat-sharing is subject to these costs, then larger prey size increases the payoff for following conventions (see also Stanford this volume). Larger prey size has this effect because the bigger the pile of meat, the more potential consumers are drawn to the bonanza. More claimants could raise the cost of making a claim, a cost even higher if some are armed. When large animals are taken, tendencies to use conventions to divide and distribute the meat would be much more strongly favored than otherwise.

Big Game Makes Hunting More Important to All

The arrival of meat in very large packages increases the payoffs for using conventions to settle contests. The same thing makes hunting an activity of much greater interest and importance in the human than in the chimpanzee case; more individuals can expect to gain more nutritional benefit from any hunter's success. The success rates for chimpanzee hunters represented by the Gombe population [0.037 prey/ hunter/day (Wrangham and Riss 1990)] are arrestingly close to those for human big game hunters represented by the Hadza [0.034 prey/hunter/day (Hawkes et al. 1991)]. But, because of the difference in prey size, Hadza hunters with success rates essentially identical to those of chimpanzees make about *thirty times* the amount of meat available for consumption that chimpanzees do.

A shift toward larger prey makes successes generally more important because more consumers can expect to get more meat, and for another reason as well: Prey size and encounter rate are inversely related (Table 11.2). When Hadza hunters are induced to take small animals, their success rates are 12 to 42 times higher than they are for big game (Hawkes et al. 1991). The relationship between prey body size and success rates is evident even within the suite of large animals Hadza hunters regularly target. Fewer animals in the very largest body size range are taken (O'Connell et al. 1990). This inverse relationship between success rate and prey size is evident in other samples as well (Table 11.2). Ache hunters, for example, capture an average of 0.66 prey/hunter/day in the size range under 10 kg. For prey from 20 to 40 kg the Ache rate falls by an order of magnitude. The two largest prey species sometimes captured by Ache hunters (Hill and Hawkes 1983), capybara (avg. 60 kg) and tapir (avg. 150 kg), are taken so rarely that no captures occurred over an observation period of 674 hunter-days (Hawkes et al. 1982). Interest in a

Table 11.2. Prey size and hunting success rates.

Case	Prey Weights (kg)	Average Success Rates	
Ache	<10	0.66 prey/hunter/day	(674 hunter-days)
Ache	20–40	0.06 prey/hunter/day	(674 hunter-days)
Ache	>40	<0.001 prey/hunter/day	(0 in 674 hunter-days)
!Kung	<10	0.17 prey/hunter/day	(83 hunter-days)
!Kung	>10	0.05 prey/hunter-day	(83 hunter-days)
!Kung	>40	<0.01 prey/hunter/day	(0 in 83 hunter-days)
"over the long run a [!Kung] hunter averages only two or three large antelope a year" (Lee 1979)			
Hadza	<10	1.21 prey/hunter/day	(102 hunter-days)
Hadza	<10	0.23 prey/hunter/day	(102 hunter-days)
Hadza	>40	0.034 prey/hunter/day	(2076 hunter-days)
Hadza	>40	0.022 prey/hunter/day	(2076 hunter-days daytime only)

Ache data from Hawkes et al.. (1982). !Kung data from Lee's (1979) work diaries. Hadza data from Hawkes et al. (1991). Hadza small game data from experimental trials. Snaring and encounter hunting results are presented. Hadza large game data cover observations days in 1985, 1986, 1988, and 1989. The whole sample includes both daytime encounter hunting and nightime ambush in the dry season. Daytime only figure includes all daytime encounter hunting and excludes the prey struck by ambush from night time blinds in the dry season.

hunter's success is thus doubly magnified by a shift toward larger prey: the bonanzas are bigger and garnered less often.

These are reasons why others would be more interested in successful hunters who target larger prey than small. Any man choosing to hunt small game or to gather plant foods instead would be successful more often, but he could control most of those resources from the start, leaving little for others to claim. The preference for association with hunters who take large animals hypothesized here arises *because* the hunter does not own the carcass and so cannot control the initial division and distribution of shares. No one can rely on his unpredictable successes, but many expect to gain from them (Hawkes 1990). By this argument others choose to join or stay with him because of the connection between him and chances to claim meat. Men may thus be hunting to show off this connection, to build and maintain their reputations as a valuable neighbors and allies (Hawkes 1991, 1993b).

Hunting Reputations

Men do earn reputations for their hunting, and good reputations earn preferential treatment in all three of the hunter-gatherer examples. Among the Hadza, better hunters are married to harder working wives (Hawkes et al. in press). This, combined with the fact that differences in the nutritional welfare of children are associated with differences in the foraging efforts of their mothers and grandmothers (Hawkes et al. 1997), suggests that better hunters are more likely to marry women who are more successful mothers. Men with better hunting reputations are married to women who have children faster and have more surviving children (Blurton Jones et al. 1997). Such men also are married to younger (and so more fertile) women (Blurton Jones et al. 1997), suggesting that with better hunting reputations they may be successful at *repeatedly* displacing other suitors for the most fertile women. The hypothesis that people preferentially associate with better hunters, choosing to side with them or join them because in their company there will be more public meat, implies an advantage for men with better hunting reputations when social divisions arise. According to this hypothesis, the mating advantages of better Hadza hunters result from greater deference to them from others, including men with poorer hunting reputations.

In the case of the Ache, where marriages dissolve much more frequently than among the Hadza (Blurton Jones et al. 1997), hunting reputation has a large effect on a man's fertility but only a weak effect on the survivorship of his children (Hill and Hurtado 1996). This is consistent with the hypothesis that others are more tolerant of the sexual adventures of better hunters. Because they are desirable companions for other reasons, both men and women may allow better hunters to more often displace competitors as current husbands to the most fertile women.

Among the !Kung, marriages are much less fragile than among the Ache, and although there are exceptions (Shostak 1983), extramarital sex is much less common as well. Hunting reputation still has a large effect on social standing. In a habitat where hunters usually bag no more than two or three large antelope in a year (Lee 1979), the hyperbole that Thomas (1958) captures in her description of one influential man indicates the value placed on hunting success. ". . . [I]t was said of him that he never returned from a hunt without having killed at least a wildebeest, if not something larger. Hence the people connected with him ate a great deal of meat and his popularity grew" (1959: 182).

In all these cases people place a high value on meat. So a reputation for supplying it attracts favorable attention. But at the same time hunters do not own their prey. So they cannot merchandize it. In criticizing elements of the argument that meat is like a public good in these cases, Hill and Kaplan (1993) compared the meat a hunter does not eat to color TVs the manufacturer does not watch, arguing that in both cases producers are motivated by the exchange value of their products. The manufacturer who owns the color TVs can transfer that ownership in exchange for something else. But if the evidence and arguments assembled here are even partially correct, this does not apply to the hunter. A different parallel between television and meat might. Like an advertiser paying for the production of a program on the public airwaves, the hunter provides a common good. The advertiser's own payoff, like the hunter's, comes from getting the attention of an audience. Viewers do not pay the advertiser to watch the show. Yet large advertising budgets attest to the benefits advertisers expect to accrue from the attention they get. They decide how to place their adds to maximize audience effects. So, the hypothesis is, hunters allocate their time to large animals for the same reason. Like the advertiser, the benefits to the hunters increase the more consumers can be drawn to the public good they supply.

If hunters owned their kills, then hunting might be like many other productive activities in which the producer's gain comes from consuming the product directly or from trading it for other goods and services. To the extent that large carcasses are more public than private goods, hunting them does not give hunters ownership rights. Sharing meat from large prey is not exchange (Woodburn 1998). This directly challenges the contrary proposition that meat-sharing is largely explained by reciprocal altruism (e.g., Cosmides and Tooby 1992). If kills are *not* the hunter's property, his gain is not in meat but in his reputation for supplying it. Although the hunter cannot own the meat, he can own the credit for it.

Practices like those of the !Kung in which the nominal ownership of a large animal is assigned to the owner of the first arrow to penetrate the animal illustrate a key point in this argument about property rights. The owner of the arrow may or may not be the hunter who shot it. Marshall observes that by this practice "the society seems to want to extinguish in every way possible the concept of the meat belong to the hunter" (1976: 287). Owning the meat is one thing; credit for the kill is something else. Men talk endlessly about hunts and hunting (Marshall 1976; Lee 1979), rehearsing the "minutest details." Lee (1979) was able to collect lifetime retrospective histories from !Kung men in which each participant enumerated all the large animals he had killed in his lifetime. Hunters themselves, and all those who listen to the storytelling, know who it was that shot the arrow.

The Storytelling Problem with Big Game Hunting Reputations

Although the success rates of Hadza big game hunters and chimpanzee monkey hunters at Gombe are strikingly similar, the direct experience of hunting success to the human audience is different from the direct experience of the chimpanzees. Among chimpanzees, hunters are members of temporary parties all traveling together. Hunting frequency is directly related to the size of that temporary group. The larger the party, and especially the more estrous females it contains, the more hunting observed (Stanford et al. 1994). Only individuals *on the scene of the hunt* (and relatively few of them) get meat.

By contrast, when people hunt large prey, consumers get meat whether or not they witnessed the kill. Large carcasses continue to be attractive to claimants long after butchery has begun. Among the Hadza, men women and children converge on kill sites to eat and to transport meat. The transported portions are themselves often large enough to attract more claimants. Most consumers arrive at the meat long after the death of the prey. A hunter's success may not be directly observed by anyone else and if it is, not by the same audience who saw the last one.

In the modern human cases discussed here, large game captures are rare (Table 11.2). Among the Hadza and the !Kung, hunters look for opportunities to strike large prey on encounter with poisoned arrows. The typical pattern is that hunters alone or in pairs travel in search of encounters with prey (Lee 1979; Woodburn 1968). Hadza hunters also use ambush tactics in the dry season, sitting in blinds (again, as singles or sometimes in pairs) on game trails or near water waiting to prey on species that visit the restricted points of surface water (Hawkes et al. 1991). Their success rates depend most obviously on the density and behavior of prey and on technology. Large-game densities in Hadza country through the 1980s were in the range predicted by annual rainfall in the arid East African tropics (O'Connell et al. 1988). Pleistocene densities in this region may have been higher, with hunting success rate increased accordingly. On the other hand, the absense of weapons as efficient for taking large ungulates as the bow and arrow would have lowered the success rates of ancestral hunters compared to the modern Hadza.

If we take the modern rates as a provisional estimate for rates in the past, they indicate substantial constraints on reputation building. Successes are too rare, and more important, they happen elsewhere too often, for any observer to rank hunters on the basis of direct visual experience. Only the pooled experiences of many, combined in telling and retelling stories of hunts recent and past, could identify and rank the cumulative success of individual hunters. If it is not meat but reputation that draws men to hunt big animals, and if reputations require story telling, then big game hunting would only spread and persist among members of our lineage with the capacity for language.

What of Early *Homo* and Lower Paleolithic Archaeology?

If big game hunting is a common practice only with the appearance of "archaic" *Homo sapiens*, what of the earlier members of our genus, especially *Homo erectus* (*ergaster*) (Wood and Collard 1999), a taxon displaying changes in body size, maturation rates, and geographical distribution long attributed to increased carnivory and specifically familial provisioning by hunting fathers? By the arguments here, the appearance and spread of genus *Homo* and all the archaeology of the Lower Paleolithic including evidence of associations between early humans and the remains of large animals must predate the appearance of regular large game hunting.

That possibility seems less remote with the result of recent work focused on plant foraging strategies (Schoeninger this volume; Sept this volume) and the life history consequences of a shift to plant resources that young juveniles cannot handle for themselves. Among chimpanzees, as with other nonhuman primates, youngsters feed themselves at weaning. Human children can be surprisingly energetic foragers at young ages (Blurton Jones et al. 1989), but they still depend on others for most of their diet after they are weaned. Linking these differences to recent modeling in life history theory suggests that a suite of changes including delayed maturation, increased body size, increases in longevity, and modified digestive anatomy could all have been systematic consequences of increased reliance on plant foods, like deeply buried tubers that young juveniles cannot handle for themselves (Hawkes et al. 1998; O'Connell et al. 1999). Many tubers, especially if they are cooked, can provide a rich and abundant nutrient source (Conklin-Brittain et al. 1998; Wrangham et al. 1999). The paleoclimatic conditions associated with changes in the available plant foods, the series of systematic shifts in life history, and the expected expansion in geographic range are all consistent with this hypothesis about the evolution of *Homo erectus* (O'Connell et al. 1999).

That taxon is most likely responsible for the rich PlioPleistocene archaeology at Olduvai and Lake Turkana (Bunn this volume). Larger bodied than Australopithecines, and in larger groups because feeding competition is reduced by reliance on resources like deeply buried tubers, *erectus* would likely have been more successful in mobbing predators than earlier hominids. Size and numbers would have allowed greater success at competitive scavenging than among previous hominids.

But successes would likely have been way too rare for the meat from large animals to make a difference in day-to-day life. The modern Hadza actively pursue competitive scavenging opportunities. Even using efficient projectile weapons, *and* absent the daunting competition of the dangerous predator guild of the African Pliopleistocene (van Valkenburgh this volume) they earn little meat this way (O'Connell et al. 1988). The Hadza large-carcass *scavenging* rate is about two large carcasses per hunter/year. If much lower rates account for the lower Pleistocene archaeology, then early humans ate more meat from large animals than Australopithecines but not enough to play much role in daily life (O'Connell et al. 1999).

Concluding Remarks

The arguments of this chapter begin with behavior common to both humans and chimpanzees. In both species hunting is largely a specialty of males, and hunters often cannot control the meat they capture. From these similarities I speculate about the social correlates of a transition from hunting small prey to large. Stiner's assessment (in press) that clear evidence of hunting is late, within the last 2–300,000 years, adds plausibility to the argument that big game hunters do it for the reputation, not the meat. If, as both qualitative and quantitative data on modern people suggest, hunters often have little, if any, control over the large prey they capture, then the nutritional benefits of widely shared resources go largely to others. The hunter's nutritional income (and so that of their own families) is a small fraction of the large prey they kill.

But hunters get other benefits. The hypothesis favored here is that men with reputations for supplying public meat become desirable neighbors and allies. But there is a catch to building such a reputation. Successes in taking large prey are widely spread in space and time in the modern ethnographic cases discussed here. If that were also true in the past, then reputations for successful large game hunting would require an accumulated record of the experiences of many. The record that arises from telling stories. Hominids without language would never have been drawn to hunting large game. By this argument, the *lack* of proprietary control makes hunting large prey a poor way to seek nutritional goals but a good way to seek favorable attention among storytellers. That would make meat less important in early human evolution but more important in the evolution of later members of genus *Homo*.

Acknowledgments   I thank H. Alvarez, N. Blurton Jones, W. McGrew, J. F. O'Connell, and C. Stanford for their good advice.

NOTES

1. It is surprising that the hunter's household share is bigger for very large prey but not otherwise. Perhaps the successful hunter and his coresidents adjust their claims in anticipation of an influx of hungry visitors. Further work on this question is needed.

2. Circumstances at the agricultural settlement differ. Houses and settlement size create opportunities for privacy that are absent in temporary foraging camps.

REFERENCES

Aureli, F., R. Cozeolino, C. Cordischi, and S. Scucchi. 1992. Kin-oriented redirection among Japanese Macaques: an expression of a revenge system? *Animal Behaviour* 44:283–291.

Barnard, A., and J. Woodburn. 1988. Property power and ideology in hunting and gathering societies: an introduction. In *Hunters and Gatherers 2: Property, Power and Ideology* (T. Ingold, D. Riches, and J. Woodburn eds.), pp. 4–31. New York: Berg.

Barzel, Y. 1997. *Economic Analysis of Property Rights*, 2nd ed. Cambridge: Cambridge University Press.

Blurton Jones, N. G. 1984. A selfish origin for food-sharing: tolerated theft. *Ethology and Sociobiology* 5:1–3.

———— 1987. Tolerated theft: suggestions about the ecology and evolution of sharing, hoarding and scrounging. *Social Science Information* 26:31–54.

Blurton Jones, N., K. Hawkes, and J. F. O'Connell. 1989. Modelling and measuring costs of children in two foraging societies. In *Comparative Socioecology: The Behavioral Ecology of Humans and Other Mammals* (V. Standen and R. Foley, eds.), pp. 367–390. London: Basil Blackwell.

———— 1997. Why do Hadza children forage? In *Uniting Psychology and Biology: Integrative perspectives on Human Development* (N. Segal, G. E. Weisfeld, and C. C. Wesifeld, eds.), pp. 279–313. Washington, DC: American Psychological Association.

Blurton Jones, N. G., L. C. Smith, J. F. O'Connell, K. Hawkes, and C. Kamazura. 1992. Demography of the Hadza, an increasing and high density population of savanna foragers. *American Journal of Physical Anthropology* 89:159–181.

Boesch, C., and H. Boesch. 1989. Hunting behavior of wild chimpanzees in the Tai National Park. *American Journal ofPhysical Anthropology* 78:547–573.

Brown, J. L. 1964. The evolution of diversity in avian territorial systems. *Wilson Bulletin* 76:160–169.

Coe, M. J., D. H. Cummings, and J. Phillipson. 1976. Biomass and production of large African herbivores in relation to rainfall and primary production. *Oecologia* 22:341–354.

Conklin-Brittain, N., R. W. Wrangham, and C. Smith. 1998. Relating chimpanzee diets to potential Australopithecus diest. Paper for ICAES conference. http://www.cast.uark.edu/local/icaes/conferences/wburg/posters/nconklin/conklin.html.

Cosmides, L., and J. Tooby. 1992. Cognitive adaptations for social exchange. In *The Adapted Mind* (J. Barkow, L. Cosmides, and J. Tooby, eds.), pp. 163–228. New York: Oxford University Press.

de Waal, F. 1982. *Chimpanzee Politics: Sex and Power Among the Apes*. New York: Harper and Row.

Erdal, D., and A. Whiten. 1994. On human egalitarianism: an evolutionary product of Machiavellian status escalation? *Current Anthropology* 35:175–178.

Fisher, H. 1992. *The Anatomy of Love: The Natural History of Monogamy, Adultery, and Divorce*. New York: Norton.

Goodall, J. 1986. *The Chimpanzees of Gombe: Patterns of Behavior*. Cambridge, MA: Harvard University Press.

Hawkes, K. 1990. Why do men hunt? Some benefits for risky strategies. In *Risk and Uncertainty in Tribal. and Peasant Economies* (E. Cashdan, ed.), pp. 145–166. Boulder, CO: Westview Press.

——— 1991. Showing off: tests of an hypothesis about men's foraging goals. *Ethology and Sociobiology* 12:29–54.

——— 1992. On sharing and work. *Current Anthropology* 33:404–407.

——— 1993a. Why hunter-gatherers work: an ancient version of the problem of public goods. *Current Anthropology* 34:341–361.

——— 1993b. reply to Hill and Kaplan. *Current Anthropology* 34(5):706–710.

——— in press. Big game hunting and the evolution of egalitarian societies. In *Hierarchies in Action: Cui Bono?* (M. Deihl, ed.). CAI Publication Series. Carbondale, IL: Southern Illinois University.

Hawkes, K., K. Hill, and J. F. O'Connell. 1982. Why hunters gather: optimal foraging and the Ache of eastern Paraguay. *American Ethnologist* 9:379–398.

Hawkes, K., J. F. O'Connell, and N. G. Blurton Jones. 1991. Hunting income patterns among the Hadza: big game, common goods, foraging goals, and the evolution of the human diet. *Philosophical Transactions of the Royal Society*, SERIES B 334:243–251.

——— 1997. Hadza women's time allocation, offspring production, and the evolution of long postmenopausal life spans. *Current Anthropology* 38(4):551–577.

——— 1998. Hunting and the evolution of nuclear families: some lessons from the Hadza about men's work. Ms. Submitted for publication.

——— in press. Hadza meat sharing. *Evolution and Human Behavior.*

Hawkes, K., J. F. O'Connell, N. G. Blurton Jones, H. Alvarez, and E. L. Charnov. 1998. Grandmothering, menopause, and the evolution of human life histories. *Proceedings of the National Academy of Sciences* USA 95(3):1336–1339.

Hill, K., and K. Hawkes. 1983. Neotropical hunting among the Ache of Eastern Paraguay. In *Adaptive Responses of Native Amazonians* (R. Hames and W. Vickers, eds.), pp. 139–188. New York: Academic Press.

Hill, K., K. Hawkes. H. Kaplan, and A. M. Hurtado. 1987. Foraging decisions among Ache hunter-gatherers: new data and implications for optimal foraging models. *Ethology and Sociobiology* 8:1–36.

Hill, K., and A. M. Hurtado. 1996. *Ache Life History: The Ecology and Demography of a Foraging People.* New York: Aldine de Gruyter.

Hill, K., and H. Kaplan. 1993.On why male foragers hunt and share food. *Current Anthropology* 34(5):701–706.

Isaac, G. Ll. 1978. The food-sharing behavior of proto human hominids. *Scientific American* 238(4): 90–108.

——— 1984. The archaeology of human origins: studies of the Lower Paleolithic in East Africa, 1971–1981. *Advances in World Archaelogy* 3:1–89.

Isaac, G. Ll. and D. Crader. 1981. To what extent were early hominids carnivorous? In *Omnivorous Primates* (R. Harding and G. Teleki, eds.), pp. 37–103. New York: Columbia University Press.

Kaplan, H. 1983. *The Evolution of Food-sharing Among Adult Conspecifics: Research With Ache Hunter-Gatherers of Eastern Paraguay.* Ph.D. Dissertation. University of Utah.

Kaplan, H., and K. Hill. 1985. Food-sharing among Ache foragers: tests of explanatory hypotheses. *Current Anthropology* 26(2):223–246.

Kaplan, H., K. Hill, K. Hawkes, and A. M. Hurtado. 1984. Food-sharing among Ache hunter-gatherers of eastern Paraguay. *Current Anthropology* 25(1):113–115.

Kaplan, H., K. Hill, and A. M. Hurtado. 1990. Risk, foraging, and food-sharing among the Ache. In *Risk and Uncertainty in Tribal and Peasant Economies* (E. Cashdan, ed.), pp. 107–143. Boulder, CO: Westview Press.

Lancaster, J., and C. Lancaster. 1983. Parental investment: the hominid adaptation. In *How Humans Adapt* (D. Ortner, ed.), pp. 33–69. Washington DC: Smithsonian Institute Press.

Lee, R. B. 1969. Eating Christmas in the Kalahari. *Natural History* (December):14–22, 60–63.

Lee, R. B. 1979. *The !Kung San: Men Women and Work in a Foraging Society*. Cambridge: Cambridge University Press.

Lovejoy, O. 1981. The origin of man. *Science* 211:341–350.

Marshall, L. 1976. *The !Kung of Nyae Nyae*. Cambridge, MA: Harvard University Press.

Maynard Smith, J. 1982. *Evolution and the Theory of Games*. Cambridge: Cambridge University Press.

Nishida, T., T. Hasegawa, H. Hayaki, Y. Takahata, and S. Uehara. 1992. Meat-sharing as a coalition strategy by an alpha male chimpanzee? In *Topics in Primatology, Vol. I, Human Origins* (T. Nishida. W. C. McGrew, P. Marler, M. Pickford, and F. B. M. deWaal, eds.), pp. 159–174. Tokyo: University of Tokyo Press.

O'Connell, J. F., K. Hawkes, and N. G. Blurton Jones. 1988. Hadza scavenging: implications for Plio-Pleistocene hominid subsistence. *Current Anthropology* 29:356–363.

——— 1990. Reanalysis of large mammal body part transport among the Hadza. *Journal of Archaeological Science* 17:301–316.

——— 1999. Grandmothering and the evolution of *Homo Erectus. Journal of Human Evolution* 36:461–485.

Peterson, N. 1993. Demand sharing: reciprocity and the pressure for generosity among foragers. *American Anthropologist* 95:860–874.

Pinker, S. 1997. *How the Mind Works*. New York: Norton.

Ridley, M. 1996. *The Origins of Virtue: Human Instincts and the Evolution of Cooperation*. New York: Viking.

Sahlins, M. D. 1972. *Stone Age Economics*. Chicago: Aldine.

Shostak, M. 1983. *Nisa: The Life and Words of a !Kung Woman*. New York: Vintage.

Stanford, C. B. 1996. Hunting ecology of chimpanzees. *American Anthropologist* 98:96–113.

Stanford, C. B., J. Wallis, E. Mpongo, and J. Goodall. 1994. Hunting decisions in wild chimpanzees. *Behaviour* 131:1–20.

Stiner, M. C. in press. Carnivory, coevolution, and the geographic spread of the genus *Homo. Journal of Archaeological Research*.

Sugden, R. 1986. *The Economics of Rights, Co-Operation and Welfare*. Oxford: Basil Blackwell Ltd.

Teleki, G. 1973. *The Predatory Behavior of Wild Chimpanzees.* Lewisburg, PA: Bucknell University Press.

Thomas, E. M. 1958. *The Harmless People*. New York: Random House/Vintage.

Tooby, J., and I. Devore. 1987. The reconstruction of hominid evolution through strategic modeling. In *The Evolution of Human Behavior: Primate Models* (W. G. Kinzey, ed.), pp. 183–237. Albany: SUNY Press.

Trivers, R. L. 1972. Parental investment and sexual selection. In *Sexual Selection and the Descent of Man, 1871–1971.* (B. Campbell, ed.), pp. 136–179. London: Heinemann.

Uehara, S., T. Nishida, M. Hamai, T. Hasegawa, H. Hayaki, M. A. Huffman, K. Kawanaka, S. Kobayashi, J. C. Mitani, Y. Takahata, H. Takasaki, and T. Tsukahara. 1992. Characteristics of predation by the chimpanzees in the Mahale Mountains National Park, Tanzania. In *Topics in Primatology, Vol. I, Human Origins* (T. Nishida. W. C.McGrew, P. Marler, M. Pickford, and F. B. M. de Waal, eds.), pp. 143–158. Tokyo: University of Tokyo Press.

Washburn, S. L., and C. S. Lancaster. 1968. The evolution of hunting, In *Man the Hunter* (R. B. Lee and I. DeVore, eds.), pp. 293–303. Chicago: Aldine.

Wiessner, P. 1996. Leveling the hunter: constraints on the status quest in foraging societies. In *Food and the Status Quest: An Interdisciplinary Perspective* (P. Wiessner and W. Schiefenhovel, eds.), pp. 171–191. Providence, RI: Berghahn Books.

Winterhalder, B. 1996. A marginal model of tolerated theft. *Ethology and Sociobiology* 17:37–53.

Wood, B., and M. Collard. 1999. The human genus. *Science* 284:65–71.

Woodburn, J. 1968. An introduction to Hadza ecology. In *Man the Hunter* (R. Lee and I deVore, eds.), pp. 49–55. Chicago: Aldine.

Woodburn, J. 1998. Sharing is not exchange. In *Property Relations: Renewing the Anthropological Tradition* (C. M. Hann, ed.), pp. 48–63. Cambridge: Cambridge University Press.

Wrangham, R. W., and E. van Z. B. Riss. 1990. Rates of predation on mammals by Gombe chimpanzees, 1972–1975. *Primates* 31:157–170.

Wrangham, R. W., J. H. Jones, G. Laden, D. Pilbeam, and N. Conklin-Brittain. 1999. The raw and the stolen: cooking and the ecology of human origins. *Current Anthropology* 40:567–594.

12

Specialized Meat-Eating in the Holocene
An Archaeological Case from the Frigid Tropics of High-Altitude Peru

John W. Rick
Katherine M. Moore

Introduction

Like many ethnographically known hunter-gatherers themselves, anthropologists spend a great deal of time conversing and arguing about meat-eating and its partial correlate, hunting. The ability to procure meat, once felt to be a hallmark of human intelligence and culture, is now highly contested at various stages of human evolution. Although primates are clearly involved in hunting, with increasingly extensive modern records of how meat procurement fits within their lives, the involvement of premodern humans with hunting has left evidence that is less clear. This volume encompasses both specific evidence (e.g., chapters by Speth and Tchernov or Pickering), and more general overviews and models of the data and processes of evolving hunting abilities (see chapter by Foley). There are few who would contest the human ability to hunt by the time of anatomical and behavioral modernity, and issues of which prey were chosen, the degree of reliance on hunted foods, and which methods of hunting were used are more relevant. As humans develop behavioral flexibility, situations emerge in which the predominance of carnivory is an option, allowing humans to become specialized predators. This chapter looks at one such case that illustrates the difference between focused human carnivory and the less intensive exploitation of animals generally seen in most premodern hominid assemblages.

In a "trial formulation" now often taken as established fact, Lee and DeVore (1968: 7) viewed modern human hunter-gatherers as dependent primarily on plant foods, a revision of many previous meat-centric views. Yet, like so many perspectives on hunter-gatherers, this attempt to stereotype hunter-gatherer existence was destined to be defied by the variability known from both the ethnographic present and the prehistoric past. Later constructions, like that of Binford (1980), retained certain features of the Lee and DeVore model but recognized the effects of varying resource structure across latitude. This accommodated the well-known, more meat-dependent high-latitude mode of hunter-gatherer existence, as seen in groups like the Inuit. Binford's low-latitude forager and high-latitude collector resource strategies improved the match between theory and actual hunter-gatherer subsistence organization, but they cannot be expected to encompass reality any better than using latitude as a simple determinate of natural environments themselves.

Many attempts have been made to predict which available resources will be used in any environment by hunter-gatherers (Bettinger 1980). Optimal foraging and other models have, if nothing else, led to a broader recognition that hunter-gatherer diets are not a random sampling of available resources but are the result of a decision-making process about what foods to obtain (Winterhalder and Smith 1981). But no matter how cogent the decisions that formulate a diet, it is inevitably predicated on the ability of the resource procurers—itself a compound of physical competence, mental abilities, stored information and technology. Given reasonably simple assumptions about human resource strategies, it should be possible to predict the approximate resource mix for a given evolutionary and technological condition.

Two difficult issues remain, however. First is the conceptually simple one of whether the obtained resources will be compatible with dietary needs and limitations of the hunter-gatherers. An optimal diet in terms of energy return will not necessarily satisfy nutritional needs. Some nutrient-based models have been formulated that potentially solve this problem. The second issue involves the dynamics and evolutionary context of the resource strategy itself. Formal models have not been overly successful in predicting the evolution of meat-procurement strategies, nor in calculating the long-term consequences of the employment of these strategies. The lack of major advances in this arena is not too surprising, given the potential variety of strategies that might be imagined, and the complexity of hunter-prey interactions in most human resource situations. The more simplistic existing models, for instance, would have trouble distinguishing between subsistence systems of *Homo erectus*, archaic *Homo sapiens*, or fully modern *Homo sapiens*. Speth, and Tappen (this volume) consider the evolutionary importance of prehistoric data related to hunting, and Klein (1998) has interpreted evolving human strategic abilities based on the composition of hunted faunal assemblages. But predictions of past hunting strategies, relying on energy-based formulations, would often argue for similar resource strategies, even when encompassing a range of technologies or evolving human abilities. Also, the long-term prey–predator situation that would evolve with any given intensity of a specific exploitation has rarely been considered. In fact, few studies consider human impacts on hunting resources, yet intensively employed, well-tuned technologies are likely to eliminate or diminish the very prey they were designed for.

When dealing with mentally modern humans, meat-eating must be seen as a behavior dependent on the ability to find and kill other animals, which is to say, *hunting*. Whereas the range of expectable hunting behaviors in an ape community may be fairly limited, and probably expedient and opportunistic with minimal intervention of technology (see contributions by Stanford and Rose this volume), modern humans have the ability to create complex strategies and technologies. But the richness of human meat-eating is precisely how choices are made between these complex strategies and technologies. Human dietary composition is at least as much a result of these as it is any sort of an outcome of basic environmental parameters evaluated through energetic currency. In other words, it is not so much what you eat per se but rather how you have gone about getting it that reflects the more analytically fascinating aspect of human forager subsistence.

A familiar refrain in hunter-gatherer studies is that the range of observable behavior, and hence hunting strategies as well, has been decreasing as the range of habitats used by hunter-gatherers shrinks. Although in many habitats there may be no simple sequence from foraging to food production, and although pure 'unaffected' hunter-gatherers may not have existed in many environments for a long period of time, it is still reasonable to assume that a greater range of hunting strategies will be found in the prehistoric record. But what specifically can that greater diversity tell us about human hunting and meat consumption? Questions that might be considered include:

1. What was the evolution of hunting abilities, both in a very long-term, global framework, and on a local, specific level?
2. What is the relationship between human mental ability and human hunting strategies?
3. What is the dietary flexibility of the human species?
4. What is the interaction between culturally enhanced hunting strategies and environments; how does the human place within ecosystems change with increasing cultural abilities?

This chapter will only deal with a small segment of such inquiry. It will show, for fully modern humans within a single environment of unusual characteristics, the local, short-term evolutionary outcome of hunting strategies. In doing so, it shows an extreme, but illustrative, example of dietary specialization in meat-eating.

Many different environmental situations and their respective hunting strategies might contribute to an examination of the evolution of meat-eating specialization. This necessarily prehistoric perspective, however, has to face the limited data samples and the interpretive difficulties in reconstructing strategies from such data. One way of simplifying these problems is to deal with an environment in which meat consumption is the primary dietary option due to resource limitation and also where the range of meat-producing species is quite limited. In such a simplified situation it may be possible to look in detail at the human interaction with a single species and observe changes over a short, continuous time—yielding insights into how a local strategy evolved.

In addition to describing a particular case of a heavily meat-oriented prehistoric society, a second goal here is to show that this adaptation did not lead to many of the stereotyped conditions expected of hunting-oriented societies. In particular, mobility in hunter-gatherers has often been tied to a need to follow game or to otherwise respond to its own mobility level (Service 1966; Steward 1972). In addition, Binford (1983) has argued that even if resource availability would have potentially permitted low hunter mobility, the response would be to reserve the known resource and explore for further ones in a pattern of extensive land use. This mobility-dependent pattern would act against intensive exploitation or management of prey species, which for some is felt to come when population growth reduces forager territory size due to circumscription imposed by surrounding groups, with the resulting need to extract food from an ever-smaller area (Hayden 1981). This, of course, can be used as an explanation both for the beginnings of species domestication and human social complexity. In the case we present here, the evolution of a very intensive utilization of a single genus, probably through a system of managed hunting, fostered a pattern of low mobility without apparent population explosion or any resulting development of complexity. Not only is a diet composed primarily of meat-eating a viable one, but the strategies providing the diet demand neither major levels of mobility nor extensive land use.

Environmental Setting

This study focuses on Preceramic Period (11,000–3600 BP) hunter-gatherers of the high altitude grassland *puna* zone of central Peru. The puna environment, located around 11 degrees south of the equator, is a special setting with climatic conditions that violate the usual suppositions that low-latitude environments are warm. Because of its 3,900–4,400-meter altitude, the puna has a very low average temperature of about 2°C, and this average does not vary much through the year. Like other tropical environments, there is limited seasonality in temperature or precipitation; in general, the drier season is one of colder nights and warmer days, centered in July–August, while the wetter season, peaking in January–February, has less extreme diurnal temperatures (ONERN 1976; Francou 1983). Because of the low temperatures, there are relatively few herbaceous plants, and the plant communities consist primarily of small-seeded bunch grasses, stunted trees and shrubs, and a variety of ground-hugging plants that invest heavily in root structures of a woody nature (Figure 12.1) (Weberbauer 1936; Tosi 1960). Heat conservation is of a major consequence for plant life, and the cold-ameliorating effects of scattered bodies of water and rock formations lead to a mosaic of less cold-tolerant species within a matrix of hardy puna grasses. While altitude is a primary structuring agent of the life zones of the Andes, the vegetation of the central puna of Peru is not strikingly altitude-stratified within its fairly narrow vertical range. In general, the structure of the puna vegetation gives the impression of relative uniformity in that there are no riparian forest belts, snowcapped peaks, or other different zones included within broad puna expanses.

Relatively few plants produce significant quantities of humanly consumable food in the puna. Small cactus fruit, a few berry- and seed-producing plants, and a few herbaceous plants or those with consumable, if tough, tubers or rhizomes are the only candidates for dietary contribution from the floral world. Thus, the first trophic level is not very productive for humans, and we must look higher in the food chain for the majority of humanly consumable resources. The most apparent wildlife are deer and camelids, which graze and browse on the abundant puna vegetation. Two deer species are present, if rare today: the huemul, or taruca (*Hippocamelus anti-*

Figure 12.1. Typical puna setting and vegetation, with the base camp site of Panaulauca in the background.

sensis), and the white-tail (*Odocoileus virginianus*) (Cowan and Holloway 1973; Merkt 1987).

More common, where protected from overhunting, is the vicuña (*Vicugna vicugna*), a deer-sized camelid whose fine fur, primary dependence on grazing, and social organization argue for a quite specific adaptation to the climatic and vegetation conditions of the puna. A second wild camelid, the guanaco (*Lama guanicoe*), like the deer, is more of a dietary and environmental generalist across broad altitude ranges, browsing and grazing on a wide variety of resources (Franklin 1976). Another important difference between the vicuña and the guanaco is that the former is an obligate drinker while the guanaco is much more drought tolerant. Other animal species are present, including both terrestrial birds and waterfowl, a few rodents, and small fish and amphibians in larger bodies of water (Moore 1989). In general, the puna is marked by a low species diversity in both the plant and animal kingdoms, and, even allowing for variance in technology, animals would have had greater potential than plants to support human hunter-gatherers.

The vicuña stands out as the resource that is simultaneously nonseasonal, common, visible, accessible, and presumably procurable with fairly standard hunter technology. It has a very consistent, non-seasonal social organization, with animals grouped into bands and troops (Koford 1957; Franklin 1974). Bands are year-round territorial groups, consisting of a single adult male and three to seven adult females, plus immature animals of less than a year in age. Most vicuña territories are found along permanent sources of water, with the primary occupied area around 200 × 200 meters, supplemented by sleeping and refuge areas. Troops are relatively unstable, nonterritorial male groups that are usually found in the vicinity of band territories. Troop males frequently violate band territorial boundaries, provoking expulsion attempts by the territorial male. Overall, the vicuña can be summarized as a moderate density, highly spatially predictable and very visible resource.

It is possible to make very approximate calculations of the potential that vicuña offered to support human hunter populations. One of us previously suggested that in simple caloric terms, an average puna vicuña density could allow a human group of 25 to subsist over an indefinite time within an area of about 250 km² (Rick 1980). This assumes, however, that humans are the overwhelming source of vicuña mortality and that hunting strategies do not interfere with vicuña reproduction in a systematic way. Essential questions of how productivity of the vicuña might vary under different hunting techniques and how hunting techniques might have evolved are equally important.

Archaeological Evidence

Two major rounds of archaeological fieldwork were undertaken in the central Peruvian puna of the Department of Junín that contributed data capable of determining if a highly vicuña-oriented subsistence system had existed. The temporal focus was the Preceramic period, which lasted from about 11,000 BP until the ceramic horizon at around 3600 BP. The first field investigations, undertaken between 1973 and 1976, concentrated on the potential base camp site of Pachamachay and the area immediately surrounding it (Figure 12.2). We were able to define five phases of Preceramic occupation followed by ceramic period Phases 6 through 8, based on changes in occupation intensity, technology, and tool style:

Phase 8: 330 B.C.–1200 A.D.
Phase 7: 1020–330 B.C.
Phase 6: 1620–1020 B.C.
Phase 5: 2640–1620 B.C.
Phase 4: 3800–2640 B.C.
Phase 3: 5080–3800 B.C.
Phases 2a and 2b: 7050–5080 B.C.
Phase 1: ca 9000–7050 B.C.

An abundance of most classes of evidence gave support for a low-mobility, hunting-based society, but despite an abundance of animal bone within such puna sites, our sampling of the intensively occupied cave mouth areas produced a relatively small Preceramic faunal sample (Kent 1982; Wing 1974). Evidently the most-used living surfaces had been kept free of large bones, which were displaced down the talus slopes in front of the cave. The lack of an adequate faunal sample severely limited our ability to understand changes in hunting-oriented subsistence strategies across time.

The second major fieldwork episode was carried out from 1979 to 1986, shifting locus slightly south to the area surrounding another likely base camp, Panaulauca (Figure 12.1) (Rick and Bocek 1985). Although political unrest in the region prematurely suspended fieldwork, we had already recovered a large sample of cultural material from a number of contexts in the site's deposits, along with samples from sites of lower occupation intensity in the surrounding area. In particular, a very large sample of animal bone was obtained, which has been extensively examined by

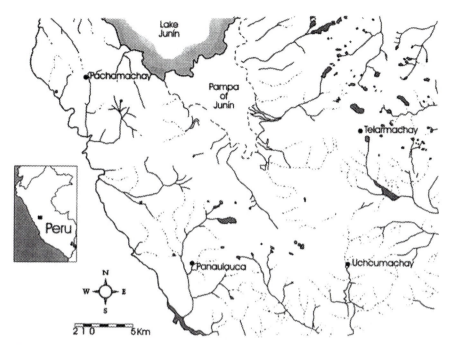

Figure 12.2 Map of the Junín puna of central Peru. Base camps mentioned in text are shown, along with Telarmachay and Uchcumachay: two sites excavated by other projects.

Moore (1989). Here we will summarize some of the more important findings of the project as they relate to an hypothesized meat-focused diet, after which we will more closely examine hypothetical hunting strategies and the corresponding archaeological correlates using simulation techniques.

Settlement Pattern

The distribution of sites across the puna landscape reflects a number of factors, but probably shelter and proximity to primary resources are the most influential. Both Pachamachay and Panaulauca base camps were placed in the most inhabitable caves of their areas: those with deep chambers, of a scale large enough to house a small band-sized group of a maximum of around 25 persons, but small enough to offer real shelter against cold puna winds. The remaining sites with preceramic deposits are concentrated in rock shelters located near concentrations of streams or regularly placed along major watercourses. Site density is notably lower in areas of volcanic bedrock, as opposed to the more common limestone substrate. The association of vicuña territories with permanent sources of water (Rick 1980) and the better grazing resources in limestone areas, along with other details, suggests that the site distribution is consistent with an exploitation pattern primarily aimed at vicuña.

Intensity of Occupation

A series of cave sites in the Junín puna are known to have exceptional densities of cultural material in their preceramic layers. In our excavations at Panaulauca and Pachamachay we have observed similar patterns of material densities across time. To date, we have no evidence for pre-Holocene human occupation or Pleistocene fauna, although some carnivore-gnawed animal remains occur in apparently pre-human levels. Both sites hint at a very early Holocene occupation of low intensity, followed by an early peak of cultural materials around 9000–8000 BP. A sharp but brief drop in occupation intensity follows, after which a still larger and longer peak of occupation seems to occur from about 6500 to around 3600 BP. Thereafter, the use of caves as habitation centers fades, undoubtedly replaced by the ceramic-age formative herding camps frequently observed in open-air contexts. Although there is variation in the amount of materials across time in these deposits, there is no stratigraphic evidence for abandonment of the sites by humans at any time during the Preceramic Period. The actual density of remains during the Preceramic Period is spectacular. Extrapolating from the proportion of the sites excavated, we can calculate that Pachamachay and Panaulauca deposits each contain on the order of 500,000 stone tools and probably in the range of 25 million pieces of stone chipping waste. When a similar pattern of high density in the animal bone assemblage is included (Moore 1998), these data argue for long-term and intensive occupation at these sites during significant segments of the Preceramic period, probably in the form of base camps of low mobility hunting groups.

Tool Industries

The stone tool assemblage from Preceramic Period levels of excavated puna sites consists primarily of chipped stone projectile points of a variety of forms, a series of unifacially retouched flakes, and larger, blunt-edged core tools. Most of the unifacial tools can be lumped into high-edge-angle tools with a round edge outline and straight-edge tools with a more acute edge angle. Roughly speaking, the function of the industry seems to break down into penetrating, scraping, and cutting tasks, mostly appropriate for hunting, hide processing, and cutting relatively soft materials such as meat. None of the chipped stone tools argues strongly for a plant-processing function, and in fact, the few food plants of the puna would not involve these stone tools in their procurement or consumption. Grinding stones, which generally have a plant-processing connotation, are extremely rare in puna sites despite an abundance of appropriate raw materials. Rock exposures appropriate for grinding facilities abound, but to date, no evidence of bedrock usage has been located. The Preceramic bone tool industry, numerically meager in relation to chipped stone tools, is composed mostly of sharp-to-blunt pointed bone fragments of varying levels of modification and antler tips and crowns showing wear. The main functions implied include hole-making in soft materials and stone flaking; again, none intrinsically suggest use on plant materials. Overall, the known technology of these sites seems heavily oriented towards hunting and processing of meat and animal products such as hides.

Rock Art

Pictographs, usually painted in red, are frequently seen in shelters where appropriate protection exists from erosive elements. Although the age of the art is far from certain, deposits of preceramic age are uniformly present in decorated shelters, while ceramic materials are present with less consistency. Red ochre is regularly found in preceramic levels of sites and is effectively absent in ceramic period strata; among other uses—including the tanning of hides—this is probably the colorant used in most puna rock art. The pictographs themselves, when sufficiently preserved to interpret, are almost always of large-bodied, long-neck animals that are clearly portraying camelids. Attempts at identifying the species of camelid have not been successful, but female characteristics, including depiction of teats and X-ray-like views of unborn fetuses, are sometimes evident. The consistent positioning of these clear females and nonfemale animals of different sizes across a number of rock art panels suggests that organizational features of the vicuna may be portrayed in the art. True hunting scenes of weapon-wielding humans in aggressive interaction with camelids are not yet known from the central Peruvian puna, nor have representations of wounded or dead animals been observed. Thus, rock art suggests a strong attention to camelids, probably one of the wild species, but a surprising lack of depiction of hunting. The art does reflect the close observation of camelid behavior that would be consistent with a strong hunting focus on these animals.

Human Remains

Compared to the intensity of occupation debris in the excavated sites, a relatively small number of human interments have been encountered: a total of 12 individuals from preceramic contexts. Our excavations leave no doubt that preceramic disposal of the dead primarily occurred in places other than the heavily utilized cave mouth areas of base camp sites. The best preserved of these 12 burials come from a very brief time interval in Panaulauca around 5500 BP; these seven interments may have taken place during a brief, stratigraphically undetectable abandonment of the site, during which it was an appropriate location for burial. Bone stable isotopes of carbon and nitrogen were studied using collagen from the powdered bone of the 12 human skeletons and a sample of animal bone collagen and food plants (Moore and Schoeninger 1987). Although it is difficult to directly compare dietary evidence from bone chemistry and archaeological remains, the nitrogen stable isotope data support a very high meat diet, as the delta N15 determinations of the human bone collagen are very close to those of obligate carnivores, such as the puma, in the same environment.

Faunal Remains

Although the analysis of animal bone from puna sites is too complex to be considered here in detail, a summary of the data will help support our basic meat-eating hypothesis. The data and analysis of the faunal remains reported here are derived from K. Moore's doctoral dissertation and subsequent publications (Moore 1988,

1989, 1998). As mentioned above, excavations at Pachamachay produced very little animal bone, even though great quantities of faunal remains were evident in the profiles of a previous excavator's trench. At Panaulauca, our more representative excavations recovered a very large amount of animal bone (Table 12.1) from a relatively small sample of the site's living floor deposits and from a very small sample (1 m²) of the bone-dense talus at the mouth of the cave. The overwhelming majority of the bones date to the preceramic period, and their density in the deposits covaries with that observed in stone tools and chipping waste.

The animal bones represent an assemblage dominated by deer and camelids with a very minor complement (generally considerably less than 1%) of small animals including birds and rodents. In the earliest two phases of occupation, deer have a significant representation, perhaps as much as half of the camelid values, but this quickly reduces across time, and camelids compose about 90% of the assemblage by Phase 2b and thereafter (Figure 12.3). In addition, the identity of guanaco and the smaller vicuña may be inferred metrically for a selection of skeletal elements and teeth for which nonoverlapping distributions have been observed in modern skeletal samples. This technique cannot unambiguously separate samples of domesticated camelids, but is reliable for the pair of wild species in this region. In the early preceramic phases, small camelids (presumed vicuña) made up 85% of the camelids and large camelids (presumed guanaco) 15%; while in the later preceramic phases, guanaco-sized animals made up 25% of the camelids. These data represent an average percent MNI of measured skeletal elements for each phase (Moore 1989: 316–384). The larger size of the guanaco would have contributed more than those proportions to meat weight.

The weathering states of the bone surfaces and the near-perfect recovery of the organic fraction of the bone during collagen preparation show that dissolution of bone was insignificant in this cold, limestone- and dolomite-derived depositional environment. The preservation of delicate fetal bones and the proportion of easily

Table 12.1 Summary of animal bone sample from Panaulauca Cave, showing the total bones, the total bones identified as *Vicugna/Lama* and the number of camelid mandibles with tooth rows that were used to create age profiles.

Phase	Total Number of Bones	NISP Camelid	MNI Aged Camelid
8	9,104	716	9
7	45,568	4,159	39
6	134,194	8,656	48
5	200,124	14,792	99
4	352,432	21,012	82
3	102,230	6,939	37
2B	66,840	5,888	26
2A	26,528	1,638	8
1	7,974	503	3

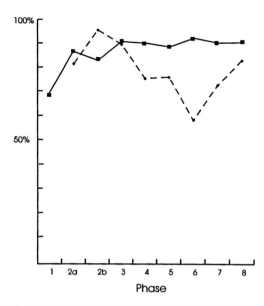

Figure 12.3. Graph of the percentage of camelids within the Panaulauca talus slope faunal assemblage (solid line) and graph of the percentage of vicuña incisors among the total camelid incisors recovered at this site. Modified from Moore (1989).

destroyed elements such as ribs and vertebrae suggest that that entire animals were returned to the site and that only limited density-mediated forces have acted on the bones. Except for a small pocket of material that we have excluded as noncultural in source, evidence for carnivore puncturing, gnawing on long bones, and digestion was sparse. The fragmentation of the bones suggests that complete series of butchering and consumption events took place in and around the cave, from dismemberment and meat-eating, marrow and bone grease preparation, and possibly, the preparation of dried meat. The number and distribution of very small bone fragments (Moore 1998) suggests that intensive use was made of individual carcasses and that occupants made near-complete recovery of within-bone fats, particularly during the later Preceramic.

Raw Materials and Species Geography

The raw materials of Preceramic artifacts from excavations were analyzed, with emphasis on the lithic resources represented. The Junín puna has abundant and diverse chert sources derived from the predominant limestone bedrock, in strong contrast to the metamorphic and igneous bedrock of lower altitude Andean formations. We found that the lithic raw materials were overwhelmingly of local origin; raw materials from nonpuna sources were effectively absent, even in the very large samples studied. Similarly, very few if any animal remains represent nonpuna species. Analysis of plant remains, not reported here due to space restrictions, did not reveal any species capable of competing with animal resources in volume, availability, or quality. Plant resources utilized in Preceramic times were again overwhelmingly of puna origin. The only two examples of clearly nonpuna materials were shell, in the form of beads of marine origin found with one burial, and a few unworked fragments of a large snail species that inhabits the tropical forests to the east of the Andes.

Summary of the Archaeological Data

These broad-ranging data consistently point to a number of aspects of puna subsistence and diet. Human distribution on the landscape is consistent with vicuña exploitation, and the dominant toolkit is composed primarily of hunting tools. Human remains reflect a very high-meat diet, and the identified plant remains do not suggest major alternate sources of diet capable of competing with meat. Faunal remains confirm the presence of an immense amount of by-product of animal exploitation, and the vicuña is the predominant animal represented in the deposits throughout the time period of interest. Thus, the presence of a highly meat-oriented subsistence system focused on a single species, the vicuña, throughout the Preceramic Period in the central puna of Peru seems an unavoidable conclusion. Also, there is minimal evidence of any contact, exchange, or time spent outside the puna region. Surveys of areas surrounding the Junín puna have shown few sites to which Preceramic populations might have gone should they have left the puna. It remains to provide detail about the specific nature of this dietary and hunting emphasis and to make observations about how this adaptation evolved over time.

Hunting Strategies for Intensive Use of Low Diversity Prey

The puna situation outlined above suggests a very narrow diet breadth focused on a species that is very predictable in both its seasonal and daily locational behavior, and very visible within an open grassland setting. Fully modern *Homo sapiens* hunters might have responded to this situation by devoting a large amount of attention to their prey in the form of information gathering and behaviors aimed at prey population maintenance, leading to the evolution of effective technologies and behaviors for utilization of this resource. Factors that might encourage this are the moderate density of the species in question, its large body size, and K-selected (high parental investment) reproductive strategy that would make overexploitation a real possibility. Few alternative resources were available in the event of severe vicuña population reduction, and they are of much lower productive potential. An expedient exploitation leading to local or regional eradication of this species, while possible with available technology, does not conform to the long-term evidence of vicuña utilization in the archaeological record, especially in combination with an increasingly intensive and low mobility human occupation. Thus, the range of exploitation strategies could range from a highly intensive, information-based management to a much more casual and opportunistic pattern that falls short of regional game decimation.

Two issues loom large in considering this range of potential strategies. First, how great would the differences be between strategies in terms of human effort, long-term ecosystem stability, and most importantly, resource productivity? Clearly, if different hunting strategies have similar outcomes, then there would be little incentive for strategies to evolve. Second, even if the specific strategy employed has implications for the long-term success of human populations, we must have specific criteria to identify these strategies in the archaeological record. The puna situation suggests that heavy vicuña exploitation was a successful lifeway for a relatively lengthy period of time, but the measures of human population density and mobility cannot specify more than a general pattern of nonextermination of this primary prey animal.

Simple calculations, such as those mentioned above, give a general sense of the productivity of a resource but cannot be used for more specific and realistic understandings of prey–predator interactions. Simulation techniques offer the possibility of understanding dynamic, long-term patterns, to the degree the simulation parameters and system approximate those of the real world. In the puna case, Rick programmed a computer simulation that established vicuña populations with the demographic characteristics of known vicuña and then subjected these to varying intensity levels of different hunting strategies. The rules for the strategies were formulated in a culturally realistic manner that controls patterns of hunter behavior, rather than specifies the animals the hunter(s) obtain(s). The relative productivity of these different hunting strategies can be evaluated by increasing hunting intensity until a maximum sustainable harvest rate is obtained for each strategy. Criteria for identification of strategies can be sought through the sex and age distributions of animals hunted in the simulations, which can be compared against archaeological assemblages for fit. Because the sex of camelid remains has not yet been regularly identified in Andean archaeological assemblages, it will not be considered further, although such identifications would greatly aid in this process.

The Simulations

To simulate vicuña hunts, we relied heavily on the field studies of Franklin (1976); Hofmann, Otte, and Ponce (1983); and Koford (1957) for basic information about vicuña social organization, reproduction, and behavior. For some population dynamics not available for vicuña, such as the relationships between recruitment, population size, and life expectancy, patterns seen in white-tail deer (*Odocoileus virginianus*) were adopted. The specific vicuña population created in the computer consists of 15 bands in a spatial patterning similar to known vicuña territories, spaced along a creek, plus animals in male troops that are not spatially located. The rate of vicuña reproduction is controlled by the number of females in a band, the band's density, and to a lesser degree that of neighboring bands, a birth survivorship factor, and a random variability factor. This formula is tuned to an optimal band size, leading these vicuña bands to approximate those known in the real world. Mortality patterns and transition of vicuña through changing yearling and adult statuses are responsive to local animal density and other factors. Too many specific rules were used to specify here, but the outcome is a reasonably accurate simulation of the life processes of the vicuña within a responsive social and natural context. These simulated populations show demographic patterns consistent with those known for actual reestablished, reproducing, and eventually density-inhibited populations in southern Peruvian reserves in recent decades (Franklin 1976).

The simulations start with an existing "average" population of vicuña with typical age structure and run for 35 years. The first 20 years are a period of adjustment in which the vicuña population accommodates the natural and cultural mortality factors specified; the last 15 years of the simulation are used to produce statistics for comparison with other simulation runs. A large amount of demographic data is output, but of most importance here are statistics on population size, the relative number of animals hunted versus those dying of natural causes, and the ages of animals taken in the hunting routines. For each hunting routine, simulations are run at steps of predation intensity that increase until the vicuña populations crash. The hunting intensity that produces the maximum sustainable yield (MSY) for any routine is easily determined, and these runs can be compared between hunting strategies. Obviously, we do not assume that hunting was uniformly carried out at MSY, but degradation of yield with either heavier or lighter predation was found to be uniform and predictable for the different strategies, and thus comparisons of the strategies at MSY are applicable to a broader intensity range.

The greatest difficulty in simulating hunting routines is in estimating differential susceptibility to predation across ages within the vicuña social groupings. If hunting is not done on a mass kill basis, the animals most vulnerable to hunters with paleolithic technology are the young, due to their lack of experience, and the old, due to their increasing infirmity with age. Without knowing the effectiveness of the technology, the degree of hunting competence, and some quantifiable estimates of increased susceptibility in vulnerable ages, there is no way to accurately simulate the outcome of hunting strategies in which vulnerability is the prime factor. There is no reliable record of vicuña predation by humans or any other predator that might give the necessary data on susceptibility. In fact, if the susceptibility of the young and old is the primary factor in hunting mortality, simulation is hardly necessary to predict approximately the outcome of this unstrategized type of hunt: the resulting mortality profiles will conform to the attritional pattern widely recognized among zooarchaeologists. The productivity of such random-kill-subject-to-susceptibility hunts will be moderate at best. Although game populations will see a beneficial reduction in older, nonreproductive animals that are increasingly being lost to natural mortality, the inefficient harvesting of undersize animals would inhibit the game population's ability to recruit new members.

Of greater interest is the effect of strategized hunting within the influential and pronounced social structure of the vicuña. Thus, Rick programmed a range of strategies running from catastrophic through random towards optimal—categories that require some explanation. Catastrophic kills involve the taking of entire social units, producing a mortality profile equivalent to the unit's age structure. Hunting techniques implied would be surround or jump strategies in which either the mobility of the animal is reduced to allow limited technologies to kill all animals, irrespective of susceptibility, or the animals' tendency to flight is used to cause them to harm themselves *en masse*. Specific catastrophic strategies included:

1. Hunting of multiple bands in sequence along the modeled drainage system.
2. Hunting of entire random bands.
3. Hunting of major segments of troop animals.

Random hunts take random individuals within social groups according to different rules but without regard to age. Stalking or use of blinds could produce this pattern of kill. Specific strategies include:

4. Simple random individual hunts with all animals in all bands equally susceptible.
5. Random hunting of individuals within largest bands.

The latter technique could reflect either increased likelihood of hunting within bigger, more visible bands or a simple management technique designed to keep bands of relatively equal size, avoiding overpopulation within band territories.

Optimal hunts are those designed to take out the individual animals least important to the reproductive future of the population. Such hunting strategies imply close monitoring of vicuña populations and very controlled predation patterns. Two variants of optimal hunts are:

6. True optimal hunts
7. Near-optimal hunts

True optimal hunts are complex strategies that do not kill any undersize individuals, remove individuals to achieve optimal band size for reproduction, kill older animals first in both troops and bands, and take nearly all troop animals. This is not at a realistic type of hunt and probably could not be achieved even with modern weapons, as sex and particularly age of vicuña are difficult to estimate at a distance from the animals. This hunt simply serves as a highest imaginable productivity comparison. The near-optimal hunts basically take random individuals from largest bands until a specific band population is achieved, and troop males are harvested in a predation rate proportional to that practiced on bands. This technique would require hunters to be aware of the size of bands, avoid kills in small bands, and be effective at producing measured kills within troops—feasible rules for capable prehistoric game managers. One potential difficulty is the relatively unpredictable location and flight-prone behavior of the nonterritorial all-male troops.

Simulation Productivity Implications

We are not emphasizing the use of simulation to estimate gross productivity of the vicuña as a resource. The simulations do suggest that the vicuña has the potential to provide a very large proportion of the diet of low-density, low-mobility puna hunter-gatherers, but of greater concern here is the relative productivity of different vicuña hunting strategies. The simulations show that there is an immense difference in the productive capacity of the vicuña between the different hunting strat-egies. Compared against the true optimal standard, the troop-kill-only strategy (3) is the worst, yielding less than 25% of optimal productivity. The near-optimal hunt MSY (7) is about 83% of the true optimal, which shows that relatively simple hunting rules could achieve a very high productivity compared to more expedient techniques. The remaining strategies range between 40% and 65% of optimal productivity (Table 12.2). The proportional productivity differences between strategies are maintained, it should be noted, even when natural vicuña mortality is varied by altering a yearly natural survivorship factor in the simulations. The MSY runs of the simulation by definition maintain long-term game populations, but any of the strategies will provide a larger number of animals for a brief period under an inten-sive predation that depletes the vicuña. This type of extermination hunting was simu-lated, and not surprisingly, its long-term productivity is much lower than any MSY simulations because the delay in repopulating vacant territories leaves grazing re-sources underutilized.

An important consideration is the vicuña population size that produces MSY for the different strategies. The true optimal (6) and near-optimal (7) hunts have rela-tively small vicuña population sizes at MSY, compared with the less productive strategies. Figure 12.4 helps explain the reasons for this: the most productive hunts maximize the percentage of overall animal mortality that contributes to the hunt-ers' diet while at the same time encouraging rapid reproduction of the prey. A younger and smaller, and thus well-nourished and highly reproductive, population is ideal. The further a hunt is from the optimal, the less is its ability to produce such an ideal population. There are two implications of this. First, optimal MSY strate-gies lead to smaller, vigorous populations that are intrinsically more stable and buffered against food shortages. Second, the difference in the proportion of the vicuña population being harvested by the different strategies is even greater than the productivity statistics would suggest. Thus, the percent-of-population hunting yield varies about 6:1 between optimal and least optimal MSY hunts.

The implications of these figures are fairly obvious; the hunting strategies adopted or developed by puna hunters would have a very strong effect on their mobility, ter-ritory size, and the likelihood of long-term occupation of single sites. Expedient hunt-

Table 12.2.

Simulation Strategy	Number of Animals Killed per Year	Avg. Vicuña Population Size	Avg. No. of Individuals Recruited per Year
1 Band sequence kill	10.7	210	17.2
2 Random band kill	13.9	197	21.7
3 Troop kill only	6.0	161	13.2
4 Random single kill	15.0	218	20.3
5 Single kill in largest band	16.0	243	24.5
6 Optimal	25.0	115	25.7
7 Near-optimal	22.0	122	23.1

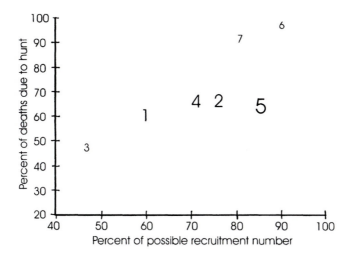

Figure 12.4. Graph of major factors effecting the productivity of different simulated hunting strategies. Numbers correspond to simulations listed in Table 12.1. Size of number symbols reflects size of animal population in simulation.

ing techniques that reduced the vicuña population would not only require frequent mobility but would also reduce the long-term, overall productivity of the puna and the stability of the natural world as well. The payoff in energetic terms and risk reduction to developing conservative hunting strategies would be great in this sort of environment, suggesting a likelihood that intensive, rather than extensive utilization patterns might occur long prior to any population growth and circumscription.

Identification Criteria for Hunting Strategies

The simulations produced data that allow construction of the age mortality profiles expected under differing intensities of the strategies. Because age-specific susceptibility was not modeled, it is not surprising that most of the profiles are similar— they all approximate the population profile of the social units under exploitation. Younger ages are generally well represented, tapering towards old age. Low intensity hunting of populations with high natural survivorship flatten this trend, because fewer young animals are incorporated into a fairly aged population. High-intensity hunting was expected to have the effect of greatly reducing the tapering old-age tail of the populations, but in fact, even populations being exploited to extinction do not show profiles notably different from intermediate levels of predation. Troop hunting has a major impact because troops lack animals younger than a year; conversely, nontroop kills will have relatively enriched yearling representation. Some variability is seen as optimal exploitation is approached due to avoidance of the very young and preference for older animals. Most notable, however, is that increased hunting intensity seems to have a greatest impact on the optimal hunts, showing a clear increase in prime age young adults. Ironically, the optimal and troop hunts have fairly similar profiles at high exploitation levels because they both extensively harvest young adults. Overall, there may be signatures of both hunting strategies and exploitation intensity embedded in the age-mortality profiles, but they are not distinctive enough to be obvious.

In attempting to match the simulations with the prehistoric record, the limitations of archaeological data are very evident. Even assuming that the relatively voluminous puna faunal data are representative of the animals hunted prehistorically, the total number of individuals composing archaeological age-mortality profiles is relatively small, and the identifiable age grades are not evenly distributed across the camelid age span (Table 12.1). Age assignments were based on tooth eruption and tooth wear compared with known-age animals (Moore 1989) and produce a minimum number of individuals of given age grades. Age profiles were constructed using complete tooth rows in mandibles only, allowing the most precise, accurate, and independent estimates possible using archaeological materials. To have samples sufficient in number to give meaningful profiles, archaeological levels were grouped within time phases (Figure 12.5). There are few close matches between most archaeological profiles from Panaulauca and the simulation data. In general, very young animals are much better represented in the archaeological profiles than in the simulations, and for many of the earlier archaeological levels, there is a notable gap in early adult ages. This is remarkable because any differential preservation would bias against the proportion of baby animals. An interesting possibility, however, is that some proportion of these young animals are the remains of scavenged stillborn or early neonate dead known to occur in vicuña birth season (Wheeler 1984). If this were the case, then the actual hunted prehistoric assemblages would more closely match our simulations. Visually analyzing these profiles is difficult, so multidimensional scaling (MDS) was used to compare the simulations and archaeological samples. MDS reduces the dimensions of variability for measured subjects to make the overall relationships between them more apparent.

The resulting placement of simulations and archaeological phases both confirms the expected and brings out some new data relationships (Figure 12.6). It is clear that MDS cannot segregate the majority of simulated hunting strategies, although optimal and troop-kill strategies are both separate from the remainder and show greater variability among simulations of different hunting intensity. The majority of the remaining techniques—random band or random individual kills—form a compact cluster of low overall variability. The archaeological levels are mostly well separated on the axis that also distinguishes optimal from random hunts. By examining the correlation of the dimensions of the MDS solution with age ranges, it is clear that the vertical axis reflects kills of central adult ages of 3 to 12 years, but primarily emphasizing the younger end, and the very young (0–9 months of age). The horizontal axis is less clear, but seems most sensitive to hunting intensity in the simulations, mainly reflecting differences in the representation of 1.5–3-year-olds.

Seen as a time sequence, archaeological phases 1 through 3 essentially demonstrate an increase along the horizontal, or intensity axis. This may be related to a somewhat seasonal signature of camelid ages in Phases 1 through 2b that could imply

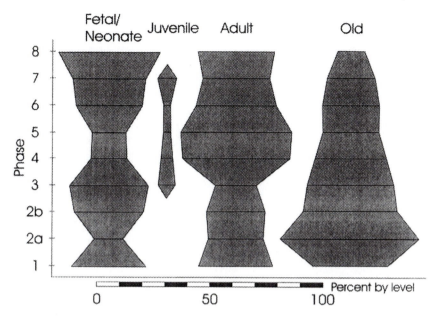

Figure 12.5. Percentage frequency chart of different camelid age categories determined from mandibles across archaeological phases in the overall Panaulauca faunal assemblage.

a less than year-round occupation of these sites in the earliest occupations. In terms of animal ages harvested, we see young and a few prime age adults, plus some quite aged animals, in an increasing pattern of exploitation intensity. Starting with Phase 4, peaking in Phase 5, and receding somewhat in Phases 6 and 7, the primary variability is along the vertical axis, getting near the variate space of the random hunting simulations. The late Phase 8 returns into the space of the earlier phases, but there is evidence that some of the animals are domesticated by this point. This vertical axis change can be described as a move away from killing the youngest animals, substituting mostly prime age adults. Some of this change could be due to a relative reduction in the seasonally available young, as occupation apparently becomes year-round, but the increase in only the prime age adults suggests an increasingly effective hunting of difficult-to-obtain animals.

The great distance between the early phases and the simulations reflects an emphasis on some age ranges representing attritional-type assemblages for the former, and a nonage-specific random distribution in the latter. The animals being increasingly taken in the earlier preceramic seem to reflect an expedient, attritional exploitation. This is also consistent with the pattern of bone fragmentation in these levels, where bone fragments are very dense, but the intensity of fragmentation (and presumably carcass use) is limited. The upward shift of the later preceramic phases argues that hunters were managing to take a more balanced cross-section of the animal population, something approaching a catastrophic profile. This could rep-

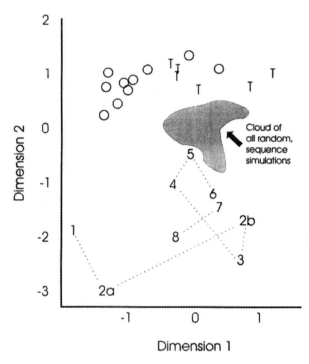

Figure 12.6. Multidimensional scaling similarity plot of Panaulauca archaeological phases' camelid age-specific mortality (numbers), and simulated hunt age-specific mortality (letters and shaded area). Os represent optimal hunts; Ts are troop kill only hunts.

resent mass killing of social groups of animals, but we suspect this is not the case. If it were, the very young ranges of animals should be even more strongly represented, and the peak of animals in mid-age range should not stand out so strongly. Barring catastrophic kills as the source of this pattern, the change suggests a greatly increased choice of and ability to kill prime age animals. The pattern of bone fragmentation and processing in the later preceramic shows intensive use of the animals taken, maximizing food yield from each carcass. The overall shift in the prehistoric record is away from an attritional pattern in the direction of optimality. Troop kills are not likely to be the predominant cause of this shift because some yearling animals continue to be present in the archaeological assemblages of the most "optimal-shifted" phases. Another strand of evidence that suggests increasing management of animal populations is a decreasing rate of toothwear experienced by camelids in the later periods. Range management experience shows that such toothwear differences may have been associated with smaller group sizes, improved pasture quality, and improved animal health and carcass weights. All these conditions would be predicted in a move towards optimality but not with an increase in troop usage.

Conclusion

A number of lines of evidence converge to suggest that, during the later phases of the Junín puna Preceramic occupation (7000–3600 BP) there was a move towards a managed hunting strategy that probably was designed to promote the productivity of wild animal populations. In Phases 4 and 5 (5800–3600 BP), a maximum intensity of site occupation is seen, along with evidence of selective hunting of animal age ranges desirable for maximum game productivity but ages that are relatively hard to kill. At the same time, the reduction in camelid tooth wear and a reduction in the aged camelids within the faunal assemblage (and thus probably within the actual population) argue that the animal populations were buffered below their own carrying capacity, probably by human exploitation. Coupled with strong evidence for year-round exploitation in the seasons represented in the fauna (Moore 1998) and evidence in stone tools for stylistic segregation of neighboring base camps (Rick 1996), it seems likely that a low mobility lifeway based on intensive and year-round use of small hunting territories came into existence. The evidence at hand argues that this intensive but apparently strategized utilization of this species did not lead to immediate domestication of the prey species. In fact, it is not clear that the vicuña were ever domesticated, and, at the very least, transitional forms between vicuña and camelid domesticates are not apparent in these puna sites.

Exactly how such a managed hunt would have been practically achieved is hard to know. It has been observed that the band-heading adult male vicuña have a tendency to defend their territories (Koford 1957), and initially lag behind female band members when an intruder is noted. Thus, it might be possible for a hunter to selectively kill only the band male, who would fairly quickly be replaced by a troop male. Two factors suggest that this was not the predominant technique used prehistorically. First, even the relatively short vacancy in a band territory that follows on the band male's death would have significantly disrupted reproduction. Second, we found that any simulated strategy that only harvests males results in disastrous overpopulation of band territories by excess females and an accompanying reduction of young animal survivorship. Abundant folklore of the Andes also suggests that band females will hover around a dead band male and be reticent to take flight. Further studies of modern vicuña behavior will help clarify exactly what characteristics these animals have that might have aided in a controlled prehistoric hunt.

In perspective, this is a rather special case of highly focused animal exploitation and, consequently, a meat-dominated diet. Puna hunters seem to have realized a potential to manage game populations, although the nature of this management remains to be understood. It is interesting to note that although occupation intensity hits its highest level in the known base camps at this time, there is no apparent increase in overall number of sites with later Preceramic occupation, with all investigated sites yielding both late and early preceramic components. This period of managed exploitation lasted at least 2,000, and perhaps as much as 3,000 years or more, with stylistic evidence of social stability. The eventual transition out of this condition seems to be coupled with both a settlement shift to open-air hamlets and a subsistence shift to herding. The forces that caused this change are not yet known, but it was not an immediate consequence of intensive use of a single species, or of reduced mobility.

The path towards the late Preceramic condition is similarly unclear, but there are some interesting hints. Both base camp records show an early peak in occupation intensity (Phases 2a , 2b) that seems to be coupled with an increase in hunting intensity, but not with a shift towards age-specific hunting selectivity. Stylistic evidence from tools (Rick 1996) suggests a greater amount of mobility or interaction between base camp groups, and the seasonality of ecofacts argues less strongly for year-round occupation, although even at this time there is little evidence for interaction with areas beyond the puna. There is a notable break in stylistic continuity that coincides with the mid-Preceramic reduction in occupation intensity, which could argue for either population replacement or some other form of social flux. It is tempting to envision an early increasing specialization in camelid use, but one that did not involve effective management techniques, eventually leading to abandonment or alteration of this regional population. This could represent a "learning experience" that might have helped lead to a managed hunting system through negative example. Belief systems compatible with and promoting of managed hunting might have emerged in this context. Although these are speculations given our current state of knowledge, it would not be surprising to see hunters dependent on one primary game species develop a range of cultural responses capable of increasing the dependability of their unique prey species.

In evolutionary terms, hunting and meat consumption may not have been the crucible of human intelligence, or the glue of social order. Yet, we find that the nature of hunting becomes increasingly familiar in primates as genealogical distance decreases, as well demonstrated by the primate chapters in this volume. In a similar way, prehistoric hominids seem to show use of their apparently increasing mental abilities across time in the way they deal with hunting prey. While Washburn and Lancaster (1968) and others may not ultimately be right that hunting served as a selective force for human intelligence, we think it is the case that evidence of prehistoric hunting will often be key to understanding changes in cultural abilities. The debate on the issue of Neandertal hunting abilities is ably elaborated by Speth and Tchernov in this volume, and it is precisely this type of specific and increasingly strategized relationship between humans and prey that can yield many major gains in understanding the evolution of culture. The puna case suggests the use of human intelligence in the form of perceptive hunting strategies that not only took good advantage of natural resources but had the potential to actually improve and stabilize the natural productivity of this environment. These are features usually imputed for food production, but it is important to realize that hunters did have possibilities to alter their environments, not always for the worst. The viability of a meat-based diet for humans is a major issue I have not dealt with here, but the puna case raises the possibility that, under certain conditions, intensive exploitation of game may have been a stable and effective way of making a living and not just a stopping point on a trajectory from expedient, extensive hunting towards food production.

Acknowledgments   The authors would like to express their appreciation to Ramiro Matos M., then of the University of San Marcos (Lima), Kent Flannery and Jeffrey Parsons of the University of Michigan, and the S.A.I.S. "Tupac Amaru" Ltda. #1 for helping make possible the fieldwork on which this article was based. Much appreciated financial support was provided by the Archaeology Program of the National Science Foundation, primarily through grant BNS 80–22748, Sigma Xi, and Stanford University, the University of Michigan, and Bentley College. Helpful comments were received from the editors and authors of this volume and an anonymous reviewer.

REFERENCES

Bettinger, R. L. 1980. Explanatory/predictive models of hunter-gatherer adaptation. In *Advances in Archaeological Method and Theory*, vol. 3, pp. 189–253. New York: Academic Press.

Binford, L. R. 1980. Willow smoke and dogs' tails: hunter-gatherer settlement systems and archaeological site formation. *American Antiquity* 45:4–20.

Binford, L. R. 1983. *Working at Archaeology*. New York: Academic Press.

Cowan, M. J. McTaggert, and C. Holloway. 1973. Threatened deer of the world: conservation status. *Biological Conservation* 5(4):243–250.

Francou, B. 1983. Les regimes thermiques et pluviometriques de Pachachaca (Andes Centrales du Perou): contribution a la connaissance des rythmes saisonniers dans le climat de la puna. *Bulletin de l'Institut Francais d'Etudes Andines* XII (1–2):17–53.

Franklin, W. L. 1976. *Socioecology of the Vicuña*. Ph.D. dissertation. Utah State University, Logan.

Franklin, W. L. 1974. The social behavior of the vicuña. In *The Behavior of Ungulates and Its Relation to Management*. (V. Geist and F. Walter, eds.), pp. 477–487. Morges, Switzerland: International Union for Conservation of Nature and Natural Resources.

Hayden, B. 1981. Research and development in the stone age: technological transitions among hunter-gatherers. *Current Anthropology* 22(5):519–548.

Hoffman, R. K., K-C. Otte, and C. F. Ponce. 1983. *El Manejo de la Vicuña Silvestre*. Tomo 1. Germany: Eschborn.

Kent, J. D. 1982. *Domestication and Exploitation of the South American Camelids: Methods of Analysis and Their Application to Circumlacustrine Archaeological Sites in Bolivia and Peru*. Ph.D. dissertation. Department of Anthropology, Washington University, University Microfilms, Ann Arbor.

Klein, R. G. 1998. Why anatomically modern people did not disperse from Africa 100,000 years ago. In *Neandertals and Modern Humans in Western Asia* (T. Akazawa, K. Aoki, and O. Bar-Yosef, eds.), pp. 509–521. New York: Plenum Press.

Koford, C. B. 1957. The vicuña and the puna. *Ecological Monographs* 27(2):152–219.

Lee, R. B., and I. DeVore, (eds.). 1968. *Man the Hunter*. Chicago: Aldine.

Merkt, J. B. 1987. Reproductive seasonality and grouping patterns of the North Andean deer or taruca (*Hippocamelus antisensis*) in southern Peru. *In Biology and Management of the Cervidae* (C. M. Wemmer, ed.), pp. 388–401. Washington, DC: Smithsonian Institution Press.

Moore, K. M. 1988. Hunting and herding economies on the Junín Puna. In *Economic Prehistory of the Central Andes* (E. S. Wing and J. C. Wheeler, eds.), pp. 154–166. B.A.R. International Series 427.

Moore, K. M. 1989. *Hunting and the Origins of Herding in Peru*. Ph.D. dissertation. Department of Anthropology, University of Michigan, Ann Arbor.

Moore, K. M. 1998. Measures of mobility and occupational intensity in highland Peru. In *Identifying Seasonality and Sedentism in Archaeological Sites: Old and New World Perspectives* (T. R. Rocek and O. Bar-Yosef, eds.), vol. 6, pp. 181–196. Cambridge, MA: Peabody Museum Bulletin.

Moore, K. M., and M. J. Schoeninger. 1987. Quantitative reconstruction of diet in prehistoric highland Peru. Presented at the 52nd annual meeting of the Society for American Archaeology, Toronto.

ONERN. 1976. *Inventario y Evaluación de los Recursos Naturales de la SAIS "Tupac Amaru."* Lima: Oficina Nacional de Evaluación de Recursos Naturales.

Rick, J. W. 1980. *Prehistoric Hunters of the High Andes.* New York: Academic Press.

———— 1996. Projectile points, style, and social process in the Preceramic of Central Peru. In *Stone Tools: Theoretical Insights Into Human Prehistory* (G. Odell, ed.), pp. 245–278. New York: Plenum Press.

Rick, J. W., and B. Bocek. 1985. La época precerámica en la Puna de Junín: investigaciones en la zona de Panaulauca. *Chungara* 13:109–127.

Service, E. R. 1966. *The Hunters.* Englewood, Cliffs, NJ: Prentice Hall.

Steward, J. H. 1972. *Theory of Culture Change.* Urbana: University of Illinois Press.

Tosi, J. A., Jr. 1960. *Zonas de Vida Natural en el Peru.* Boletin Tecnico No. 5 271. Instituto Interamericano de Ciencias Agrícolas de la OEA, Zona Andina.

Washburn, S. L., and C. S. Lancaster. 1968. The evolution of hunting. In *Man the Hunter*, (R. B. Lee and I. DeVore, eds.), pp. 293–303. Chicago: Aldine.

Weberbauer, A. 1936. Phytogeography of the Peruvian Andes: flora of Peru. *Field Museum of Natural History Botanical Series* 13(1):13–80.

Wheeler, J. C. 1984. On the origin and early development of camelid pastoralism in the Andes. In *Animals and Archaeology 3: Early Herders and Their Flocks* (J. Clutton Brock and C. Grigson, eds.), pp. 395–410. BAR International Series 202.

Wing, E. S. 1974. Informe preliminar acerca de los restos de fauna de la cueva de Pachamachay, en Junín, Peru. *Revista del Museo Nacional* 41:78–80.

Winterhalder, B., and E. A. Smith, eds. 1981. *Hunter-Gatherer Foraging Strategies: Ethnographic and Archaeological Analyses.* Chicago: University of Chicago Press.

13

Mutualistic Hunting

Michael S. Alvard

Every moving thing that liveth shall be meat for you.
God speaking to Noah, Genesis 9:3

Introduction

The problems involved with living in complex social groups have emerged as important prime movers for hominid adaptation. In *H. sapiens*, social complexity is associated with a number of interesting traits. One of the more interesting is the cooperative large-game acquisition and the distribution of the meat resource. Sometime during the last 5 million or so years, hominids went from a chimpanzee-like subsistence pattern to one where meat was a substantial proportion of the diet. In fact, the proportion of meat in the diet is one characteristic that sets humans apart from other primates.

It is not surprising that social complexity and foraging for meat are related. Indeed, many important aspects of human nature revolve around common problems associated with acquiring, defending, and distributing resources. Social scientists have long understood the importance of resource production and transfers (Winterhalder 1997). The entire field of economics is based on the acquisition of scarce resources and their transfer between conspecifics. It is increasingly evident that foraging constraints, as well as competition and cooperation with conspecifics selected for increased intelligence in our primate ancestors (Byrne and Whiten 1988; King 1994; Whiten and Byrne 1997; Dunbar 1998). The human large game-focused foraging strategy is linked to a suite of adaptive traits related to social cognitive skills. Many specific cognitive tools for dealing with risk and reward likely evolved in a context of resource acquisition and distribution during our evolutionary past—during the so-called environment of evolutionary adaptedness (EEA). The cognitive skills required for cooperative hunting, for example, are usefully viewed as adaptations to associated problems such as cheater and cooperator detecting

(Cosmides and Tooby 1992) and the accounting required for distribution and consumption. The EEA is the set of environmental conditions under which human mental abilities evolved (Symons 1979; Tooby and Cosmides 1992), often considered the Plio-Pleistocene for many important traits, although the time period depends on the trait in question. Recent evidence suggests that enhanced hominid carnivory, whether from hunting or scavenging, may have developed as early as 2.5 millions years ago (de Heinzelin et al. 1999).

It is in this context that meat has played an important role in the evolution of humanity in ways independent of its otherwise significant and concentrated nutritional contribution. Meat is usually rare relative to plant food, giving it increased value. It is also often difficult and dangerous to obtain, increasing its value even more. When individuals obtain it, meat is often obtained in quantities that create short-term surpluses, creating inequalities between those that have it and those that do not (Winterhalder 1997). It also often requires cooperation to obtain, defend, and distribute.

Cooperative hunting and meat-sharing has received much attention since the Man the Hunter Conference in 1966 (Lee and Devore 1968). It is conceivable that the cooperative acquisition of meat (Bunn and Ezzo 1993) and its defense (Rose and Marshall 1996) opened a niche that was otherwise unavailable to a solitarily foraging primate, whether or not it was the original reason for the evolution of hominid sociality. Many of the potential meat resources present in the environment of hominids were only available if cooperative effort was made to obtain them. In fact, much meat harvested by extant hunter-gathers is obtained through cooperative acquisition (e.g., !Kung, Lee 1979; Mbuti Pygmies, Ichikawa 1983; Inujjuamiut, Smith 1991). A number of researchers (Washburn and Lancaster 1968; Lovejoy 1981; Lancaster and Lancaster 1983; and others) have argued the well-known idea that male hunting and provisioning of females and dependent young were watershed adaptations that formed the basis for a suite of human social characters. Although this scenario has been justifiably questioned (for a recent critique, see Hawkes 1993), the fact remains that many important aspects of human nature revolve around solving problems related to the cooperative acquisition, defense, and distribution of hunted resources—whether or not the meat was distributed to provision families or to obtain additional matings, as suggested by Hawkes (1993).

A hominid subsistence strategy focusd on large game presents two important and related challenges. Because large prey types are unavailable to individual foragers, the first problem is for individuals to cooperate sufficiently to acquire the resource in the short term. The second problem is related to distribution. Those involved in its cooperative acquisition must obtain a satisfactory payoff from the carcass to ensure cooperation will continue in the long term. The two problems are related because cooperative acquisition is more likely if participants have sufficient certainty that they will receive a payoff during the distribution.

These are complex issues, and a number of sophisticated analytic tools are available to understand cooperative behavior like those associated with big game hunting and meat distribution. Among the most popular are game theoretical approaches. Game theory attempts to model how organisms make decisions when outcomes are contingent on what others do, and recent applications have incorporated evolutionary perspectives (Maynard-Smith 1982; Hawkes 1992). As I will discuss below, the well-known game called Prisoner's Dilemma (PD) has dominated game theory research on cooperation. The iterated PD (the PD game played over multiple turns) presents intellectually challenging obstacles to cooperation while at the same time it provides a good model for understanding reciprocity. Reciprocity involves non-simultaneous exchange of benefits, is thought to be common in nature, and is often presented as a mechanism to explain food-sharing in humans (Kaplan and Hill 1985; Winterhalder 1986). While reciprocity and the Prisoner's Dilemma are useful for understanding resource sharing, these models are not be sufficient for understanding many types of cooperation involved in resource acquisition.

Mutualism has been suggested as an alternative to explain many cases of cooperation not readily understood as reciprocity (West-Eberhard 1975; see also Brown 1983; Conner 1986; Mesterton-Gibbons and Dugatkin 1992; Dugatkin 1997; Winterhalder 1997). Although reciprocity involves a short-term cost, mutual cooperation provides immediate benefits to the individual. It may be a particularly important mechanism to explain cooperative hunting/ scavenging where the common enemy is a prey item that a solitary individual cannot kill or defend (Earl 1987; Packer and Ruttan 1988; Scheel and Packer 1991). In this chapter, I review the similarities and differences between mutualistic and reciprocal cooperation and the ecological circumstances that favor one behavioral response over the other. I will go on to discuss mutualism in a context of big game hunting and finally introduce some preliminary data from a case study of extant Indonesian whale hunters.

Altruism and Cooperation

Altruism has proven to be an essential concept within the evolutionary study of social behavior, but in many ways it has been a strawman. Altruism is a behavior that increases the fitness of others and decreases the fitness of the actor—and by definition will be selected out of a population. Much of the last 40 years of research in evolutionary ecology has been devoted to showing that the bulk of altruistic behavior is only apparently so. For example, Hamilton (1964) introduced the concept of inclusive fitness to show that help to kin is not altruism because relatives share genes. Cooperation is conceptually related to altruism but differs in important ways. Clements and Stephens (1995) have recently stressed the point that cooperation need not be altruistic at all. In fact, *none* of the hypotheses current in the literature evoke genuine altruism to explain cooperative behavior. Dugatkin (1997: 37–38) defines cooperation as an activity requiring collective action by at least two individuals that results in a "good" outcome for the members of the group. "Good" is measured by an appropriate proxy currency to fitness. Clements and Stephens (1995) define cooperation as joint action for mutual benefit. Altruism is a behavior that favors others over self and, as a result, will not evolve. In contrast, cooperative behavior maintains an element of self-interest. Cooperation favors self *and* others and for this reason can evolve.

Political and economic theories note that there are obstacles to cooperation where the good produced is a public one (Olsen 1965). The primary obstacle is the conflict of interest that often exists between the individuals that make up a group and the interests of the group as a whole. While a good or mutually beneficial outcome might be obtained through cooperative hunting, for example, an *individual* can often obtain even higher payoffs by consuming the good and allowing others to pay the costs of acquisition—assuming the good produced is a public one. Public goods include resources that individuals can consume regardless of whether they have paid for them or not (Hawkes 1992). These sorts of problems have been variously termed collective action problems (Olson 1965), free riding (Kim and Walker 1984), and social dilemmas (Dawes 1980). Hardin (1968) provided the "tragedy of the commons" as the metaphor to describe the outcome where a public good is destroyed because of selfish behavior by individuals.

The same sorts of conundrums have been postulated for the evolution of animal and human societies. The common interpretation is that it is difficult for cooperation to evolve because it involves self-sacrifice, yet is it relatively common in animal societies, particularly in human and nonhuman primate societies. Indeed, recent evolutionarily guided research with primates shows that these animals exhibit the spectrum of behaviors from cooperative to corruptive, often within the same species (see, e.g., de Waal 1989; Wrangham and Peterson 1996). What explains this variability?

Reciprocity

Trivers (1971) described reciprocity as one mechanism to explain how cooperation could evolve between unrelated individuals. He termed the process reciprocal altruism. Reciprocity involves the nonsimultaneous exchange of resources between individuals. Reciprocity is apparently altruistic in the short term because individuals relinquish resources to others without any immediate return. Trivers argued that this could be selected for if the long-term reciprocated benefits outweigh the short-term costs. In its simplest form, reciprocity occurs when an individual pays a short-term cost to benefit another because of expected reciprocation in the future. Note that if the future benefit outweighs the present cost, the behavior is not altruism in the true sense. It should also be noted that if the initial act is not costly, the behavior is mutualism, not reciprocity (Conner 1986; see below). For example, imagine that at time *t* individual *X* has more resource than individual *Y*. *X* transfers resources to *Y* and thus suffers a cost from the act, and *Y* benefits by avoiding a shortfall. At some time *t* + 1, *Y* may have a surplus and *X* a shortfall. *X* benefits by receiving resources transferred by *Y*.

Reciprocity is a mechanism that reduces variation in resource consumption and hence risk. In a subsistence context, risk is defined as the likelihood of a resource shortfall—that is, dropping below some minimum quantity of a resource (e.g., R_{min}; Winterhalder 1997). Reciprocity minimizes time-unit to time-unit variation as resources flow from haves to have-nots one time, and back another, as the roles of giver and receiver change due to random variation in individual foraging returns.

A classic example of reciprocity from the ethnographic literature is Eskimo food-sharing partnerships as reported by Damas (1972). Sharing partnerships were common in many Inuit hunting and gathering bands, notably the Copper and Netsilik. Shares of meat, most often ringed seal, were exchanged between dyads of hunters who had agreed beforehand to participate in the long-term arrangement. Ringed seal was the most important prey item in the diet—in fact, ringed seal may have been the limiting food item. Shares consisted of parts like the neck, heart, ribs, back, or other part of the seal. A partnership might work the following way: when hunter X harvested a seal, his partner Y got a fin; when Y harvested a seal, X got a fin. While Damas did not test the idea, such sharing surely reduced day-to-day variance in the quantity of food consumed in an otherwise stochastic environment. Hunters had multiple partners (one hunter reported having 19 during his lifetime— but it is unclear whether they were all concurrent).

An important aspect of this type of adaptive environment is that the best decision from an individual's point of view depends critically on the behavior of other strategizing conspecific actors. As has been made abundantly clear from a variety of analytic works, cooperation by reciprocity is open to exploitation by cheater strategies (Olson 1965; Hardin 1968; Dawes 1980; Kim and Walker 1984; Hawkes 1992). A cheater in this case accepts the benefits in the shortterm, but fails to reciprocate adequately in the future. For the seal partners, cheating might consist of accepting the fin from one's partner but not providing a fin in return. Cheating may also be as subtle as a hunter simply not hunting enough to reciprocate equivalent amounts to partners. While cooperating with another cooperator results in high returns, cheating with a cooperator pays an even higher return. If my partner is selected to maximize returns, he will cheat, and I should base my decision on that fact and defect myself.

It is this social feature of the environment that makes game theory useful for analyzing cooperative problems, and the Prisoner's Dilemma particularly appealing as a model for reciprocal exchange. Game theory attempts to model how organisms make optimal decisions when these are contingent on what others do (Brams 1994). The classic Prisoner's Dilemma (PD) model captures much of the essence of problems associated with cooperation. The game is usually formulated in the following way. Two individuals have committed a crime. Both are caught and are being held prisoners in separate cells in a jail. Each is interrogated by police and is given the following set of choices. If neither confesses (that is, they both cooperate), they are given a 5-year sentence for carrying weapons. If each confesses (defect), each receives a penalty of 10 years. If one defects (turns states evidence) and implicates the other, the defector goes free while the other gets the maximum jail term of 20 years. Volumes have been written on this simple game, and its study has dominated inquiry into cooperation (e.g., Von Nuemann and Morgenstein 1953; Axelrod and Hamilton 1981; Maynard-Smith 1982; Boyd 1988; Dugatkin 1997;). In the simplest form of the model, two individuals can either cooperate (C = cooperate) or act selfishly (D = defect) during a single turn. The actor plays a row strategy against the choice of his opponent who selects a column. The four possible combinations are indicated in Figure 13.1.

The payoff to each depends on what the other does. The two prisoners each have a higher return if they both cooperate than if they both cheat ($R > P$; 5 years in jail is better than 10 years in jail). However, confessing (defection) has a higher return

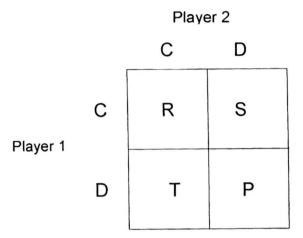

Figure 13.1. The payoff matrix for a two person game.
C = cooperate, D = defect. The cells indicate the payoff
to player 1. For example, if player 1 cooperates and player
2 defects, player 1 receives S units as payoff.

than cooperating with a cooperating partner ($T > R$; going free is better than 5 years in jail) or another defector ($P > S$; 10 years in jail is better than 20 years in jail). $S < P < R < T$ defines the prisoner's dilemma game, and defection is the optimal strategy in the game. In terms of evolutionary game theory, defection is an ESS (Evolutionary Stable Strategy; Maynard-Smith 1982). An ESS is a strategy that cannot be replaced via natural selection when common in the population.

Much of the work involving the PD tries to reconcile its solution with the fact that cooperation is relatively common in nature.

This problem has generated a wealth of theoretical work to find a solution (for a recent review, see Dugatkin 1997). Most studies have focused on the iterated version of the game, played over several turns. The work of Axelrod and Hamilton (1981) reported on the well-known Tit-for-Tat strategy (TFT) and emphasized that reciprocity is more likely if participants have a high probability of repeated encounters. Additional theoretical developments have also generated successful cooperative strategies such as Contrite Tit-for-Tat (CTFT—Boyd 1989), Generous Tit-for-Tat, and Pavlov (Nowak and Sigmund 1992).

Mutualism, Social Foraging, and Big Game Hunting

Despite of its intellectual fascination, recent work has suggested that the Prisoner's Dilemma and the associated pay-off schedule that defines the game may not be the best paradigm for understanding many cases of cooperation (Maynard Smith 1983; Clements and Stephens 1995; Corning 1996; Dugatkin, 1997). This is because the PD payoff schedule, that is, the costs and benefits of alternative decisions, does not conform to all social-ecological contexts. For example, in a hunting context, the payoffs for a player playing the row can be interpreted as follows. The R cell can be understood as cooperative hunting for larger game. The T cell is solitary small game hunting. The S cell represents solitary hunting for large game. P is also solitary small game hunting. If the returns to individuals from cooparative large game hunting are greater than from pursuing small game alone ($R > T$), the game is not the PD.

As an alternative, mutualism has been proposed as a model that may more parsimoniously explain much cooperation including cooperative meat acquisition in humans (West-Eberhard 1975; Brown 1983; Conner 1986; Mesterton-Gibbons and Dugatkin 1992; Dugatkin 1997; Winterhalder 1997). There are two types of mutualism, each defined by their particular pay-off matrix that differs from PD. According to Brown (1983), by-product mutualism is behaviors that the ego must accomplish regardless of whether others are present or not. Brown uses the term "by-product" because the benefits that accrue to others are incidental to the ego's behavior. Economists refer to such benefits (or costs) as externalities and define them as the indirect effect of consumption or production activity on the consumption or production of others (Laffont 1987).

As discussed above, in the PD an individual does better by cheating than by cooperating when paired with either a cooperator *or* a another cheater. In a game of by-product mutualism (also referred to as pseudoreciprocity—Conner 1986), the payoffs are different (Dugatkin 1997: 31–34). The obstacles to cooperation in the PD arise because the payoffs for cheating are sufficiently high. Selection favors mutualism in circumstances where *not* cooperating inflicts a cost on the cheater. For example, a hunter that does not cooperate in the hunt for large game reduces his own returns if the returns from solitary foraging are less.

One way to think about how mutualism and PD differ is with respect to the cost of cooperating. Mutualism has often been defined as no-cost cooperating—that is, there is no cost to cooperating because there are no opportunities for cheaters to take advantage (Dugatkin 1997). The flip side of this has been termed the "boomerang factor" by Dugatkin and Mesterton-Gibbons (1992). The boomerang factor is the probability that a cheater will be the victim of his or her own cheating, expressed through the opportunity costs of not cooperating. This occurs when $R > T$ (cooperating with a cooperater is better than defecting) and $S > P$ (cooperating with a defector is also better than defecting) In this case, cooperate is an ESS. In the PD there is no boomerang factor because $T > R$ and $P > S$. Cheating always does better. Dugatkin (1997) offers the payoff matrix in Figure 13.2 as an example of a payoff that would lead to by-product mutualism.

Brown (1983) offers hunting as an example of by-product mutualism because it is often more profitably done cooperatively than alone. This satisfies the $R > T$ requirement. But, by-product mutualism is not a good model if hunting is impossible to do alone, as might be the case when large game is the prey. In this case, S is not larger than P! Whale hunting, for example, is not something a hunter can accomplish unless he is in a group. While easily construed as mutualistic because cheating does not pay, such hunting is not "done regardless of the presence of others" (Brown 1983: 30).

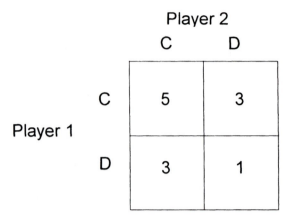

Figure 13.2. Dugatkin (1997) offers the above pay-off matrix as an example of by-product mutualism (also referred to as no-cost cooperation).

A second kind of mutualistic cooperation is known as synergistic mutualism (Maynard-Smith 1983; see also Corning 1996), where the ESS solution is to either defect *or* cooperate. Synergy refers to situations where the combined effect of individuals working together is greater than the sum of their individual efforts. In this case, $R > T$, but $P > S$ and the final outcome depends on initial conditions. Maynard Smith and Szathmary (1995) present a heuristic model for comparing PD situations with synergistic mutualism. They define two boating situations—rowing and sculling. In the simplest case, sculling involves two individuals sitting in a boat—one person in front and the other just behind the first, both facing the same direction. Each have two oars on both sides of the boat. Sculling is presented as a Prisoner's Dilemma. Each crew member does better if both row than if both defect and rest $(R > P)$. Individuals do better by cheating (resting), however, when paired with either a defector or a rower.

Rowing differs from sculling in that each of the two players has only one oar on opposite sides of the boat. Because of this structural change, the payoffs are different, and rowing can result in mutualism (Figure 13.3). The fastest speed is obtained if both actors row (cooperation). If both defect and neither rows, the boat sits there, but neither exhausts themselves. But if one actor rows and the other does not, the boat goes in circles *and* the cooperator exhausts himself.

The difference between synergistic hunting and by-product hunting lies with the returns obtained from solitary large game hunting relative to the returns obtained from solitary small game hunting. In a by-product situation, individuals play the cooperate move and pursue large game because it gives higher returns to the individual than does small game hunting, no matter what others do. In a synergistic context, returns rates increase significantly when hunting occurs in a group but is unproductive alone. In this case, the payoffs of hunting large game alone are lower than small game alone.

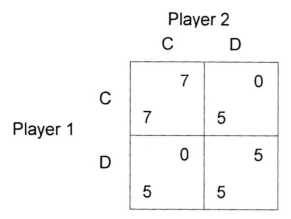

Figure 13.3. The rowing game from Maynard-Smith and Szathmary (1995: 262). The payoffs are presented for both players (player 1 on the lower left, player 2 in the upper right of each cell). The fastest speed (seven units) is obtained if both actors row (both cooperate). If both defect and neither rows, the boat sits, but neither exhausts themselves (five units). If one actor rows and the other does not, the boat goes in circles. In this case, the cooperator exhausts himself (0 units). The defector goes nowhere as well but is, at least, resting while doing so.

Dugatkin et al. (1992) created a model that describes the relationship between the PD game and both kinds of mutualism as a function of environmental adversity (see Figure 13.4). Note that $R - T$ (R minus T) measures the payoff differential between a cooperating strategy and a defecting strategy for the actor when his partner cooperates; $S - P$ measures the payoff differential between cooperating and defecting when the partner defects. Dugatkin et al. assume that in increasingly adverse environments both $R - T$ and $S - P$ will increase. When both $R - T$ and $S - P$ are negative, the game is the Prisoner's Dilemma, and defect is the ESS. As the environment becomes increasingly adverse, the payoff increases for the ego to cooperate. This is obtained if both $R - T$ and $S - P$ are positive; in this case, cooperation is the solution and the model is by-product mutualism. The ego should cooperate regardless of what his partner does—even if it provides an unreciprocated payoff to the partner. If $R - T > 0$ and $S - P < 0$, both cheat and cooperate are ESS solutions—this is the equivalent of Maynard Smith and Szathmary's rowing game. A sufficiently adverse ecology produces what has been termed by Mesterton-Gibbons (1991) as a "common enemy." In the case of hunters, the common enemy can be conceived of as a large and difficult-to-catch prey. Packer and Ruttan (1988) come to similar conclusions when they show that cooperative hunting can be a solution when group hunting increases hunting success or prey encounter rates or decreases hunting costs sufficiently to overcome the costs of having to distribute the harvest among the hunters.

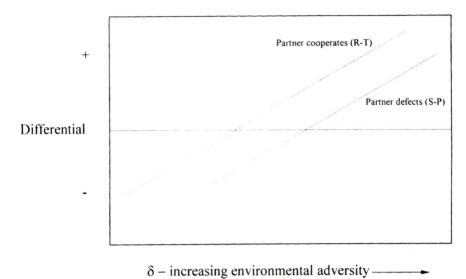

Figure 13.4. Dugatkin et al. (1992) model of the "common enemy." The model describes the relationship between the PD game and mutualism as a function of environment adversity. R-T is the payoff differential between a cooperating strategy and defecting strategy for the actor when his partner cooperates; S-P measures the payoff differential between cooperating and defecting when the partner defects. In increasingly adverse environments, both R-T and S-P increase. When R-T and S-P are negative, the game is the Prisoners Dilemma and defect is the ESS. As the environment becomes increasingly adverse and both R-T and S-P are positive, the game becomes by-product mutualism and player 1 should cooperate, regardless of what player 2 does—even if it means providing a public good. If R-T<0 and S-P>0, the game is synergistic mutualism; both cheat and cooperate are possible.

Recent work with nonhuman predators supports this conclusion. East African lions hunt cooperatively, but the degree of cooperation depends on how easily specific prey types can be killed by a solitary hunter. As the probability of success by a solitary hunter declines, the likelihood of cooperation increases. Cooperation is much less likely with prey that lone hunters can take with assurance (Scheel and Packer 1991). Scheel and Packer (1991) found that lions are significantly more likely to cooperatively hunt prey that are difficult and dangerous, such as zebra and buffalo, than prey such as warthog and wildebeest, which are often taken by lone hunters. The same pattern is found for spotted hyenas in Ngorongoro Crater, who often hunt Thomson's gazelles alone, but cooperate to hunt zebras (Kruuk 1972).

It is apparent that it is largely the ecology of the subsistence situation that sets the payoff matrix. For example, there is evidence that environmental differences exist between the Tai forest and Gombe that make colobus monkey hunting by chimpanzees more difficult at Tai Forest (Bshary and Noe 1997). The forest canopy is high and less broken at Tai Forest. This creates a context where the colobus monkeys can more easily find escape routes, and thus hunting is more difficult than at Gombe where the canopy is low and broken. This has been suggested to pattern the chimpanzee hunting strategies at the two sites. Tai chimpanzees cooperate in about 66% of all hunts (Boesch 1994). A common cooperative strategy involves individuals positioning themselves at escape routes from trees where monkeys are cornered. One hunter then climbs the tree, driving the prey into waiting partners. At Gombe, where the environment makes it difficult for colobus monkeys to escape solitary hunters, chimpanzees cooperate much less—about 7% of all hunts.

An Example of Mutualistic Large Game Acquisition: The Lamalara Whale Hunters

As discussed above, synergistic mutualism may be an apt model for cooperative large game hunting. Synergistic mutualism can be identified by examining the payoffs between partners as indicated in the cells of the model matrix. The following section presents preliminary payoff data collected from an ongoing study of the cooperative hunting practices of traditional Indonesian whalers. The data were collected from October through December 1998. The hunting data are limited (only two hunts consisting of 14 boats), and inconclusive at the moment but suggest how big game hunting is modeled as synergistic mutualism.

The village of Lamalera is located on the island of Lembata, in the province of Nusa Tenggara Timor, Indonesia. The village population is approximately 2,000 individuals, divided into 21 clans (see Barnes 1996 for the detailed ethnography). The inhabitants are Lamaholot speakers, sharing a system of patrilineal descent and a tripartite asymmetric marriage alliance between clans. Although whaling occurs throughout the year, two separate seasons are recognized. *Lefa* refers to the primary whaling season of May until September. During *lefa* boats go out daily, weather permitting. *Baleo* refers to the opportunistic pursuit of whales during the balance of the year. Because of sea conditions, boats are kept in their sheds, and hunts occur only if prey are spotted from shore. The primary prey for both seasons is sperm whale (*Physeter catadon*) and ray (*Mantis birostris*, *Mobula kuhlii*, and *Mobula diabolus*).

Various clans are associated with corporations that own, maintain, and operate whaling operations focused around ~10 meter-long vessels called *tena*, which are propelled by oars and large rectangular woven palm sails. Killing prey with a *tena* is a manifestly cooperative activity, impossible to accomplish solitarily. The average crew size for the 14 observed *tena* was 13.5 (range 10–16). During the whaling season, a fleet of *tena* leaves daily at sunrise (weather permitting) and searches an area directly to the south of the coast at a distance of several kilometers from the shore. When a whale is sighted, for example, the sails are lowered and the crew rows furiously to catch up with the whale. Once the boat is in range, the harpooner leaps from the small harpooner's platform on the bow to drive the harpoon into the back of the whale. The whale then dives or tows the ship about until it is exhausted.

The *tena* travel in a diffuse group, and cooperation between boats is common. Large whales (e.g., adult male sperm whales) are difficult animals to catch, and more than one boat is often required to subdue one. During generalized search, boats forage gregariously but seem to search independently. The boat that first sights a prey item has priority to the kill. Boats that provide help receive full shares in the kill. Once a whale is killed, it must be towed back to the village, a task sometimes undertaken by several ships (Barnes 1996). Returns can be up into the thousands of kilograms of edible produce [a typical sperm whale yields over 3,000 kg (Barnes 1996: 310)], but variance on a daily basis is high.

The ecology of meat acquisition at Lamalera offers men few choices. Besides whaling, there are few alternatives for acquiring meat or other forms of animal protein. Little animal husbandry is practiced. Some goats and pigs are kept, but grazing is poor because the village is located on the lava flows of an extinct volcano. Nor does corn, the staple carbohydrate for the island, do well on the lava beds. The common alternative to whaling is the relatively noncooperative hook-and-line or net fishing with small boats called *sapã*. *Sapã* fishing occurs commonly during the *baleo* season, but also during the *lefa* season if men feel *tena* hunting is not productive. Some men also specialize in *Sapã* fishing year around. *Sapã* fishing is accomplished alone or in teams of two. The average group size for 95 observed *sapã* events was 1.6 men.

The choices of whaling and *Sapã* fishing offer men two alternatives that can be modeled in terms of a payoff matrix equivalent to synergistic mutualism. Keep in mind that the model is caricature—whaling is not a two-person game. The model is nonetheless heuristically useful as a starting point for thinking about big game hunting in terms of mutualism. The matrix is presented in Figure 13.5, where payoffs to both players are shown. The R cell (both cooperate) can be understood as cooperative hunting for whales as a crewmember. The T cell is solitary *sapã* fishing by Player 1 who defects to fish alone while Player 2 pursues whales). The S cell represents solitary, noncooperative whale hunting by Player 1. The P cell represents solitary *sapã* fishing by both players. Cooperating as a crewmember provides the highest return to an individual. Preliminary analysis from the sample of two *baleo* whale hunts indicates that a crewmember's share is approximately 25–35 kg, or approximately 3 kg per hour of hunting (unpublished data). Note that these figures are a rough estimated based on only 2 days of opportunistic baleo hunts. The critical fact is that returns from cooperative whaling are greater than the alternative of *sapã* fishing, which returns approximately 0.39 kg per hour per person ($N = 95$ fishing trips, unpublished data). The other key is that whaling returns 0.0 kg per hour if attempted alone; participation among *tena* crewmembers is mutualistic in the sense that no one hunter can take a whale on his own. Because $R > T$, the game is not the Prisoner's Dilemma.

One essential feature of the analysis is that Lamalaran whaling is mutualistic only to the extent that the payoffs are guaranteed to the participants. What prevents defection after the whale is brought back to the village? How does a crewmember know that he will get his share? What prevents cheaters from absconding with others' shares? If defectors do not do worse than cooperators, the case for mutualism becomes tenuous.

Once a whale is brought ashore, distribution of the meat is widespread, but not group-wide, as has been reported for other subsistence hunters (Kaplan and Hill 1985). The preliminary data indicate the whale may not be a public good, as Hawkes

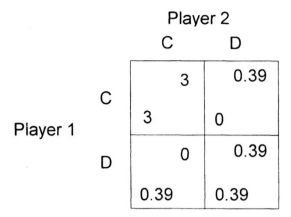

Figure 13.5. The payoff schedule for Lamalera whale hunters in kilograms of fish or whale per hour. Cooperating to capture a whale gives the highest return to an individual—approximately 3 kg per hour. The alternative (*sapã* hook and line, or net fishing) returns approximately 0.39 kg per hour. Whaling returns 0.0 kg per hour if attempted alone. The ESS is either to cooperatively whale or fish alone using *sapã*, depending on initial conditions.

(1993) suggests may be common for big game hunters. Distributions are regulated by a very complex set of unwritten norms, and only a limited number of people share. In a very real sense, shares are owned according to the set of norms. Following Barnes (1996), crewmembers receive shares according to their role, and corporate members receive shares as part of hereditary rights. In addition, shares go to specialists—the carpenter, sail maker, and smith—who may or may not be clan members or crew. Barnes (1996: 179–200) describes the distribution rules in some detail. This type of systematic sharing of game animals is common among hunting people (Gould 1967; Damas 1972; Robbe 1975; Ichikawa 1983; Altman 1987; Cassell 1988). Secondary distributions may be more widespread than the initial distributions to share holders, although data have not been analyzed at this time.

The distribution norms seem designed to facilitate a fair partitioning of resources among hunt participants and clan members. A fair distribution can be defined as one where the share quantities are proportional to the share owners' contributions to the hunt's success. The entire system is premised on the assumption of fair shares and crewmembers seem to participate with the implicit assumption that they will receive the payoff prescribed by the norm. What provides a crewmember with such assurance? What would happen if someone were denied their share?

At this point, speculation is required to tentatively answer these questions. It should first be noted that covert cheating would be extremely difficult to conceal. Butchering and distribution occur on the public beach, and all interested parties participate and monitor activities. As a result, Lamaleran crewmembers could only be disenfranchised from their shares by overt cheating. Because such behavior has not been observed, it is difficult to say what such an event would be like. Almost all men carry sharp butchering tools during distributions, and it is likely that if a crewmember were denied his due share, violence and disruption of the entire subsistence system would ensue.

Although such confrontation may seem costly, there is evidence that shows people are nonetheless willing to pay significant costs when others act "unfairly" (Forsythe et al. 1994; Roth 1995). Indeed, norm enforcement is a critical mechanism in the maintenance of many types of cooperation (Bowles and Gintis 1998a, 1998b). There is substantial evidence that even in situations where social dilemmas exist, groups "have repeatedly shown their capacity to organize themselves, establish credible commitments, monitor each others behavior, and impose sanctions on those who break their commitments" (Ostrom et al. 1992: 405). Winterhalder (1997: 137) notes that by-product mutualism combined with norm enforcement through the implicit threat of punishment can stabilize reciprocity. If so, it can stabilize synergistic mutualism as well. The work of Boyd and Richerson (1992) shows that punishers who induce cooperation in others for personal benefits can additionally provide a public good as a by-product (see also Clutton-Brock and Parker 1995). If *not*, punishing can have a sufficiently severe boomerang effect (see Dugatkin 1997), and a variety of collective action outcomes become possible (see, e.g., Sethi and Somanathan 1996). The high payoffs for cooperative whaling relative to the payoffs from noncooperative *sapā* fishing may provide incentive for many actors to pay the costs of enforcement and act as punishers if needed. As a result, shareowners behave as if they have certainty approaching 100% that they will receive the share they are expecting.

Conclusion

> Our models may have been too pessimistic about the constraints on errant behavior in cooperative relationships. In effect, the games may have been unintentionally "rigged." Consider some of the common assumptions in Prisoner's Dilemma games: The games are always voluntary and "democratic"; each player is free to choose his/her own preferred strategy, and the opposing player has no means available for coercing choices or compliance. Also, the players are not allowed to communicate with one another in an effort to reduce the uncertainties in the interactions. Furthermore, defectors are usually rewarded handsomely for cheating while the cooperators are denied the power to prevent defectors from enjoying the rewards, much less punishing them for defection. Such "grade inflation" for defection biases the game in favor of cheating. Worse yet, in iterative games the players are forced to continue playing; they cannot exclude or ostracize a defector. They can only retaliate by themselves defecting and hoping thereby to penalize the other player. (Corning 1996: 185)

Peter Corning aptly describes some of the limitation of the Prisoner's Dilemma-centric view of cooperation. Note, however, that he is lamenting the constraints on the PD game, not that the PD is almost exclusively used to model cooperative interactions. Maynard-Smith and Szathmary (1995: 261) go further and state, "The intellectual fascination of the Prisoner's Dilemma game may have led us to overestimate its evolutionary importance." More work needs to be done to see if this is the case.

With respect to the cooperative acquisition of meat, future work must involve delineating models that more realistically reflect the ecology and subsistence strategies of our subjects—be they our ancient ancestors, chimpanzees, or contemporary whale hunters. Mutualism can be usefully considered as either an alternative or complementary hypothesis to explain many aspects of cooperation, particularly cooperative large game hunting. All hunting is not mutualistic, but many types of cooperative big game hunting represent a payoff structure that more closely matches what is predicted to produce mutualistic cooperation.

I emphasized one additional point in this chapter. Norms are increasingly being viewed as critical to our understanding of cooperation. Culturally transmitted distribution norms are what make the difference between the chaotic type of post-acquisition meat distribution that Hawkes (this volume) describes for chimpanzees and the relatively organized distribution described for the whale hunters. It is difficult to imagine how hunt participants would be willing to invest the time and effort and risk involved in hunting a whale if they did not have confidence that the effort would pay off. At some point in the last five million years, hominids developed the cognitive tools and social complexity required for norm formation and enforcement. These tools allowed hominids to take advantage of the mutualistic payoffs common to big game hunting and substantially increase the quantity of meat in their diet.

REFERENCES

Altman, J. 1987. Hunter-gatherers today: an aboriginal economy of North Australia. *American Institute of Aboriginal Studies*. 35:701–709.
Axelrod, R., and W. Hamilton. 1981. The evolution of cooperation. *Science* 211:1390–1396.
Barnes, R. H. 1996. *Sea Hunters of Indonesia*. Oxford: Clarendon Press.
Boesch, C. 1994. Cooperative hunting in wild chimpanzees. *Animal Behavior* 48:653–667.
Boyd, R. 1988. Is the repeated prisoner's dilemma a good model of reciprocal altruism? *Ethology and Sociobiology* 9:211–222.
Boyd, R. 1989. Mistakes allow evolutionary stability in the repeated Prisoner's Dilemma game. *Journal of Theoretical Biology* 136:147–156.
Boyd, R., and P. Richerson. 1992. Punishment allows the evolution of cooperation (or anything else) in sizable groups. *Ethology and Sociobiology* 13:171–195.
Bowles, S., and H. Gintis. 1998a. Mutual monitoring in teams: the effects of residual claimancy and reciprocity. Santa Fe Institute Working Paper #98-08-074E.
Bowles, S., and H. Gintis. 1998b. The evolution of strong reciprocity. Santa Fe Institute Working Paper #98-08-073E.
Brams, S. 1994. *Theory of Moves*. Cambridge: Cambridge University Press.
Brown, J. 1983. Cooperation: a biologist's dilemma. *Advances in the Study of Behavior*. 13:1–37.
Bshary, B., and R. Noe. 1997. Anti-predation behavior of red colobus monkeys in the presence of chimpanzees. *Behavioral Ecology and Sociobiology* 41:321–333

Bunn, H., and E. Ezzo. 1993. Hunting and scavenging by Plio-pleistocene hominids: nutritional constraints, archeological patterns and behavioral implications. *Journal of Archaeological Science* 20:365–398.

Byrne, R., and A. Whiten. 1988. *Machiavellian Intelligence: Social Expertise and the Evolution of Intellect in Monkeys, Apes and Humans*. Oxford: Clarendon Press.

Cassell, M. S. 1988. Farmers on the northern ice: relations of production in the traditional north Alaskan Inupiat whale hunt. *Research in Economic Anthropology* 10:89–116.

Clements, K., and D. Stephens. 1995. Testing models of non-kin cooperation; mutualism and the Prisoner's dilemma. *Animal Behavior* 50:527–535.

Clutton-Brock, T., and G. Parker. 1995. Punishment in animal societies. *Science* 373:209–216.

Conner, R. 1986. Pseudoreciprocity: investing in mutualism. *Animal Behavior* 34:1562–1584.

Corning, P. 1996. The co-operative gene: the role of synergy in evolution. *Evolutionary Theory* 11:183–207.

Cosmides, L., and J. Tooby. 1992. Cognitive adaptations for social exchange. In *The Adapted Mind* (J. Barkow, L. Cosmides, and J. Tooby, eds.), pp. 163–228. New York: Oxford University Press.

Damas, D. 1972. Central Eskimo systems of food-sharing. *Ethnology* 11:220–239.

Dawes, R. 1980. Social dilemmas. *Annual Review of Psychology* 31:169–193.

de Heinzelin, J., J. Desmond Clark, T. White, W. Hart, P. Renne, G. WoldeGabriel, and Y. Beyene. 1999. Environment and behavior of 2.5-million-year-old bouri hominids. *Science* 284:625–629.

de Waal, F. 1989. Food-sharing and reciprocal obligations among chimpanzees. *Human Evolution* 18:433–459.

Dugatkin, L. 1997. *Cooperation Among Animals: An Evolutionary Perspective*. Oxford: Oxford University Press.

Dugatkin, L., M. Mesterton-Gibbons, and A. Houston. 1992. Beyond the prisoner's dilemma: towards models to discriminate among mechanisms of cooperation in nature. *Trends in Ecology and Evolution* 7:202–205.

Dunbar, R. 1998. The social brain hypothesis. *Evolutionary Anthropology* 6:178–189.

Earl, M. 1987. A flexible body mass in social carnivores. *American Naturalist* 129:755–760.

Forsythe, R., J. Horowitz, N. Savin, and M. Sefton. 1994. Replicability, fairness and pay in experiments with simple bargaining games. *Games and Economic Behaviour* 6:347–369.

Gould, R. A. 1967. Notes on hunting, butchering, and sharing of game among the Ngatatjara and their neighbors in the West Australian Desert. *Kroeber Anthropology* 36:41–66.

Hamilton W. 1964. The genetical evolution of social behaviour. *Journal of Theoretical Biology* 7:1–16.

Hardin, G. 1968. The tragedy of the commons. *Science* 162:1243–1248.

Hawkes, K. 1992. Sharing and collective action. In *Evolutionary Ecology and Human Behavior* (E. A. Smith and B. Winterhalder, eds.), pp. 269–300. New York: Aldine de Gruyter.

Hawkes, K. 1993. Why hunter-gatherers work: an ancient version of the problem of public goods. *Current Anthropology.* 34:341–361.

Ichikawa, M. 1983. An examination of the hunting-dependent life of the Mbuti Pygmies, Eastern Zaire. *African Study Monographs* 4:55–76.

Kaplan, H., and K. Hill. 1985. Food-sharing among Ache foragers: tests of explanatory hypotheses. *Current Anthropology* 26:223–246.

Kim, O., and M. Walker. 1984. The free rider problem: experimental evidence. *Public Choice* 43:3–24.

King, B. 1994. *Information Continuum: Evolution of Social Information Transfer in Monkeys, Apes and Hominids*. Santa Fe, NM: School of American Research.

Kruuk, H. 1972. *The Spotted Hyena: A Study of Predation and Social Behavior*. Chicago: University of Chicago Press.

Laffont, J. 1987. Externalities. In *The New Palgrave: A Dictionary of Economics* (J. Eatwell, M. Millgate, and P. Newman, eds.). London: Macmillan.

Lancaster, J., and C. Lancaster. 1983. Parental investment: the hominid adaptation. In *How Humans Adapt* (D. Ortner, ed.), pp. 33–69. Washington, DC: Smithsonian Institution Press.

Lee, R. 1979. *The !Kung San: Men, Women, and Work in a Foraging Society*. Cambridge: Cambridge University Press.

Lee, R., and I. Devore, eds. 1968. *Man the Hunter*. New York: Aldine Press.

Lovejoy, O. 1981. The origin of Man. *Science* 211:341–350.

Maynard-Smith, J. 1982. *Evolution and the Theory of Games*. Cambridge: Cambridge University Press.

Maynard-Smith, J. 1983. Game theory and the evolution of cooperation. In *Evolution From Molecules to Men* (D. S. Bendell, ed.), pp. 445–456. Cambridge: Cambridge University Press.

Maynard-Smith, J., and E. Szathmary. 1995. *The Major Transitions in Evolution*. Oxford: W. H. Freeman.

Mesterton-Gibbons, M. 1991. An escape from the prisoner's dilemma. *Journal of Mathematical Biology* 29:251–269.

Mesterton-Gibbons, M., and L. Dugatkin. 1992. Cooperation among unrelated individuals: evolutionary factors. *Quarterly Review of Biology* 67:276–281.

Nowak, M., and K. Sigmund. 1992. Tit for tat in heterogeneous populations. *Nature* 355:250–252.

Olson, M. 1965. *The Logic of Collective Action: Public Goods and the Theory of Groups*. Cambridge, MA: Harvard University Press.

Ostrom, E., W. Walker, and R. Gardner. 1992. Covenants with and without a sword: self-governance is possible. *American Political Science Review* 86:404–417.

Packer C., and L. Ruttan. 1988. The evolution of cooperative hunting. *American Naturalist* 132:159–198.

Packer, C., L. Herbst, A. Pusey, D. Bygott, J. Hanby, and M. Borgerhoff Mulder. 1988. Reproductive success of Lions. In *Reproductive Success* (T. Clutton-Brock, ed.), pp. 363–383. Chicago: University of Chicago Press.

Robbe, P. 1975. Partage du gibier chez les Ammassalimiut observe en 1972 dans un village de Tileqilaq. *Objects et Monde* 15:209–222.

Rose, L., and F. Marshall. 1996. Meat eating, hominid sociality, and home bases revisited. *Current Anthropology* 37:307–338.

Roth, A. 1995. Bargaining experiments. In *The Handbook of Experimental Economics* (J. Kagel and A. Roth, eds.), pp. 253–348. Princeton, NJ: Princeton University Press.

Scheel, D., and C. Packer. 1991. Group hunting behaviour of lions: a search for cooperation. *Animal Behavior* 41:697–709.

Sethi, R., and E. Somanathan. 1996. The evolution of social norms in common property resource use. *The American Economic Review* 86:766–788.

Smith, E. 1991. *Inujjuamiut Foraging Strategies: Evolutionary Ecology of an Arctic Hunting Economy*. New York: Aldine.

Smith, E., and B. Winterhalder. 1992. Natural selection and decision making: some fundamental principles. In *Evolutionary Ecology and Human Behavior* (E. Smith and B. Winterhalder, eds.), pp. 25–60. New York: Aldine de Gruyter.

Symons, D. 1979. *The Evolution of Human Sexuality*. Oxford: Oxford University Press.

Tooby, J., and L. Cosmides. 1992. The psychological foundations of culture. In *The Adapted Mind* (J. Barkow, J. Tooby, and L. Cosmides, eds.), pp. 19–136. New York: Oxford University Press.

Trivers, R. 1971. The evolution of reciprocal altruism. *Quarterly Review of Biology* 46:35–57.

von Nuemann, J., and O. Morgenstien. 1953. *Theory of Games and Economic Behavior*. Princeton, NJ: Princeton University Press.

Washburn, S., and C. Lancaster. 1968. The evolution of hunting. In *Man and the Hunter* (R. Lee and I. Devore, eds.), pp. 293–303. New York: Aldine Press.

West-Eberhard, M. 1975. The evolution of social behavior by kin selection. *Quarterly Review of Biology* 50:1–33.

Whiten, A., and R. Byrne, eds. 1997. *Machiavellian Intelligence II: Extensions and Evaluations*. Cambridge: Cambridge University Press.

Winterhalder, B. 1986. Diet choice, risk, food-sharing in a stochastic environment. *Journal of Anthropological Archaeology* 5:369–392.

Winterhalder, B. 1997. Gifts given, gifts taken: the behavioral ecology of nonmarket, intragroup exchange. *Journal of Archaeological Research* 5:121–168.

Wrangham, R., and D. Peterson. 1996. *Demonic Males*. New York: Houghton Mifflin.

14

Intragroup Resource Transfers
Comparative Evidence, Models, and Implications for Human Evolution

Bruce Winterhalder

Introduction

The notion that early hominid social groups might have engaged in routine sharing of meat or other highly valued food-stuffs apparently is seen by paleoanthropologists as a bit romantic and wholly naïve. The site-level empiricism that fueled Isaac's (1978a, 1978b, 1984) promotion of the idea has given way to taphonomic caution (Binford 1985). Alternative interpretations—such as the putative living sites may have been stone caches used briefly for secondary processing of animal parts removed from kill sites (Potts 1984)—have become available. The ethnographic analogy with extant hunter-gatherers that seemed to Isaac and others to offer decisive comparative confirmation is now viewed with skepticism. Prehistorians no longer willingly suffer the "tyranny of the ethnographic record" (Wobst 1978).

The rejection of sharing as an important feature of hominid socioecology is unfortunate. I say this even as one who endorses the cautionary, methodological lessons of taphonomy and who applauds certain kinds of skepticism about ethnographic analogy. Binford and other critics almost certainly were correct about weaknesses in Isaac's argument (see Blumenshine 1991). However, they almost certainly were mistaken in their negative appraisal of his emphasis on sharing. There are other and ultimately much better reasons than those offered by Isaac to think that routine sharing might have characterized hominid subsistence adaptations. Those reasons, their linkage to archaeologically visible patterns of food selection (e.g., consumption of meat versus vegetable items), and some of their implications are the subject of this chapter. The topic is important because it is central to socioecological reconstruction of hominid subsistence behavior and evolution, the larger subject of this volume.

I begin with the presumption that hominids, whatever their species, were *social* foragers, living in relatively stable, multiadult units. The size, composition, and turnover in the residential group, the subgroups that formed for task-specific activities, and other features of social organization presumably were no less diverse than those known from primate studies or ethology more generally. I also begin with some semantic conventions. I will use *transfer* as a generic, inclusive term for movement of food and other goods or services among individuals. Transfer thus refers broadly to behaviors described as scrounging, sharing, giving and taking, distribution, exchange, trade, etc. A key lesson of recent behavioral ecology work is that such transfers can take various behavioral forms for diverse evolutionary reasons. We can no longer think of food movement within a group as one, undifferentiated behavior; the food-sharing hypothesis has become a bundle of analytically distinct possibilities. We will be unable to talk intelligibly about hominid socioecology unless more specific terms become aligned with the variety of particular forms transfer behaviors can take (Winterhalder 1996c; Hames 1998). Throughout the remainder of this chapter I will use quotations ("sharing") when I refer to the broad and undifferentiated use found, for instance, in most ethnographies.

Evolutionary Concepts and Models Explaining Transfers

Through the same period that paleoanthropologists grew wary of the "sharing" hypothesis, behavioral ecologists were developing a variety of tools for analyzing transfers. They show that most evolutionary mechanisms have the potential to generate intragroup food allocation (reviews in Kaplan and Hill 1985b; Winterhalder 1996b, 1996c). I begin with these models rather than case studies because concepts and terminology developed in this literature are necessary to accurately and succinctly describe and interpret the examples that follow.

Tolerated theft

One of the most basic of these models is tolerated theft (Blurton Jones 1984, 1987), or scrounging (Giraldeau et al. 1990). Tolerated theft and the subsequent models reviewed here begin with an assumption about the resource environment. One or more food items important to a social forager occur in divisible *packets* of intermediate size, susceptible to transfer. In physical terms a packet is an item or patch larger than can be consumed in a few mouthfuls. It also must be smaller than would sate all members of the group. In analytical terms, it is a resource unit large enough to be subject to diminishing marginal value (fitness or utility) to an individual consuming it. Holders of a packet garner a weak form of possession (Kummer 1991). Possession itself implies a further constraint on size; a packet must be a resource that can be clutched, carried, or otherwise defended or sequestered from group members. For hominids, a 6-kg mammal meets this condition. Ripe fruit scattered throughout the canopy of a large tree that is encountered by the entire group while foraging together probably does not. However, the same fruit located by an individual and carried in quantity back to a residential camp in a string basket presumably would meet it. Encounters with this type of resource are likely to be unsynchronized and unpredictable to greater or lesser degree.

From the perspective of the fortunate individual who located and is growing sated from consuming a packet, its surplus or residual portions rapidly diminish in value. Those same residual portions have a high value to a hungry onlooker. The possessor has little incentive to defend what the other has high incentive to contest and acquire. The fitness of both individuals is enhanced if harmful conflict without compensating benefits can be avoided. Evolutionary self-interest is expressed in this circumstance as willingness to hazard forceful acquisition of high value food portions and as reluctance to mount a defense of portions with limited value. Holders of a packet will cede low-value portions, and supplicants will take them until there is an equilibrium of their interests. Winterhalder (1996a) uses marginal analysis to show in greater detail how the balance of costs and benefits affecting tolerated theft are affected by resource availability and qualities, individual procurement behavior, and group size.

Producing, Scrounging, and Opportunism

Behavioral ecologists have given tolerated theft, or scrounging in their terminology, close analysis using game theory (Giraldeau et al. 1990; Caraco and Giraldeau, 1991; Vickery et al. 1991). This technique aids in understanding the complex social dynamics that can arise when the optimal behavior of an individual depends on how others in the group respond (Smith and Winterhalder 1992).

In a representative model there are three tactics (Vickery et al. 1991). *Producers* expend the time and energy to locate the food packets they consume while *scroungers* avoid these costs by appropriating portions of the packet that a producer has already located. Scroungers will do well as long as they are rare. However, as they increase in frequency, more and more of them compete for the take of fewer and fewer producers, and their relative advantage disappears. This creates frequency-dependent selection—each tactic has the advantage when it is uncommon—generating a stable equilibrium mix of producers and scroungers in the group. A third, *opportunist* tactic produces or scrounges as the occasion arises but with a slight handicap relative to the two pure options. This handicap arises because the mixed or generalist tactic likely entails extra costs or compromises in conceptual skills. Three variables determine the equilibrium mix of the three tactics: producer priority (the degree to which the individual locating a resource can monopolize its consumption), opportunists' handicap, and group size.

If the opportunist handicap is substantial, opportunists will be eliminated from the equilibrium. Producers and scroungers will occur together as long as the scroungers' share of a packet is greater than the inverse of group size (or, $1/n$). If the scroungers' total share is less than $(1/n)$, producers will eliminate scroungers. There are two important effects of these conditions. Greater producer priority in the consumption of a packet lowers the likelihood that scroungers will occur alongside producers. Larger group size increases the likelihood they will occur. On the other hand, if the opportunists' handicap is not substantial, then they enter the equilibrium mix, either alone or in combination with producers or scroungers. As the opportunist handicap diminishes to zero, opportunists will come to dominate the group.

The boundary conditions that mark shifts among these combinations of tactics are best appreciated graphically (see Vickery et al. 1991, Figure 2; Winterhalder 1996c, Box 2). Generally, the model makes the important point that groups of social foragers will evolve to contain opportunists and/or scroungers along with producers. They will do so under a wide variety of conditions. The mix may be expressed in two ways: (1) by the relative proportion of individuals in a group, each of whom practices one tactic exclusively (e.g., three producers and three scroungers); or (2) by the frequency with which all group members practice each tactic (e.g., each is a producer 50% of the time and an scrounger 50% of the time).

Risk Sensitive Subsistence

In the ethnographic literature on hunter-gatherers, it is commonplace to see the proposal that intragroup food transfers lower the likelihood of subsistence short-falls. Group members who pool and divide their catch consume a daily ration of food that is subject to much less variance than the daily yield of their individual foraging efforts. The importance of pooling (or "sharing") grows as the group becomes increasingly dependent on large, unpredictably acquired packets. Its effectiveness can be quite high in small groups, as long as encounters with packets are not synchronized among group members (Winterhalder 1986, 1990; Winterhalder et al. 1998). Unpredictability in the subsistence quest sharply increases the marginal value of food to the temporarily unlucky, heightening the benefit-to-cost differentials that promote food transfers.

Pseudo-reciprocity or By-product Mutualism

In pseudo-reciprocity (Connor 1995), individual A undertakes a behavior for benefits that will be enhanced if, intentionally or inadvertently, individual B can be induced to cooperate and share in it. Mesterton-Gibbons and Dugatkin (1992; Dugatkin et al. 1992) call this situation by-product mutualism. Pseudo-reciprocity differs from altruistic reciprocity (Trivers 1971) in that the immediate structure of the situation guarantees that cooperation produces a relative gain to both the donor and receiver. There is no temptation to cheat (see "altruistic reciprocity," below) because a cheater who opts out of reciprocity when the occasion arises does so at its own expense. For example, when initiating pursuit of a large prey item a predator might signal the prey's presence to an unrelated conspecific. If joint pursuit has a significantly higher likelihood of success, the signal giver who shares this opportunity realizes a net gain along with the benefactor. Brown (1983: 30–31) argues that by-product mutualism may be common in nature; Alvard (this volume) provides a more complete review.

Altruistic Reciprocity

In reciprocal altruism (Trivers 1971) individual A performs an action at some small cost to itself but at a greater benefit to individual B. *Should* B reciprocate, both individuals realize a net fitness gain from the paired actions and reciprocity will evolve by natural selection. However, the structure of the situation offers no guarantee that B *will* reciprocate in the future when their roles are reversed. A self-interested B may do better by cheating; accepting the benefit but avoiding the reciprocity when A is in need. Such cheating will impede the evolution of reciprocally altruistic acts except under certain circumstances (see below). Because the classical ethnographic vision of hunter-gatherer "sharing" is one of reciprocal altruism, this problem of defection by cheaters or free riders has made behavioral ecologists skeptical of some ethnographic claims about it (Hawkes 1992a).

The literature on reciprocal altruism is large and highly technical. Classic papers by Axelrod and coauthors (Axelrod and Hamilton, 1981; Axelrod and Dion, 1988), and more recent reviews by Sigmund (1993) and Nowak et al. (1995), provide authoritative and accessible summaries. The tactic of tit-for-tat reciprocity enjoins cooperation as long as you encounter cooperation and defection on encountering defection. It will expand and sustain itself in a population only (1) after group members reach a certain threshold frequency of reciprocal (cooperative) interactions; and (2) under certain, narrowly defined environmental conditions. Initially, these restrictions appear to create a stringent impediment to the evolution of cooperation. However, it has been shown that tolerated theft (Blurton Jones 1984, 1987), kin selection (Axelrod and Hamilton 1981), and the "clustering" of reciprocators (Nowak and Sigmund 1992) all can prime the evolution of reciprocal altruism, thus obviating condition (1). With respect to point (2), the conditions required to sustain reciprocity are, in fact, common among social foragers. Individuals must: (a) encounter and interact with one another frequently; (b) experience regular role reversals between giver and taker; (c) face an indefinite future of such interactions; (d) recognize one another and draw on memory to exclude or sanction cheaters; (e) live in a small group; and (f) make few errors (see Axelrod and Dion 1988; Wilkinson 1988). The ability to establish social norms leading to punishment of defectors (and of individuals who tolerate them) helps as well (Boyd and Richerson 1989, 1992). For instance, Nettle and Dunbar (1997) use a simulation to show that stable reciprocity evolves much more easily when reciprocators are able to use language dialect differentiation to recognize one another and to exclude cheaters.

Since the triumph of tit-for-tat, more effective and more cooperative tactics have been identified (Nowak and Sigmund 1992, 1993). Once tit-for-tat reciprocity establishes itself in a population, it will be supplanted in sequential fashion by these more effective tactics. Self-interest can "turn the table" on cheating. Under the right conditions, "Cooperation evolves even in a totally selfish population. . . . Reciprocity flourishes in a variety of environments, and it even acts to create an environment to its taste. It is a self-promoting policy" (Sigmund 1993: 201).

Trade/Exchange and Showing Off

Transfers of food might also represent flows within exchange networks involving other (not-in-kind) resources or services. If individuals hold different resources or capacities subject to diminishing marginal returns, such exchanges will occur because they are advantageous to both parties. Transfers completed simultaneously in both directions are relatively straightforward. Both parties presumably gain an immediate advantage. If there is a delay before a return completes the transaction, then analysis must take account of the possibility of cheating and that of discounting (Rogers 1994).

Hawkes (1991, 1992b, 1993a, 1993b, this volume; see also Dwyer and Minnegal 1993; Hill and Kaplan 1993; Thiel 1994) has developed an exchange proposal within the rubric of sexual selection: the "show off" hypothesis. According to Hawkes, the potential for reproductive advantages will lead some male foragers to seek high-prestige, high-variance game resources. Although obtained sporadically, these game represent bonanzas of highly desired foods. When distributed widely, they capture social attention for their provider. Hawkes argues that this attention can be exchanged for enhanced fitness. In effect, some males trade a willingness to provide a public good—the capture and group wide distribution of an especially attractive food—for indirect, diffuse, and sometimes delayed social advantages accorded them by the group members. This show off proposal has the advantage that it collects under one model three routine observations about hunter-gatherers. It helps explain (1) why large game is pursued, (2) why some males might find it advantageous to contribute more resources to transfer networks than they receive from them, and (3) why males typically hunt and females gather (when both most likely could increase their foraging efficiency by mixing these activities to a greater extent; see Hill et al. 1987).

Kin, Interdemic, and Cultural Selection

A complete behavioral ecology explanation undertakes a dual obligation to describe (1) the ecological setting in which a behavior is expected and (2) the evolutionary process(es) thought to generate it. The first obligation generates models of circumstance. These specify how environmental constraints determine the costs and benefits of various behavioral tactics. Meeting the second obligation requires models of mechanism. These specify the processes by which selection acts on the evolution of the behavior. Attention to mechanisms is especially important because not all costs and benefits that might be cited in a functionalist argument (Elster 1983) are likely to have causal salience in an evolutionary analysis.

In a separate article (Winterhalder 1996b), I provide a concordance between models of circumstance and mechanism that have been proposed for explaining food transfers. It reveals that we do not yet have models of circumstance specifically associated with some potentially important evolutionary mechanisms. Among them are kin or nepotistic selection, group-level or interdemic selection (Wilson 1998), and cultural selection or dual inheritance models like those developed by Boyd and Richerson (1985) and Durham (1990).

Empirical Evidence: Ethological and Ethnographic

From bats to killer whales to extant human hunter-gatherers, field and experimental evidence indicate that food transfers are common in social foragers. Transfers take a variety of species- or population-specific forms. In the survey that follows, I have two reasons for beginning with cases taxonomically distant from our own order (Table 14.1). The minor one is that these cases draw attention to an ethological literature full of unrealized comparative possibilities. The major reason is that they give substance and specificity to the theoretical models just examined.

The Ethology of Social Foragers

Songbirds

Colonial nesting cliff swallows (*Hirundo pyrrhonota*) forage in loose, widely spaced groups for compact aerial clusters of insects (Brown et al. 1991). Poor foraging conditions on cool, calm days stimulate a distinctive squeak call that individuals use to alert related and unrelated conspecifics that an insect swarm has been discovered. Experimentation shows that such calls increase when birds are presented with insect swarms (flushed from ground cover by investigators), and call playbacks quickly draw nonforaging birds to the source. By actively recruiting other birds to their discovery, individuals presumably are able to track the swarm longer, enhancing their own foraging success. If this interpretation is correct, use of the squeak call represents an instance of pseudo-reciprocity.

In two separate laboratory experiments with flocks of spice finches (*Lonchura punctulata*), Giraldeau et al. (1994) increased the proportion of scroungers in the group (treatment 1) and, separately, elevated the difficulty faced by producers in obtaining a food packet (treatment 2). Scroungers were conditioned to eat from the food discoveries of producers, as happens under natural conditions, but to avoid foraging themselves. Producers were conditioned to locate food packets. The authors found that birds would respond to the first treatment by shifting toward producing. They responded to the second by shifting toward scrounging. In effect, spice finches are able to opportunistically change their foraging tactics as a function of local socioecological conditions and the tactics of fellow flock members, as predicted by producer-scrounger models.

Bats

Vampire bats (*Desmodus rotundus*) exhibit one of the better studied instances of reciprocity "sharing" (Wilkinson 1987, 1988, 1990). Their feeding ecology—nightly foraging from a central roost for a mammalian blood meal—is unusually precarious. They will die from weight loss and metabolic collapse if they go more than 60 hours without a meal. Yet, individuals fail to secure a meal on 7% to 30% of nights, the higher figure characteristic of inexperienced juveniles. Based on the lower 7% nightly failure rate of adults, annual mortality should be about 82%. It actually is around 24%.

Food transfers forestall the predicted level of starvation in this species. Individuals that have fallen to a less than 24-hour metabolic reserve solicit and receive regurgitated blood from roost mates whose foraging was successful. Both relatedness and long-term prior association without relatedness lead to this transfer behavior. Unrelated individuals seem to form stable, dyadic relationships, "individuals who regurgitate almost exclusively to each other" (Wilkinson 1990: 80). Careful study

Table 14.1. Ethological case studies.

Species; Citation; Study Type	Effective Subsistence Environment	Social Organization	Transfer Behavior	Inferred or Known Evolutionary Mechanism
Common vampire bat (*Desmodus rotundus*); Wilkinson (1990); Naturalistic and field experiment.	High risk foraging conditions; bats cannot survive more than 2 consecutive nights without a meal, yet 7% to 30% fail to feed on any given night.	Long-term, fluid social associations among 8–12 females, comprising several matrilines, and an equal number of offspring. Dyadic preferences among nonrelated females.	Unsuccessful foragers solicit regurgitated blood meal; sharing occurs preferentially among long-term roost mates who may or may not be related. Unrelated roost mates appear to develop a sharing "buddy system."	Transfers due to a mix of kin selection and reciprocal altruism, the latter predominating.
Killer whales (*Orcinus orca*); Hoelzel (1991); Naturalistic.	Coordinated group foraging on seals (2%) and sea lions (97%), with preference for restricted capture sites and efficiently captured prey, most often pups.	Three pods observed, 2–7 individuals, composed of two adults (male and/or female) and subadults. Close genetic relationship known for one pod; inferred for remainder.	Within-pod food-sharing could be confirmed for 27% to 86% of captures, depending on pod. One individual dominated the active hunting and capture, then provisioned others.	Transfers enhance inclusive fitness of related group members in an environment in which high quality feeding sites are limited. No discussion of other possible mechanisms.
Rhesus macaques (*Macaca mulatta*); Hauser and Marler (1993a, 1993b); Naturalistic observations and experimentation on free-ranging, provisioned populations, Cayo Santiago Island.	Although provisioned daily for over 50% of their diet, macaques also forage for coconut; small fruits such as berries; insects; and flowers.	Studies were conducted on 10 focal females and 12 focal males living in group "L," which totaled approximately 300 individuals.	Distinctive "calling" vocalizations (warbles, harmonic arches, chirps) given on discovery and possession of rare, preferred food patches; calls attract nearby individuals.	Kin selection suggested females call rate correlated (positively with number of nearby kin, who then may share in it or perhaps provide coalition defense of it); reciprocity altruism is suggested by social sanctions directed at hoarding.
Common ravens (*Corvus corax*); Heinrich and Marzluff (1995); Naturalistic and experimental field observations.	Difficult winter scavenging of partially consumed moose or deer carcasses, an unpredictable and short lived but very rich feeding opportunity.	Normally territorial, during the winter ravens actively communicate location of such a feeding opportunity, aggregating up to 100 or more unrelated individuals from distances as great as 30 miles.	Juvenile and vagrant ravens exchange information about feeding sites through communal roosts and soaring displays.	Reciprocal altruism: "... food-sharing turns out to be a successful strategy for maximizing survival in an environment where food is sparsely and unevenly distributed in space and time, and where young birds must cooperate in order to defend and feed on a carcass at the same time" (p. 342).

Cliff swallow;(*Hirundo pyrrhonota*); Brown et al. (1991); Naturalistic and experimental field observations.	Signaling behavior during breeding season more likely if foraging conditions for aerial insect swarms are poor (calm, cool, sunless days), those in which insect swarms are relatively inactive.	Colonial nesting, social passerines; kin relationships in the foraging groups that practice squeak calls are unknown.	A vocal "squeak call" is used exclusively to recruit conspecifics to food discoveries when foraging in flocks spread over a wide area, away from the colony. This call augments passive information transfer at the colony itself.	Pseudoreciprocity: individuals issuing a call probably benefit from enhanced foraging success, as conspecifics make it easier to track or reestablish the position of the erratically flying swarms.
Chimpanzee (*Pan troglodytes*); Stanford (1995, 1998); Naturalistic field.	Hunting of small mammals (red colobus monkeys make up 80% of the prey) and meat consumption focused on relatively lean, dry-season months, when food shortages lead to weight loss.	Loosely structured, fission–fusion residential groups, in which hunting parties may vary from 1 to 35 individuals, predominantly male.	Meat may be "exchanged" for political support and/or sexual access; production of surviving offspring may be greater for females receiving more meat.	Exchange of valuable food for indirect and direct fitness-enhancing benefits.
Chimpanzee (*Pan troglodytes*); de Waal (1989); Seminaturalistic enclosure, provisioning experiments.	Provision of concentrated food bundles of medium attractiveness.	24 m × 30 m outdoor colony of one adult male and eight adult females with subadults, totaling 19 animals, adults predominantly unrelated.	Of 4,653 food interactions observed, 50.4% were food transfers. Most transfers resulted from relaxed claims and cofeeding.	Reciprocity of food-for-social favors, such as grooming, indicating a concept of "trade." Food transfers (selective relinquishment) among adults showed a high level of long-term symmetry. Short-term transfers were mediated by social relationships (e.g., were not necessarily tit-for-tat reciprocity, from one event to the next). Tolerated theft not supported.
Spice finch (*Lonchura punctulata*); Giraldeau et al. 1994; Laboratory, experimental.	Experimeters manipulated either (1) the proportion of scroungers in a feeding flock, or (2) the cost of being a producer.	Spice finches form egalitarian social groups, in which they "scramble" to take advantage of each other's food discoveries.	Birds adjusted their use of producing and scrounging, as predicted, in response to local foraging conditions.	Individual-level selection, creating behavioral plasticity sensitive to rate-maximizing options under local socio-ecological conditions.

Table 14.1. (continued)

Species; Citation; Study Type	Effective Subsistence Environment	Social Organization	Transfer Behavior	Inferred or Known Evolutionary Mechanism
Lion (*Panthera leo*); Packer et al. (1990); Naturalistic observations.	Seasonally abundant migratory game (Thomson's gazelle, wildebeest, zebra) alternating with scarcity (warthog and buffalo); high levels of inter-pride competition.	Stable, territorial prides of related females, with fission-fusion formation of situation-specific subgroups (foraging groups, reproductive crèche, etc.).	Egalitarian consumption of prey by members of foraging groups, irrespective of participation in pursuit.	Cooperative hunting apparently a secondary consequence of reproductive patterns and grouping for defense of cubs and territory among related individuals.
White-faced capuchin monkey (*Cebus capucinus*); Perry and Rose (1994), Rose (1997); Naturalistic observations	Tropical dry forest; seasonal rainfall and differences in food and water availability between sites; occasional nest predation on squirrels and coatis pups.	Stable multimale, multifemale social group; female bonded, without exclusive male–female consortships.	At Santa Rosa, a low food site, the acquirer generally consumed all of a coatis pup; at a richer subsistence site, Lomas Barbudal, the capturing capuchin became sated and residual portions were subject to transfer.	Begging (tolerated food transfer to "theft") by individuals attracted to the kill; weak or nonexistent kin or dominance effects on likelihood of meat transfer.

documents that this species meets the conditions necessary for the evolution of reciprocal altruism: stable, long-term association among reciprocators; regular, donor–recipient role reversals; high short term benefit-to-cost ratio for transfers; and the ability to detect and control cheaters.

Ravens

Common ravens (*Corvux corax*) survive the New England winter feeding as scavengers from deer and moose carcasses (Heinrich and Marzluff 1995). Such feeding opportunities are rare and quite difficult to locate. They may be camouflaged by predators or covered incidentally by snowfall. Daylight is short, and ravens have the further handicap that they can eat only after the hide of a moose or deer has been breached by larger carnivores. Once located, a feeding opportunity usually is massive relative to an individual raven's requirements, but it may be ephemeral. In a scene observed repeatedly by Heinrich and Marzluff, one or two juvenile ravens flying alone will locate a dead deer or moose. Without eating, they fly off to a communal roosting site. From this assembly location, they return a few days later at dawn, leading a company of 40 to 100 other ravens who feed cooperatively for several days to a week.

It is telling that individual ravens forgo immediate feeding in order to actively communicate the location of the opportunity to a large number of nonkin. DNA studies show that such aggregations have no higher degrees of relationship than randomly captured individuals. High rates of turnover at the feeding site, the large numbers of birds involved, and their wide range reduce the odds that instances of "sharing" are reciprocated between individual pairs of birds. The roost assembly is not an ongoing social group. Heinrich and Marzluff propose that self-interested reciprocal altruism—principally for the benefits of risk minimization in an unpredictable feeding environment—operates here without stable social associations among the participating individuals. The cost of "sharing" is minimal, as an individual raven can eat its fill and scarcely dent the supply. The benefits—chiefly reduced uncertainty of subsequent meals—are great. Further, the subadults that most readily engage in this behavior must arrive at a feeding site with the force of numbers to overcome its defense by adult ravens.

Whales

Killer whales (*Orcinus orca*), observed at Punta Norte on the Argentinian coast, live in loosely structured "pods" (Hoelzel 1991). These social groups are composed of two adults (males, females, or both) and a variable number of subadult individuals (maximum observed = 5). Southern sea lions (*Otario flavescens*) constitute 97% of observed prey captures. Whales focus their hunting effort at spatially restricted sites where shallow water and bottom relief enhances success rates, and they selectively pursue sea lion groups containing pups, the most readily captured prey type. Within each pod one individual makes 70% to 100% of the active hunts and captures. Other pod members mill nearby. The hunter then joins pod mates before the group consumes the catch. Conservative estimates, based on cases observable on the surface, indicate that between 27% and 86% of the captured prey were transferred in this manner.

Hoelzel infers that transfers occur because of genetic relationships, some of which are known and some inferred, among pod members. Subadults may be fed by a parent until they gain the experience required to effectively strand seal pups themselves, raising the inclusive fitness of the provider. Provisioning may be extended to less direct relations because good hunting sites are rare, and competition for them is more costly than cooperation in their use.

Rhesus Macaques

On Cayo Santiago, troops of rhesus macaques (*Macaca mulatta*) separate to forage. Frequently they are out of sight of one another in the foliage. Individuals, especially females, give food calls that signal discovery of a particularly rich patch of food to macaques in the surrounding area (Hauser and Marler 1993a, 1993b). Females' call rates are positively correlated with the number of kin in the vicinity, but nonkin are among those responding. When a macaque that did not signal is detected eating in one of these patches, she is aggressively punished. Hauser and Marler are able to show that, because of this punishment, nonsignalers who are detected eat less from their discoveries than those who call and share it with their fellows. However, in the rare case of a discoverer that did not call and was not detected, he or she eats more than discoverers who were joined by surrounding macaques.

The rare instance of successful hoarding shows that it is a cost-benefit temptation. The more common instances of unsuccessful hoarding (detection despite failure to call) show that social sanctions can effectively eliminate the immediate benefit and help to control frequency of cheating. Although Hauser and Marler do not explicitly compare causal possibilities, it would appear that both kin selection and reciprocal altruism are operating here.

Macaques are not unique among monkeys in these types of behavior. White-faced capuchins (*Cebus capucinus*) "share" portions of coatis pups captured from their nests (Perry and Rose 1994; Rose 1997, this volume; Table 14.1; see also de Waal 1997b on food transfers in brown capuchins). Adult, buffy-headed marmosets (*Callithrix flaviceps*) share large insects and vertebrate prey with nondescendent infants and juveniles (Ferrari 1987).

Lions

Group living, cooperative hunting, and food "sharing" in the social carnivores has made them attractive models for hominid adaptations (e.g., Thompson 1975, 1976). The same species have been subject to extensive study by behavioral ecologists (e.g., Packer and Ruttan 1988). Lions make an instructive case, with a long interpretive history (see Packer et al. 1990). When game is seasonally abundant, per capita consumption and consumption variance are unrelated to foraging group size. Cooperative hunting itself provides no subsistence advantage. However, during the period of seasonal food shortages two group sizes optimize hunting success, measured as per capita intake. Lions do best either by foraging alone or by foraging cooperatively in a group of five to six. Groups of two to four, by contrast, suffer significantly reduced intakes. Per capita success rates with different size classes of prey create this bimodal pattern.

Observations show that actual foraging group size deviates from these two optima in an interesting pattern. Individuals in prides whose total membership exceeds five or six adults can do equally well by foraging alone or with four to five others, but they very rarely are seen hunting alone. Individuals living in prides whose membership is four or fewer would do best hunting alone but nearly always are found hunting in the largest group allowed by the size of the pride (e.g., two, three, or four). In both cases, solitary hunting is avoided in favor of cooperation, even if, as in small prides, it means suboptimal capture rates. In light of this, Packer et al.'s (1990) present data indicate that female lions hunt in groups primarily to better defend themselves, their territories, and their cubs. They hunt in groups of a size that optimizes success only when that goal is consistent with defense, that is, in the larger prides. Cooperative hunting and food transfer in lions are secondary to other adaptive constraints.

Chimpanzees

Group hunting, meat-eating, and meat transfer are common among Gombe National Park chimpanzees (Stanford 1995, 1998, this volume; see also Boesch-Achermann and Boesch 1994). Hunting episodes peak during the dry season months of August and September, a period of vegetable food shortage when chimpanzees normally lose weight. Males do 90% of the hunting. Capture success grows with the size of the hunting group, from 30% for the lone individual to 70–80% for groups of 10 or more. Presence of an estrous female increases the likelihood of a hunt and, independently, an increase in the number of estrous females present increases the size of the hunting group. Meat transferred by males to females in exchange for sexual access appears also to increase female reproductive success by elevating offspring survivorship in ways not yet understood. Anecdotal evidence hints that meat transferred to other males gains their political support. Food transfers in this species appear to be sexually and politically charged matters of exchange, like those posited in the show off hypothesis. Stanford notes that one male, Frodo, was an especially prolific hunter. Like killer whales, individual chimpanzees may vary in the intensity and success of their hunting efforts.

Experimental provisioning studies by de Waal (1989) confirm the potential of chimpanzees for reciprocity. Adults provisioned with medium sized, moderately attractive plant food bundles transfer portions to others. These food movements are regular, symmetrical in frequency within dyads, and generally peaceable instances of "selective relinquishment." On a short-term basis, turn taking in such relationships frequently intersperses social favors, such as grooming, with transfers of vegetable foods. Sanctioning also occurs. "Stingy" individuals are subject to significantly more aggression from group members. Because of the not-in-kind nature of the transfers, de Waal describes them as "trade" (1989: 454).

In a follow-up study, de Waal (1997a) confirmed that reciprocity in these exchange partnerships is not due to simple frequency of dyadic association. Rather, a supplicant meets lessened resistance to a food transfer if he or she has earlier engaged in grooming the possessor. Reciprocity is contingent on earlier service from the partner. Chimpanzees apparently are keeping mental records of favors received and acting in response to a particular history of interaction. In the absence of a significant cost to the donor, de Waal stops short of calling these interactions reciprocal *altruism*, preferring instead to speak of "social exchange."

The Ethnography of Social Foragers

The ethnographic literature on hunter-gatherer food transfers ("sharing") is large, predominantly qualitative and, in many cases, anecdotal. It also is well known to most anthropologists. For these reasons, and because of my introductory claim that a strong argument for prehistoric food transfers can be made in the absence of ethnographic analogy, my summary of this literature will be brief. Key review articles on human food "sharing" include Price (1975), Feinman (1979), Gould (1981), Woodburn (1982), Kaplan and Hill (1985b), Smith (1988), Peterson (1993), Winterhalder (1996b, 1996c) and Hawkes (this volume). Representative ethnographic case studies of foragers and horticulturalist/foragers include those for the Pilagá (Henry 1951), the Mamaindê (Aspelin 1979), the !Kung San (Wiessner 1982), the Nata River Basarwa (Cashdan 1985), the G/wi, G//ana and Kua Basarwa of Kutse (Kent 1993), and the Kubo (Dwyer and Minnegal 1993).

The rationales for food "sharing" given by most ethnographers fall into two categories. There are functionalist claims that it enhances social solidarity or promotes egalitarianism. And, there are adaptationist arguments that it lowers the "risk" of a diet dependent at least partially on the acquisition of unpredictable resources, especially game. Only the latter possibility is clearly consistent with behavioral ecology. Although we can confidently claim that food transfer behavior is ubiquitous within extant hunter-gatherer groups, few ethnographic studies provide the kinds of data needed to evaluate specific behavioral ecology models. Most anthropological studies were conducted under the theoretical sponsorship of group-level functionalism and well before behavioral ecology models, with their more exacting data requirements, were available. I elaborate on a small set of recent studies (Table 14.2) that explicitly address one or more of the possible causal circumstances and mechanisms of behavioral ecology.

The Aché of Paraguay were mobile foragers until the mid-1970s, when they aggregated around mission settlements and took up swidden agriculture (Hill and Hurtado 1996). Periodically, they resume hunting and gathering on forest treks of several weeks' duration, some of which were documented by Kaplan, Hill, Hawkes and Hurtado (Kaplan et al. 1984; Kaplan and Hill 1985a, 1985b; Hill et al. 1987). As predicted by scrounging, reciprocity, and risk-minimization models, the frequency of Aché transfers correlates positively with specific food qualities. Larger and more valuable foods, asynchronously and unpredictably acquired, are more frequently shared. Despite this consistency, these researchers reject tolerated theft or reciprocity as explanations because food transfers are not overtly contested or evenly balanced (cf. Winterhalder 1996a, 1996c). Instead, indirect evidence indi-

Table 14.2. Ethnographic case studies.

Group; Citation; Study Type	Effective Subsistence Environment	Social Organization	Transfer Behavior	Inferred or Known Evolutionary Mechanism
Aché Kaplan et al. (1984); Kaplan and Hill (1985a, 1985b); Naturalistic/ethnographic	Lowland subtropical forest, eastern Paraguay. Non-domesticated resources include game, honey, fruits, plant foods, and insects.	Now living in a residential settlement, Aché were until the mid-1970s mobile, band-level foragers. Data gathered from task groups of 15–28 individuals, on 1- to 2-week treks away from the settlement for hunting and gathering.	Sharing is common for highly valued resources acquired asynchronously and in packets (game, honey) and uncommon for plant foods.	Transfer behaviors are not patterned by kinship (relatedness), and while consistent with reciprocity and variance reduction, are unbalanced to a degree, suggesting delayed trade for social or reproductive benefits.
Ifaluk Betzig and Turke (1986); Naturalistic/ethnographic	Pacific islets (western Carolines); predominantly a subsistence economy based on fishing and horticulture (taro, breadfruit, coconuts).	Fifty-six households belonging to ranked clans.	Routine interhousehold transfers of prepared foods.	Kin selection; transfer patterns generally follow expectations based on relatedness and cost-to-benefit ratios between givers and receivers.
Meriam Bliege Bird and Bird (1997); Naturalistic/ethnographic	Small volcanic islands in the Torres Strait; subhumid tropical savanna zone; maritime foraging for marine fish, turtles, and mammals. Supplemented by yam, banana, and manioc, plus small amounts of domestic animals.	Formerly dispersed kin-based groups have coalesced to a single permanent village of 400; shortages of land put a premium social status and political alliances.	Distribution of low cost, nesting season turtles to nearby households; donation of high cost mating season turtle to public feasting.	Distribution of turtle meat consistent with tolerated theft, suggesting that males seek this resource in exchange for socio-political or reproductive benefits in a competitive resource environment.
Yanomamö Hames (1998); Naturalistic/ethnographic	Egalitarian, horticultural/foraging population living in lowland Venezuela.	Village level, tribal social organization, 50 to 100 residents.	Interhousehold exchange of foodstuffs, predominantly among subvillage sets of families who cultivate dyadic relationships (their kinship relationships not analyzed).	Exchange patterns more consistent with self-interested reciprocal altruism and risk reduction than with the "egalitarian" exchange model of social anthropology.

cates that food donors gain reproductive benefits through more frequent mating and higher offspring survival rates. This would make Aché transfers a form of trade.

The horticulturalist/foragers of Ifaluk (Western Caroline Islands) regularly prepare food in greater abundance than can be consumed within the family. Portions are then allocated to other households. Betzig and Turke (1986) analyzed these transfers from the perspective of Hamilton's (1964a, 1964b) kin selection equation. They found that cost-benefit ratios and degree of relatedness correlated in the expected ways with transfer patterns. For instance, households transferring food had higher degrees of relatedness than would be found between randomly chosen household pairs, and the threshold relatedness necessary for transfer grew as transportation costs increased. Because Betzig and Turke (1986) examined only the predictions of kin selection, we do not know the importance of other evolutionary mechanisms in this case.

Bliege Bird and Bird (1997) use seasonal changes in the acquisition costs of turtles among the Meriam horticulturalist/foragers (Torres Straight) to analyze distribution patterns for evidence of evolutionary causation. Turtle hunting occurs in two circumstances, each with its associated distribution pattern. Open ocean encounter hunts during the feeding/mating season (May to September) are costly. They also are dangerous and physically demanding. Participation is limited to younger males, success is uncertain, and synchrony of captures is low. When turtles are captured in this season, their meat is consumed in public feasting. Because of this wide distribution, the hunter receives at most an individual share of the meat. By contrast, in the nesting season (October to April) Meriam foragers intercept egg-laying turtles on the beaches. This is a much less demanding and dangerous procedure, and it involves a broader sex-age segment of the population. The catch is larger and more synchronous. Nesting turtles are butchered and portions are parceled out to neighbors (who may be represented only by a bucket left at the butchery site).

Bliege Bird and Bird argue that hypotheses derived from kinship and reciprocity (risk) models of food transfers are not supported by this evidence. Trade/exchange could not be securely tested. By contrast, tolerated theft is supported, leading the authors to suggest that benefits like those predicted in the show off hypothesis must be the motivating factor in much male turtle hunting. This is especially evident for the ocean hunts, for which the catch is distributed at public feasts.

Hames (1998) compares two "sharing" hypotheses using data from four Yanomamö villages. Under the *egalitarian* model common in sociocultual anthropology, transfers in unranked societies are thought to be determined by the capacity to give and the need to receive. Because food producers are not equally skilled, and households exhibit different dependency ratios, this hypothesis predicts unbalanced flows among households. By contrast, under a model of reciprocity altruism, donations are given in the expectation of compensation through delayed return. Outflows should be independent of a household's productivity and inflows independent of a household's needs. By examining Yanomamö distribution patterns with respect to their frequency and balance, the demographic features of donor and recipient households, and village size, Hames shows that transfer patterns are more consistent with the reciprocity/variance reduction model. Despite their egalitarian tendencies, Yanomamö households do not preferentially transfer from high-production to high-consumption households.

Discussion

Given this summary of models and cases, the following inferences seem sound.

Intragroup food transfers are common among social foragers. They regularly occur in nonhuman as well as human populations. These include various songbirds, whales, ravens, bats, social carnivores, macaques, chimpanzees, and other primates. At least within vertebrates, the examples are not confined to advanced evolutionary grades.

This fact greatly expands the comparative possibilities for hypothesis generation and testing. Vampire bats offer a working instance of the traditional view that hunter-gatherer "sharing" is a case of risk minimizing based on reciprocal altruism. Ravens give us a behavioral ecology model of transfers by a wide-ranging scavenger that depends on group behavior to usurp more adept predators. Killer whales show us how physically constrained sites for harvest opportunities may lead to transfers. Lions demonstrate that cooperative hunting and food transfers may be suboptimal but occur anyway as a result of other selective pressures for group living. Swallows and ravens force us to confront the critical but subtle differences between pseudo- and altruistic-reciprocity. Studies of free-ranging macaques and chimpanzees may help us to understand how certain foraging behaviors combine with plant or animal properties to make resources act as packets.

Among primates, Boesch (1994) compares chimpanzee cooperative hunting and meat "sharing" at Gombe Stream and Taï National Park, Côte de'Ivoire. The reviews by Rose (1997, this volume) of capuchin, chimpanzee, and human predation and food transfer are a model for the comparative approach. Paleoanthropologists will have to immerse themselves in behavioral ecology to a degree not apparent in the contemporary literature on hominid evolution if they are to realize the analytical potential of this kind of evidence (O'Connell 1995; Winterhalder 1996c).

Intragroup food transfers are ubiquitous among social foragers having in common a particular suite of socioecological features. Asynchronous harvesting and weak possession of intermediate-sized food packets by members of relatively stable and contiguous social units is common to nearly all of the models and examples cited. Marginal valuation and risk sensitivity add to evolutionary pressures for transfers. The disparity between a raven-sized stomach and a moose-sized banquet highlights the potential significance of the former; the metabolic urgency of bat foraging points to the importance of the latter. Where this suite of resource conditions pertains, intragroup food transfers appear to be common. Because the generating conditions are material, well identified, and fairly limited in number, they should be observable archaeologically. However, it is important to add that packets are sometimes defined by their functional qualities (see also Winterhalder 1996a). A roost-mate's stomach, distended with a recent blood meal, is a packet to a vampire bat. A swarm of insects is a packet to a swallow. Fruit may or may not qualify as a packet depending on how it is harvested by macaques.

In evolutionary terms, food transfer behavior among social foragers is subject to multiple causation. Within the suite of subsistence features cited immediately above, food transfers can come about through a variety of evolutionary mechanisms (Tables 14.1 and 14.2; Winterhalder 1996b). Transfers are likely to result from overlapping causes; more than one of these mechanisms can operate concurrently. In fact, multiple causation may in part be responsible for the ubiquity of transfers. The balance struck among the forces of tolerated theft/scrounging, marginal valuation, risk sensitivity, pseudo- and altruistic-reciprocity, exchange, and showing off presumably is determined by local features of social structure and environment. As the latter vary, the specific forms of transfer behavior are predicted to vary as well.

Wilkinson (1987) presents methods for discriminating between kin selection and reciprocal altruism. His evidence on vampire bats points to mixed causation, with reciprocity predominating: "the increase in individual survivorship due to reciprocal food-sharing events in this species provides a greater increase in inclusive fitness than can be attributed to aiding relatives" (Wilkinson 1988: 85). This finding echoes a preliminary result from ethnographic studies: in foragers, it typically has been difficult to show that intragroup distribution patterns are directed preferentially to relatives (compare Betzig and Turke 1986, and Kaplan and Hill 1985b). Reciprocity can dominate the concurrent operation of kin selection in the evolution of transfers.

Each of the four ethnographic cases attributes primary causal influence to a different evolutionary mechanism: individual selection for trade in the Aché, kin selection in the Ifaluk, tolerated theft and showing off in the Miriam, and reciprocity selection among the Yanomamö. Even if we treat these conclusions as preliminary—the data required to reliably assess the importance of differing causes exceed what is available in the best of studies—it is nonetheless suggestive in that they invoke nearly the full range of possible models as primary determinants.

Food transfer behavior takes diverse forms. Transfers can be active, passive, or both. Swallows in the field alert distant flock members to insect swarms with a special squeak call. They also use passive observations at their colonial nesting site to follow successful foragers to bountiful feeding sites (see Brown et al. 1991). Transfers may entail food and/or information about food. Food may transfer against itself (in-kind) or against other resources, social allegiance and political support, reproductive access, or other services or benefits (not in kind), as is seen in captive (de Waal 1989, 1997a) and wild (Stanford 1995) populations of chimpanzees. In the Stanford (1995) study, meat appears to be a rudimentary exchange commodity, at least in the spheres of sexual relationships and political alliances. Transfers may be symmetrical or asymmetrical, immediate or delayed. They may be embedded in social events that range from barely disguised thievery to gifts, forcibly given. Risk may be high (bats) or low (macaques). Transfer may involve related or unrelated individuals living in relatively stable social groups (e.g., bats), or it may occur among unrelated individuals with no ongoing associations (e.g., ravens) (Table 14.1).

Ethnographic studies show similar intergroup diversity among extant hunter-gatherers. As with other species, this diversity presumably arises from environment (e.g., degree of dependence on resource packets, the stability and size of the social unit, etc.) and from differing balances among the evolutionary mechanisms operating in each case. To repeat an introductory observation, "sharing" is no longer just sharing.

Intragroup diversity may also characterize the evolution of transfers. Models of scrounging and evidence from spice finches show that groups of social foragers might well contain stable mixes of different tactics. Producers and opportunists may exist alone, producers may coexist with scroungers or with opportunists, and opportunists may coexist with scroungers. At equilibrium no individual can gain by switching its tactic (or the frequency with which it uses various tactics). We can predict that groups of social foragers will contain individuals who adopt unlike economic roles or who switch among economic roles. This indicates that differential foraging efforts by males may also be multiply caused by some balance between evolutionary tendencies for showing off and those for producing/scrounging.

Conclusions

The food "sharing" hypothesis was rejected in part because paleoanthropologists were made to feel uncomfortable projecting "modern" human behavior onto the Plio-Pleistocene past (Binford 1985). At the time, this was a laudable caution. However, we now know that in wider comparative perspective it has the unfortunate and indefensible consequence of denying to hominids the socioecological transfer capacities of ravens and bats. While we may be obliged to avoid seeing "signs of modern humanity in the activities of these early ancestors" (Potts 1984: 347), we are not under any similar analytical compulsion to treat our hominid ancestors as less behaviorally sophisticated in their food production and allocation than other vertebrates.

Along with Rose and Marshall (1996), I believe it is time to revive the food "sharing" hypothesis. My approach nonetheless differs from Rose and Marshall in at least three respects. I think it is evident that: (1) we must look to nonprimate as well as primate species and extant foragers for ideas and comparative information. Primate and ethnographic examples are too limited in number and confounded by phylogenetic association to trust as our only source of comparative evidence; (2) careful taphonomy is not enough for behavioral reconstruction. The archaeological and other evidence must be interpreted through the variables and models of behavioral ecology, that is through conceptual models (Tooby and DeVore 1987; O'Connell 1996). Glynn Isaac was prescient in this as well; he argued that, to imagine what cannot be directly observed in prehistoric archaeology, we will need "a knowledge of ecology and an understanding of alternative strategies for exploiting the economy of nature . . ." (1986, quoted in Blumenschine 1991: 321); and (3) one step in that direction will be recognizing that transfer behaviors in groups of social foragers are common, linked to clearly specifiable environmental circumstances, diverse in their behavioral manifestations, and caused by a variety of evolutionary mechanisms, some of which we are beginning to understand through analyses using behavioral ecology models.

REFERENCES

Aspelin, P. L. 1979. Food distribution and social bonding among the Mamaindê of Mato Grosso, Brazil. *Journal of Anthropological Research* 35:309–327.
Axelrod, R., and D. Dion. 1988. The further evolution of cooperation. *Science* 242:1385–1390.

Axelrod, R., and W. D. Hamilton. 1981. The evolution of cooperation. *Science* 211:1390–1396.

Betzig, L. L., and P. W. Turke. 1986. Food-sharing on Ifaluk. *Current Anthropology* 27:397–400.

Binford, L. R. 1985. Human ancestors: changing views of their behavior. *Journal of Anthropological Archaeology* 4:292–327.

Bliege Bird, R. L., and D. W. Bird. 1997. Delayed reciprocity and tolerated theft: the behavioral ecology of food-sharing strategies. *Current Anthropology* 38:49–78.

Blumenschine, R. J. 1991. Breakfast at Olorgesailie: the natural history approach to Early Stone Age archaeology. *Journal of Human Evolution* 21:307–327.

Blurton Jones, N. G. 1984. A selfish origin for human food-sharing: tolerated theft. *Ethology and Sociobiology* 5:1–3.

Blurton Jones, N. G. 1987. Tolerated theft, suggestions about the ecology and evolution of sharing, hoarding and scrounging. *Social Science Information* 26:31–54.

Boesch, C. 1994. Cooperative hunting in wild chimpanzees. *Animal Behaviour* 48:653–667.

Boesch-Achermann, H., and C. Boesch. 1994. Hominization in the rainforest: the chimpanzee's piece of the puzzle. *Evolutionary Anthropology* 3:9–16.

Boyd, R., and P. J. Richerson. 1985. *Culture and the Evolutionary Process*. Chicago: University of Chicago Press.

Boyd, R., and P. J. Richerson. 1989. The evolution of indirect reciprocity. *Social Networks* 11:213–236.

Boyd, R., and P. J. Richerson. 1992. Punishment allows the evolution of cooperation (or anything else) in sizable groups. *Ethology and Sociobiology* 13:171–195.

Brown, C. R., M. B. Brown, and M. L. Shaffer. 1991. Food-sharing signals among socially foraging cliff swallows. *Animal Behaviour* 42:551–564.

Brown, J. L. 1983. Cooperation—a biologist's dilemma. *Advances in the Study of Behavior* 13:1–37.

Caraco, T., and L.-A. Giraldeau. 1991. Social foraging: producing and scrounging in a stochastic environment. *Journal of Theoretical Biology* 153:559–583.

Cashdan, E. A. 1985. Coping with risk: reciprocity among the Basarwa of Northern Botswana. *Man (N.S.)* 20:454–474.

Connor, R. C. 1995. Altruism among non-relatives: alternatives to the 'prisoner's dilemma.' *Trends in Ecology and Evolution* 10:84–86.

de Waal, F. B. M. 1989. Food-sharing and reciprocal obligations among chimpanzees. *Journal of Human Evolution* 18:433–459.

de Waal, F. B. M. 1997a. The chimpanzee's service economy: food for grooming. *Evolution and Human Behavior* 18:375–386.

de Waal, F. B. M. 1997b. Food transfers through mesh in brown capuchins. *Journal of Comparative Psychology* 111:370–378.

Dugatkin, L. A., M. Mesterton-Gibbons, and A. I. Houston. 1992. Beyond the prisoner's dilemma: toward models to discriminate among mechanisms of cooperation in nature. *Trends in Ecology and Evolution* 7:202–205.

Durham, W. H. 1990. Advances in evolutionary culture theory. *Annual Review of Anthropology* 19:187–210.

Dwyer, P. D., and M. Minnegal. 1993. Are Kubo hunters 'show offs'? *Ethology and Sociobiology* 14:53–70.

Elster, J. 1983. *Explaining Technical Change: A Case Study in the Philosophy of Science.* Cambridge: Cambridge University Press.

Feinman, S. 1979. An evolutionary theory of food-sharing. *Social Science Information* 18:695–726.

Ferrari, S. F. 1987. Food transfer in a wild marmoset group. *Folia Primatologica* 48:203–206.

Giraldeau, L.-A., Hogan, and M. J. Clinchy. 1990. The payoffs to producing and scrounging: what happens when patches are divisible? *Ethology* 85:132–146.

Giraldeau, L.-A., C. Soos, and G. Beauchamp. 1994. A test of the producer-scrounger foraging game in captive flocks of spice finches, *Lonchura punctulata. Behavioral Ecology and Sociobiology* 34:251–256.

Gould, R. A. 1981. Comparative ecology of food-sharing in Australia and northwest California. In: *Omnivorous Primates: Gathering and Hunting in Human Evolution* (R. S. O. Harding and G. Teleki, eds.), pp. 422–454. New York: Columbia University Press.

Hames, R. In press. Reciprocal altruism in Yanomamö food exchange. In *Human Behavior and Adaptation: An Anthropological Perspective* (N. Chagnon, L. Cronk, and W. Irons, eds.).

Hamilton, W. D. 1964a. The genetical evolution of social behaviour. I. *Journal of Theoretical Biology* 7:1–16.

Hamilton, W. D. 1964b. The genetical evolution of social behaviour. II. *Journal of Theoretical Biology* 7:17–51.

Hauser, M. D., and P. Marler. 1993a. Food-associated calls in rhesus macaques (*Macaca mulatta*): I. Socioecological factors. *Behavioral Ecology* 4:194–205.

Hauser, M. D., and P. Marler. 1993b. Food-associated calls in rhesus macaques (*Macaca mulatta*): II. Costs and benefits of call production and suppression. *Behavioral Ecology* 4:206–212.

Hawkes, K. 1991. Showing off: tests of an hypothesis about men's foraging goals. *Ethology and Sociobiology* 12:29–54.

Hawkes, K. 1992a. Sharing and collective action. In *Evolutionary Ecology and Human Behavior* (E. A. Smith and B. Winterhalder, eds.), pp. 269–300. Hawthorne, NY: Aldine de Gruyter.

Hawkes, K. 1992b. On sharing and work. *Current Anthropology* 33:404–407.

Hawkes, K. 1993a. Why hunter-gatherers work: an ancient version of the problem of public goods. *Current Anthropology* 34:341–361.

Hawkes, K. 1993b. Reply. *Current Anthropology* 34:706–710.

Heinrich, B., and J. Marzluff. 1995. Why ravens share. *American Scientist* 83:342–349.

Henry, J. 1951. The economics of Pilagá food distribution. *American Anthropologist* 53:187–219.

Hill, K., and A. M. Hurtado. 1996. *Ache Life History: The Ecology and Demography of a Foraging People.* Hawthorne, NY: Aldine de Gruyter.

Hill, K., and H. Kaplan. 1993. On why male foragers hunt and share food. *Current Anthropology* 34:701–706.

Hill, K., H. Kaplan, K. Hawkes, and A. M. Hurtado. 1987. Foraging decisions among Aché hunter-gatherers: new data and implications for optimal foraging models. *Ethology and Sociobiology* 8:1–36.

Hoelzel, A. R. 1991. Killer whale predation on marine mammals at Punta Norte, Argentina; food-sharing, provisioning and foraging strategy. *Behavioral Ecology and Sociobiology* 29:197–204.

Isaac, G. 1978a. Food-sharing and human evolution: archaeological evidence from the Plio-Pleistocene of East Africa. *Journal of Anthropological Research* 34:311–325.

Isaac, G. 1978b. The food-sharing behavior of protohuman hominids. *Scientific American* 238(4):90–108.

Isaac, G. 1984. The archaeology of human origins: studies of the lower Pleistocene in East Africa 1971–1981. *Advances in World Archaeology* 3:1–87.

Kaplan, H., and K. Hill. 1985a. Hunting ability and reproductive success among male Ache foragers: preliminary results. *Current Anthropology* 26:131–133.

Kaplan, H., and K. Hill. 1985b. Food-sharing among Ache foragers: tests of explanatory hypotheses. *Current Anthropology* 26:223–246.

Kaplan, H., K. Hill, K. Hawkes, and A. Hurtado. 1984. Food-sharing among Ache hunter-gatherers of eastern Paraguay. *Current Anthropology* 25:113–115.

Kent, S. 1993. Sharing in an egalitarian community. *Man (N.S.)* 28:479–514.

Kummer, H. 1991. Evolutionary transformations of possessive behavior. In *To Have Possessions: A Handbook on Ownership and Property* (R. W. Rudmin, ed.), pp. 75–83. Corte Madera, CA: Select Press.

Mesterton-Gibbons, M., and L. A. Dugatkin. 1992. Cooperation among unrelated individuals: evolutionary factors. *The Quarterly Review of Biology* 67:267–281.

Nettle, D., and R. I. M. Dunbar. 1997. Social markers and the evolution of reciprocal exchange. *Current Anthropology* 38:93–99.

Nowak, M. A., and K. Sigmund. 1992. Tit for tat in heterogeneous populations. *Nature* 355:250–253.

Nowak, M. A., and K. Sigmund. 1993. A strategy of win-stay, lose-shift that outperforms tit-for-tat in the Prisoner's Dilemma game. *Nature* 364:56–58.

Nowak, M. A., R. M. May, and K. Sigmund. 1995. The arithmetics of mutual help. *Scientific American* 272(6):76–81.

O'Connell, J.F. 1995. Ethnoarchaeology needs a general theory of behavior. *Journal of Archaeological Research* 3:205–255.

Packer, C., and L. Ruttan. 1988. The evolution of cooperative hunting. *The American Naturalist* 132:159–198.

Packer, C., D. Scheel, and A. E. Pusey. 1990. Why lions form groups: food is not enough. *The American Naturalist* 136:1–19.

Perry, S., and L. Rose. 1994. Begging and transfer of coati meat by white-faced capuchin monkeys, *Cebus capucinus*. *Primates* 35:409–415.

Peterson, N. 1993. Demand sharing: reciprocity and the pressure for generosity among foragers. *American Anthropologist* 95:860–874.

Potts, R. 1984. Home bases and early hominids. *American Scientist* 72:338–347.

Price, J. A. 1975. Sharing: the integration of intimate economics. *Anthropologica* XVII:3–27.

Rogers, A. 1994. Evolution of time preference by natural selection. *American Economic Review* 84:460–481.

Rose, L. M. 1997. Vertebrate predation and food-sharing in *Cebus* and *Pan*. *International Journal of Primatology* 18:727–765.

Rose, L., and F. Marshall. 1996. Meat-eating, hominid sociality, and home bases revisited. *Current Anthropology* 37:307–338.

Sigmund, K. 1993. *Games of Life: Explorations in Ecology, Evolution and Behaviour.* London: Penguin.

Smith, E. A. 1988. Risk and uncertainty in the "original affluent society": evolutionary ecology of resource-sharing and land tenure. In *Hunter-Gatherers, Volume I: History, Evolution and Social Change* (T. Ingold, D. Riches, and J. Woodburn, eds.), pp. 222–251. New York: Berg.

Smith, E. A., and B. Winterhalder. 1992. Natural selection and decision-making: some fundamental principles. In *Evolutionary Ecology and Human Behavior* (E. A. Smith, and B. Winterhalder, eds.), pp. 25–60. New York: Aldine de Gruyter.

Stanford, C. B. 1995. Chimpanzee hunting behavior and human evolution. *American Scientist* 83:256–261.

Stanford, C. B. 1998. *Chimpanzee and Red Colobus: The Ecology of Predator and Prey.* Cambridge, MA: Harvard University Press.

Thiel, B. 1994. Further thoughts on why men share meat. *Current Anthropology* 35:440–441.

Thompson, P. R. 1975. A cross-species analysis of carnivore, primate, and hominid behaviour. *Journal of Human Evolution* 4:113–124.

Thompson, P. R. 1976. A behavior model for *Australopithecus africanus. Journal of Human Evolution* 5:547–558.

Tooby, J., and I. DeVore. 1987. The reconstruction of hominid behavioral evolution through strategic modeling. In *The Evolution of Human Behavior: Primate Models* (W. G. Kinzey, ed.), pp. 183–237. Albany, NY: State University of New York Press.

Trivers, R. L. 1971. The evolution of reciprocal altruism. *Quarterly Review of Biology* 46:35–57.

Vickery, W. L., L.-A. Giraldeau, J. J. Templeton, D. L. Kramer, and C. A. Chapman. 1991. Producers, scroungers, and group foraging. *The American Naturalist* 137:847–863.

Wiessner, P. 1982. Risk, reciprocity and social influences on !Kung San economics. In *Politics and History in Band Societies* (E. Leacock, and R. Lee, eds.), pp. 61–84. Cambridge: Cambridge University Press.

Wilkinson, G. S. 1987. Altruism and co-operation in bats. In *Recent Advances in the Study of Bats* (M. B. Fenton, P. Racey, and J. M. V. Rayner, eds.), pp. 299–323. Cambridge: Cambridge University Press.

Wilkinson, G. S. 1988. Reciprocal altruism in bats and other mammals. *Ethology and Sociobiology* 9:85–100.

Wilkinson, G. S. 1990. Food-sharing in vampire bats. *Scientific American* 262(2):76–82.

Wilson, D. S. 1998. Hunting, sharing, and multilevel selection: the tolerated-theft model revisited. *Current Anthropology* 39:73–97.

Winterhalder, B. 1986. Diet choice, risk, and food-sharing in a stochastic environment. *Journal of Anthropological Archaeology* 5:369–392.

Winterhalder, B. 1990. Open field, common pot: harvest variability and risk avoidance in agricultural and foraging societies. In *Risk and Uncertainty in Tribal and Peasant Economies* (E. Cashdan, ed.), pp. 67–87. Boulder, CO: Westview Press.

Winterhalder, B. 1996a. A marginal model of tolerated theft. *Ethology and Sociobiology* 17:37–53.

Winterhalder, B. 1996b. Gifts given, gifts taken: the behavioral ecology of nonmarket, intragroup exchange. *Journal of Archaeological Research* 5:121–168.

Winterhalder, B. 1996c. Social foraging and the behavioral ecology of intragroup resource transfers. *Evolutionary Anthropology* 5:46–57.

Winterhalder, B., F. Lu, and B. Tucker. 1999. Risk-sensitive subsistence tactics: models and evidence from subsistence studies in biology and anthropology. *Journal of Archaeological Research* 7:301–348.

Wobst, H. M. 1978. The archaeo-ethnology of hunter-gatherers or the tyranny of the ethnographic record in archaeology. *American Antiquity* 43:303–309.

Woodburn, J. 1982. Egalitarian societies. *Man (N.S.)* 17:431–451.

Part IV

Theoretical Considerations

15

The Evolutionary Consequences of Increased Carnivory in Hominids

Robert Foley

Introduction

The relatively high level of carnivory in living humans compared to other extant primates has long been a subject of anthropological, archaeological, and evolutionary discussion. Some have assigned enormous ecological, behavioral, and cognitive or social significance to more meat-eating (e.g., Ardrey 1961), while others have either questioned its empirical base (e.g., Binford 1981) or consider it to be little more than a minor ecological shift or addition to the hominid dietary base that remained stubbornly based on gathering (Dahlberg 1981). In recent years there has been a vigorous debate on issues related to the timing and nature of early hominid meat-eating, arising from Isaac's food-sharing (Isaac 1978) model, Binford's (1981) and others' critique, and subsequent methodological and empirical developments (Bunn 1981; Potts 1984; Blumenschine 1986; Rose and Marshall 1996).

However, meat-eating has many other aspects when considered from a broader evolutionary perspective, and it is some of these that I shall address in this chapter. The approach adopted is that of using evolutionary and ecological theory derived from comparative studies to make predictions about changes in adaptation and behavior in response to changing costs and benefits. This approach has been developed elsewhere and applied to early hominid foraging behavior, including meat-eating (Foley 1987; Shipman and Walker 1989). Three questions are central: (1) what factors are likely to influence the increase or decrease in the amount of meat in a diet? (2) What are the physiological, anatomical and behavioral correlates of meat-eating? and (3) what are the consequences of meat-eating for higher level evolutionary and ecological mechanisms such as speciation, extinction, and population dispersals, distribution, and density? The first section of the chapter looks at the nature of meat as a resource, the levels of carnivory that might be involved, and the phylogenetic context for considering its development in human evolution. In the second part, the evolutionary correlates of increased carnivory are outlined as the basis for considering where in the fossil record these correlates can be found. This discussion then forms the third section.

Primates, Humans, and Meat

Meat

As a preliminary gesture towards definitions, "meat" is taken here to be a short-hand for animal-derived dietary resources, primarily from vertebrates (but see McGrew this volume). For the most part, this can be expected to be muscle tissue but would also extend to other edible elements. What is of greater importance than the anatomical elements involved from the perspective adopted here is the general characteristics of meat as a resource. The key element is that, for an anthropoid primate, it may be considered as a high quality resource, providing high nutritional returns (high energy/protein, low digestive costs) (Harding 1981; Fleagle 1988). Meat would be more similar to fruits as a major element in most anthropoid diets and less similar to leaves (Chivers et al. 1984). This is not the same as saying that it would automatically fall within any optimal diet, as this would depend upon the costs and benefits of both the search/acquisition as well as the processing/feeding of the resource, but simply that, other things being equal, it is nutritionally valu-able. In considering the implications of a high-quality resource for the evolution-ary ecology of a primate, this aspect is a useful starting point. As an illustration, a small antelope (e.g., Thompson's gazelle) would yield approximately 52,000 kilo-joules (kJ), 200 g of fat, and 2,600 g of protein (Leung 1968; Kingdon 1997). A very rough estimate indicates that this is the equivalent of eating nearly 300 figs (a favored food among chimpanzees) for energy, 2,000 figs for protein, and 666 figs for fat (Wrangham et al. 1993; Conklin and Wrangham 1994). The difference be-tween these two resources comes when it is taken into account that there are many more figs (1,000 kg in a single tree when fruiting) in a forest than gazelles, and therefore, search costs are very different.

The other characteristics of meat (which are frequent correlates of high quality foods in general) that would impinge on evolutionary processes are that, by and large, animals are patchily distributed in an environment, certainly through space and frequently over time as well (e.g., seasonal variation in biomass), and they are often unpredictable within the environment (Schoener 1971; Krebs and Davies 1984). This last characteristic is the hardest to formulate precisely, as to some ex-tent predictability of a resource is as much a function of the characteristics of the predatory species as an inherent quality of the prey. Thus, in shaping evolutionary responses, meat will be considered here as a patchy, unpredictable and high-quality resource. To place this in a comparative context, leaves for a forest dwelling pri-mate might be considered to be evenly distributed, predictable, and low quality, but obviously these are relative and locally variable scales.

Significant Carnivory?

The second problem that needs to be clarified at the outset is the level of meat-eating that is being discussed. Among mammals as a whole, there is a clear contrast between compulsive, specialized, and exclusive carnivores such as lions, and total herbivores such as antelopes. Much of the discussion on carnivory in hominids has been ambiguous as to the levels involved, and in particular, what would constitute a "significant" amount of carnivory. It has been estimated that the common chimpanzee may acquire around 5% of its food from meat (see Stanford this volume), and possibly some individuals up to 10%; among contemporary human populations meat-eating may vary from zero (e.g., some religious sects) to almost 100% (among high latitude hunter-gatherers) (Lee and DeVore 1968b; Kelly 1995). Among ethnographically observed hunter-gatherers, the level of meat-eating varies with latitude and environment (Lee and DeVore 1968b). For tropical populations living in environments not dissimilar to those of the African Pliocene, estimates may be as low as 20% (Lee and DeVore 1968a), or more than 50% (Hawkes et al. 1991). Furthermore, there may be seasonal variations and periods when meat may not be eaten at all or may be the primary source of food.

In this chapter I would consider "significant" increases in meat-eating to be greater than that found in chimpanzee populations, but it would not be necessary for this to be the predominant element of the diet. In practice it could be argued that any community that obtains between 20% and 50% of their diet from animals would have its distribution, structure, density, and behavior significantly influenced over evolutionarily meaningful time periods. Furthermore, such evolutionary shifts can occur where the behavior is not general to the population as a whole but may relate to one sex or to age-specific categories, as is the case for hunting among chimpanzees (Stanford 1996; Stanford et al. 1994). Thus, in considering the shift from an essentially eclectic hominoid type of diet to one more similar to living humans, it is in the shift from around 10% to around 20%, and possibly at times as much as 40–50%, that I would consider to be of major interest. In this context, furthermore, it is the level of meat-eating that is of more importance than the means by which it is acquired, and even whether the food comes from smaller or larger animals.

Phylogenetic Context and Diet

In discussing what levels of meat-eating might be evolutionarily significant it was proposed that levels well below that of full specialized carnivory would have had a major evolutionary effect. A more theoretical basis for this proposition can be found by considering hominids in their phylogenetic context. While environments, operating through natural selection, shape the behavior and adaptations of lineages, they do so in specific phylogenetic contexts. The same environment or the same resources will have differential effects according to the phylogenetic "raw material" on which selection operates. It is necessary, therefore, to specify the nature of the evolutionary heritages that the first hominids would have possessed.

The most significant of these is that as anthropoid primates the hominids would have been compulsively social, relatively large brained, with a diet focused primarily on fruits (Harding 1981; Fleagle 1988). Across the range of the anthropoids, fruit is the major resource; in adapting to local conditions different species will extend that frugivorous preference in any number of directions—seeds and grasses (gelada), leaves (colobines and mountain gorillas), meat (chimpanzees, baboons), shellfish (chacma baboons), nuts (orangs, chimpanzees, uakari), and insects (chimpanzees, capuchins, squirrel monkeys) (Smuts et al. 1987). Such extensions might be in the direction of either lower quality or higher quality resources. However, the key element is that primates on the whole have a preference for relatively high quality resources.

More specifically, it has been established that hominids are the sister clade of *Pan* (Goodman et al. 1983) and that the earliest australopithecines are more similar to chimpanzees in overall morphology than to living *Homo* (White et al. 1994). It can be inferred, therefore, that the last common ancestor (LCA) may have been relatively similar to the chimpanzee (at this level whether this is *P. paniscus* or *P. troglodytes/verus* is not strictly important, although the differences are interesting). If that is the case, then we can postulate a number of traits that would have been present in the earliest hominids (Wrangham 1987; Foley 1987, 1989, 1996). Obviously, the first of these might be that meat-eating is itself a plesiomorphy of the *Pan/Australopithecus-Homo* clade and that some level of meat-eating has characterized all hominids. Associated with this might be tool use and manufacture (stone and wood). At a social level, chimpanzees and humans live by and large in relatively large communities with multiple adult males and females, as well as young, and have predominantly female dispersal and male residence and kin bonding. Using the *Pan* comparative context, communities may have been relatively antagonistic to each other, if not actually hostile. In addition, it can be expected that life history strategies may have been markedly skewed in the direction associated with K-selected strategies.

Table 15.1 lists characters that can be considered to be part of the early hominid phylogenetic heritage (i.e., are plesiomorphic to the clade), and therefore, part of the evolutionary raw material that would have been modified by natural selection during the Pliocene and Pleistocene. Perhaps from the point of view of the issues to be discussed here it should be stressed that all early hominids were likely to have hunted and used tools of some sort, and they would have lived in stable and complex social groups .

Evolutionary Correlates of Carnivory

The discussion of phylogenetic context and the nature of meat as a resource provides a means of constraining the nature of the evolutionary correlates of carnivory. It is not necessarily meat per se but the resource characteristics of meat for a social animal with high reproductive costs that are interesting. Although carnivores have been used for hominid foraging models (Kruuk and Turner 1967; Caro 1989), fundamental phylogenetic differences impose major limitations on their use. The key question here is what would the consequences be for a large-brained primate if it increased the intake of a high-quality resource such as meat (Foley 1987; Shipman and Walker 1989).

Table 15.1. Hominid plesiomorphies that may be expected to be already present in the first hominids, based on their presence in other primate clades.

Catarrhines (and Possibly Other Anthropoids	Great Apes	African Apes	Pan/Homo-Australopithecus
Compulsive sociality	Female dispersal	Male residence	Manufacture of simple wooden tools
High levels of maternal care	Larger body size	(Semi)terrestriality	Use of wood for tools
K selected life history strategy	EQ of approximately 2	Prolonged dependence of young on mother	Stones used as hammers(?)
High quality dietary preference	Increased longevity		Male kin-bonding and alliance formation
	Marked sexual dimorphism		Intergroup hostility and intercommunity violence
			Hunting of vertebrates (including mammals and primates)
			High cognitive levels (communication, political activity, deception, coordination, etc.)

Only those directly relevant to the issues discussed here are presented (see Groves 1989) for a more morphologically oriented list, and Foley (1996), Wrangham (1987), and Di Fiore and Randall (1994) for further discussion. Attributing traits as plesiomorphies in two closely related clades in which one (humans) has evolved very markedly is problematic, and the alternative hypothesis (that they are homoplasies) is generally considered less parsimonious. Some traits such as certain types of tool use in chimpanzees are populationally variable, and this may indicate that they are not genuine plesiomorphies. However, a list such as this indicates the initial characteristics already present in the hominid clade and hence does not require special explanation. Some must be considered more speculative than others; for example, high sexual dimorphism is considered to be a plesiomorphy for hominoids, as orangs, gorillas, and most australopithecines are dimorphic, while humans and *Pan* are less so. Alternative polarities are possible. Traits not shared across these lineages (stone tool manufacture, scavenging, higher levels of meat consumption, language, etc.) may be considered hominid apomorphies and thus require explanation.

Energetics, Behavior, and Socioecology

In the light of the discussion of the characteristics of meat provided above, a shift towards more carnivory would essentially be towards higher quality food that was more patchily distributed and less predictable in both time and space. Variation in these characteristics has long been the basis for models of socioecology, and these can be used to generate some expected correlations of increased meat-eating among hominids.

Animals that exploit higher quality resources are associated with a number of things. First among these is simply a good level of nutrition. As meat is easily assimilated and requires little mastication or digestion, there would be reduced costs in terms of processing, both in terms of energy expenditure and time (this is independent of the higher search costs, which relate to patchiness—see below). There may well have been benefits in terms of the size of the digestive tract, with energy available for either other tissues or for other activity budgets (Milton 1981, 1987, 1993; Milton and Demment 1988).

Energetic, behavioral, or socioecological consequences would also arise out of the patchiness of animal resources. Different species of herbivorous mammals obviously have a diversity of densities and distributions. Nonetheless, it is fair to say that medium-sized herbivores are not evenly distributed across a landscape. Many are herd/harem animals and so live in small groups, which itself creates patchiness. Even where they are more solitary, they are widely dispersed and, hence, would be hard to find. A "patch" such as a solitary lesser kudu (175,000 kJ) would occur relatively rarely, as would a dead elephant (2 million kJ). A consequence of this is that hominids searching for animals (either alive or dead) would have large ranging distances (day range length), and larger home ranges as well (Foley 1987; Shipman and Walker 1989). To cover larger areas would involve both higher energy expenditure and more time, and thus there would be selective pressures leading to greater (terrestrial) locomotor efficiency, and to selection for being able to cope with time stressed foraging budgets. An alternative perspective would relate the shift to carnivory to bipedalism. Carnivory is associated with large home ranges (McNab 1963) and would, therefore, require a more efficient means of terrestrial locomotion, and bipedalism might thus have been a condition upon which a dietary shift was based (Foley 1987, 1992).

Apart from being more patchy in space, meat resources are also more patchy in time. Most African herbivorous mammals are seasonally variable in their distribution, and biomass can change very markedly due either to migration or dispersal/concentration. Sinclair et al. (1986) have suggested that this would have led to a migratory (herd-following) strategy on the part of more carnivorous hominids, but this is likely to be incompatible with the inferred territorial and social behavior of hominids. Altricial young, such as would be expected for hominoids, would be a major constraint on rapid mobility, and intergroup hostility such as is proposed by Wrangham (Wrangham 1987; Foley and Lee 1995) for the basal hominids (see below) would make long-distance fissioning for hunting or scavenging a risky strategy. A more likely response is that meat-eating would be seasonally variable, depending upon resource abundance (Foley 1987, 1993; Stanford et al. 1994), and, hence, would be part of a flexible foraging strategy with high levels of dietary variability.

Patchiness of food is not just a question of how it is distributed but also the size of the patches. Meat from African mammals occurs in relatively large patches, and this will have major consequences for socioecological patterns. It has been proposed and demonstrated in a number of examples that where resources exist in large (especially high quality) patches, the animals exploiting those resources will aggregate and, when social, form groups (Crook 1970; Wrangham 1980). As anthropoid primates are inherently social, the issue is not the aggregations but their size and degree of within-group bonding, association and substructure, and relationships with other groups.

Two elements can be considered here. The first is group size and structure. If hominids were acquiring relatively large animals or patches of smaller animals, either as scavenged carcasses or as kills, then there may be a shift towards larger communities and groups. In the phylogenetic context of something like the last common ancestor described above, this could operate in two ways. The first is that communities that have access to meat resources will grow and be relatively large, either through the acquisition of (female) immigrants, or additionally through higher reproductive rates and success. Communities may thus vary in size according to abundance of local resources. The second way will not affect overall community size, but its substructure. Chimpanzee communities have a fission–fusion structure, as on a daily basis they split up into smaller units for foraging and patrolling (Goodall 1983, 1986). The size of these parties is strongly influenced by resource availability; exploitation of large patches of high quality foods such as an animal carcass might be expected to result in larger foraging parties. This in turn might mean that there is a greater probability of the "sharing" of resources at any particular predatory or scavenging event (Winterhalder 1996).

The second element is that large patches of high quality resources are more likely to be defended (Brown 1964). Such a territorial strategy, in the context of male kin-bonded groups (see Table 15.1) which are already territorial with regard to males, would place an emphasis on both the size of the groups (larger groups would be at an advantage) and the quality of the relationships within them. Defense of high-quality territories may be a factor in strengthening intragroup alliances. It may also impose selection for larger body size among males. A further consideration is that where groups are highly territorial and hostile to each other, there may be a tendency for certain groups to grow and fission at the expense of other groups. This may have effects both on the demography of the populations and the genetic structure.

The daily, seasonal, and annual variation in animal distributions means that they are also less predictable than most plant-based resources. Lack of predictability is likely to act as a selective pressure on a number of aspects of hominid behavior. Some of these will mimic or reinforce those associated with the patchy distribution of meat, such as flexibility of response to resource availability, time stressed foraging, and larger ranging distances. Others may add another dimension. One such is greater cognitive faculties. Lake (1995) has shown through simulations that where information about carcass distribution can be transmitted between individuals, then under certain conditions (primarily related to environmental stability) (see also Boyd and Richerson 1985) there would be a higher return rate. Even on an individual basis, greater powers of observation, memory, and association would enhance success. Greater use of technology would be another cognitively related strategy that would have the effect of increasing the probability of returns for a more carnivorous hominid.

Another such dimension would relate to behavior in relation to risk. Unpredictability implies a risk of not finding any food on a particular day, and risk-buffering strategies would be essential (Cashdan 1985). A number might be suggested: physiological storage of energy (fat deposition) would be one for coping with lean times; in a complementary way, the ability to gorge on very large quantities would be another [modern humans have been recorded as being able to consume 2–3 kilos of meat at a sitting, particularly if fat content is high (O'Dea 1991)]. Changes in metabolic rate would thus be an expected outcome. Second, in social terms the costs of "free riders" would be higher—those who consume resources at a rate disproportionate to their acquisition of food. Mechanisms for detecting such free riders and imposing additional costs on group membership such as have been proposed by Aunger (1996) would provide an advantage. These would most likely take the form of increased levels of social bonding (grooming, etc.), although a trend to-wards more human systems (such as language, group identifiers, and exchange systems) may be a longer term pattern. These mechanisms would be bound up with elements of resource sharing and transfer within a group (Winterhalder 1996). A final strategy might be in a different direction, towards more risk-prone behavior. Hawkes (1991) has suggested that among the Hadza the benefits accrued from hunting behavior relates as much to male reproductive strategies directly as from the direct resource acquisition. Such behavior may be analogous to what Zahavi (1975) has referred to as the handicap principle, where males in particular exhibit risk-prone behavior as a way of attracting mates. Male hominids (the successful ones at least!) pursuing a more carnivorous foraging strategy may have benefited in terms of sexual selection from this more risk-prone behavior.

Life History and Encephalization

The key characteristic of meat that has been emphasized here is that it is a high-quality resource, relative to other elements of an orthodox primate's diet; this is not necessarily the same as a high-ranked diet in optimal foraging terms but resources that provide a high level of energetic and other nutritional intake when acquired. High-quality resources are an integral part of a number of comparative biological relationships, of which the most relevant here relate to brain size. Brains constitute tissues that are expensive to grow and maintain (10 times more energy for maintenance than most other tissues), and thus the observed relationships between brain size and other biological characteristics are based not so much on the benefits of a high level of cognition, but on the energetic costs involved (Martin 1980). This energetic perspective has led to a number of models and observations on the evolution of larger brains. Martin (1980) (but see also Harvey and Krebs 1990, for a critique) has shown that across taxa brain size scales with metabolic rate [(i.e. brain size and metabolic rate are allometrically scaled to body size at the same coefficient (0.75)], leading to his maternal constraint hypothesis that the size of any taxa's brain is limited by the energy available to the mother during pregnancy and lactation (most brain growth in most species occurs in utero). From this basis Martin argued that larger brains occurred only in species that had a good resource base. Foley and Lee (1991) showed that across the primates as a whole, and using a phylogenetically controlled analysis, larger brained taxa tended to have a much higher quality diet (i.e., high percentage of fruit and meat). This was extended to argue that hominid brain enlargement occurred in the context of a high-quality diet, and it was proposed that increased meat-eating was the critical development (Foley and Lee 1991). Aiello and Wheeler (1995) added a further dimension by arguing that the costs of larger brains could be offset by smaller guts (another expensive tissue), something that would occur with increased carnivory, as meat-eaters have smaller relative guts than frugivores or folivores. Vasey and Walker (this volume) have also considered the effects in terms of prenatal genomic conflicts.

The key evolutionary inference is that the evolution of relatively larger brains is dependent upon energetics as much as the actual selective pressures leading to an advantage of having a large brain. In this sense, the so-called "social" and "ecological" hypotheses of intelligence among mammals are not mutually exclusive. The former can be the direct selective pressure (the advantages of intelligence are that they enhance social strategies and, hence, survivorship and reproduction), while the latter might be the necessary preconditions upon which the growth and maintenance of larger brains is dependent (Foley and Lee 1991; Foley 1992). A shift to higher quality resources would be an expected correlate of larger brains and, indeed, a precondition.

Brain size is also correlated with a number of other life history variables (Harvey and Clutton-Brock 1985; Harvey et al. 1987). Animals with larger brains tend to have longer life spans, slower growth rates, later ages of first reproduction, and fewer offspring with longer interbirth intervals. To some extent these are all in turn related to the overall costs of being effectively "K-selected"—individuals/offspring are "expensive," constituting a major investment on the part of mothers, with a consequent high level of selection for parental care, offspring survival, and adult longevity (Clutton-Brock 1991). The evolution of larger brains among hominids would be expected to correlate with changes in life history, and there would thus be a series of adaptive/biological changes that would occur in association with the proposed expansion of the diet to include more meat.

A question that arises in relation to these associations is a quantitative one—how much additional energy is required to account for encephalization, or to put it another way, how much "meat" would make a sufficient difference. Estimates indicate that during the first few years of life, when all brain growth occurs, the large size of the human brain would add approximately 10% to an infant's overall nutritional needs, compared to that of a chimpanzee infant of the same size. In effect this means that the costs of larger brains amount to increased energetic costs of approximately 10% (Foley and Lee 1991). If this is the case, then only a relatively small amount of a high-quality resource such as meat could make a sufficient difference, particularly if associated with a reduction in other costs, such as reduced gut size, or in particular contexts such as additional weaning energy or prolonging a mother's ability to lactate. Small incremental increases rather than a major change in foraging behavior can have significant evolutionary consequences.

Spatial Distribution and Evolutionary Patterns

A well-established observation is that the population density is lower for animals higher up the trophic level and that as a corollary their home ranges tend to be larger (McNab 1963). This is simply explained in terms of the reduced availability of resources. A further association exists in terms of species range area; carnivores tend to be less speciose and to have much larger ranges (Figure 15.1) (Foley 1991). The mechanism underlying this is that carnivores are likely to be less habitat and resource specific; although populations may specialize locally, across the species range diversity can occur. Furthermore, the differences between one prey type and

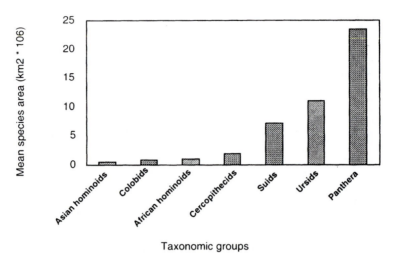

Figure 15.1. Species range areas for catarrhine primates and carnivores (data from Foley 1991). Animals with more meat components to their diet have significantly larger species range areas than those, such as primates, which are essentially plant eaters.

another are unlikely to be sufficiently great to reduce carnivore effectiveness. In contrast, plants are often highly specific in their antipredator strategies, and habitats can differ quite sharply so that specialized herbivores are likely to be much more spatially constrained. The fact that carnivores are forced to forage widely means that each population is likely to range over several habitats and, hence, be less affected by environmental boundaries. The evolutionary effect will be wide-ranging species. Classic examples can be found among the large cats, brown bears, and several canids (Leney 1997), which historically could be found with relatively little taxonomic distinction across several continents—lions, leopards, and cheetahs all had very wide Palaeoarctic distributions and in some cases occurred in the New World as well. Most herbivore distributions tend to be subcontinental, and among the bovids, for example, speciation occurs locally in many cases. Non-human primates conform to the herbivore pattern—the average anthropoid species range is approximately one million square kilometres (Foley 1991); there are virtually no primates with distributions across more than one continent (*Macaca sylvestris* and *Papio hamadryas* being very limited exceptions), and very few can be found as a single species across an entire continental range (an exception being *Cercopithecus aethiops,* depending on taxonomy).

An increase in levels of carnivory can thus be expected to affect the distribution of hominids (Foley 1987, 1991; Shipman and Walker 1989) and, in turn, the way in which evolutionary mechanisms operate. Increased levels of meat-eating would result in reduced rather than increased population densities and more dispersed and scattered communities. At a very simple level carnivory would result in reduced reproductive success, although this statement would need to be qualified in terms of what the alternative strategy might produce—i.e., maintained herbivory may have resulted in extinction and thus even lower reproductive success! However, as stated above, hominids shifting to a more meat-based diet do so in the context of their primate heritage, and two points were emphasized. The first was that hominids are highly social and so, unlike most carnivores, are unlikely to disperse in the same way—individualistically, across very large areas. Their local density would always be community based, even if these communities were themselves relatively rare. The extremes of carnivore spatial patterns are unlikely to have occurred. The second is that in most of the discussion relating to early hominids, while there may have been an increase in levels of meat-eating, specialized carnivory is not thought to have occurred, and thus patterns for more omnivorous taxa are likely to be a more appropriate model. However, among such groups—e.g., pigs and bears—species range areas are intermediate between carnivores and herbivores, suggesting that the trend in spatial patterns is relevant and thus that some increase in geographical range per taxonomic unit would be expected.

In sum, more carnivorous hominids should be more widely dispersed, more tolerant of habitat differences, and more likely to occur across major biomes with relatively little taxonomic differentiation. The key link is in terms of speciation, the implication being that such hominids are less likely to speciate. This, in turn, hinges on definitions of species and ideas about speciation. Most models are drawn from studies of invertebrates and plants, and relatively little is known about speciation in larger and more social mammals. The best studied groups—the savanna baboons—seem to show that even where there are relatively clear-cut species in morphological terms, they are not necessarily true biological species in the sense used by Mayr (1963). Hybrid zones have been documented, especially between *Papio hamadryas* and *P. anubis* (Phillips-Conroy et al. 1992), and it has also been shown that there are important socio-ecological elements affecting admixture. It may be suggested that this too is part of the tendency for speciation to be a less clear-cut process among more habitat tolerant and omnivorous primates, such as savanna-dwelling baboons. For vertebrates in general, speciation, where it does occur, is mostly based on allopatry. This might, therefore, only occur where there is major geographical separation, such as where populations are dispersed across major continental zones. Leney (1997) has argued that carnivore evolution is largely driven by resource-based competition, as habitat variation is not experienced as a selection pressure by large-bodied predators to the same extent as among herbivores. The consequence is that carnivores end up as polytypic species with local variants evolved to meet the pressures of the local carnivore community, whereas primates as a whole are both subject to a finer grained selection pressure based on environmental variation and tend to become isolated in local pockets and undergo allopatric speciation on a narrower scale.

More speculatively, it can be suggested that population density among more carnivorous hominids would be relatively low, on average, across large areas, although made up of rather uneven distributions according to local resource distribution. This overall population structure would have implications for models of the genetic structure of global human populations and levels of observed taxonomic diversity.

In summary (see Table 15.2), the following evolutionary outcomes of increased carnivory can be expected as a signature of a shift in foraging behavior among early

Table 15.2 Summary of expected evolutionary and ecological consequences of increased carnivory among hominids.

Expected Correlates of Increased Carnivory in Hominids	Ecological or Evolutionary Factor Responsible
Physical Characteristics	
Reduced gut size	• meat is easily digestible tissue, with energy available for allocation to other tissues and/or activities
Increased brain size	• high (protein) quality of meat can be used to fuel costs of growth and maintenance of larger brains
Reduced molar teeth	• reduced masticatory requirements
Increased locomotor efficiency and changes in body proportions	• hunting/scavenging demands greater ranging distances, both day ranges and home ranges • selection for improved efficiency of locomotion over terrestrial ranges would occur
Increased body size	• body size is influenced by range size requirements; locomotor efficiency increases with body size • the demands of strength for bringing down prey, carrying carcasses, or competing with other predators may also be a factor in pushing up body size • intergroup competition
Physiological (metabolic) adaptations for "feast or famine"	• meat comes in relatively large packages or not at all
Increased sexual dimorphism/larger males	• intergroup competition
Life History Traits	
Longer life spans, slower growth rates, later ages of first reproduction, fewer offspring with longer interbirth intervals, and prolonged longevity	• Outcome of selection for larger brains (social complexity) and availability of high-quality resources for "expensive offspring"
Time Budgets	
Reduced feeding time	• once acquired, meat is easily digestible
Increased travel time	• animal resources are more thinly and unevenly distributed, and more unpredictable
Time stressed daily activity schedule	• animal resources are more thinly and unevenly distributed, and more unpredictable
Seasonally variable activity schedule	• animal resources in tropical African environments are seasonally very variable
Socioecology and Population Structure	
Larger social communities	• larger patches of high quality foods promotes social groups • conflict and hostility between groups would select for larger groups
Greater variation in community size between groups	• local and regional differences in animal resource availability (more for animal than plant resources?) • locally variable rates of female transfer in relation to hunting/scavenging success
Higher rates of within community sharing (transfer) of resources	• large "package" size of animals combined with lower probability of individual foraging success

Table 15.2 (Continued)

Expected Correlates of Increased Carnivory in Hominids	Ecological or Evolutionary Factor Responsible
Higher rates of intergroup territoriality, hostility and conflict	• effect of defensibility of animal resources or territories in relation to male-kin-bonded groups
Stronger within community alliances and structure	• higher rates of resource sharing • within-community interdependence arising from intergroup conflicts
More dispersed communities at lower densities	• dispersed resources and effect of tropic structure
Extinction and absorption of declining communities, expansion and fissioning of growing communities	• variation in resource availability
Cognition and Behavior	
Intelligence (observation, memory, association) for flexible foraging behavior	• high variability in resource distribution and abundance • low predictability of animal resources • risk buffering
Horizontal transmission of information (culture)	• exchange of information about patchy and unpredictable resource distribution
Social intelligence and strategies for complex resource distribution monitoring within communities	• detection of free riders and maintenance of group cohesion in context of "sharing" large packets of food
Risk prone behavior(?)	• sexual selection for risk prone behavior among hunting/scavenging males (handicap principle)
Evolutionary Diversity and Mechanisms	
Larger species ranges	• habitat tolerance arising from increased carnivory • effect of increased ranging in response to dispersed resources
Reduced rates of speciation and lower levels of evolutionary diversity (continental scale)	• Wide-ranging behavior or more carnivorous species associated with low speciation rates
Reduced ecological diversity	• local competitive exclusion
Eurytopy (habitat tolerance)	• carnivorous foraging strategies and more likely to be general rather than prey and habitat specific
Allopatric speciation	• range overlap and low level of morphological, behavioral (and genetic?) variation

hominids: larger day and home ranges, more time spent traveling, less time spent feeding, with selection for locomotor efficiency. Gut size may be reduced, with an increased potential to store energy and to survive periods of shortage. There may be an increase in brain size, with a concomitant shift in other life history traits, including slower rates of maturation and prolonged longevity. Socioecological factors will result in larger communities with higher levels of territoriality, and the development of means of testing group membership and detecting cheats. Finally, geographical distributions and habitat tolerance may be expanded, with relatively low levels of diversification and speciation.

The Hominid Fossil Record in the Context
of the Correlates of Carnivory

The discussion above sets out a series of traits that might be expected to be associated with the expansion of meat-eating among early hominids. The next stage is to see whether there is any evidence for these in the fossil and archaeological records or if such associations can be inferred by other means.

Australopithecines

The earliest hominids can broadly be considered as the australopithecines, of which there may be four or more species. In addition a very early hominid, *Ardipithecus ramidus*, may be adaptively similar but has yet to be published in full (White et al. 1994). As a group, they occur in the Pliocene and are confined to sub-Saharan Africa. Morphologically, they are characterized by bipedalism, anthropoid-sized brain (see Figure 15.2), a trend towards larger molars and premolars that suffer intense wear, and retain characteristics such as relatively prognathic faces. In terms of body size, they fall within the range 30–70 kg, although most indicators suggest that 40–55 kg would be the size of a typical early australopithecine, and it has been proposed that levels of sexual dimorphism were high (McHenry 1992).

There is no direct evidence linking any australopithecines with meat-eating activities—toothwear, dental morphology, associations with technology, associations with animal bones and cutmarks have all proven to be ambiguous or absent. In general it has been accepted in recent years that the South African cave sites are best interpreted in terms of australopithecines being prey items rather than predators (Brain 1981; see Pickering this volume). Does this mean that the australopithecines were exclusive plant/fruit feeders? Although caution should be exercized, a better reconstruction of their behavior would be that they were almost certainly as carnivorous as chimpanzees, as they were living in an environment with more animal resources and poorer plants. Assuming a common ancestry with *Pan*, and in the light of the discussion above (see Table 15.1 and associated text), hunting of small mammals can be considered to be a hominid plesiomorphy, and thus the australopithecines would be expected to have obtained a small percentage of their nutrition from animals. The habitats in which the australopithecines lived, even if they were partially wooded, were unlikely to have higher levels of fruit abundance than typical chimpanzee habitats and would almost certainly have had higher densities of mammals (Reed 1997). Australopithecines would have been opportunistic, occasionally carnivorous, highly social bipedal apes living in relatively dry environments. The morphological evidence is consistent with this as the dentition is relatively generalized.

There are a number of reasons, however, for not inferring more than occasional opportunistic consumption of meat among the early hominids. The first of these is that reconstructions of the thorax of australopithecines indicate that the rib cage was similar to that of an ape—i.e., expanded in the lower regions (Schmid 1983). This may be seen as an indication of a relatively large gut, similar to that found in chimps, and hence indicative of a largely herbivorous diet. Second, the australo-

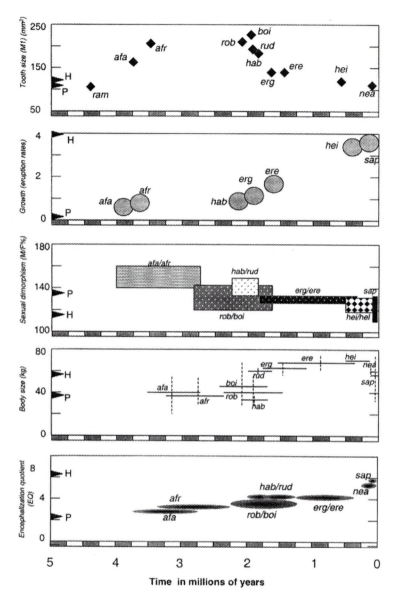

Figure 15.2. Summary of the adaptive trends over time (in millions of years) of the hominids inferred from the fossil record (from Foley 1999, and sources therein). In all graphs P indicates the value for *Pan*, and H for *Homo sapiens*. (A) The occulusal surface area (in mm²) of first molars: (B) The second graph shows inferred changes in growth based on dental enamel secretion patterns, using the deviation from chipanzee standards as a measure: (C) Sexual dimorphism (male weight/female weight *100) in body size, based on body weight estimates, as shown in (D) Body size ranges for hominids (in kg); and (E) encephalization quotients (EQ) for hominid taxa.

pithecines do appear to have been subject themselves to high levels of predation (Brain 1981), which, while not mutually exclusive from being predators themselves, might imply that carcass sites would have been dangerous places. Third, the australopithecines are confined to the drier parts of Africa, and each of the known species appear to be relatively restricted in their distribution. None occurs in both east and south Africa, so that species' ranges are within the range of other primates. The patterns of diversity are, in other words, more similar to those of other primates than to more omnivorous or carnivorous lineages (Foley 1991, in press). And finally, the most apparent directional trend found in the evolution of the australopithecines is towards increased molar size as large, flat, grinding surfaces, or in other words, a trend towards megadonty. This would imply that the primary selective pressure in terms of diet would have been more efficient processing of hard, course, brittle plant foods rather than meat (Walker 1981; Kay 1985; Kay and Grine 1988). Megadontic hominids will be considered in more detail below, but if hominid evolution were viewed entirely from the perspective of Pliocene hominids, then the processing of dry savanna plant foods seems to have acted as a greater selective pressure than that of meat.

There are, of course, some elements of the australopithecine fossil record that may be found among the expected correlates of increased carnivory, especially the increase in body size compared to chimpanzees and the change in locomotion. The shift to bipedalism certainly relates to more efficient terrestrial locomotion (Foley 1992; Rodman and McHenry 1980; Steudel 1994). Models exploring the costs and benefits of bipedalism suggest that bipedalism is effective compared to ape-like quadrupedalism when approximately 60% of foraging time is spent on the ground (Foley and Elton 1998). Travel between trees and feeding on terrestrial plant resources would be a sufficient factor in driving the hominids towards a bipedal adaptation. Furthermore, such a shift would be enhanced by increases in day range, as would be expected to occur in drier environments regardless of whether plants or animals were exploited (Foley 1992). In addition, it has been repeatedly claimed that the australopithecines show the retention of levels of arboreal activity (Jungers 1982; Susman et al. 1985), and this is more likely to be associated with feeding off fruits and leaves, rather than arboreal predation.

Megadontic Hominids

From 2.6 My, the australopithecines exhibit higher levels of posterior megadonty. There is no clear-cut line between earlier and more megadontic hominids, and many of the specimens currently assigned to A. africanus overlap in dental size with the so-called robust australopithecines. Furthermore, there is no consensus on whether the robust australopithecines are a monophyletic group, or whether, for example, A. aethiopicus and A. boisei represent convergent trends. Apart from larger molars and premolars, the robust australopithecines are characterized by shorter and more orthognathic faces (except A. aethiopicus), the presence of cranial superstructures, and very reduced and crowded anterior dentitions. Very little is known about their postcranial anatomy. They are probably in general larger in body size than the earlier australopithecines (McHenry 1992), but again, the contrast implied by the distinction between the "robust" and "gracile" australopithecines is not as marked as might be inferred. Their encephalization quotients (EQs) are marginally greater than those of earlier hominids (McHenry 1992), implying some trend toward encephalization. Two species are recognized in eastern Africa and one, or possibly two, in the south.

It is generally accepted that a better interpretation is that the large and usually very worn teeth of the robust australopithecines reflect a hard, small-object, plant-based diet. The robust australopithecines, found in more arid and open environments (Reed 1997), appear to have been moving into a low-quality plant-food niche. There is some evidence, furthermore, that the robust australopithecine teeth erupted early and quickly, suggesting that there was a need for teeth to be in occlusion relatively early in life (Beynon and Dean 1988). This is a long way from a carnivorous adaptation. Three additional points regarding the adaptations of the robust australopithecines can be made. First, isotopic analyses of some of the South African robust australopithecines have shown a chemical signature that can be interpreted in terms of some meat intake (Sillen 1992; Lee-Thorpe et al. 1994; Sponheimer and Lee-Thorpe 1999; and see Schoeninger this volume). However, although the teeth of the robusts indicate plant foods, as hominids it is probable that they were also opportunistic hunters, and their diets are likely to have been eclectic. What the teeth indicate is not a uniform diet but that the ability to consume hard coarse foods at certain times was critical to their survival. Indeed, the megadonty may reflect the importance of certain key resources during the dry seasons while diet breadth may have been much greater during other seasons. Second, there may be convergence with some of the expected correlates of increased carnivory. In particular, the implied diet is one that is likely to result in increased feeding time, and robust australopithecines may have shared with later *Homo* a relatively time-stressed adaptation. And third, the patterns of taxonomic diversity, with a separation of east and south African taxa, are again those expected for primates in general (Foley 1991, 1994, in press).

In summary, the fossil evidence does not indicate a significant increase in carnivory among the earliest hominids. Australopithecines are best interpreted as bipedal African savanna apes with diets that incorporated meat as part of a *Pan*-Hominid plesiomorphy but remained essentially frugivorous. What is striking, however, is that for the Pliocene, and for what were clearly the most abundant hominids, the observable ecological trend is towards low-quality plant foods. It can be suggested that this was a primary set of adaptations to seasonally dry environments and, in particular, to dry season food shortages. It is also very divergent from trends in later hominid evolution.

Early Homo

The genus *Homo* is usually characterized in terms of enlargement of the brain, reduction of the face and teeth, and the presence of a protuberant nose. Although these are relatively clear-cut in Pleistocene hominids, Pliocene *Homo* is far more difficult to identify. Two species have been recognized as belonging to early *Homo*— *H. habilis* and *H. rudolfensis*. These taxa are contemporary with the robust australopithecines. Many have associated the appearance of early *Homo* with a more carnivorous way of life, particularly in the light of (a) their possible association with stone tools (Leakey 1972); (b) their possible association with cutmarks and animal bones found with artefacts (Bunn and Kroll 1986; Domínguez-Rodrigo 1997); (c) their larger brains; and (d) their less specialized dentition. However, recent analyses have cast doubt on some of these associations. Body size corrected EQs, for some at least, do not show much of a change in brain size (Collard and Wood in press); some, especially those assigned to *H. rudolfensis*, have some level of megadonty; some, especially OH62, are very small and have very primitive postcrania (Johanson et al. 1987). Furthermore, the specimens associated with early *Homo* are very variable, and evidence for as many as three species across Africa and no clear East-South conspecifics (Foley in press) might be taken as evidence for an essentially australopithecine grade of adaptation.

Although these specimens may belong to the *Homo* clade (and even this may be questioned), they do not show a very marked shift away from other australopithecines. The lack of megadonty in *Homo habilis* is perhaps the only strong evidence for an adaptive departure, and for a "new" evolutionary trend among hominids.

Homo Ergaster *and Later Hominids*

The next hominid known in the fossil record is *Homo ergaster*, represented by KNM-ER 3733, KNM-ER 3883, and more completely by KNM-WT 15000. There is no dispute about this taxon's membership of *Homo*, and some would sink it into *Homo erectus* or even *Homo sapiens*. A number of significant changes are evident. First, there is an increase in body size (to around 60 kg for males) and a change in body shape and proportions (Ruff and Walker 1993). Judging by WT15000, *Homo ergaster* is linear and long limbed with a shift in the shape of the thorax towards that found in modern humans. The brain size is larger (EQ = ~4). Studies of its growth patterns suggest that although it did not mature as slowly as modern humans, there was a shift away from the more ape-like patterns found in the australopithecines (Smith 1994). By association *H. ergaster* has been linked with Mode 1 Oldowan technology and the appearance around 1.6 Myr with Mode 2 industries and the greater abundance of stone tools and butchered carcasses (some with cutmarks). *H. ergaster* is also known to have occurred in both South and East Africa, possibly in Georgia (Dmnisi); the Asian species, *H. erectus*, thought to be derived from *H. ergaster* or conspecific with it, is also known at this time in parts of Asia.

Overall, *H. ergaster/erectus*, appears to show a number of evolutionary shifts that would be expected to occur as a result of a more carnivorous foraging strategy; these include increased body size, reduced gut size, a more specialized terrestrial locomotor strategy (full bipedalism), changes in life history parameters towards slower rates of maturation, larger brain sizes, greater use of technology, larger geographical ranges, and relatively low taxonomic diversity (one or two species over Africa and southern Asia). A similar pattern is found in the transition between the vegetarian cave bear and the modern brown bear, in the evolution of the Upper Pleistocene superpredator bears, in the late Devensian of Britain (Banwell Cave), the Polar Bear, and the similarly cursorial and carnivorous Kodiak variant (Leney and Foley 1998). These bears have long gracile limbs, reduced body mass for stature, and possibly reduced gut size and a more meat-based diet.

Three questions arise from these observations. First, can the timing of this shift be pinpointed more precisely? The full morphological traits associated with *H. ergaster* are known by 1.7 Myr. There is some postcranial evidence that may indicate that this taxon was present in East Africa by 1.9 Myr, and there is evidence for hominids in SE Asia broadly belonging to this clade by 1.9 Myr. Stone tools, if they are associated with *H. ergaster,* rather than *Homo* more generally, are known from 2.6 Myr, although the earliest documentation of Mode 2 industries is considerably later (1.4 Myr). It is therefore possible that the change in hominid evolution away from the generalized australopithecine or megadontic patterns occurred as early as 2.6 Myr, although a date closer to 2.0 Myr is more likely. If the earliest Asian dates are accepted, then it is possible that the appearance of *H. ergaster* was associated with a rapid dispersal across and beyond Africa, although only in warmer tropical regions. Expansion into colder parts of Eurasia is unknown prior to approximately 1.0 Myr.

The second question is what environmental conditions may have prompted this change. The major climate changes of the period 2.7–2.3 Myr (Vrba 1996) would appear to be too early. Conditions around 2.0 million years are not significantly different from those preceding it. However, it is possible that the very unstable conditions of the period greater than 2.3 Myr years produced conditions in which hominid populations were isolated, and that this generated the diversity of hominids seen around 2.0 million years ago. Certainly from this period more arid environments were occupied (Reed 1997). Foley (1987) argued that meat-eating was a specific response to more seasonal conditions and, in particular, was a strategy that would have been appropriate during dry seasons in areas where large mammals congregated. Meat would thus have been a fallback strategy for periods of intense plant food shortages but one that could only be pursued locally. The divergent trends towards megadonty/low-quality plant exploitation and more meat-eating would thus be alternative solutions to dry season conditions.

The third question, however, is whether the same evolutionary responses could have been brought about by other ecological strategies. This will be briefly considered hereafter.

Alternative Resource-Based Explanations

This last question concerns equifinality, or the issue of whether other factors are likely to have resulted in the same evolutionary outcomes; in other words, could such characteristics as changes in brain size and body size, or expansion of geographical range, have occurred as a result of other behavioral, environmental, or physiological shifts. This problem may be broken down into two categories. The first of these is changes that are not directly or even indirectly related to changes in resource relationships. It is possible that the evolution of human evolutionary traits occurred as a result of purely exaptive elements, or through pleiotropic or even chance evolutionary events, and that the search for an ecological basis for human evolution is misled. This possibility should be kept in mind, and links to major questions in evolutionary theory, but will not be pursued here. The justification for taking this position here is that some of the changes in human evolution, such as the increase in body size and brain size, do involve additional energetic costs, and it is difficult to see how these could have arisen through selection were there not some ecological basis. It is this possibility that forms the second category—changes in ecology that have major evolutionary consequences but are not tied to increased carnivory. Two alternative strategies can be proposed.

Roots, Plants, and Digging Sticks

One alternative strategy would have been a shift within the use of plant foods. A number can be suggested but perhaps the most likely is access to underground plant resources, in particular, underground storage organs (USOs). Most baboons make limited use of these, and theropithecines are sometimes very dependent upon them; modern hunter-gatherers have been documented as making extensive use of roots and tubers and in some cases depending very substantially upon them for a large part of their regular daily nutritional intake (Hawkes et al. 1982). They provide a significant source of food, especially in the dry season. The development of a simple digging stick technology would be sufficient. According to this model, greater access to underground plants provided the nutritional security for costs associated with encephalization and would be a far less risk prone strategy. Hawkes et al. (1982) have also argued that this is more in keeping with optimality models and with the role of females in provisioning and have proposed the "grandmother hypothesis" (see Hawkes this volume) as a part of this. According to this hypothesis, the appearance of more meat-eating, as indicated by the archaeological record, would be of greater behavioral than ecological significance.

Dependence upon USOs could perhaps account for some aspects of the grade shift from australopithecines to *Homo ergaster*—for example, tool use, and possibly parenting strategies (see Hawkes this volume). Others are less easily linked. USOs are likely to be highly abrasive and tough, especially without processing, and would not have led to dental reduction, although increases in body size would not be directly related to USO usage. It would also be less easily linked to the changes in evolutionary pattern and the expansion of geographical range across Africa and Asia. Underground resources occur very unevenly across large areas of Africa (see Peters et al. 1984; Peters 1987), for a discussion of plant food distributions), and the elaboration of technology after 1.4 Myr would not be an expected outcome. These considerations lead to the conclusion that more extensive use of USOs might well have occurred and been an important part of the overall change in hominid behavior, but in conjunction with meat-eating rather than instead of it.

Aquatic Resources

Aquatic resources have also been linked with encephalization (Crawford and Marsh 1990). Fish and molluscs are high-quality foods, and provide both fats and protein, as well as energy, and it has been suggested that the biochemical pathways involved are particularly conducive to the development of neural tissue. Many of the life history strategy changes and the rapid expansion, especially along rivers and coasts, would be very compatible with an aquatic resource hypothesis. However, the nature of the technology observed in the Pliocene and early Pleistocene is not obviously aquatically oriented, and there is, by and large, very little archaeological evidence for use of aquatic resources until the last interglacial period and the appearance of modern humans. This, of course, may be a taphonomic effect associated with changes in lake and sea levels, but it is perhaps more an indication that the impact of a shift to marine and freshwater resources is linked not to the early grade shift in *Homo*, but to the evolution of modern humans in the late middle Pleistocene.

Conclusions

This chapter has attempted to place the evolution of increased carnivory among hominids into a broader evolutionary context. It has been less concerned with focusing on the evidence for hominid meat-eating, nor the causes for it, but how a change in foraging behavior and diet will affect the broader patterns of adaptation and evolution. There are two main conclusions that can be drawn: (1) if carnivory became a significant part of a hominid diet, then evolutionary and ecological theory predicts far-reaching changes (Foley 1987; Shipman and Walker 1989); meat-eating thus needs to be considered as more than just a question of calories and niche space. (2) The predictions associated with some level of carnivory are most apparent with the appearance of *H. ergaster*, and this may be the closest to a grade shift in the earlier parts of hominid evolution, representing the key change from a more orthodox primate way of life (Figure 15.3).

In a cladistics-dominated world of evolutionary biology, grades are not very fashionable concepts, but they still represent an important part of the apparatus of evolutionary theory. A grade is a shared level of biological and behavioral organization, usually based on some adaptive strategy. Grades are significant in that they constrain the way comparative analyses are used. For example, a comparison of brain size/body size relationships among vertebrates would yield very different results if grades were not taken into account; in regression terms, the slopes may be similar, but the intercepts differ according to grade, and meaningful relationships can be lost by ignoring this fact (Martin 1983). At the lower taxonomic level discussed here, grades are unlikely to be as clear-cut, but it can be argued that *H. ergaster* does represent a significant shift in adaptation from the other hominids. *H. ergaster* displays a related set of novel features, covering encephalization, life history, locomotion, and range, as well as inferred behavior. Such a shift needs accounting for, and it has been argued here that an increased level of carnivory is a good candidate for one of the factors involved.

However, in conclusion, it should be emphasized that the identification of a grade shift at the beginning of the Pleistocene, and its linkage with more meat-eating, does not necessarily imply full, modern, hunter-gatherer behavior. Early technological (Modes 1 and 2 in Clark's terminology, Oldowan and Acheulean industries) and

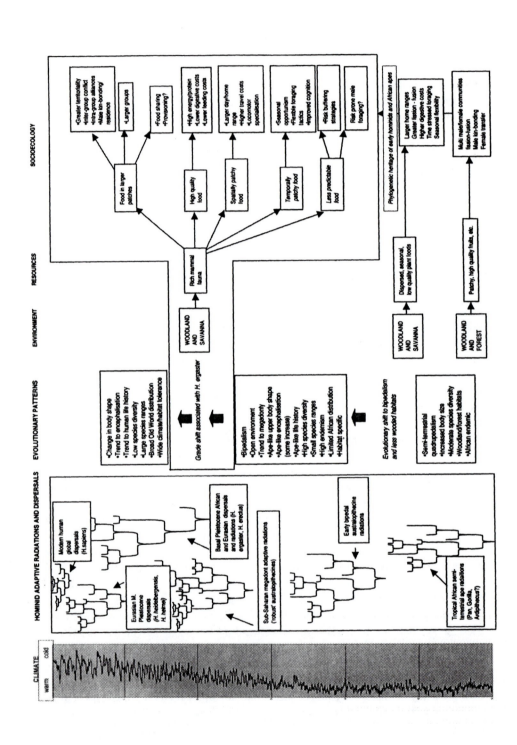

morphological conservatism and stability and the clear impact of Mode 3 (prepared core) and Mode 4 technologies (blade technologies) later in human evolution (from 300 Kyr) (Foley and Lahr 1997) indicate that there almost certainly was at least one other additional major shift in hominid evolution, and foraging—including hunting—may have played a major part in this. However, the lines of evidence and reasoning put forward here strongly suggest that meat-eating has played a significant role in the evolution of *Homo*, not just *Homo sapiens*.

Acknowledgments I thank Sarah Elton, Marta Lahr, and Mark Leney for helpful suggestions on an earlier draft, and the contributors to the conference for much stimulating discussion and comment.

REFERENCES

Aiello, L. C., and Wheeler, P. 1995. The expensive tissue hypothesis. *Current Anthropology* 36:199–222.

Ardrey, R. 1961. *African Genesis*. London: Atheneum.

Aunger, R. 1996. Acculturation and the persistence of indigenous food avoidances in the Ituri Forest, Zaire. *Human Organisation* 55:206–218.

Beynon, A. D., and M. C. Dean. 1988. Distinct dental development patterns in early fossil hominids. *Nature* 335:509–514.

Binford, L. R. 1981. *Bones: Ancient Men and Modern Myths*. New York: Academic Press.

Blumenschine, R. 1986. Carcass consumption sequences and archaeological distinction of hunting and scavenging. *Journal of Human Evolution* 15:639–660.

Boyd, R., and P. Richerson. 1985. *Culture and the Evolutionary Process*. Chicago: University of Chicago Press.

Brain, C. K. 1981. *The Hunters or the Hunted: An Introduction to African Cave Taphonomy*. Chicago: University of Chicago Press.

Brown, J. L. 1964. The evolution of diversity in avian territorial systems. *Wilson Bulletin* 76:160–169.

Bunn, H. T. 1981. Archaeological evidence for meat-eating by Plio-Pleistocene hominids from Koobi Fora and Olduvai Gorge. *Nature* 291:575–577.

Bunn, H. T., and E. M. Kroll. 1986. Systematic butchery by Plio/Pleistocene hominids at Olduvai Gorge, Tanzania. *Current Anthropology* 27:431–452.

Caro, T. M. 1989. Determinants of asociality in felids. In *Comparative Socioecology* (V. Standen and R. A. Foley, eds.), pp. 41–74. Oxford: Blackwell.

Cashdan, E. A. 1985. Coping with risk: reciprocity among the Basarwa of northern Botswana. *Man* 20:454–474.

Figure 15.3. Summary of the evolutionary and socioecological consequences of meat-eating in relation to the hominid fossil record. The left-hand box shows the pattern of climatic change derived from the marine isotope cores. The next box provides a schematic representation of the pattern of radiations and dispersals of the hominids. The inferred major evolutionary and adaptive changes associated with each period are shown in the third column. The shaded area shows the links proposed for increased carnivory associated with the evolution of *Homo ergaster*. See text for full discussion of these.

Chivers, D. J., B. A. Wood, and A. Bilsborough. 1984. *Food Acquisition and Processing in Primates*. New York: Plenum Press.

Clutton-Brock, T. H. 1991. *The Evolution of Parental Care*. Princeton, NJ: Princeton University Press.

Collard, M., and B. A. Wood, in press. Adaptive grades in early African hominds. In *African Biogeography and Hominid Evolution* (T. Bromage and F. Schrinke, eds.). Oxford: Oxford University Press.

Conklin, N. L., and R. W. Wrangham. 1994. The value of figs to a hind-gut fermenting frugivore: a nutritional analysis. *Biochemical Ecology and Systematics* 22:137–151.

Crawford, M., and D. Marsh. 1989. *The Driving Force: Food, Evolution and the Future*. London: Heinemann.

Crook, J. H. 1970. The socio-ecology of primates. In *Social Behavior in Birds and Mammals* (J. H. Crook, ed.). London: Academic Press.

Dahlberg, F. 1981. *Women the Gatherer*. New Haven, CT: Yale University Press.

Difiore, A., and D. Rendall. 1994. Evolution of social organization: a reappraisal for primates using phylogenetic analysis. Proceedings of the *National Academy of Science* 91:9941–9945.

Domínguez-Rodrigo, M. 1997. Meat-eating by early hominids at the FLK 22 *Zinjanthropus* site, Olduvai Gorge (Tanzania): an experimental approach using cutmark data. *Journal of Human Evolution* 33:669–690.

Fleagle, J. 1988. *Primate Adaptations and Evolution*. London: Academic Press.

Foley, R. A. 1987. *Another Unique Species: Patterns of Human Evolutionary Ecology*. Harlow, England: Longman.

Foley, R. A. 1989. The evolution of hominid social behavior. In *Comparative Socioecology: The Behavioral Ecology of Humans and Other Mammals* (V. Standen and R. A. Foley, eds.), pp. 474–493. Oxford: Blackwell Scientific Publications.

Foley, R. A. 1991. How many hominid species should there be? *Journal of Human Evolution* 20:413–427.

Foley, R. A. 1992. Evolutionary ecology of fossil hominids. In *Evolutionary Ecology and Human Behavior* (E. A. Smith and B. Winterhalder, eds.), pp. 131–164. Chicago: Aldine de Gruyter.

Foley, R. A. 1993. The influence of seasonality on hominid evolution. In *Seasonality and Human Ecology* (S. J. Ulijaszek and S. Strickland, eds.), pp. 17–37. Cambridge: Cambridge University Press.

Foley, R. A. 1994. Speciation, extinction and climatic change in hominid evolution. *Journal of Human Evolution* 26:275–289.

Foley, R. A. 1995. *Humans Before Humanity: An Evolutionary Perspective*. Oxford: Blackwell Publishers.

Foley, R. A. 1996. An evolutionary and chronological framework for human social behavior. *Proceedings of the British Academy* 88:95–117.

Foley, R. A., in press, Evolutionary geography of Pliocene African hominids. In *African Biogeogrphy and Hominid Evolution* (T. Bromage and F. Schrinke, eds.). New York: Oxford University Press.

Foley, R. A., and S. E. Elton. 1998. Time and energy: the ecological context for the evolution of bipedalism. In *Primate Locomotion* (E. Strasser, J. Fleagle, A. Rosenberger, and H. McHenry, eds.), pp. 419–433. New York: Plenum Press.

Foley, R. A., and M. M. Lahr. 1997. Mode 3 technologies and the evolution of modern humans. *Cambridge Journal of Archaeology* 7:3–32.

Foley, R. A., and P. C. Lee. 1991. Ecology and energetics of encephalization in hominid evolution. *Philosophical Transactions of the Royal Society, London Series B* 334:223–232.

Foley, R. A., and P. C. Lee. 1995. Finite social space and the evolution of human social behavior. In *The Archaeology of Human Ancestry* (J. Steele and S. Shennan, eds.), pp. 47–66. London: Routledge.

Goodall, J. 1983. Population dynamics during a 15–year period in one community of free-living chimpanzees in the Gombe National Park, Tanzania. *Zeitschrift fur Tierpsychologie* 61:1–60.

Goodall, J. 1986. *The Chimpanzees of Gombe: Patterns of Behavior*. Cambridge, MA: Harvard University Press.

Goodman, M., M. L. Baba, and L. L. Darga. 1983. The bearing of molecular data on the cladogenesis and times of divergence of hominoid lineages. In *New Interpretations of Ape and Human Ancestry* (R. Ciochon and R. S. Corruccini, eds.), pp. 67–86. New York: Plenum Press.

Groves, C. P. 1989. *A Theory of Human and Primate Evoluation*. Oxford: Clarendon Press.

Harding, R. S. O. 1981. An order of omnivores: non-human primate diets in the wild. In *Omnivorous Primates* (R. S. O. Harding and G. Teleki, eds.), pp. 191–214. New York: Columbia University Press.

Harvey, P. H., and T. H. Clutton-Brock. 1985. Life history variation in primates. *Evolution* 39:559–581.

Harvey, P. H., and J. R. Krebs. 1990. Comparing brains. *Science* 249:140–146.

Harvey, P. H., R. D. Martin, and T. H. Clutton-Brock. 1987. Life histories in comparative perspective. In *Primate Societies* (B. B. Smuts, D. L. Cheney, R. M. Seyfarth, R. W. Wrangham, and T. T. Struhsaker, eds.), pp. 181–196. Chicago: University of Chicago Press.

Hawkes, K. 1991. Showing off: test of an hypothesis about men's foraging goals. *Ethology and Sociobiology* 12:29–54.

Hawkes, K., K. Hill, and J. F. O'Connell. 1982. Why hunters gather: optima foaging and the Ache of eastern Paraguay. *American Ethnologist* 9:379–380.

Hawkes, K., J. F. O'Connell, and N. G. Blurton-Jones. 1991. Hunting income patterns among the Hadza: big game, common goods, foraging goals and the evolution of the human diet. *Philosophical Transactions of the Royal Society of London B* 334:243–251.

Isaac, G. L. 1978. The food-sharing behavior of protohuman hominids. *Scientific American* 238:90–108.

Johanson, D., F. T. Masao, G. G. Eck, T. D. White, R. C. Walter, W. H. Kimbel, B. Asfaw, P. Manega, P. Ndessokia, and G. Suwa. 1987. New partial skeleton of *Homo habilis* from Olduvai Gorge, Tanzania. *Nature* 327:205–209.

Jungers, W. L. 1982. Lucy's limbs: skeletal allometry and locomotion in *Australopithecus afarensis*. *Nature* 297:676–678.

Kay, R. 1985. Dental evidence for the diet of Australopithecus. *Annual Review of Anthropology* 14:315–343.

Kay, R. F., and F. Grine. 1988. Tooth morphology, wear and diet in *Australopithecus* and *Paranthropus*. In *Evolutionary History of the "Robust" Australopithecines* (F. Grine, ed.), pp. 427–447. New York: Aldine de Gruyter.

Kelly, R. 1995. *The Foraging Spectrum*. Washington, DC: Smithsonian Institution.

Kingdon, J. 1997. *Field Guide to African Mammals*. London: Collins.

Krebs, J., and N. B. Davies. 1984. *Behavioral Ecology*. Oxford: Blackwell.

Kruuk, H., and M. Turner. 1967. Comparative notes on predation by lion, leopard, cheetah and wild dog in the Serengeti area, East Africa. *Mammalia* 31:1–27.

Lake, M. W. 1995. *Computer Simulation Modelling of Early Hominid Subsistence Activities*. Ph.D. thesis. University of Cambridge.

Leakey, M. D. 1972. *Olduvai Gorge. Volume 3*. Cambridge: Cambridge University Press.

Lee, R. B., and I. DeVore. 1968a. *Man the Hunter.* Chicago: Aldine.

Lee, R. B., and I. DeVore. 1968b. Problems in the studies of hunters and gatherers. In *Man the Hunter* (R. B. Lee and I. DeVore, eds.), pp. 3–12. Chicago: Aldine.

Lee-Thorp, J., N. J. Van der Merwe, and C. K. Brain. 1994. Diet of *Australopithecus robustus* at Swartkrans from stable carbon isotope analysis. *Journal of Human Evolution* 27:361–372.

Leney, M. 1997. *Morphology and Microevolution in Pleistocene Carnivores.* Ph.D. thesis. University of Cambridge.

Leney, M. D., and R. A. Foley. 1998. Competition ecology: Pleistocene hominids and the carnivore community. In *Lifestyles and Survival Strategies in Pliocene and Pleistocene Hominids* (H. Ulrich, ed.). Schwelm: Arhaea.

Leung, W. W. 1968. *Food Composition Table for Use in Africa.* Rome: FAO.

Martin, R. A. 1980. Body mass and basal metabolism of extinct mammals. *Comparative Biochemistry & Physiology* 66:307–314.

Martin, R. D. 1983. Human brain evolution in an ecological context. In *52nd James Arthur Lecture on the Evolution of the brain.* New York: American Museum of Natural History.

Mayr, E. 1963. *Animal Species and Evolution.* Cambridge, MA: Harvard University Press.

McHenry, H. M. 1992, How big were early hominids? *Evolutionary Anthropology* 1:15–20.

McNab, B. K. 1963. Bioenergetics and the determination of home range size. *American Naturalist* 97:130–140.

Milton, K. 1981. Distribution patterns of tropical plant foods as an evolutionary stimulus to primate mental development. *American Anthropologist* 117:496–505.

Milton, K. 1987. Primate diets and gut morphology: implications for hominid evolution. In *Food and Evolution.* (M. Harris and E. B. Ross, eds.). Philadelphia: Temple University Press.

Milton, K. 1993. Diet and primate evolution. *Scientific American* 292:1–7.

Milton, K., and M. W. Demment. 1988. Digestion and passage kinetics of chimpanzees fed high and low-fiber diets and comparison with human data. *Journal of Nutrition* 118:1082–1088.

O'Dea, K. 1991. Traditional diet and food preferences of Australian aboriginal hunter-gatherers. *Philosophical Transactions of the Royal Society of London Series B* 334:233–241.

Peters, C. R. 1987. Nut-like oil seeds: food for monkeys, chimpanzees, humans and probably ape-men. *American Journal of Physical Anthropology* 73:333–363.

Peters, C. R., E. M. O'Brien, E. M., and E. O. Box. 1984. Plant types and seasonality of wild plant foods, Tanzania to southwestern Africa: resources for models of the natural environment. *Journal of Human Evolution* 13:397–414.

Phillips-Conroy, J., C. J. Jolly, P. Nystrom, and H. A. Hemmalin. 1992. Migration of male Hamadryas baboons into Anubis groups in the Awash National Park, Ethiopia. *International Journal of Primatology* 13(4):455–476.

Potts, R. 1984. Hominid hunters? Problems of identifying the earliest hunter/gatherers. In *Hominid Evolution and Community Ecology: Prehistoric Human Adaptation in Biological Perspective* (R. Foley, ed.), pp. 129–166. London: Academic Press.

Reed, K. E. 1997. Early hominid evolution and ecological change through the African Plio-Pleistocene. *Journal of Human Evolution* 32:289–322.

Rodman, P. S., and H. M. McHenry. 1980. Bioenergetics and origins of bipedalism. *American Journal of Physical Anthropology* 52:103–106.

Rose, L. M., and F. Marshall. 1996. Meat-eating, hominid sociality and home bases revisited. *Current Anthropology* 37:307–338.

Ruff, C., and A. C. Walker. 1993. Body size and shape. In *The Nariokotome Skeleton* (A. C. Walker and R. E. Leakey, eds.), pp. 234–265. Cambridge, MA: Harvard University Press.

Schmid, P. 1983. Eine Reconstruktion ded Skelettes von AL 288 (Hadar) und daren Konsequenzen. *Folia Primatologica* 40:283–306.

Schoener, T. W. 1971. Theory of feeding strategies. *Annual Review of Ecology and Systematics* 2:369–404.

Shipman, P., and A. Walker. 1989. The costs of becoming a predator. *Journal of Human Evolution* 18:373–392.

Sillen, A. 1992. Strontium/calcium ratios (Sr/Ca) of *Australopithecus robustus* and associated fauna from Swartkrans. *Journal of Human Evolution* 23:495–516.

Smith, B. H. 1994. Patterns of dental development on *Homo, Australopithecus, Pan* and *Gorilla. American Journal of Physical Anthropology* 94:307–325.

Smuts, B. B., D. L. Cheney, R. M. Seyfarth, R. W. Wrangham, and T. T. Struhsaker. 1987. *Primate Societies.* Chicago: University of Chicago Press.

Sponheimer, M., and J. A. Lee-Thorpe. 1999. Isotopic evidence for the diet of an early hominid, *Australopithecus africanus. Science* 283: 368–370.

Stanford, C. B. 1996. The hunting ecology of wild chimpanzees: implications for the behavioral ecology of Pliocene hominids. *American Anthropologist* 98:96–113.

Stanford, C. B., J. Wallis, H. Matama, and J. Goodall. 1994. Patterns of predation by chimpanzees on red colobus monkeys in Gombe National Park, 1982–1991. *American Journal of Physical Anthropology* 94:213–228.

Steudel, K. 1994. Locomotor energetics and hominid evolution. *Evolutionary Anthropology* 3:42–48.

Susman, R. L., J. T. Stern, and W. L. Jungers. 1985. Locomotor adaptations in the Hadar hominids. In *Ancestors: The Hard Evidence* (E. Delson, ed.), pp. 184–192. New York: Alan Liss.

Vrba, E. 1996. *Palaeoclimate and Neogene Evolution.* New Haven, CT: Yale University Press.

Walker, A. C. 1981. Dietary hypotheses on human evolution. *Philosophical Transactions of the Royal Society, London* B292:47–64.

White, T. D., G. Suwa, and B. Asfaw. 1994. *Australopithecus ramidus*, a new species of early hominid from Aramis, Ethiopia. *Nature* 366:261–265.

Winterhalder, B. 1996. Social foraging and the behavioral ecology of intra-group transfers. *Evoluitonary Anthropology* 5:46–57.

Wrangham, R. W. 1980. An ecological model of female-bonded primate groups. *Behavior* 75:262–299.

Wrangham, R. W. 1987. The significance of African Apes for reconstructing human social evolution. In *The Evolution of Human Behavior: Primate Models* (W. G. Kinzey, ed.), pp. 51–71. Albany, NY: State University of New York Press.

Wrangham, R. W., N. L. Conklin, G. Etot, J. Obua, K. Hunt, M. D. Hauser, and A. P. Clark. 1993. The value of figs to chimpanzees. *International Journal of Primatology* 14:423–256.

Zahavi, A. 1975. Mate selection—a selection for handicap. *Journal of Theoretical Biology* 53:205–214.

16

Neonate Body Size and Hominid Carnivory

Natalia Vasey
Alan Walker

Introduction

In a fascinating discussion of genetic conflict between human mothers and their offspring, Haig (1993) put forward the idea that the placenta intervenes between the fetus and the mother causing escalation in a struggle for resources between them. Although individual nutritional requirements of fetus and mother are usually met, placental actions sometimes result in illness, pathology, and death. Haig's ideas give a theoretical underpinning to understanding the observations of Portmann (1939, 1941, 1952, 1962, 1965, 1990), followed by those of Martin (1983), that the human full-term fetus, although grown with about the same gestation period as those of great apes, is both relatively and absolutely large and yet is secondarily altricial.

The secondarily altricial condition in human newborns is due to the immature state of the brain at birth. Yet neonate brain and body size are large in humans relative to great apes (Martin 1983; Portmann 1990). To advance humans to a higher baseline of brain and body weight at birth, Martin (1983) has hypothesized that the energetic investment must be made prenatally, while the fetus can take advantage of the mother's higher total metabolic turnover. Maternal investment is mediated by a highly invasive type of placenta in humans and other haplorhine primates. Total metabolic turnover is a function not only of the rate of investment (e.g., metabolic rate) but also the time over which investment takes place (e.g., gestation) and the number of offspring invested in per litter. Primates give birth to infants with large brains relative to other mammals by a decrease in resources devoted to fetal body development (Sacher 1982; Martin 1983; Martin and MacLarnon 1988).

As relative prenatal growth rates do not differ significantly between humans and other haplorhines (Ross and MacLarnon 1995), we propose that during evolution of the genus *Homo*, mothers must have begun acquiring foods of higher nutritional value. This must have involved a change in trophic level (i.e., their position in the food chain) and may explain the introduction of animal protein and fat into the human diet, a relatively rare acquisition among the primarily vegetarian Order Primates, and carried out to a much greater extent in humans than in any other large primate.

In this chapter we examine whether human neonates are relatively larger than those of other primates using the most comprehensive data currently available for the Order (Smith and Jungers 1997; Smith and Leigh 1998). We also provide a review and synthesis of placentation, genomic imprinting, and reproductive energetics as they pertain to the evolution of human brain and body size increases in the newborn. Based upon anatomical evidence and the distribution of early *Homo* fossils, we contend that the secondarily altricial condition of human neonates was progressively established beginning with the earliest members of the genus *Homo*. We hypothesize that the ecological and behavioral correlates of this reproductive pattern included systematic acquisition of animal protein and fat, alloparenting, and novel ranging and dispersal patterns. For the type of escalation proposed by Haig (1993) to mount, nutritionally dense foods (such as protein and fat) would have to be accessible. Sufficient access may have occurred only about 2 million years ago with the advent of significant hunting skills.

The Secondarily Altricial Condition of Human Neonates

Precocial and altricial are terms describing two basic life history patterns observed among mammals and birds (Portmann 1990). Altricial mammals produce litters of poorly developed young after relatively short gestation periods. Young are born with little or no body hair and poorly developed organs of special sense (i.e., ears, eyes) that are sealed by membranes. Often young are placed in nests as their homeothermic capacity is not fully developed. The forelimbs are more developed than the hindlimbs, and overall body proportions of altricial mammals are less like that of the adult than in mammals that are precocial at birth. In contrast, precocial mammals produce small litters of well-developed offspring (usually singletons) after a relatively long gestation period and rarely use nests because newborns are fully capable of regulating their own body temperature. They are born fully furred with ears and eyes open. The body proportions and locomotor skills of the young resemble those of the adult. Whereas altricial mammals generally invest little time or energy caring for rapidly growing litters of young, precocial mammals invest more time and energy in caring for a single offspring.

Primates as an order are highly precocial, with their relatively long gestation periods, small litters, and well-developed newborns with adult-like body proportions (Portmann 1990). They also give birth to larger young and begin reproducing relatively later in life (Martin 1983; Martin and MacLarnon 1985; Portmann 1990). Humans present an extreme among precocial primates in producing enormous neonates (Martin 1983; Portmann 1990) relatively late in life, which they then indulge with an extended infancy and adolescence (Schultz 1960). Yet human infants are born helpless, lacking the body proportions, motor skills, and locomotor patterns of adults, as is typical of other precocial primates. Human newborns, therefore, appear superficially altricial. But they are not altricial. Rather, they are born physiologically early; fetal brain growth rates persist for 1 year after birth, at which time the human infant has the body proportions and motor skills we would expect to see in precocial mammals of similar body weight (Martin 1983; Portmann 1990). For these reasons, Portmann bestowed the term "secondarily altricial" to describe the human newborn.

In precocial mammals, brain growth slows down at or near birth, whereas in altricial mammals fetal brain growth rates continue after birth. By the time they attain adult brain size, precocial neonates have increased their brain size by a factor of 2.5 whereas altricial neonates have increased their brain size by a factor of 7.5. Human neonates fall in between, increasing their brain size by a factor of 3.5 (Martin 1983). Precocial mammals leave the accelerated period of brain growth to uterine life where the mother's higher metabolic turnover can take on most of the energetic cost (Martin 1983). Human females cannot grow their infants internally beyond 9 months: beyond this point in time, infants are too large to pass through the pelvic inlet, which is compromised by mechanical constraints of bipedalism. Consequently, despite fitting the precocial pattern in other respects, human fetal brain growth rates persist after birth as in altricial mammals. Hence, the secondarily altricial condition in human neonates is due to the immature state of the brain at birth (Martin 1983; Portmann 1990). In turn, the immature state of the brain at birth is due to relatively large neonate mass, which may be an adjustment of the fetal body to neonatal brain size (Portmann 1990: 48).

Relative Body Mass of the Human Neonate

Previous analyses of human neonate mass relative to other primates are limited to great apes alone and demonstrate that human neonates are two times as heavy as ape neonates (Martin 1983; Portmann 1990). Although analyses of neonate mass across primates (Martin 1992) and placental mammals (e.g., Martin 1984) have been done, the position of humans relative to nonhuman primates was not specifically examined. Also, individual neonate mass was used instead of litter mass as the author was concerned with scaling relationships of neonate and mother with respect to metabolic turnover and gestation length (Martin 1998: 57).

Using the recently compiled data on adult and neonatal body mass in primates (Smith and Jungers 1997; Smith and Leigh 1998), we quantify whether human neonates are large relative to hominoids, catarrhines, haplorhines, and all primates. We use species means for adult female body mass and for the heaviest neonate (e.g., male or female) in reduced major axis regression analyses. Human babies in this sample are from Canada, and adult human females are from Denmark. We have yet to find a good dataset of human females and babies from the same area of the world that is not confounded by problems such as maternal weight additions due to pregnancy and the inclusion of premature infant weights. We correct for litter size by multiplying the mean number of neonates per litter by mean neonate body mass. Data on litter size were taken from the following: Rasmussen 1985, Bearder 1987,

Harvey et al. 1987, Rowe 1996, and the Duke University Primate Center Web site. There is no published data on litter size for various strepsirhine and New World monkey species for which Smith and Leigh (1998) provide neonate body mass (*Galago moholi, Nycticebus pygmaeus, Callithrix humeralifer, Saguinas labiatus, S. leucopus,* and *S. mystax*). The latter species were therefore not included in our analysis. A total of 103 primate species make up the dataset.

Our results confirm that human neonates are relatively large (Table 16.1). This is true for our sample of haplorhines, shown in Figure 16.1, [residual for *H. sapiens* (0.15) is exceeded only by *Cercopithecus wolfi* (0.21)], catarrhines [residual for *H. sapiens* (0.17) is exceeded only by *Cercopithecus wolfi* (0.18)], and hominoids [residual is greatest for *H. sapiens* at (0.11)]. Human neonates also appear relatively large when compared only to haplorhines weighing over 5,000 grams [residual value for *H. sapiens* (0.10) is exceeded only by *Cercocebus atys* (0.18) and *Cercocebus torquatus* (0.12)]. It should be noted that samples sizes for mean neonatal mass are often small (e.g., $n = 1$ for *Cercocebus atys* and *Cercocebus torquatus*) and in several cases unknown (e.g., *Cercopithecus wolfi*).

In the sample containing all primates, residuals for various groups of primates exceed those of *H. sapiens.* In large part, this is due to fitting a regression line to a sample that contains two distinct grades (i.e., two separate linear relationships that may represent two fundamentally different types of biological organization). When neonate mass is expressed as a proportion of maternal mass, strepsirhine and haplorhine lineages are clearly separated (Figure 16.2). At any given body mass, haplorhine mothers give birth to heavier litters than strepsirhines. This is also true when individual neonate mass is used instead of litter mass (Leutenegger 1973; Martin 1992). The presence of these two grades suggests that regression analyses at or within the haplorhine grade is most appropriate.

Despite the relatively large size of the human neonate, prenatal and postnatal growth rates in humans fall within range of other haplorhines (Ross and MacLarnon 1995). Postnatally, growth rates can remain similar because postnatal growth is prolonged over a longer period of time in humans; lactation lasts longer with weaning occurring at a relatively later age, whereas weaning weight is relatively similar to other primates (Lee et al. 1991). Gestation length in humans, on the other hand, is only slightly longer than expected relative to other placental mammals when scaled with body size (Martin and MacLarnon 1985, 1988). Thus, gestation poses a puzzle. How are relatively much larger human newborns produced at growth rates similar

Table 16.1. Reduced major axis regression statistics for neonatal litter mass (LM) on adult female body mass (FM).

Taxon	Regression equation	r^2	p	n
Primates	$\log_{10} LM = 0.84.\log_{10} FM - 0.55$	0.898	< 0.001	103
Haplorhines	$\log_{10} LM = 0.72.\log_{10} FM - 0.05$	0.957	< 0.001	77
Haplorhines > 5 kg	$\log_{10} LM = 0.80.\log_{10} FM - 0.41$	0.888	< 0.001	42
Catarrhines	$\log_{10} LM = 0.68.\log_{10} FM + 0.10$	0.885	< 0.001	49
Hominoids	$\log_{10} LM = 0.81.\log_{10} FM - 0.44$	0.955	< 0.001	8

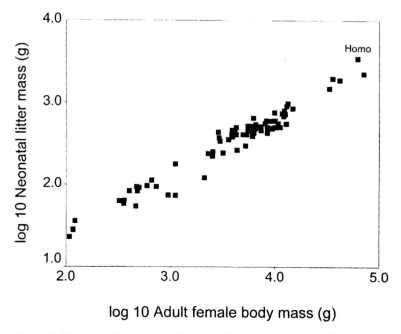

Figure 16.1. Logarithmic plot of neonatal litter mass on adult female body mass in haplorhine primates.

to other haplorhine primates when their gestation lengths are roughly similar? In the following three sections we provide a review and synthesis of placentation, genomic imprinting, and reproductive energetics as they bear on the evolution of relative brain and body size increase in the human newborn.

Placentation

Various aspects of placentation allow development of large and secondarily altricial neonates including type of placenta, scaling factors in maternal–fetal nutrient transport (Hill 1932; and Martin 1990), and the role of the placenta in maternal–fetal physiological conflicts. Haplorhine primates possess a hemochorial placenta. This is the most invasive type of placenta, as the fetus derives most of its nutrition by establishing a direct connection with the maternal blood vascular system (Figure 16.3). (For a review of placentation see Grosser 1909, 1927; Mossman 1987; Martin 1990.) Haig (1993) demonstrates how the placenta plays a critical role in creating physiological imbalances in the maternal–fetal nutrient transport system in human pregnancy. These imbalances appear to result from placental actions meant to reduce the probability of miscarriage or that increase the nutrient content or volume of maternal blood flowing to the fetus. Such placental actions are evident in immunological activity, allocrine hormones (placental hormones acting on the maternal system), and in the hemodynamics of pregnancy (forces on blood circu-

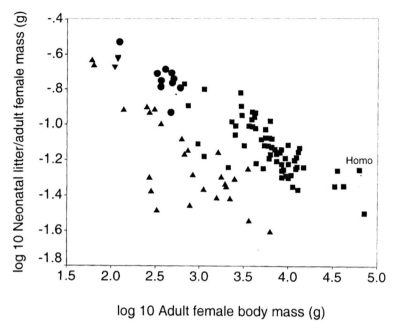

Figure 16.2. Logarithmic plot of neonatal litter mass/adult female body mass on adult female body mass in primates. Strepsirhine primates have a lower ratio (i.e., smaller infants) at any given maternal body mass. Key: Strepsirhines (s), tarsiers (t), callitrichids (l), and all other haplorhines (n). At the interface of the two grades are *Callimico*, *Callicebus*, and *Varecia* ($n \geq 7$ for neonate mass in all three taxa).

lation). Various illnesses and pathologies that occur in preparation for or during human pregnancy are offered by Haig as evidence in support of the hypothesis that mother and fetus, with their different genomes, have conflicting claims on limited maternal resources. Included are gestational diabetes, hydatidiform moles, and preeclampsia (pregnancy-induced high blood pressure accompanied by excessive protein in maternal urine). We suggest that the highly invasive human placentation pattern is uniquely sheltered from natural selection as it is an ephemeral organ that contributes to the development of offspring over a relatively short period of time (see also Mossman 1937). As with runaway sexual selection, placental/fetal adaptations can proceed without natural selection and risk, becoming maladaptive in humans as they are geared toward short-term effects.

Genomic Imprinting and Regional Expansions of the Brain and Conceptus

Although scaling factors and maternal–fetal physiological conflicts during pregnancy illustrate the critical role of the human placenta in obtaining nutrients to grow

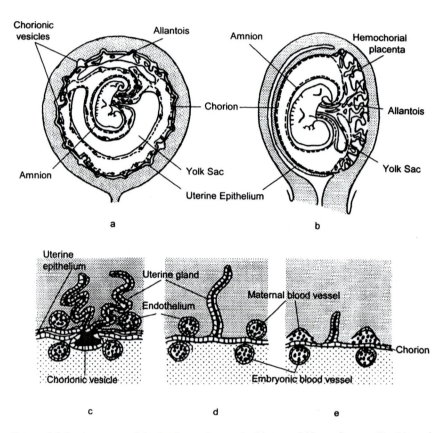

Figure 16.3. Anatomy of the fetal membranes in (a) strepsirhine primates (*Loris*), and (b) haplorhine primates (*Homo*). Cross sections illustrating the type of interface between the uterine epithelium and the placental chorionic membrane in (c) epitheliochorial placentation, (d) endotheliochorial, and (e) hemochorial placentation. Embryonic tissues (light stippling) and maternal tissues (dark stippling). Note the relative development of the uterine glands in each type and disintegration of the endothelium of maternal blood vessels in hemochorial placentation such that the chorion is directly bathed in maternal blood. The amnion is the innermost of four fetal membranes. It forms a fluid-filled sac around the embryo. The yolk sac contains nutrients. Blood vessels develop within it to transfer nutrients to the embryo. The allantois is an outgrowth of the embryonic gut that eventually fuses with the chorion. It contains blood vessels (allantoic or umbilical) that are the chief respiratory organ of the fetus. The chorion is the outermost fetal membrane. The outer layer of the chorion (trophoblast) initiates attachment to the uterus and invasion of maternal tissues. Drawings after Mossman 1987 and Martin 1990.

large-brained and large-bodied infants, the genetic basis of these traits probably plays a more fundamental role. Recent research on mammals has demonstrated that maternal and paternal genomes make different contributions to the brain, the placenta, and overall body mass. Such processes are known as genomic imprinting. Genomic imprinting refers to cases where certain autosomal alleles (i.e., alleles occurring on chromosomes other than sex chromosomes) are only expressed when derived from sperm (maternal contribution silenced, referred to as maternally imprinted), whereas others are only expressed when inherited from the egg (paternal contribution silenced, referred to as paternally imprinted) (Solter 1988; Surani et al. 1988; Reik 1989).

Many mammalian imprinted genes of known function support a theory advanced by Haig and Westoby (1989) that parents have different interests concerning growth rate of offspring. Paternal genes silence maternal counterparts that rein in growth, resulting in larger bodied "vigorous" offspring, whereas maternal genes silence their paternal counterparts to moderate growth, thereby protecting the mother and ensuring survival of current and future offspring. A variety of placental functions appear to be mediated by imprinted genes, including the production of allocrine hormones and those governing the growth of placental versus fetal mass (Haig and Westoby 1989; Hall 1990; Moore and Haig 1991; Haig 1993). Genomic imprinting may ultimately explain the pathological occurrence of complete hydatidiform moles that are conceptuses showing massive proliferation of placental cells without an associated fetus. They have only paternal chromosomes.

Studies of genomic imprinting and brain development (Fundele and Surani 1994) and experimental studies (Allen et al. 1995; Kerverne et al. 1996a) on mice reveal that areas of forebrain expansion (neocortex and striatum) are those to which the maternal genome makes a substantial developmental contribution, whereas areas of forebrain reduction (hypothalamus) are those to which the paternal genome makes a substantial contribution. The neocortex and striatum are areas of the forebrain concerned with anticipation, forward planning, and execution ("executive brain"), whereas the hypothalamus and septum are areas of the forebrain concerned with physiological homeostasis, sexual behavior, and parental behavior, all of which are largely under hormonal control. From insectivores to prosimians to anthropoids, the neocortex and striatum increase in size relative to the rest of the brain and body, while the hypothalamus, septum, and other regions decrease in size (Kerverne et al. 1996b). These data suggest that during development and over an evolutionary time scale for mammals, genomic imprinting has facilitated a rapid, nonlinear expansion of the brain, especially the neocortex and striatum. Whereas maternal metabolic turnover appears to be responsible for overall increase in brain and body size in the human neonate, paternally imprinted genes (i.e., those inherited from the mother) appear to be responsible for regional expansions of the brain and conceptus, and for limiting somatic fetal growth. Studies of genomic imprinting substantiate the hypothesis that the mammalian mother plays a special role in the development of her offspring's brain and in the evolution of brain size (see also Martin 1996). These findings highlight the need to examine human reproductive energetics in a comparative perspective.

Reproductive Energetics

Measures of Maternal Energy Investment and Cost During Gestation and Lactation

Measures of maternal energy investment during gestation and lactation can be direct or indirect. Direct methods of maternal energy investment during gestation consist of assaying ground-up fetuses or newborn infants for water content, fat, and protein (e.g., Tilden and Oftedal 1995). Direct methods of maternal energy investment during lactation consist of measuring milk energy concentration (water content, protein, nonprotein nitrogen, fat, and total sugar) and milk yields (e.g., Tilden and Oftedal 1997). Direct methods also include assessment of uterine, placental, and mammary tissue. Indirect methods of estimating maternal energy investment during gestation and lactation consist of examining prenatal and postnatal growth rates. For gestation, frequently used variables are litter mass, or mass gain relative to gestation length, and maternal body mass and metabolic rate (e.g., Martin and MacLarnon 1988, 1990). For lactation, a frequently used variable is average postnatal growth rate calculated as weight gain of total litter from birth to weaning divided by weaning age (e.g., Ross and MacLarnon 1995).

Energetic costs of gestation and lactation are commonly examined by monitoring caloric intake or maternal metabolic rate relative to maternal and offspring mass, but behavioral compensation can be extremely important in minimizing energy costs during various reproductive stages (Gittleman and Thompson 1988). This may involve energy conservation tactics such as reduced maternal activity levels or increased feeding rates, time spent feeding, or food selectivity during one or more reproductive stages. Basal metabolic rate (BMR) represents cubic centimeters of oxygen consumed per gram body mass per hour for fasting, adult animals within their thermoneutral zone. Most wild and domesticated mammals show little or no increase in maternal resting metabolic rates during gestation and lactation (Nicoll and Thompson 1987). Fat deposition prior to breeding or during gestation helps meet the higher costs of gestation and lactation, especially for larger mammals, and can affect litter size, sex ratio, offspring size, and brain size at weaning (refs. in Gittleman and Thompson 1988).

For all of the above reasons, relative energetic costs of gestation and lactation can be difficult to compare accurately between taxonomic groups and between reproductive stages. Nonetheless, energetic costs are generally considered to be higher during lactation than gestation. Primates require more food energy during lactation than during any other reproductive stage (e.g., Kirkwood and Underwood 1984; Sauther and Nash 1987). The primary reason for higher energetic costs during lactation than gestation is that energy and nutrient transfer is less direct, and therefore less efficient, after birth, at which time milk must be synthesized and transferred to offspring to sustain their growth and maintenance. After birth the infant is, in fact, at a higher trophic level than the mother and loses a large part of the energy available in the milk during the transfer between levels. In addition, the newborn undergoes more thermoregulatory stress and is more active than the fetus.

Energetic Investment and Cost of Pregnancy and Lactation in Human Females

Human females show many parallels to other mammals as well as some unique features in energetic costs of pregnancy and lactation. The discrepancy between estimates of energy requirements and estimates of intake during pregnancy and lactation has been explained by assuming that physical activity decreases in pregnancy and that human females are capable of energy-conserving alterations in metabolism and fat mobilization. In "healthy populations" increases in BMR are relatively high compared to other mammals during the last two trimesters (7% and 19%, respectively) but not during the first (4%) (reviewed in Prentice et al. 1996). On the other hand, resting metabolic rate does not increase significantly during lactation. The efficiency of converting dietary energy to milk energy, whether measured in terms of biochemical (91–94%) or calorimetric efficiency (80–85%), is high in humans relative to many other mammals due to the low level of fat synthesis in human milk (Prentice et al. 1996). Humans, like other anthropoid primates and most lemurs, produce dilute milks that are relatively low in fat and protein concentration (Martin 1984; Oftedal 1984).

Like many other mammals, human females gain weight during pregnancy (reviewed in Prentice et al. 1996). Most of the energy cost for tissue deposition (72%) is due to fat accumulation, although amounts vary between women from developed and developing countries. During pregnancy, protein synthesized by the mother is predominantly deposited in the conceptus (fetus 44%; placenta 10%), whereas fat deposition occurs mainly in maternal adipose tissue (85%) followed by the fetus (14%). Most mammals are born lean at birth, whereas human babies accumulate large amounts of fat during the final weeks of pregnancy and may contain 3 to 4 weeks of energy requirements in fat when born (Girard and Ferre 1982; Ziegler et al. 1976). Maternal fat loss can make an enormous contribution to the daily and overall energy costs of lactation in humans relative to other mammals, although it is not considered a biologically programmed part of normal lactation in humans and varies in developed versus developing countries (Prentice et al. 1996).

It is usual in contemporary Western societies for people to be aware of the dangers of eating too much animal fat, but fat is needed as much as protein in a full diet, and growth and maintenance of infants is dependent on a proper intake of fat. Speth and Spielmann (1983) long ago pointed out that a diet high in lean meat can cause severe deficiencies in essential fatty acids, especially in cases where the mother is malnourished and the infant weaned onto a low-fat diet.

The human brain is about one-third lipid, and this has to be taken from the mother by the fetus via the placenta and by the infant via mother's milk. It is worth noting that pregnant women lose 3–5% of brain volume during the last trimester of pregnancy (Holdcroft et al. 1997), and that this lost volume is likely to be essential fatty acids (Horrobin 1998).

Continuation of the fetal pattern of brain growth (Portmann 1990) requires changes in lactation (Martin 1983). Martin himself postulated that human milk fat would be unique in composition but could only refer to work comparing cows' milk to human milk. The critical detailed comparison, though, would be between human milk and that of African great apes.

Prenatal Growth Rates, Gestation, and Metabolism in Human Females

When examining indirect measures of energetic investment (i.e., growth rates), a broad sample of comparative data is available. Whether examined in relation to a vast array of eutherian mammals (Martin and MacLarnon 1985, 1988, 1990) or in relation to haplorhine primates alone (Ross and MacLarnon 1995), humans do not depart significantly from these groups in gestation length or prenatal growth rates relative to body mass or maternal metabolic rate. Gestation length is only slightly above expected in humans. Indeed, gestation length appears to be relatively invariant when scaled with body size. Despite these similarities, human females give birth to infants that are substantially larger than would be predicted by adult body size (Figure 16.1), a point advanced earlier based upon a data base consisting of just the great apes (Martin 1983; Portmann 1990). It may be that a small relative increase in human gestation length may have an enormous effect on neonate mass. But there are two points that would suggest otherwise. First, ranges for gestation length in gorillas (*Gorilla gorilla gorilla*, mean = 256 days, range = 237–285 days) and orangutans (*Pongo pygmaeus*, mean = 260 days; *Pongo abelli*, range = 223–267 days) overlap the mean for *Homo sapiens* at 267 days (data from Harvey et al. 1987 and Rowe 1996). Second, data on human fetal growth (Hytten and Leitch 1971) do not show a growth spurt in late gestation.

Portmann (1990) has suggested that the relatively large body mass of human neonates is an adjustment of the entire body to the size of the brain at birth. Attempting a functional explanation, Martin (1983, 1996) suggested that it is energetically more efficient for brain growth to take place during fetal life as long as possible because brain tissue is expensive to make and maintain, and the metabolic turnover of the mother is greater than her fetus. Martin and MacLarnon (1988, 1990) have demonstrated a consistent relationship between BMR and prenatal growth rates in primates and proposed that maternal metabolic rate constrains the rate of fetal development in addition to past and present ecological factors. In effect, the cost of growing a larger newborn with a relatively larger brain is borne by the mother. The most recent review of BMR in human females indicates that, unlike most mammals with a standard BMR, there are small incremental increases in BMR throughout pregnancy (Prentice et al. 1996). In addition to a slightly longer gestation length, increases in BMR may also enhance maternal investment in neonate brain and body mass.

Attributing the large brain and body size of human neonates to the greater metabolic turnover of a mother relative to her fetus and to slight increases in relative gestation length and BMR may explain how the adaptation is maintained. However, it does not explain how humans (or human ancestors) were advanced to a higher baseline of brain and body weight to begin with. Other factors must be at work. It has been cogently argued that type of placentation does not seem to exert any measurable influence on prenatal somatic growth rates (Martin and MacLarnon 1988; Martin 1990).

The least invasive type of placenta (epitheliochorial) is found among hoofed mammals (ungulates) and dolphins, yet these precocial mammals produce neonates that are relatively heavier than those of haplorhine primates. Also, once gestation length, maternal body mass and metabolic rate are accounted for, strepsirhine primates, with their epitheliochorial placenta, show considerable overlap with haplorhines in rates of fetal development. Thus, we cannot conclude that hemochorial placentas are more efficient in transferring resources from mother to fetus. However, in light of Haig's (1993) work, it can be argued that the invasive hemochorial placenta gives the fetus more control and access to specific nutrients that ultimately advance the human neonate to a higher baseline of brain and body mass. We suggest that attaining the new baseline requires not only that the energetic investment be made prenatally while the fetus can take advantage of the mother's greater metabolic turnover but also that the fetus has control and access to nutrients in the mother's circulatory system mediated by the highly invasive haplorhine placenta.

As relative prenatal growth rates do not differ significantly between humans and other haplorhines, it appears that various factors, some of which may not be significant standing alone (i.e., gestation length, BMR), unite to produce large-brained, large-bodied neonates. One factor that can be singled out is that the human mother must acquire foods of relatively higher nutritional value than other haplorhines to cover the costs of growing such a large infant, given the constraints of gestation length and growth rate. This must have involved a change in trophic level. Furthermore, the maternal digestive system must be able to derive nutrients from such foods, and the placenta must be able to transfer them to the fetus. This hypothesized change in trophic level may explain the introduction of animal protein and fat into the human diet, a relatively rare occurrence among the primarily vegetarian Order Primates. Milton (1999) offers a complementary view. Considering the ecological environment of early hominids with its probable patchy distribution of high-quality plant foods, Milton (1999) suggests that increased energetic requirements for foraging, in combination with large body size, may have precipitated exploitation of a second trophic level. Milton suggests that an increase in the relative size of the small intestine in modern humans belies ingestion of nutritionally dense and volumetrically concentrated animal products in our ancestors. Such low-bulk foods contain a large complement of minerals, trace elements, and vitamins, in addition to protein and fat, which would allow hominids to rely on plant foods mainly for energy.

One factor that may support the hypothesis of a change in trophic level is that humans show no major increase in relative metabolic rate, although slight increases are detectable during the second and third trimesters of pregnancy (Prentice et al. 1996). Human metabolism facilitates growth of newborns of high brain and body mass without deviating from the mammalian scaling pattern, where BMR is proportional to the 0.75 power of body mass (Kleiber 1932). Metabolic rate may be constrained to prevent disruption of optimal body temperature for protein synthesis, which is especially important during both gestation and lactation (McNab 1980). Human females can circumvent this constraint by increasing intake of nutritionally dense foods that are high in protein and fat. Alternative strategies taken by other precocial mammals whose infants grow large brains in utero include increasing gut volume. This is seen in many small herbivores (see Thompson 1992 for a review). Humans have not taken this approach. To the contrary, modern humans are characterized by a relatively reduced gut size and the gut anatomy of frugivores with faunivorous tendencies (Martin et al. 1985; Sussman 1987). Although there are many confounding factors in trying to reconstruct the "natural" diet of humans by examining modern human populations (Sussman 1987), it is nonetheless likely that the transition from great apes to humans, specifically from *Australopithecus* to *Homo* (Schmid 1983), involved a reduction in gut size and that this reduction correlates with a trophic shift in diet. The internal organs, like brain tissue, are metabolically expensive to grow and maintain, and the metabolic requirements of relatively large brains may have, in part, been offset by a corresponding reduction of the gut (Aiello and Wheeler 1995).

Postnatal Growth Rates, Life History, and Social Factors

Although relative postnatal somatic growth rates in humans do not depart significantly from those of other primates or mammals, the brain continues to grow at accelerated fetal rates for an additional 12 months after birth (Martin 1983; Portmann 1990). Life history correlates that explain this relatively expensive postnatal growth period, without perturbing relative somatic growth rates, include a relatively longer lactation period and later weaning age. Relative weaning weight in humans does not differ from other primates or other mammals (Lee et al. 1991).

Social factors also appear to play a role in postnatal growth. Bearing altricial young that are nonclinging and highly dependent provides a setting for the cooperative care of young found in many modern human populations. Cooperative care of young may be particularly beneficial to females during lactation, allowing them to allocate time and energy so as to compensate for or meet the high energetic requirements of nursing large-bodied and large-brained infants. These features of the human newborn and their coadapted consequences probably characterized early *Homo*. Nonclinging, helpless infants are thought to have become possible in fully terrestrial hominids (early *Homo*), in combination with cooperative social behavior and advanced tool use that enhanced predator avoidance and food acquisition (Stanley 1992). In early *Homo*, cooperative care of young may have enhanced foraging success for mothers, or alternatively, permitted provisioning of young by other community members. Carnivores show some parallels to humans in that species with communal care patterns and/or distinct diets permit a high rate of energy transfer from lactating females to young, which in turn affects growth rate and litter mass (Gittleman and Oftedal 1987).

Models in Reproductive Energetics

Two models used to examine reproductive energetics in mammals can now be examined to help place humans in perspective. The BMR-speed prediction holds total energy allocated to reproduction constant and reduces the duration of reproduction, whereas the BMR-reproductive effort prediction holds the duration of reproduction more or less constant and opts for an increase in the total energy expended for reproduction (Thompson 1992). As gestation length in humans does not depart much from expectations relative to body size, the BMR-reproductive effort model appears to apply at this reproductive stage. The slightly elevated metabolic rate of pregnant human females during the relatively fixed gestation length lends further support to the contention that human females are investing relatively more energy in biosynthesis of fetal tissues and fat during gestation. During lactation, neither model applies. Human females do not hold lactation constant or shorten it. Rather, they lengthen this reproductive phase and proceed to nourish their costly infants over a relatively protracted period until they can be weaned at an optimal weight. As with gestation, nursing such costly young may have required a diet containing more animal protein and fat. In addition, this protracted period of energetically costly care appears to have required cooperative care of young, given the altricial state of offspring at birth and their high nutritional requirements. In sum, we contend that during the course of human evolution, females maximized energy allocation during reproduction through behavioral compensation (e.g., reduced locomotion, better thermoregulation, or the availability of alloparental care) as well as by incorporating more animal protein and fat into the diet.

Evidence for Secondarily Altricial Newborns in the Genus *Homo*

Maternal pelvic limitations on increased fetal brain development appear to have been reached before the emergence of *Homo erectus*, in tandem with the appearance of early *Homo*. Allowing for growth to maturity and sex differences, Walker and Ruff (1993) estimated that a *Homo erectus* neonate would resemble a modern human at 32–33 weeks of age and have a brain weighing approximately 200–240 g. Assuming a human pattern of brain growth, a *H. erectus* neonate with a brain weighing 200 g would have an adult brain weighing 750 g, and a *H. erectus* neonate with a brain weighing 240 g would have an adult brain weighing 840 g (increase in size by a factor of 3.5). The latter is very similar to the estimated brain size in KNM-WT 15,000 (909 cubic centimeters) and virtually the same as the threshold value of 850 cc considered by Martin (1983) to require postnatal continuation of fetal growth patterns.

Given the estimates of neonatal and adult brain size in KNM-WT 15000, *H. erectus* appears to have evolved the prenatal and postnatal brain growth patterns found in modern humans. By extension, they probably bore secondarily altricial young much like those of modern humans. Thus, *H. erectus* appears to have obtained an adult brain size of sufficient size (750–1060 cc for early African *H. erectus*) such that its corresponding neonatal brain size would have breached pelvic inlet diameter if allowed to continue beyond 9 months. This increase in neonate size would have required earlier delivery and continuation of fetal brain growth rates outside the mother's body. As this reconstruction is based upon one of the geologically earlier finds of *H. erectus*, it is likely that even earlier members of the genus *Homo* had already become secondarily altricial. Behavioral implications are that infants of early *Homo* were highly in need of adult care, as they remained helpless for long periods of time. If the accompanying trophic shift in diet were also in place, these novel adaptations may have precipitated the geographic dispersal of early *Homo* beyond the African continent (Shipman and Walker 1989; see also Foley this volume).

Conclusions

This review examines some of the underlying processes by which a primate species might come to be large brained. Humans manage this by starting with a large-brained, large-bodied infant, making a substantially greater energetic investment in the developing fetus than in any other primate. It has been pointed out that there is competition for resources between the fetus and the mother, and because the fetus is on the receiving end of the system, increased resources can only come about by substantial biochemical or dietary changes, behavioral changes, or a combination of all three factors. We suggest that increased access to animal protein and fat enabled early hominids to break free from constraints that limit the prenatal brain growth of other haplorhines. But it is not enough to merely claim that increased dietary fat and protein can lead to big-brained, large infants—we doubt that even the best-fed chimpanzee, bonobo, or gorilla could ever grow a very large brain. The placenta, the organ that mediates energy transfer between mother and fetus, must have changed in the human lineage. It can have changed in several ways, ranging from increased invasiveness at the microscopic level, to major changes in the pathways of nutrient metabolism at the biochemical level (the placenta is not a passive organ). Differences between the placentas of African apes and humans at the detailed anatomical, physiological, and biochemical levels, including studies of placental gene expression, would make a fruitful area of research and help us understand one of the most profound of human adaptations—our large brains. We expect that major differences will be found in the metabolic pathways and/or efficiency of production of essential fatty acids. There is some evidence from the fossil record to suggest that secondary altriciality was in place by 1.6 million years ago and plenty of evidence from the archaeological record for increased consumption of meat and fat from hunting and power scavenging by 1.75 million years ago (see Bunn this volume). Although brain-to-body size relationships for early hominids are not yet securely documented, a grade shift from an australopithecine-sized brain to a *H. habilis/H. erectus* one seems a likely correlation with the shift to increased use of animal resources.

Acknowledgments We thank David Haig, Jim Latham, Bob Martin, and Rich Smith for their contributions to this chapter. We also thank Craig Stanford and Henry Bunn for inviting us to participate in the symposium, and the Wenner-Gren Foundation for sponsorship.

REFERENCES

Aiello, L. C., and P. Wheeler. 1995. The expensive tissue hypothesis: the brain and digestive system in human and primate evolution. *Current Anthropology* 36:199–221.

Allen, N., K. Logan, G. Lally, M. Norris, and E. B. Keverne. 1995. Distribution of parthenogenetic cells in the mouse brain and their influence on brain development and behaviour. *Proceedings of the National Academy of Sciences, USA* 92:10782–10786.

Bearder, S. K. 1987. Lorises, bushbabies, and tarsiers: diverse societies in solitary foragers. In *Primate Societies* (B. B. Smuts, D. L. Cheney, R. M. Seyfarth, R. W. Wrangham, and T. T. Struhsaker, eds.), pp. 11–24. Chicago: University of Chicago Press.

Fundele, R. H., and A. Surani. 1994. Experimental embryological analysis of genetic imprinting in mouse development. *Developmental Genetics* 15:515–522.

Girard, J., and P. Ferre. 1982. Metabolic and hormonal changes around birth. In *The Biochemical Development of the Fetus and Neonate* (C. T. Jones, ed.), pp. 517–551. Amsterdam: Elsevier.

Gittleman, J. L., and O. T. Oftedal. 1987. Comparative growth and lactation energetics in carnivores. *Symposium of the Zoological Society of London* 57:41–77.

Gittleman, J. L., and S. D. Thompson. 1988. Energy allocation in mammalian reproduction. *American Zoologist* 28:863–875.

Grosser, O. 1909. *Vergleichende Anatomie und Entwicklungsgeschichte der Eihäute und der Placenta*. Vienna: Wilhelm Braumüller.

Grosser, O. 1927. *Frühentwicklung, Eihaubtbildung und Placentation des Menschen und der Säugetiere*. Munich: J. F. Bergmann.

Haig, D. 1993. Genetic conflicts in human pregnancy. *Quarterly Review of Biology* 68:495–532.

Haig, D., and M. Westoby. 1989. Parent-specific gene expression and the triploid endosperm. *American Naturalist* 134:147–155.

Hall, J. G. 1990. Genomic imprinting: review and relevance to human disease. *American Journal of Human Genetics* 46:857–873.

Harvey, P. H., R. D. Martin, and T. H. Clutton-Brock. 1987. Life histories in comparative perspective. In *Primate Societies* (B. B. Smuts, D. L. Cheney, R. M. Seyfarth, R. W. Wrangham, and T. T. Struhsaker, eds.), pp. 181–196. Chicago: University of Chicago Press.

Hill, J. P. 1932. The developmental history of the primates. *Philosophical Transactions of the Royal Society of London B* 221:45–178.

Holdcroft, A., A. Oatridge, J. V. Hajnal, and G. M. Bydder. 1997. Changes in brain size in normal human pregnancy. *Journal of Physiology* 498P:80P–81P (abstract).

Horrobin, D.F. 1998. Schizophrenia: the illness that made us human. *Medical Hypotheses* 50:269–288.

Hytten, F., and I. Leitch. 1971. *The Physiology of Human Pregnancy*, 2nd ed. Oxford: Blackwell.

Keverne, E. B., R. Fundele, M. Narashimha, S. C. Barton, and M. A. Surani. 1996a. Genomic imprinting and the differential roles of parental genomes in brain development. *Developmental Brain Research* 92:91–100.

Keverne, E. B., F. L. Martel, and C. M. Nevison. 1996b. Primate brain evolution: genetic and functional considerations. *Proceedings of the Royal Society of London* 262:689–696.

Kirkwood, J. K., and S. J. Underwood. 1984. Energy requirements of captive cotton-top tamarins (*Saguinas oedipus oedipus*). *Folia Primatologica* 42:180–187.

Kleiber, M. 1932. Body size and metabolism. *Hilgardia* 6:315–353.

Lee, P. C., P. Majluf, and I. J. Gordon. 1991. Growth, weaning, and maternal investment from a comparative perspective. *Journal of Zoology London* 225:99–114.

Leutenegger, W. 1973. Maternal–fetal weight relationships in primates. *Folia Primatologica* 20:280–293.

Martin, R. D. 1983. Human brain evolution in an ecological context. *Fifty-Second James Arthur Lecture on the Evolution of the Human Brain*. New York: American Museum of Natural History.

Martin, R. D. 1984. Scaling effects and adaptive strategies in mammalian lactation. *Symposium of the Zoological Society of London* 51:87–117.

Martin, R. D. 1990. *Primate Origins and Evolution: A Phylogenetic Reconstruction*. Princeton, NJ: Princeton University Press.

Martin, R. D. 1992. Goeldi and the dwarfs: the evolutionary biology of the small New World monkeys. *Journal of Human Evolution* 22:367–393

Martin, R. D. 1996. Scaling of the mammalian brain: the maternal energy hypothesis. *News in Physiological Science* 11:149–156.

Martin, R. D. 1998. Comparative aspects of human brain evolution: scaling, energy costs and confounding variables. In *The Origin and Diversification of Language* (N. G. Jablonski and L. C. Aiello, eds.), pp. 35–68. San Francisco: Memoirs of the California Academy of Sciences 24.

Martin, R. D., D. J. Chivers, A. M. MacLarnon, and C. M. Hladik. 1985. Gastrointestinal allometry in primates and other mammals. In *Size and Scaling in Primate Biology* (W. L. Jungers, ed.), pp. 61–89. New York: Plenum Press.

Martin, R. D., and MacLarnon A. M. 1985. Gestation period, neonatal size and maternal investment in placental mammals. *Nature* 313:220–223.

Martin, R. D., and A. M. MacLarnon. 1988. Comparative quantitative studies of growth and reproduction. *Symposium of the Zoological Society of London* 60:39–80.

Martin, R. D., and A. M. MacLarnon. 1990. Reproductive patterns in primates and other mammals: the dichotomy between altricial and precocial offspring. In *Primate Life History and Evolution* (C. Jean-De Rousseau, ed.), pp. 47–79. New York: Wiley-Liss.

McNab, B. K. 1980. Food habits, energetics, and the population biology of mammals. *American Naturalist* 116:106–124.

Milton, K. 1999. A hypothesis to explain the role of meat-eating in human evolution. *Evolutionary Anthropology* 8:11–21.

Moore, T., and D. Haig. 1991. Genomic imprinting in mammalian development: a parental tug-of-war. *Trends in Genetics* 7:45–49.

Mossman, H. W. 1937. Comparative morphogenesis of the fetal membranes and accessory uterine structures. In *Contributions to Embryology*, vol. 26, pp. 129–246. Washington, DC: Carnegie Institute.

Mossman, H. W. 1987. *Vertebrate Fetal Membranes*. New Brunswick, NJ: Rutgers University Press.

Nicoll, M. E., and S. D. Thompson. 1987. Basal metabolic rates and energetics of reproduction in therian mammals: marsupials and placentals compared. *Symposium of the Zoological Society of London* 57:7–27.

Oftedal, O. T. 1984. Milk composition, milk yield and energy output at peak lactation: a comparative review. *Symposium of the Zoological Society of London* 51:33–85.

Portmann, A. 1939. Nesthocker und Nestflüchter als Entwicklungszustände von verschiedener Wertigkeit bei Vögeln und Säugern. *Revue Suisse de Zoologie* 46:386–390.

Portmann, A. 1941. Die Tragzeiten der Primaten und die Dauer der Schwangerschaft beim Menschen: ein Problem der vergleichenden Biologie. *Revue Suisse de Zoologie* 48:511–518.

Portmann, A. 1952. Besonderheiten und Bedeutung der menschlichen Brutflege. *Ciba-Zeitschrift* 11:4758–4763.

Portmann, A. 1962. Cerebralisation und Ontogenese. *Medizinar. Grundlagenforsch.* 4:1–62.

Portmann, A. 1965. Über die Evolution der Tragzeit bei Säugetieren. *Revue Suisse de Zoologie* 72:658–666.

Portmann, A. 1990. *A Zoologist Looks at Human Kind*. New York: Columbia University Press.

Prentice, A. M., C. J. K. Spaaij, G. R. Goldberg, S. D. Poppitt, J. M. A. van Raaij, M. Totton, D. Swann, and A. E. Black 1996. Energy requirements of pregnant and lactating women. *European Journal of Clinical Nutrition* 50 (Supplement 1):S82–S111.

Rasmussen, D. T. 1985. A comparative study of breeding seasonality and litter size in eleven taxa of captive lemurs (*Lemur* and *Varecia*). *International Journal of Primatology* 6:501–517.

Reik, W. 1989. Genomic imprinting and genetic disorders in man. *Trends in Genetics* 5:331–336.

Ross, C., and A. MacLarnon. 1995. Ecological and social correlates of maternal expenditure on infant growth in haplorhine primates. In *Motherhood in Human and Nonhuman Primates* (C. R. Pryce, R. D. Martin, and D. Skuse, eds.), pp. 37–46. Basel: Karger.

Rowe, N. 1996. *The Pictorial Guide to the Living Primates*. East Hampton, NY: Pogonias Press.

Sacher, G. A. 1982. The role of brain maturation in the evolution of the primates. In *Primate Brain Evolution* (E. Armstrong and d. Falk, eds.), pp. 97–112. New York: Plenum.

Sauther, M. L., and L. T. Nash. 1987. Effect of reproductive state and body size on food consumption in captive *Galago senegalensis braccatus*. *American Journal of Physical Anthropology* 73:81–88.

Schmid, P. 1983. Eine Rekonstruktion des Skelettes von AL 288 (Hadar) und daren Konsequenzen. *Folia Primatologica* 40:283–306.

Schultz, A. H. 1960. Age changes in primates and their modification in man. In *Human Growth* (J. M. Tanner, ed.), pp. 1–20. Oxford: Pergamon.

Shipman, P., and A. Walker. 1989. The costs of becoming a predator. *Journal of Human Evolution* 18:373–392.

Smith, R. J., and W. L. Jungers. 1997. Body mass in comparative primatology. *Journal of Human Evolution* 32:523–559.

Smith, R. J., and S. R. Leigh. 1998. Sexual dimorphism in primate neonatal body mass. *Journal of Human Evolution* 34:173–201.

Solter, D. 1988. Differential imprinting and expression of maternal and paternal genomes. *Annual Review of Genetics* 22:127–146.

Speth, J. D., and K. A. Speilmann. 1983. Energy source, protein metabolism and hunter-gatherer subsistence strategies. *Journal of Anthropological Archeology* 2:1–31.

Stanley, S. M. 1992. An ecological theory for the origin of *Homo*. *Paleobiology* 18:237–257.

Surani, M. A., W. Reik, and N. D. Allen. 1988. Transgenes as molecular probes for genomic imprinting. *Trends in Genetics* 4:59–61.

Sussman, R. W. 1987. Species-specific dietary patterns in primates and human dietary adaptations. In *The Evolution of Human Behavior: Primate Models* (W. G. Kinzey, ed.), pp. 151–179. Albany, NY: SUNY Press.

Thompson, S. D. 1992. Gestation and lactation in small mammals: basal metabolic rate and the limits of energy use. In *Mammalian Energetics: Interdisciplinary Views of Metabolism and Reproduction* (T. E. Tomasi and R. H. Horton, eds.), pp. 213–259. Ithaca, NY: Comstock.

Tilden, C. D., and O. T. Oftedal. 1995. Bioenergetics of reproduction in prosimian primates: is it related to female dominance? In *Creatures of the Dark* (L. Alterman, G. A. Doyle, and M. K. Izard, eds.), pp. 119–128. New York: Plenum.

Tilden, C. D., and O. T. Oftedal. 1997. Milk composition reflects pattern of maternal care in prosimian primates. *American Journal of Primatology* 41:195–211.

Walker, A. C., and C. B. Ruff. 1993. The reconstruction of the pelvis. In *The Nariokotome Homo Erectus Skeleton* (A. C. Walker and R. Leakey, eds.), pp. 221–233. Cambridge, MA: Harvard University Press.

Ziegler, E. E., A. M. O'Donnell, S. E. Nelson, and S. J. Fomon. 1976. Body composition of the reference fetus. *Growth* 40:329–341.

Conclusions

Research Trajectories on Hominid Meat-Eating

Henry T. Bunn

Craig B. Stanford

The chapters in this volume provide informative views on the physique and physiology of ancient hominids, on the dynamics of the ecosystems in which they lived, on the archaeological remains of their foraging behavior, and on analog-based studies that facilitate reconstructions of the foraging strategies and behavior of ancient hominids. The common theoretical link among all of those approaches is behavioral ecology, as most explicitly addressed in the chapters by Foley and by Winterhalder. From that perspective, the biological composition of particular hominid taxa can be juxtaposed with the dynamic ecological parameters of the landscapes in which they lived to derive behavioral reconstructions of their probable adaptations. Diverse analogs provide the necessary insights on the dynamics involved, and in this volume the analogs range from vampire bats and other taxa (Winterhalder), modern savanna ecosystems (Tappen and Sept), modern carnivores (Van Valkenburgh), modern nonhuman primates (McGrew, Rose, Schoeninger et al., and Stanford), to modern and prehistoric Holocene human foragers (Alvard, Bunn, Hawkes, Rick, Schoeninger et al., and Stanford).

A consistent theme of the volume is that all such analog-based information must be applied cautiously and with the most appropriate ancient counterpart in mind. Thus, no one modern ecosystem, for example, can be expected to provide a specific picture of the Plio-Pleistocene landscape; all modern examples available should be examined to best define the operative dynamics and the range of likely responses by ancient hominids (e.g., Tooby and DeVore 1987). Similarly, analogs based on humans and nonhuman primates must be directed at clarifying the behavioral ecology of the most appropriate ancient hominid, as defined in part by shared similarities in biology, phylogeny, and ecological constraints. The consensus view among the authors of this volume was that chimpanzees and other nonhuman primate analogs reveal most about likely adaptations of australopithecines, while analogs based on modern foragers and prehistoric *Homo sapiens* are best applied to understanding earlier taxa in the genus *Homo*.

Stanford and Allen (1991) argued that the distinction between analogic and nonanalogic models of human origins is a false dichotomy; even the most broad-based model using information from a range of sources is ultimately a set of overlapping analogs. Among the nonhuman primates, those species that share either a close phylogenetic relationship or a habitat similar to those in which early hominids evolved have been most used to model early hominid behavioral ecology. For this reason early anthropological field studies of nonhuman primates focused on baboons (DeVore and Washburn 1963) and chimpanzees (Goodall 1968). As savanna-living Old World monkeys, baboons fit the conception of the 1960s of early humans inhabiting open grassland, and the importance of dominance and aggression among this species seemed applicable to early hominid social behavior as well. Later, Goodall's fieldwork on chimpanzees brought this ape to the fore as the prime exemplar of Pliocene hominid behavior.

It would be simplistic to imagine early australopithecines as bipedal chimpanzees; many aspects of the ecology, positional behavior, and social behavior differ profoundly between the two species. The value of chimpanzees lies in what they tell us about the potential range of adaptations likely to have been present in the australopithecines. Four decades of chimpanzee field studies have documented a wealth of diversity among chimpanzee populations in cultural traditions ranging from tool use (Whiten et al. 1999) to hunting (Stanford 1996, 1998). We know that chimpanzees in Tanzania may hunt for wild pigs, while those of another population 2,000 km to the west ignore pigs. Chimpanzees in one forest in Tanzania use stick tools to fish for termites, while those in another population only 160 km away fail to do so. These cultural traditions tell us that we should expect similar, if not greater, degrees of local variability in the behavior of australopithecines and early *Homo*. While one hominid population in the Pliocene may have hunted avidly for prey, another population only a few hundred kilometers away may not have hunted at all or may have scavenged in addition to hunting. The value of primate models is, thus, that they teach us to recognize the potential possibilities for intraspecific and interspecific variation in meat-eating as well as other key adaptive behaviors visible in the fossil record.

The Man the Hunter paradigm and the Home Base and Food-Sharing model were revisited often during the conference upon which this volume is based, and it is instructive to do so again here. Our intent is not to attempt to reinstate verbatim either of those models from the 1960s and 1970s, but, instead, to use them as a baseline against which to measure current findings on hominid foraging adaptations. In the home base model, Isaac (e.g., 1971, 1978, 1984) reasoned that the cooccurrences of stone tools and fossil bones of a variety of animals resembled the discarded remains at modern forager base camps, indicating that a human-like behavioral package involving a gender-based division of labor, cooperation, food transport, and food-sharing, all existed by the beginning of the Pleistocene. When Isaac developed his model, Man the Hunter still loomed large as the pivotal, though increasingly criticized, behavior leading to modern humanity.

Decoupling the Plio-Pleistocene evidence from the home base model, a new research trajectory that Isaac himself helped to initiate by the mid-1970s, provided a wide-open framework for new research, including more site-oriented excavations (e.g., Isaac and Harris 1978; Bunn et al. 1980; Isaac et al. 1981), landscape-oriented surface transects and excavation (e.g., Isaac 1981; Blumenschine and Masao 1991; Bunn 1994; Stern 1993); and analog-based ethnoarchaeological, ethological, and experimental approaches (e.g., Binford 1981; Bunn 1981; Keeley and Toth 1981; Potts and Shipman 1981; Vincent 1984; Blumenschine 1987, 1988; Behrensmeyer et al. 1986; Binford et al. 1988; Bunn et al. 1988; O'Connell et al. 1988; McGrew 1992; Blumenschine and Marean 1993; Sept 1994; Tappen 1990). There is, of course, a plethora of other Africanist and non-Africanist research on these topics (e.g., Brain 1981; Hudson 1993; Lyman 1994).

A diversity of analytical approaches and reinterpretations of early Pleistocene Africa emerged from that period of research. Some of the more novel reinterpretations of the so-called home base sites include: repeated kill sites and feeding sites of large carnivores, from which hominids scavenged for marginal tid-bits of meat (e.g., Binford 1981, 1988); stone cache sites where hominids intentionally stockpiled stone raw material for later use during fleeting visits to butcher carcasses (Potts 1984, 1988); average locations on the paleolandscape in terms of the density of recovered artifacts and bones, indicating, therefore, that "home bases, or repeatedly visited focal locations for *multiple* hominid activities, have not been shown to exist during basal Bed II times" (Blumenschine and Masao 1991: 458); time-averaged palimpsests of stone and bone that accumulated over tens of thousands of years and are no different in composition (except density of remains) than the sparser remains across the paleolandscape, indicating, once again, that the sites were not locations of diverse hominid activities occurring within the restricted time frame implied by the home base label (Stern 1993). Isaac himself dropped the home base term in favor of central place foraging site, but all of the behavioral ingredients of the original Home Base Model were retained as a viable working hypothesis (Isaac 1984), in which the sites themselves may have simply functioned as convenient, secure areas with climbable shade trees for repeated, leisurely diurnal visits (Kroll and Isaac 1984; Kroll 1997). The most recent reinterpretation of the home base sites has usefully merged primatological and archaeological evidence as the Resource Defense Model (Rose and Marshall 1996).

Notably, after all of the taphonomically oriented research and conflicting reinterpretations that have followed Isaac's Home Base Model, the basic building blocks of evidence, the bones and the stone tools, have remained in place. The concentrations of bones at home base/central place sites that were initially assumed to be residues of hominid hunting, scavenging, carcass transport, meat-eating, and of subsequent carnivore feeding, have been demonstrated beyond reasonable doubt to be just about that. Judging from evidence from FLK Zinj. and other key sites in East Africa, of abundant butchery damage to bones, of skeletal proportions and minimum numbers of animals at the same sites, and of unweathered to lightly weathered bones, indicating a maximum period of a few months or years for site formation (e.g., Bunn and Kroll 1986), the foraging strategies of early Pleistocene hominids, and probably early *Homo erectus*, in East Africa, included some combination

of hunting and scavenging, systematic butchery for meat and fat, and repeated transport of meaty carcass portions to favored, central locations on the paleolandscape.
Winterhalder (this volume) suggests that food-sharing was probably also a component of the foraging adaptation of early hominids.

As the other class of archaeological evidence from home base sites, the Oldowan
tools have proven to be much more than the "smashed rocks" that Binford (1983:
57) imagined. Judging from the abundant butchery damage on bones from FLK
Zinj. and from microwear damage on a sample of Oldowan flakes from Koobi Fora
(Keeley and Toth 1981), hominids used flakes as cutting tools to skin, dismember,
and deflesh carcasses, to cut soft plant material, and to scrape and saw hard wood,
and they used hammerstones and other core tools to pound open marrow-rich limb
bones and mandibles. Refitting evidence from Koobi Fora indicates that hominids
transported flakes and cores to and from home base sites, and they conducted significant stone-knapping at the sites (Kroll and Isaac 1984; Isaac 1997; Kroll 1997).
In regions of the Koobi Fora paleolandscape lacking stone raw material and discarded tools, hominids transported stone cutting tools at least 15 km to butcher
carcasses, and they carried the stone tools with them when they left the area (Bunn
1997).

This summary of the East African Plio-Pleistocene evidence, which has evolved
from Isaac's home base model, provides a useful perspective for comparison with
other contexts in Africa and Eurasia. In southern Africa, the principal paleoanthropological evidence of Plio-Pleistocene age derives from five dolomitic cave systems in South Africa that are well known for their admixture of abundant fossil
remains of hominids and diverse fauna, with uncommon but locally abundant stone
and even bone tools (Brain 1981, 1993; Kuman 1994). Interpretations include the
view of gracile australopithecines as violent, bloodthirsty predators (Dart 1953,
1957), of hominids as prey items of large felids, hyenas, and raptors (Brain 1981,
1993), and of early *Homo* and robust australopithecines as hunters, scavengers, and
users of stone tools, bone tools, and fire (Brain et al. 1988; Susman 1988, 1994).
The detailed taphonomic analyses by Pickering (1999; this volume), however, reveal
little evidence to support a functional, behavioral association between the fauna, the
tools, and any of the hominids actually recovered from the deposits at Sterkfontein
or Swartkrans, where the most intriguing behavioral reconstructions had been developed in prior research. Judging from the clear behavioral associations between
fauna and tools at open-air contexts of comparable age in East Africa, it thus appears likely that more will be learned about the behavioral ecology of hominids in
southern Africa from the recovery of evidence from open-air sites than from the
cave deposits themselves.

In Eurasia, paleoanthropological evidence of a hominid presence appeared by
approximately 1.4 million years ago, if not earlier (Swisher et al. 1994). Stiner (in
press) provides an insightful and timely summary of early and middle Pleistocene
archaeological and paleoecological evidence, particularly from Europe, that indicates an initial reliance on the scavenging of megafauna by small and highly mobile hominid groups, followed during the middle Pleistocene by the development
of hunting weapons (wooden spears) and a foraging adaptation based on the hunting and scavenging of a more diverse and generally smaller fauna, and on the use

of home base/central place types of sites. Stiner's reconstruction of the evolution of hominid foraging strategies in Eurasia is consistent with the current evidence of early Eurasian sites involving megafauna death/butchery sites with associated stone tools and a scant archaeological and hominid fossil record in general. But again, judging from the older, Plio-Pleistocene record in East Africa, where a more familiarly human-like foraging pattern of megafauna death/butchery sites and a scant archaeological record exist on the same paleolandscape with home base types of sites (as at Koobi Fora), there is a distinct possibility that the available early Eurasian pattern results from a preservational bias against home bases and/or incomplete field survey in appropriate depositional settings. Only future research can reveal whether or not there is more diversity to the early Eurasian record than is currently documented.

Although the inherent incompleteness of the fossil and archaeological record is a given, several contributions to the volume provide timely messages on just how limited the prehistoric record is relative to the actual dynamics of hominid foraging behavior and diet, and those help to define a workable trajectory for future research. McGrew (this volume) emphasizes the paleontologically invisible invertebrate component in chimpanzee diet. Speth and Tchernov (this volume) describe the sophisticated hunting strategies of Neanderthals at Kebara Cave in Israel, and they suggest that researchers may be seriously underestimating the behavioral capabilities of that taxon. A similar likelihood exists for *Homo erectus* and early *Homo sapiens* in Eurasia, and for early *Homo erectus* and australopithecines in Africa. The contributions by Rick on prehistoric foragers in the Andes, by Alvard on whale hunters in Indonesia, and by Hawkes on Hadza foragers in Tanzania, while all fascinating stand-alone studies in their own right, also illustrate the complex dynamics of foraging adaptations among modern *Homo sapiens*. Much of that behavioral complexity would be invisible in the ancient archaeological and fossil record, even if it existed. Future paleoanthropological research needs to address that constraint by defining research questions and analytical methods at an appropriate scale of resolution—questions that are answerable, given the incomplete nature of the evidence, and methods that allow for the recognition of more detailed, complex behaviors when they appear in the archaeological and fossil record.

Since the meat-eating conference convened several months ago, there have been several relevant developments in paleoanthropology. First, Wood and Collard (1999) have redefined the genus *Homo* in a manner that still includes *Homo ergaster*, or early African *Homo erectus*, which now appears in the record by 1.9 million years ago, but that excludes both *Homo habilis* and *Homo rudolfensis* from the genus *Homo*. From a behavioral perspective, that generic redefinition has little impact on the interpretation of the archaeological record postdating 1.9 million years ago, which, since the discovery of *Homo habilis* (Leakey et al. 1964), has been commonly linked to that taxon or its immediate derivatives. But as the antiquity of early African *Homo erectus* has been pushed back progressively in time (e.g., Feibel et al. 1989), there has been a corresponding increase in attributions of the archaeological record from Olduvai Gorge and Koobi Fora, all of which postdates 1.9 million years ago, to early *Homo erectus*. The most emphatic statements attributing at least some of the archaeological record postdating 1.9 million years ago, to *Paranthropus*, have been made by researchers at Swartkrans (Brain et al. 1988; Susman 1988, 1994).

With the redefinition of *Homo*, the attribution of the archaeological record predating 1.9 million years ago becomes more challenging. The discovery at multiple localities of progressively older stone artifacts [e.g., at the Omo by 2.3 million years ago (Merrick 1976), at West Turkana by 2.3 million years ago (Kibunjia 1994), at Hadar by 2.4 million years ago (Roche and Tiercelin 1980; Harris 1983)], occurred alongside progressively older discoveries of early *Homo* [e.g., in Malawi by 2.4 million years ago (Schrenk et al. 1993), at Baringo by 2.4 million years ago (Hill et al. 1992), at Hadar by 2.3 million years ago (Kimbel et al. 1996)]. In that context, the common view could be maintained that earliest *Homo* developed habitual meat-eating, which selected for larger, energy-demanding brains, and that earliest *Homo* made the oldest tools, particularly flake tools to butcher carcasses. The proposed exclusion of *Homo habilis* and *Homo rudolfensis* from the genus *Homo* (Wood and Collard 1999) prevents the attribution of the oldest flaked stone tools to *Homo*. As redefined, *Australopithecus habilis* and *A. rudolfensis* may still have been tool makers, but a likely ingredient in future research on the behavioral ecology of all species of late Pliocene hominids will be the adaptive advantages that tool use may have provided.

A second recent discovery, from Bouri at the Middle Awash (Asfaw et al. 1999; de Heinzelin et al. 1999), appears to confirm the manufacture of flaked stone tools 2.5 million years ago by a new species of *Australopithecus* and to demonstrate their use in the defleshing of animal carcasses. Although based on a small, preliminary sample of fossil and archaeological evidence, the Bouri material provides satisfying confirmation that the oldest known flaked tools were used to deflesh meat-bearing limbs of large carcasses and to break open marrow-yielding bones. Based on current evidence, the Bouri location may also document on-the-spot meat-eating, and thus, it may predate the habitual, repeated transport of multiple carcass portions to home base types of sites that are a familiar part of the record by the beginning of the Pleistocene.

A third recent development provides a striking alternative to the dominant theme of this volume that increased meat-eating was influential in the early evolution of the *Homo* clade. Papers by Wrangham et al. (1999) and by O'Connell et al. (1999) rediscover the tuber hypothesis of Hatley and Kappelman (1980) and expand it into the cooked-tuber hypothesis, with claims of early Pleistocene digging sticks, controlled fire, and a greatly enhanced energetic value in the cooked tubers acquired and processed by those new technologies. To do so, the authors have had to downplay or simply ignore the abundant documented evidence of carcass acquisition, transport, butchery, and increased meat-eating by early *Homo*, and they have chosen to accept at face value and rely on highly problematic evidence of bone digging tools from Swartkrans (Brain et al. 1988), of controlled fire from Koobi For a and Chesowanja (Bellomo 1994; Clark and Harris 1985), and of extravagant overestimates of the energetic and nutritional yields of cooked tubers (e.g., Schoeninger et al. this volume). Simply stated, the Swartkrans tools are predominantly short, several centimeter-long splinters of bone designed to scratch in the topsoil for the same shallow tubers that are eaten by baboons, not the heavy, several foot-long digging sticks used by modern foragers to access deeply buried tubers. The timing in human prehistory of the control of fire and its use to cook food is not well established. Finally, the food value of particular tubers is likely to be reduced significantly when bioavailability is taken into account properly.

Whether or not tubers were a dominant component in the diet of early Pleistocene *Homo*, there is a consensus that hominid diets were primarily plant based, as they are among modern tropical foragers. High-quality meat was a rewarding but inherently risky supplement that, nevertheless, increased in significance during the evolution of the *Homo* clade. How and when did that shift occur? In addressing that major question, perhaps it would be most productive to avoid the polarizations that occur when issues are dichotomized into hunting versus scavenging, meat versus fat, tubers versus meat, and so on, and, instead, to accept the likelihood that the foraging adaptations and diet of Plio-Pleistocene hominids were characterized by diversity. If, as in some modern foraging societies, gathering plants in general supported less reliable foraging for meat in the Plio-Pleistocene, then it is probably not coincidence that such a complementary foraging strategy actually approximates the basics of the adaptations envisioned all along in the home base model. Within that general framework, current evidence indicates that the acquisition and consumption of meat may not have made us hominids, but there is compelling evidence that meat-eating had a major, influential role in making us human.

REFERENCES

Asfaw, B., T. White, O. Lovejoy, B. Latimer, S. Simpson, and G. Suwa. 1999. *Australopithecus garhi:* a new species of early hominid from Ethiopia. *Science* 284:629–635.

Behrensmeyer, A. K., K. D. Gordon, and G. T. Yanagi. 1986. Trampling as a cause of bone surface damage and pseudo-cut marks. *Nature* 319:768–771.

Bellomo, R. V. 1994. Methods of determining early hominid behavioral activities associated with the controlled use of fire at FxJj 20 Main, Koobi Fora, Kenya. In *Early Hominid Behavioral Ecology (Journal of Human Evolution, Vol. 27)* (J. S. Oliver, N. E. Sikes, and K. M. Stewart, eds.), pp. 173–195. London: Academic Press.

Binford, L. R. 1981. *Bones: Ancient Men and Modern Myths.* New York: Academic Press.

Binford, L. R. 1983. *In Pursuit of the Past: Decoding the Archaeological Record.* New York: Thames and Hudson.

Binford, L. R. 1988. Fact and fiction about the *Zinjanthropus* floor: data, arguments, and interpretations. *Current Anthropology* 29(1):123–135.

Binford, L. R., M. G. L. Mills, and N. M. Stone. 1988. Hyena scavenging behavior and its implications for the interpretation of faunal assemblages from FLK 22 (the *Zinj* Foor) at Olduvai Gorge. *Journal of Anthropological Archaeology* 7:99–135.

Blumenschine, R. J. 1987. Characteristics of an early hominid scavenging niche. *Current Anthropology* 28:383–407.

Blumenschine, R. J. 1988. An experimental model of the timing of hominid and carnivore influence on archaeological bone assemblages. *Journal of Archaeological Science* 15:483–509.

Blumenschine, R. J., and F. T. Masao. 1991. Living sites at Olduvai Gorge, Tanzania? Preliminary landscape archaeology results in the basal Bed II lake margin zone. *Journal of Human Evolution* 21:451–462.

Blumenschine, R. J., and C. W. Marean. 1993. A carnivore's view of archaeological bone assemblages. In *From Bones to Behavior: Ethnoarchaeological and Experimental Contributions to the Interpretation of Faunal Remains, Center for Archaeological Investigations Occasional Paper No. 21.* (J. Hudson, ed.), pp. 273–300. Carbondale: Southern Illinois University.

Brain, C. K. 1981. *The Hunters or the Hunted? An Introduction to African Cave Taphonomy.* Chicago: University of Chicago Press.

Brain, C. K. 1993. *Swartkrans: A Cave's Chronicle of Early Man.* Pretoria: Transvaal Museum.

Brain, C. K., C. S. Churcher, J. D. Clark, F. E. Grine, P. Shipman, R. L. Susman, A. Turner, and V. Watson. 1988. New evidence of early hominids, their culture and environment from the Swartkrans cave, South Africa. *South African Journal of Science* 84:828–835.

Bunn, H. T. 1981. Archaeological evidence for meat-eating by Plio-Pleistocene hominids from Koobi Fora and Olduvai Gorge. *Nature* 291:574–577.

Bunn, H. T. 1997. The bone assemblages from the excavated sites. In *Koobi For a Research Project. Volume 5. Plio-Pleistocene Archaeology,* (G. Ll. Isaac, ed.), pp. 402–458. Oxford: Clarendon Press.

Bunn, H. T., and E. M. Kroll. 1986. Systematic butchery by Plio/Pleistocene hominids at Olduvai Gorge, Tanzania. *Current Anthropology* 27(5):431–452.

Bunn, H. T., and E. M. Kroll. 1988. Reply to "Fact and Fiction" by L. R. Binford. *Current Anthropology* 29(1):135–149.

Bunn, H. T., J. W. K. Harris, G. Ll. Isaac, Z. Kaufulu, E. Kroll, K. Schick, N. Toth, and A. K. Behrensmeyer. 1980. FxJj 50: an early Pleistocene site in northern Kenya. *World Archaeology* 12:109–136.

Bunn, H. T., L. E. Bartram, and E. M. Kroll. 1988. Variability in bone assemblage formation from Hadza hunting, scavenging, and carcass processing. *Journal of Anthropological Archaeology* 7:412–457.

Clark, J. D. and J. W. K. Harris. 1985. Fire and its role in early hominid lifeways. *African Archaeological Review* 3:3–27.

Dart, R. A. 1953. The predatory transition from ape to man. *International Anthropological and Linguistic Review* 1:201–218.

Dart, R. A. 1957. *The Osteodontokeratic Culture of* Australopithecus prometheus. *Transvaal Museum Memoir No. 10.* Pretoria: Transvaal Museum.

De Heinzelin, J., J. D. Clark, T. White, W. Hart, P. Renne, G. WoldeGabriel, Y. Beyene, and E. Vrba. 1999. Environment and behavior of 2.5-million-year-old Bouri hominids. *Science* 284:625–629.

DeVore, I., and S.L. Washburn. 1963. Baboon ecology and human evolution. In *African Ecology and Human Evolution* (F. C. Howell and F. Bourliere, eds.), pp. 335–367. Chicago: Aldine.

Feibel, C. S., F. H. Brown, and I. McDougall. 1989. Stratigraphic context of fossil hominids from Omo Group deposits: northern Turkana basin, Kenya and Ethiopia. *American Journal of Physical Anthropology* 78:595–622.

Goodall, J. 1968 Behaviour of free-living chimpanzees of the Gombe Stream area. *Animal Behaviour Monographs* 1:163–311.

Harris, J. W. K. 1983. Cultural beginnings: Plio-Pleistocene arcaheological occurrences from the Afar, Ethiopia. *African Archaeological Review* 1:3–31.

Hatley, T., and J. Kappelman. 1980. Bears, pigs, and Plio-Pleistocene hominids: a case for the exploitation of below ground food resources. *Human Ecology* 8:371–387.

Hill, A., A. Ward, A. Deino, G. Curtis, and R. Drake. 1992. Earliest *Homo. Nature* 355:719–722.

Hudson, J., (ed). 1993. *From Bones to Behavior: Ethnoarchaeological and Experimental Contributions to the Interpretation of Faunal Remains. Center for Archaeological Investigations Occasional Paper No. 21.* Carbondale: Southern Illinois University.

Isaac, G. Ll. 1971. The diet of early man: aspects of archaeological evidence from lower and middle Pleistocene sites in East Africa. *World Archaeology* 2:279–298.

Isaac, G. Ll. 1978. The food-sharing behaviour of proto-human hominids. *Scientific American* 238(4):90–108.

Isaac, G. Ll. 1981. Stone Age visiting cards: approaches to the study of early land use patterns. In *Patterns of the Past: Essays in Honour of D. L. Clarke* (I. Hodder, G. Ll. Isaac, and N. Hammond, eds.), pp. 131–155. Cambridge: Cambridge University Press.

Isaac, G. Ll. 1984. The archaeology of human origins: studies of the lower Pleistocene in East Africa, 1971–1981. In *Advances in World Archaeology, Vol. 3* (F. Wendorf and A. E. Close, eds.), pp. 1–87. Orlando, FL: Academic Press.

Isaac, G. Ll. (ed.). 1997. *Koobi Fora Research Project, Volume. 5. Plio-Pleistocene Archaeology.* Oxford: Clarendon Press.

Isaac, G. Ll., and J. W. K. Harris. 1978. Archaeology. In *Koobi Fora Research Project, Vol. 1. The fossil hominds and an introduction to their context, 1968–1974* (M. G. Leakey and R. E. Leakey, eds.), pp. 64–85. Oxford: Clarendon Press.

Isaac, G. Ll., J. W. K. Harris, and F. Marshall. 1981. Small is informative: the application of the study of mini-sites and least-effort criteria in the interpretation of the early Pleistocene archaeological record at Koobi Fora. In *Las industrias mas antiguas, comision VI, X Congreso* (J. D. Clark and G. Ll. Isaac, eds.), pp. 101–119. Mexico City: Union Internacional de Ciencias Prehistoricas y Protohistoricas.

Keeley, L. H., and N. Toth. 1981. Microwear polishes on early stone tools from Koobi Fora, Kenya. *Nature* 293:464–465.

Kimbel, W. H., R. C. Walter, D. C. Johanson, and K. E. Reed, et al. 1996. Late Pliocene *Homo* and Oldowan tools from the Hadar Formation (Kada Hadar Member), Ethiopia. *Journal of Human Evolution* 31(6):549–561.

Kibunjia, M. 1994. Pliocene archaeological occurrences in the Lake Turkana basin. *Journal of Human Evolution* 27:159–171.

Kroll, E. M. 1997. Lithic and faunal distributions at eight archaeological excavations. In *Koobi Fora Research Project, Volume. 5. Plio-Pleistocene Archaeology* (G Ll. Isaac, ed.), pp. 459–543. Oxford: Clarendon Press.

Kroll, E. M., and G.Ll. Isaac. 1984. Configurations of artifacts and bones at early Pleistocene sites in East Africa. In *Intrasite Spatial Analysis in Archaeology* (H. J. Hietala, ed.), pp. 4–31. Cambridge: Cambridge University Press.

Kuman, K. 1994. The archaeology of Sterkontein—past and present. *Journal of Human Evolution* 27:471–495.

Leakey, L. S. B., P. V. Tobias, and J. R. Napier. 1964. A new species of the genus *Homo* from Olduvai Gorge. *Nature* 202:7–9.

Lyman, R. L. 1994. *Vertebrate Taphonomy.* Cambridge: Cambridge University Press.

McGrew, W. C. 1992. *Chimpanzee Material Culture: Implications for Human Evolution.* Cambridge: Cambridge University Press.

Merrick, H. V. 1976. Recent archaeological research in the Plio-Pleistocene deposits of the Lower Omo Valley, Southwestern Ethiopia. In *Human Origins: Louis Leakey and the East African Evidence* (G. Ll. Isaac and E. R. McCown, eds.), pp. 461–481. Menlo Park, CA: W. A. Benjamin, Inc.

O'Connell, J. F., K. Hawkes, and N. G. Blurton Jones. 1988. Hadza hunting, butchering, and bone transport and their archaeological implications. *Journal of Anthropological Research* 44:113–162.

O'Connell, J. F., K. Hawkes, and N.G. Blurton Jones. 1999. Grandmothering and the evolution of *Homo erectus*. *Journal of Human Evolution* 36:461–485.

Pickering, T. R. 1999. *Taphonomic Interpretations of the Sterkfontein Early Hominid Site (Gauteng, South Africa) Reconsidered in Light of Recent Evidence*. Ph.D. Dissertation. Department of Anthropology, Madison: University of Wisconsin.

Potts, R. B. 1984. Home bases and early hominids. *American Scientist* 72:338–347.

Potts, R. B. 1988. *Early Hominid Activities at Olduvai*. New York: Aldine de Gruyter.

Potts, R. B., and P. Shipman. 1981. Cutmarks made by stone tools on bones from Olduvai Gorge, Tanzania. *Nature* 291:577–580.

Roche, H., and J. J. Tiercelin. 1980. Industries lithiques de la formation Plio-Pleistocene d'Hadar Ethiopia (campaigne 1976). In *Proceedings of the 8th Panafrican Congress of Prehistory and Quaternary Studies, Nairobi, 1977* (R. E. F. Leakey and B. Ogot, eds.), pp. 194–199. Nairobi: The International Louis Leakey Memorial Institute for African Prehistory.

Rose, L., and F. Marshall. 1996. Meat eating, hominid sociality, and home bases revisited. *Current Anthropology* 37(2):307–338.

Schrenk, F., T. Bromage, C. Betzler, U. Ring, and Y. Juwayeyi. 1993. Oldest *Homo* and Pliocene biogeography of the Malawi Rift. *Nature* 265:833–836.

Sept, J. 1994. Beyond bones: archaeological sites, early hominid subsistence, and the costs and benefits of exploiting wild plant foods in east African riverine landscapes. *Journal of Human Evolution* 27:295–320.

Stanford, C. B. 1996. The hunting ecology of wild chimpanzees: implications for the behavioral ecology of Pliocene hominids. *American Anthropologist* 98:96–113.

Stanford, C. B. 1998. *Chimpanzee and Red Colobus: The Ecology of Predator and Prey*. Cambridge, MA: Harvard University Press.

Stanford, C. B., and J. S. Allen. 1991. Strategic storytelling: current models of human behavioral evolution. *Current Anthropology* 32:58–61.

Stern, N. 1993. The structure of the Lower Pleistocene archaeological record. *Current Anthropology* 34(3):201–226.

Stiner, M. C. in press. Carnivory, coevolution, and the geographic spread of the genus *Homo*. *Journal of Archaeological Research*.

Susman, R. L. 1988. New postcranial remains from Swartkrans and their bearing on the functional morphology and behavior of *Paranthropus robustus*. In *Evolutionary History of the "Robust" Australopithecines* (F. E. Grine, ed.), pp. 149–172. New York: Aldine de Gruyter.

Susman, R. L. 1994. Fossil evidence for early hominid tool use. *Science* 265:1570–1573.

Swisher, C. C., III, G. H. Curtis, T. Jacob, A. G. Getty, A. Suprijo, and A. Widiasmoro. 1994. Age of the earliest known hominids in Java, Indonesia. *Science* 263:1118–21.

Tappen, M. 1990. Savanna ecology and natural bone deposition: implications for early hominid site formation, hunting, and scavenging. *Current Anthropology* 36(2):223–260.

Tooby, J., and I. DeVore. 1987. The reconstruction of hominid behavioral evolution through strategic modeling. In *The Evolution of Human Behavior: Primate Models* (W. G. Kinzey, ed.), pp. 183–237. Albany, NY: State University of New York.

Vincent, A. 1984. Plant foods in savanna environments: a preliminary report of tubers eaten by the Hadza of northern Tanzania. *World Archaeology* 17:131–148.

Whiten, A., J. Goodall, W. C. McGrew, R. W. Wrangham, and C. Boesch 1999. Cultures in chimpanzees. *Nature* 399:682–687.

Wood, B., and M. Collard. 1999. The human genus. *Science* 284(2):65–71.

Wrangham, R. W., J. Holland Jones, G. Laden, D. Pilbeam, and N. Conklin-Brittain. 1999. The raw and the stolen: cooking and the ecology of human origins. *Current Anthropology* 40(5):567–594.

Index

Printed in the United States
68616LVS00002B/34

9 780195 131390